Beginning PHP and MySQL E-Commerce

From Novice to Professional

SECOND EDITION

Cristian Darie and Emilian Balanescu

Beginning PHP and MySQL E-Commerce: From Novice to Professional, Second Edition

Copyright © 2008 by Cristian Darie and Emilian Balanescu

ISBN-13 (paperback): 978-1-59059-864-1

ISBN-13 (electronic): 978-1-4302-0291-2

Printed and bound in the United States of America (POD)

Lead Editors: Jason Gilmore and Tom Welsh
Technical Reviewers: Bogdan Brinzarea-Iamandi, Sharon Dempsey, Audra Hendrix
Editorial Board: Clay Andres, Steve Anglin, Ewan Buckingham, Tony Campbell, Gary Cornell,
    Jonathan Gennick, Kevin Goff, Matthew Moodie, Joseph Ottinger, Jeffrey Pepper, Frank Pohlmann,
    Ben Renow-Clarke, Dominic Shakeshaft, Matt Wade, Tom Welsh
Senior Project Manager: Tracy Brown Collins
Copy Editors: Heather Lang, Kim Wimpsett
Associate Production Director: Kari Brooks-Copony
Production Editor: Laura Esterman
Compositor: Kinetic Publishing Services, LLC
Proofreader: Liz Welch
Indexer: Broccoli Information Management
Artists: April Milne, Kinetic Publishing Services, LLC
Cover Designer: Kurt Krames
Manufacturing Director: Tom Debolski

Distributed to the book trade worldwide by Springer-Verlag New York, Inc., 233 Spring Street, 6th Floor, New York, NY 10013. Phone 1-800-SPRINGER, fax 201-348-4505, e-mail orders-ny@springer-sbm.com, or visit http://www.springeronline.com.

For information on translations, please contact Apress directly at 2855 Telegraph Avenue, Suite 600, Berkeley, CA 94705. Phone 510-549-5930, fax 510-549-5939, e-mail info@apress.com, or visit http://www.apress.com.

Apress and friends of ED books may be purchased in bulk for academic, corporate, or promotional use. eBook versions and licenses are also available for most titles. For more information, reference our Special Bulk Sales–eBook Licensing web page at http://www.apress.com/info/bulksales.

The source code for this book is available to readers at http://www.apress.com.

Contents at a Glance

PART 1 ■ ■ ■ Phase I of Development

PART 2 ■ ■ ■ Phase II of Development

PART 3 ■ ■ ■ Phase III of Development

Contents

PART 2 ■ ■ ■ Phase II of Development

Part 3 ■ ■ ■ Phase III of Development

About the Authors

CRISTIAN DARIE is a software engineer working as a senior application architect for Netbridge Development S.R.L., maintaining and extending the largest Romanian e-commerce web site, OKazii.ro.

Cristian is the author of numerous technical books, and he's studying distributed application architectures for his PhD at the Politehnica University of Bucharest, Romania. He's getting involved with various commercial and research projects, and when not planning to buy Google, he enjoys his bit of social life. If you want to say "hi," you can reach Cristian through his personal web site at http://www.cristiandarie.ro.

EMILIAN BALANESCU is a programmer experienced in many technologies, such as PHP, Java, .NET, PostgreSQL, MySQL, and Microsoft SQL Server. He is a Microsoft Certified Technology Specialist, currently working as a senior web developer at SoftNET Business Services S.R.L., where he helps in developing a collaboration tool for small and medium-sized businesses. You can reach Emilian at http://www.emilianbalanescu.ro.

About the Technical Reviewers

BOGDAN BRINZAREA-IAMANDI has a strong background in computer science, holding a master's and bachelor's degree from the Automatic Control and Computers Faculty of the Politehnica University of Bucharest, Romania, and another master's degree from the computer science department of Ecole Polytechnique in Paris, France. His main interests are new web technologies and distributed and mobile computing.

SHARON DEMPSEY is a writer and entrepreneur who is developing an online publication of locally focused financial information. A desire to create a web site with a searchable database and e-commerce capabilities led to her involvement with this book. Sharon tested the procedures in this volume within the Windows XP environment and offered critique from the perspective of a do-it-yourselfer who is not a computer expert.

AUDRA HENDRIX is adjusting to life in America after her recent return from France where she spent five years living in Paris and working as an independent consultant. Fluent in French, she focused her expertise on needs assessment, application development and deployment, and future growth planning for a variety of import/export and retail system clientele. She was educated at Northwestern University in Evanston, Illinois, and began her computer career with Hewlett-Packard. She currently consults as development advisor and technology liaison for small to medium-sized businesses. While her client roster includes the Fortune 500, she prefers the challenge of working and developing small and medium-sized businesses that are struggling to institute or transition their technology solutions. She also assists in the development of a full array of marketing strategies with a niche focus on web presence and services.

Acknowledgments

The authors would like to thank the following people for their invaluable assistance with the production of this book:

Tracy Brown Collins, our project manager, for guiding everyone through the process of building this book. The challenges we've faced during one year of work have transformed this book into an organizational nightmare, but Tracy has kept us on track, helping us finish the project successfully.

Heather Lang and Kim Wimpsett for their wonderful edits, which somehow made our copy sound like it was written by someone who actually knows English (and knows it well!).

Laura Esterman and the rest of the production team for transforming the documents we've written and the graphics we've submitted into the book that you hold in your hands right now.

Bogdan Brinzarea-Iamandi, Sharon Dempsey, and Audra Hendrix for testing the code, verifying the technical accuracy of this book, and suggesting many important improvements that have significantly improved the quality of this book and eliminated many potential sources of frustration for readers.

Family and friends of both Cristian and Emilian for the fantastic emotional support they've offered while writing this book.

Introduction

Welcome to the second edition of *Beginning PHP and MySQL E-Commerce: From Novice to Professional!*

This book is a practical, step-by-step PHP and MySQL tutorial that teaches you real-world development practices. Guiding you through every step of the design and build process, this tutorial will teach you how to create high-quality, fully featured, extendable e-commerce web sites.

Over the course of this book, you will develop the necessary skills to get your business up on the Web and available to a worldwide audience. In each chapter, you will implement and test new features of your e-commerce web site, and you will learn the theoretical foundations required to understand the implementation details. The features are presented in increasing complexity as you advance throughout this book, so that your journey will be as pleasant and painless as possible. By the end, you'll understand the concepts, and you'll have the knowledge to create your own powerful web sites.

Owners of the first edition will find that a large part of the book has been rewritten and many features have been added, as a result of the advances in the web development scene and the extensive feedback we've received from the readers of the first edition. Now, you'll find the book teaches you AJAX techniques, how to implement search engine optimization and product attributes, and many other exciting features.

The case study is presented in three phases of development. The first phase focuses on getting the site up and running as quickly as possible and at a low cost. Although not yet fully featured, at the conclusion of this phase, your site will have a fully functional, searchable product catalog and will be capable of accepting PayPal payments, enabling you to begin generating revenue immediately.

The second phase concentrates on increasing revenue by improving the shopping experience. In this phase, you'll learn how to proactively encourage customers to buy more by implementing a dynamic product recommendations mechanism. You'll also implement your own custom shopping cart to replace the PayPal one we'll implement initially, and you'll add AJAX features to your site.

In the third phase, we'll show you how to increase your profit margins by reducing costs through automating and streamlining order processing and administration and by handling credit card transactions yourself. You also learn how to integrate external functionality through web services and improve your customer's shopping experience by adding product review functionality.

We hope you'll enjoy reading our book, and that you'll find it useful and relevant to your development projects!

Who This Book Is For

Beginning PHP and MySQL E-Commerce: From Novice to Professional, Second Edition is aimed at developers looking for a tutorial approach to building a full e-commerce web site from design to deployment. The book teaches most of the necessary concepts and guides you through all the implementation steps, but it's assumed that you have some basic knowledge of building web sites with PHP and MySQL. W. Jason Gilmore's *Beginning PHP and MySQL: From Novice to Professional, Second Edition* (Apress, 2006) can provide this foundation knowledge for you.

The code in this book has been tested with PHP 5 and MySQL 5. The code is *not* compatible with older versions of PHP, which lack the object-oriented programming (OOP) support required to implement the presented code architecture.

Information regarding the compatibility with newer versions of PHP and MySQL will be kept updated on the book's support page at Cristian Darie's web site at http://www.cristiandarie.ro/php-mysql-ecommerce-2/.

How This Book Is Structured

This book is divided into three parts containing 22 chapters total. We cover a wide variety of topics and showing you how to

- Build a product catalog that can be browsed and searched

- Implement the catalog administration pages that allow adding, modifying, and removing products, categories, and departments, and other administrative features

- Create your own shopping basket and check-out mechanism in PHP

- Increase sales by implementing product recommendations and product reviews

- Handle payments using PayPal, DataCash, and Authorize.net

- Implement a customer accounts system

- Integrate Amazon.com web services to sell Amazon.com items through your web site

While implementing these features, you'll learn how to

- Design relational databases and write MySQL queries and stored procedures

- Use the MySQL full-text search feature to implement product searching

- Use the Smarty templating engine to write structured and extensible PHP code

- Implement search engine optimization features

- Use AJAX to improve the users' experience utilizing your web site

- Integrate external web services

The following brief roadmap highlights how we'll take you from novice to professional in these topics.

Phase I of Development

The first phase of development consists of the first 11 chapters of the book, and it concentrates on establishing the basic framework for the site and putting a product catalog online. We'll start by putting together the basic site architecture and deciding how the different parts of the application will work together. We'll then build the product catalog into this architecture.

Chapter 1: Starting an E-Commerce Site

In this chapter, we'll introduce some of the principles of e-commerce in the real world. You see the importance of focusing on short-term revenue and keeping risks down. We look at the three basic ways in which an e-commerce site can make money. We then apply those principles to a three-phase plan that provides a deliverable, usable site at each phase of this book.

Chapter 2: Laying Out the Foundations

The first chapter offered an overview of e-commerce in the real world. Now that you've decided to develop a web site, we start to look in more detail at laying down the foundations for its future. We'll talk about what technologies and tools you'll use, and even more importantly, how you'll use them.

Chapter 3: Starting the TShirtShop Project

In this chapter, you'll prepare the ground for developing the TShirtShop project—the e-commerce web site you'll be creating throughout the book. You'll be guided through installing and configuring the necessary software on your development machine, including the Apache web server and the MySQL database server. You'll also write a bit of code for the foundations of your project, and you will create the MySQL database that will store the web site's data.

Chapter 4: Creating the Product Catalog: Part 1

After learning about the three-tier architecture and implementing a bit of your web site's main page, it's time to continue your work by starting to create the TShirtShop product catalog. Because the product catalog is composed of many components, you'll create it over two chapters. In Chapter 4, you'll create the first database table, your first MySQL stored procedure, and implement the PHP code that accesses that stored procedure. By the end of this chapter, you'll have something dynamically generated on your web page.

Chapter 5: Creating the Product Catalog: Part 2

In Chapter 4, you created a selectable list of departments for TShirtShop. However, a product catalog is much more than a list of departments. In Chapter 5, you'll add the rest of the product catalog features, creating category pages, product lists, and product details pages. While designing the data structure that supports these features, you'll learn how to implement relationships between data tables and how to use parameterized MySQL stored procedures.

Chapter 6: Product Attributes

Many online stores allow shoppers to customize the products they buy. For example, when selling t-shirts (as TShirtShop does), it's common to let your customer choose the size and color of the t-shirt—sparing them the fashion risk of one-size-and-one-color fits all. In this chapter, we'll implement the product attributes feature in TShirtShop.

Chapter 7: Search Engine Optimization

Search engine optimization, or simply SEO, refers to the practices employed to increase the number of visitors a web site receives from organic (unpaid) search engine result pages. Today, the search engine is the most important tool people use to find information and products on the Internet. Needless to say, having your e-commerce web site rank well for the relevant key-words will help drive visitors to your site and increase the chances that visitors will buy from you and not the competition! In this chapter, we'll update TShirtShop so that its core architecture will be search engine friendly, which will help marketers in their efforts.

Chapter 8: Searching the Catalog

In the preceding chapters, you will have implemented a functional product catalog for TShirtShop. However, the site still lacks the all-important search feature. The goal in this chapter is to allow the visitor to search the site for products by entering one or more keywords. You'll learn how to implement search results rankings and how to implement functionality to browse through the search results page by page. You'll see how easy it is to add new features to a working site by integrating the new components into the existing architecture.

Chapter 9: Receiving Payments Using PayPal

Your e-commerce web site needs a way to receive payments from customers. The preferred solution for established companies is to open a merchant account, but many small businesses choose to start with a solution that's simpler to implement, where they don't have to process credit card or payment information themselves.

A number of companies and web sites exist to help individuals or small businesses that don't have the resources to process credit card and wire transactions, and these companies can be used to process the payment between companies and their customers. In this chapter, we'll demonstrate some of the functionality provided by one such company, PayPal.

Chapter 10: Catalog Administration: Departments and Categories

The final detail to take care of before launching a web site is to create its administrative inter-face. Although this is a part visitors will never see, it's still key to delivering a quality web site to your client. In this chapter and the following one, you implement a catalog administration page. In Chapter 10, we deal with administering departments and categories.

Chapter 11: Catalog Administration: Products and Attributes

This chapter completes the catalog administration features by implementing products and product attributes management features. Once this chapter is complete, your site administra-tors will be able to create products, assign products to new departments or categories, create or delete product attributes, and so on.

Phase II of Development

The second phase of development teaches you how to increase revenue by improving the shopping experience. In this phase, you'll learn how to proactively encourage customers to buy more by implementing a dynamic product recommendations mechanism, and you'll also implement AJAX and search engine optimization features.

Chapter 12: Creating Your Own Shopping Cart

With this chapter, you enter the second phase of development, where you start improving and adding new features to the already existing, fully functional e-commerce site. In Chapter 12, you'll implement the custom shopping cart, which stores its data in the local database. This provides you with more flexibility than the PayPal shopping basket, over which you have limited control and which you can't save into your database for further processing and analysis.

Chapter 13: Implementing AJAX Features

In this chapter, we'll enhance our fully functional shopping cart and product catalog using the technology that made web development headlines in 2005. This technology is called AJAX, and it allows you to make your web applications easier and more pleasant to use for your visitors.

Chapter 14: Accepting Customer Orders

The good news is that the brand-new shopping cart implemented in Chapter 12, and then AJAXified in Chapter 13, looks good and is fully functional. The bad news is that it doesn't allow the visitor to place an order yet, making it totally useless in the context of a production system. As you have probably already guessed, you'll deal with that problem in Chapter 14, in two separate stages. In the first part of the chapter, you'll implement the client-side part of the order-placement mechanism. In the second part of the chapter, you'll implement a simple order administration page where the site administrator can view and handle pending orders.

Chapter 15: Product Recommendations

One of the most important advantages of an Internet store, compared to a brick-and-mortar location, is the capability to customize the web site for each visitor based on his or her preferences or on preferences based on data gathered from similar visitors. If your web site knows how to suggest additional products in a clever way, your visitors might end up buying more than initially planned. You have undoubtedly already seen this strategy in action on many successful e-commerce sites, and there is a reason for that—it increases profits. In this chapter, you'll implement a simple but efficient dynamic product recommendations system in your TShirtShop web store.

Phase III of Development

In the third phase of development, you'll learn how to increase your profit margins by reducing costs through automating and streamlining order processing and administration and by handling credit card transactions yourself. You also learn how to integrate external functionality through web services and improve your customer's shopping experience by adding product review functionality.

Chapter 16: Managing Customer Details

In the first two stages of development, you've built a basic (but functional) site and hooked it into PayPal for taking payments and confirming orders. In the third section of this book, you'll take things a little further. By cutting out PayPal from the ordering process, you can gain better control as well as reduce overhead. This isn't as complicated as you might think, but you must be careful to do things right. Chapter 16 lays the groundwork by implementing a customer account system, as well as looking into the security aspects of exchanging and storing customer and credit card details.

Chapter 17: Storing Customer Orders

In Chapter 16, we added customer account management capabilities, and we're now securely keeping track of customer addresses and credit card information. However, we're not currently using this information in our order-tracking system, which was created in Phase II of development. We currently don't associate an order with the account of the customer who placed that order.

In this chapter, we'll make the modifications required for customers to place orders that are associated with their user profiles. The main modification here is that the customer associated with an order will be identified by a new piece of information in the orders' table, and much of the rest of the modifications in this book will be made to use this information.

These changes will allow us to track into our database the orders placed by a particular customer and represent a base for implementing the order pipeline and credit card transactions in the following chapters.

Chapter 18: Implementing the Order Pipeline: Part 1

Order pipeline functionality is an extremely useful capability for an e-commerce site. Order pipeline functions let us keep track of orders at every stage in the process and provide auditing information that we can refer to later or if something goes wrong during the order processing. We can do all this without relying on a third-party accounting system, which can also reduce costs.

Implementing the order pipeline is the first step we're making toward creating a professional order management system. In this and the next chapter, we'll build our own order-processing pipeline that deals with credit card authorization, stock checking, shipping, e-mail notification, and so on. We'll leave the credit card–processing specifics for Chapter 20, but in this chapter, we'll show you where this process fits into the picture.

Chapter 19: Implementing the Order Pipeline: Part 2

In this chapter, you'll add the required pipeline sections so that you can process orders from start to finish, although you won't be adding full credit card transaction functionality until the next chapter. We'll also look at the web administration of orders by modifying the order administration pages added earlier in the book to take into account the new order-processing system.

Chapter 20: Processing Credit Card Transactions

The last thing you need to do before launching the e-commerce site is enable credit card processing. In this chapter, we'll look at how you can build this into the pipeline you created in

Chapters 13 and 14. You'll see how to use two popular credit card gateways to do this, DataCash and Authorize.net. By the end of this chapter, TShirtShop will be a fully functioning, secure, and usable e-commerce application.

Chapter 21: Product Reviews

At this point, you have a complete and functional e-commerce web site. However, this doesn't stop you from adding even more features to your site, making it more useful and pleasant for visitors. By adding a product review system, you increase the chances that visitors will return to your site, either to write a review for a product they bought or to see what other people think about that product.

Chapter 22: Using Amazon.com Web Services

So far in this book, you've learned how to integrate external functionality provided PayPal, DataCash, and Authorize.net to process payments from your customers. In this chapter, you'll learn new possibilities for integrating features from external sources through web services. Knowing how to interact with third-party web services can offer you an important advantage over your competitors. In Chapter 22, you'll learn how to use Amazon.com functionality from and through web services.

Downloading the Code

The code for this book can be downloaded in zip file format from the Downloads section of the Apress web site. You can find the code, errata, and other resources related to the book also on Cristian Darie's web site at `http://www.cristiandarie.ro/php-mysql-ecommerce-2/`.

Contacting the Authors

You can contact Cristian Darie through his web site at `http://www.cristiandarie.ro` and Emilian Balanescu through his at `http://www.emilianbalanescu.ro`.

## PART 1

Phase I of Development

■ ■ ■

## CHAPTER 1

Starting an E-Commerce Site

The word "e-commerce" has had a remarkable fall from grace in the past few years. Just the idea of having an e-commerce web site was once enough to get many businesspeople salivating in anticipation. But now, it's no longer enough to say, "E-commerce is the future—get online or get out of business." You now need compelling, realistic, and specific reasons to take your business online.

If you want to build an e-commerce site today, you must answer some tough questions. Here are a few things to ask yourself:

- Many big e-commerce sites have failed. What can e-commerce possibly offer me in today's tougher environment?

- Most e-commerce companies seem to need massive investment. How can I produce a site on my limited budget?

- Even successful e-commerce sites expect to take years before they turn a profit. My business can't wait that long. How can I make money now?

We'll take a shot at answering these questions in this chapter.

Deciding Whether to Go Online

Although there are hundreds of possible reasons to go online, they tend to fall into the following groups:

- Retain existing customers and get new customers

- Encourage existing customers to spend more money

- Reduce the costs of fulfilling orders

We'll look at each of these in the following sections.

Get More Customers

Getting more customers is immediately the most attractive reason to go online. With an e-commerce site, even small businesses can reach customers all over the world. This reason can also be the most dangerous, however, because many people set up e-commerce sites assuming that the site will reach customers immediately. It won't. In the offline world, you need to know a shop exists before you can go into it. This is still true in the world of e-commerce—people must know your site exists before you can hope to get a single order.

Addressing this issue is largely a question of making your site known. Aside from advertising, methods of getting more customers to visit include registering the web site with the popular search engines and directory listings, optimizing the site for search-engine ranking, creating forums, sending newsletters, and so on.

In this book, we don't cover the aspects of selling your site; we focus on ways to sell the products listed on your site. But this book does include some basic search engine optimization techniques (to attract visitors), and it provides a well-designed presentation that will sell the site once your customers visit it.

Encourage Customers to Spend More

Assuming your company already has customers, you probably wish that they bought more. What stops them? If the customers don't want any more of a certain product, there's not a lot that e-commerce can do, but there are other roadblocks on the sales path that can be removed, such as these:

- Getting to the physical location of the shop or placing an order by mail is a hassle.

- Some of the things you sell can be bought from more convenient places.

- You're mostly open while your customers are at work.

- It's harder to implement an efficient product recommendation system in a physical store.

A quality e-commerce site can increase your business revenue. The convenience of being online also means that people are more likely to choose you over other local suppliers. Because your site is online 24 hours a day, rather than the usual 9 to 5, your customers can shop with you outside of their working hours. Having an online store brings a double blessing to you if your customers work in offices, because they can indulge in retail therapy directly from their desks.

People with Internet access will find placing an order online far easier than any other method—meaning that when the temptation to buy strikes, it's much easier for them to give in. Skillful e-commerce design can encourage your customers to buy things they wouldn't usually think of. Special offers to regular shoppers, suggested impulse purchases before or during checkout, useful accessories presented alongside the main product, and showing a more expensive alternative to the one they're considering encourage customers to buy more. You can easily update your site to suggest items of particular seasonal interest, to announce interesting new products, or to recommend products similar to what a specific customer has already bought.

You'll learn how to use some of these methods in later chapters; by the end of this book, you'll have a good idea of how to add more features for yourself.

Finally, it's much easier to learn about your customers via e-commerce than in face-to-face shops or even with mail order. Even if you just gather e-mail addresses, you can use these to send out updates and news. More sophisticated sites can automatically analyze a customer's buying habits to make suggestions on other products the customer might like to buy.

Another related benefit of e-commerce is that there's no real cost in having people browse without buying. In fact, getting people to visit the site as often as possible can be valuable. You should consider building features into the site that are designed purely to make people visit regularly; for example, you might include community features such as forums or free content related to the products you're selling.

Reduce the Costs of Fulfilling Orders

A well-built e-commerce site will be much less expensive to run than a comparable offline business. Under conventional business models, a staff member must feed an order into the company's order-processing system. With e-commerce, the customer can do this for you—the gateway between the site and the order processing can be seamless.

Of course, after your e-commerce site is up and running, the cost of actually taking orders gets close to zero—you don't need to pay for checkout staff, assistants, security guards, or rent in a busy shopping mall.

If you have a sound business idea, and you execute the site well, you can receive these benefits without a massive investment. What's important is to always focus on the almighty dollar: Will your site, or any particular feature of it, really help you get more customers, retain existing customers, and get customers to spend more, or will it reduce costs and therefore increase your margins?

Now it's time to introduce the site we'll be using as the example in this book and see just how all of these principles relate to our own shop.

Let's Make Money

We're going to build an e-commerce store that sells t-shirts. On e-commerce sites, there's always a trade-off to make between building an amazing site that everybody will love and creating a site on a limited budget that will make money. Usually, I'm on the all-the-bells-and-whistles-really-amazing-site side, but I'm always grateful that my ambitions are reined in by the actual business demands. If you're designing and building the site for yourself and you are the client, then you have a challenge—keeping your view realistic while maintaining your enthusiasm for the project.

This book shows you a logical way to build an e-commerce site that will deliver what it needs to be profitable. However, when designing your own site, you need to think carefully about exactly who your customers are, what they need, how they want to place orders, and what they are most likely to buy. Consider the following points before you start to visualize or design the site and certainly before you start programming:

Getting customers: How will you get visitors to the site in the first place?

Offering products: What will you offer, and how will you expect customers to buy? Will they buy in bulk? Will they make a lot of repeat orders? Will they know what they want before they visit, or will they want to be inspired? These factors will influence how you arrange your catalog and searching as well as what order process you use. A shopping basket is great if people want to browse. If people know exactly what they want, then they might prefer something more like an order form.

Processing orders: How will you turn a customer order into a parcel ready for mailing? Your main consideration here is finding an efficient way to process payments and deliver orders to whoever manages your stocks or warehouse. How will you give your customers confidence in your ability to protect their data and deliver their purchases on time?

Serving customers: Will customers require additional help with products that they buy from you? Do you need to offer warranties, service contracts, or other support services?

Bringing customers back: How will you entice customers back to the site? Are they likely to only visit the site to make a purchase, or will there be e-window-shoppers? Are your products consumables, and can you predict when your customers will need something new?

After you've answered these questions, you can start designing your site, knowing that you're designing for your customers—not just doing what seems like a good idea at the time. The example site presented in this book has taken a deliberate generic approach to show you the most common e-commerce techniques.

To really lift yourself above the competition, however, you don't need fancy features or Flash movies—you just need to understand, attract, and serve your customers better than anybody else. This book will help you do that.

Risks and Threats

All this might make it sound as if your e-commerce business can't possibly fail. Well, it's time to take a cold shower and realize that even the best-laid plans often go wrong. Some risks are particularly relevant to e-commerce companies, such as

- Hacking

- Credit card scams

- Hardware failures

- Unreliable shipping services

- Software errors

- Changing laws

You can't get rid of these risks, but if you know about them, you can defend your site from them.

An important way to protect your site from many risks is to maintain backups. You already know backups are important. But if you're anything like us, when it gets to the end of the day, saving five minutes and going home earlier seems even more important. When you have a live web site, this simply isn't an option. Two words: Back up (your web site). Every day.

We don't talk much about the legal side of e-commerce in this book because we are programmers, not lawyers. However, if you are setting up an e-commerce site that goes much beyond an online garage sale, you'll need to look into these issues before putting your business online.

While we're on the subject of risks and threats, one issue that can substantially damage your e-commerce site's reputation is unreliable order fulfillment. This book shows you how to construct a web site that offers products, takes customer orders, and communicates those orders to the owner. An essential part of the process is delivering the products, and to do this, you need a good logistics network set up before launching your shop. If your store doesn't deliver the goods, customers won't come back or refer their *friends*.

■Tip Webmonkey provides an excellent general e-commerce tutorial, which covers taxation, shipping, and many of the issues you'll face when designing your site, at `http://www.webmonkey.com/webmonkey/ e-business/building/tutorials/tutorial3.html`. Check this out before you start designing your site.

Designing for Business

Building an e-commerce site requires a significant investment. If you design the site in phases, you can reduce the initial investment and therefore cut your losses if the idea proves unsuccessful. You can use the results from an early phase to assess whether it's worthwhile to add extra features and even use revenue from the site to fund future development. If nothing else, planning to build the site in phases means that you can get your site online and receiving orders much earlier than if you build every possible feature into the first release.

Even after you've completed your initial planned phases, things generally do not end there. When planning a large software project, it's important to design in a way that makes inevitable future growth easy. In Chapter 2, where we'll start dealing with the technical details of building e-commerce sites, you'll learn how to design the web site architecture to allow for long-term development flexibility.

If you're building sites for clients, they will like to keep their options open. Planning the site, or any other software, in phases will help your clients feel comfortable doing business with you. They will be able to see that you are getting the job done and can decide to end the project at the end of any phase if they feel—for whatever reason—that they don't want to continue to invest in development.

Phase I: Getting a Site Up

Chapters 2 through 11 concentrate on establishing the basic framework for the site and putting a product catalog online. We'll start by putting together the basic site architecture and deciding how the different parts of the application will work together. We'll then build the product catalog into this architecture. You'll learn how to

- Design a database for storing a product catalog containing departments, categories, and products

- Write the Structured Query Language (SQL) and Hypertext Preprocessor (PHP) code for accessing that data and making the product catalog functional

- Add data to the product catalog that defines product attributes, such as color and size

- Provide a product search engine

- Implement basic techniques to make your web site search engine friendly and reduce URL link and redirect errors

- Receive payments through PayPal Website Payments Standard

- Give the site's administrators a private section of the site where they can administer the catalog online

After you've built this catalog, you'll see how to offer the products for sale by integrating it with PayPal's shopping cart and order-processing system, which will handle credit card transactions for you and e-mail you with details of orders. These orders will be processed manually, but in the early stages of an e-commerce site, the time you lose processing orders will be less than the time it would have taken to develop an automated system.

Phase II: Creating Your Own Shopping Cart

Using PayPal's shopping cart is OK and very easy, but it does mean you miss out on a lot of advantages. For example, you can't control the look and feel of PayPal's shopping cart, whereas if you use your own, you can make it an integral part of the site.

This is a significant advantage, but it's superficial compared to some of the others. For example, with your own shopping cart, you can store complete orders in the database as part of the order process and use that data to learn about the customers. With additional work, you also can use the shopping basket and checkout process as a platform for selling more products. How often have you been tempted by impulse purchases near the checkout of your local store? Well, impulse shopping also works with e-commerce. Having your own shopping cart and checkout gives you the option of offering low-cost special offers from the shopping cart at checkout. You can even analyze the contents of the cart and make suggestions based on this.

Chapters 12 through 15 show you how to

- Build your own shopping cart

- Pass a complete order through to PayPal for credit card processing

- Add AJAX features to your product catalog and shopping cart to enhance the user experience

- Create an order administration page

- Implement a product recommendation system

Once again, at the end of Phase II, our site will be fully operational. You can leave it as it is or add features within the existing PayPal-based payment system. But when the site gets serious, you'll want to start processing orders and credit cards yourself. This is the part where things get complicated, and you need to be serious and careful about your site's security.

Phase III: Processing Orders and Adding Features

The core of e-commerce—and the bit that really separates it from other web-development projects—is handling orders and credit cards. PayPal has helped us put this off, but there are many good reasons why—eventually—you'll want to part company with PayPal:

Cost: PayPal is not expensive, but the extra services it offers must be paid for somehow. Moving to a simpler credit card processing service can mean lower transaction costs (this is not a rule though), although developing your own system will obviously incur upfront costs.

Freedom: PayPal has a fairly strict set of terms and conditions and is designed for residents of a limited number of countries. By taking on more of the credit card processing responsibility yourself, you can better control the way your site works. As an obvious example, you can accept payment using regional methods such as the Switch debit cards common in the United Kingdom.

Integration: If you deal with transactions and orders using your own system, you can integrate your store and your warehouse to whatever extent you require. You could even automatically contact a third-party supplier and have the supplier ship the goods straight to the customer.

Information: When you handle the whole order yourself, you can record and collate all the information involved in the transaction—and then use it for marketing and research purposes.

By integrating the order processing with the warehouse, fulfillment center, or suppliers, you can reduce costs significantly. This might reduce the need for staff in the fulfillment center or allow the business to grow without requiring additional staff.

Acquiring information about customers can feed back into the whole process, giving you valuable information about how to sell more. For example, using that data, you could e-mail customers with special offers or just keep in touch with a newsletter. You also could analyze buying patterns and use that data to formulate targeted marketing campaigns.

During Phase III, which is covered in Chapters 16 through 22, you will learn how to

- Build a customer accounts module so that customers can log in and retrieve their details every time they make an order

- Allow customers to add product reviews

- Integrate Amazon.com products into your web site using XML Web Services

- Establish secure connections using Secure Socket Layer (SSL) so that data sent by users is encrypted on its travels across the Internet

- Charge credit cards using DataCash, Authorize.net, and PayPal Website Payments Pro (formerly known as VeriSign Payflow Pro)

- Store credit card numbers securely in a database

This third phase is the most involved and requires some hard and careful work. By the end of Phase III, however, you will have an e-commerce site with a searchable product catalog, shopping cart, secure checkout, and complete order-processing system.

TShirtShop

As we said earlier, we're going to build an online shop called TShirtShop (which will sell, surprisingly enough, t-shirts). Figure 1-1 shows how TShirtShop will look at some point during the second stage of development.

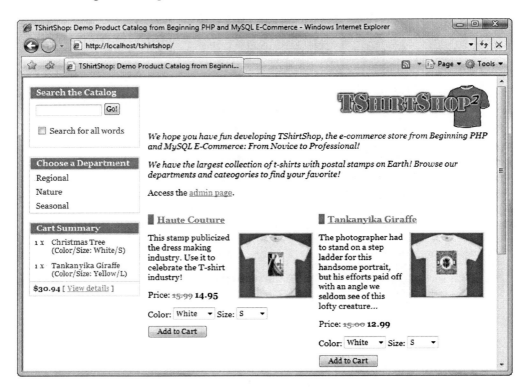

Figure 1-1. *TShirtShop during Phase II of development*

■**Tip** You can find a link to an online version of TShirtShop at http://www.cristiandarie.ro/php-mysql-ecommerce-2/. Many thanks go to the folks at Going Postal (http://www.goingpostal.cc) who allowed us to use some of their products to populate our virtual TShirtShop store.

For the purposes of this book, we'll assume that the client already exists as a mail-order company and has a good network of customers. The company is not completely new to the business and wants the site to make it easier and more enjoyable for its existing customers to buy—with the goal that customers will end up buying more.

Knowing this, we suggest the building and opening the TShirtShop web site in phases for the following reasons:

- The company is unlikely to get massive orders initially—we should keep the initial cost of building the web site down as much as possible.

- The company is accustomed to manually processing mail orders, so manually processing orders e-mailed by PayPal will not introduce many new problems.

- The company doesn't want to invest all of its money in a massive e-commerce site only to find that people actually prefer mail order after all! Or it might find that, after Phase I, the site does exactly what it wants, and there's no point in expanding it further. Either way, we hope that offering a lower initial cost gives our bid the edge (it might also mean we can get away with a higher total price).

Because this company is already a mail-order business, it probably already has a merchant account and can process credit cards. Therefore, moving on to Phase III as soon as possible would be best for this company, so it can benefit from the preferential card-processing rates.

Summary

In this chapter, we've discussed the positive financial and customer service aspects of including e-commerce in your business operation. In the real and sometimes hostile commercial world, where it's important to focus on raising short-term revenue and minimizing risk, an e-commerce site will help you by

- Increasing your customer base

- Persuading your customers to spend more

- Lowering your fulfillment costs

We've applied those principles to a three-phase plan that provides a deliverable, usable site at each stage and continues to expand throughout this book.

At this point, you've presented your plan to the owners of the t-shirt shop. In the next chapter, you'll put on your programming hat and start to design and build the web site (assuming you got the contract, of course).

CHAPTER 2

■■■

Laying Out the Foundations

Now that you've convinced the client that you can create a cool web site to complement his or her activity, it's time to stop celebrating and start thinking about how to put into practice all the promises you've made. As usual, when you lay down on paper the technical requirements you must meet, everything starts to seem a bit more complicated than initially anticipated.

To ensure this project's success, you need to come up with a smart way to implement what you agreed to when you signed the contract. You want to develop the project smoothly and quickly, but the ultimate goal is to make sure the client is satisfied with your work. Consequently, you should aim to provide your site's increasing number of visitors with a positive web experience by creating a pleasant, functional, and responsive web site.

The requirements are high, but this is normal for an e-commerce site today. To maximize the chances of success, we'll analyze and anticipate as many of the technical requirements as possible and implement solutions in a way that supports changes and additions with minimal effort. Your goals for this chapter are to

- Analyze the project from a technical point of view

- Analyze and choose the architecture for your application

- Decide which technologies, programming languages, and tools to use

- Consider naming and coding conventions

Note Be warned that this and the next few chapters are dense, and you may find them pretty challenging if you don't have much experience with PHP or MySQL. Books such as *Beginning PHP and MySQL 5: From Novice to Professional, Second Edition* (W. Jason Gilmore. Apress, 2006.) do a good job of preparing you to build your first e-commerce web site.

Also, we strongly recommend that you consistently follow an efficient project management methodology to maximize the chances of the project's success, on budget and on time. Most project management theories imply that you and your client have signed an initial requirements/specifications document containing the details of the project you're about to create. You can use this document as a guide while creating the solution; it also allows you to charge extra if the client brings new requirements or requests changes after development has started.

Designing for Growth

The word "design" in the context of a web application can mean many things. Its most popular usage probably refers to the visual and user interface design of a web site.

This aspect is crucial because, let's face it, the visitor is often more impressed with how a site looks and how easy it is to use than about which technologies and techniques are used behind the scenes or what operating system the web server is running. If the site is slow, hard to use, or easy to forget, it just doesn't matter what rocket science was used to create it.

Unfortunately, this truth makes many inexperienced programmers underestimate the importance of the way the invisible part of the site is implemented—the code, the database, and so on. The visual part of a site gets visitors interested to begin with, but its functionality makes them come back. A web site can sometimes be implemented very quickly based on certain initial requirements, but if not properly architected, it can become difficult, if not impossible, to change.

For any project of any size, some preparation must be done before starting to code. Still, no matter how much preparation and design work is done, the unexpected does happen, and hidden catches, new requirements, and changing rules always seem to work against deadlines. Even without these unexpected factors, site designers are often asked to change or add functionality many times after the project is finished and deployed. This will also be the case for TShirtShop, which will be implemented in three separate stages, as discussed in Chapter 1.

You will learn how to create the web site so that the site (or you) will not fall apart when functionality is extended or updates are made. Because this is a programming book, instead of focusing on how to design the user interface or on marketing techniques, we'll pay close attention to designing the code that makes them work.

The phrase "designing the code" can have different meanings; for example, we'll need to have a short talk about naming conventions. Yet, the most important aspect that we need to take a look at is the application architecture. The architecture refers to the way you split the code into smaller components (for example, the product search feature) for a simple piece of functionality. Although it might be easier to implement that functionality as quickly and as simply as possible in a single component, you gain great long-term advantages by creating smaller, more simple components that work together to achieve the desired result.

Before talking about the architecture itself, you must determine what you want from this architecture.

Meeting Long-Term Requirements with Minimal Effort

Apart from the fact that you want a fast web site, each of the phases of development we talked about in Chapter 1 brings new requirements that must be met.

Every time you proceed to a new stage, you want to be able to *reuse* most of the already existing solution. It would be very inefficient to redesign the whole site (not just the visual part but the code as well!) just because you need to add a new feature. You can make it easier to reuse a solution by planning ahead, so any new functionality that needs to be added can be plugged in with ease, rather than each change causing a new headache.

When building the web site, implementing a *flexible architecture* composed of pluggable components allows you to add new features—such as the shopping cart, the departments list, or the product search feature—by coding them as separate components and plugging them into the existing application. Achieving a good level of flexibility is one of the main goals regarding the application's architecture, and this chapter shows how you can put this into practice.

You'll see that the flexibility level is proportional to the amount of time required to design and implement it, so we'll try to find a compromise that will provide the best gains without complicating the code too much.

Another major requirement that is common to all online applications is having a *scalable architecture*. Scalability is defined as the capability to increase resources to yield a linear increase in service capacity. In other words, ideally, in a scalable system, the ratio (proportion) between the number of client requests and the hardware resources required to handle those requests is constant, even when the number of clients increases. An unscalable system can't deal with an increasing number of clients, no matter how many hardware resources are provided. Because we're optimistic about the number of customers, we must be sure that the site will be capable of delivering its functionality to a large number of clients without throwing out errors or performing sluggishly.

Reliability is also a critical aspect for an e-commerce application. With the help of a coherent error-handling strategy and a powerful relational database, you can ensure data integrity and ensure that noncritical errors are properly handled without bringing the site to its knees.

The Magic of the Three-Tier Architecture

Generally, the architecture refers to the way we split the code that implements a feature of the application into separate components based on what they do and grouping each kind of component into a single logical tier.

In particular, the three-tier architecture refers to an architecture that is based on these tiers:

- The presentation tier

- The business tier

- The data tier

The *presentation tier* contains the user interface elements of the site and includes all the logic that manages the interaction between the visitor and the client's business. This tier makes the whole site feel alive, and the way you design it has a crucial importance for the site's success. Because your application is a web site, its presentation tier is composed of dynamic web pages.

The *business tier* (also called the *middle tier*) receives requests from the presentation tier and returns a result to the presentation tier depending on the business logic it contains. Almost any event that happens in the presentation tier usually results in the business tier being called (utilized), except events that can be handled locally by the presentation tier, such as simple input data validation, and so on. For example, if the visitor is doing a product search, the presentation tier calls the business tier and says, "Please send me back the products that match this search criterion." Most of the time, the business tier needs to call the data tier for information to be able to respond to the presentation tier's request.

The *data tier* (sometimes referred to as the *database tier*) is responsible for managing the application's data and sending it to the business tier when requested. For the TShirtShop e-commerce site, you'll need to store data about products (including their categories and their departments), users, shopping carts, and so on. Almost every client request finally results in the data tier being interrogated for information (except when previously retrieved data has been cached at the business tier or presentation tier levels), so it's important to have a fast database system. In Chapters 4 and 5, you'll learn how to design the database for optimum performance.

These tiers are purely logical—there is no constraint on the physical location of each tier. In theory, you are free to place all of the application, and implicitly all of its tiers, on a single server machine, or you can place each tier on a separate machine if the application permits this. Chapter 22 explains how to integrate functionality from other web sites using XML Web Services. XML Web Services permit easy integration of functionality across multiple servers without the hassle of customized code.

An important constraint in the three-tier architecture model is that information must flow in sequential order among tiers. The presentation tier is only allowed to access the business tier, and it can never directly access the data tier. The business tier is the brain in the middle that communicates with the other tiers and processes and coordinates all the information flow. If the presentation tier directly accessed the data tier, the rules of three-tier architecture programming would be broken.

These rules may look like limitations at first, but when utilizing an architecture, you need to be consistent and obey its rules to reap the benefits. Sticking to the three-tier architecture ensures that your site remains easily updated or changed and adds a level of control over who or what can access your data. This may seem to be unnecessary overhead for you right now; however, there is a substantial future benefit of adhering to this system whenever you need to change your site's functioning or logic.

Figure 2-1 is a simple representation of the way data is passed in an application that implements the three-tier architecture.

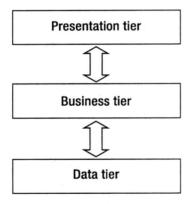

Figure 2-1. *Simple representation of the three-tier architecture*

A Simple Example Using the Three-Tier Architecture

It's easier to understand how data is passed and transformed between tiers if you take a closer look at a simple example. To make the example even more relevant to our project, let's analyze a situation that will actually happen in TShirtShop. This scenario is typical for three-tier applications.

Like most e-commerce sites, TShirtShop will have a shopping cart, which we will discuss later in the book. For now, it's enough to know that the visitor will add products to the shopping cart by clicking an Add to Cart button. Figure 2-2 shows how the information flows through the application when that button is clicked.

At step 1, the user clicks the Add to Cart button for a specific product. At step 2, the presentation tier (which contains the button) forwards the request to the business tier, "Hey, I want this product added to my shopping cart!" At step 3, the business tier receives the request, understands that the user wants a specific product added to the shopping cart, and handles the request by telling the data tier to update the visitor's shopping cart by adding the selected product. The data tier needs to be called, because it stores and manages the entire web site's data, including users' shopping cart information.

At step 4, the data tier updates the database and eventually returns a success code to the business tier. At step 5, the business tier handles the return code and any errors that might have occurred in the data tier while updating the database and then returns the output to the presentation tier.

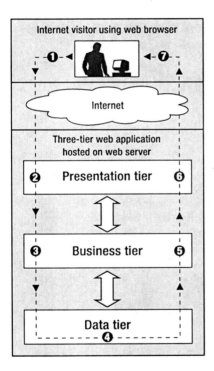

Figure 2-2. *Internet visitor interacting with a three-tier application*

At step 6, the presentation tier generates an updated view of the shopping cart. At step 7, the results of the execution are wrapped up by generating a Hypertext Markup Language (HTML) web page that is returned to the visitor where the updated shopping cart can be seen in the visitor's web browser.

Note that, in this simple example, the business tier doesn't do a lot of processing, and its business logic isn't very complex. However, if new business rules appear for your application, you would change the business tier. If, for example, the business logic specified that a product could be added to the shopping cart only if its quantity in stock was greater than zero, an additional data tier call would have been made to determine the quantity. The data tier would be requested to update the shopping cart only if products are in stock. In any case, the presentation tier is informed about the status and provides human-readable feedback to the visitor.

What's in a Number?

It's interesting to note how each tier interprets the same piece of information differently. For the data tier, the numbers and information it stores have no significance because this tier is an engine that saves, manages, and retrieves numbers, strings, or other data types—to the data tier this data is just arbitrary information, not product quantities or product names. In the context of the previous example, a product quantity of zero represents a simple, plain number without any meaning to the data tier (it is simply zero, a 32-bit integer).

The data only gains significance when the business tier reads it. When the business tier asks the data tier for a product quantity and gets a "0" result, this is interpreted by the business tier as, "Hey, no products in stock!" This data is finally wrapped in a nice, visual form by the presentation tier, such as a label reading, "Sorry, at the moment this product cannot be ordered."

Even if it's unlikely that you want to forbid a customer from adding a product to the shopping cart if the product is not in stock, the example (described in Figure 2-3) is good enough to present in yet another way how each of the three tiers has a different purpose.

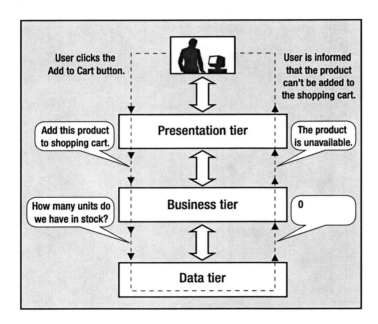

Figure 2-3. *Example of information exchange among application tiers*

The Right Logic for the Right Tier

Because each layer contains its own logic, sometimes it can be tricky to decide where exactly to draw the lines between tiers. In the previous scenario, instead of reading the product's quantity in the business tier and deciding whether the product is available based on that number (resulting ultimately in two database calls), you could have a single stored procedure named `add_product_if_available` that adds the product to the shopping cart only if it's available in stock.

In this scenario, some logic is transferred from the business tier to the data tier. In many other circumstances, you might have the option to place some logic in one tier or another or maybe in both. In most cases, there is no single best way to implement the three-tier architecture, and you'll need to make a compromise or a choice based on personal preference or external constraints.

Furthermore, there are occasions in which even though you know the *right* way (in respect to the architecture) to implement something, you might choose to break the rules to get a performance gain. As a general rule, if performance can be improved this way, it is OK to break the strict limits between tiers *just a little bit* (for example, add some of the business rules to the data tier or vice versa), *if* these rules are not likely to change in time. Otherwise, keeping all the business rules in the middle tier is preferable, because it generates a cleaner application that is easier to maintain.

Finally, don't be tempted to access the data tier directly from the presentation tier. This is a common mistake that is the shortest path to a complicated, hard-to-maintain, and inflexible system. In many data access tutorials or introductory materials, you'll be shown how to perform basic database operations using a simple user interface application. In these kinds of programs, all the logic is probably written in a short, single file, instead of separate tiers. Although the materials might be very good, keep in mind that most of these texts are meant to teach you how to do different individual tasks (for example, access a database), and not how to correctly create a flexible and scalable application.

A Three-Tier Architecture for TShirtShop

Implementing a three-tier architecture for the TShirtShop web site will help achieve the goals listed at the beginning of the chapter. The coding discipline, imposed by a system that might seem rigid at first sight, allows for excellent levels of flexibility and extensibility in the long run.

Splitting major parts of the application into separate smaller components encourages reusability. More than once when adding new features to the site, you'll see that you can reuse some of the already existing bits. Adding a new feature without needing to change much of what already exists is, in itself, a good example of reusability.

Another advantage of the three-tiered architecture is that, if properly implemented, the overall system is resistant to changes. When bits in one of the tiers change, the other tiers usually remain unaffected, sometimes even in extreme cases. For example, if for some reason the back-end database system is changed (say, the manager decides to use PostgreSQL instead of MySQL), you only need to update the data tier and maybe just a little bit of the business tier.

Why Not Use More Tiers?

The three-tier architecture we've been talking about so far is a particular (and the most popular) version of the *n*-tier architecture. *n-tier architecture* refers to splitting the solution into a number (*n*) of logical tiers. In complex projects, sometimes it makes sense to split the business layer into more than one layer, thus resulting in architecture with more than three layers. However, for our web site, it makes the most sense to stick with the three-layered design, which offers most of the benefits while not requiring too many hours of design or a complex hierarchy of framework code to support the architecture.

Maybe with a more involved and complex architecture, you could achieve even higher levels of flexibility and scalability for the application, but you would need much more time for design before starting to implement anything. As with any programming project, you must find a fair balance between the time required to design the architecture and the time spent to implement it. The three-tier architecture is best suited to projects with average complexity, such as the TShirtShop web site.

You also might be asking the opposite question, "Why not use fewer tiers?" A two-tier architecture, also called *client-server* architecture, can be appropriate for less complex projects. In short, a two-tier architecture requires less time for planning and allows quicker development in the beginning; however, it generates an application that's harder to maintain and extend in the long run. Because we're expecting to have to extend the application in the future, the client-server architecture is not appropriate for our application, so it won't be discussed further in this book.

Now that the general architecture is known, let's see what technologies and tools you will use to implement it. We'll have a brief discussion of the technologies, and in Chapter 3, you'll create the foundation of the presentation and data tiers by creating the first page of the site and the back-end database. You'll start implementing real functionality in each of the three tiers in Chapter 4 when you start creating the web site's product catalog.

Choosing Technologies and Tools

No matter which architecture is chosen, a major question that arises in every development project is which technologies, programming languages, and tools are going to be used, bearing in mind that external requirements can seriously limit your options.

In this book, we're creating a web site using PHP 5, MySQL 5, and related technologies. We really like these technologies, but it doesn't necessarily mean they're the best choice for any kind of project, in any circumstances. Additionally, there are many situations in which you must use specific technologies because of client requirements. The Requirements Analysis stage that is present in most software development process will determine which technologies you must use for creating the application.

Although the book assumes some previous experience with PHP and MySQL, we'll take a quick look at them and see how they fit into our project and into the three-tier architecture.

Using PHP to Generate Dynamic Web Content

PHP is an open source technology for building dynamic, interactive web content. Its short description (on the official PHP web site, http://www.php.net) is "PHP is a widely-used general-purpose scripting language that is especially suited for web development and can be embedded into HTML."

PHP stands for PHP: Hypertext Preprocessor (yes, it's a recursive acronym) and is available for free download at its official web site. The story of PHP, having its roots somewhere in 1994, is a successful one. Among the factors that led to its success are the following:

- PHP is free; especially when combined with Linux server software, PHP can prove to be a very cost-efficient technology to build dynamic web content.

- PHP has a shorter learning curve than other scripting languages.

- The PHP community is agile. Many useful helper libraries or new versions of the existing libraries are being developed (such as those you can find in the PEAR repository or at http://www.phpclasses.org), and new features are added frequently.

- PHP works very well on a variety of web servers and operating systems (Unix-like platforms, Windows, and Mac OS).

However, PHP is not the only server-side scripting language around for creating dynamic web pages. Among its most popular competitors are JavaServer Pages (JSP), Perl, ColdFusion, and ASP.NET. Among these technologies are many differences but also some fundamental similarities. For example, pages written with any of these technologies are composed of basic HTML, which draws the static part of the page (the template), and code that generates the dynamic part.

■**Note** You might want to check out *Beginning ASP.NET 2.0 E-Commerce in C# 2005* (Cristian Darie and Karli Watson. Apress, 2005.), which explains how to build e-commerce web sites with ASP.NET 2.0, C#, and SQL Server 2005.

Using Smarty to Separate Layout from Code

Because PHP is simple and easy to start with, it has always been tempting to start coding without properly designing an architecture and framework that would be beneficial in the long run.

What makes things even worse is that the straightforward method of building PHP pages is to mix PHP instructions with HTML because PHP doesn't have, by default, an obvious technique of separating the PHP code from the HTML layout information.

Mixing the PHP logic with HTML has two important disadvantages:

- This technique often leads to long, complicated, and hard-to-manage code. Maybe you have seen those kilometric source files with an unpleasant mixture of PHP and HTML, which are hard to read and impossible to understand after a week.

- These mixed files are the subject of both designers' and programmers' work, which complicates the collaboration more than necessary. This also increases the chances of the designer creating bugs in the code logic while working on cosmetic changes.

These kinds of problems led to the development of template engines, which offer frameworks separating the presentation logic from the static HTML layout. Smarty (http://smarty.php.net) is the most popular and powerful template engine for PHP. Its main purpose is to offer you a simple way to separate application logic (PHP code) from its presentation code (HTML).

This separation permits the programmer and the template designer to work independently on the same application. The programmer can change the PHP logic without needing to change the template files, and the designer can change the templates without caring how the code that makes them alive works.

Figure 2-4 shows the relationship between the Smarty design template file and its Smarty plug-in file.

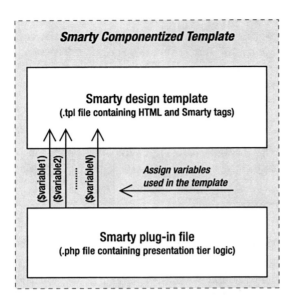

Figure 2-4. *Smarty componentized template*

The Smarty design template (a `.tpl` file containing the HTML layout and Smarty-specific tags and code) and its Smarty plug-in file (a `.php` file containing the associated code for the template) form a *Smarty componentized template*.

In practice, we'll not create a Smarty plug-in file for each template, as shown in Figure 2-4. Instead, we'll create a generic Smarty plug-in that integrates with all your Smarty templates, loading the necessary presentation objects. Presentation objects are classes that provide the template files with the data they need.

You'll learn more about how Smarty works while you're building the e-commerce web site. For a concise introduction to Smarty, read the Smarty Crash Course at `http://smarty.php.net/crashcourse.php`. For a detailed reference, we recommend *Smarty PHP Template Programming and Applications* (Hasin Hayder, J. P. Maia, and Lucian Gheorghe. Packt Publishing, 2006.).

■**Note** Adding Smarty or another templating engine to a web application's architecture adds some initial coding effort and also implies a learning curve. However, you should try it anyway, because the advantages of using such a modern development technique will prove to be significant later in the process.

What About the Alternatives?

Smarty is not the only template engine available for PHP. You can find many others by Googling for "PHP template engines." You can find the most popular of them nicely listed by Justin Silverton in his article "Top 25 PHP Template Engines" (your favorite search engine will help you, once again, find the article).

Although all template engines follow the same basic principles, we chose to use Smarty in the PHP e-commerce project for this book because of its very good performance results, powerful features (such as template compilation and caching), and wide acceptance in the industry.

Using MySQL to Store Web Site Data

Most of the data your visitors will see while browsing the web site will be retrieved from a relational database. A relational database management system (RDBMS) is a complex software program, the purpose of which is to store, manage, and retrieve data as quickly and reliably as possible. For the TShirtShop web site, it will store all data regarding the products, departments, users, shopping carts, and so on.

Many RDBMSs are available for you to use with PHP, including MySQL, PostgreSQL, Oracle, and so on. However, both formal surveys and real-world practice show MySQL is truly the leading database choice for PHP-driven projects.

MySQL is the world's most popular open source database, and it's a free (for noncommercial use), fast, and reliable database. Another important advantage is that many web hosting providers offer access to a MySQL database, which makes your life easier when going live with your newly created e-commerce web site. We'll use MySQL as the back-end database when developing the TShirtShop e-commerce web site.

The language used to communicate with a relational database is SQL (SQL Query Language, or, according to older specifications, Structured Query Language). However, each database engine recognizes a particular dialect of this language. If you decide to use a different RDBMS than MySQL, you'll probably need to update some of the SQL queries.

Getting in Touch with MySQL

You talk with the database server by formulating an SQL query, sending it to the database engine, and retrieving the results. The SQL query can say anything related to the web site data, or its data structures, such as "give me the list of departments," "remove product number 223," "create a data table," or "search the catalog for yellow t-shirts."

No matter what the SQL query says, we need a way to send it to MySQL. MySQL ships with a simple, text-based interface (named mysql) that permits executing SQL queries and gets back the results. If you find it difficult to use, don't worry; there are alternatives to the command-line interface. Several free, third-party database administration tools allow you to manipulate data structures and execute SQL queries via an easy-to-use graphical interface. Many web-hosting companies offer database access through phpMyAdmin (which is the most widely used MySQL web client interface), which is another good reason for you to get familiar with this tool. However, you can use the visual client of your choice. A popular desktop tool for interacting with MySQL databases is Toad for MySQL (http://www.quest.com/toad-for-mysql/).

Apart from needing to interact with MySQL via a direct interface to its engine, you also need to learn how to access MySQL programmatically from PHP code. This requirement is obvious, because the e-commerce web site will need to query the database to retrieve catalog information (departments, categories, products, and so on) when building pages for the visitors.

As for querying MySQL databases through PHP code, the tool you'll rely on here is the PHP Data Objects (PDO) extension.

Implementing Database Integration Using PDO

PDO (PHP Data Objects) is a native data-access abstraction library that ships with PHP starting from version 5.1 and is offered as a PECL extension for PHP 5.0 (PECL is a repository of PHP extensions, located at http://pecl.php.net/). The official PDO manual, together with installation instructions, is available at http://php.net/pdo.

PDO offers a uniform way to access a variety of data sources. Using PDO increases your application's portability and flexibility, because if the back-end database changes, the effects on your data-access code are kept to a minimum (in many cases, all that needs to change is the connection string for the new database).

After you become familiar with the PDO data-access abstraction layer, you can use the same programming techniques on other projects that might require a different database solution.

To demonstrate the difference between accessing the database using the old PHP functions and PDO, let's take a quick look at two short PHP code snippets.

▮**Note** If you aren't familiar with how the code works, don't worry—we'll analyze everything in greater detail in the following chapters.

The following shows database access using PHP native (MySQL-specific) functions:

```
// Connecting to MySQL
$link = mysql_connect('localhost', $username, $password);

if (!$link)
{
   die ('Could not connect: ' . mysql_error());
}

$db_selected = mysql_select_db('tshirtshop', $link);

if (!$db_selected)
{
   die ('Could not select database : ' . mysql_error());
}

// Execute SQL query
$queryString = 'SELECT * FROM product';

$result = mysql_query($queryString);

if (!$result)
{
   die ('Query failed : ' . mysql_error());
}

// Close connection
mysql_close($link);
```

Note If you are still planning to use PHP MySQL extension instead of PDO in your projects, you should consider using the PHP MySQL improved extension (mysqli). You can find more details about the PHP MySQL improved extension at http://www.php.net/manual/en/ref.mysqli.php.

Next, the same action is shown, this time using PDO:

```
try
{
  // Create a new PDO instance
  $database_handler =
    new PDO('mysql:host=localhost;dbname=tshirtshop',
            $username, $password);

  // Build the SQL query
  $sqlQuery = 'SELECT * FROM product';

  // Execute SQL query
  $statement_handler = $database_handler->query($sqlQuery);

  // Fetch data
  $result = $statement_handler->fetchAll(PDO::FETCH_ASSOC);

  // Clear the PDO object instance
  $database_handler = null;
}
catch (PDOException $e)
{
  /* If something goes wrong we catch the exception thrown by
     the object, print the message, and stop the execution of
     script */
  print 'Error! <br />' . $e->getMessage() . '<br />';

  exit;
}
```

The version of the code that uses PDO is longer, but it includes a powerful error-handling mechanism—a very helpful tool when debugging your application If these concepts sound foreign, once again, wait until the later chapters where we'll put PDO to work, and you'll learn more about it there.

Also, when using PDO, you won't need to change the data access code if, for example, you decide to use PostgreSQL instead of MySQL. On the other hand, the first code snippet, which uses MySQL-specific functions, would need to change completely (use pg_connect and pg_query instead of mysql_connect and mysql_query, and so on). In addition, some PostgreSQL-specific functions have different parameters than the similar MySQL functions.

When using a database abstraction layer (such as PDO), you'll probably only need to change the connection string when changing the database back end. Note that here we're only talking about the PHP code that interacts with the database. In practice, you might also need to update some SQL queries if the database engines support different dialects of SQL.

Note To keep your SQL queries as portable as possible, keep their syntax as close as possible to the SQL-92 standard. You'll learn more about SQL details in Chapter 4.

MySQL and the Three-Tier Architecture

It is clear by now that MySQL is somehow related to the data tier. However, if you haven't worked with databases until now, it might be less than obvious that MySQL is more than a simple store of data. Apart from the actual data stored inside, MySQL is also capable of storing logic in the form of stored procedures, to maintain table relationships, to ensure various data integrity rules are obeyed, and so on.

You can communicate with MySQL through SQL, which is a language used to interact with the database. SQL is used to transmit to the database instructions such as "send me the last 10 orders" or "delete product number 123."

Although it's possible to compose SQL statements in your PHP code and then submit them for execution, this is generally a *bad practice*, because it incurs security, consistency, and performance penalties. In our solution, we'll store all data tier logic using *database functions*.

The code presented in this book was tested with MySQL 5.0 and MySQL 5.1. The role of the MySQL server in the three-tier architecture is described in Figure 2-5.

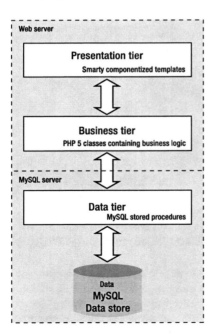

Figure 2-5. *The technologies you'll use to develop TShirtShop*

Choosing Naming and Coding Standards

Although coding and naming standards might not seem that important at first, they definitely shouldn't be overlooked. Not following a set of rules for your code will almost always result in code that's hard to read, understand, and maintain. On the other hand, when you follow a consistent way of coding, you can almost say your code is already half documented, which is an important contribution toward the project's maintainability, especially when multiple people are working on the same project at the same time.

Tip Some companies have their own policies regarding coding and naming standards, whereas in other cases, you'll have the flexibility to use your own preferences. In either case, the golden rule to follow is *be consistent in the way you code*. Commenting your code is another good practice that improves the long-term maintainability of your code.

Naming conventions refer to many elements within a project, simply because almost all of a project's elements have names: the project itself, files, classes, variables, methods, method parameters, database tables, database columns, and so on. Without some discipline when naming all those elements, after a week of coding, you won't understand a single line of what you've written.

When developing TShirtShop, we followed a set of naming conventions that are popular among PHP developers. Some of the most important rules are summarized here and in the piece of code that follows:

- Class names and method names should be written using Pascal casing (uppercase letters for the first letter in every word), such as WarZone.

- Public class attribute names follow the same rules as class names but should be prepended with the character "m". So, valid public attribute names look like this: $mSomeSoldier.

- Private class attribute names follow the same rules as public class attribute names, except they're also prepended with an underscore, such as in $_mSomeOtherSoldier.

- Method argument names should use camel casing (uppercase letters for the first letter in every word except the first one), such as $someEnemy, $someOtherEnemy.

- Variable names should be written in lowercase, with an underscore as the word separator, such as $master_of_war.

- Database objects use the same conventions as variable names (the department_id column).

- Try to indent your code using a fixed number of spaces (say, four) for each level. (The code in this book uses two spaces because of physical space limitations.)

Here's a sample code snippet:

```
class WarZone
{
  public  $mSomeSoldier;
  private $_mSomeOtherSoldier;

  function SearchAndDestroy($someEnemy, $someOtherEnemy)
  {
    $master_of_war = 'Soldier';

    $this->mSomeSoldier = $someEnemy;
    $this->_mSomeOtherSoldier = $someOtherEnemy;
  }
}
```

Among the decisions that need to be made is whether to use quotes for strings. JavaScript, HTML, and PHP allow using both single quotes and double quotes. For the code in this book, we'll use double quotes in HTML and JavaScript code, and we'll use single quotes in PHP. Although for JavaScript it's a matter of taste (you can use single quotes, as long as you use them consistently), in PHP, the single quotes are processed faster, are more secure, and are less likely to cause programming errors. Learn more about PHP strings at http://php.net/ types.string. You can find two useful articles on PHP strings at http://www.sitepoint.com/print/ quick-php-tips and http://www.jeroenmulder.com/weblog/2005/04/php_single_and_double_ quotes.php.

Summary

Hey, we covered a lot of ground in this chapter, didn't we? We talked about the three-tier architecture and how it helps you create great flexible and scalable applications. We also saw how each of the technologies used in this book fits into the three-tier architecture.

If you feel overwhelmed, please don't worry. In the next chapter, we will begin to create the first part of our site. We will explain each step as we go, so you will have a clear understanding of each element of the application.

CHAPTER 3

■ ■ ■

Starting the TShirtShop Project

Now that the theoretical foundations of the project have been laid, it's time to start putting them to work. In this chapter, we'll implement the first page for the TShirtShop web site. In this chapter, you will

- Install and configure the necessary software on your development machine

- Create the basic structure of the web site

- Implement an error-handling routine and a reporting routine in the site skeleton

- Set up the database that will be used to store catalog data, customer orders, and so on

Subsequent chapters will build on this foundation to create the product catalog with department and category navigation, product lists, product details pages, and much more.

Note Be warned that this and the next few chapters are dense, and you may found them pretty challenging if you don't have much experience with PHP or MySQL 5. Books such as *Beginning PHP and MySQL 5: From Novice to Professional, Second Edition* (W. Jason Gilmore. Apress, 2006) do a good job at preparing you to build your first e-commerce web site.

So far, we have dealt with theory regarding the application you're going to create. It was fun, but it's going to be even more interesting to put into practice what you've learned up until now. The code in this book has been tested with

- PHP 5.2

- Apache 2.2

- MySQL 5

Caution The code is most likely to be compatible with newer versions of the mentioned software, but it won't work with versions of PHP older than PHP 5.

Most of this project should work with other web servers as well, as long as they're compatible with PHP (see http://www.php.net/manual/en/installation.php). The URL rewriting feature makes use of mod_rewrite, which is an Apache module. If you decide to use another web server, you may need to make changes to the URL rewriting code you'll find in Chapter 7. Apache, however, is the web server of choice for the vast majority of PHP projects.

Getting a Code Editor

Before writing the first line of code, you'll need to install a code editor, if you don't already have a favorite on your machine. Many free editors are available, and there is an ever longer list of commercial editors. The one you use is a matter of taste and money. You can find a list of PHP editors at http://www.php-editors.com. Here are a few of the most popular:

- Zend Studio (http://www.zend.com/products/zend_studio) is the most powerful integrated development environment (IDE) available for developing PHP web applications.

- phpEclipse (http://www.phpeclipse.net) is an increasingly popular environment for developing PHP web applications. Zend is also a member of the Eclipse foundation.

- Emacs (http://www.gnu.org/software/emacs/) is, as defined on its web site, an "extensible, customizable, self-documenting real-time display editor." Emacs is a very powerful, free, and cross-platform editor.

- SciTe (http://scintilla.sourceforge.net/SciTEDownload.html) is a free and cross-platform editor.

- PSPad (http://www.pspad.com/) is a freeware editor popular among Windows developers. The editor knows how to highlight the syntax for many existing file formats. Additional plug-ins can add integrated CSS editing functionality and spell checking.

- PHP Designer 2006 (http://www.mpsoftware.dk) is a Windows editor that contains an integrated debugger.

Installing XAMPP

XAMPP is a package created by Apache Friends (http://www.apachefriends.org), which includes Apache, PHP, MySQL, and many other goodies. If you don't have these already installed on your machine, the easiest way to have them running is to install XAMPP. XAMPP ships in Linux, Windows, Mac OS X, and Solaris versions.

If you prefer to install Apache, PHP, and MySQL yourself, you will also need to install and configure the following modules, which are needed in various stages of TShirtShop development: PDO, PDO driver for MySQL, cURL, mcrypt, and mhash. Additionally, for the third stage of development, when you start working with your customers' credit card and personal information, you will need to install SSL support in Apache.

Tip Our web-hosting friends at http://nexcess.net are offering special discount prices for the readers of this book. Their servers are also configured to run TShirtShop.

Follow the steps of the exercise to install XAMPP on your Windows machine. The installation instructions for Linux are presented afterward, in a separate exercise. Mac OS X users can find their version of the software, together with installation instructions, at http://www.apachefriends.org/en/xampp-macosx.html.

For more information about installing XAMPP, you can check out its Installation wiki page at http://www.installationwiki.org/XAMPP.

Exercise: Installing XAMPP on Windows

Here are the steps you should follow:

1. Visit http://www.apachefriends.org/en/xampp-windows.html, and download the XAMPP installer package, which should be an executable file named something like xampp-win32-version-installer.exe.

2. Execute the installer executable. Leave the default options for the first few setup screens. We recommend that you install XAMPP in the root folder of your drive, such as C:\xampp. When asked, choose to install Apache and MySQL as services, as shown in Figure 3-1. Then click Install.

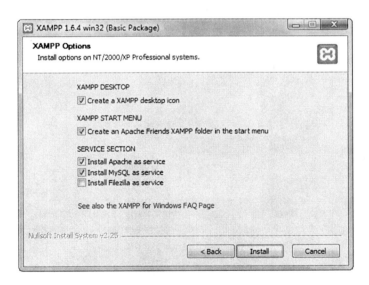

Figure 3-1. *Setting XAMPP installation options*

3. Next, you'll be asked to confirm the installation of each of these as services. You don't need to install the FileZilla FTP server, because we're not using it in this book, but do install Apache and MySQL as services.

■**Note** You can't have more than one web server working on port 80 (the default port used for HTTP communication). If you already have a web server on your machine, such as IIS, you should make it use another port, uninstall it, or deactivate it. Otherwise, Apache won't work. To make Apache work on another port, you should edit C:\xampp\apache\conf\httpd.conf and locate lines containing Listen 80 and ServerName localhost:80, and replace the value 80 with the port number of your choice (8080 is a typical choice for a second web server).

4. In the end, confirm the execution of the XAMPP Control Panel, which can be used for administering the installed services. Figure 3-2 shows the XAMPP Control Panel.

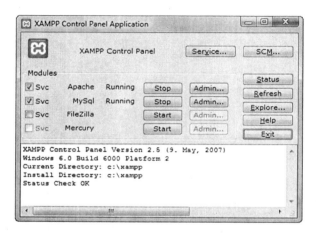

Figure 3-2. *The XAMPP Control Panel*

5. To test that Apache installed correctly, load http://localhost/ (or http://localhost:8080/ if Apache works on port 8080) using your web browser. The XAMPP welcome screen like the one in Figure 3-3 should load.

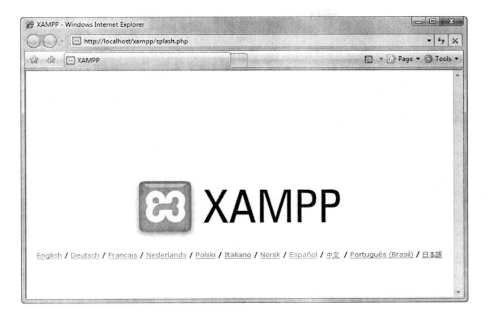

Figure 3-3. *Testing XAMPP installation*

Exercise: Installing XAMPP on Linux

Here are the steps you should follow:

1. Visit http://www.apachefriends.org/en/xampp-linux.html, and download the XAMPP package, which should be an archive file named something like xampp-linux-X.Y.Z.tar.gz.

2. Execute the following command from a Linux shell logged as the system administrator root:

   ```
   tar xvfz xampp-linux-X.Y.Z.tar.gz -C /opt
   ```

   This will extract the downloaded archive file to /opt.

■**Note** You can't have more web servers working on port 80 (the default port used for HTTP communication). If you already have a web server on your machine, you should make it use another port, uninstall it, or deactivate it. Otherwise, Apache won't work. To make Apache work on another port, you should edit /opt/lampp/etc/httpd.conf, locate the lines containing Listen 80 and ServerName localhost:80, and replace the value 80 with the port number of your choice (usually the 8080 is used).

3. To start XAMPP simply call the following command:

   `/opt/lampp/lampp start`

   To restart XAMPP replace `start` in the previous command with `restart`, and to stop XAMPP, replace it with `stop`.

4. To test that Apache installed correctly, load `http://localhost/` (or `http://localhost:8080/` if Apache works on port 8080) using your web browser. The XAMPP welcome screen like the one in Figure 3-3 should load.

Preparing the tshirtshop Alias

One of the advantages of working with open source, platform-independent technologies is that you can choose the operating system to use for development. You should be able to develop and run TShirtShop on Windows, Unix, Linux, Mac OS, and others. However, this also means that you may struggle a little bit while setting up your environment, especially if you're a beginner.

When setting up the project's folder, a few details differ depending on the operating system (mostly because of the different file paths), so we'll cover them separately for Windows and for Linux systems in the following pages. However, the main steps are the same for all platforms:

1. Create a folder `tshirtshop` on your disk (we use lowercase for folder names), which will contain the TShirtShop project's files (such as PHP code, image files, and so on).

2. Edit Apache's configuration file (`httpd.conf`) to create an alias named `tshirtshop` that points to the `tshirtshop` physical folder created earlier. This way, when pointing a web browser to `http://localhost/tshirtshop`, the project in the `tshirtshop` physical folder will be loaded. This functionality is implemented in Apache using aliases, which are configured through the `httpd.conf` configuration file. The syntax of an alias entry is as follows:

   `Alias alias_name real_folder_name`

▓**Tip** The `httpd.conf` configuration file is well self-documented, but you can also check the Apache 2 documentation available at `http://httpd.apache.org/docs-2.0/`.

If you're working on Windows, use the steps in the following exercise to configure your `tshirtshop` working folder. The steps for Linux systems will follow after this exercise.

Exercise: Preparing the tshirtshop Alias on Windows

1. Create a new folder named tshirtshop, which will be used for all the work you'll do in this book. We assume that you create it in the root folder C:\ (because we'll use relative paths in the project, you can choose any location that can be accessed by your Apache folder).

2. The default place used by Apache (in XAMPP setup) to serve client requests from is C:\xampp\htdocs. This location is defined by the DocumentRoot directive in the Apache configuration file, which is located in C:\xampp\apache\conf\httpd.conf.

   Because we want to use our folder instead of the default folder mentioned by DocumentRoot, we need to create an alias named tshirtshop that points to the tshirtshop physical folder you created in Step 1. Open the Apache configuration file (httpd.conf), find the aliases section (which is defined by the <IfModule alias_module> configuration tag), and add the following lines:

```
<IfModule alias_module>
  # ...
  # Configure the tshirtshop alias
  Alias /tshirtshop/ "C:/tshirtshop/"
  Alias /tshirtshop "C:/tshirtshop"
</IfModule>
<Directory "C:/tshirtshop">
  Options Indexes FollowSymLinks
  AllowOverride All
  Order allow,deny
  Allow from all
</Directory>
```

   After adding these lines and restarting the Apache web server, a request for http://localhost/tshirtshop or http://localhost/tshirtshop/ will load the application in the tshirtshop folder (once it exists).

3. Create a file named test.php in the tshirtshop folder, with the following line inside:

```
<?php phpinfo(); ?>
```

4. Restart the Apache web server (the easiest way to do this is by using the XAMPP Control Panel). Restarting the server is necessary, because we've made changes to the Apache configuration file.

5. Load http://localhost/tshirtshop/test.php (or http://localhost:8080/tshirtshop/test.php if Apache works on port 8080) in a web browser.

Exercise: Preparing the tshirtshop Alias on Linux Systems

1. Create a new folder named tshirtshop, which will be used for all the work you'll do in this book. You might find it easiest to create it in your home directory (in which case the complete path to your tshirtshop folder will be something like /home/username/tshirtshop), but because we'll use relative paths in the project, feel free to create it in any location.

2. The default place used by Apache to serve client requests from is usually something like /opt/lampp/htdocs. This location is defined by the DocumentRoot directive in the Apache configuration file, whose complete path is usually /opt/lampp/etc/httpd.conf.

   Because we want to use our folder instead of the default folder mentioned by DocumentRoot, we need to create an alias named tshirtshop that points to the tshirtshop physical folder you created in Step 1. Open the Apache configuration file (httpd.conf), find the aliases section (which is defined by the <IfModule alias_module> configuration tag), and add the following lines:

```
<IfModule alias_module>
  # ...
  # Configure the tshirtshop alias
  Alias /tshirtshop/ "/home/username/tshirtshop/"
  Alias /tshirtshop "/home/username/tshirtshop"
</IfModule>
<Directory "/home/username/tshirtshop">
  Options Indexes FollowSymLinks
  AllowOverride All
  Order allow,deny
  Allow from all
</Directory>
```

   After adding these lines, a request for http://localhost/tshirtshop or http://localhost/tshirtshop/ will result in the application in the tshirtshop folder (once it exists) being executed.

3. Create a file named test.php in the tshirtshop folder, with the following line inside:

```
<?php phpinfo(); ?>
```

4. Restart the Apache web server (this is necessary because we've made changes to the Apache configuration file). Then load http://localhost/tshirtshop/test.php (or http://localhost:8080/tshirtshop/test.php if Apache works on port 8080) in a web browser.

How It Works: Preparing the tshirtshop Alias on Windows and Linux

This first step toward building the TShirtShop e-commerce site is a small but a very important one, because it allows you to test that Apache, PHP, and the tshirtshop alias work OK. If you have problems running the test page, make sure you followed the previous XAMPP installation steps correctly.

No matter whether you're working on Windows or a Linux flavor, loading test.php in a web browser should give you the PHP information returned by the phpinfo() function as shown in Figure 3-4.

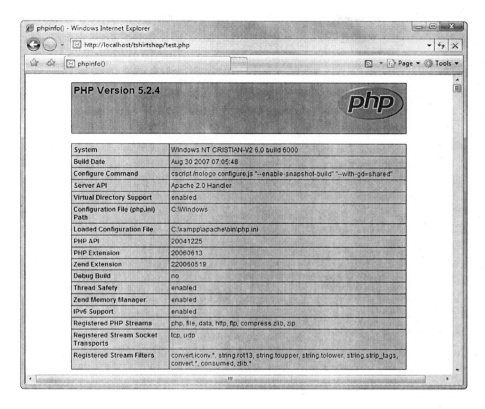

Figure 3-4. *Testing PHP and the tshirtshop alias*

You also ensured that the tshirtshop directory and all its contents can be accessed properly by the web server.

Installing Smarty

Installing Smarty requires simply copying the Smarty PHP classes to your project's folder. Many web-hosting companies provide these classes for you, but it's better to have your own installation for two reasons:

- It's always preferable to make your project independent of the server's settings, when possible.

- Even if the hosting system has Smarty installed, that company's version might be changed in time, perhaps without notice, possibly affecting your web site's functionality.

In the following exercise, you'll install Smarty into a subfolder of the tshirtshop folder named libs. The steps should work the same no matter what operating system you're running.

Exercise: Installing Smarty

1. Create a folder named `libs` inside the `tshirtshop` folder, and then create a folder named `smarty` inside the `libs` folder.

2. Download the latest stable release of Smarty from `http://smarty.php.net/download.php`. The archive is a `.tar.gz` file. To open it under Windows, you'll need a program such as WinRar (`http://www.rarlabs.com`) or WinZip (`http://www.winzip.com`).

3. Open the downloaded Smarty archive, and copy *the contents* of the `Smarty-2.X.Y/libs` directory from the archive to the folder you created earlier (`tshirtshop/libs/smarty`). You only need to copy the contents of the mentioned `libs` folder, nothing more. (With Smarty 2.6.18, the latest version of Smarty we've used for our tests, your `tshirtshop/libs/smarty` folder contains four `.php` files, and two other folders: `internals` and `plugins`.)

4. To operate correctly, Smarty needs three working folders, which you need to create: `templates`, `templates_c`, and `configs`. Create a folder named `presentation` inside the `tshirtshop` directory, and in this folder, create the two folders named `templates` and `templates_c`. The `presentation` folder will contain all the files of the TShirtShop presentation layer.

5. Create a folder named `include` in the `tshirtshop` folder. This folder will store all the configuration files of the application. Inside this folder, create a folder named `configs`; we'll use this latter one to store Smarty-specific configuration data.

6. If you're using a Linux or Unix operating system, you also need to ensure that Apache has write access to the `templates_c` directory, where the Smarty engine needs to save its compiled template files (you'll learn more about this a bit later). Execute the following command to ensure that your Apache server can access your project's files and has write permissions to the `templates_c` directory:

```
chmod a+w /home/username/tshirtshop/presentation/templates_c
```

▩Note Setting permissions on a Linux or Unix system as shown here allows any user with a shell account on your Linux box to view the source code of any files in your folder, including PHP code and other data (which might include sensitive information such as database passwords, keys used to encrypt/decrypt credit card information, and so on). To fine-tune the security settings, consult your system administrator.

7. Check the errata page of this book for updated instructions about Smarty installation and configuration. This way we make sure you don't run into trouble, should any future version of Smarty break any existing TShirtShop functionality. You can find a link to the errata page at `http://www.cristiandarie.ro/php-mysql-ecommerce-2/` or at `http://www.apress.com`.

How It Works: The Smarty Installation

In this exercise, you created these three folders used by Smarty:

- The `templates` folder will contain the Smarty templates for your web site (`.tpl` files).

- The `templates_c` folder will contain the compiled Smarty templates. These are `.php` files that Smarty generates automatically when parsing the `.tpl` templates. The compiled templates are regenerated whenever the source `.tpl` templates are modified.

- The `configs` folder will contain configuration files you might need for templates.

After adding these folders, your folder structure should look like this:

```
tshirtshop/
  include/
    configs/
  libs/
    smarty/
      internals/
      plugins/
  presentation/
    templates/
    templates_c/
```

Implementing the Site Skeleton

The visual design of the site is usually agreed on after a discussion with the client and in collaboration with a professional web designer. Alternatively, you can buy a web site template from one of the many companies that offer this kind of service for a reasonable price.

There is an incredible amount of literature available to help with visual design, layout, CSS, usability, findability, and other aspects related to web development. Each of these topics is critical in today's highly competitive online world. This being a programming book, our primary focus will regard the technical aspects of building TShirtShop. However, as a responsible web developer, you should not lose sight of the other essential elements of the Web ecosystem. If you haven't already, we strongly recommend you check at least some of these resources:

- *Don't Make Me Think: A Common Sense Approach to Web Usability*, Second Edition, by Steve Krug (New Riders Press, 2005)

- *Prioritizing Web Usability* by Jakob Nielsen and Hoa Loranger (New Riders Press, 2006)

- *Designing Interfaces: Patterns for Effective Interaction Design* by Jenifer Tidwell (O'Reilly, 2005)

- *Web Accessibility: Web Standards and Regulatory Compliance* by Andrew Kirkpatrick, Richard Rutter, Christian Heilmann, Jim Thatcher, and Cynthia Waddell (friends of ED, 2006)

- *Ambient Findability* by Peter Morville (O'Reilly, 2005)

- *Bulletproof Web Design*, Second Edition, by Dan Cederholm (New Riders Press, 2007)

- *Professional Search Engine Optimization with PHP: A Developer's Guide to SEO* by Cristian Darie and Jaimie Sirovich (Wrox Press, 2007)

For TShirtShop, we will implement a simple, yet friendly and usable design, which will allow for easy customization and will allow you to focus on the technical details of the site. To help us keep our focus on the technical aspects of TShirtShop, when creating the web site's layout, we'll be using a framework called Yahoo User Interface Library (YUI). This will allow us to implement our simple interface, which looks the same in today's modern browsers, even if we are not experts in CSS. The official web site of YUI is located at http://developer.yahoo.com/yui/. All pages in TShirtShop, including the first page, will have the structure shown in Figure 3-5.

Although the detailed structure of the product catalog is covered in the next chapter, right now, we know that a main list of departments needs to be displayed on every page of the site. When the visitor clicks a department, the list of categories for that department will appear below the department list. The site also has a search box that will allow visitors to perform product searches. At the top of the page, the site header will be visible on any page the visitor browses.

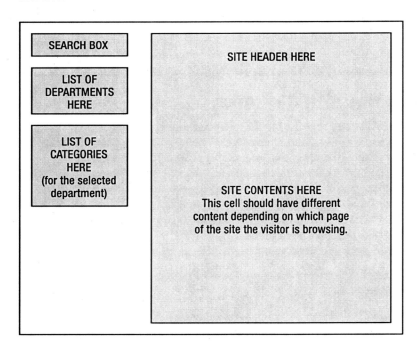

Figure 3-5. *Structure of web pages in TShirtShop*

To implement this structure as simply as possible, we'll use Smarty componentized templates (or simple Smarty design templates) to create the separate parts of the page as shown in Figure 3-6.

▊Note What we call a Smarty componentized template is the combination of a Smarty design template (the `.tpl` file) with an associated Smarty plug-in file (a `.php` file). We add the Smarty plug-in to the scene when your template needs to display data dynamically—in which case the plug-in contains the presentation logic that gathers the necessary data and feeds it to the template. When you need to display static content such functionality isn't needed, and a Smarty design template would suffice. You'll learn how to work with Smarty plug-ins in Chapter 4. Their official documentation page is `http://smarty.php.net/manual/en/plugins.php`.

In Figure 3-6, you can see some of the Smarty componentized templates you'll build in the next few chapters. The site contents box will be generated by a simple Smarty design template, named `store_front.tpl`, that you'll build later in this chapter. In Chapter 4, you'll extend it to a Smarty componentized template, when you'll need to generate dynamic content.

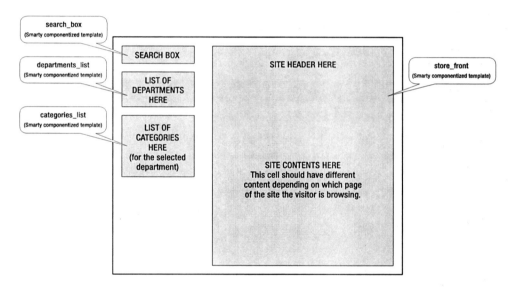

Figure 3-6. *Using Smarty to generate content*

Using Smarty templates to implement different pieces of functionality provides the benefits discussed in Chapter 2. Having different, unrelated pieces of functionality logically separated from one another gives you the flexibility to modify them independently and even reuse them in other pages without having to write their code again. It's also extremely easy to change the place in the parent web page of a feature implemented as a Smarty template.

The list of departments and search box are elements that will be present in every page of the site. The list of categories appears only when the visitor selects a department from the list. The contents cell is a dynamic part of the web site that will update itself with varying content depending on the site location (Home, About Us, Products, etc.) requested by the visitor. There are two main options for implementing that cell: add a componentized template that changes itself depending on the location or use different componentized templates to populate the cell depending on the location being browsed. There is no rule of thumb about which method to use, because the decision mainly depends on the specifics of the project. For TShirtShop, we will use the second option and create a number of componentized templates that will fill that location.

In the remainder of this chapter, you will

- Create the front page of TShirtShop
- Implement the foundations of the error-handling system in TShirtShop
- Create the tshirtshop database

Building TShirtShop's Front Page

The front page in TShirtShop will be generated by the files index.php and store_front.tpl.

You'll write the store_front.tpl Smarty template with placeholders for the three major parts of the site—the header, the table of departments, and the page contents cell. As mentioned earlier, we'll use YUI and the YUI grid builder to help us generate a professional CSS-based layout for our store.

Implement the main page in the following exercise, and we'll discuss the details in the "How It Works" section thereafter.

Exercise: Implementing the First Page

1. Create a new folder named images inside the tshirtshop folder.

2. Copy the files in image_folders/images from the Source Code/Download web page of the book (which you can find at the book details page on http://www.cristiandarie.ro) to tshirtshop/images (the folder you just created).

3. Create a file named site.conf in the tshirtshop/include/configs folder (used by the Smarty templates engine), and add the following line to it:

   site_title = "TShirtShop: Demo Product Catalog from Beginning PHP and MySQL E-Commerce"

4. Create a new folder named styles in the project root folder (tshirtshop).

5. Download the latest YUI package from http://developer.yahoo.com/yui/download/. Open the archive, and copy the yui_2.X.Y/build/reset/rest-min.css, yui_2.X.Y/build/base/base-min.css , yui_2.X.Y/build/fonts/fonts-min.css, and yui_2.X.Y/build/grids/grids-min.css files to your tshirtshop/styles folder.

6. Load the YUI CSS Grid Builder at http://developer.yahoo.com/yui/grids/builder/, and select the Toolbox options as described in Table 3-1. After setting these options, your grid builder page should look as shown in Figure 3-7.

Table 3-1. *YUI CSS Grid Builder Options*

Grid setting	Value
Body	750px.
Body columns	Sidebar left 180px.
Split content	Leave one row at "1 Column (100)" and click Add Another Row to add a new row.

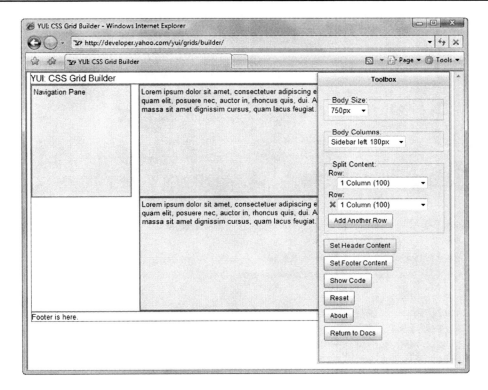

Figure 3-7. *Using the YUI CSS Grid Builder*

7. Click the Show Code button of the grid builder to have the tool generate the code for your grid. The code will be displayed in a window such as the one shown in Figure 3-8.

■**Note** Using the YUI CSS Grid Builder helps generating the HTML layout for you, but using this tool is optional. If, for any reason, you can't or don't want to use the YUI CSS Grid Builder, simply skip to the next step of the exercise, where you can type the necessary code yourself.

Figure 3-8. *The code generated by the YUI CSS Grid Builder*

8. Create a file named store_front.tpl in tshirtshop/presentation/templates, and add the following code to it. Note that we've used here the code the YUI CSS Grid Builder generated for us earlier.

```
{* smarty *}
{config_load file="site.conf"}
<!DOCTYPE html PUBLIC "-//W3C//DTD XHTML 1.0 Transitional//EN"
 "http://www.w3.org/TR/xhtml1/DTD/xhtml1-transitional.dtd">
<html>
  <head>
    <title>{#site_title#}</title>
    <meta http-equiv="Content-Type" content="text/html; charset=UTF-8" />
    <link type="text/css" rel="stylesheet" href="styles/tshirtshop.css" />
  </head>
  <body>
    <div id="doc" class="yui-t2">
      <div id="bd">
        <div id="yui-main">
          <div class="yui-b">
            <div id="header" class="yui-g">
              <a href="index.php">
                <img src="images/tshirtshop.tif" alt="tshirtshop logo" />
              </a>
            </div>
            <div id="contents" class="yui-g">
```

```
                Place contents here
              </div>
            </div>
          </div>
          <div class="yui-b">
            Place list of departments here
          </div>
        </div>
      </div>
    </body>
  </html>
```

9. Create a file named tshirtshop.css in the tshirtshop/styles folder, and write this code:

```css
@import "reset-min.css";
@import "base-min.css";
@import "fonts-min.css";
@import "grids-min.css";

body {
  font-size: 85%;
  font-family: "georgia";
}

.yui-t2, #bd, #yui-main {
  z-index: -5;
}

.yui-b, .yui-g {
  z-index: auto;
}

#header {
  margin-top: 15px;
  text-align: right;
}

.error_box {
  background-color: #ffffcc;
  border: 1px solid #dc143c;
  color: #DC143C;
  margin: 0 auto;
  overflow: auto;
  padding: 5px;
  position: relative;
  text-align: left;
  width: 90%;
  z-index: 5;
}
```

10. Add a file named config.php to the tshirtshop/include folder, with the following contents:

```php
<?php
// SITE_ROOT contains the full path to the tshirtshop folder
define('SITE_ROOT', dirname(dirname(__FILE__)));

// Application directories
define('PRESENTATION_DIR', SITE_ROOT . '/presentation/');
define('BUSINESS_DIR', SITE_ROOT . '/business/');

// Settings needed to configure the Smarty template engine
define('SMARTY_DIR', SITE_ROOT . '/libs/smarty/');
define('TEMPLATE_DIR', PRESENTATION_DIR . 'templates');
define('COMPILE_DIR', PRESENTATION_DIR . 'templates_c');
define('CONFIG_DIR', SITE_ROOT . '/include/configs');
?>
```

Before moving on, let's see what is happening here. dirname(__FILE__) returns the parent directory of the current file; naturally, dirname(dirname(__FILE__)) returns the parent of the current file's directory. This way our SITE_ROOT constant will be set to the full path of tshirtshop. With the help of the SITE_ROOT constant, we set up absolute paths of Smarty folders.

11. Create a file named application.php in the tshirtshop/presentation folder, and add the following contents to it:

```php
<?php
// Reference Smarty library
require_once SMARTY_DIR . 'Smarty.class.php';

/* Class that extends Smarty, used to process and display Smarty
   files */
class Application extends Smarty
{
  // Class constructor
  public function __construct()
  {
    // Call Smarty's constructor
    parent::Smarty();

    // Change the default template directories
    $this->template_dir = TEMPLATE_DIR;
    $this->compile_dir = COMPILE_DIR;
    $this->config_dir = CONFIG_DIR;
  }
}
?>
```

In application.php, you extend the Smarty class with a wrapper class named Application, which changes Smarty's default behavior. The Application class uses its constructor to configure the Smarty folders you created earlier.

Tip As mentioned earlier, Smarty requires three folders to operate: `templates`, `templates_c`, and `configs`. In the constructor of the `Application` class, we set a separate set of these directories for our application. If you want to turn on caching, then Smarty also needs a directory named `cache`. We will not be using Smarty caching for TShirtShop, but you can read more details about this in the Smarty manual at `http://smarty.php.net/manual/en/caching.php`.

12. Add the `index.php` file to the `tshirtshop` folder. The role of this file is to load the `store_front.tpl` template by using the `Application` class you created earlier. Here's the code for `index.php`:

```php
<?php
// Include utility files
require_once 'include/config.php';

// Load the application page template
require_once PRESENTATION_DIR . 'application.php';

// Load Smarty template file
$application = new Application();

// Display the page
$application->display('store_front.tpl');
?>
```

13. Now it's time to see some output from this thing. Load `http://localhost/tshirtshop/` in your favorite web browser, and admire the results, shown in Figure 3-9.

Tip At this early point of the development process it is probably a good idea to bookmark your `tshirtshop` location in your web browser (or browsers) that you use for development. This makes things easier when repeatedly reviewing your work in progress.

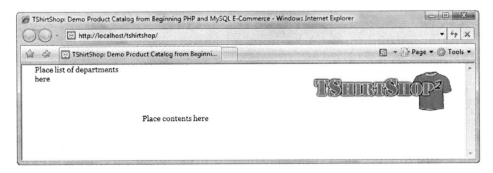

Figure 3-9. *Running TShirtShop*

How It Works: The First Page of TShirtShop

The main web page contains three major sections. There are two table cells that you'll fill with componentized templates—one for the list of departments and one for the page contents—in the following chapters.

Notice the departments list on the left side: the header at the top, and the contents cell filled with information regarding the first page. As previously mentioned, this contents cell is the only one that changes while browsing the site; the other two cells will look exactly the same no matter what page is visited. This implementation eases your life as a programmer and keeps a consistent look and feel for the web site.

Before you move on, it's important to understand how the Smarty template works. Everything starts from index.php, so you need to take a close look at it. Here's the code again:

```php
<?php
// Include utility files
require_once 'include/config.php';

// Load the application page template
require_once PRESENTATION_DIR . 'application.php';

// Load Smarty template file
$application = new Application();

// Display the page
$application->display('store_front.tpl');
?>
```

At this moment, this file has very simple functionality. First, it loads config.php, which sets some global variables, and then it loads the Smarty template file, which will generate the actual HTML content when a client requests index.php.

The standard way to create and configure a Smarty page is shown in the following code snippet:

```php
<?php
// Load the Smarty library
require_once SMARTY_DIR . 'Smarty.class.php';

// Create a new instance of the Smarty class
$smarty = new Smarty();
$smarty->template_dir = TEMPLATE_DIR;
$smarty->compile_dir = COMPILE_DIR;
$smarty->config_dir = CONFIG_DIR;
?>
```

In TShirtShop, we created a class named Application that inherits from Smarty, which contains the initialization procedure in its constructor. This makes working with Smarty templates easier. Here's again the code of the Application class:

```php
/* Class that extends Smarty, used to process and display Smarty
   files */
class Application extends Smarty
```

```
{
  // Class constructor
  public function __construct()
  {
    // Call Smarty's constructor
    parent::Smarty();

    // Change the default template directories
    $this->template_dir = TEMPLATE_DIR;
    $this->compile_dir = COMPILE_DIR;
    $this->config_dir = CONFIG_DIR;
  }
}
```

■**Note** The notion of constructor is specific to object-oriented programming terminology. The constructor of a class is a special method that executes automatically when an instance of that class is created. In PHP, the constructor of a class is called __construct(). Writing that code in the constructor of the Application class guarantees that it gets executed automatically when a new instance of Application is created.

The Smarty template file (store_front.tpl), except for a few details, contains simple HTML code. Those details are worth analyzing. In store_front.tpl, before the HTML code begins, the configuration file site.conf is loaded.

```
{* smarty *}
{config_load file="site.conf"}
```

■**Tip** Smarty comments are enclosed between {* and *} marks.

At this moment, the only variable set inside the site.conf file is site_title, which contains the name of the web site. The value of this variable is used to generate the title of the page in the HTML code:

```
<!DOCTYPE html PUBLIC "-//W3C//DTD XHTML 1.0 Transitional//EN"
 "http://www.w3.org/TR/xhtml1/DTD/xhtml1-transitional.dtd">
<html>
  <head>
    <title>{#site_title#}</title>
    <meta http-equiv="Content-Type" content="text/html; charset=UTF-8" />
    <link href="styles/tshirtshop.css" type="text/css" rel="stylesheet" />
  </head>
```

Variables that are loaded from the configuration files are referenced by enclosing them within hash marks (#), or with the smarty variable $smarty.config, as in:

```
<head>
  <title>{$smarty.config.site_title}</title>
  <meta http-equiv="Content-Type" content="text/html; charset=UTF-8" />
  <link href="styles/tshirtshop.css" type="text/css" rel="stylesheet" />
</head>
```

We loaded the site.conf configuration file using {config_load file="site.conf"} and accessed the site_title variable with {#site_title#}, which you'll use whenever you need to obtain the site title. If you want to change the site title, all you have to do is edit site.conf.

Last, it's worth noting that we're using cascading style sheets (CSS). CSS is a powerful language used to describe the appearance of the elements of a web page. CSS definitions can be stored in one or more files with the .css extensions, or even included in the HTML file, allowing web designers to detach the CSS styling definitions from the HTML document structure. If the job is done right, and CSS is used consistently in a web site, CSS will allow you to make visual changes to the entire site (or parts of the site) with very little effort, just by editing the CSS file.

In our case, we used three CSS files from the YUI library, and we have defined one of our own as well. It's not necessary to investigate the details of the YUI CSS files, although you can do that by studying the product documentation. As far as we are concerned, it's enough to say that using YUI helps us create a simple and valid layout that renders fine on all modern browsers.

If you've never worked with CSS before, don't worry. It's rather straightforward, and you will be able to harness much of its power quickly. However, when getting down to its details, CSS is a vast subject. There are many books and tutorials you can find on CSS, including the free ones you can find at http://www.w3.org/Style/CSS/ and http://www.csstutorial.net. Many useful CSS-related resources can be found at http://www.csszengarden.com/. The Wikipedia page on CSS contains useful information about the history of CSS and about its current state and limitations.

You'll see much more action with CSS in Chapter 4.

Handling and Reporting Errors

Although the code will be written to run without any unpleasant surprises, there's always a possibility that something might go wrong when processing client requests. The best strategy to deal with these unexpected problems is to find a centralized way to handle these errors and perform certain actions when they do happen.

PHP is known for its confusing error messages. If you've worked with other programming languages, you probably appreciate the information you can get from displaying the stack trace when you have an error. Tracing information is not displayed by default when you have a PHP error, so you'll want to change this behavior. In the development stage, tracing information will help you debug the application, and in a release version, the error message must be reported to the site administrator. Another problem is the tricky E_WARNING error message type, because it's hard to tell whether it's fatal or not for the application.

Tip If you don't remember or don't know what a PHP error message looks like, try adding the following line in your `index.php` file:

```
require_once 'inexistent_file.php';
```

Load the web site in your favorite browser, and notice the error message you get. If you do this test, make sure to remove the problematic line afterward!

In the context of a live web application, errors can happen unexpectedly for various reasons, such as software failures (operating system or database server crashes, viruses, and so on) and hardware failures. It's important to be able to log these errors and eventually inform the web site administrator (perhaps by sending an e-mail message), so the error can be taken care of as fast as possible.

For these reasons, we'll start establishing an efficient error-handling and reporting strategy. You'll create a class named `ErrorHandler` that will manage the error handling. In this class, you'll create a static, user-defined error-handler method named `Handler()`, which will get executed anytime a PHP error happens during runtime. In PHP, you define a custom error handler using the `set_error_handler()` function.

Caution As you'll see, the second parameter of `set_error_handler()` is used to specify the error types that the specified handler function should handle. However, this second parameter is supported only since PHP 5. Read more details at `http://www.php.net/set_error_handler`. You can also find more info about PHP errors and logging in the PHP manual at `http://www.php.net/manual/en/ref.errorfunc.php`.

Serious error types (`E_ERROR`, `E_PARSE`, `E_CORE_ERROR`, `E_CORE_WARNING`, `E_COMPILE_ERROR`, and `E_COMPILE_WARNING`) cannot be intercepted and handled by `ErrorHandler::Handler()`, but the other types of PHP errors (`E_WARNING` for example) can be.

The error-handling method, `Handler()`, will behave like this:

- It creates a detailed error message.

- If the method is configured to do so, the error is e-mailed to the site administrator.

- If the method is configured to do so, the error is logged to an errors log file.

- If the method is configured to do so, the error is shown in the response web page.

- Serious errors will halt the execution of the page. The other ones will allow the page to continue processing normally.

Let's implement the `ErrorHandler` class in the next exercise.

Exercise: Implementing the ErrorHandler Class

1. Add the following error-handling configuration variables to `include/config.php`:

```php
<?php
// SITE_ROOT contains the full path to the tshirtshop folder
define('SITE_ROOT', dirname(dirname(__FILE__)));

// Application directories
define('PRESENTATION_DIR', SITE_ROOT . '/presentation/');
define('BUSINESS_DIR', SITE_ROOT . '/business/');

// Settings needed to configure the Smarty template engine
define('SMARTY_DIR', SITE_ROOT . '/libs/smarty/');
define('TEMPLATE_DIR', PRESENTATION_DIR . 'templates');
define('COMPILE_DIR', PRESENTATION_DIR . 'templates_c');
define('CONFIG_DIR', SITE_ROOT . '/include/configs');

// These should be true while developing the web site
define('IS_WARNING_FATAL', true);
define('DEBUGGING', true);

// The error types to be reported
define('ERROR_TYPES', E_ALL);

// Settings about mailing the error messages to admin
define('SEND_ERROR_MAIL', false);
define('ADMIN_ERROR_MAIL', 'Administrator@example.com');
define('SENDMAIL_FROM', 'Errors@example.com');
ini_set('sendmail_from', SENDMAIL_FROM);

// By default we don't log errors to a file
define('LOG_ERRORS', false);
define('LOG_ERRORS_FILE', 'c:\\tshirtshop\\errors_log.txt'); // Windows
// define('LOG_ERRORS_FILE', '/home/username/tshirtshop/errors.log'); // Linux
/* Generic error message to be displayed instead of debug info
   (when DEBUGGING is false) */
define('SITE_GENERIC_ERROR_MESSAGE', '<h1>TShirtShop Error!</h1>');
?>
```

2. In the `tshirtshop` folder, create a subfolder named `business`.

3. In the `business` folder, create a file named `error_handler.php` file, and write the following code:

```php
<?php
class ErrorHandler
{
  // Private constructor to prevent direct creation of object
  private function __construct()
  {
  }
```

```php
/* Set user error-handler method to ErrorHandler::Handler method */
public static function SetHandler($errTypes = ERROR_TYPES)
{
  return set_error_handler(array ('ErrorHandler', 'Handler'), $errTypes);
}

// Error handler method
public static function Handler($errNo, $errStr, $errFile, $errLine)
{
  /* The first two elements of the backtrace array are irrelevant:
      - ErrorHandler.GetBacktrace
      - ErrorHandler.Handler */
  $backtrace = ErrorHandler::GetBacktrace(2);

  // Error message to be displayed, logged, or mailed
  $error_message = "\nERRNO: $errNo\nTEXT: $errStr" .
                   "\nLOCATION: $errFile, line " .
                   "$errLine, at " . date('F j, Y, g:i a') .
                   "\nShowing backtrace:\n$backtrace\n\n";

  // Email the error details, in case SEND_ERROR_MAIL is true
  if (SEND_ERROR_MAIL == true)
    error_log($error_message, 1, ADMIN_ERROR_MAIL, "From: " .
            SENDMAIL_FROM . "\r\nTo: " . ADMIN_ERROR_MAIL);

  // Log the error, in case LOG_ERRORS is true
  if (LOG_ERRORS == true)
    error_log($error_message, 3, LOG_ERRORS_FILE);

  /* Warnings don't abort execution if IS_WARNING_FATAL is false
     E_NOTICE and E_USER_NOTICE errors don't abort execution */
  if (($errNo == E_WARNING && IS_WARNING_FATAL == false) ||
      ($errNo == E_NOTICE || $errNo == E_USER_NOTICE))
  // If the error is nonfatal ...
  {
    // Show message only if DEBUGGING is true
    if (DEBUGGING == true)
      echo '<div class="error_box"><pre>' . $error_message . '</pre></div>';
  }
  else
  // If error is fatal ...
  {
    // Show error message
    if (DEBUGGING == true)
      echo '<div class="error_box"><pre>'. $error_message . '</pre></div>';
    else
      echo SITE_GENERIC_ERROR_MESSAGE;
```

```php
      // Stop processing the request
      exit();
    }
  }

  // Builds backtrace message
  public static function GetBacktrace($irrelevantFirstEntries)
  {
    $s = '';
    $MAXSTRLEN = 64;
    $trace_array = debug_backtrace();

    for ($i = 0; $i < $irrelevantFirstEntries; $i++)
      array_shift($trace_array);
    $tabs = sizeof($trace_array) - 1;

    foreach ($trace_array as $arr)
    {
      $tabs -= 1;
      if (isset ($arr['class']))
        $s .= $arr['class'] . '.';
      $args = array ();

      if (!empty ($arr['args']))
        foreach ($arr['args']as $v)
        {
          if (is_null($v))
            $args[] = 'null';
          elseif (is_array($v))
            $args[] = 'Array[' . sizeof($v) . ']';
          elseif (is_object($v))
            $args[] = 'Object: ' . get_class($v);
          elseif (is_bool($v))
            $args[] = $v ? 'true' : 'false';
          else
          {
            $v = (string)@$v;
            $str = htmlspecialchars(substr($v, 0, $MAXSTRLEN));
            if (strlen($v) > $MAXSTRLEN)
              $str .= '...';
            $args[] = '"' . $str . '"';
          }
        }

      $s .= $arr['function'] . '(' . implode(', ', $args) . ')';
      $line = (isset ($arr['line']) ? $arr['line']: 'unknown');
      $file = (isset ($arr['file']) ? $arr['file']: 'unknown');
      $s .= sprintf(' # line %4d, file: %s', $line, $file);
```

```
        $s .= "\n";
    }

    return $s;
    }
}
?>
```

> ■**Note** You'll learn more about object-oriented programming concepts and PHP in the following chapters. For now, we'd like just to draw attention to the class constructor, a special function named __construct(). If you type in this code by hand, notice the function name is prefixed by two underscore symbols, not one. Overlooking this detail is a common source of errors in PHP 5 scripts.

4. Modify the index.php file to include the newly created error_handler.php file, and set the error handler:

```
<?php
// Include utility files
require_once 'include/config.php';
require_once BUSINESS_DIR . 'error_handler.php';

// Set the error handler
ErrorHandler::SetHandler();

// Load the application page template
require_once PRESENTATION_DIR . 'application.php';
```

5. Great! You just finished writing the new error-handling code. Let's test it. First, load the web site in your browser to see that you typed in everything correctly. If you get no errors, test the new error-handling system by adding the following line to index.php:

```
<?php
// Include utility files
require_once 'include/config.php';
require_once BUSINESS_DIR . 'error_handler.php';

// Sets the error handler
ErrorHandler::SetHandler();

// Load the application page template
require_once PRESENTATION_DIR . 'application.php';

// Display the page
$application->display('store_front.tpl');

// Try to load inexistent file
require_once 'inexistent_file.php';
?>
```

Now, reload index.php in your browser, and admire your brand-new error message, shown in Figure 3-10.

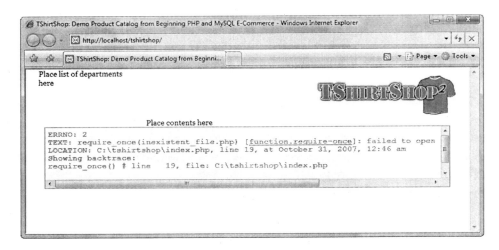

Figure 3-10. *Error message showing backtrace information*

■**Caution** Don't forget to remove the buggy line from index.php before moving on.

How It Works: Error Handling

The method that intercepts web site errors and deals with them is ErrorHandler::Handler() (located in error_handler.php). The code that registers the ErrorHandler::Handler() function as the one that handles errors in your site is in the ErrorHandler::SetHandler() method, which is invoked in index.php:

```
/* Set user error handler method to ErrorHandler::Handler method */
public static function SetHandler($errTypes = ERROR_TYPES)
{
  return set_error_handler(array ('ErrorHandler', 'Handler'), $errTypes);
}
```

■**Note** The second parameter of set_error_handler() specifies the range of errors that should be intercepted. E_ALL specifies all types of errors, including E_NOTICE errors, which should be reported during web site development.

When called, ErrorHandler::Handler() constructs the error message with the help of a method named ErrorHandler::GetBacktrace() and forwards the error message to the client's browser, a log file, the administrator (by e-mail), or a combination of these; the forwarding behavior can be configured by editing config.php.

GetBacktrace() gets the backtrace information from the debug_backtrace() function (introduced in PHP 4.3.0) and changes its output format to generate an HTML error message similar to a Java error. It isn't important to understand every line in GetBacktrace() unless you want to personalize the backtrace displayed in case of an error. The 2 parameter sent to GetBacktrace() specifies that the backtrace results should omit the first two entries (the calls to ErrorHandler::Handler() and ErrorHandler::GetBacktrace()).

You build the detailed error string in ErrorHandler::Handler(), including the backtrace information:

```
$backtrace = ErrorHandler::GetBacktrace(2);

// Error message to be displayed, logged or mailed
$error_message = "\nERRNO: $errNo\nTEXT: $errStr" .
                 "\nLOCATION: $errFile, line " .
                 "$errLine, at " . date('F j, Y, g:i a') .
                 "\nShowing backtrace:\n$backtrace\n\n";
```

Depending on the configuration options from the config.php file, you decide whether to display, log, and/or e-mail the error. Here we use PHP's error_log() function, which knows how to e-mail or write the error's details to a log file:

```
    // Email the error details, in case SEND_ERROR_MAIL is true
    if (SEND_ERROR_MAIL == true)
      error_log($error_message, 1, ADMIN_ERROR_MAIL, "From: " .
                SENDMAIL_FROM . "\r\nTo: " . ADMIN_ERROR_MAIL);

    // Log the error, in case LOG_ERRORS is true
    if (LOG_ERRORS == true)
      error_log($error_message, 3, LOG_ERRORS_FILE);
```

■**Note** If you want to be able to send an error mail to a localhost mail account (your_name@localhost), then you should have a Simple Mail Transfer Protocol (SMTP) server started on your machine. On a Red Hat (or Fedora) Linux distribution, you can start an SMTP server with the following command:

```
service sendmail start
```

Also, on Windows systems, you should check in IIS (Internet Information Services) Manager for Default SMTP Virtual Server and make sure it's started.

While you are developing the site, the DEBUGGING constant should be set to true, but after launching the site in the wild, you should make it false, causing a user-friendly error message to be displayed instead of the debugging information in case of serious errors and no message to be shown at all in case of nonfatal errors.

The errors of type E_WARNING are pretty tricky, because you don't know which of them should stop the execution of the request. The IS_WARNING_FATAL constant set in config.php decides whether this type of error should be considered fatal for the project. Also, errors of type E_NOTICE and E_USER_NOTICE are not considered fatal:

```
/* Warnings don't abort execution if IS_WARNING_FATAL is false
   E_NOTICE and E_USER_NOTICE errors don't abort execution */
if (($errNo == E_WARNING && IS_WARNING_FATAL == false) ||
    ($errNo == E_NOTICE || $errNo == E_USER_NOTICE))
// If the error is nonfatal ...
{
  // Show message only if DEBUGGING is true
  if (DEBUGGING == true)
    echo '<div class="error_box"><pre>' . $error_message . '</pre></div>';
}
else
// If error is fatal ...
{
  // Show error message
  if (DEBUGGING == true)
    echo '<div class="error_box"><pre>' . $error_message . '</pre></div>';
  else
    echo SITE_GENERIC_ERROR_MESSAGE;

  // Stop processing the request
  exit();
}
```

In the following chapters, you'll need to manually trigger errors using the trigger_error() PHP function, which lets you specify the kind of error to generate. By default, it generates E_USER_NOTICE errors, which are not considered fatal but are logged and reported by ErrorHandler::Handler() code.

Preparing the Database

The final step in this chapter is to create the MySQL database, although you won't use it until the next chapter. We will show you the steps to create your database and create a user with full privileges to it using phpMyAdmin that ships with XAMPP, but you can use other visual interfaces such as Toad (http://www.quest.com/toad-for-mysql) or even the MySQL text-mode console.

Before moving on, make sure you have MySQL started. On Windows, you can start MySQL from the XAMPP Control Panel, and on Linux, it usually starts when you start XAMPP (the command to start XAMPP on Linux is /opt/lamp/lamp start). Follow the steps in the exercise to create the database and a new user account.

Exercise: Creating the tshirtshop Database and a New User Account

1. Load the phpMyAdmin page in your favorite web browser (http://localhost/phpmyadmin); type **tshirtshop** in the "Create new database" text box; and choose the utf8_unicode_ci collation, as shown in Figure 3-11.

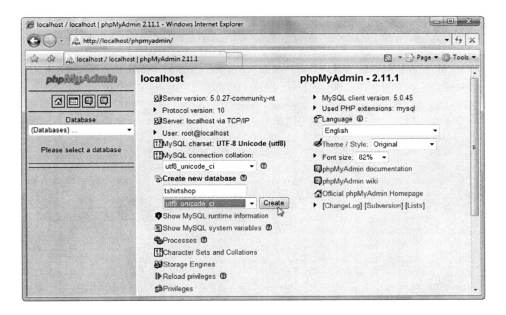

Figure 3-11. *Creating the tshirtshop database using phpMyAdmin*

2. Click the Create button to create the new database. In the screen that follows (see Figure 3-12), you're shown the SQL query phpMyAdmin used to create your database.

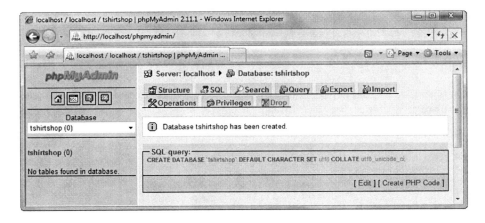

Figure 3-12. *Editing your database using phpMyAdmin*

■**Note** You'll learn more about SQL queries in Chapter 4. SQL is the language used to interact with the database. However, you can accomplish many tasks, such as creating databases and data tables, using a web interface such as phpMyAdmin, which generates the SQL queries for you.

3. Now add a new user to the database. Our data tier access code will access the TShirtShop database using this user's credentials. You'll create a user named tshirtshopadmin (with the password tshirtshopadmin), who will have full access inside the TShirtShop database but not to any other database. You have more alternatives to achieve the same results, and for more details, see the MySQL documentation at `http://dev.mysql.com/doc/refman/5.1/en/account-management-sql.html`.

Now, click the SQL tab, and type the SQL query shown in Figure 3-13.

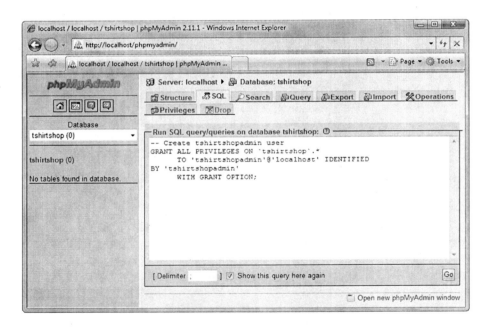

Figure 3-13. *Creating a new database user*

4. After entering the SQL query as shown, click the Go button. You should be informed that the SQL query has been executed successfully (see Figure 3-14).

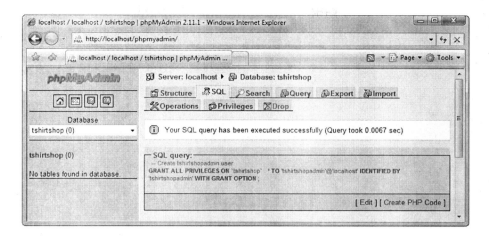

Figure 3-14. *The new user has been successfully created in the database.*

Downloading the Code

You can find the latest code downloads and a link to an online version of TShirtShop at the authors' web sites at http://www.cristiandarie.ro or http://www.emilianbalanescu.ro or in the Source Code/Download section of the Apress web site at http://www.apress.com. It should be easy to read through this book and build your solution as you go; however, if you want to check something from our working version, you can. Instructions on loading the chapters are available in the welcome.html document in the download.

Summary

It's time to put your feet up on your desk and admire your work! In this chapter, you learned about the benefits of using the right architecture for an application. So far, we have a very flexible and scalable application, because it doesn't have much functionality, and you'll feel the real advantages of using a disciplined way of coding in the next chapters.

In this chapter, you have coded the basic, static part of the presentation tier, implemented a bit of error-handling code, and created the tshirtshop database, which is the support for the data tier. In the next chapter, you'll start implementing the product catalog and learn a lot about how to dynamically generate visual content using data stored in the database with the help of the middle tier and with smart and fast controls and components in the presentation tier.

■ ■ ■

## CHAPTER 4

Creating the Product Catalog: Part 1

After learning about the three-tier architecture and implementing a bit of your web site's main page, you're ready to start creating the TShirtShop product catalog.

Because the product catalog is composed of many components, you'll create it over two chapters. In this chapter, you'll create the first data table, implement access methods in the middle tier, and learn how to deal with the data tier. By the end of this chapter, you'll finally have something dynamically generated on your web page. In Chapter 5, you'll finish building the product catalog by adding support for categories, product lists, a product details page, and more!

The main topics we'll cover in this chapter are

- Analyzing the structure of the product catalog and the functionality it should support

- Creating the database structures for the catalog and the data tier of the catalog

- Implementing the business tier objects required to make the catalog run

- Implementing a functional user interface for the product catalog

Showing Your Visitors What You've Got

One of the essential features required in any e-store is to allow the visitor to easily browse through the products. Just imagine what Amazon.com would be like without its excellent product catalog!

Whether your visitors are looking for something specific or just browsing, it's important to make sure their experiences with your site are pleasant ones. After all, you want your visitors to find what they are looking for as easily and painlessly as possible. This is why you'll want to add search functionality to the site and also find a clever way of structuring products into categories so they can be quickly and intuitively accessed.

Depending on the size of the store, it might be enough to group products under a number of categories, but if there are a lot of products, you'll need to find even more ways to categorize and structure the product catalog.

Determining the structure of the catalog is one of the first tasks to accomplish in this chapter. Keep in mind that, in a professional approach, these details would have been established before starting to code when building the requirements document for the project. However, for the purposes of this book, we prefer to deal with things one at a time.

After the structure of the catalog is established, you'll start writing the code that makes the catalog work as planned.

What Does a Product Catalog Look Like?

Today's web surfers are more demanding than they used to be. They expect to find information quickly on whatever product or service they have in mind, and if they don't find it, they are likely to go to the competition before giving the site a second chance. Of course, you don't want this to happen to *your* visitors, so you need to structure the catalog to make it as intuitive and helpful as possible.

Because the e-store will start with around 100 products and will probably have many more in the future, it's not enough to just group them in categories. The store also has a number of departments, and each department will contain a number of categories. Each category can then have any number of products attached to it.

▪**Note** Later in the book, you'll also create the administrative part of the web site, often referred to as the *control panel*, which allows the client to update department, category, and product data. Until then, you'll manually fill in the database with data (or you can "cheat" by using the SQL scripts provided in the Source Code/Download section of the Apress web site at `http://www.apress.com`, as you'll see).

Another particularly important detail that you need to think about is whether a category can exist in more than one department and whether a product can exist in more than one category. As you might suspect, this is the kind of decision that has implications on the way you code the product catalog, so you need to consult your client on this matter.

For the TShirtShop product catalog, each category can exist in only one department, but a product can exist in more than one category. For example, in our catalog, the product Kat Over New Moon will appear in both Animal and Christmas categories. This decision will have implications in the way you'll design the database, and we'll highlight those implications when we get there.

Finally, apart from having the products grouped in categories, you also want to have featured products. For this web site, a product can be featured either on the front page or in the department pages. The next section shows a few screenshots that explain this.

Previewing the Product Catalog

Although you'll have the fully functional product catalog finished by the end of Chapter 5, taking a look at it right now will give you a better idea about where you're heading. In Figure 4-1, you can see the TShirtShop front page and two of its featured products.

Note the departments list in the upper-left corner of the page. The list of departments is dynamically generated with data gathered from the database; you'll implement the list of departments in this chapter.

When site visitors click a department in the departments list, they go to the main page of the specified department. This replaces the store's list of catalog-featured products with a page containing information specific to the selected department—including the list of featured products for that department. In Figure 4-2, you see the page that will appear when the Seasonal department is clicked.

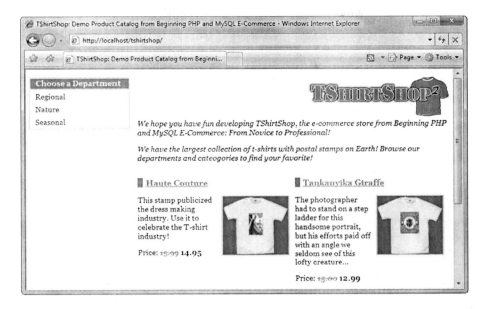

Figure 4-1. *TShirtShop front page and two of its featured products*

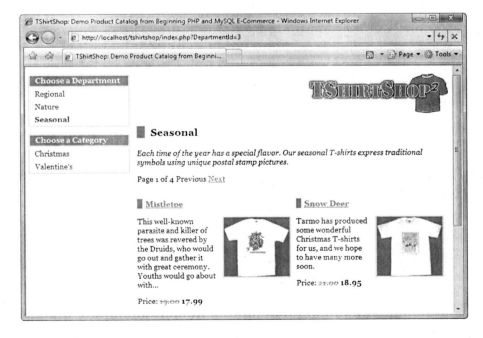

Figure 4-2. *Visiting the Seasonal department*

Under the list of departments, you can now see the list of categories that belong to the selected department. On the right side of the screen, you can see the name of the selected department, its description, and its featured products. When a particular page must display a larger number of products than a predefined value, the products will be split into more sub-pages, and a pager shows up to allow the navigation between these pages. You can see this pager in Figure 4-2.

We decided to list only the featured products in the department page, and let the visitors browse all the products by navigating to category pages. On a department page, the text above the list of products is the description for the selected department, which means you'll need to store both a name and a description for each department in the database. When selecting a category from the categories list, all of its products are listed, along with the category title and description. Clicking a product's image or title takes you to a product details page, which you can see in Figure 4-3. The department and category boxes must retain their state when a product is selected; this is a navigational aid for the visitor. A Continue Shopping link also shows up, helping the visitor go back to the page he or she was visiting prior to selecting a product.

Figure 4-3. *Visiting a product details page*

When a category is selected, all its products are listed—you no longer see featured products. Note that the description text also changes. This time, this is the description of the selected category.

Roadmap for This Chapter

As you can see, the product catalog, although not very complicated, has more parts that need to be covered. In this chapter, you'll only create the departments list (see Figure 4-4).

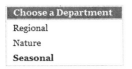

Figure 4-4. *The departments list*

The departments list will be the first dynamically generated data in your site (the names of the departments will be extracted from the database).

In this chapter, you'll implement just the departments list part of the web site. After you understand how this list works, you'll be able to quickly implement the other components of the product catalog in Chapter 5.

In Chapter 2, we discussed the three-tiered architecture that you'll use to implement the web application. The product catalog part of the site is no exception to the rule, and its components (including the departments list) will be spread over the three logical layers. Figure 4-5 previews what you'll create in this chapter at each tier to achieve a functional departments list.

So far, you've only played a bit with the presentation and business tiers in Chapter 3. Now, when building the catalog, you'll finally meet the final tier and work further with the tshirtshop database (depending on whom you ask, the data store may or may not be considered an integral part of the three-tiered architecture).

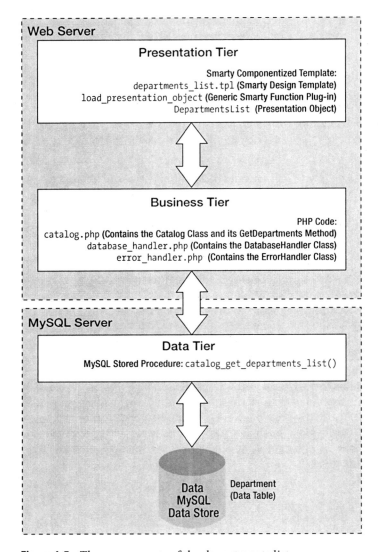

Figure 4-5. *The components of the departments list*

These are the main steps you'll take toward having your own dynamically generated department list. Note that you start with the database and make your way to the presentation tier:

1. Create the department table in the database. This table will store data regarding the store's departments. Before adding this table, you'll learn the basic concepts of working with relational databases.

2. Write a MySQL stored procedure named catalog_get_departments_list, which returns the IDs and names of the departments from the department table. PHP scripts will call this stored procedure to generate the departments list for your visitor. MySQL stored procedures are logically located in the data tier of your application. At this step, you'll learn how to speak to your relational database using SQL.

3. Create the `DatabaseHandler` class, which will be your helper class that performs common database interaction operations. `DatabaseHandler` is a wrapper class for some PDO methods and includes consistent error-handling techniques that deal with database-related errors.

4. Create the business tier components of the departments list (the `Catalog` class and its `GetDepartments()` method). You'll see how to communicate with the database, through the `DatabaseHandler` helper class, to retrieve the necessary data.

5. Implement the `departments_list` Smarty componentized template, the `load_presentation_object` Smarty plug-in that glues the templates and their associated presentation objects. The `DepartmentList` presentation object is needed by the `departments_list` template.

So, let's start by creating the `department` table.

Storing Catalog Information

The vast majority of web applications, e-commerce web sites being no exception, live around the data they manage. Analyzing and understanding the data you need to store and process is an essential step in successfully completing your project.

The typical data storage solution for this kind of application is a relational database. However, this is not a requirement—you have the freedom to create your own data access layer and have whatever kind of data structures you want to support your application.

■**Note** In some particular cases, it may be preferable to store your data in plain text files or XML files instead of databases, but these solutions are generally not suited for applications such as TShirtShop, so we won't cover them in this book. However, it's good to know your options.

Although this is not a book about databases or relational database design, you'll learn all you need to know to understand the product catalog and make it work.

Essentially, a relational database is made up of *data tables* and the *relationships* that exist among them. Because you'll work with a single data table in this chapter, we'll cover only the database theory that applies to the table as a separate, individual database item. In the next chapter, when you'll add the other tables to the picture, we'll take a closer look at the theory behind relational databases by analyzing how the tables relate to each other and how MySQL helps you deal with these relationships.

■**Note** In a real-world situation, you would probably design the whole database (or at least all the tables relevant to the feature you build) from the start. In this book, we chose to split the development over two chapters to maintain a better balance of theory and practice.

So, let's start with a little bit of theory, after which you'll create the department data table and the rest of the required components:

Understanding Data Tables

This section provides a quick database lesson covering the essential information you need to know to design simple data tables. We'll briefly discuss the main parts that make up a database table:

- Primary keys

- MySQL data types

- UNIQUE columns

- NOT NULL columns and default values

- Autoincrement columns

- Indexes

■**Note** If you have previous experience with MySQL, you might want to skip this section and go directly to the "Creating the department Table" section.

A data table is made up of columns and rows. Columns are also referred to as *fields*, and rows are sometimes also called *records*.

Because this chapter covers the only departments list, you'll only need to create one data table: the department table. This table will store your departments' data and is one of the simplest tables you'll work with.

With the help of the MySQL client console interface, it's easy to create a data table in the database *if* you know for sure what kind of data it will store. When designing a table, you must consider which fields it should contain and which data types should be used for those fields. Besides a field's data type, there are a few more properties to consider, which you'll learn about in the following pages.

To determine which fields you need for the department table, write down a few examples of records that would be stored in that table. Remember from the previous figures that there isn't much information to store about a department—just the name and description for each department. The table containing the departments' data might look like Figure 4-6 (you'll implement the table in the database later, after we discuss the theory).

name	description
Regional	Proud of your country? Wear a T-shirt with a national symbol stamp!
Nature	Find beautiful T-shirts with animals and flowers in our Nature department!
Seasonal	Each time of the year has a special flavor. Our seasonal T-shirts express traditional symbols using unique postal stamp pictures.

Figure 4-6. *Data from the department table*

From a table like this, the names would be extracted to populate the list in the upper-left part of the web page, and the descriptions would be used as headers for the featured products list.

Primary Keys

The way you work with data tables in a relational database is a bit different from the way you usually work on paper. A fundamental requirement in relational databases is that each data row in a table must be *uniquely identifiable*. This makes sense because you usually save records into a database so that you can retrieve them later; however, you can't always do that if each table row doesn't have something that makes it unique. For example, suppose you add another record to the department table shown previously in Figure 4-6, making it look like the table shown in Figure 4-7.

name	description
Regional	Proud of your country? Wear a T-shirt with a national symbol stamp!
Nature	Find beautiful T-shirts with animals and flowers in our Nature department!
Seasonal	Each time of the year has a special flavor. Our seasonal T-shirts express traditional symbols using unique postal stamp pictures.
Seasonal	Ooops! Don't try this at home!

Figure 4-7. *Two departments with the same name*

Look at this table, and tell me the description of the Seasonal department! Yep, we have a problem—we have two departments with the same name Seasonal (the name isn't unique). If you queried the table using the name column, you would get two results. Sometimes getting multiple results for a query is what you expect—but other times you want the rows to be uniquely identifiable depending on the value of a column, which is supposed to be unique.

This problem is addressed, in the world of relational database design, using the concept of the *primary key*, which allows you to uniquely identify a specific row out of many rows. Technically, the primary key is not a column itself. Instead, the PRIMARY KEY is a *constraint* that when applied on a column guarantees that the column will have unique values across the table.

Constraints are rules that apply to data tables and make up part of the *data integrity* rules of the database. The database takes care of its own integrity and makes sure these rules aren't broken. If, for example, you try to add two identical values for a column that has a PRIMARY KEY constraint, the database refuses the operation and generates an error. We'll do some experiments later in this chapter to show this.

■**Note** A primary key is not a column but a constraint that applies to that column; however, from now on and for convenience, when referring to the primary key, we'll be talking about the column that has the PRIMARY KEY constraint applied to it.

Back to the example, setting the name column as the primary key of the department table would solve the problem because two departments would not be allowed to have the same name. If name is the primary key of the department table, searching for a product with a specific name will always produce exactly one result if the name exists, or no results if no records have the specified name.

■**Tip** This is common sense, but it has to be said: a primary key column will never allow NULL values.

An alternative solution, and usually the preferred one, is to have an additional column in the table, called an ID column, to act as its primary key. With an ID column, the department table would look like Figure 4-8.

department_id	name	description
1	Regional	Proud of your country? Wear a T-shirt with a national symbol stamp!
2	Nature	Find beautiful T-shirts with animals and flowers in our Nature department!
3	Seasonal	Each time of the year has a special flavor. Our seasonal T-shirts express traditional symbols using unique postal stamp pictures.

Figure 4-8. *Adding an ID column as the primary key of department*

The primary key column is named department_id. We'll use this naming convention for primary key columns in all data tables we'll create. In this scenario, having departments with the same name is now acceptable, because they would have different IDs. (To guard against unique column values for columns that are not the primary key you'd need to use the UNIQUE constraint, which is discussed next.)

There are two main reasons it's better to create a separate numerical primary key column than to use the name (or another existing column) as the primary key:

Performance: The database engine handles sorting and searching operations much faster with numerical values than with strings. This becomes even more relevant in the context of working with multiple related tables that need to be frequently joined (you'll learn more about this in Chapter 5).

Department name changes: If you need to rely on the ID value being stable in time, creating an artificial key solves the problem because it's unlikely you'll ever want to change the ID.

In Figure 4-8, the primary key is composed of a single column, but this is not a requirement. If the primary key is set on more than one column, the group of primary key columns (taken as a unit) is guaranteed to be unique, but the individual columns that form the primary key can have repeating values in the table. In Chapter 5, you'll see an example of a multivalued primary key. For now, it's enough to know that they exist.

■**Note** Applying a PRIMARY KEY constraint on a field also generates a unique index created on it by default. Indexes are objects that improve performance of many database operations, dramatically speeding up your web application (you'll learn more about this later in the "Indexes" section of this chapter).

Unique Columns

UNIQUE is yet another kind of constraint that can be applied to table columns. This constraint is similar to the PRIMARY KEY constraint in that it doesn't allow duplicate data in a column. Still, there are differences. Although there is only one PRIMARY KEY constraint per table, you are allowed to have as many UNIQUE constraints as you like.

Columns that have the UNIQUE constraint are useful when you already have a primary key but still have columns (or groups of columns) for which you want to have unique values. You can set name to be unique in the department table if you want to forbid repeating values.

The facts that you need to remember about UNIQUE constraints follow:

- The UNIQUE constraint forbids having identical values on the field.

- You can have more than one UNIQUE field in a data table.

- A UNIQUE field is allowed to accept NULL values, in which case it will accept any number of them.

- Indexes are automatically created on UNIQUE and PRIMARY KEY columns.

Columns and Data Types

Each column in a table has a particular data type. By looking at the department table shown in Figure 4-8, you can see that department_id has a numeric data type, whereas name and description contain text.

It's important to consider the many data types that MySQL Server supports so that you'll be able to make correct decisions about how to create your tables. Table 4-1 isn't an exhaustive list of MySQL data types, but it focuses on the main types you might come across in your project. Refer to the MySQL documentation for a more detailed list at http://www.mysql.org/doc/refman/5.1/en/data-types.html.

■**Tip** For more information about any specific detail regarding MySQL or PHP, including MySQL data types, you can always refer to W. Jason Gilmore's *Beginning PHP and MySQL 5: From Novice to Professional, Second Edition* (Apress, 2006), which is an excellent reference.

To keep the table short, under the Data Type heading, we have listed the types used in this project, while similar data types are explained under the Description and Notes headings. You don't need to memorize the list, but you should get an idea of which data types are available.

Table 4-1. *MySQL Server Data Types for Use in TShirtShop*

Data Type	Size in Bytes	Description and Notes
int	4	Stores integer numbers from –2,147,483,648 to 2,147,483,647. Related types are bigint, mediumint, smallint, and tinyint. A bit data type is able to store values of 0 and 1.
decimal (M,N)	M+2 bytes if N > 0	One character for each digit of the value, the decimal point (if the scale is greater than 0), and the negative sign (for negative numbers).
	M+1 bytes if N = 0	decimal is a numeric data type you'll use to store monetary information because of its exact precision. To preserve the decimal precision of these numbers, MySQL stores decimal values internally as strings. M represents the precision (the number of significant decimal digits that will be stored for values), and N is the scale (the number of digits after the decimal point). If N is 0, decimal will only store integer values.
datetime	8 bytes	Supports date and time data from 1000-01-01 00:00:00 to 9999-12-31 23:59:59.
varchar	variable	Stores variable-length character data from 0 to 65,535. The dimension you set represents the maximum length of strings it can accept.
text (blob)	L+2 bytes, where L < 2^16	A column with a maximum length of 65,535 (2^16 – 1) characters.

Keep in mind that data type names are case insensitive, so you might see them capitalized differently depending on the database console program you're using.

Now, let's get back to the department table and determine which data types to use. Don't worry that you don't have the table yet in your database; you'll create it a bit later. Figure 4-9 shows the fields of the department table. department_id is an int data type, and name and description are varchar data types.

Field	Type	Collation	Attributes	Null	Default	Extra
department_id	int(11)			No		auto_increment
name	varchar(100)	utf8_unicode_ci		No		
description	varchar(1000)	utf8_unicode_ci		No		

Figure 4-9. *Designing the department table*

For varchar, the associated dimension—such as in varchar(100)—represents the maximum length of the stored strings. We'll choose to have 100 characters available for the department's name and 1,000 for the description. An integer record, as shown in the table, always occupies 4 bytes.

NOT NULL Columns and Default Values

For each column of the table, you can specify whether it is allowed to be NULL. The best and shortest definition for NULL is "undefined." For example, in your department table, only department_id and name are really required, whereas description is optional—meaning that you are allowed to add a new department without supplying a description for it. If you add a new row of data without supplying a value for columns that allow nulls, NULL is automatically supplied for them.

Especially for character data, there is a subtle difference between the NULL value and an empty value. If you add a product with an empty string for its description, this means that you actually set a value for its description; it's an empty string, not an undefined (NULL) value.

The primary key field never allows NULL values. For the other columns, it's up to you to decide which fields are required and which are not.

In some cases, instead of allowing NULLs, you'll prefer to specify default values. This way, if the value is unspecified when creating a new row, it will be supplied with the default value. The default value can be a literal value (such as 0 for a salary column or "unknown" for a description column), a system value, or a function.

Autoincrement Columns

Autoincrement columns are automatically numbered columns. When a column is set as an autoincrement column, MySQL automatically provides values for it when inserting new records into the table. Usually if max is the largest value currently in the table for that column, then the next generated value will be max + 1.

This way, the generated values are always unique, which makes them especially useful when used in conjunction with the PRIMARY KEY constraint. You already know that primary keys are used on columns that uniquely identify each row of a table. If you set a primary key column to also be an autoincrement column, the MySQL server automatically fills that column with values when adding new rows (in other words, it generates new IDs), ensuring that the values are unique.

When setting an autoincrement column, the first value that the MySQL server provides for that column is 1, but you can change this before adding data to your table with an SQL statement like the following:

```
ALTER TABLE your_table_name AUTO_INCREMENT = 1234;
```

This way, your MySQL server will start generating values with 1234.

The table structure you saw in Figure 4-9 shows that department_id in your department table is an autoincrement column.

■**Note** Unlike other database servers, MySQL still allows you to manually specify for an autonumbered field when adding new rows, if you want.

For more details about the autoincrement columns, see its official documentation at http://www.mysql.org/doc/refman/5.1/en/example-auto-increment.html.

Indexes

Indexes are related to MySQL performance tuning, so we'll mention them only briefly here. *Indexes* are database objects meant to increase the overall speed of database operations. Indexes work on the presumption that the vast majority of database operations are read operations. Indexes increase the speed of search operations but slow down insert, delete, and update operations. Usually, the gains of using indexes considerably outweigh the drawbacks.

On a table, you can create one or more indexes, with each index working on one column or on a set of columns. When a table is indexed on a specific column, its rows are either indexed or physically arranged based on the values of that column and the type of index. This makes search operations on that column very fast. If, for example, an index exists on department_id and then you do a search for the department with the ID value 934, the search would be performed very quickly.

The drawback of indexes is that they can slow down database operations that add new rows or update existing ones because the index must be actualized (or the table rows rearranged) each time these operations occur.

You should keep the following in mind about indexes:

- Indexes greatly increase search operations on the database, but they slow down operations that change the database (delete, update, and insert operations).

- Having too many indexes can slow down the general performance of the database. The general rule is to set indexes on columns frequently used in WHERE, ORDER BY, and GROUP BY clauses or used in table joins.

- By default, unique indexes are automatically created on primary key table columns.

You can use dedicated tools to test the performance of a database under stress conditions with and without particular indexes; in fact, a serious database administrator will want to run some of these tests before deciding on a winning combination for indexes.

■**Note** You learned about some data table properties in the previous pages. For more details about each of them, refer to the MySQL online manual at http://dev.mysql.com/doc/ or Jason Gilmore's *Beginning PHP and MySQL 5: From Novice to Professional, Second Edition* (Apress, 2006).

Creating the department Table

You created the tshirtshop database in Chapter 3. In the following exercise, you'll add the department table to it using the phpMyAdmin web client interface.

■**Note** Alternatively, you can use the SQL scripts from the Source Code/Download section of the Apress web site to create and populate the department table. You can find the database creation scripts in the Database folder for this chapter in the code download for this book. You can also find the files on the authors' web sites.

Exercise: Creating the department Table

1. Point your web browser to your phpMyAdmin location (`http://localhost/phpmyadmin/`), like you did in Chapter 3 when creating the `tshirtshop` database.

2. Select the `tshirtshop` database from the Database combo box in the left side of the window. Type **department** in the Name text box of the "Create a new table on database tshirtshop" section, and type **3** in the "Number of fields" text box, as shown in Figure 4-10.

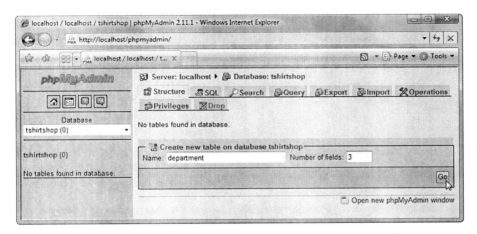

Figure 4-10. *Adding the department table to the database*

3. Click Go. You'll be presented with a screen where you need to specify the details for each of the three table columns as shown in Figure 4-11.

If you prefer to type the SQL code yourself instead of using the visual builder of phpMyAdmin, here's the code you need (you can find it in the source code download as well):

```
-- Create deparment table
CREATE TABLE `department` (
  `department_id` INT          NOT NULL  AUTO_INCREMENT,
  `name`          VARCHAR(100) NOT NULL,
  `description`   VARCHAR(1000),
  PRIMARY KEY (`department_id`)
) ENGINE=MyISAM;
```

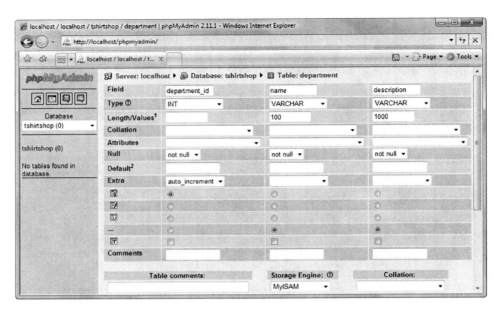

Figure 4-11. *Designing the department table*

4. Click Save. You'll be shown a page with many details about the table you just created. There, you can see the SQL code that was generated to create the table and various other details, such as confirmation that an index was indeed created automatically for the primary key field.

5. Now, you can add some sample data in the department table. Click the SQL tab, type the following query, and then click Go to execute it. The command should add three records to the department table you created earlier.

```
-- Populate department table
INSERT INTO `department` (`department_id`, `name`, `description`) VALUES
      (1, 'Regional', 'Proud of your country? Wear a T-shirt with a national
symbol stamp!'),
      (2, 'Nature', 'Find beautiful T-shirts with animals and flowers in our
Nature department!'),
      (3, 'Seasonal', 'Each time of the year has a special flavor. Our seasonal
T-shirts express traditional symbols using unique postal stamp pictures.');
```

How It Works: Creating MySQL Data Tables

You have just created your first database table! You also filled the table with some data using the INSERT SQL command, which we use to add records to a database table. You'll learn more about it soon.

As you can see, as soon as you have a clear idea about the structure of a table, it's relatively easy to use the phpMyAdmin web interface to create it into your database. Let's move on!

Communicating with the Database

Now that you have a table filled with data, let's do something useful with it! The ultimate goal with this table is to get the list of department names from a PHP page and populate the Smarty template with that list.

To get data from a database, you first need to know how to communicate with the database. Relational databases understand dialects and variants of *SQL*. The usual way of communicating with MySQL is to write an SQL command, send it to the MySQL server, and get the results back.

In practice, as you'll see later, we prefer to centralize the data access code using MySQL *stored procedures*, but before you can learn about them, you need to know the basics of SQL.

The Structured Query Language (SQL)

SQL is the language used to communicate with modern relational database management systems (RDBMSs). However, we haven't seen a database system yet that supports exactly the SQL 99 and SQL 2003 standards. This means that in many cases, the SQL code that works with one database will not work with the other. Currently, MySQL supports most of SQL 92 and an important part of SQL 99.

The most commonly used SQL commands are SELECT, INSERT, UPDATE, and DELETE. These commands allow you to perform the most basic operations on the database.

The basic syntax of these commands is very simple, as you'll see in the following pages. However, keep in mind that SQL is a very flexible and powerful language and can be used to create much more complicated and powerful queries than what you see here. You'll learn more while building the web site, but for now, let's take a quick look at the basic syntax. For more details about any of these commands, you can always refer to their official documentation:

- http://www.mysql.org/doc/refman/5.1/en/select.html

- http://www.mysql.org/doc/refman/5.1/en/insert.html

- http://www.mysql.org/doc/refman/5.1/en/update.html

- http://www.mysql.org/doc/refman/5.1/en/delete.html

SELECT

The SELECT statement is used to query the database and retrieve selected data that match the criteria you specify. Its basic structure is

```
SELECT <column list>
[FROM <table name(s)>]
[WHERE <restrictive condition(s)>]
```

■Note In this book, the SQL commands and queries appear in uppercase for consistency and clarity although SQL is not case sensitive. The WHERE and FROM clauses appear in brackets because they are optional.

The following command returns the name of the department that has the department_id of 1. In your case, the returned value is Regional, but you would receive no results if there was no department with an ID of 1.

```
SELECT name FROM department WHERE department_id = 1;
```

Tip You can easily test these queries to make sure they actually work by using the MySQL console interface or phpMyAdmin.

If you want more columns to be returned, you simply list them, separated by commas. Alternatively, you can use an asterisk (*), which means "all columns." However, for performance reasons, if you need only certain columns, you should list them separately instead of asking for them all. Using * is not advisable even if at a particular moment you do want all the columns for a query, because in the future, you may add even more columns to the table, and your query would end up asking for more data than is needed. Finally, using * doesn't guarantee the order in which the columns are returned, as the order of the columns in a table may change (although this is not likely to happen). For these reasons, we don't use * in this book.

With your current department table, the following two statements return the same results:

```
SELECT department_id, name, description
FROM    department
WHERE   department_id = 1;

SELECT * FROM department WHERE department_id = 1;
```

Tip You can split an SQL query on more lines, if you prefer—MySQL won't mind.

If you don't want to place any condition on the query, simply remove the WHERE clause, and you'll get all the rows. The following SELECT statement returns all rows and all columns from the department table:

```
SELECT * FROM department;
```

Tip If you are impatient and can't wait until later in the chapter, you can test the SQL queries right now by using the phpMyAdmin web client interface! Be careful, though, because in the rest of the book, we'll assume the data in your department table is the same as shown previously in the chapter.

Unless a sorting order is specified, the order in which the rows are returned by a SELECT clause can't be determined. Moreover, executing the same query twice could generate different results! To sort the results, you use ORDER BY. The following query will return the list of departments sorted alphabetically by the department name:

```
SELECT    department_id, name, description
FROM      department
ORDER BY name;
```

INSERT

The INSERT statement is used to insert a row of data into the table. Its syntax is as follows:

```
INSERT INTO <table name> [(column list)] VALUES (column values)
```

Tip Although the column list is optional (if you don't include it, column values are assigned to columns in the order in which they appear in the table's definition), you should always include it. This ensures that changing the table definition doesn't break the existing INSERT statements.

The following INSERT statement adds a department named Zodiac T-Shirts Department to the department table:

```
INSERT INTO department (name) VALUES ('Zodiac T-Shirts Department');
```

No value was specified for the description field, because it was marked to allow NULLs in the department table. This is why you can omit specifying a value, if you want to. Also, you're allowed to omit specifying a department ID, because the department_id column was created with the AUTO_INCREMENT option, which means the database takes care of automatically generating a value for it when adding new records. However, you're allowed to manually specify a value, if you prefer.

Tip Because department_id is the primary key column, trying to add more records with the same ID would cause the database to generate an error. The database doesn't permit having duplicate values in the primary key field.

When letting MySQL generate values for AUTO_INCREMENT columns, you can obtain the last generated value using the LAST_INSERT_ID() function. Here's an example of how this works:

```
INSERT INTO department (name) VALUES ('Some New Department');
SELECT LAST_INSERT_ID();
```

Tip In MySQL, the semicolon (;) is the delimiter between SQL commands.

UPDATE

The UPDATE statement is used to modify existing data and has the following syntax:

```
UPDATE   <table name>
SET <column name> = <new value> [, <column name> = <new value> ... ]
[WHERE <restrictive condition>]
```

The following query changes the name of the department with the ID of 43 to Cool Department. If there were more departments with that ID, all of them would have been modified, but because department_id is the primary key, you can't have more departments with the same ID.

```
UPDATE department SET name='Cool Department' WHERE department_id = 43;
```

Be careful with the UPDATE statement, because it makes messing up an entire table easy. If the WHERE clause is omitted, the change is applied to every record of the table, which you usually don't want to happen. MySQL will be happy to change all of your records; even if all departments in the table would have the same name and description, they would still be perceived as different entities because they have different department_id values.

DELETE

The syntax of the DELETE command is actually very simple:

```
DELETE FROM <table name>
[WHERE <restrictive condition>]
```

Most of the time, you'll want to use the WHERE clause to delete a single row:

```
DELETE FROM department WHERE department_id = 43;
```

As with UPDATE, be careful with this command, because if you forget to specify a WHERE clause, you'll end up deleting all of the rows in the table. The table itself isn't deleted by the DELETE command; for that purpose, you'd use DROP TABLE (http://dev.mysql.com/doc/refman/5.0/en/drop-table.html).

The following query deletes all the records in department:

```
DELETE FROM department;
```

MySQL Stored Procedures

A stored procedure is a named set of SQL commands stored in the MySQL server. Similar to functions in PHP, stored procedures can receive parameters and return data. Stored procedures in MySQL 5.1 follow the ANSI SQL 2003 specification. Their official documentation page is http://www.mysql.org/doc/refman/5.1/en/stored-procedures.html.

You don't need to use stored procedures if you want to perform database operations. You can directly send SQL commands from an external application (such as a PHP script of your TShirtShop application) to your MySQL database. When using stored procedures, instead of passing the SQL code you want executed, you just call the stored procedure and the values for any parameters it might have. Using stored procedures for data operations has the following advantages:

- Performance can be better, because MySQL generates an execution plan for the queries in the stored procedure when it's first executed, and then reuses the same plan on subsequent executions of the procedure.

- Using stored procedures allows for better maintainability of the data access and manipulation code, which is stored in a central place, and permits easier implementation of the three-tier architecture (the database stored procedures forming the data tier).

- Security can be better controlled, because MySQL permits setting different security permissions for each stored procedure.

- SQL queries created ad hoc in PHP code are more vulnerable to SQL injection attacks, which is a major security threat (many Internet resources cover this security subject, and you can find the most popular of them by Googling for "SQL injection attack").

- This might be a matter of taste, but separating the SQL logic from the PHP code keeps the PHP code cleaner and easier to manage; it simply looks better to execute a stored procedure than to build SQL queries by joining strings in PHP.

When developing TShirtShop, we'll save all the data access code as MySQL stored procedures inside the tshirtshop database. The syntax for creating stored procedures is

```
DELIMITER $$
CREATE PROCEDURE <name>(<param1 type>, <param2 type> ... )
BEGIN
  <code>
END$$

DELIMITER;
```

Note that the delimiter can be defined as something other than $$. The key is to define it as something different than the default delimiter, the semicolon.

You can't create a stored procedure if your database already has a procedure with the same name. To remove an existing stored procedure, you use the DROP PROCEDURE command. To change the body or parameters of an existing procedure, you need to delete it using DROP PROCEDURE and create it again. MySQL supports a command named ALTER PROCEDURE, but unlike with other database applications, it can't be used to update the body or parameters of an existing procedure.

For the data tier of the departments list, you need to create stored procedure called catalog_get_departments_list. This procedure returns a list with the IDs and names of the departments in TShirtShop, and it will be called by business tier methods that need this data. Let's implement catalog_get_departments_list in the following exercise.

Exercise: Creating MySQL Stored Procedures

1. Load phpMyAdmin (http://localhost/phpmyadmin/) into your favorite browser. Select the tshirtshop database from the Database combo box in the left side of the window.

2. Select the SQL tab, and change the delimiter to $$ as shown in Figure 4-12.

3. Execute the following code, which creates the catalog_get_departments_list stored procedure:

```
-- Create catalog_get_departments_list stored procedure
CREATE PROCEDURE catalog_get_departments_list()
BEGIN
  SELECT department_id, name FROM department ORDER BY department_id;
END$$
```

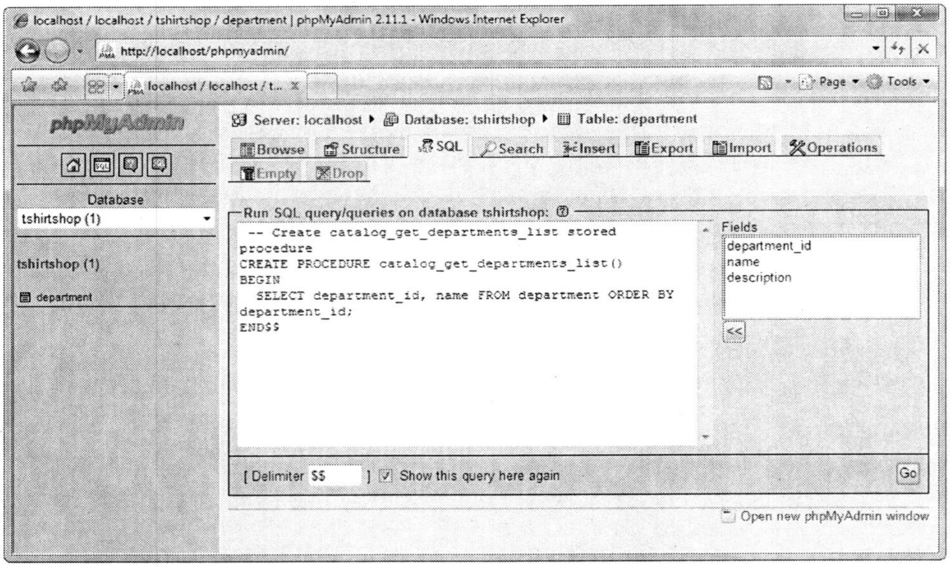

Figure 4-12. *Creating the catalog_get_deparments_list stored procedure*

How It Works: MySQL Stored Procedures

Let's break down in parts the `catalog_get_departments_list` stored procedure. On the first line, we're defining the stored procedure name:

```
PROCEDURE catalog_get_departments_list()
```

The body of the stored procedure is between `BEGIN` and `END$$`. The following code snippet represents the typical way we'll code our stored procedures. The bold line represents the query we're interested in, and the rest is auxiliary code required to define the body of the stored procedure.

```
BEGIN
  SELECT department_id, name FROM department ORDER BY department_id;
END$$
```

So what happens here? The code that performs the actual functionality is written between `BEGIN` and `END$$`. The syntax may look weird at first, but what it does is pretty straightforward.

The stored procedure executes the `SELECT` statement and returns the results.

Adding Logic to the Site

The business tier (or middle tier) is said to be the brains of the application, because it manages the application's business logic. However, for simple tasks such as getting a list of departments from the data tier, the business tier doesn't have much logic to implement. It just requests the data from the database and passes it along. Usually, there will be a presentation tier object that will request this data, but it could be another business tier method that needs the data to implement some more complex functionality.

In this chapter, we're building the foundation of the business tier, which includes the functionality to open and close database connections, store data logic as MySQL stored procedures, and access these stored procedures from PHP.

For the business tier of the departments list, you'll implement two classes:

- `DatabaseHandler` will store the common functionality that you'll reuse whenever you need to access the database. Having this kind of generic functionality packed in a separate class saves keystrokes and avoids bugs in the long run.

- `Catalog` contains product-catalog-specific functionality, such as the `GetDepartments()` method that will retrieve the list of departments from the database.

Connecting to MySQL

The SQL queries you write must be sent somehow to the database engine for execution. As you learned in Chapter 2, you'll use PHP PDO to access the MySQL server.

Before writing the business tier code, you need to analyze and understand the possibilities for implementation. The important questions to answer before writing any code include the following:

- What strategy should you adopt for opening and closing database connections when you need to execute an SQL query?

- Which methods of PHP PDO should you use for executing database stored procedures and returning the results?

- How should you handle possible errors and integrate the error-handling solution with the error-handling code you wrote in Chapter 3?

Let's have a look at each of these questions one by one, and then we'll start writing some code.

Opening and Closing Connections to the MySQL Server

There are two main possible approaches you can take for this. The first is illustrated by the following sequence of actions, which needs to be executed each time the database needs to be accessed.

1. *Open* a connection to the database immediately before you need to execute a command on the database.

2. *Execute* the SQL query (or the database stored procedure) using the open connection, and get back the results. At this stage, you also need to handle any possible errors.

3. *Close* the database connection immediately after executing the command.

This method has the advantage that you don't keep database connections for a long time (which is good because database connections consume server resources), and it is also encouraged for servers that don't allow many simultaneous database connections. The disadvantage is the overhead implied by opening and closing the database connection every time, which can be partially reduced by using persistent connections.

▓**Note** "Persistent connections" refers to a technology that attempts to improve the efficiency of opening and closing database connections with no impact on functionality. You can learn more about this technology at http://www.php.net/manual/en/features.persistent-connections.php.

The alternative solution, and the one you'll use when implementing TShirtShop, is like this:

1. *Open* a connection to the database the first time you need to access the database during a request.

2. *Execute* all database stored procedures (or SQL queries) through that connection without closing it. Here, you also need to handle any possible errors.

3. *Close* the database connection when the client request finishes processing.

Using this method, all database operations that happen for a single client request (which happens each time a user visits a new page of our site) will go through a single database connection, avoiding opening and closing the connection each time you need something from the database. You'll still use persistent connections to improve the efficiency of opening a new database connection for each client request.

This solution is the one you will use for data access in the TShirtShop project.

Using PHP PDO for Database Operations

Now, we'll talk about how to put this in practice—opening and closing database connections and executing queries using those connections—using PHP PDO.

As explained in Chapter 2, you won't access MySQL through PHP's MySQL extension functions, but through a database abstraction layer (PHP PDO). The PDO classes permit accessing various data sources using the same application programming interface (API), so you won't need to change the PHP data access code or learn different data-access techniques when working with database systems other than MySQL (but you might need to change the SQL code itself if the database you migrate to uses a different dialect). Using PHP PDO is the modern way to interact with your database, and it makes your life as a programmer easier in the long run.

The important PHP PDO class you'll work with is PDO, which provides methods for performing various database operations. We can take advantage of the many methods already in the PDO class to process data, make connections to the DB, and for many other common tasks; we are spared having to write the code for these common tasks, because they are already included in the PDO class. It is a good idea to be familiar with the methods that are made available to you through the PDO class—you don't have to understand exactly how they work, but knowing that the functionality is already available can save you hours of painstakingly reinventing the wheel.

> ■**Note** In this book, you'll learn about the PHP PDO functionality as used in TShirtShop. For more details about PHP PDO, see the *PHP Manual* documentation at http://www.php.net/manual/en/ref.pdo.php.

The PDO class provides the functionality to connect to the MySQL server and execute SQL queries. The method that opens a database connection is PDO's constructor, which receives as parameters the connection string to the database server and an optional parameter that specifies whether the connection is a persistent connection. The connection string contains the data required to connect to the database server. You create a new PDO object like this:

```
$dbh = new PDO('mysql:dbname=' . $db_name . ';host=' . $db_host,
               $db_user,
               $db_pass,
               array(PDO::ATTR_PERSISTENT => $persistent));
```

> ■**Note** The constructor of the PDO class returns an initialized database connection object (which is specific to the type of database you're connecting to, such as mysql) if the connection is successful; otherwise, an exception is thrown.

The previous code snippet shows the standard data you need to supply when connecting to a MySQL server and uses five variables:

- $db_user represents the username.

- $db_pass represents the user's password.

- $db_host is the hostname of your MySQL server.

- $db_name is the name of the database you're connecting to.

- $persistent is true if we want to create a persistent database connection or false otherwise.

To disconnect from the database, you need to make $dbh equal null ($dbh = null).

The following code snippet demonstrates how to create, open, and then close a MySQL database connection and also catch any exceptions that are thrown:

```
try
{
  // Open connection
  $dbh = new PDO('mysql:dbname=' . $db_name . ';host=' . $db_host,
                 $db_user, $db_pass);

  // Close connection
  $dbh = null;
}
```

```
catch (PDOException $e)
{
  echo 'Connection failed: ' . $e->getMessage();
}
```

The try and catch keywords are used to handle *exceptions*.

PHP 5 EXCEPTION HANDLING

In Chapter 3, you implemented the code that intercepts and handles (and eventually reports) errors that happen in the TShirtShop site. *PHP errors* are the standard mechanism that you can use to react with an error happening in your PHP code. When a PHP error occurs, the execution stops; you can, however, define an error-handling function that is called just before the execution is terminated. You added such a function in Chapter 3, where you obtained as many details as possible about the error and logged them for future reference. Having those details, a programmer can fix the code to avoid the same error happening in the future.

PHP 5 introduced, along with other object-oriented programming (OOP) features, a new way to handle runtime errors: enter exceptions. Exceptions represent the modern way of managing runtime errors in your code and are much more powerful and flexible than PHP errors. Exceptions are a very important part of the OO (object oriented) model, and PHP 5 introduces an exception model resembling that of other OOP languages, such as Java and C#. However, exceptions in PHP coexist with the standard PHP errors in a strange combination, and you can't solely rely on exceptions for dealing with runtime problems. Some PHP extensions, such as PDO, can be configured to generate exceptions to signal problems that happen at runtime, whereas in other cases, your only option is to deal with standard PHP errors.

The advantages of exceptions over errors lay in the flexibility you're offered in handling them. When an exception is generated, you can handle it locally and let your script continue executing normally, or you can pass the exception to another class for further processing. With exceptions, your script isn't terminated like it is when a PHP error appears. When using exceptions, you place the code that you suspect could throw an exception inside a try block and handle potential exceptions in an associated catch block:

```
try
{
  // Code that could generate an exception that you want to handle
}
catch (Exception $e)
{
  // Code that is executed when an exception is generated
  // (exception details are accessible through the $e object)
}
```

When an exception is generated by any of the code in the try block, the execution is passed directly to the catch block. Unless the code in the catch block rethrows the exception, it is assumed that it handled the exception, and the execution of your script continues normally. This kind of flexibility allows you to prevent many causes that could make your pages stop working, and you'll appreciate the power exceptions give you when writing PHP code!

A PHP 5 exception is represented by the Exception class, which contains the exception's details. You can generate (throw) an exception yourself using the throw keyword. The Exception object that you throw is propagated through the call stack until it is intercepted using the catch keyword. The *call stack* is the list of methods being executed. So if a function A() calls a function B(), which in turn calls a function C(), then the call stack will be formed of these three methods. In this scenario, an exception that is raised in function C() can be handled in the same function, provided the offending code is inside a try-catch block. If this is not the case, the exception propagates to method B(), which has a chance to handle the exception, and so on. If no method handles the exception, the exception is finally intercepted by the PHP interpreter, which transforms the exception into a PHP Fatal Error.

In our database-handling code, we'll catch the potential exceptions that could be generated by PDO. Although it doesn't do it by default, PDO can be instructed to generate exceptions in case something goes wrong when executing an SQL command or opening a database connection, like this:

```
// Create a new PDO class instance
$handler = new PDO( ... );

// Configure PDO to throw exceptions
self::$_mHandler->setAttribute(PDO::ATTR_ERRMODE,
                               PDO::ERRMODE_EXCEPTION);
```

We catch any exceptions the data access code may throw, and we pass the error details to the error-handling code you wrote in Chapter 3. The following code snippet shows a short method with this functionality implemented:

```
// Wrapper method for PDOStatement::fetch()
public static function GetRow($sqlQuery, $params = null,
                             $fetchStyle = PDO::FETCH_ASSOC)
{
  // Initialize the return value to null
  $result = null;

  // Try to execute an SQL query or a stored procedure
  try
  {
    // Get the database handler
    $database_handler = self::GetHandler();

    // Prepare the query for execution
    $statement_handler = $database_handler->prepare($sqlQuery);

    // Execute the query
    $statement_handler->execute($params);

    // Fetch result
    $result = $statement_handler->fetch($fetchStyle);
  }
```

```
    // Trigger an error if an exception was thrown when executing the SQL query
    catch(PDOException $e)
    {
      // Close the database handler and trigger an error
      self::Close();
      trigger_error($e->getMessage(), E_USER_ERROR);
    }

    // Return the query results
    return $result;
  }
```

Issuing Commands Using the Connection

After opening the connection, you're now at the stage we've been aiming for from the start: executing SQL commands through the connection.

You can execute the command in many ways, depending on the specifics. Does the SQL query you want to execute return any data? If so, what kind of data and in which format? The PDO methods that we'll use to execute SQL queries follow:

- PDOStatement::execute() is used to execute an INSERT, UPDATE, or DELETE queries that don't return any data.

- PDOStatement::fetch() is used to retrieve one row of data from the database.

- PDOStatement::fetchAll() is used to retrieve multiple rows of data from the database.

- PDO::prepare() prepares an SQL query to be executed, creating a so-called prepared statement.

A *prepared statement* is a parameterized SQL query whose parameter values are replaced by either parameter markers (?) or named variables (:variable_name), like in these examples:

```
$query1 = "SELECT name FROM department WHERE department_id = ?"
$query2 = "SELECT name FROM department WHERE department_id = :dept_id"
```

To execute a prepared statement, you supply the parameter values to the functions that execute your query, which take care of building the complete SQL query for you. To implement the list of departments, you won't need to work with parameters, but you'll learn how to handle them in Chapter 5.

In this book, we'll always use prepared statements, because they bring two important benefits:

- Parameter values are checked to prevent injection attacks.

- The query will likely execute faster with prepared statements, because the database server can reuse the access plan it builds for a prepared statement.

To be able to reuse more of the database-handling code and to have a centralized error-handling mechanism for the database code, we won't be using the PDO methods directly from the business tier of our application. Instead, we'll wrap the PDO functionality into a class named DatabaseHandler, and we'll use this class from the other classes of the business tier.

Writing the Business Tier Code

OK, let's write some code! You'll start by writing the DatabaseHandler class, which will be a support class that contains generic functionality needed in the other business tier methods. Next, you'll create a business tier class named Catalog, which uses the DatabaseHandler class to provide the functionality required by the presentation tier. The Catalog class will contain methods such as GetDepartments() (which will be used to generate the list of departments), GetCategories(), and so on. The only method we'll need to add to the Catalog class in this chapter is GetDepartments().

Although in this chapter we won't need all this functionality, we'll write the complete code of the DatabaseHandler class. DatabaseHandler will have the following methods:

- Execute() executes a stored procedure that doesn't return records from the database, such as INSERT, DELETE, or UPDATE statements.

- GetAll() is used to execute queries that return more rows of data, such as when requesting the list of departments.

- GetRow() is used to execute queries that return a row data.

- GetOne() returns a single value from the database. We can use this method to call database stored procedures that return a single value, such as one that returns the subtotal of a shopping cart.

Exercise: Creating and Using the DatabaseHandler Class

1. Add the database login information at the end of tshirtshop/include/config.php, modifying the constants' values to fit your server's configuration. The following code assumes you created the admin user account as instructed in Chapter 3:

```
// Database connectivity setup
define('DB_PERSISTENCY', 'true');
define('DB_SERVER', 'localhost');
define('DB_USERNAME', 'tshirtshopadmin');
define('DB_PASSWORD', 'tshirtshopadmin');
define('DB_DATABASE', 'tshirtshop');
define('PDO_DSN', 'mysql:host=' . DB_SERVER . ';dbname=' . DB_DATABASE);
```

2. Create a new file named database_handler.php in the tshirtshop/business folder, and create the DatabaseHandler class as shown in the following code listing. At this moment, we only included its constructor (which is private, so the class can't be instantiated), and the static GetHandler() method, which creates a new database connection, saves it into the $_mHandler member, and then returns this object (find more explanations about the process in the upcoming "How it Works" section).

```
<?php
// Class providing generic data access functionality
class DatabaseHandler
{
  // Hold an instance of the PDO class
  private static $_mHandler;
```

```php
    // Private constructor to prevent direct creation of object
    private function __construct()
    {
    }

    // Return an initialized database handler
    private static function GetHandler()
    {
      // Create a database connection only if one doesn't already exist
      if (!isset(self::$_mHandler))
      {
        // Execute code catching potential exceptions
        try
        {
          // Create a new PDO class instance
          self::$_mHandler =
            new PDO(PDO_DSN, DB_USERNAME, DB_PASSWORD,
                    array(PDO::ATTR_PERSISTENT => DB_PERSISTENCY));

          // Configure PDO to throw exceptions
          self::$_mHandler->setAttribute(PDO::ATTR_ERRMODE,
                                          PDO::ERRMODE_EXCEPTION);
        }
        catch (PDOException $e)
        {
          // Close the database handler and trigger an error
          self::Close();
          trigger_error($e->getMessage(), E_USER_ERROR);
        }
      }

      // Return the database handler
      return self::$_mHandler;
    }
  }
?>
```

3. Add the Close() method to the DatabaseHandler class. This method will be called to close the database connection:

```php
    // Clear the PDO class instance
    public static function Close()
    {
      self::$_mHandler = null;
    }
```

4. Add the Execute() method to the DatabaseHandler class. This method uses the PDOStatement::
execute() to run queries that don't return records (INSERT, DELETE, or UPDATE queries):

```
// Wrapper method for PDOStatement::execute()
public static function Execute($sqlQuery, $params = null)
{
  // Try to execute an SQL query or a stored procedure
  try
  {
    // Get the database handler
    $database_handler = self::GetHandler();

    // Prepare the query for execution
    $statement_handler = $database_handler->prepare($sqlQuery);

    // Execute query
    $statement_handler->execute($params);
  }
  // Trigger an error if an exception was thrown when executing the SQL query
  catch(PDOException $e)
  {
    // Close the database handler and trigger an error
    self::Close();
    trigger_error($e->getMessage(), E_USER_ERROR);
  }
}
```

5. Add the GetAll() method, which is the wrapper method for PDOStatement::fetchAll(). You'll call
this method for retrieving a complete result set from a SELECT query:

```
// Wrapper method for PDOStatement::fetchAll()
public static function GetAll($sqlQuery, $params = null,
                             $fetchStyle = PDO::FETCH_ASSOC)
{
  // Initialize the return value to null
  $result = null;

  // Try to execute an SQL query or a stored procedure
  try
  {
    // Get the database handler
    $database_handler = self::GetHandler();

    // Prepare the query for execution
    $statement_handler = $database_handler->prepare($sqlQuery);

    // Execute the query
    $statement_handler->execute($params);
```

```
      // Fetch result
      $result = $statement_handler->fetchAll($fetchStyle);
    }
    // Trigger an error if an exception was thrown when executing the SQL query
    catch(PDOException $e)
    {
      // Close the database handler and trigger an error
      self::Close();
      trigger_error($e->getMessage(), E_USER_ERROR);
    }


    // Return the query results
    return $result;
  }
```

6. Add the GetRow() method, which is the wrapper class for PDOStatement::fetch(), as shown. This will be used to get a row of data resulted from a SELECT query:

```
// Wrapper method for PDOStatement::fetch()
public static function GetRow($sqlQuery, $params = null,
                             $fetchStyle = PDO::FETCH_ASSOC)
{
  // Initialize the return value to null
  $result = null;

  // Try to execute an SQL query or a stored procedure
  try
  {
    // Get the database handler
    $database_handler = self::GetHandler();

    // Prepare the query for execution
    $statement_handler = $database_handler->prepare($sqlQuery);

    // Execute the query
    $statement_handler->execute($params);

    // Fetch result
    $result = $statement_handler->fetch($fetchStyle);
  }
  // Trigger an error if an exception was thrown when executing the SQL query
  catch(PDOException $e)
  {
    // Close the database handler and trigger an error
    self::Close();
    trigger_error($e->getMessage(), E_USER_ERROR);
  }
```

```
      // Return the query results
      return $result;
  }
```

7. Add the GetOne() method, which is the wrapper class for PDOStatement::fetch(), as shown. This will be used to get a single value resulted from a SELECT query:

```
// Return the first column value from a row
public static function GetOne($sqlQuery, $params = null)
{
  // Initialize the return value to null
  $result = null;

  // Try to execute an SQL query or a stored procedure
  try
  {
    // Get the database handler
    $database_handler = self::GetHandler();

    // Prepare the query for execution
    $statement_handler = $database_handler->prepare($sqlQuery);

    // Execute the query
    $statement_handler->execute($params);

    // Fetch result
    $result = $statement_handler->fetch(PDO::FETCH_NUM);

    /* Save the first value of the result set (first column of the first row)
       to $result */
    $result = $result[0];
  }
  // Trigger an error if an exception was thrown when executing the SQL query
  catch(PDOException $e)
  {
    // Close the database handler and trigger an error
    self::Close();
    trigger_error($e->getMessage(), E_USER_ERROR);
  }

  // Return the query results
  return $result;
}
```

8. Create a file named catalog.php file inside the business folder. Add the following code into this file:

```php
<?php
// Business tier class for reading product catalog information
```

```
class Catalog
{
  // Retrieves all departments
  public static function GetDepartments()
  {
    // Build SQL query
    $sql = 'CALL catalog_get_departments_list()';

    // Execute the query and return the results
    return DatabaseHandler::GetAll($sql);
  }
}
?>
```

9. You need to include the newly created database_handler.php in index.php to make the class available for the application. To do this, add the highlighted code to the index.php file:

```
<?php
// Include utility files
require_once 'include/config.php';
require_once BUSINESS_DIR . 'error_handler.php';

// Sets the error handler
ErrorHandler::SetHandler();

// Load the application page template
require_once PRESENTATION_DIR . 'application.php';

// Load the database handler
require_once BUSINESS_DIR . 'database_handler.php';
```

10. At the end of index.php, add the highlighted code that closes the database connection:

```
// Load Smarty template file
$application = new Application();

// Display the page
$application->display('store_front.tpl');

// Close database connection
DatabaseHandler::Close();
?>
```

How It Works: The Business Tier Code

After adding the database connection data to include/config.php, you created the DatabaseHandler class. This class contains a number of wrapper methods that access PDO methods and provide the functionality needed for the rest of the business tier methods.

The DatabaseHandler class has a *private constructor*, meaning that it can't be instantiated; you can't create DatabaseHandler objects, but you can execute the *static methods* for the class. Static class members and methods, as opposed to instance members and methods, are owned not by a particular instance of the class but by the class as a whole. In other words, to execute an SQL query using GetAll(), we wouldn't create a new class instance, like in the following example (and we couldn't do it not only because there's no instance version of the GetAll() method but also because the private constructor prevents us from instantiating the DatabaseHandler class):

```
$myHandler = new DatabaseHandler();
$results = $myHandler->GetAll($sql);
```

Instead, static methods are called directly using the class name (using the :: notation) as follows, instead of an object of the class (which uses the -> notation):

```
DatabaseHandler::GetAll($sql);
```

Static members of a class are internally stored by PHP using a global instance of the class. In our PDO scenario, the advantage of storing the database connection in a static member (private static $_mHandler) is that all database operations our site makes during one web request go through this one database connection. As explained earlier, for performance, we prefer to use this technique instead of creating a new database connection for each query that needs to be executed, and the support of static members of PHP allows us to implement it.

Note Static members are OOP-specific features that aren't supported by PHP 4 and older versions. You can find a very good introduction to the OOP features in PHP 5 at http://php.net/manual/en/ language.oop5.php.

The methods that execute database stored procedures have a standard structure, taking advantage of the fact that PDO has been configured to throw exceptions. Let's take a closer look at the GetRow() method:

```
// Wrapper method for PDOStatement::fetch()
public static function GetRow($sqlQuery, $params = null,
                              $fetchStyle = PDO::FETCH_ASSOC)
{
  // Initialize the return value to null
  $result = null;

  // Try to execute an SQL query or a stored procedure
  try
  {
    // Get the database handler
    $database_handler = self::GetHandler();

    // Prepare the query for execution
    $statement_handler = $database_handler->prepare($sqlQuery);
```

```
    // Execute the query
    $statement_handler->execute($params);

    // Fetch result
    $result = $statement_handler->fetch($fetchStyle);
  }
  // Trigger an error if an exception was thrown when executing the SQL query
  catch(PDOException $e)
  {
    // Close the database handler and trigger an error
    self::Close();
    trigger_error($e->getMessage(), E_USER_ERROR);
  }

  // Return the query results
  return $result;
}
```

This method generates an error (using the `trigger_error()` function) if the database command didn't execute successfully. The error is captured by the error-handling mechanism you implemented in Chapter 3.

Because of the way you implemented the error-handling code in Chapter 3, generating an E_USER_ERROR error freezes the execution of the request, eventually logging and/or e-mailing the error data, and showing the visitor a nice "Please come back later" message (if there is such thing as a nice "Please come back later" message, anyway).

Note that before the error is generated, we also close the database connection to ensure that we're not leaving any database resources occupied by the script.

By default, if you don't specify to `trigger_error()` the kind of error to generate, an E_USER_NOTICE message is generated, which doesn't interfere with the normal execution of the request (the error is eventually logged, but execution continues normally afterward).

The functionality in the DatabaseHandler class is meant to be used in the other business tier classes, such as Catalog. At this moment, Catalog contains a single method: GetDepartments().

```
// Business tier class for reading product catalog information
class Catalog
{
  // Retrieves all departments
  public static function GetDepartments()
  {
    // Build SQL query
    $sql = 'CALL catalog_get_departments_list()';

    // Execute the query and return the results
    return DatabaseHandler::GetAll($sql);
  }
}
```

Because it relies on the functionality you've already included in the DatabaseHandler class and in the database functions in place, the code in Catalog is very simple and straightforward. The GetDepartments() method will be called from the presentation tier, which will display the returned data to the visitor. It starts by building the SQL query, and then calling the appropriate DatabaseHandler method to execute the query. In this case, we're calling GetAll() to retrieve the list of departments.

Right now, the database connection is opened when index.php starts processing and is closed at the end. All database operations that happen in one iteration of this file will be done through this connection.

Displaying the List of Departments

Now that everything is in place in the other tiers, all you have to do is create the presentation tier part—this is the final goal that we've been aiming toward from the beginning of this chapter. As shown previously, the departments list needs to look something like the one shown in Figure 4-13 when the site is loaded in the browser.

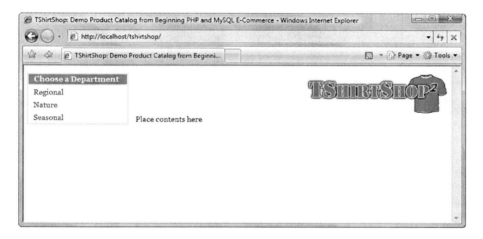

Figure 4-13. *TShirtShop with a dynamically generated list of departments*

You'll implement this functionality as a separate componentized template named departments_list. You'll then just include departments_list.tpl in the main Smarty template (templates/store_front.tpl).

The departments_list componentized template is made up of three files: the Smarty design template (templates/departments_list.tpl), the presentation object (presentation/departments_list.php), and the Smarty plug-in file (presentation/smarty_plugins/function.load_presentation_object.php). The Smarty plug-in file is a generic plug-in that will be used by all Smarty templates to load presentation objects.

Using Smarty Plug-ins

The *Smarty plug-in* is the Smarty technique we'll use to implement the logic behind Smarty design template files (with the `.tpl` extension). This is not the only way to store the logic behind a Smarty design template, but it's the way the Smarty documentation recommends at `http://smarty.php.net/manual/en/tips.componentized.templates.php`.

The layout and presentation in our project is generated using Smarty design templates. When a certain component is more complex and needs PHP code to supply it with additional data or functionality, we use a Smarty componentized template, which is composed of

- *Smarty design template*: This is a `.tpl` file containing HTML and Smarty-specific tags. For the departments list, the design template is named `departments_list.tpl`.

- *Smarty plug-in function*: The Smarty plug-in function is referenced from the Smarty design template, and its role is to supply the template with data it needs to display. In our project, the same Smarty plug-in function (`function.load_presentation_object.php`) will be loaded by all Smarty design templates. However, the Smarty plug-in function will return different results depending on the parameters it is invoked with.

- *Presentation object*: This is a class that returns the data required by a Smarty design template. In the case of the departments list, this class will be named `DepartmentsList`. This class reads the list of departments and stores it into a public member that can then be accessed by the Smarty design template.

Smarty plug-in files and functions must follow strict naming conventions to be located by Smarty. Smarty plug-in files must be named as `type.name.php` (in our case, `function.load_presentation_object.php`), and the functions inside these files must be named as `smarty_type_name` (in our case, `smarty_function_load_presentation_object`). The official page for Smarty plug-ins naming conventions is `http://smarty.php.net/manual/en/plugins.naming.conventions.php`. You can learn more about Smarty plug-ins at `http://smarty.php.net/manual/en/plugins.php`.

After the Smarty plug-in file is in place, you can reference it from the Smarty design template file (`departments_list.tpl`) with a line like this:

```
{load_presentation_object filename="departments_list" assign="obj"}
```

Given the correct naming conventions where used, this line is enough to get Smarty to load the plug-in file, which at its turn will load the presentation object mentioned through the `filename` parameter, and assign the loaded object to a template variable (in our example the name of the variable will be `obj`). The Smarty design template file can then access the variables populated by the plug-in function like this:

```
{$obj->mDepartments[i].name}
```

To understand how the whole mechanism works, let's create the `departments_list` componentized template, and all the other pieces required to have it working. We'll continue to use CSS for defining the visual styles of our presentation. While CSS is very powerful, learning the basics of its use is straightforward and easy—and even fun!

Exercise: Creating the departments_list Componentized Template

1. Open the tshirtshop.css file in the tshirtshop/styles folder, and add the following code listing. These styles refer to the way department names should look inside the departments list when they are unselected, unselected but with the mouse hovering over them, or selected.

```
div.yui-b div.box {
  color: #333333;
  border: 1px solid #c6e1ec;
  margin-top: 15px;
}

div.yui-b div p.box-title {
  background: #0590C7;
  border-bottom: 2px solid #c6e1ec;
  color: #FFFFFF;
  display: block;
  font-size: 93%;
  font-weight: bold;
  margin: 1px;
  padding: 2px 10px;
}

a {
  color: #0590C7;
}

a:hover {
  color: #ff0000;
}

a.selected {
  font-weight: bold;
}

div.yui-b div ul {
  margin: 0;
}

div.yui-b div ul li {
  border-bottom: 1px solid #fff;
  list-style-type: none;
}

div.yui-b div ul li a {
  color: #333333;
  display: block;
```

```css
   text-decoration: none;
   padding: 3px 10px;
}

div.yui-b div ul li a:hover {
   background: #c6e1ec;
   color: #333333;
}
```

2. Edit the `presentation/application.php` file, and add the following two lines to the constructor of the Application class. These lines configure the plug-in folders used by Smarty. The first one is for the internal Smarty plug-ins, and the second specifies the `smarty_plugins` folder you'll create to hold the plug-ins you'll write for TShirtShop.

```php
/* Class that extends Smarty, used to process and display Smarty
   files */
classApplication extends Smarty
{
  // Class constructor
  public function __construct()
  {
    // Call Smarty's constructor
    parent::Smarty();

    // Change the default template directories
    $this->template_dir = TEMPLATE_DIR;
    $this->compile_dir = COMPILE_DIR;
    $this->config_dir = CONFIG_DIR;
    $this->plugins_dir[0] = SMARTY_DIR . 'plugins';
    $this->plugins_dir[1] = PRESENTATION_DIR . 'smarty_plugins';
  }
}
```

3. Now, create the Smarty template file for the `departments_list` componentized template. Write the following lines in `presentation/templates/departments_list.tpl`. This will create the presentation or visual layout of the departments list.

```smarty
{* departments_list.tpl *}
{load_presentation_object filename="departments_list" assign="obj"}
{* Start departments list *}
<div class="box">
  <p class="box-title">Choose a Department</p>
  <ul>
  {* Loop through the list of departments *}
  {section name=i loop=$obj->mDepartments}
    {assign var=selected value=""}
    {* Verify if the department is selected to decide what CSS style
       to use *}
    {if ($obj->mSelectedDepartment ==
```

```
                    $obj->mDepartments[i].department_id)}
          {assign var=selected value="class=\"selected\""}
      {/if}
      <li>
        {* Generate a link for a new department in the list *}
        <a {$selected} href="{$obj->mDepartments[i].link_to_department}">
          {$obj->mDepartments[i].name}
        </a>
      </li>
    {/section}
    </ul>
  </div>
{* End departments list *}
```

4. Create a folder named `smarty_plugins` in the `presentation` folder. This will contain the Smarty plug-in files.

5. Inside the `smarty_plugins` folder, create a file named `function.load_presentation_object.php`, and add the following code to it:

```php
<?php
// Plug-in functions inside plug-in files must be named: smarty_type_name
function smarty_function_load_presentation_object($params, $smarty)
{
  require_once PRESENTATION_DIR . $params['filename'] . '.php';

  $className = str_replace(' ', '',
                           ucfirst(str_replace('_', ' ',
                                               $params['filename'])));

  // Create presentation object
  $obj = new $className();

  if (method_exists($obj, 'init'))
  {
    $obj->init();
  }

  // Assign template variable
  $smarty->assign($params['assign'], $obj);
}
?>
```

6. Inside the `presentation` folder, create a file named `departments_list.php`, and add the following code to it:

```php
<?php
// Manages the departments list
class DepartmentsList
{
```

```
/* Public variables available in departments_list.tpl Smarty template */
public $mSelectedDepartment = 0;
public $mDepartments;

// Constructor reads query string parameter
public function __construct()
{
  /* If DepartmentId exists in the query string, we're visiting a
     department */
  if (isset ($_GET['DepartmentId']))
    $this->mSelectedDepartment = (int)$_GET['DepartmentId'];
}

/* Calls business tier method to read departments list and create
   their links */
public function init()
{
  // Get the list of departments from the business tier
  $this->mDepartments = Catalog::GetDepartments();

  // Create the department links
  for ($i = 0; $i < count($this->mDepartments); $i++)
    $this->mDepartments[$i]['link_to_department'] =
      'index.php?DepartmentId=' . $this->mDepartments[$i]['department_id'];
}
}
?>
```

7. Modify the index.php file to include a reference to the Catalog business tier class:

```
// Load the application page template
require_once PRESENTATION_DIR . 'application.php';

// Load the database handler
require_once BUSINESS_DIR . 'database_handler.php';

// Load Business Tier
require_once BUSINESS_DIR . 'catalog.php';

// Load Smarty template file
$application = new Application();
```

8. Make the following modification in presentation/templates/store_front.tpl to load the newly created departments_list componentized template. Search for the following code:

```
    <div class="yui-b">
      Place list of departments here
    </div>
```

and replace it with this:

```
<div class="yui-b">
  {include file="departments_list.tpl"}
</div>
```

9. Examine the result of your work with your favorite browser by loading http://localhost/tshirtshop/
   index.php (refer to Figure 4-13). Play a little with the page to see what happens when you click a department or place the mouse over a link.

■**Note** If you don't get the expected output, make sure your machine is configured correctly and all PHP
required modules, such as PDO, were loaded successfully. Many errors will be reported in the Apache error
log file (by default, C:\xampp\apache\logs\error.log on Windows or /opt/lampp/logs/error_log on
Linux). Also, make sure to check the book's errata page, which we'll keep updated with solutions to potential
problems you may run into.

How It Works: The departments_list Smarty Template

If the page worked as expected from the start, you're certainly one lucky programmer! Most of the time, errors
happen because of typos, so watch out for them! Database access problems are also common, so make sure you
correctly configured the tshirtshop database and the tshirtshopadmin user, as shown in Chapter 3. In any
case, we're lucky to have a good error-reporting mechanism, which shows a detailed error report if something goes
wrong. Figure 4-14 shows the error message I received when mistyping the database password in config.php.
The error message shows up in the box that generated it (to be able to read the message, you need to select it in
the box it was generated, and paste it in another document).

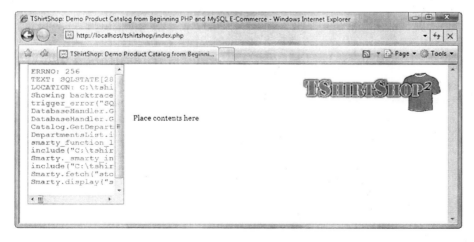

Figure 4-14. *The error-handling code you've written in Chapter 2 is helpful for debugging.*

If everything goes right, however, you'll get the neat page containing a list of departments generated using
a Smarty template. Each department name in the list is a link to the department's page, which, in fact, is a link to

the index.php page with a DepartmentId parameter in the query string that specifies which department was selected. Here's an example of such a link:

http://localhost/tshirtshop/index.php?DepartmentId=3

When clicking a department's link, the selected department will be displayed using a different CSS style in the list (see Figure 4-15).

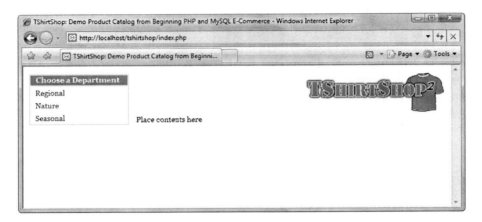

Figure 4-15. *Selecting a department*

It is important to understand how the Smarty template file (presentation/templates/departments_list.tpl) and the plug-in file (presentation/smarty_plugins/function.load_presentation_object.php) work together to generate the list of departments and to use the correct style for the currently selected one.

The processing starts at function.load_presentation_object.php, which is included in the store_front.tpl file. The first line in departments_list.tpl loads the DepartmentList presentation object through the Smarty plug-in:

{load_presentation_object filename="departments_list" assign="obj"}

The smarty_function_load_presentation_object() plug-in function creates and initializes a DepartmentsList object (this class is included in presentation/departments_list.php), which is then assigned to the obj variable accessible from the Smarty design template file:

```
// Plug-in functions inside plug-in files must be named: smarty_type_name
function smarty_function_load_presentation_object($params, $smarty)
{
  require_once PRESENTATION_DIR . $params['filename'] . '.php';

  $className = str_replace(' ', '',
                      ucfirst(str_replace('_', ' ',
                                      $params['filename'])));

  // Create presentation object
  $obj = new $className();
```

```
  if (method_exists($obj, 'init'))
  {
    $obj->init();
  }

  // Assign template variable
  $smarty->assign($params['assign'], $obj);
}
```

The init() method in DepartmentsList populates a public member of the class ($mDepartments) with an array containing the list of departments and another public member containing the index of the currently selected department ($mSelectedDepartment).

Back to the Smarty code now—inside the HTML code that forms the layout of the Smarty template (presentation/templates/departments_list.tpl), you can see the Smarty tags that do the magic:

```
{* Loop through the list of departments *}
{section name=i loop=$obj->mDepartments}
  {assign var=selected value=""}
  {* Verify if the department is selected to decide what CSS style
     to use *}
  {if ($obj->mSelectedDepartment == $obj->mDepartments[i].department_id)}
    {assign var=selected value="class=\"selected\""}
  {/if}
  <li>
    {* Generate a link for a new department in the list *}
    <a {$selected} href="{$obj->mDepartments[i].link_to_department}">
      {$obj->mDepartments[i].name}
    </a>
  </li>
{/section}
```

Smarty template sections are used for looping over arrays of data. In this case, you want to loop over the departments array kept in $obj->mDepartments:

```
{section name=i loop=$obj->mDepartments}
  ...
{/section}
```

Inside the loop, you verify whether the current department in the loop ($obj->mDepartments[i].department_id) has the ID that was mentioned in the query string ($obj->mSelectedDepartment). Depending on this, you decide what style to apply to the name by saving the style name (selected or default style) to a variable named selected.

This variable is then used to generate the link:

```
    <a {$selected} href="{$obj->mDepartments[i].link_to_department}">
      {$obj->mDepartments[i].name}
    </a>
```

Creating the Link Factory

In a well-constructed web site, all the links must have a consistent format. For example, in PHP, you read query string parameters by name rather than ordinal, so the following two links would normally have the same output:

- `http://localhost/index.php?DepartmentId=3&CategoryId=5`

- `http://localhost/index.php?CategoryId=5&DepartmentId=3`

In many cases, the case of parts of an URL can be changed without affecting the output. To have all the URLs in our web site follow a consistent style, we'll create a class that creates links.

This class will prove to be very useful in the long term. In Chapter 7, we'll update the URLs in our web site, so that they will be more friendly to search engines and human visitors browsing your site. Having a central place that generates links will make this feature easy to implement.

Also, at some point in the development process, you'll want certain pages of your site to be accessible only through secured HTTPS connections to ensure the confidentiality of the data passed from the client to the server and back. Such sensitive pages include user login forms, pages where the user enters credit card data, and so on. We don't get into much detail here. However, what you do need to know is that pages accessed through HTTPS occupy much of a server's resources, and we only want to use a secure connection when visiting secure pages. Once again, the link factory can come in handy, as it can be configured to generate HTTPS links only for the sections of the web site that need increased security.

Our link factory will always generate absolute links. Most of the time, it's more comfortable to use relative links inside the web site. For example, it's typical for the header image of a site to contain a link to `index.php` rather than the full URL, such as `http://www.example.com/index.php`. In this case, clicking the header image from a secured page would redirect the user to `https://www.example.com/index.php`, so the visitor would end up accessing through a secure connection a page that isn't supposed to be accessed like that (and, in effect, consumes much more server resources than necessary).

To avoid this problem and other similar ones, we'll write a bit of code that makes sure all the links in the web site are absolute links.

Exercise: Creating the Link Factory

1. Create a new file named `link.php` in the `presentation` folder, and add the following code to it:

```php
<?php
class Link
{
  public static function Build($link)
  {
    $base = 'http://' . getenv('SERVER_NAME');
```

```php
      // If HTTP_SERVER_PORT is defined and different than default
      if (defined('HTTP_SERVER_PORT') && HTTP_SERVER_PORT != '80')
      {
        // Append server port
        $base .= ':' . HTTP_SERVER_PORT;
      }

      $link = $base . VIRTUAL_LOCATION . $link;

      // Escape html
      return htmlspecialchars($link, ENT_QUOTES);
    }

    public static function ToDepartment($departmentId)
    {
      $link = 'index.php?DepartmentId=' . $departmentId;

      return self::Build($link);
    }
  }
?>
```

2. Add two new constants to include/config.php:

```php
// Server HTTP port (can omit if the default 80 is used)
define('HTTP_SERVER_PORT', '80');
/* Name of the virtual directory the site runs in, for example:
   '/tshirtshop/' if the site runs at http://www.example.com/tshirtshop/
   '/' if the site runs at http://www.example.com/ */
define('VIRTUAL_LOCATION', '/tshirtshop/');
```

3. Modify the init() method from the DepartmentsList class in presentation/departments_list.php as shown in the highlighted code:

```php
  /* Calls business tier method to read departments list and create
     their links */
  public function init()
  {
    // Get the list of departments from the business tier
    $this->mDepartments = Catalog::GetDepartments();

    // Create the department links
    for ($i = 0; $i < count($this->mDepartments); $i++)
      $this->mDepartments[$i]['link_to_department'] =
        Link::ToDepartment($this->mDepartments[$i]['department_id']);
  }
```

4. Create a new file named `store_front.php` in the `presentation` folder, and add the following code to it. This is the presentation object that we'll use for the `store_front` template, and it builds a link to the main page of the site.

```php
<?php
class StoreFront
{
  public $mSiteUrl;

  // Class constructor
  public function __construct()
  {
    $this->mSiteUrl = Link::Build('');
  }
}
?>
```

5. Modify `presentation/templates/store_front.tpl` like this:

```
{* smarty *}
{config_load file="site.conf"}
{load_presentation_object filename="store_front" assign="obj"}
<!DOCTYPE html PUBLIC "-//W3C//DTD XHTML 1.0 Transitional//EN"
 "http://www.w3.org/TR/xhtml1/DTD/xhtml1-transitional.dtd">
<html>
  <head>
    <title>{#site_title#}</title>
    <meta http-equiv="Content-Type" content="text/html; charset=UTF-8" />
    <link type="text/css" rel="stylesheet"
    href="{$obj->mSiteUrl}styles/tshirtshop.css" />
  </head>
  <body>
    <div id="doc" class="yui-t2">
      <div id="bd">
        <div id="yui-main">
          <div class="yui-b">
            <div id="header" class="yui-g">
              <a href="{$obj->mSiteUrl}">
                <img src="{$obj->mSiteUrl}images/tshirtshop.png"
                alt="tshirtshop logo" />
              </a>
            </div>
            <div id="contents" class="yui-g">
              Place contents here
            </div>
          </div>
        </div>
        <div class="yui-b">
          {include file="departments_list.tpl"}
```

```
        </div>
      </div>
    </div>
  </body>
</html>
```

6. Open index.php, and add a reference to the Link class as shown in the highlighted code:

```php
<?php
// Include utility files
require_once 'include/config.php';
require_once BUSINESS_DIR . 'error_handler.php';

// Sets the error handler
ErrorHandler::SetHandler();

// Load the application page template
require_once PRESENTATION_DIR . 'application.php';
require_once PRESENTATION_DIR . 'link.php';

// Load the database handler
require_once BUSINESS_DIR . 'database_handler.php';
```

7. Load TShirtShop, and make sure it still works as expected. This exercise isn't supposed to alter our existing functionality but to implement an improvement that will prove to be of great help when extending the site in the following chapters.

How It Works: Using the Link Factory

First of all, make sure the new entry you added to config.php is configured correctly. If you're running your web site on a different port than the default of 80 (say, if you're using port 8080), make sure you specify the correct port in the HTTP_SERVER_PORT constant. Now, let's see how the link factory works. The Link presentation object is used as shown by the modifications you've implemented in store_front.tpl and departments_list.tpl, and it transforms the relative links received as parameters to absolute links.

■**Note** In case you aren't using the tshirtshop alias as explained in Chapter 3, you'll need to modify the VIRTUAL_LOCATION constant in config.php to reflect the real location of your web application.

Note that the Build() method doesn't add the port if the HTTP_SERVER_PORT constant isn't defined or if it contains the default port 80:

```php
// If HTTP_SERVER_PORT is defined and different than default
if (defined('HTTP_SERVER_PORT') && HTTP_SERVER_PORT != '80')
{
  // Append server port
  $base .= ':' . HTTP_SERVER_PORT;
}
```

However, you should add the HTTP_SERVER_PORT to config.php anyway to make it easier to modify in case you move the application to a server that runs on another port. If HTTP_SERVER_PORT would be, for example, 8080, the links to index.php specified earlier would be transformed to

```
<a href="http//www.example.com:8080/index.php">
```

Summary

This long chapter was well worth the effort when you consider how much theory you've learned and applied to the TShirtShop project! In this chapter, you accomplished the following:

- You created the department table and populated it with data.

- You learned how to access this data from the data tier using PDO and then how to access the data tier method from the business tier.

- You learned how to use PHP 5 exceptions.

- You implemented the user interface using a Smarty template.

In the next chapter, you will finish creating the product catalog by displaying the site's categories and products! After that's accomplished, we'll have the opportunity to review the structure our web site is built on and the theory you've learned so far.

CHAPTER 5

■ ■ ■

Creating the Product Catalog: Part 2

In the previous chapter, you implemented a selectable list of departments for the TShirtShop web site. However, a product catalog is much more than that list of departments. In this chapter, you'll add many new product catalog features, including displaying product lists and a product details.

Review Figures 4-1, 4-2, and 4-3 to get a visual feeling of the new functionality you'll implement in this chapter. More specifically, in this chapter, you will

- Learn about relational data and the types of relationships that occur among data tables and then create the new data structures in your database.

- Learn how to join related data tables and even more theory about MySQL stored procedures and techniques.

- Complete the business tier to work with the new MySQL stored procedures, send parameters, and pass requested data to the presentation tier.

- Complete the presentation tier to show your visitor details about the catalog's categories, products, and more.

Storing the New Data

Given the new functionality you are adding in this chapter, it's not surprising that you need to add more data tables to the database. However, this isn't just about adding new data tables. You also need to learn about relational data and the relationships that you can implement among the data tables so that you can obtain more significant information from your database.

What Makes a Relational Database

It's no mystery that a database is something that stores data. However, today's modern Relational Database Management Systems (RDBMS), such as MySQL, PostgreSQL, SQL Server, Oracle, DB2, and others, have extended this basic role by adding the capability to store and manage relational data. This is a concept that deserves some attention.

So what does *relational data* mean? It's easy to see that every piece of data ever written in a real-world database is somehow related to some already existing information. Products are related to categories and departments; orders are related to products and customers, and so on. A relational database keeps its information stored in data tables but is also aware of the relationships between the tables.

These related tables form the *relational database*, which becomes an object with a significance of its own, rather than simply being a group of unrelated data tables. It is said that *data* becomes *information* only when we give significance to it, and establishing relations with other pieces of data is an ideal means of doing so.

Look at the product catalog to see what pieces of data it needs and how you can transform this data into information. For the product catalog, you'll need at least three data tables: one for departments, one for categories, and one for products. It's important to note that physically each data table is an independent database object, even if logically it's part of a larger entity—in other words, even though we say that a category *contains* products, the table that contains the products is not inside the table that contains categories. This is not in contradiction with the relational character of the database.

Figure 5-1 depicts a simple representation of three data tables, including some selected sample data.

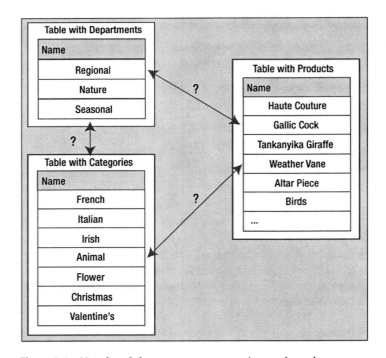

Figure 5-1. *Unrelated departments, categories, and products*

When two tables are said to be related, this more specifically means that the *records* of those tables are related. So, if the products table is related to the categories table, this translates into each product record being somehow related to one of the records in the categories table.

Figure 5-1 doesn't show the physical representation of the database, so we didn't list the table names there. Diagrams like this are used to decide *what* needs to be stored in the database. After you know *what* to store, the next step is to decide *how* the listed data is related, which leads to the physical structure for the database. Although Figure 5-1 shows three kinds of data that you want to store, you'll learn later that to implement this structure in the database, you'll actually use four tables.

So, now that you know the data you want to store, let's think about how the three parts relate to each other. Apart from knowing that the records of two tables are related *somehow*, you also need to know *the kind of relationship* between them. Let's now take a closer look at the different ways in which two tables can be related.

Relational Data and Table Relationships

To continue exploring the world of relational databases, let's further analyze the three logical tables we've been looking at so far. To make life easier, let's give them names now: the table containing products is product; the table containing categories is category; and the last one is our old friend, department. No surprises here! Luckily, these tables implement the most common kinds of relationships that exist between tables, the *one-to-many* and *many-to-many* relationships, so you have the chance to learn about them.

Note Some variations of these two relationship types exist, as well as the less popular *one-to-one* relationship. In the one-to-one relationship, each row in one table matches exactly one row in the other. For example, in a database that allowed patients to be assigned to beds, you would hope that there would be a one-to-one relationship between patients and beds! Database systems don't support enforcing this kind of relationship, because you would have to add matching records in both tables at the same time. Moreover, two tables with a one-to-one relationship can be joined to form a single table.

One-to-Many Relationships

The one-to-many relationship happens when one record in a table can be associated with multiple records in the related table but not vice versa. In our case, this happens for the department-category relation. A specific department can contain any number of categories, but each category belongs to *exactly one* department. Figure 5-2 better represents the one-to-many relationship among departments and categories.

Another common scenario in which you see the one-to-many relationship is with the order-order_detail tables, where order contains general details about the order (such as date, total amount, and so on) and order_detail contains the products related to the order.

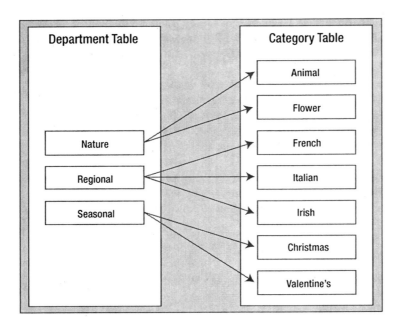

Figure 5-2. *A one-to-many relationship among departments and categories*

The one-to-many relationship is implemented in the database by adding an extra column in the table at the *many* side of the relationship, which references the ID column of the table in the *one* side of the relationship. Simply said, in the `category` table, you'll have an extra column (called `department_id`) that will hold the ID of the department the category belongs to. You'll implement this in your database a bit later, after you learn about the many-to-many relationships and foreign key constraints.

Many-to-Many Relationships

The other common type of relationship is the many-to-many relationship. This kind of relationship is implemented when records in both tables of the relationship can have multiple matching records in the other. In our scenario, this happens for the `product` and `category` tables, because we know that a product can exist in more than one category (*one* product with *many* categories), and a category can have more than one product (*one* category with *many* products).

This happens because we decided earlier that a product could be in more than one category. If a product could only belong to a single category, you would have another one-to-many relationship, just like the one that exists among departments and categories (where a category can't belong to more than one department).

If you represent this relationship with a picture, as shown previously in Figure 5-2, but with generic names this time, you get something like what is shown in Figure 5-3.

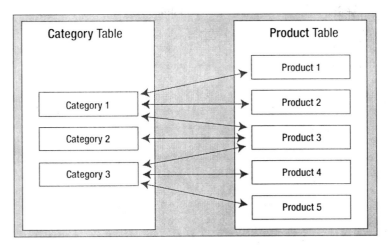

Figure 5-3. *The many-to-many relationship between categories and products*

Although logically the many-to-many relationship happens between two tables, databases (including MySQL databases) don't have the means to physically implement this kind of relationship by using just two tables, so we cheat by adding a third table to the mix. This third table, called a *junction table* (also known as a *linking table* or *associate table*) and two one-to-many relationships will help achieve the many-to-many relationship. The junction table is used to associate products and categories, with no restriction on how many products can exist for a category or to how many categories a product can be added. Figure 5-4 shows the role of the junction table.

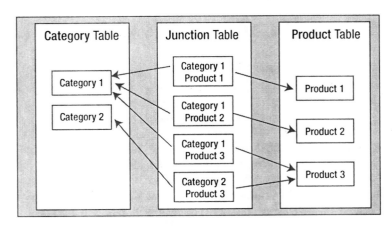

Figure 5-4. *The many-to-many relationship among categories and products*

Note that each record in the junction table links one category with one product. You can have as many records as you like in the junction table, linking any category to any product. The linking table contains two fields, each one referencing the primary key of one of the two linked tables. In our case, the junction table will contain two fields: a category_id field and a product_id field.

Each record in the junction table will consist of a product and category ID pair (product_id, category_id), which will be used to associate a particular product with a particular category. By adding more records to the product_category table, you can associate a product with more categories or a category with more products, effectively implementing the many-to-many relationship.

Because the many-to-many relationship is implemented using a third table that makes the connection between the linked tables, there is no need to add additional fields to the related tables in the way that we added the department_id to the category table for implementing the one-to-many relationship.

There's no definitive naming convention to use for the junction table. Most of the time it's OK to just join the names of the two linked tables—in this case, the junction table is named product_category.

Enforcing Table Relationships Using Foreign Keys

Relationships among tables can be physically enforced in the database using FOREIGN KEY constraints, or simply *foreign keys*.

You learned in the previous chapter about the PRIMARY KEY and UNIQUE constraints. We covered them there, because they apply to the table as an individual entity. Foreign keys, on the other hand, occur between two tables: the table in which the foreign key is defined (the *referencing table*) and the table the foreign key references (the *referenced table*).

■**Tip** Actually, the referencing table and the referenced table can be one and the same. This isn't seen too often in practice, but it's not unusual either. For example, you can have a table with employees, where each employee references the employee that is his or her boss (in this scenario, the big boss's row would probably reference itself).

A *foreign key* is a column or combination of columns used to enforce a link between data in two tables (usually representing a one-to-many relationship). Foreign keys are used both as a method of ensuring data integrity and to establish a relationship between tables.

To enforce database integrity, the foreign keys, like the other types of constraints, apply certain restrictions. Unlike PRIMARY KEY and UNIQUE constraints that apply restrictions to a single table, the FOREIGN KEY constraint *applies restrictions on both the referencing and referenced tables*. For example, if you enforce the one-to-many relationship between the department and category tables by using a FOREIGN KEY constraint, the database will include this relationship as part of its integrity. It will not allow you to add a category to a nonexistent department, nor will it allow you to delete a department if there are categories that belong to it.

There's good news and bad news about the FOREIGN KEY constraint and MySQL. The bad news is that the default storage engine in most MySQL instances—MyISAM—doesn't support enforcing FOREIGN KEY constraints. The alternative to MyISAM is the InnoDB storage engine, but InnoDB tables don't support full-text searching, which will be needed when implementing the search feature (in Chapter 8).

The good news is that you can have different types of tables inside a single database, so you can use MyISAM for tables that don't need free-text searching and/or foreign keys and InnoDB for the others. You must be extra careful when manipulating data from MyISAM tables, however, because you can't rely on the database to enforce its integrity on its own.

■**Note** Foreign keys can be programmatically implemented for the storing engines types that don't support them, with the aid of *triggers*. You can find a good tutorial about this technique at `http://dev.mysql.com/tech-resources/articles/mysql-enforcing-foreign-keys.html`.

Before implementing the rest of the product catalog tables, we need to explain more about the various types of MySQL table types.

MySQL Table Types

MySQL supports several storage engines that can be used to store your data. When creating a new data table, if not specified otherwise, the default table type (MyISAM) is used. Following are three important table types supported by MySQL:

MyISAM is the default storage engine when creating new tables since MySQL 3.23 (when it replaced its older version, ISAM). It is the fastest table type in MySQL, at the cost of not supporting foreign keys, `CHECK` constraints, transactions, and some other advanced features. However, unlike the other table types, it supports full-text searching, which is very helpful when implementing the searching capability in the web site.

InnoDB is a very popular and powerful database engine for MySQL that, among other features, supports transactions, has great capability to handle many simultaneous update operations, and can enforce `FOREIGN KEY` constraints. The engine is developed independently of MySQL, and its home page is `http://www.innodb.com`.

HEAP is a special kind of table type in that it is constructed in system memory. It cannot be used to reliably store data (in case of a system failure, all data is lost and cannot be recovered), but it can be a good choice when working with tables that need to be very fast with data that can be easily reconstructed if accidentally lost.

To learn more about these storage engines, and about the other storage engines supported by MySQL, see the manual page at `http://dev.mysql.com/doc/refman/5.0/en/storage-engines.html`.

■**Note** For the TShirtShop product catalog, you'll be using MyISAM tables mainly because you need their full-text search feature. If you change your mind about the type of a table, you can easily change it with the `ALTER TABLE` command. The following line of code would make the department table an InnoDB table:

```
ALTER TABLE department ENGINE=InnoDB;
```

Creating and Populating the New Data Tables

Now, it's time to create the three new tables to complete our product catalog:

- category
- product
- product_category

Adding Categories

The process of creating the category table is pretty much the same as for the department table you created in Chapter 3. The category table will have four fields, described in Table 5-1.

Table 5-1. *Designing the category Table*

Field Name	Data Type	Description
category_id	int	An autoincrement integer that represents the unique ID for the category. It is the primary key of the table, and it doesn't allow NULLs.
department_id	int	An integer that represents the department the category belongs to. It doesn't allow NULLs.
name	varchar(100)	Stores the category name. It does not allow NULLs.
description	varchar(1000)	Stores the category description. It allows NULLs.

There are two ways to create the category table and populate it: either execute the SQL scripts from the Source Code/Download section of the Apress web site (http://www.apress.com/) or follow the steps in the following exercise.

Exercise: Creating the category Table

1. Using phpMyAdmin, navigate to your tshirtshop database.

2. Click the SQL button in the top menu, and use the form to execute the following SQL query, which creates the category table (alternatively, you can use phpMyAdmin to create the table by specifying the fields using a visual interface as you did in Chapter 4 for the department table).

```
-- Create category table
CREATE TABLE 'category' (
    'category_id'    INT              NOT NULL  AUTO_INCREMENT,
    'department_id'  INT              NOT NULL,
    'name'           VARCHAR(100)     NOT NULL,
    'description'    VARCHAR(1000),
    PRIMARY KEY ('category_id'),
    KEY 'idx_category_department_id' ('department_id')
) ENGINE=MyISAM;
```

3. Now, let's populate the table with some data. Execute the following SQL script:

```
-- Populate category table
INSERT INTO 'category' ('category_id', 'department_id', 'name',
'description') VALUES
        (1, 1, 'French', 'The French have always had an eye for beauty. One look
at the T-shirts below and you''ll see that same appreciation has been applied
abundantly to their postage stamps. Below are some of our most beautiful and
colorful T-shirts, so browse away! And don''t forget to go all the way to the
bottom - you don''t want to miss any of them!'),
        (2, 1, 'Italian', 'The full and resplendent treasure chest of art,
literature, music, and science that Italy has given the world is reflected
splendidly in its postal stamps. If we could, we would dedicate hundreds of
T-shirts to this amazing treasure of beautiful images, but for now we will
have to live with what you see here. You don''t have to be Italian to love
these gorgeous T-shirts, just someone who appreciates the finer things in
life!'),
        (3, 1, 'Irish', 'It was Churchill who remarked that he thought the Irish
most curious because they didn''t want to be English. How right he was! But
then, he was half-American, wasn''t he? If you have an Irish genealogy you
will want these T-shirts! If you suddenly turn Irish on St. Patrick''s Day,
you too will want these T-shirts! Take a look at some of the coolest T-shirts
we have!'),
        (4, 2, 'Animal', ' Our ever-growing selection of beautiful animal T-
shirts represents critters from everywhere, both wild and domestic. If you
don''t see the T-shirt with the animal you''re looking for, tell us and
we''ll find it!'),
        (5, 2, 'Flower', 'These unique and beautiful flower T-shirts are just
the item for the gardener, flower arranger, florist, or general lover of
things beautiful. Surprise the flower in your life with one of the beautiful
botanical T-shirts or just get a few for yourself!'),
        (6, 3, 'Christmas', ' Because this is a unique Christmas T-shirt that
you''ll only wear a few times a year, it will probably last for decades (unless
some grinch nabs it from you, of course). Far into the future, after you''re
gone, your grandkids will pull it out and argue over who gets to wear it. What
great snapshots they''ll make dressed in Grandpa or Grandma''s incredibly
tasteful and unique Christmas T-shirt! Yes, everyone will remember you forever
and what a silly goof you were when you would wear only your Santa beard and
cap so you wouldn''t cover up your nifty T-shirt.'),
        (7, 3, 'Valentine''s', 'For the more timid, all you have to do is wear
your heartfelt message to get it across. Buy one for you and your sweetie(s)
today!');
```

How It Works: Populating the categories Table

Adding data to your table should be a trivial task, given that you know the data that needs to be inserted. As pointed out earlier, you can find the SQL scripts in the book's code in the Source Code/Download section of the Apress web site (http://www.apress.com). Figure 5-5 shows data from the category table as shown by phpMyAdmin.

←T→			category_id	department_id	name	description
☐	✎	✕	1	1	French	The French have always had an eye for beauty. One ...
☐	✎	✕	2	1	Italian	The full and resplendent treasure chest of art, li...
☐	✎	✕	3	1	Irish	It was Churchill that remarked that he thought the...
☐	✎	✕	4	2	Animal	Our ever-growing selection of beautiful animal T-...
☐	✎	✕	5	2	Flower	These unique and beautiful flower T-shirts are jus...
☐	✎	✕	6	3	Christmas	Because this is a unique Christmas T-shirt that y...
☐	✎	✕	7	3	Valentine's	For the more timid, all you have to do is wear you...

Figure 5-5. *Data from the category table*

In the SQL code, note how we escaped the special characters in the category descriptions, such as the single quotes, that need to be doubled, so MySQL will know to interpret those as quotes to be added to the description, instead of as string termination characters.

Adding Products and Relating Them to Categories

You'll now go through the same steps as earlier, but this time, you'll create a slightly more complicated table: product. The product table has the fields shown in Table 5-2.

Table 5-2. *Designing the product Table*

Field Name	Data Type	Description
product_id	int	An integer that represents the unique ID for the category. It is the primary key of the table and an autoincrement field.
name	varchar(100)	Stores the product name. It doesn't allow NULLs.
description	varchar(1000)	Stores the category description. It allows NULLs.
price	numeric(10, 2)	Stores the product price.
discounted_price	numeric(10, 2)	Stores the discounted product price. Will store 0.00 if the product doesn't have a current discount price.
image	varchar(150)	Stores the name of the product's picture file (or eventually the complete path), which gets displayed on the product details page. You could keep the picture directly in the table, but in most cases, it's much more efficient to store the picture files in the file system and have only their names stored into the database. If you have a high-traffic web site, you might even want to place the image files in a separate physical location (for example, another hard disk) to increase site performance. This field allows NULLs.
image_2	varchar(150)	Stores the name of a second picture of the product, which gets displayed on the product details page. It allows NULLs.

Field Name	Data Type	Description
thumbnail	varchar(150)	Stores the name of the product's thumbnail picture. This image gets displayed in product lists when browsing the catalog.
display	smallint	Stores a value specifying in what areas of the catalog this product should be displayed. The possible values are 0 (default), meaning the product is listed only in the page of the category it's a part of); 1, which indicates that the product is also featured on the front catalog page; 2, indicating the product is also featured in the departments it's a part of; and 3, which means the product is also featured on both the front and the department pages. With the help of this field, the site administrators can highlight a set of products that will be of particular interest to visitors at a specific season, holiday, and so on. Also, if you want to promote products that have a discounted price, this feature is just what you need.

The product_category table is the linking table that allows implementing the many-to-many relationship between the product and category tables. It has two fields that form the primary key of the table: product_id and category_id.

Follow the steps of the exercise to create the product table in your database.

Exercise: Creating the product Table

1. Using phpMyAdmin, execute the following command to create the product table:

```
-- Create product table
CREATE TABLE `product` (
   `product_id`        INT           NOT NULL AUTO_INCREMENT,
   `name`              VARCHAR(100)  NOT NULL,
   `description`       VARCHAR(1000) NOT NULL,
   `price`             NUMERIC(10, 2) NOT NULL,
   `discounted_price`  NUMERIC(10, 2) NOT NULL DEFAULT 0.00,
   `image`             VARCHAR(150),
   `image_2`           VARCHAR(150),
   `thumbnail`         VARCHAR(150),
   `display`           SMALLINT      NOT NULL DEFAULT 0,
   PRIMARY KEY (`product_id`)
) ENGINE=MyISAM;
```

2. Now, create the product_category table by executing this query:

```
-- Create product_category table
CREATE TABLE `product_category` (
   `product_id`  INT NOT NULL,
   `category_id` INT NOT NULL,
   PRIMARY KEY (`product_id`, `category_id`)
) ENGINE=MyISAM;
```

3. Use the populate_product.sql script from the code download to populate the product table with sample data.

4. Use the populate_product_category.sql script from the code download to populate the product_category table with sample data.

How It Works: Many-to-Many Relationships

Many-to-many relationships are created by adding a third table, called a junction table, which is named product_category in this case. This table contains product_id and category_id pairs, and each record in the table associates a particular product with a particular category. So, if you see a record such as (1, 4) in product_category, you know that the product with the ID of 1 belongs to the category with the ID of 4.

This is also the first time that you set a primary key consisting of more than one column. The primary key of product_category is formed by both its fields: product_id and category_id. This means that you won't be allowed to have two identical (product_id, category_id) pairs in the table. However, it's perfectly legal to have a product_id or category_id appear more than once, as long as it is part of a unique (product_id, category_id) pair. This makes sense because you don't want to have two identical records in the product_category table. A product can be associated with a particular category or not; it cannot be associated with a category multiple times.

Using Database Diagrams

All the theory about table relationships can be a bit confusing at first, but you'll get used to it. To understand the relationship more clearly, you can get a picture by using database diagrams.

A number of tools allow you to build database structures visually, implement them physically in the database for you, and generate the necessary SQL script. Although we won't present any particular tool in this book, it's good to know that they exist. You can find a list of the most popular tools at http://www.databaseanswers.com/modelling_tools.htm.

Database diagrams also have the capability to implement the relationships between tables. For example, if you had implemented the relationships among your four tables so far, the database diagram would look something like Figure 5-6.

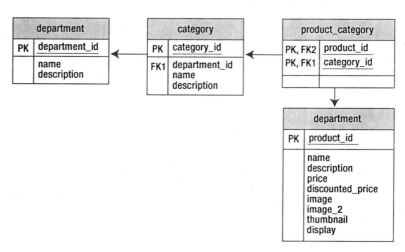

Figure 5-6. *Viewing tables and relationships using a database diagram*

In the diagram, the primary keys of each table are marked with "PK." Foreign keys are marked with "FK" (because there can be more of them in a table, they're numbered). The arrows between two tables point toward the table in the *one* part of the relationship.

Querying the New Data

Now, you have a database with a wealth of information just waiting to be read by somebody. However, the new elements bring with them a set of new things you need to learn.

For this chapter, the data tier logic is a little bit more complicated than in the previous chapter, because it must answer to queries like "give me the second page of products from the Cartoons category" or "give me the products on promotion for department *X*." Before moving on to writing the stored procedures that implement this logic, let's first cover the theory about

- Retrieving short product descriptions

- Joining data tables

- Implementing paging

Let's deal with these tasks one by one.

Getting Short Descriptions

In the product lists that your visitor sees while browsing the catalog, we won't display full product descriptions, only a portion of them. In TShirtShop, we'll display the first 150 characters of every product description, after which, if the description has a greater length, we concatenate (append) ellipses (. . .) to the end of the description. Of course, you can decide if you would like more or less of the description to display by simply changing this length (150 in our design) to whatever number you choose; be sure to verify that this displays well by previewing your changes in your browser of choice.

We'll use the LEFT(str, len) MySQL function to extract the first *N* (len) characters from the product description, where *N* is the number of characters to be extracted. The following SELECT command returns products' descriptions trimmed at 30 characters, with ". . ." appended to the end if the description has a length greater than 30 characters:

```
SELECT   name,
         IF(LENGTH(description) <= 30, description,
             CONCAT(LEFT(description, 30), '...')) AS description
FROM     product
ORDER BY name;
```

The new column generated by the CONCAT(LEFT(description, 30), '...') expression doesn't have a name by default, so we create an alias for it using the AS keyword. With your current data, this query would return something like this:

name	description
A Partridge in a Pear Tree	The original of this beautiful...
Adoration of the Kings	This design is from a miniatur...
Afghan Flower	This beautiful image was issue...
Albania Flower	Well, these crab apples starte...
Alsace	It was in this region of Franc...
...	...

Joining Data Tables

Because your data is stored in several tables, all of the information you'll need might not be one table. Take a look at the following list, which contains data from both the department and category tables:

Department Name	Category Name
Regional	French
Regional	Italian
Regional	Irish
Nature	Animal
Nature	Flower
Seasonal	Christmas
Seasonal	Valentine's

In other cases, all the information you need is in just one table, but you need to place conditions on it based on the information in another table. You cannot get this kind of result set with simple queries such as the ones you've used so far. Needing a result set based on data from multiple tables is a good indication that you might need to use *table joins*.

When extracting the products that belong to a category, the SQL query isn't the same as when extracting the categories that belong to a department. This is because products and categories are linked through the product_category linking table.

To get the list of products in a category, you first need to look in the product_category table and get all the (product_id, category_id) pairs where category_id is the ID of the category you're looking for. That list contains the IDs of the products in that category. Using these IDs, you'll be able to generate the required product list from the product table. Although this sounds pretty complicated, it can be done using a single SQL query. The real power of SQL lies in its capability to perform complex operations on large amounts of data using simple queries.

Joining one table with another results in the columns (not the rows) of those tables being joined. When joining two tables, there always must be a common column on which the join will be made. Tables are joined in SQL using the JOIN clause. You'll learn how to make table joins by analyzing the product and product_category tables and by analyzing how you can get a list of products that belong to a certain category.

Suppose you want to get all the products where category_id = 5. The query that joins the product and product_category tables is as follows:

```
SELECT     product_category.product_id,
           product_category.category_id,
           product.name
```

```
FROM       product_category
INNER JOIN product
      ON product.product_id = product_category.product_id
ORDER BY   product.product_id;
```

The result will look something like this (to save space, the listing doesn't include all returned rows and columns):

product_id	category_id	name
1	1	Arc d'Triomphe
2	1	Chartres Cathedral
3	1	Coat of Arms
4	1	Gallic Cock
5	1	Marianne
6	1	Alsace
7	1	Apocalypse Tapestry
8	1	Centaur
9	1	Corsica
10	1	Haute Couture
11	1	Iris
12	1	Lorraine
13	1	Mercury
14	1	County of Nice
15	1	Notre Dame
16	1	Paris Peace Conference
17	1	Sarah Bernhardt
18	1	Hunt
19	2	Italia
20	2	Torch
...		

The resultant table is composed of the requested fields from the joined tables synchronized on the product_id column, which was specified as the column to make the join on. You can see that the products that exist in multiple categories are listed more than once, once for each category they belong in, but this problem will go away after we filter the results to get only the products for a certain category.

Note that in the SELECT clause, the column names are prefixed by the table name. *This is a requirement if the columns exist in more tables that participate in the table join,* such as product_id in our case. For the other column, prefixing its name with the table name is optional, although it's a good practice to avoid confusion.

The query that returns only the products that belong to category 5 is

```
SELECT     product.product_id, product.name
FROM       product_category
```

```
INNER JOIN product
        ON product.product_id = product_category.product_id
WHERE        product_category.category_id = 5;
```

The results follow:

product_id	name
65	Afghan Flower
66	Albania Flower
67	Austria Flower
68	Bulgarian Flower

A final thing worth discussing here is the use of *aliases*. Aliases aren't necessarily related to table joins, but they become especially useful (and sometimes necessary) when joining tables, and they assign different (usually) shorter names for the tables involved. Aliases are necessary when joining a table with itself, in which case, you need to assign different aliases for its different instances to differentiate them. The following query returns the same products as the query before, but it uses aliases:

```
SELECT      p.product_id, p.name
FROM        product_category pc
INNER JOIN product p
        ON p.product_id = pc.product_id
WHERE       pc.category_id = 5;
```

Showing Products Page by Page

If certain web sections need to list large numbers of products, it's useful to let the visitor browse them page by page, with a predefined (or configurable by the visitor) number of products per page.

Depending on the tier on your architecture where paging is performed, there are three main ways to implement paging:

Paging at the data tier level: In this case, the database returns only a single page of products, the page needed by the presentation tier.

Paging at the business tier level: The business tier requests the complete page of products from the database, performs filtering, and returns to the presentation tier only the page of products that needs to be displayed.

Paging at the presentation tier level: In this scenario, the presentation tier receives the complete list of products and extracts only the page that needs to be displayed for the visitor.

Paging at the business tier and presentation tier levels has potential performance problems, especially when dealing with large result sets, because they imply transferring unnecessarily large quantities of data from the database to the presentation tier. Additional data also needs to be stored on the server's memory, unnecessarily consuming server resources.

In our web site, we'll implement paging at the data tier level, not only because of its better performance but also because it allows you to learn some tricks about database programming that you'll find useful when developing your web sites.

To implement paging at the data tier level, we need to know how to build a SELECT query that returns just a portion of records (products) from a larger set, and each database language seems to have different ways of doing this. To achieve this functionality in MySQL, you need to use the LIMIT keyword with the SELECT statement. LIMIT takes one or two arguments. The first argument specifies the index of the first returned record, and the second specifies how many rows to return.

The following SQL query tells MySQL to return the rows 15, 16, 17, 18, and 19 from the list of products ordered by their IDs (remember that an index starts at zero for the first record, so we ask for *row 15* by asking for the *index 14*—the row number minus one):

```
SELECT    name
FROM      product
ORDER BY  product_id
LIMIT     14, 5;
```

With the current database you should get these results:

```
name
- - - - - - - - - - - - - - - - - - - - - - - - - - - - - - - - - - - - - - - - - - - - - - - - - - - - -
Notre Dame
Paris Peace Conference
Sarah Bernhardt
Hunt
Italia
```

You'll use the LIMIT keyword to specify the range of records you're interested in when retrieving lists of products. For more details, you can always refer to the official documentation at http://dev.mysql.com/doc/refman/5.1/en/select.html.

Writing the New Database Stored Procedures

Now that you are familiar with how to query the database, you can implement the data tier stored procedures, which will return data from the database. First, you'll implement the MySQL stored procedures that retrieve department and category information:

- catalog_get_department_details

- catalog_get_categories_list

- catalog_get_category_details

Afterward, you'll write the stored procedures that deal with products. Only four stored procedures ask for products, but you'll also implement three helper functions (catalog_count_products_in_category, catalog_count_products_on_department, and catalog_count_products_on_catalog) to assist in implementing the paging functionality. The complete list of stored procedures you need to implement follows:

- catalog_count_products_in_category
- catalog_get_products_in_category
- catalog_count_products_on_department
- catalog_get_products_on_department
- catalog_count_products_on_catalog
- catalog_get_products_on_catalog
- catalog_get_product_details
- catalog_get_product_locations

Notice that we have named our stored procedures in such a way that the name tells you what the stored procedure does. This is called *self-documenting* or *self-describing* code and is a good habit to form when coding; it will help you—or anyone else who needs to work on your site—to quickly understand what each of your stored procedures does without having to look inside them. Many a programmer has learned the hard way that two weeks from now you will not remember what a particular function does, and naming it function_one tells you absolutely nothing about its purpose; following a self-documenting style will, in the long run, save hours during debugging and redesign.

In the following sections, you'll be shown the code of each stored procedure. We won't go though individual exercises to create these stored procedures. Use phpMyAdmin to add them to your database, using the SQL tab *and changing the* DELIMITER *to* $$, as shown in Figure 5-7.

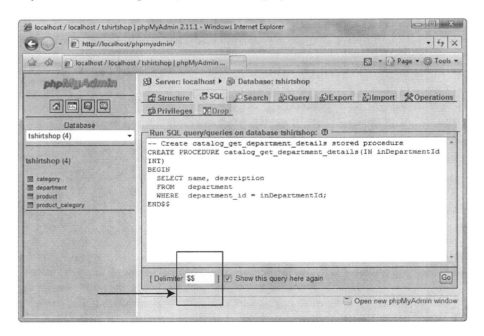

Figure 5-7. *Changing the SQL delimiter in phpMyAdmin*

> **Caution** Don't forget to set the delimiter when you create *each* stored procedure!

catalog_get_department_details

The catalog_get_department_details stored procedure returns the name and description for a given department whose ID is received as parameter. This is needed when the user selects a department in the product catalog, and the database must be queried to find out the name and the description of the particular department.

Next is the SQL code that creates the catalog_get_department_details stored procedure. Execute it using phpMyAdmin. *Don't forget to set the* $$ *delimiter!*

```
-- Create catalog_get_department_details stored procedure
CREATE PROCEDURE catalog_get_department_details(IN inDepartmentId INT)
BEGIN
  SELECT name, description
  FROM   department
  WHERE  department_id = inDepartmentId;
END$$
```

As you can see, a stored procedure is very much like a PHP function, in that it receives parameters, executes some code, and returns the results. In this case, we have a single input (IN) parameter named inDepartmentId, whose data type is int. Take note of the naming convention we've chosen for parameter names; the name of the parameter includes the parameter direction (in), and uses camel casing.

MySQL also supports output (OUT) parameters and input-output (INOUT) parameters. You'll see examples of using these a little later. The official documentation page for the CREATE PROCEDURE command, which contains the complete details about using parameters with stored procedures, is located at http://dev.mysql.com/doc/refman/5.1/en/create-procedure.html.

The catalog_get_department_details stored procedure returns the names and descriptions of all departments whose department_ids match the one specified by the inDepartmentId input parameter. The WHERE clause (WHERE department_id = inDepartmentId) is used to request the details of that specific department.

catalog_get_categories_list

When a visitor selects a department, the categories that belong to that department must be displayed. The categories will be retrieved by the catalog_get_categories_list stored procedure, which returns the list of categories in a specific department. The stored procedure needs to know the ID of the department for which to retrieve the categories.

```
-- Create catalog_get_categories_list stored procedure
CREATE PROCEDURE catalog_get_categories_list(IN inDepartmentId INT)
BEGIN
  SELECT    category_id, name
  FROM      category
  WHERE     department_id = inDepartmentId
  ORDER BY category_id;
END$$
```

catalog_get_category_details

When the visitor selects a particular category, we need to display its name and description. Execute this code, *using the* $$ *delimiter*, to create the procedure:

```
-- Create catalog_get_category_details stored procedure
CREATE PROCEDURE catalog_get_category_details(IN inCategoryId INT)
BEGIN
  SELECT name, description
  FROM    category
  WHERE   category_id = inCategoryId;
END$$
```

catalog_count_products_in_category

This function returns the number of products in a category. This data will be necessary when paginating the lists of products, and we'll need to be able to calculate how many pages of products we have in a category.

Note that, unlike the previous procedures you've written, this time, we return a single value rather than a set of data. That value is calculated using COUNT, which returns the number of records that match a particular query.

```
-- Create catalog_count_products_in_category stored procedure
CREATE PROCEDURE catalog_count_products_in_category(IN inCategoryId INT)
BEGIN
  SELECT     COUNT(*) AS categories_count
  FROM       product p
  INNER JOIN product_category pc
             ON p.product_id = pc.product_id
  WHERE      pc.category_id = inCategoryId;
END$$
```

catalog_get_products_in_category

This stored procedure returns the products that belong to a certain category. To obtain this list of products, you need to join the product and product_category tables, as explained earlier in this chapter. We also trim the product's description.

The stored procedure receives four parameters:

- inCategoryID is the ID for which we're returning products.

- inShortProductDescriptionLength is the maximum length allowed for the product's description. If the description is longer than this value, it will be truncated and "..." will be added at the end. Note that this is only used when displaying product lists; in the product details page, the description won't be truncated. You will declare the global value of this variable later on in config.php, but for now, it is enough to know that it exists and what its value will be set to: in our case 150 characters.

- inProductsPerPage is the maximum number of products our site can display on a single catalog page. If the total number of products in the category is larger than this number, we return only a page containing the number of inProductsPerPage products. Again, this variable's value will be declared globally in config.php later on; for now, you only need to know that for our project we will set this to 4.

- inStartItem is the index of the first product to return. So, for example, when the visitor visits the *second page* of products—using pagination and displaying four products per page—inStartItem will be 4 and inProductsPerPage will be 4. With these values, the catalog_get_products_in_category function will return the products from the fifth to ninth rows of results.

```
-- Create catalog_get_products_in_category stored procedure
CREATE PROCEDURE catalog_get_products_in_category(
  IN inCategoryId INT, IN inShortProductDescriptionLength INT,
  IN inProductsPerPage INT, IN inStartItem INT)
BEGIN
  -- Prepare statement
  PREPARE statement FROM
    "SELECT      p.product_id, p.name,
                 IF(LENGTH(p.description) <= ?,
                    p.description,
                    CONCAT(LEFT(p.description, ?),
                           '...')) AS description,
                 p.price, p.discounted_price, p.thumbnail
    FROM         product p
    INNER JOIN   product_category pc
                    ON p.product_id = pc.product_id
    WHERE        pc.category_id = ?
    ORDER BY     p.display DESC
    LIMIT        ?, ?";

  -- Define query parameters
  SET @p1 = inShortProductDescriptionLength;
  SET @p2 = inShortProductDescriptionLength;
  SET @p3 = inCategoryId;
  SET @p4 = inStartItem;
  SET @p5 = inProductsPerPage;

  -- Execute the statement
  EXECUTE statement USING @p1, @p2, @p3, @p4, @p5;
END$$
```

In this procedure, you can find a demonstration of using *prepared statements*, which represent query templates that contain input parameters whose values you supply right before executing the statement.

The reason we need to use prepared statements is that they allow adding parameters to the LIMIT clause of a SELECT query. MySQL 5, at the time of this writing, doesn't allow using an input parameter to set the value of LIMIT except when using prepared statements.

We created a prepared statement that retrieves the necessary products using the PREPARE command. The statement variables are marked with a question mark (?) in the query. When executing the query with EXECUTE, we provide the values of those parameters as parameters of the EXECUTE command. The prepared statement contains five parameters, so we supply five parameters to EXECUTE (@p1, @p2, @p3, @p4, @p5).

Prepared statements are also useful for performance (because the same statement can be executed multiple times) and security reasons (because the data types for parameters can be checked for data type compliancy). However, in our case, we're using PDO to implement these features, so we're really using prepared statements only so that we can supply parameters to LIMIT.

We'll use the same technique on the other procedures that use LIMIT as well.

catalog_count_products_on_department

This stored procedure counts the number of products that are to be displayed in the page of a given department. Note that all the department's products aren't listed on the department's page, but only those products whose display value is 2 (product on department promotion) or 3 (product on department and catalog promotion).

```
-- Create catalog_count_products_on_department stored procedure
CREATE PROCEDURE catalog_count_products_on_department(IN inDepartmentId INT)
BEGIN
  SELECT DISTINCT COUNT(*) AS products_on_department_count
  FROM            product p
  INNER JOIN      product_category pc
                    ON p.product_id = pc.product_id
  INNER JOIN      category c
                    ON pc.category_id = c.category_id
  WHERE           (p.display = 2 OR p.display = 3)
                  AND c.department_id = inDepartmentId;
END$$
```

The SQL code is almost the same as the one in catalog_get_products_on_department, which we're discussing next.

catalog_get_products_on_department

When the visitor selects a particular department, apart from needing to list its name, description, and list of categories (you wrote the necessary code for these tasks earlier), you also want to display the list of featured products for that department.

catalog_get_products_on_department returns all the products that belong to a specific department and has the display set to 2 (product on department promotion) or 3 (product on department and catalog promotion).

In catalog_get_products_in_category, you needed to make a table join to find out the products that belong to a specific category. Now that you need to do this for departments, the task is a bit more complicated, because you can't directly know what products belong to each department.

You know how to find categories that belong to a specific department (you did this in catalog_get_categories_list), and you know how to get the products that belong to a specific category (you did that in catalog_get_products_in_category). By combining these pieces of information, you can generate the list of products in a department. For this, you need two table joins.

You will also use the DISTINCT clause to filter the results to avoid getting the same record multiple times. This can happen when a product belongs to more than one category, and these categories are in the same department. In this situation, you would get the same product returned for each of the matching categories, unless the results are filtered using DISTINCT.

```
-- Create catalog_get_products_on_department stored procedure
CREATE PROCEDURE catalog_get_products_on_department(
  IN inDepartmentId INT, IN inShortProductDescriptionLength INT,
  IN inProductsPerPage INT, IN inStartItem INT)
BEGIN
  PREPARE statement FROM
    "SELECT DISTINCT p.product_id, p.name,
                    IF(LENGTH(p.description) <= ?,
                       p.description,
                       CONCAT(LEFT(p.description, ?),
                              '...')) AS description,
                    p.price, p.discounted_price, p.thumbnail
    FROM            product p
    INNER JOIN      product_category pc
                      ON p.product_id = pc.product_id
    INNER JOIN      category c
                      ON pc.category_id = c.category_id
    WHERE           (p.display = 2 OR p.display = 3)
                    AND c.department_id = ?
    ORDER BY        p.display DESC
    LIMIT           ?, ?";

  SET @p1 = inShortProductDescriptionLength;
  SET @p2 = inShortProductDescriptionLength;
  SET @p3 = inDepartmentId;
  SET @p4 = inStartItem;
  SET @p5 = inProductsPerPage;

  EXECUTE statement USING @p1, @p2, @p3, @p4, @p5;
END$$
```

▪**Tip** If the way table joins work looks too complicated, try following them on the diagram shown earlier in Figure 5-6. The more you work with DBs and queries, the easier it is to do; even experts sometimes struggle with creating the perfect query or get bogged down keeping track of the joins and so forth, so take heart and keep at it. It really is a case of practice makes perfect!

catalog_count_products_on_catalog

The catalog_count_products_on_catalog stored procedure returns the count of the number of products to be displayed on the catalog's front page. These are products whose display fields have the value of 1 (product is promoted on the first page) or 3 (product is promoted on the first page and on the department pages).

```
-- Create catalog_count_products_on_catalog stored procedure
CREATE PROCEDURE catalog_count_products_on_catalog()
BEGIN
  SELECT COUNT(*) AS products_on_catalog_count
  FROM   product
  WHERE  display = 1 OR display = 3;
END$$
```

catalog_get_products_on_catalog

The catalog_get_products_on_catalog stored procedure returns the actual products to be displayed on the catalog's front page. These are products whose display fields have the value of 1 (product is promoted on the first page) or 3 (product is promoted on the first page and on the department pages). The product description is trimmed at a specified number of characters. The pagination is implemented the same way as in the previous two stored procedures that return lists of products.

```
-- Create catalog_get_products_on_catalog stored procedure
CREATE PROCEDURE catalog_get_products_on_catalog(
  IN inShortProductDescriptionLength INT,
  IN inProductsPerPage INT, IN inStartItem INT)
BEGIN
  PREPARE statement FROM
    "SELECT   product_id, name,
              IF(LENGTH(description) <= ?,
                 description,
                 CONCAT(LEFT(description, ?),
                        '...')) AS description,
              price, discounted_price, thumbnail
     FROM     product
     WHERE    display = 1 OR display = 3
     ORDER BY display DESC
     LIMIT    ?, ?";

  SET @p1 = inShortProductDescriptionLength;
  SET @p2 = inShortProductDescriptionLength;
  SET @p3 = inStartItem;
  SET @p4 = inProductsPerPage;

  EXECUTE statement USING @p1, @p2, @p3, @p4;
END$$
```

catalog_get_product_details

The catalog_get_product_details stored procedure returns detailed information about a product and is called to get the data that will be displayed on the product's details page.

```
-- Create catalog_get_product_details stored procedure
CREATE PROCEDURE catalog_get_product_details(IN inProductId INT)
BEGIN
  SELECT product_id, name, description,
         price, discounted_price, image, image_2
  FROM   product
  WHERE  product_id = inProductId;
END$$
```

catalog_get_product_locations

The catalog_get_product_locations stored procedure returns the categories and departments a product is part of. This will help us display the "Find similar products in our catalog" feature in the product details pages.

This is also the first time we're using subqueries in this book. In the following code, we have highlighted the subqueries to make them easier to read. As you can see, a subquery is just like a simple query, except it's written inside another query.

An interesting detail about subqueries is that most of the time they can be used instead of table joins to achieve the same results. Choosing one solution over the other is, in many cases, a matter of preference. In mission-critical solutions, depending on the circumstances, you may choose one over the other for performance reasons. However, this is an advanced subject that we'll let you learn from specialized database books or tutorials.

```
-- Create catalog_get_product_locations stored procedure
CREATE PROCEDURE catalog_get_product_locations(IN inProductId INT)
BEGIN
  SELECT c.category_id, c.name AS category_name, c.department_id,
         (SELECT name
          FROM   department
          WHERE  department_id = c.department_id) AS department_name
         -- Subquery returns the name of the department of the category
  FROM   category c
  WHERE  c.category_id IN
            (SELECT category_id
             FROM   product_category
             WHERE  product_id = inProductId);
             -- Subquery returns the category IDs a product belongs to
END$$
```

Well, that's about it. Right now, your data store is ready to hold and process the product catalog information. To make sure you haven't missed creating any of the stored procedures, you can execute the following command, which shows the stored procedures you currently have in your database:

```
SHOW PROCEDURE STATUS
```

By writing the stored procedures, you've already implemented a significant part of your product catalog! It's time to move to the next step: implementing the business tier of the product catalog.

Completing the Business Tier Code

In the business tier, you'll add some new methods that will call the previously created stored procedures in the data tier. Recall that you started working on the Catalog class (located in the business/catalog.php file) in Chapter 4. The new methods that you'll add here follow:

- GetDepartmentDetails()

- GetCategoriesInDepartment()

- GetCategoryDetails()

- HowManyPages()

- GetProductsInCategory()

- GetProductsOnDepartment()

- GetProductsOnCatalog()

- GetProductDetails()

- GetProductLocations()

Defining Product List Constants and Activating Session

Before writing the business tier methods, let's first update the include/config.php file by adding the SHORT_PRODUCT_DESCRIPTION_LENGTH and PRODUCTS_PER_PAGE constants. These allow you to easily define the product display of your site by specifying the length of product descriptions and how many products to be displayed per page. These are the values the business tier methods will supply when calling stored procedures that return pages of products, such as catalog_get_products_on_catalog.

```
...
// Server HTTP port (can omit if the default 80 is used)
define('HTTP_SERVER_PORT', '80');
/* Name of the virtual directory the site runs in, for example:
   '/tshirtshop/' if the site runs at http://www.example.com/tshirtshop/
   '/' if the site runs at http://www.example.com/ */
define('VIRTUAL_LOCATION', '/tshirtshop/');

// Configure product lists display options
define('SHORT_PRODUCT_DESCRIPTION_LENGTH', 150);
define('PRODUCTS_PER_PAGE', 4);
?>
```

Then, modify index.php by adding these lines to it:

```php
<?php
// Activate session
session_start();

// Include utility files
require_once 'include/config.php';
require_once BUSINESS_DIR . 'error_handler.php';

// Set the error handler
ErrorHandler::SetHandler();
...
```

The SHORT_PRODUCT_DESCRIPTION_LENGTH constant specifies how many characters from the product's description should appear when displaying product lists. The complete description gets displayed in the product's details page, which you'll implement at the end of this chapter.

PRODUCTS_PER_PAGE specifies the maximum number of products that can be displayed in any catalog page. If the visitor's selection contains more than PRODUCTS_PER_PAGE products, the list of products is split into subpages, accessible through the navigation controls.

We also enabled the PHP session, which will help us improve performance when navigating through pages of products.

Note Session handling is a great PHP feature that allows you to keep track of variables specific to a certain visitor accessing the web site. While the visitor browses the catalog, the session variables are persisted by the web server and associated to a unique visitor identifier (which is stored by default in the visitor's browser as a *cookie*). The visitor's session object stores (name, value) pairs that are saved at server-side and are accessible for the visitor's entire session. In this chapter, we'll use the session feature for improving performance. When implementing the paging functionality, before requesting the list of products, you first ask the database for the total number of products that are going to be returned, so you can show the visitor how many pages of products are available. This number will be saved in the visitor's session, so if the visitor browses the pages of a list of products, the database wouldn't be queried multiple times for the total number of products on subsequent calls; this number will be directly read from the session (this functionality is implemented in the HowManyPages() method that you'll implement later). In this chapter, you'll also use the session to implement the Continue Shopping buttons in product details pages.

Let's work through each business tier method. All these methods need to be added to the Catalog class, located in the business/catalog.php file that you started writing in Chapter 4.

GetDepartmentDetails

GetDepartmentDetails() is called from the presentation tier when a department is clicked to display its name and description. The presentation tier passes the ID of the selected department, and you need to send back the name and the description of the selected department.

The needed data is obtained by calling the `catalog_get_department_details` stored procedure that you've written earlier. Just as planned, the business tier acts, in this case, as a buffer between the presentation tier and the data tier.

```
// Retrieves complete details for the specified department
public static function GetDepartmentDetails($departmentId)
{
  // Build SQL query
  $sql = 'CALL catalog_get_department_details(:department_id)';

  // Build the parameters array
  $params = array (':department_id' => $departmentId);

  // Execute the query and return the results
  return DatabaseHandler::GetRow($sql, $params);
}
```

GetCategoriesInDepartment

The `GetCategoriesInDepartment()` method is called to retrieve the list of categories that belong to a department. Add this method to the `Catalog` class:

```
// Retrieves list of categories that belong to a department
public static function GetCategoriesInDepartment($departmentId)
{
  // Build SQL query
  $sql = 'CALL catalog_get_categories_list(:department_id)';

  // Build the parameters array
  $params = array (':department_id' => $departmentId);

  // Execute the query and return the results
  return DatabaseHandler::GetAll($sql, $params);
}
```

GetCategoryDetails

`GetCategoryDetails()` is called from the presentation tier when a category is clicked to display its name and description. The presentation tier passes the ID of the selected category, and you need to send back the name and the description of the selected category.

```
// Retrieves complete details for the specified category
public static function GetCategoryDetails($categoryId)
{
  // Build SQL query
  $sql = 'CALL catalog_get_category_details(:category_id)';

  // Build the parameters array
  $params = array (':category_id' => $categoryId);
```

```
  // Execute the query and return the results
  return DatabaseHandler::GetRow($sql, $params);
}
```

HowManyPages

As you know, our product catalog will display a fixed number of products in every page. When a catalog page contains more than an established number of products, we display navigation controls that allow the visitor to browse back and forth through the subpages of products. You can see the navigation controls in Figure 4-2 in Chapter 4.

When displaying the navigation controls, you need to calculate the number of subpages of products you have for a given catalog page; for this, we're creating the HowManyPages() helper method.

This method receives as an argument a SELECT query that counts the total number of products of the catalog page ($countSql) and returns the number of subpages. This will be done by simply dividing the total number of products by the number of products to be displayed in a subpage of products; this latter number is configurable through the PRODUCTS_PER_PAGE constant in include/config.php.

To improve the performance when a visitor browses back and forth through the subpages, after we calculate the number of subpages for the first time, we're saving it to the visitor's session. This way, the SQL query received as parameter won't need to be executed more than once on a single visit to a catalog page.

This method is called from the other data tier methods (GetProductsInCategory(), GetProductsOnDepartment(), GetProductsOnCatalog()), which we'll cover next.

Add HowManyPages() to the Catalog class:

```
/* Calculates how many pages of products could be filled by the
   number of products returned by the $countSql query */
private static function HowManyPages($countSql, $countSqlParams)
{
  // Create a hash for the sql query
  $queryHashCode = md5($countSql . var_export($countSqlParams, true));

  // Verify if we have the query results in cache
  if (isset ($_SESSION['last_count_hash']) &&
      isset ($_SESSION['how_many_pages']) &&
      $_SESSION['last_count_hash'] === $queryHashCode)
  {
    // Retrieve the the cached value
    $how_many_pages = $_SESSION['how_many_pages'];
  }
  else
  {
    // Execute the query
    $items_count = DatabaseHandler::GetOne($countSql, $countSqlParams);
```

```
  // Calculate the number of pages
  $how_many_pages = ceil($items_count / PRODUCTS_PER_PAGE);

  // Save the query and its count result in the session
  $_SESSION['last_count_hash'] = $queryHashCode;
  $_SESSION['how_many_pages'] = $how_many_pages;
}


// Return the number of pages
return $how_many_pages;
}
```

Let's analyze the function to see how it does its job.

The method is private, because you won't access it from within other classes—it's a helper class for other methods of Catalog.

The method verifies whether the previous call to it was for the same SELECT query. If it was, the result cached from the previous call is returned. This small trick improves performance when the visitor is browsing subpages of the same list of products because the actual counting in the database is performed only once.

```
// Create a hash for the sql query
$queryHashCode = md5($countSql . var_export($countSqlParams, true));

// Verify if we have the query results in cache
if (isset ($_SESSION['last_count_hash']) &&
    isset ($_SESSION['how_many_pages']) &&
    $_SESSION['last_count_hash'] === $queryHashCode)
{
  // Retrieve the cached value
  $how_many_pages = $_SESSION['how_many_pages'];
}
```

The number of pages associated with the received query and parameters is saved in the current visitor's session in a variable named how_many_pages. If the conditions aren't met, which means the results of the query aren't cached, we calculate them and save them to the session:

```
else
{
  // Execute the query
  $items_count = DatabaseHandler::GetOne($countSql, $countSqlParams);

  // Calculate the number of pages
  $how_many_pages = ceil($items_count / PRODUCTS_PER_PAGE);

  // Save the query and its count result in the session
  $_SESSION['last_count_hash'] = $queryHashCode;
  $_SESSION['how_many_pages'] = $how_many_pages;
}
```

In the end, no matter if the number of pages was fetched from the session or calculated by the database, it is returned to the calling function:

```
// Return the number of pages
return $how_many_pages;
```

GetProductsInCategory

GetProductsInCategory() returns the list of products that belong to a particular category. Add the following method to the Catalog class in business/catalog.php:

```
// Retrieves list of products that belong to a category
public static function GetProductsInCategory(
                        $categoryId, $pageNo, &$rHowManyPages)
{
  // Query that returns the number of products in the category
  $sql = 'CALL catalog_count_products_in_category(:category_id)';
  // Build the parameters array
  $params = array (':category_id' => $categoryId);

  // Calculate the number of pages required to display the products
  $rHowManyPages = Catalog::HowManyPages($sql, $params);
  // Calculate the start item
  $start_item = ($pageNo - 1) * PRODUCTS_PER_PAGE;

  // Retrieve the list of products
  $sql = 'CALL catalog_get_products_in_category(
                :category_id, :short_product_description_length,
                :products_per_page, :start_item)';

  // Build the parameters array
  $params = array (
    ':category_id' => $categoryId,
    ':short_product_description_length' =>
      SHORT_PRODUCT_DESCRIPTION_LENGTH,
    ':products_per_page' => PRODUCTS_PER_PAGE,
    ':start_item' => $start_item);

  // Execute the query and return the results
  return DatabaseHandler::GetAll($sql, $params);
}
```

This function has two purposes:

- Calculate the number of subpages of products and return this number through the &$rHowManyPages parameter. To calculate this number, the HowManyPages() method you added earlier is used. The SQL query that is used to retrieve the total number of products calls the catalog_count_products_in_category database stored procedure that you added earlier to your databases.

- Return the list of products in the mentioned category.

▓**Note** The ampersand (&) before a function parameter means it is passed by reference. When a variable is passed by reference, an alias of the variable is passed instead of creating a new copy of the value. This way, when a variable is passed by reference and the called function changes its value, its new value will be reflected in the caller function, too. Passing by reference is an alternative method to receiving a return value from a called function and is particularly useful when you need to get multiple return values from the called function. CreateSubpageQuery() returns the text of a SELECT query through its return value and the total number of subpages through the $rHowManyPages parameter that is passed by reference.

GetProductsOnDepartment

The GetProductsOnDepartment() method returns the list of products featured for a particular department. The department's featured products must be displayed when the customer visits the home page of a department. Put it inside the Catalog class:

```
// Retrieves the list of products for the department page
public static function GetProductsOnDepartment(
                      $departmentId, $pageNo, &$rHowManyPages)
{
  // Query that returns the number of products in the department page
  $sql = 'CALL catalog_count_products_on_department(:department_id)';
  // Build the parameters array
  $params = array (':department_id' => $departmentId);

  // Calculate the number of pages required to display the products
  $rHowManyPages = Catalog::HowManyPages($sql, $params);
  // Calculate the start item
  $start_item = ($pageNo - 1) * PRODUCTS_PER_PAGE;

  // Retrieve the list of products
  $sql = 'CALL catalog_get_products_on_department(
              :department_id, :short_product_description_length,
              :products_per_page, :start_item)';

  // Build the parameters array
  $params = array (
    ':department_id' => $departmentId,
    ':short_product_description_length' =>
      SHORT_PRODUCT_DESCRIPTION_LENGTH,
    ':products_per_page' => PRODUCTS_PER_PAGE,
    ':start_item' => $start_item);

  // Execute the query and return the results
  return DatabaseHandler::GetAll($sql, $params);
}
```

GetProductsOnCatalog

The `GetProductsOnCatalog()` method returns the list of products featured on the catalog's front page. It goes inside the `Catalog` class:

```
// Retrieves the list of products on catalog page
public static function GetProductsOnCatalog($pageNo, &$rHowManyPages)
{
  // Query that returns the number of products for the front catalog page
  $sql = 'CALL catalog_count_products_on_catalog()';

  // Calculate the number of pages required to display the products
  $rHowManyPages = Catalog::HowManyPages($sql, null);
  // Calculate the start item
  $start_item = ($pageNo - 1) * PRODUCTS_PER_PAGE;

  // Retrieve the list of products
  $sql = 'CALL catalog_get_products_on_catalog(
                :short_product_description_length,
                :products_per_page, :start_item)';

  // Build the parameters array
  $params = array (
    ':short_product_description_length' =>
      SHORT_PRODUCT_DESCRIPTION_LENGTH,
    ':products_per_page' => PRODUCTS_PER_PAGE,
    ':start_item' => $start_item);

  // Execute the query and return the results
  return DatabaseHandler::GetAll($sql, $params);
}
```

GetProductDetails

Add the `GetProductDetails()` method to the `Catalog` class:

```
// Retrieves complete product details
public static function GetProductDetails($productId)
{
  // Build SQL query
  $sql = 'CALL catalog_get_product_details(:product_id)';

  // Build the parameters array
  $params = array (':product_id' => $productId);

  // Execute the query and return the results
  return DatabaseHandler::GetRow($sql, $params);
}
```

GetProductLocations

Finally, add the GetProductLocations() method, which calls the catalog_get_product_locations stored procedure, to extract the categories and departments that a product is part of:

```
// Retrieves product locations
public static function GetProductLocations($productId)
{
  // Build SQL query
  $sql = 'CALL catalog_get_product_locations(:product_id)';

  // Build the parameters array
  $params = array (':product_id' => $productId);

  // Execute the query and return the results
  return DatabaseHandler::GetAll($sql, $params);
}
```

Implementing the Presentation Tier

Believe it or not, right now the data and business tiers of the product catalog are complete for this chapter. All that is left to do is use their functionality in the presentation tier. In this final section, you'll create a few Smarty templates and integrate them into the existing project.

Execute the TShirtShop project (or load http://localhost/tshirtshop/ in your favorite web browser) to see once again what happens when the visitor clicks a department. After the page loads, click one of the departments. The main page (index.php) is reloaded, but this time with a query string at the end of the URL:

http://localhost/tshirtshop/index.php?DepartmentId=1

Using this parameter, DepartmentId, you can obtain any information about the selected department, such as its name, description, list of products, and so on. In the following sections, you'll create the controls that display the list of categories associated with the selected department and the products for the selected department, category, or main web page.

Displaying Department and Category Details

The componentized template responsible for showing the contents of a particular department is named department, and you'll build it in the exercise that follows. You'll first create the componentized template and then modify the store_front componentized template to load it when DepartmentId is present in the query string. After this exercise, when clicking a department in the list, you should see a page like the one in Figure 5-8.

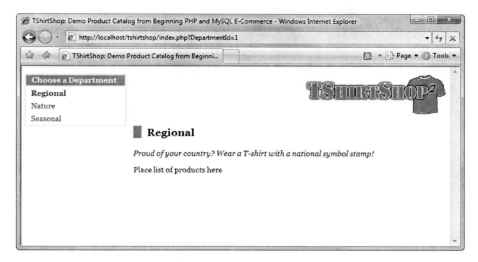

Figure 5-8. *Selecting the Regional department*

Exercise: Displaying Department Details

1. Add the following two styles to the `tshirtshop.css` file from the `styles` folder. You'll need them for displaying the department's title and description:

```
.title {
  border-left: 15px solid #0590C7;
  padding-left: 10px;
}

.description {
  font-style: italic;
}
```

2. Create a new template file named `blank.tpl` in the `presentation/templates` folder with the following contents:

```
{* Smarty blank page *}
```

Yes, this is a blank Smarty template file, which contains just a comment. You'll use it a bit later. *Make sure you add that comment to the file*; if you leave it empty, you'll get an error when trying to use the template—and that's never fun.

3. Create a new template file named `department.tpl` in the `presentation/templates` folder, and add the following code to it:

```
{* department.tpl *}
{load_presentation_object filename="department" assign="obj"}
<h1 class="title">{$obj->mName}</h1>
<p class="description">{$obj->mDescription}</p>
Place list of products here
```

The two presentation object members, $obj->mName and $obj->mDescription, contain the name and description of the selected department. The Department presentation object is created by the presentation/smarty_plugins/function.load_presentation_object.php plug-in.

4. Let's now create the Department presentation object for department.tpl. Create the presentation/department.php file, and add the following code to it:

```php
<?php
// Deals with retrieving department details
class Department
{
  // Public variables for the smarty template
  public $mName;
  public $mDescription;

  // Private members
  private $_mDepartmentId;
  private $_mCategoryId;

  // Class constructor
  public function __construct()
  {
    // We need to have DepartmentId in the query string
    if (isset ($_GET['DepartmentId']))
      $this->_mDepartmentId = (int)$_GET['DepartmentId'];
    else
      trigger_error('DepartmentId not set');

    /* If CategoryId is in the query string we save it
       (casting it to integer to protect against invalid values) */
    if (isset ($_GET['CategoryId']))
      $this->_mCategoryId = (int)$_GET['CategoryId'];
  }

  public function init()
  {
    // If visiting a department ...
    $department_details =
      Catalog::GetDepartmentDetails($this->_mDepartmentId);

    $this->mName = $department_details['name'];
    $this->mDescription = $department_details['description'];

    // If visiting a category ...
    if (isset ($this->_mCategoryId))
    {
      $category_details =
        Catalog::GetCategoryDetails($this->_mCategoryId);
```

```
        $this->mName = $this->mName . ' &raquo; ' .
                    $category_details['name'];
        $this->mDescription = $category_details['description'];
      }
    }
  }
?>
```

5. Now, let's modify presentation/templates/store_front.tpl and presentation/store_front.php to load the newly created componentized template when DepartmentId appears in the query string. If the visitor is browsing a department, you set the $mContentsCell member in the StoreFront presentation object to the componentized template you have just created so that the products you've chosen to display on the store front appear.

   Modify presentation/store_front.php as shown:

```php
<?php
class StoreFront
{
  public $mSiteUrl;
  // Define the template file for the page contents
  public $mContentsCell = 'blank.tpl';

  // Class constructor
  public function __construct()
  {
    $this->mSiteUrl = Link::Build('');
  }

  // Initialize presentation object
  public function init()
  {
    // Load department details if visiting a department
    if (isset ($_GET['DepartmentId']))
    {
      $this->mContentsCell = 'department.tpl';
    }
  }
}
?>
```

6. Open presentation/templates/store_front.tpl, and replace the text Place contents here with

   `{include file=$obj->mContentsCell}`

7. Load your web site in a browser, and select one of the departments to ensure everything works as expected, as shown earlier in Figure 5-8.

■**Caution** Certain versions of PHP 5 have a bug that generates an error when loading the site at this stage, which reads "General error: 2014 Cannot execute queries while other unbuffered queries are active." The bug is documented at http://bugs.php.net/bug.php?id=39858. Consult the book's errata page for solutions to this problem.

How It Works: The Department Componentized Template

Congratulations! If your little list of departments functions as described, you've just made it past the toughest part of this book. Make sure you understand very well what happens in the code before moving on.

After implementing the data and business tiers, adding the visual part was a fairly easy task. After adding the CSS styles and creating the blank template file, you created the Smarty template file department.tpl, which contains the HTML layout for displaying a department's data. This template file is loaded in the contents cell, just below the header, in store_front.tpl:

```
<div id="yui-main">
  <div class="yui-b">
    <div id="header" class="yui-g">
      <a href="{$obj->mSiteUrl}">
        <img src="{$obj->mSiteUrl}images/tshirtshop.png"
         alt="tshirtshop logo" />
      </a>
    </div>
    <div id="contents" class="yui-g">
      {include file=$obj->mContentsCell}
    </div>
  </div>
</div>
```

The $mContentsCell field of the presentation object is populated in store_front.php, depending on the query string parameters. At the moment, if the DepartmentId parameter is found in the query string, the page contents cell is populated with the department.tpl template file you just wrote. Otherwise (such as when you're on the first page), the blank.tpl template file is used, since we haven't yet implemented the contents cell template (you'll change this when creating a template to populate the contents cell for the first page).

This is the code in store_front.php that assigns a value to $mContentsCell when a department is selected:

```
// Initialize presentation object
public function init()
{
  // Load department details if visiting a department
  if (isset ($_GET['DepartmentId']))
  {
    $this->mContentsCell = 'department.tpl';
  }
}
```

The first interesting aspect to know about department.tpl is the way it loads the Department presentation object with the help of load_presentation_object Smarty plug-in function.

```
{* department.tpl *}
{load_presentation_object filename="department" assign="obj"}
```

This allows you to access the instance of the Department class (which we'll discuss next) and its public members ($mName and $mDescription) from the template file (department.tpl), like this:

```
<h1 class="title">{$obj->mName}</h1>
<p class="description">{$obj->mDescription}</p>
Place list of products here
```

The next step now is to understand how the presentation object, department.php, does its work to obtain the department's name and description. The file contains the Department class. The two public members of Department are the ones you access from the Smarty template (the department's name and description). The final role of this class is to populate these members, which are required to build the output for the visitor:

```
// Deals with retrieving department details
class Department
{
  // Public variables for the smarty template
  public $mName;
  public $mDescription;
```

There are also two private members that are used for internal purposes. $_mDepartmentId and $_mCategoryId will store the values of the DepartmentId and CategoryId query string parameters:

```
  // Private members
  private $_mDepartmentId;
  private $_mCategoryId;
```

Next comes the constructor. In any object-oriented language, the constructor of the class is executed when the class is instantiated, and the constructor is used to perform various initialization procedures. In our case, the constructor of Department reads the DepartmentId and CategoryId query string parameters into the $_mDepartmentId and $_mCategoryId private class members. You need these because if CategoryId actually exists in the query string, then you also need to display the name of the category and the category's description instead of the department's description.

```
  // Class constructor
  public function __construct()
  {
    // We need to have DepartmentId in the query string
    if (isset ($_GET['DepartmentId']))
      $this->_mDepartmentId = (int)$_GET['DepartmentId'];
    else
      trigger_error('DepartmentId not set');

    /* If CategoryId is in the query string we save it
       (casting it to integer to protect against invalid values) */
    if (isset ($_GET['CategoryId']))
      $this->_mCategoryId = (int)$_GET['CategoryId'];
  }
```

The real functionality of the class is hidden inside the init() method. In our solution, the init() method is always executed immediately after the constructor, because it's called immediately after the object is created, in the load_presentation_object Smarty plug-in function (as you know from Chapter 4, this plug-in function is used by all Smarty templates to load their presentation objects).

The init() method populates the $mName and $mDescription public members with information from the business tier. The GetDepartmentDetails() method of the business tier Catalog class is used to retrieve the details of the department; if necessary, the GetCategoryDetails() method is also called to retrieve the details of the category (the details of the department need to be retrieved even when visiting a category, because in that case, we display both the department name and the category name).

```
public function init()
{
  // If visiting a department ...
  $department_details =
    Catalog::GetDepartmentDetails($this->_mDepartmentId);

  $this->mName = $department_details['name'];
  $this->mDescription = $department_details['description'];

  // If visiting a category ...
  if (isset ($this->_mCategoryId))
  {
    $category_details =
      Catalog::GetCategoryDetails($this->_mCategoryId);

    $this->mName = $this->mName . ' &raquo; ' .
                   $category_details['name'];
    $this->mDescription = $category_details['description'];
  }
}
```

Displaying the List of Categories

When a visitor selects a department, the categories that belong to that department must appear. For this, you'll implement a new Smarty template named categories_list. categories_list is very similar to the department_list componentized template. It consists of a template section used for looping over the array of categories data (category name and category ID). This template section will contain links to index.php, but this time, their query string will also contain a CategoryId showing that a category has been clicked, like this:

```
http://localhost/tshirtshop/index.php?DepartmentId=1&CategoryId=2
```

The steps in the following exercise are very much like the ones for the departments_list componentized template (created at the end of Chapter 4), so we'll move a bit more quickly this time.

Exercise: Creating the categories_list Componentized Template

1. Create the Smarty template for the `categories_list` componentized template. Write the following lines in presentation/templates/categories_list.tpl:

```
{* categories_list.tpl *}
{load_presentation_object filename="categories_list" assign="obj"}
{* Start categories list *}
<div class="box">
  <p class="box-title">Choose a Category</p>
  <ul>
  {section name=i loop=$obj->mCategories}
    {assign var=selected value=""}
    {if ($obj->mSelectedCategory == $obj->mCategories[i].category_id)}
      {assign var=selected value="class=\"selected\""}
    {/if}
    <li>
      <a {$selected} href="{$obj->mCategories[i].link_to_category}">
        {$obj->mCategories[i].name}
      </a>
    </li>
  {/section}
  </ul>
</div>
{* End categories list *}
```

2. Create the presentation/categories_list.php file, and add the following code to it:

```php
<?php
// Manages the categories list
class CategoriesList
{
  // Public variables for the smarty template
  public $mSelectedCategory   = 0;
  public $mSelectedDepartment = 0;
  public $mCategories;

  // Constructor reads query string parameter
  public function __construct()
  {
    if (isset ($_GET['DepartmentId']))
      $this->mSelectedDepartment = (int)$_GET['DepartmentId'];
    else
      trigger_error('DepartmentId not set');

    if (isset ($_GET['CategoryId']))
      $this->mSelectedCategory = (int)$_GET['CategoryId'];
  }
```

```php
    public function init()
    {
      $this->mCategories =
        Catalog::GetCategoriesInDepartment($this->mSelectedDepartment);

      // Building links for the category pages
      for ($i = 0; $i < count($this->mCategories); $i++)
        $this->mCategories[$i]['link_to_category'] =
          Link::ToCategory($this->mSelectedDepartment,
                          $this->mCategories[$i]['category_id']);
    }
  }
?>
```

3. Open the presentation/link.php file, and add the ToCategory() method shown below to Link class. This method creates categories links.

```php
public static function ToCategory($departmentId, $categoryId)
{
  $link = 'index.php?DepartmentId=' . $departmentId .
          '&CategoryId=' . $categoryId;

  return self::Build($link);self::Build($link);
}
```

4. Modify presentation/store_front.php like this:

```php
<?php
class StoreFront
{
  public $mSiteUrl;
  // Define the template file for the page contents
  public $mContentsCell = 'blank.tpl';
  // Define the template file for the categories cell
  public $mCategoriesCell = 'blank.tpl';

  // Class constructor
  public function __construct()
  {
    $this->mSiteUrl = Link::Build('');
  }

  // Initialize presentation object
  public function init()
  {
    // Load department details if visiting a department
    if (isset ($_GET['DepartmentId']))
    {
```

```
        $this->mContentsCell = 'department.tpl';
        $this->mCategoriesCell = 'categories_list.tpl';
      }
    }
  }
  ?>
```

5. Now include the `categories_list` componentized template in presentation/templates/store_front.tpl just below the list of departments. Note that we include `$obj->mCategoriesCell` and not `categories_list.tpl`, because the list of categories needs to show up only when a department is selected. When no department is selected, `$obj->mCategoriesCell` is set to `blank.tpl` in `store_front.php`.

```
    {include file="departments_list.tpl"}
    {include file=$obj->mCategoriesCell}
```

6. Load TShirtShop in a web browser. When the page loads, click one of the departments. You'll see the categories list appear in the chosen place. Selecting a category displays the category description, as shown in Figure 5-9.

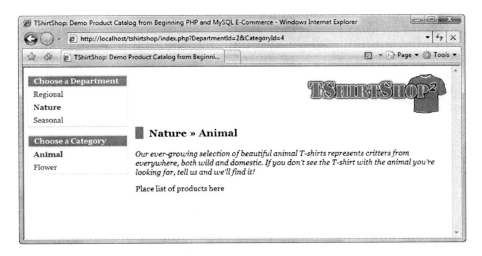

Figure 5-9. *Selecting the Animal category*

How It Works: The categories_list Componentized Template

The `categories_list` componentized template works similarly to the `departments_list`. The `CategoriesList` class (located in the `presentation/categories_list.php` presentation object file) has three public members that can be accessed from the template file (`categories_list.tpl`):

```
// Public variables for the smarty template
public $mSelectedCategory   = 0;
public $mSelectedDepartment = 0;
public $mCategories;
```

$mSelectedCategory retains the category that is selected, which must be displayed with a different style than the other categories in the list. The same is true with $mSelectedDepartment. $mCategories is the list of categories you populate the categories list with. This list is obtained with a call to the business tier.

The links in the categories list are created using the Link::ToCategory() method to ensure the consistency of the links across the site and to ensure they're also properly escaped (& is transformed to &, and so on).

Displaying Product Lists

Whether on the main web page or browsing a category, some products should appear instead of the "Place list of products here" text. Here, you create the products_list componentized template, which is capable of displaying a list containing detailed information about the products. When a large number of products need to be presented, navigation links will appear (see Figure 5-10).

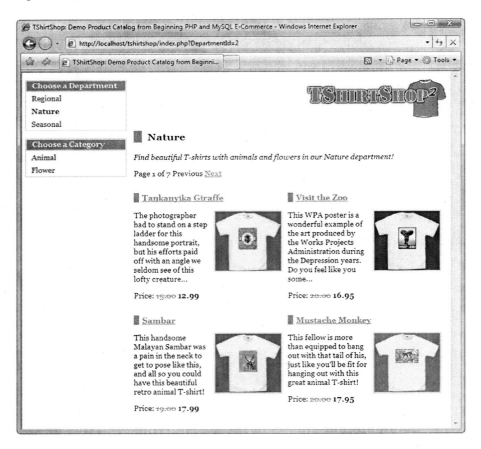

Figure 5-10. *The products_list componentized template with paging*

This componentized template will be used in multiple places within the web site. On the main page, it displays the products that have the display field set to 1 or 3. When a visitor selects a particular department, the products_list componentized template displays the products featured for the selected department. Finally, when the visitor clicks a category, the componentized template displays all the products that belong to that category. Due to the way the database is implemented, you can feature a product in the departments it belongs to but not on the main page or vice versa. If a product belongs to more than one department, it will appear on the main page of each of these departments.

The componentized template chooses which products to display after analyzing the query string. If both DepartmentId and CategoryId parameters are present in the query string, this means the products of that category should be listed. If only DepartmentId is present, the visitor is visiting a department, so its featured products should appear. If DepartmentId is not present, the visitor is on the main page, so the catalog featured products should appear.

To integrate the products_list componentized template with the first page, you'll need to create an additional template file (first_page_contents.tpl), which you'll implement later. After creating products_list in the following exercise, you'll be able to browse the products by department and by category. Afterward, you'll see how to add products to the main web page.

Exercise: Creating the products_list Componentized Template

1. Copy the product_images directory from the code archive of the book to your project's tshirtshop folder.

2. Add the following styles to the tshirtshop.css file, from the styles folder:

```css
.product-list tbody tr td {
  border: none;
  padding: 0;
  width: 50%;
}

.product-list tbody tr td p img {
  border: 2px solid #c6e1ec;
  float: right;
  margin: 0 10px;
  vertical-align: top;
}

.product-title {
  border-left: 10px solid #0590C7;
  padding-left: 5px;
}

.section {
  display: block;
}

.price {
  font-weight: bold;
}
```

```
.old-price {
  color: #ff0000;
  font-weight: normal;
  text-decoration: line-through;
}
```

3. Create a new Smarty design template named `products_list.tpl` inside the `presentation/templates` folder, and add the following code to it:

```
{* products_list.tpl *}
{load_presentation_object filename="products_list" assign="obj"}
{if $obj->mrTotalPages > 1}
<p>
  Page {$obj->mPage} of {$obj->mrTotalPages}
  {if $obj->mLinkToPreviousPage}
  <a href="{$obj->mLinkToPreviousPage}">Previous</a>
  {else}
  Previous
  {/if}
  {if $obj->mLinkToNextPage}
  <a href="{$obj->mLinkToNextPage}">Next</a>
  {else}
  Next
  {/if}
</p>
{/if}
{if $obj->mProducts}
<table class="product-list" border="0">
  <tbody>
  {section name=k loop=$obj->mProducts}
    {if $smarty.section.k.index % 2 == 0}
    <tr>
    {/if}
      <td valign="top">
        <h3 class="product-title">
          <a href="{$obj->mProducts[k].link_to_product}">
            {$obj->mProducts[k].name}
          </a>
        </h3>
        <p>
          {if $obj->mProducts[k].thumbnail neq ""}
          <a href="{$obj->mProducts[k].link_to_product}">
            <img src="{$obj->mProducts[k].thumbnail}"
            alt="{$obj->mProducts[k].name}" />
          </a>
          {/if}
          {$obj->mProducts[k].description}
        </p>
```

```
          <p class="section">
            Price:
            {if $obj->mProducts[k].discounted_price != 0}
              <span class="old-price">{$obj->mProducts[k].price}</span>
              <span class="price">{$obj->mProducts[k].discounted_price}</span>
            {else}
              <span class="price">{$obj->mProducts[k].price}</span>
            {/if}
          </p>
        </td>
      {if $smarty.section.k.index % 2 != 0 && !$smarty.section.k.first ||
          $smarty.section.k.last}
      </tr>
      {/if}
    {/section}
    </tbody>
  </table>
  {/if}
```

4. Now, you must create the presentation object file for the products_list.tpl template. Create a new file named products_list.php in the presentation folder, and add the following code to it:

```php
<?php
class ProductsList
{
  // Public variables to be read from Smarty template
  public $mPage = 1;
  public $mrTotalPages;
  public $mLinkToNextPage;
  public $mLinkToPreviousPage;
  public $mProducts;

  // Private members
  private $_mDepartmentId;
  private $_mCategoryId;

  // Class constructor
  public function __construct()
  {
    // Get DepartmentId from query string casting it to int
    if (isset ($_GET['DepartmentId']))
      $this->_mDepartmentId = (int)$_GET['DepartmentId'];

    // Get CategoryId from query string casting it to int
    if (isset ($_GET['CategoryId']))
      $this->_mCategoryId = (int)$_GET['CategoryId'];

    // Get Page number from query string casting it to int
```

```php
    if (isset ($_GET['Page']))
      $this->mPage = (int)$_GET['Page'];

    if ($this->mPage < 1)
      trigger_error('Incorrect Page value');
  }

  public function init()
  {
    /* If browsing a category, get the list of products by calling
       the GetProductsInCategory() business tier method */
    if (isset ($this->_mCategoryId))
      $this->mProducts = Catalog::GetProductsInCategory(
        $this->_mCategoryId, $this->mPage, $this->mrTotalPages);
    /* If browsing a department, get the list of products by calling
       the GetProductsOnDepartment() business tier method */
    elseif (isset ($this->_mDepartmentId))
      $this->mProducts = Catalog::GetProductsOnDepartment(
        $this->_mDepartmentId, $this->mPage, $this->mrTotalPages);

    /* If there are subpages of products, display navigation
       controls */
    if ($this->mrTotalPages > 1)
    {
      // Build the Next link
      if ($this->mPage < $this->mrTotalPages)
      {
        if (isset($this->_mCategoryId))
          $this->mLinkToNextPage =
            Link::ToCategory($this->_mDepartmentId, $this->_mCategoryId,
                             $this->mPage + 1);
        elseif (isset($this->_mDepartmentId))
          $this->mLinkToNextPage =
            Link::ToDepartment($this->_mDepartmentId, $this->mPage + 1);
      }

      // Build the Previous link
      if ($this->mPage > 1)
      {
        if (isset($this->_mCategoryId))
          $this->mLinkToPreviousPage =
            Link::ToCategory($this->_mDepartmentId, $this->_mCategoryId,
                             $this->mPage - 1);
        elseif (isset($this->_mDepartmentId))
          $this->mLinkToPreviousPage =
            Link::ToDepartment($this->_mDepartmentId, $this->mPage - 1);
      }
    }
```

```php
      // Build links for product details pages
      for ($i = 0; $i < count($this->mProducts); $i++)
      {
        $this->mProducts[$i]['link_to_product'] =
          Link::ToProduct($this->mProducts[$i]['product_id']);

        if ($this->mProducts[$i]['thumbnail'])
          $this->mProducts[$i]['thumbnail'] =
            Link::Build('product_images/' . $this->mProducts[$i]['thumbnail']);
      }
    }
  }
}
?>
```

5. Modify presentation/link.php as highlighted here to add a new method to the Link class called ToProduct(), which creates links to product pages. Also, we'll add the parameter $page to the two existing methods, ToDepartment() and ToCategory(), and the code needed for pagination.

```php
  public static function ToDepartment($departmentId, $page = 1)
  {
    $link = 'index.php?DepartmentId=' . $departmentId;

    if ($page > 1)
      $link .= '&Page=' . $page;

    return self::Build($link);
  }

  public static function ToCategory($departmentId, $categoryId, $page = 1)
  {
    $link = 'index.php?DepartmentId=' . $departmentId .
            '&CategoryId=' . $categoryId;

    if ($page > 1)
      $link .= '&Page=' . $page;

    return self::Build($link);
  }

  public static function ToProduct($productId)
  {
    return self::Build('index.php?ProductId=' . $productId);
  }
}
?>
```

6. Open `presentation/templates/department.tpl` and replace

   `Place list of products here`

   with

   `{include file="products_list.tpl"}`

7. Load your project in your favorite browser; navigate to one of the departments; and then select a category from a department. Also, find a category with more than four products to test that the paging functionality works, as shown earlier in Figure 5-10.

How It Works: The products_list Componentized Template

Because most functionality regarding the products list has already been implemented in the data and business tiers, this task was fairly simple. The Smarty design template file (`products_list.tpl`) contains the layout to be used when displaying products, and its presentation object file (`presentation/products_list.php`) gets the correct list of products to display.

The constructor in `products_list.php` (the `ProductsList` class) creates a new instance of the business tier object (`Catalog`) and retrieves `DepartmentId`, `CategoryId`, and `Page` from the query string, casting them to `int` as a security measure. These values are used to decide which products to display:

```
// Class constructor
public function __construct()
{
  // Get DepartmentId from query string casting it to int
  if (isset ($_GET['DepartmentId']))
    $this->_mDepartmentId = (int)$_GET['DepartmentId'];

  // Get CategoryId from query string casting it to int
  if (isset ($_GET['CategoryId']))
    $this->_mCategoryId = (int)$_GET['CategoryId'];

  // Get Page number from query string casting it to int
  if (isset ($_GET['Page']))
    $this->mPage = (int)$_GET['Page'];

  if ($this->mPage < 1)
    trigger_error('Incorrect Page value');
}
```

The `init()` method, which continues the constructor's job, starts by retrieving the requested list of products. It decides what method of the business tier to call by analyzing the `$_mCategoryId` and `$_mDepartmentId` members (which, thanks to the constructor, represent the values of the `CategoryId` and `DepartmentId` query string parameters).

If `CategoryId` is present in the query string, it means the visitor is browsing a category, so `GetProductsInCategory()` is called to retrieve the products in that category. If only `DepartmentId` is present, `GetProductsOnDepartment()` is called to retrieve the department's featured products.

```
public function init()
{
  /* If browsing a category, get the list of products by calling
     the GetProductsInCategory() business tier method */
  if (isset ($this->_mCategoryId))
    $this->mProducts = Catalog::GetProductsInCategory(
      $this->_mCategoryId, $this->mPage, $this->mrTotalPages);
  /* If browsing a department, get the list of products by calling
     the GetProductsOnDepartment() business tier method */
  elseif (isset ($this->_mDepartmentId))
    $this->mProducts = Catalog::GetProductsOnDepartment(
      $this->_mDepartmentId, $this->mPage, $this->mrTotalPages);
```

The next part of the function takes care of paging. If the business tier call tells you there is more than one page of products (so there are more products than what you specified in the PRODUCTS_PER_PAGE constant), you need to show the visitor the current subpage of products being visited, the total number of subpages, and the Previous and Next page links. The comments in code should make the functionality fairly clear, so we won't reiterate the code here.

In the final part of the function, you added the link_to_product and thumbnail data to each $mProducts record, which contain, respectively, the link to the product's page and its thumbnail file name. These values are used in the template file to display the product images and create links to the product pages on the products' names and pictures. The links are created using the Link::ToProduct() and Link::Build() methods:

```
// Build links for product details pages
for ($i = 0; $i < count($this->mProducts); $i++)
{
  $this->mProducts[$i]['link_to_product'] =
    Link::ToProduct($this->mProducts[$i]['product_id']);

  if ($this->mProducts[$i]['thumbnail'])
    $this->mProducts[$i]['thumbnail'] =
      Link::Build('product_images/' . $this->mProducts[$i]['thumbnail']);
}
```

We've also modified the methods of the Link class to add the Page parameter to the query string, if the page number is greater than 1. This is now necessary since adding product lists to our catalog implies supporting the paging functionality.

```
if ($page > 1)
  $link .= '?Page=' . $page;
```

Displaying Front Page Contents

Apart from general information about the web site, you also want to show some promotional products on the first page of TShirtShop.

If the visitor browses a department or a category, the department Smarty template is used to build the output. For the main web page, we'll create the first_page_contents componentized template that will build the output.

Remember the StoreFront class in presentation/store_front.php, where you have a member named $mContentsCell that you fill with different details depending on what part of the site is being visited? When a department or a category is being visited, the department componentized template is loaded, and it takes care of filling that space. We still haven't done anything with that cell for the first page, when no department or category has been selected.

In the following exercise, you'll write a template file that contains some information about the web site and shows the products that have been set up as promotions on the first page. Remember that the product table contains a field named display. Site administrators will set this field to on_catalog for products that need to be displayed in the first page.

Exercise: Creating the first_page_contents Componentized Template

1. Start by creating the Smarty design template file. The presentation/templates/first_page_contents.tpl file should have these contents:

```
{* first_page_contents.tpl *}
<p class="description">
  We hope you have fun developing TShirtShop, the e-commerce store from
  Beginning PHP and MySQL E-Commerce: From Novice to Professional!
</p>
<p class="description">
  We have the largest collection of t-shirts with postal stamps on Earth!
  Browse our departments and cateogories to find your favorite!
</p>
{include file="products_list.tpl"}
```

2. Modify the presentation/store_front.php file, as highlighted in the following code:

```
<?php
class StoreFront
{
  public $mSiteUrl;
  // Define the template file for the page contents
  public $mContentsCell = 'first_page_contents.tpl';
  // Define the template file for the categories cell
  public $mCategoriesCell = 'blank.tpl';
```

This way, when no DepartmentId and CategoryId are in the query string, store_front.php will load the first_page_contents componentized template.

3. Modify the init() method from the ProductsList class located in the presentation/products_list.php file, as highlighted:

```
public function init()
{
  /* If browsing a category, get the list of products by calling
     the GetProductsInCategory() business tier method */
  if (isset ($this->_mCategoryId))
    $this->mProducts = Catalog::GetProductsInCategory(
      $this->_mCategoryId, $this->mPage, $this->mrTotalPages);
```

```
/* If browsing a department, get the list of products by calling
   the GetProductsOnDepartment() business tier method */
elseif (isset ($this->_mDepartmentId))
  $this->mProducts = Catalog::GetProductsOnDepartment(
    $this->_mDepartmentId, $this->mPage, $this->mrTotalPages);
/* If browsing the first page, get the list of products by
   calling the GetProductsOnCatalog() business
   tier method */
else
  $this->mProducts = Catalog::GetProductsOnCatalog(
                       $this->mPage, $this->mrTotalPages);

/* If there are subpages of products, display navigation
   controls */
if ($this->mrTotalPages > 1)
{
  // Build the Next link
  if ($this->mPage < $this->mrTotalPages)
  {
    if (isset($this->_mCategoryId))
      $this->mLinkToNextPage =
        Link::ToCategory($this->_mDepartmentId, $this->_mCategoryId,
                         $this->mPage + 1);
    elseif (isset($this->_mDepartmentId))
      $this->mLinkToNextPage =
        Link::ToDepartment($this->_mDepartmentId, $this->mPage + 1);
    else
      $this->mLinkToNextPage = Link::ToIndex($this->mPage + 1);
  }

  // Build the Previous link
  if ($this->mPage > 1)
  {
    if (isset($this->_mCategoryId))
      $this->mLinkToPreviousPage =
        Link::ToCategory($this->_mDepartmentId, $this->_mCategoryId,
                         $this->mPage - 1);
    elseif (isset($this->_mDepartmentId))
      $this->mLinkToPreviousPage =
        Link::ToDepartment($this->_mDepartmentId, $this->mPage - 1);
    else
      $this->mLinkToPreviousPage = Link::ToIndex($this->mPage - 1);
  }
}
```

4. Open the `link.php` file located in the `presentation` folder, and add the following method to the `Link` class:

```php
public static function ToIndex($page = 1)
{
  $link = '';

  if ($page > 1)
    $link .= 'index.php?Page=' . $page;

  return self::Build($link);
}
```

5. Load your project in your favorite browser. The result should look like Figure 5-11.

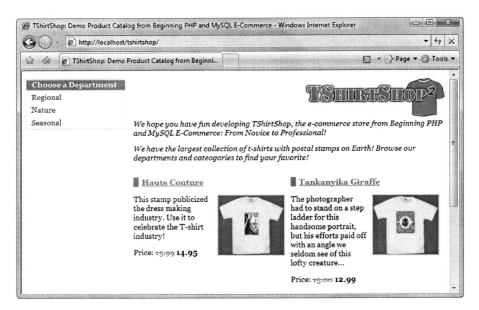

Figure 5-11. *The front page of TShirtShop*

How It Works: The first_page_contents Componentized Template

The actual list of products is still displayed using the `products_list` Smarty componentized template, which you built earlier in this chapter. However, this time, it isn't loaded from `department.tpl` (like it loads when browsing a department or a category) but from a new template file named `first_page_contents.tpl`.

We added new functionality to the `init()` method in the `ProductsList` class for displaying the products to be featured on the first page of the site. Also, we created the `ToIndex()` method in the `Link` class to support pagination for the first page of the site.

Showing Product Details

The last bit of code you'll implement in this chapter is about displaying product details. When a visitor clicks any product, he or she will be forwarded to the product's details page, which shows the product's complete description and the secondary product image. In later chapters, you'll add more features to this page, such as product recommendations or product reviews.

On this page, we'll also implement the Continue Shopping functionality. This consists of a Continue Shopping link at the bottom of the product details page, which links to the page the visitor was prior to looking at a product's detail page. If the visitor arrives to that page by browsing directly, or from a search engine, the Continue Shopping button will link to the home page of the shop. Let's do this in the following exercise.

Exercise: Creating the product Componentized Template

1. Add the following styles to `styles/tshirtshop.css`:

```css
.product-image {
  border: 2px solid #c6e1ec;
}

ol {
  margin: 0px;
  padding: 0px 0px 0px 5px;
}

ol li {
  color: #0590C7;
  list-style-type: none;
  margin: 0px;
  padding: 5px 0px;
}
```

2. Now, get in touch with your artistic side, and use these CSS definitions in the product details page. Create the `product.tpl` file in the `presentation/templates` folder. Feel free to go wild and customize this page as you want.

```
{load_presentation_object filename="product" assign="obj"}
<h1 class="title">{$obj->mProduct.name}</h1>
{if $obj->mProduct.image}
<img class="product-image" src="{$obj->mProduct.image}"
 alt="{$obj->mProduct.name} image" />
{/if}
{if $obj->mProduct.image_2}
<img class="product-image" src="{$obj->mProduct.image_2}"
 alt="{$obj->mProduct.name} image 2" />
{/if}
<p class="description">{$obj->mProduct.description}</p>
```

```
<p class="section">
  Price:
  {if $obj->mProduct.discounted_price != 0}
    <span class="old-price">{$obj->mProduct.price}</span>
    <span class="price">{$obj->mProduct.discounted_price}</span>
  {else}
    <span class="price">{$obj->mProduct.price}</span>
  {/if}
</p>
{if $obj->mLinkToContinueShopping}
<a href="{$obj->mLinkToContinueShopping}">Continue Shopping</a>
{/if}
<h2>Find similar products in our catalog:</h2>
<ol>
{section name=i loop=$obj->mLocations}
  <li class="navigation">
    {strip}
    <a href="{$obj->mLocations[i].link_to_department}">
      {$obj->mLocations[i].department_name}
    </a>
    {/strip}
    &raquo;
    {strip}
    <a href="{$obj->mLocations[i].link_to_category}">
      {$obj->mLocations[i].category_name}
    </a>
    {/strip}
  </li>
{/section}
</ol>
```

3. OK, now create the componentized template for the product details page in which the product with full description and a second image will display. Create a file named product.php in the presentation folder with the following contents:

```php
<?php
// Handles product details
class Product
{
  // Public variables to be used in Smarty template
  public $mProduct;
  public $mProductLocations;
  public $mLinkToContinueShopping;
  public $mLocations;

  // Private stuff
  private $_mProductId;
```

```php
// Class constructor
public function __construct()
{
  // Variable initialization
  if (isset ($_GET['ProductId']))
    $this->_mProductId = (int)$_GET['ProductId'];
  else
    trigger_error('ProductId not set');
}

public function init()
{
  // Get product details from business tier
  $this->mProduct = Catalog::GetProductDetails($this->_mProductId);

  if (isset ($_SESSION['link_to_continue_shopping']))
  {
    $continue_shopping =
      Link::QueryStringToArray($_SESSION['link_to_continue_shopping']);

    $page = 1;

    if (isset ($continue_shopping['Page']))
      $page = (int)$continue_shopping['Page'];

    if (isset ($continue_shopping['CategoryId']))
      $this->mLinkToContinueShopping =
        Link::ToCategory((int)$continue_shopping['DepartmentId'],
                         (int)$continue_shopping['CategoryId'], $page);
    elseif (isset ($continue_shopping['DepartmentId']))
      $this->mLinkToContinueShopping =
        Link::ToDepartment((int)$continue_shopping['DepartmentId'], $page);
    else
      $this->mLinkToContinueShopping = Link::ToIndex($page);
  }

  if ($this->mProduct['image'])
    $this->mProduct['image'] =
      Link::Build('product_images/' . $this->mProduct['image']);

  if ($this->mProduct['image_2'])
    $this->mProduct['image_2'] =
      Link::Build('product_images/' . $this->mProduct['image_2']);
```

```
        $this->mLocations = Catalog::GetProductLocations($this->_mProductId);

        // Build links for product departments and categories pages
        for ($i = 0; $i < count($this->mLocations); $i++)
        {
          $this->mLocations[$i]['link_to_department'] =
            Link::ToDepartment($this->mLocations[$i]['department_id']);

          $this->mLocations[$i]['link_to_category'] =
            Link::ToCategory($this->mLocations[$i]['department_id'],
                             $this->mLocations[$i]['category_id']);
        }
      }
    }
  }
?>
```

4. Add the following method to presentation/link.php. This function creates an associative array with the elements of the query string. We'll use this functionality to implement the Continue Shopping feature.

```
    public static function QueryStringToArray($queryString)
    {
      $result = array();

      if ($queryString != '')
      {
        $elements = explode('&', $queryString);

        foreach($elements as $key => $value)
        {
          $element = explode('=', $value);
          $result[urldecode($element[0])] =
              isset($element[1]) ? urldecode($element[1]) : '';
        }
      }

      return $result;
    }
```

5. Modify presentation/products_list.php as shown in the following code snippet. This new code saves the last catalog page accessed. When displaying a product details page, this address will be used to create the Continue Shopping link.

```
    // Class constructor
    public function __construct()
    {
    ...
    ...
```

```
    if ($this->mPage < 1)
      trigger_error('Incorrect Page value');

    // Save page request for continue shopping functionality
    $_SESSION['link_to_continue_shopping'] = $_SERVER['QUERY_STRING'];
  }
```

6. Modify presentation/departments_list.php by adding the highlighted code, which is also required for the Continue Shopping functionality:

```
// Constructor reads query string parameter
public function __construct()
{
  /* If DepartmentId exists in the query string, we're visiting a
     department */
  if (isset ($_GET['DepartmentId']))
    $this->mSelectedDepartment = (int)$_GET['DepartmentId'];
  elseif (isset($_GET['ProductId']) &&
          isset($_SESSION['link_to_continue_shopping']))
  {
    $continue_shopping =
      Link::QueryStringToArray($_SESSION['link_to_continue_shopping']);

    if (array_key_exists('DepartmentId', $continue_shopping))
      $this->mSelectedDepartment =
        (int)$continue_shopping['DepartmentId'];
  }
}
```

7. Modify presentation/categories_list.php to load the department ID and category ID parameters from the Continue Shopping data saved in the session:

```
// Constructor reads query string parameter
public function __construct()
{
  if (!isset($_GET['ProductId']))
  {
    if (isset ($_GET['DepartmentId']))
      $this->mSelectedDepartment = (int)$_GET['DepartmentId'];
    else
      trigger_error('DepartmentId not set');

    if (isset ($_GET['CategoryId']))
      $this->mSelectedCategory = (int)$_GET['CategoryId'];
  }
```

```
    else
    {
      $continue_shopping =
        Link::QueryStringToArray($_SESSION['link_to_continue_shopping']);

      if (array_key_exists('DepartmentId', $continue_shopping))
        $this->mSelectedDepartment =
          (int)$continue_shopping['DepartmentId'];
      else
        trigger_error('DepartmentId not set');

      if (array_key_exists('CategoryId', $continue_shopping))
        $this->mSelectedCategory =
          (int)$continue_shopping['CategoryId'];
    }
  }
```

8. Edit presentation/store_front.php to load the product.tpl template using the $mContentsCell member if the ProductId parameter exists in the query string. Also, if we've arrived to the product page from a department or category catalog page, we display the list of categories as well. This is a small feature but an important one for improving the catalog navigation experience of your visitor. Add the boldfaced lines to the store_front.php file as shown in the following code:

```
public function init()
{
  // Load department details if visiting a department
  if (isset ($_GET['DepartmentId']))
  {
    $this->mContentsCell = 'department.tpl';
    $this->mCategoriesCell = 'categories_list.tpl';
  }
  elseif (isset($_GET['ProductId']) &&
          isset($_SESSION['link_to_continue_shopping']) &&
          strpos($_SESSION['link_to_continue_shopping'], 'DepartmentId', 0)
          !== false)
  {
    $this->mCategoriesCell = 'categories_list.tpl';
  }

  // Load product details page if visiting a product
  if (isset ($_GET['ProductId']))
    $this->mContentsCell = 'product.tpl';
  }
}
?>
```

9. Load the web site, and click the picture or name of any product. You should be forwarded to its details page. Figure 5-12 shows an example details page.

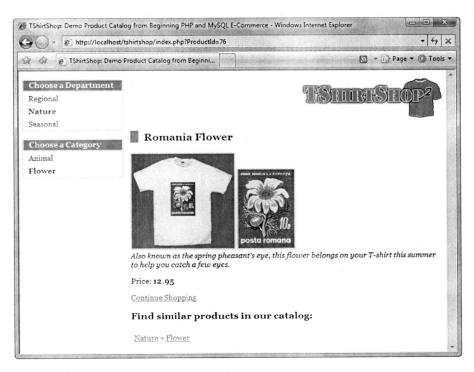

Figure 5-12. *A product details page in TShirtShop*

How It Works: The product Componentized Template

As expected, the steps to implement the product details page were quite straightforward, since we only wrote or updated code that is already structured in a logical and consistent fashion. Implementing such features will become easier as you get used to the project structure in the following chapters.

What's interesting to note about this exercise are the way we used the session to implement the Continue Shopping link and the way we display the list of categories in the product details page. Whether a product page is visited from the front page of the catalog, is loaded directly in your browser, or is navigated to from an external web site, the list of categories doesn't show up. On the other hand, if you browsed a department or a category before loading a product details page, the department and category navigation elements show up in the product details page as well.

The code was explained throughout the exercise, so we'll not revisit it again. Read it again, and make sure you understand it clearly before moving on to the next chapter.

Summary

Congratulations! You've done a lot of work in this chapter! You finished building the product catalog by implementing the necessary logic in the data, business, and presentation tiers. On the way, you learned a great deal of theory, including

- Relational data and the types of relationships that can occur between tables

- How to obtain data from multiple tables in a single result set using JOIN and how to filter the results using WHERE

- How to display the list of categories and products depending on what page the visitor is browsing

- How to display a product details page and implement the Continue Shopping functionality

- How to implement paging in the products list when browsing pages containing many products

It's OK if you found much of the code quite complex, because it really is. Unless you're a PHP guru already, you should feel really proud of creating successfully a functional product catalog that features paging, categories and departments, product details pages, and many more smaller but equally important features!

Chapter 6 will be at least as exciting as this one, because you'll learn how to add attributes to products in your web site!

CHAPTER 6

■■■

Product Attributes

Many online stores allow shoppers to customize the products they buy. For example, when selling t-shirts, it's common to let your customer choose the size and color of the t-shirt—sparing them the fashion risk of one-size-one-color-fits-all. In this chapter, we'll implement the product attributes feature in TShirtShop (see Figure 6-1).

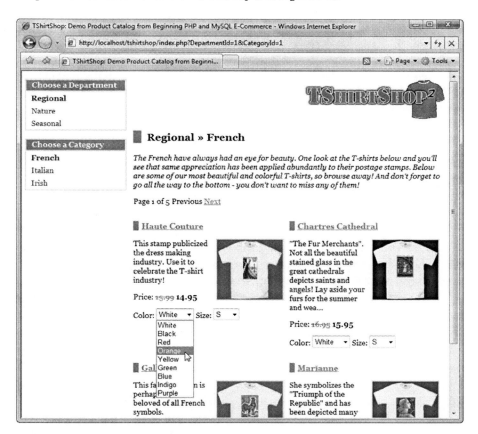

Figure 6-1. *Products with attributes*

We'll do this starting with the data tier, where you'll create data tables and a stored procedure, then write the business tier code that calls that procedure, and finally use this functionality to update the Smarty template for the user interface. At the end of this chapter, our catalog will allow customers to choose the size and color of the t-shirt, as shown in Figure 6-1. Since the attributes data is stored in the database, you can add your own attributes and attribute values.

Implementing the Data Tier

The data tier components that support the product attributes feature include three data tables (attribute, attribute_value, and product_attribute) and a stored procedure named catalog_get_product_attributes.

The three data tables follow:

- attribute stores the name of the attributes, such as Size and Color.

- attribute_value contains the possible attribute values for each attribute group. There is a one-to-many relationship between attribute and attribute_value. Each attribute, take Color for example, can have several values associated with it—Red, Orange, Yellow, and so on. We need this table to help us to link the attribute_id (like 1 for Color) to its attribute_value_ids for its possible values (Red, Orange, Yellow, and so on). So, it will contain three columns: attribute_id, which is found in the attribute table and tells us what kind of attribute we are talking about (e.g., a color or a size); attribute_value_id, the integer we assign to uniquely identify the items in the attribute_value table itself; and value, which will hold the text description like Orange, Red, S (for small), M (for medium), and so on.

- product_attribute is an associate table implementing a many-to-many relationship between the product and attribute_value tables, with (product_id, attribute_value_id) pairs (the attribute_value table will allow us to quickly and easily populate this table).

■**Note** The system you're implementing doesn't permit an attribute to change the price of the product. For example, a white t-shirt will always have the same price as a black t-shirt. If you need to have different product prices, you need to create different products. If you need to support attributes that affect the product price, one option would be to extend the product_attribute table by including data about the change in the product price and making many other changes and additions to the business tier and presentation tier code. We advise you not to make any changes at this time, as they would propagate to the following chapters as well, making the task of following the book more difficult.

You learned in Chapter 5 that database diagrams can help in understanding the relationships among data tables. A visual representation of these tables and of the relationships among the attribute tables can be seen in Figure 6-2. The relationship between the product table and the other tables is shown in Figure 5-6. If you are new to databases, you should take a moment to study this diagram so that the following code is easier for you to negotiate and understand.

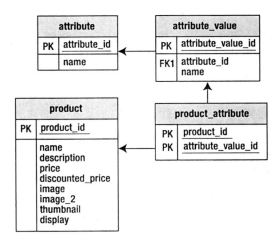

Figure 6-2. *Diagram describing the relationships among the data tables required to implement product attributes*

Let's start by updating the tshirtshop database and then implement the new stored procedure catalog_get_product_attributes in the following exercise.

1. Open phpMyAdmin, and execute the following code, which creates and populates the attribute table:

```
-- Create attribute table (stores attributes such as Size and Color)
CREATE TABLE `attribute` (
  `attribute_id` INT         NOT NULL  AUTO_INCREMENT,
  `name`         VARCHAR(100) NOT NULL, -- E.g. Color, Size
  PRIMARY KEY (`attribute_id`)
) ENGINE=MyISAM;


-- Populate attribute table
INSERT INTO `attribute` (`attribute_id`, `name`) VALUES
      (1, 'Size'), (2, 'Color');
```

2. Continue by creating and populating the attribute_value table, using the following SQL code:

```
-- Create attribute_value table (stores values such as Yellow or XXL)
CREATE TABLE `attribute_value` (
  `attribute_value_id` INT         NOT NULL  AUTO_INCREMENT,
  `attribute_id`       INT         NOT NULL, -- The ID of the attribute
  `value`              VARCHAR(100) NOT NULL, -- E.g. Yellow
  PRIMARY KEY (`attribute_value_id`),
  KEY `idx_attribute_value_attribute_id` (`attribute_id`)
) ENGINE=MyISAM;
```

```
-- Populate attribute_value table
INSERT INTO `attribute_value` (`attribute_value_id`, `attribute_id`, `value`)
VALUES
        (1, 1, 'S'), (2, 1, 'M'), (3, 1, 'L'), (4, 1, 'XL'), (5, 1, 'XXL'),
        (6, 2, 'White'),  (7, 2, 'Black'), (8, 2, 'Red'), (9, 2, 'Orange'),
        (10, 2, 'Yellow'), (11, 2, 'Green'), (12, 2, 'Blue'),
        (13, 2, 'Indigo'), (14, 2, 'Purple');
```

3. Create and populate the product_attribute table, using the code in the following listing:

```
-- Create product_attribute table (associates attribute values to products)
CREATE TABLE `product_attribute` (
  `product_id`         INT NOT NULL,
  `attribute_value_id` INT NOT NULL,
  PRIMARY KEY (`product_id`, `attribute_value_id`)
) ENGINE=MyISAM;


-- Populate product_attribute table
INSERT INTO `product_attribute` (`product_id`, `attribute_value_id`)
      SELECT `p`.`product_id`, `av`.`attribute_value_id`
      FROM   `product` `p`, `attribute_value` `av`;
```

4. Execute the following SQL code, which creates the catalog_get_product_attributes stored procedure. This stored procedure will associate the attributes assigned to a product. *Don't forget to set the
   delimiter to $$ before executing the code.*

```
-- Create catalog_get_product_attributes stored procedure
CREATE PROCEDURE catalog_get_product_attributes(IN inProductId INT)
BEGIN
  SELECT     a.name AS attribute_name,
             av.attribute_value_id, av.value AS attribute_value
  FROM       attribute_value av
  INNER JOIN attribute a
               ON av.attribute_id = a.attribute_id
  WHERE      av.attribute_value_id IN
               (SELECT attribute_value_id
                FROM   product_attribute
                WHERE  product_id = inProductId)
  ORDER BY   a.name;
END$$
```

How It Works: Data Logic for Product Attributes

Here, we'll discuss the code used to populate the product_attribute table and the catalog_get_product_
attributes stored procedure. Before proceeding, please make sure you understand the purpose of each field of
the attribute and attribute_value tables and the code used to populate these tables. It may take a while to
understand the table structure exactly. We will not reiterate the theory here, but feel free to refer to Chapters 4 and 5,
where we've discussed in detail the major concepts of relational database design.

When populating product_attribute, the goal is to associate all the existing attribute values (via the attribute_value_id field) to each of our products (via the product_id field). In our site, our products are t-shirts, and we want to sell each of them in all possible sizes and colors. The code that populates the product_attribute table uses the INSERT INTO command to insert a number of records produced by a SELECT query:

```
INSERT INTO `product_attribute` (`product_id`, `attribute_value_id`)
```

In our case, the SELECT query that generates the data to be inserted into product_attribute is a *cross join*. This type of JOIN makes a Cartesian product between two data sets. The result is a list that contains all the possible combinations between the records of the first data set and the records of the second data set.

For example, the Cartesian product between {1, 2, 3} and {a, b, c}, which is mathematically written as $\{1, 2, 3\} \times \{a, b, c\}$, is the following set of data: { {1, a}, {1, b}, {1, c}, {2, a}, {2, b}, {2, c}, {3, a}, {3, b}, {3, c} }.

In our case, if we make a Cartesian product between the IDs of the existing products and the IDs of the existing attribute values, we obtain a list formed of (product_id, attribute_value_id) elements, which is exactly the list we want to add to the product_attribute table. The syntax to implement this cross join operation with MySQL highlighted:

```
INSERT INTO `product_attribute` (`product_id`, `attribute_value_id`)
    SELECT `p`.`product_id`, `av`.`attribute_value_id`
    FROM   `product` `p`, `attribute_value` `av`;
```

This is certainly a nice way of creating many records into our database with minimal effort. The sample data of our database contains 14 possible attribute values and 101 products. The cross join operation that associates all attribute values to all products generates 1,414 (which is 14 multiplied by 101) records into the product_attribute table.

Note that the use of SELECT to create the cross join is not standard SQL; if you want to implement such an operation with other database servers, you may need to use different syntax. The "official" syntax to implement cross joins specifies the use of the CROSS JOIN syntax.

There are a few alternative methods to using the cross join to populate the product_attribute table with the necessary data. One method that we think is worth discussing here is to use UNION, because it's quite frequently used in such situations. UNION sums up the results of multiple SELECT statements into a single result set. For example, if you use UNION for two queries that return five records each, you get a result set of ten records. Of course, for UNION to work, all the queries involved must return the same number of columns of compatible data types. We won't go into more details about UNION, but if you're curious to see the UNION-based implementation of the cross join, here it is. It necessitates more keystrokes, but the query offers you more flexibility; for example, using UNION, you could add only certain attribute values to your products.

```
-- Populate product_attribute table
INSERT INTO `product_attribute` (`product_id`, `attribute_value_id`)
        SELECT       product_id, 1 AS attribute_value_id FROM product
        UNION SELECT product_id, 2 AS attribute_value_id FROM product
        UNION SELECT product_id, 3 AS attribute_value_id FROM product
        UNION SELECT product_id, 4 AS attribute_value_id FROM product
        UNION SELECT product_id, 5 AS attribute_value_id FROM product
        UNION SELECT product_id, 6 AS attribute_value_id FROM product
        UNION SELECT product_id, 7 AS attribute_value_id FROM product
        UNION SELECT product_id, 8 AS attribute_value_id FROM product
```

```
UNION SELECT product_id, 9  AS attribute_value_id FROM product
UNION SELECT product_id, 10 AS attribute_value_id FROM product
UNION SELECT product_id, 11 AS attribute_value_id FROM product
UNION SELECT product_id, 12 AS attribute_value_id FROM product
UNION SELECT product_id, 13 AS attribute_value_id FROM product
UNION SELECT product_id, 14 AS attribute_value_id FROM product;
```

Finally, let's take a look at the `catalog_get_product_attributes` stored procedure. This stored procedure receives as a parameter the ID of a product and returns a list of that product's attributes. This is the handy little device that the business tier will call to get the list of attributes for our products so our customers can choose a size and color for each t-shirt:

```
-- Create catalog_get_product_attributes stored procedure
CREATE PROCEDURE catalog_get_product_attributes(IN inProductId INT)
BEGIN
```

The SQL code in this procedure returns a list with the `attribute_name`, `attribute_value_id`, and `attribute_value` for all the attributes of the mentioned product:

```
SELECT     a.name AS attribute_name,
           av.attribute_value_id, av.value AS attribute_value
FROM       attribute_value av
INNER JOIN attribute a
             ON av.attribute_id = a.attribute_id
WHERE      av.attribute_value_id IN
             (SELECT attribute_value_id
              FROM   product_attribute
              WHERE  product_id = inProductId)
ORDER BY   a.name;
```

To test that the procedure works as it should, you can execute the code of the stored procedure using phpMyAdmin, replacing the parameter names with their values. For example, you could take the preceding SQL code, replace `inProductId` with the ID of a product, and then execute the code in phpMyAdmin.

Alternatively, you can call the stored procedure itself, but this operation is not supported by phpMyAdmin at the time of this writing. To execute a stored procedure you can use the MySQL console. To start the console in Windows, you need to execute the following command in `C:\xampp\mysql\bin` (assuming that you have installed XAMPP as explained in Chapter 1).

```
mysql -u root
```

If your MySQL server is secured with a password (with the default XAMPP installation, it is not), you'll need to use the `-p` parameter as well, in which case you'll be asked for the password:

```
mysql -u root -p
```

After connecting to your MySQL server, you need to connect to the `tshirtshop` database:

```
USE tshirtshop;
```

Once tshirtshop is selected, you can execute the catalog_get_product_attributes procedure, by supplying 1 as parameter, like this:

```
CALL catalog_get_product_attributes (1);
```

When executing the stored procedure like this, you get all the attributes and attribute values for the product with the ID of 1 in your database:

```
+----------------+--------------------+-----------------+
| attribute_name | attribute_value_id | attribute_value |
+----------------+--------------------+-----------------+
| Color          |                  6 | White           |
| Color          |                  7 | Black           |
| Color          |                  8 | Red             |
| Color          |                  9 | Orange          |
| Color          |                 10 | Yellow          |
| Color          |                 11 | Green           |
| Color          |                 12 | Blue            |
| Color          |                 13 | Indigo          |
| Color          |                 14 | Purple          |
| Size           |                  1 | S               |
| Size           |                  2 | M               |
| Size           |                  3 | L               |
| Size           |                  4 | XL              |
| Size           |                  5 | XXL             |
+----------------+--------------------+-----------------+
```

Implementing the Business Tier

The business tier bit of the product attributes feature is very straightforward—we only need to write the code that calls the catalog_get_product_attributes stored procedure. Add the following code to the Catalog class, in business/catalog.php:

```php
// Retrieves product attributes
public static function GetProductAttributes($productId)
{
  // Build SQL query
  $sql = 'CALL catalog_get_product_attributes(:product_id)';

  // Build the parameters array
  $params = array (':product_id' => $productId);

  // Execute the query and return the results
  return DatabaseHandler::GetAll($sql, $params);
}
```

Implementing the Presentation Tier

Creating the presentation tier implies adding controls that allow choosing a value from the list of product attribute values. As you will see, attributes are not hard-coded in the templates. Instead, the attributes (such as Size and Color) and their values (such as L, XL, White, Green, and so on) are read from the database

You can already see how making changes to the attributes for all of your products is far easier this way. You simply change the data in the attributes tables and voilà—the changes are automatically reflected on your site!

Let's implement the presentation code, and we'll discuss it afterward. To aid comprehension, remember to correlate the code you're typing now with the results you expect from the catalog_get_product_attributes stored procedures. You saw some sample output of this procedure a little earlier in this chapter.

Exercise: Implementing the Product Attributes Presentation

1. Add the following highlighted code to presentation\templates\products_list.tpl:

```
<p class="section">
  Price:
  {if $obj->mProducts[k].discounted_price != 0}
    <span class="old-price">{$obj->mProducts[k].price}</span>
    <span class="price">{$obj->mProducts[k].discounted_price}</span>
  {else}
    <span class="price">{$obj->mProducts[k].price}</span>
  {/if}
</p>

{* Generate the list of attribute values *}
<p class="attributes">

{* Parse the list of attributes and attribute values *}
{section name=l loop=$obj->mProducts[k].attributes}

  {* Generate a new select tag? *}
  {if $smarty.section.l.first ||
      $obj->mProducts[k].attributes[l].attribute_name !==
      $obj->mProducts[k].attributes[l.index_prev].attribute_name}
    {$obj->mProducts[k].attributes[l].attribute_name}:
  <select name="attr_{$obj->mProducts[k].attributes[l].attribute_name}">
  {/if}

    {* Generate a new option tag *}
    <option value="{$obj->mProducts[k].attributes[l].attribute_value}">
      {$obj->mProducts[k].attributes[l].attribute_value}
    </option>
```

```
        {* Close the select tag? *}
        {if $smarty.section.l.last ||
            $obj->mProducts[k].attributes[l].attribute_name !==
            $obj->mProducts[k].attributes[l.index_next].attribute_name}
        </select>
        {/if}

      {/section}
      </p>
    </td>
  {if $smarty.section.k.index % 2 != 0 && !$smarty.section.k.first ||
      $smarty.section.k.last}
  </tr>
  {/if}
{/section}
</tbody>
</table>
{/if}
```

2. Add the highlighted piece of code to the init() method in presentation/products_list.php. This
   displays the list of attributes for each product in the list.

```
// Build links for product details pages
for ($i = 0; $i < count($this->mProducts); $i++)
{
  $this->mProducts[$i]['link_to_product'] =
    Link::ToProduct($this->mProducts[$i]['product_id']);

  if ($this->mProducts[$i]['thumbnail'])
    $this->mProducts[$i]['thumbnail'] =
      Link::Build('product_images/' . $this->mProducts[$i]['thumbnail']);

  $this->mProducts[$i]['attributes'] =
    Catalog::GetProductAttributes($this->mProducts[$i]['product_id']);
  }
 }
}
?>
```

3. Open the presentation/templates/product.tpl file, and add the highlighted code, which generates
   the list of attribute values for the product details page:

```
<p class="section">
  Price:
  {if $obj->mProduct.discounted_price != 0}
    <span class="old-price">{$obj->mProduct.price}</span>
    <span class="price">{$obj->mProduct.discounted_price}</span>
  {else}
    <span class="price">{$obj->mProduct.price}</span>
```

```
      {/if}
   </p>

   {* Generate the list of attribute values *}
   <p class="attributes">

   {* Parse the list of attributes and attribute values *}
   {section name=k loop=$obj->mProduct.attributes}

     {* Generate a new select tag? *}
     {if $smarty.section.k.first ||
        $obj->mProduct.attributes[k].attribute_name !==
        $obj->mProduct.attributes[k.index_prev].attribute_name}
       {$obj->mProduct.attributes[k].attribute_name}:
     <select name="attr_{$obj->mProduct.attributes[k].attribute_name}">
     {/if}

        {* Generate a new option tag *}
        <option value="{$obj->mProduct.attributes[k].attribute_value}">
          {$obj->mProduct.attributes[k].attribute_value}
        </option>

     {* Close the select tag? *}
     {if $smarty.section.k.last ||
        $obj->mProduct.attributes[k].attribute_name !==
        $obj->mProduct.attributes[k.index_next].attribute_name}
     </select>
     {/if}

   {/section}
   </p>
   {if $obj->mLinkToContinueShopping}
   <a href="{$obj->mLinkToContinueShopping}">Continue Shopping</a>
   {/if}
```

4. Add the highlighted code to the init() method of the Product class from
   presentation/product.php:

```
        if ($this->mProduct['image_2'])
          $this->mProduct['image_2'] =
            Link::Build('product_images/' . $this->mProduct['image_2']);

        $this->mProduct['attributes'] =
          Catalog::GetProductAttributes($this->mProduct['product_id']);

        $this->mLocations = Catalog::GetProductLocations($this->_mProductId);
```

5. Add the following style to `styles/tshirtshop.css`:

```css
.attributes {
  clear: both;
  display: block;
  padding-top: 5px;
}
```

6. Load `http://localhost/tshirtshop/`, and admire your new product attributes in action. Figure 6-3 displays the product attributes in the product details page. Figure 6-1 shows product attributes in a product listing.

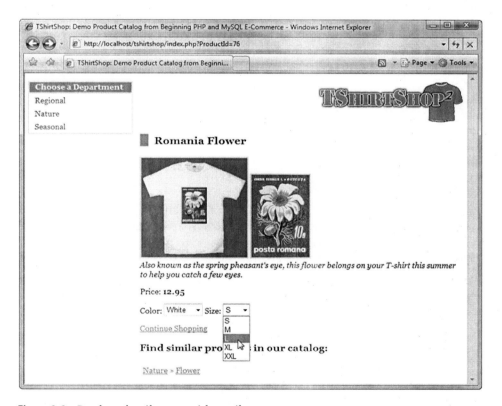

Figure 6-3. *Product details page with attributes*

How It Works: Presenting Product Attributes

You created the user interface for product attributes in two steps. You called the `Catalog::GetProductAttributes()` method of the business tier to get the list of attributes for the specified product. Then you updated the `products_list.tpl` template to display the list of attributes for each product.

At the moment, these attributes don't make much of a difference for a customer, because the products can't be ordered yet—but that detail will be taken care of in subsequent chapters.

The challenge of the exercise consists in understanding how the product attributes are displayed on the product details page and on the product lists. A useful strategy to understand how the Smarty code works is to analyze the input data received by Smarty and the code it generates. Let's once again look at the attributes data the catalog_ get_product_attributes procedure returns for the product with the ID of 1:

```
+----------------+--------------------+-----------------+
| attribute_name | attribute_value_id | attribute_value |
+----------------+--------------------+-----------------+
| Color          |                  6 | White           |
| Color          |                  7 | Black           |
| Color          |                  8 | Red             |
| Color          |                  9 | Orange          |
| Color          |                 10 | Yellow          |
| Color          |                 11 | Green           |
| Color          |                 12 | Blue            |
| Color          |                 13 | Indigo          |
| Color          |                 14 | Purple          |
| Size           |                  1 | S               |
| Size           |                  2 | M               |
| Size           |                  3 | L               |
| Size           |                  4 | XL              |
| Size           |                  5 | XXL             |
+----------------+--------------------+-----------------+
```

Now, let's look at the HTML source code generated for the details page of that product. You can load that page at http://localhost/tshirtshop/index.php?ProductId=1, and you can see its HTML source by right-clicking an empty area of the page and selecting View Source (in Internet Explorer) or View Page Source (in Firefox).

Here's what you'll find. We've deleted several options to make the listing easier to read, and we've added the Smarty comments to help you correlate the source template with the output, although the comments don't make it in the actual output:

```
{* Generate the list of attribute values *}
<p class="attributes">

{* Parse the list of attributes and attribute values *}
  {* Generate a new select tag? *}
     Color:
  <select name="attr_Color">

    {* Generate a new option tag *}
    <option value="White">
      White
    </option>

  {* Close the select tag? *}
```

```
{* Generate a new select tag? *}

  {* Generate a new option tag *}
  <option value="Black">
    Black
  </option>

{* Close the select tag? *}

{* Generate a new select tag? *}

  {* Generate a new option tag *}
  <option value="Red">
    Red
  </option>

{* Close the select tag? *}

{* Generate a new select tag? *}

...
...

  {* Close the select tag? *}
    </select>

{* Generate a new select tag? *}
    Size:
<select name="attr_Size">

  {* Generate a new option tag *}
  <option value="S">
    S
  </option>

{* Close the select tag? *}

{* Generate a new select tag? *}

  {* Generate a new option tag *}
  <option value="M">
    M
  </option>

...
...
```

```
{* Close the select tag? *}
  </select>
</p>
```

So how is this output calculated? The key is the Smarty logic included in the `product.tpl` and `products_list.tpl` templates. This code parses the list of attributes that's loaded by the business tier. This data is, in fact, the data returned by the `catalog_get_product_attributes` stored procedure:

```
{section name=k loop=$obj->mProduct.attributes}
```

For each element of that list, several steps are made to decide what kind of output to generate. Take, for example, the following code snippet, which is an `{if}` conditional statement that returns `true` for the first element and for the elements whose attribute name is different than the attribute name of the previous element:

```
{* Generate a new select tag? *}
{if $smarty.section.k.first ||
    $obj->mProduct.attributes[k].attribute_name !==
    $obj->mProduct.attributes[k.index_prev].attribute_name}
```

In short, this condition returns `true` each time a new attribute (such as Size and Color) needs to be displayed. When this happens, we generate a new `<select>` element, starting a new selection element:

```
{$obj->mProduct.attributes[k].attribute_name}:
<select name="attr_{$obj->mProduct.attributes[k].attribute_name}">
{/if}
```

The rest of the code follows along the same lines. Take a few minutes to make sure you understand it all, and then congratulate yourself for completing yet another important feature of your TShirtShop web site!

Summary

In this little chapter, we've added attributes to our products! From now on, our customers will be able to choose the colors and sizes of their t-shirts. Also, it's very easy to add your own attribute groups and attribute values, as you see fit.

Our t-shirt shop is really shaping up! But we won't compete well on the Internet if the search engines have a hard time understanding and ranking our site. Worse, if we don't carefully craft our site for search engines, we could actually lose ranking instead of gaining it! Because it can be very difficult to retrofit a site for search engine optimization, it's important that we begin addressing it early on in our design and development. In some cases, trying to retrofit a site is so difficult developers decide to simply start again from scratch! But we know that we need to plan from the beginning, so let's proceed to improving our catalog for search engine optimization right now.

CHAPTER 7

■ ■ ■

Search Engine Optimization

After adding product attributes to your site, you're probably eager to add new features as well, such as accepting user payments, product searching, or the shopping cart. We'll do that soon, we promise! Before that, there's one detail to take care of: we need to prepare the web site foundation to support our *search engine optimization* efforts. This is an important topic, because it *directly affects the profitability* of a web site, so let's get started!

Search engine optimization, or simply SEO, refers to the practices employed to increase the number of visitors a web site receives from organic (unpaid) search engine result pages. Today, the search engine is the most important tool people use to find information and products on the Internet. Needless to say, having your e-commerce web site rank well for the relevant keywords will help drive visitors to your site and increase the chances that visitors will buy from you and not the competition!

Although not (yet) rocket science, search engine optimization is a complex subject in the even larger subject of search engine marketing. In this chapter, we'll update TShirtShop so that its core architecture will be search engine friendly, which will help marketers in their efforts.

Note If you're serious about search engine optimization—and you should be!—we recommend that you continue your studies with more detailed books on this subject, because this single chapter cannot cover it in much depth. *Search Engine Optimization for Dummies* (Peter Kent. For Dummies, 2004) and *Search Engine Optimization: An Hour a Day* (Jennifer Grappone and Gradiva Couzin. Sybex, 2006) are two excellent resources that will teach you more about the basics of SEO. *Professional Search Engine Optimization with PHP: A Developer's Guide to SEO* by Cristian Darie and Jaimie Sirovich (Wrox, 2007) is your comprehensive guide into the world of SEO with PHP and explains, with many more details, all the topics covered in this chapter. Reading usability and user psychology books, such as *Prioritizing Web Usability* (Jakob Nielsen and Hoa Loranger. New Riders Press, 2006) and *Don't Make Me Think: A Common Sense Approach to Web Usability* (Steve Krug. New Riders Press, 2005), is highly recommended as well; they will help you understand the fine balance between search engine optimization, accessibility, and usability.

Optimizing TShirtShop

So what can be improved in TShirtShop to make it more search engine friendly? Well, it may come as a surprise to you to hear this, since TShirtShop is so small and young, but there's a lot to improve about it already! Fortunately, we've designed its structure in such a way that adding the new features will be painless, and the newly created structure will be there to last.

In this chapter, we will

- Implement keyword-rich URLs through URL rewriting and the mod_rewrite Apache module. This way, instead of requesting index.php using various query string parameters, our site will support URLs that look better both to humans and to search engines, such as http://www.example.com/mickey-mouse-t-shirt.html. At this step, the web site must be updated to use the new links internally.

- Properly redirect old URLs or mistyped URLs to the correct URLs. This is particularly important if your old URLs have been online for a while, and they have pages linking to them. This step will help to ensure that you don't lose any rankings that the pages on your old site may have already gained (their link equity) or incur penalties for false duplicate pages on your new site. We will also ensure that no matter how your URL is typed—www.yoursite.com or yoursite.com—search engines will understand that variations of your URL are, in fact, the same site. To a human, those may look like the same web site but to a search engine, this could be two different ones! This process of converting various forms of a URL to a standard form is called *URL canonicalization*, and we will talk more about it later.

- Redirect requests to index.php and index.html to /. This is important, because we don't want the same content duplicated in different URLs of your web site. As you'll learn, this can lead to implicit or explicit search engine penalties.

- Dynamically generate the page titles to reflect the contents of their pages. Right now, all pages have the same <title>, which is a no-no if search engine rankings and usability are of any importance (and of course they are).

- Update the pagination in all catalog pages (such as category and department pages) to include links to all the subpages, not only Previous and Next links. This makes pages of products easier to access by both search engines and humans.

- Use the 404 (page not found) and 500 (server error) status codes correctly to reflect problems with pages in the site.

We will make more SEO-related efforts in later parts of the book, but with these changes, we'll have the basics covered. The fact that the site is already structured properly certainly helps. The following SEO-related details have already been implemented:

- We correctly used page headings and other markup, so that search engines will be able to identify the page's important copy.

- We don't have duplicate content. The catalog doesn't contain identical pages, or page fragments, which can incur search engine penalties.

- The product, department, and category pages are easily reachable.

- We didn't use (and will not use) technologies such as Flash and AJAX, whose content is unreadable by search engines, to generate content. Later in this book, you'll see an example of using AJAX in a way that doesn't affect search engine visibility.

Supporting Keyword-Rich URLs

Have a look at the following URLs, and choose the one you like better:

- `http://localhost/tshirtshop/index.php?index.php?product_id=87`

- `http://localhost/tshirtshop/christmas-tree.html`

Of course, you want to have URLs such as the second one in your web site. Not only do they contain keywords that are relevant for the content of the page, which can impact search engine rankings, but they're also more appealing to a human visitor. We'll call the first URL a *dynamic URL* and the second a *keyword-rich URL*.

Long story short, we want our site to contain keyword-rich URLs. In the Apache and PHP world, this is implemented using an Apache module named mod_rewrite, which can intercept URLs that follow a certain pattern and *rewrite* the requests to another URL that can be processed by your application. This process is called *URL rewriting*.

Even when doing URL rewriting, the final file that gets executed is a script, such as index.php in our case. But the same script can be accessed using a nicer-looking URL.

Figure 7-1 shows a simple example of URL rewriting. As you can see, the mod_rewrite module intercepts the URL requested by the visitor and rewrites it to a dynamic URL that your application can understand. The PHP script executes, and the results are sent back to our users, who are (obviously) very happy to get the content they want.

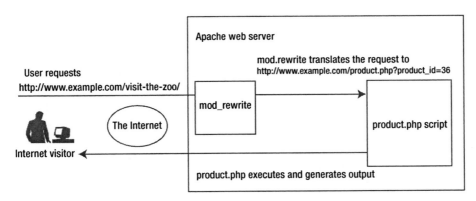

Figure 7-1. *A URL rewriting example with Apache and mod_rewrite*

There are several ways to translate the keyword-rich URL to its dynamic version for execution. In TShirtShop, we'll apply a technique that is both effective and simple to implement: we'll hide the item ID in the keyword-rich version of the URLs, such as in `http://localhost/tshirtshop/visit-the-zoo-p36/`. This keyword-rich URL contains the product ID hidden inside in a way that doesn't hinder its readability for humans and search engines alike.

In this chapter, we'll implement the support for the URLs types listed in Table 7-1. In each case, "X" is used as placeholder for department, category, product IDs, and "P" is a page number.

Table 7-1. *URL Formats Supported by TShirtShop*

URL Type	URL Format
Front page URL	`http://www.example.com/`
Front page URL if paginated	`http://www.example.com/page-P/`
Department URL	`http://www.example.com/department-name-dX/`
Department URL if paginated	`http://www.example.com/department-name-dX/page-P/`
Category URL	`http://www.example.com/dept-name-dX/cat-name-cX/`
Category URL if paginated	`http://www.example.com/dept-name-dX/cat-name-cX/page-P/`
Product URL	`http://www.example.com/product-name-pX/`

There are more details you need to learn to fully support such URLs, but we're taking things one at a time. Follow the exercise to implement support for keyword-rich URLs, and we'll discuss the details afterward.

Exercise: Supporting Keyword-Rich URLs

1. The first step is to make sure that mod_rewrite is enabled on your Apache installation. If you're working with a web hosting account, most likely mod_rewrite is already enabled. If you've installed Apache yourself, you may need to enable mod_rewrite manually. Fortunately, this is a simple task. Open the Apache configuration file, httpd.conf, and make sure the following line isn't commented by being prefixed by a hash sign (#). If it is, remove the hash, save the file, and *restart Apache*.

```
LoadModule rewrite_module modules/mod_rewrite.so
```

■**Tip** The Apache configuration file is located, by default, in `C:\xampp\apache\conf\` on a Windows XAMPP installation. On a typical Linux installation, you'll find it in `/opt/lampp/etc/`. Don't forget to restart Apache after making any changes to httpd.conf! If you get any errors, check the Apache error logs to find more details about the error.

2. Create a file named .htaccess in your project's root folder (C:\tshirtshop), and type the following code in (we will discuss it in detail later):

```
<IfModule mod_rewrite.c>

  # Enable mod_rewrite
  RewriteEngine On
```

```
# Specify the folder in which the application resides.
# Use / if the application is in the root.
RewriteBase /tshirtshop

# Rewrite to correct domain to avoid canonicalization problems
# RewriteCond %{HTTP_HOST} !^www\.example\.com
# RewriteRule ^(.*)$ http://www.example.com/$1 [R=301,L]

# Rewrite URLs ending in /index.php or /index.html to /
RewriteCond %{THE_REQUEST} ^GET\ .*/index\.(php|html?)\ HTTP
RewriteRule ^(.*)index\.(php|html?)$ $1 [R=301,L]

# Rewrite category pages
RewriteRule ^.*-d([0-9]+)/.*-c([0-9]+)/page-([0-9]+)/?$ index.php?Depart
mentId=$1&CategoryId=$2&Page=$3 [L]
RewriteRule ^.*-d([0-9]+)/.*-c([0-9]+)/?$ index.php?DepartmentId=$1&Cate
goryId=$2 [L]

# Rewrite department pages
RewriteRule ^.*-d([0-9]+)/page-([0-9]+)/?$ index.php?DepartmentId=$1&Pag
e=$2 [L]
RewriteRule ^.*-d([0-9]+)/?$ index.php?DepartmentId=$1 [L]

# Rewrite subpages of the home page
RewriteRule ^page-([0-9]+)/?$ index.php?Page=$1 [L]

# Rewrite product details pages
RewriteRule ^.*-p([0-9]+)/?$ index.php?ProductId=$1 [L]

</IfModule>
```

■**Tip** If you don't have a friendly code editor, creating a file that doesn't have a name but just an extension, such as .htaccess, can prove to be problematic in Windows. The easiest way to create this file is to open Notepad, type the contents, go to Save As, and type ".htaccess" for the file name, including the quotes. The quotes prevent the editor from automatically appending the default file extension, such as .txt for Notepad.

3. At this moment, your web site should correctly support keyword-rich URLs, in the form described prior to starting this exercise. For example, try loading http://localhost/tshirtshop/nature-d2/. The result should resemble the page shown in Figure 7-2.

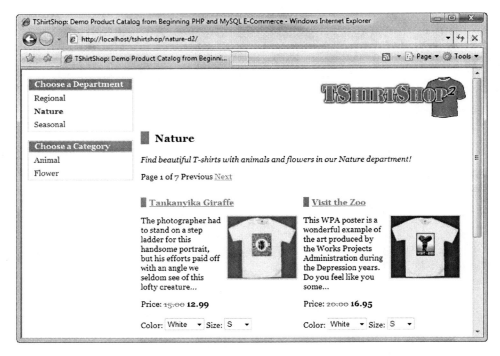

Figure 7-2. *Testing keyword-rich URLs*

How It Works: Supporting Keyword-Rich URLs

At this moment, you can test all kinds of keyword-rich URLs that are currently known by your web site: department pages and subpages, category pages and subpages, the front page and its subpages, and product details links. Note, however, that the links currently generated by your web site are still old, dynamic URLs. Updating the links in your site will be the subject of the next exercise.

The core of the functionality you've just implemented lies in the .htaccess file. We've used this Apache folder-based configuration file to store the rewriting rules for mod_rewrite. The httpd.conf Apache configuration file can also be used, but we've chosen .htaccess because many web hosting scenarios will not allow you to modify the httpd.conf file. Also, modifying .htaccess doesn't require you to restart the web server for the new settings to take effect, because the file is parsed on every request, which makes it ideal for development purposes.

The first command in .htaccess is the one that enables the rewriting engine. If you didn't configure mod_rewrite correctly, this line will cause an error:

```
RewriteEngine On
```

Next, we used the RewriteBase command to specify the name of the tshirtshop folder. Note that if you keep your application in the root folder, you should replace /tshirtshop with /.

```
RewriteBase /tshirtshop
```

Then, the real fun begins. A number of RewriteRule commands follow, which basically describe what URLs should be rewritten and to what they should be rewritten. Sometimes, the RewriteRule commands are accompanied by

RewriteCond, which specifies a condition that must be met in order for the following RewriteRule command to be executed.

A RewriteRule command contains at least two parameters. The first string that follows RewriteRule is a *regular expression* that describes the structure of the matching incoming URLs. The second describes what the URL should be rewritten to.

mod_rewrite and Regular Expressions

Regular expressions are one of those topics that programmers tend to either love or hate. A regular expression, commonly referred to as *regex*, is a text string that uses a special format to describe a text pattern. Regular expressions are used to define rules that match or transform groups of strings, and they represent one of the most powerful text manipulation tools available today. Find a few details about them at the Wikipedia page at http://en.wikipedia.org/wiki/Regular_expression.

Regular expressions are particularly useful in circumstances when you need to manipulate strings that don't have a well-defined format (as XML documents have, for example) and cannot be parsed or modified using more specialized techniques. For example, regular expressions can be used to extract or validate e-mail addresses, find valid dates in strings, remove duplicate lines of text, find the number of times a word or a letter appears in a phrase, find or validate IP addresses, and so on.

In the previous exercise, you used mod_rewrite rules, using regular expressions, to match incoming keyword-rich URLs and obtain their rewritten, dynamic versions. A bit later in this chapter, we'll use a regular expression that prepares a string for inclusion in the URL, by replacing unsupported characters with dashes and eliminating duplicate separation characters.

Regular expressions are supported by many languages and tools, including the PHP language and the mod_rewrite Apache module, and the implementations are similar. A regular expression that works in PHP will work in Java or C# without modifications most of the time. When you want to do an operation based on regular expressions, you usually must provide at least three key elements:

- The source string that needs to be parsed or manipulated

- The regular expression to be applied on the source string

- The kind of operation to be performed, which can be either obtaining the matching substrings or replacing them with something else

Regular expressions use a special syntax based on regular characters, which are interpreted literally, and metacharacters, which have special matching properties. A regular character in a regular expression matches the same character in the source string, and a sequence of such characters matches the same sequence in the source string. This is similar to searching for substrings in a string. For example, if you match "or" in "favorite color", you'll find two matches for it.

A regular expression can contain metacharacters, which have special properties, and it's their power and flexibility that makes regular expressions so useful. For example, the question mark (?) metacharacter specifies that the preceding character is optional. So if you want to match "color" and "colour", your regular expression would be colou?r.

As pointed out earlier, regular expressions can become extremely complex when you get into their more subtle details. In this section, you'll find explanations for the regular expressions we're using, and we suggest that you continue your regex training using a specialized book or tutorial.

Table 7-2 contains the description of the most common regular expression metacharacters. You can use this table as a reference for understanding the rewrite rules.

Table 7-2. *Metacharacters Commonly Used in Regular Expressions*

Metacharacter	Description
^	Matches the beginning of the line. In our case, it will always match the beginning of the URL. The domain name isn't considered part of the URL, as far as RewriteRule is concerned. It is useful to think of ^ as anchoring the characters that follow to the beginning of the string, that is, asserting that they are the first part.
.	Matches any single character.
*	Specifies that the preceding character or expression can be repeated *zero* or more times, that is, not at all to infinity.
+	Specifies that the preceding character or expression can be repeated *one* or more times. In other words, the preceding character or expression must match at least once.
?	Specifies that the preceding character or expression can be repeated *zero or one* time. In other words, the preceding character or expression is optional.
{m,n}	Specifies that the preceding character or expression can be repeated between m and n times; m and n are integers, and m needs to be lower than n.
( )	The parentheses are used to define a captured expression. The string matching the expression between parentheses can then be read as a variable. The parentheses can also be used to group the contents therein, as in mathematics, and operators such as *, +, or ? can then be applied to the resulting expression.
[ ]	Used to define a character class. For example, [abc] will match any of the characters a, b, or c. The hyphen character (-) can be used to define a range of characters. For example, [a-z] matches any lowercase letter. If the hyphen is meant to be interpreted literally, it should be the last character before the closing bracket,]. Many metacharacters lose their special function when enclosed between brackets and are interpreted literally.
[^]	Similar to [ ], except it matches everything except the mentioned character class. For example, [^a-c] matches all characters except a, b, and c.
$	Matches the end of the line. In our case, it will always match the end of the URL. It is useful to think of it as anchoring the previous characters to the end of the string, that is, asserting that they are the last part.
\	The backslash is used to escape the character that follows. It is used to escape metacharacters when you need them to be taken for their literal value, rather than their special meaning. For example, \. will match a dot, rather than any character (the typical meaning of the dot in a regular expression). The backslash can also escape itself—so if you want to match C:\Windows, you'll need to refer to it as C:\\Windows.

To understand how these metacharacters work in practice, let's analyze one of the rewrite rules in TShirtShop: the one that rewrites category page URLs. For rewriting category pages, we have two rules—one that handles paged categories and one that handles nonpaged categories. The following rule rewrites categories with pages, and the regular expression is highlighted:

```
# Redirect category pages
RewriteRule ^.*-d([0-9]+)/.*-c([0-9]+)/page-([0-9]+)/?$
index.php?DepartmentId=$1&CategoryId=$2&Page=$3 [L]
```

This regular expression is intended to match URLs such as http://localhost/tshirtshop/regional-d1/french-c1/page-2 and extract the ID of the department, the ID of the category, and the page number from these URLs. In plain English, the rule searches for strings that start with some characters followed by -d and a number (which is the department ID), followed by a forward slash, some other characters, -c and another number (which is the category ID), followed by /page- and a number, which is the page number.

Using Table 7-2 as a reference, let's analyze the regular expression technically. The expression starts with the ^ character, matching the beginning of the requested URL (the URL doesn't include the domain name). The characters .* match any string of zero or more characters, because the dot means any character, and the asterisk means that the preceding character or expression (which is the dot) can be repeated zero or more times.

The next characters, -d([0-9]+), extract the ID of the department. The [0-9] bit matches any character between 0 and 9 (that is, any digit), and the + that follows indicates that the pattern can repeat one or more times, so you can have a multidigit number rather than just a single digit. The enclosing parentheses around [0-9]+ indicate that the regular expression engine should store the matching string (which will be the department ID) inside a variable called $1. You'll need this variable to compose the rewritten URL.

The same principle is used to save the category ID and the page number into the $2 and $3 variables. Finally, you have /?, which specifies that the URL can end with a slash, but the slash is optional. The regular expression ends with $, which matches the end of the string.

■**Note** When you need to use symbols that have metacharacter significance as their literal values, you need to escape them with a backslash. For example, if you want to match index.php, the regular expression should read index\.php. The \ is the escaping character, which indicates that the dot should be taken as a literal dot, not as any character (which is the significance of the dot metacharacter).

The second argument of RewriteRule, index.php?DepartmentId=$1&CategoryId=$2&Page=$3, plugs in the variables that you extracted using the regular expression into the rewritten URL. The $1, $2, and $3 variables are replaced by the values supplied by the regular expression, and the URL is loaded by our application.

A rewrite rule can also contain a third argument, which is formed of special flags that affect how the rewrite is handled. These arguments are specific to the RewriteRule command and aren't related to regular expressions. Table 7-3 lists the possible RewriteRule arguments. These rewrite flags must always be placed in square brackets at the end of an individual rule.

Table 7-3. *RewriteRule Options*

RewriteRule Option	Significance	Description
R	Redirect	Sends an HTTP redirect.
F	Forbidden	Forbids access to the URL.
G	Gone	Marks the URL as gone.
P	Proxy	Passes the URL to mod_proxy.
L	Last	Stops processing further rules.
N	Next	Starts processing again from the first rule, but using the current rewritten URL.
C	Chain	Links the current rule with the following one.
T	Type	Forces the mentioned MIME type.
NS	Nosubreq	Applies only if no internal subrequest is performed.
NC	Nocase	URL matching is case insensitive.
QSA	Qsappend	Appends a query string part to the new URL instead of replacing it.
PT	Passthrough	Passes the rewritten URL to another Apache module for further processing.
S	Skip	Skips the next rule.
E	Env	Sets an environment variable.

RewriteRule commands are processed in sequential order as they are written in the configuration file. If you want to make sure that a rule is the last one processed in case a match is found for it, you need to use the [L] flag.

This flag is particularly useful if you have a long list of RewriteRule commands, because using [L] improves performance and prevents mod_rewrite from processing all the RewriteRule commands that follow once a match is found. This is usually what you want regardless.

Our final note on the .htaccess rules regards the following code:

```
# Redirect to correct domain to avoid canonicalization problems
#RewriteCond %{HTTP_HOST} !^www\.example\.com
#RewriteRule ^(.*)$ http://www.example.com/$1 [R=301,L]
```

As you can see, the RewriteCond and RewriteRule commands are commented out using the # character. We commented these lines, because you should change www.example.com to the location of your web site before uncommenting them (while working on localhost, leave these rules commented out).

RewriteCond is a mod_rewrite command that places a condition for the rule that follows. In this case, you're interested in verifying that the site has been accessed through www.example.com. If it hasn't, you do a 301 redirect to www.example.com. This technique implements domain name canonicalization. If your site can be accessed through multiple domain names (such as www.example.com and example.com), establish one of them as the main domain and redirect all the others to it, avoiding duplicate content penalties from the search engines. You'll learn more about 301 redirects a bit later in this chapter.

Building Keyword-Rich URLs

In the previous exercise, you achieved a great thing: you've started supporting keyword-rich URLs in TShirtShop! However, note that

- Your site supports dynamic URLs as well.

- All links in your web site use the dynamic versions of the URLs.

With these two drawbacks, the mere fact that we do support keyword-rich URLs doesn't bring any significant benefits. This leads us to a second exercise related to our URLs. This time, we'll change the dynamic links in our site to keyword-rich URLs.

In the earlier chapters, we've been wise enough to use a centralized class named Link that generates all of the site's links. This means that, now, updating all the links in our site is just a matter of updating that Link class. We'll also need to build some data tier and business tier infrastructure to support the new functionality, which consists of methods that return the name of a department, category, or product if we supply the ID.

Exercise: Generating Keyword-Rich URLs

1. Use phpMyAdmin to connect to your tshirtshop database, and execute the following code, which creates three stored procedures. These are simple procedures that return the name of a department, a category, or a product given its ID. Don't forget to set $$ as the delimiter before executing the code.

```
-- Create catalog_get_department_name stored procedure
CREATE PROCEDURE catalog_get_department_name(IN inDepartmentId INT)
BEGIN
  SELECT name FROM department WHERE department_id = inDepartmentId;
END$$


-- Create catalog_get_category_name stored procedure
CREATE PROCEDURE catalog_get_category_name(IN inCategoryId INT)
BEGIN
  SELECT name FROM category WHERE category_id = inCategoryId;
END$$


-- Create catalog_get_product_name stored procedure
CREATE PROCEDURE catalog_get_product_name(IN inProductId INT)
BEGIN
  SELECT name FROM product WHERE product_id = inProductId;
END$$
```

2. We'll now add the business tier code that accesses the stored procedures created earlier. Add the following code to the Catalog class in business/catalog.php:

```
// Retrieves department name
public static function GetDepartmentName($departmentId)
{
  // Build SQL query
  $sql = 'CALL catalog_get_department_name(:department_id)';
```

```php
    // Build the parameters array
    $params = array (':department_id' => $departmentId);

    // Execute the query and return the results
    return DatabaseHandler::GetOne($sql, $params);
  }

  // Retrieves category name
  public static function GetCategoryName($categoryId)
  {
    // Build SQL query
    $sql = 'CALL catalog_get_category_name(:category_id)';

    // Build the parameters array
    $params = array (':category_id' => $categoryId);

    // Execute the query and return the results
    return DatabaseHandler::GetOne($sql, $params);
  }

  // Retrieves product name
  public static function GetProductName($productId)
  {
    // Build SQL query
    $sql = 'CALL catalog_get_product_name(:product_id)';

    // Build the parameters array
    $params = array (':product_id' => $productId);

    // Execute the query and return the results
    return DatabaseHandler::GetOne($sql, $params);
  }
```

3. Open presentation/link.php, and modify its code like this:

```php
public static function ToDepartment($departmentId, $page = 1)
{
  $link = self::CleanUrlText(Catalog::GetDepartmentName($departmentId)) .
          '-d' . $departmentId . '/';

  if ($page > 1)
    $link .= 'page-' . $page . '/';

  return self::Build($link);
}

public static function ToCategory($departmentId, $categoryId, $page = 1)
{
```

```php
        $link = self::CleanUrlText(Catalog::GetDepartmentName($departmentId)) .
                '-d' . $departmentId . '/' .
                self::CleanUrlText(Catalog::GetCategoryName($categoryId)) .
                '-c' . $categoryId . '/';

        if ($page > 1)
          $link .= 'page-' . $page . '/';

        return self::Build($link);
    }

    public static function ToProduct($productId)
    {
      $link = self::CleanUrlText(Catalog::GetProductName($productId)) .
              '-p' . $productId . '/';

      return self::Build($link);
    }

    public static function ToIndex($page = 1)
    {
      $link = '';

      if ($page > 1)
        $link .= 'page-' . $page . '/';

      return self::Build($link);
    }
```

4. Continue working on the Link class by adding the following method, CleanUrlText(), which is called by the methods you've updated earlier to remove bad characters from the links:

```php
    // Prepares a string to be included in an URL
    public static function CleanUrlText($string)
    {
      // Remove all characters that aren't a-z, 0-9, dash, underscore or space
      $not_acceptable_characters_regex = '#[^-a-zA-Z0-9_ ]#';
      $string = preg_replace($not_acceptable_characters_regex, '', $string);

      // Remove all leading and trailing spaces
      $string = trim($string);

      // Change all dashes, underscores and spaces to dashes
      $string = preg_replace('#[-_ ]+#', '-', $string);

      // Return the modified string
      return strtolower($string);
    }
```

5. Load TShirtShop, and notice the new links. In Figure 7-3, the link to the Visit the Zoo product, `http://localhost/tshirtshop/visit-the-zoo-p36/`, is visible in Internet Explorer's status bar.

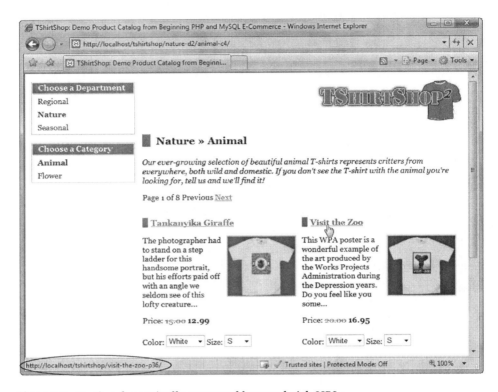

Figure 7-3. *Testing dynamically generated keyword-rich URLs*

How It Works: Generating Keyword-Rich URLs

In this exercise, you modified the `ToIndex()`, `ToDepartment()`, `ToCategory()`, and `ToProduct()` methods of the `Link` class to build keyword-rich URLs instead of dynamic URLs. To support this functionality you created infrastructure code (business tier methods and database stored procedures) that retrieves the names of departments, products, and categories from the database.

You also implemented a method named `CleanUrlText()`, which uses regular expressions to replace the characters that we don't want to include in URLs with dashes. This method transforms a string such as "Visit the Zoo" to a URL-friendly string such as "visit-the-zoo."

Make sure all the links in your site are now search engine-friendly, and let's move on to the next task for this chapter.

URL Correction with 301 Redirects

One potential problem with our site now is that the same page can be reached using many different links. Take, for example, the following URLs:

```
http://localhost/tshirtshop/nature-d2/
http://localhost/tshirtshop/TYPO-d2/
```

Because content is retrieved based on the hidden ID in the links, which in these examples is 2, both links would load the Nature department, whose correct link is `http://localhost/tshirtshop/nature-d2/`.

This flexibility happens to have potentially adverse effects on your search engine rankings. If, for any reason, the search engines reach the same page using different links, they'd think you have lots of different pages with identical content on your site and may incorrectly assume that you have a spam site. In such an extreme case, your site as a whole, or just parts of it, may be penalized.

Even in the absence of explicit penalization from search engines, having content equity divided through multiple URLs can reduce search engine rankings by itself.

The solution we recommend to avoid penalization is to properly use the HTTP status codes to redirect all the pages with identical content to a single, standard URL.

HTTP STATUS CODES

The HTTP status codes are codes that are sent as a response to a web request, together with the requested content, and they indicate the status of the request. As a web developer, you're probably familiar with the 200 status code, which indicates the request was successful, and with the 404 code, which indicates that the requested resource could not be found.

Among the HTTP status codes, there are a few that specifically address redirection issues. The most common of these redirection status codes is 301, which indicates that the requested resource has been *permanently* moved to a new location, and 302, which indicates that the relocation is only *temporary*.

When a web browser or a search engine makes a request whose response contains a redirection status code, they continue by browsing to the indicated location. The web browser will request the new URL and will update the address bar to reflect the new location.

The default redirection status code is 302. This is important to know, because when doing search engine optimization, you'll usually want to use 301 redirects. In regards to SEO, 301 redirects are preferable because they (should) also transfer the *link equity* from the old URL to the new URL.

This means that if your old URL was ranking well for certain keywords, if 301 is used, then the new URL will rank just like the old one, after search engines take note of the redirect. In practice, abuse of 301 isn't desirable, because there's no guarantee that the link equity will be completely transferred—and even if it does, it may take a while until you'll rank well again for the desired keywords.

You can learn the more subtle details of redirection and HTTP status codes from *Professional Search Engine Optimization with PHP: A Developer's Guide to SEO*, by Cristian Darie and Jaimie Sirovich (Wrox, 2007).

Our goal for the next exercise is to create a standard ("proper") URL version for each page on our site. When that page loads, we compare the known, standard URL of the page with the one requested by the visitor. If they don't match, we do a 301 redirect to the proper version of the URL.

As pointed out earlier, URL correction is useful when somebody types a URL with a typo, such as `http://localhost/tshirtshop/natureTYPO-d2/`, or when you change the name of a product, category, or department, which causes URL changes as well.

Exercise: Implementing URL Correction

1. URL correction and other features we implement in this chapter involve working with the HTTP headers. To avoid any problems setting the headers, we need to make this change in `index.php`. Add the following highlighted code to your `index.php` file:

```php
<?php
// Activate session
session_start();

// Start output buffer
ob_start();

// Include utility files
require_once 'include/config.php';
require_once BUSINESS_DIR . 'error_handler.php';
```

2. At the end of `index.php`, add the following code:

```php
// Close database connection
DatabaseHandler::Close();

// Output content from the buffer
flush();
ob_flush();
ob_end_clean();
?>
```

3. Add the `CheckRequest()` method to the `Link` class in the `presentation/link.php` file:

```php
// Redirects to proper URL if not already there
public static function CheckRequest()
{
  $proper_url = '';

  // Obtain proper URL for category pages
  if (isset ($_GET['DepartmentId']) && isset ($_GET['CategoryId']))
  {
    if (isset ($_GET['Page']))
      $proper_url = self::ToCategory($_GET['DepartmentId'],
                       $_GET['CategoryId'], $_GET['Page']);
    else
      $proper_url = self::ToCategory($_GET['DepartmentId'],
                                $_GET['CategoryId']);
  }
```

```php
    // Obtain proper URL for department pages
    elseif (isset ($_GET['DepartmentId']))
    {
      if (isset ($_GET['Page']))
        $proper_url = self::ToDepartment($_GET['DepartmentId'],
                                         $_GET['Page']);
      else
        $proper_url = self::ToDepartment($_GET['DepartmentId']);
    }
    // Obtain proper URL for product pages
    elseif (isset ($_GET['ProductId']))
    {
      $proper_url = self::ToProduct($_GET['ProductId']);
    }
    // Obtain proper URL for the home page
    else
    {
      if (isset($_GET['Page']))
        $proper_url = self::ToIndex($_GET['Page']);
      else
        $proper_url = self::ToIndex();
    }

    /* Remove the virtual location from the requested URL
       so we can compare paths */
    $requested_url = self::Build(str_replace(VIRTUAL_LOCATION, '',
                                    $_SERVER['REQUEST_URI']));

    // 301 redirect to the proper URL if necessary
    if ($requested_url != $proper_url)
    {
      // Clean output buffer
      ob_clean();

      // Redirect 301
      header('HTTP/1.1 301 Moved Permanently');
      header('Location: ' . $proper_url);

      // Clear the output buffer and stop execution
      flush();
      ob_flush();
      ob_end_clean();
      exit();
    }
}
```

4. Open index.php, and call this method like this:

```
// Load the database handler
require_once BUSINESS_DIR . 'database_handler.php';

// Load Business Tier
require_once BUSINESS_DIR . 'catalog.php';

// URL correction
Link::CheckRequest();

// Load Smarty template file
$application = new Application();

// Display the page
$application->display('store_front.tpl');

// Close database connection
DatabaseHandler::Close();
```

5. Load `http://localhost/tshirtshop/natureTYPO-d2/`, and notice that page redirects to `http://localhost/tshirtshop/nature-d2/`. Using a tool such as the LiveHTTPHeaders Firefox extension (`http://livehttpheaders.mozdev.org/`), you can see the type of redirect used was 301; see Figure 7-4.

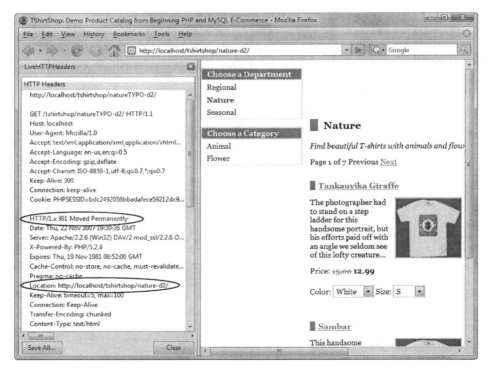

Figure 7-4. *Testing the response status code using LiveHTTPHeaders*

▓**Note** Other tools you can use to view the HTTP headers are the Web Development Helper and Fiddler for Internet Explorer and FireBug or the Web Developer plug-in for Firefox.

How It Works: Using 301 for Redirecting Content

The code follows some simple logic to get the job done. The CheckRequest() method of the Link class verifies if a request should be redirected to another URL, and if so, it does a 301 redirection. The PHP way of performing the redirection is by setting the HTTP header like this:

```
// 301 redirect to the proper URL if necessary
if ($requested_url != $proper_url)
{
  // Clean output buffer
  ob_clean();

  // Redirect 301
  header('HTTP/1.1 301 Moved Permanently');
  header('Location: ' . $proper_url);

  // Clear the output buffer and stop execution
  flush();
  ob_flush();
  ob_end_clean();
  exit();
}
```

We call CheckRequest() in index.php to make sure it checks all incoming requests.

We also altered index.php by adding output control code to ensure that we will be able to flush the output and change the output headers whenever necessary, as the headers can't be changed after sending any output to the client. Read more about the output control functions of PHP at http://php.net/outcontrol. A useful article on the subject can be found at http://www.phpit.net/article/output-buffer-fun-php/.

Customizing Page Titles

One of the common mistakes web developers make is to set the same title for all the pages on a web site. This is too bad, since the page title is, in the opinion of many SEO authorities, the most important factor in search engines' ranking algorithm. This is confirmed by the article at http://www.seomoz.org/article/search-ranking-factors.

Right now, all the pages in TShirtShop have the same title, which is defined in site.conf. In the following exercise, you'll see that it's easy to update the site to display customized page titles for each area of the site.

Exercise: Generating Customized Page Titles

1. Open presentation/store_front.php, and add the highlighted member to the StoreFront class:

```php
<?php
class StoreFront
{
  public $mSiteUrl;
  // Define the template file for the page contents
  public $mContentsCell = 'first_page_contents.tpl';
  // Define the template file for the categories cell
  public $mCategoriesCell = 'blank.tpl';
  // Page title
  public $mPageTitle;
```

2. In the same class, StoreFront, add the following code at the end of the init() method:

```php
    // Load product details page if visiting a product
    if (isset ($_GET['ProductId']))
      $this->mContentsCell = 'product.tpl';

    // Load the page title
    $this->mPageTitle = $this->_GetPageTitle();
  }
```

3. Continue updating the StoreFront class by adding the following private method:

```php
    // Returns the page title
    private function _GetPageTitle()
    {
      $page_title = 'TShirtShop: ' .
        'Demo Product Catalog from Beginning PHP and MySQL E-Commerce';

      if (isset ($_GET['DepartmentId']) && isset ($_GET['CategoryId']))
      {
        $page_title = 'TShirtShop: ' .
          Catalog::GetDepartmentName($_GET['DepartmentId']) . ' - ' .
          Catalog::GetCategoryName($_GET['CategoryId']);

        if (isset ($_GET['Page']) && ((int)$_GET['Page']) > 1)
          $page_title .= ' - Page ' . ((int)$_GET['Page']);
      }
      elseif (isset ($_GET['DepartmentId']))
      {
        $page_title = 'TShirtShop: ' .
          Catalog::GetDepartmentName($_GET['DepartmentId']);

        if (isset ($_GET['Page']) && ((int)$_GET['Page']) > 1)
          $page_title .= ' - Page ' . ((int)$_GET['Page']);
      }
```

```
    elseif (isset ($_GET['ProductId']))
    {
      $page_title = 'TShirtShop: ' .
        Catalog::GetProductName($_GET['ProductId']);
    }
    else
    {
      if (isset ($_GET['Page']) && ((int)$_GET['Page']) > 1)
        $page_title .= ' - Page ' . ((int)$_GET['Page']);
    }

    return $page_title;
  }
```

4. Update presentation/templates/store_front.tpl like this:

```html
<html>
  <head>
    <title>{$obj->mPageTitle}</title>
    <meta http-equiv="Content-Type" content="text/html; charset=UTF-8" />
    <link href="{$obj->mSiteUrl}styles/tshirtshop.css" type="text/css"
      rel="stylesheet" />
  </head>
```

5. Load a page other than the front page in TShirtShop and notice its new, customized page title, which is highlighted in Figure 7-5 (the title of the front page remains the same).

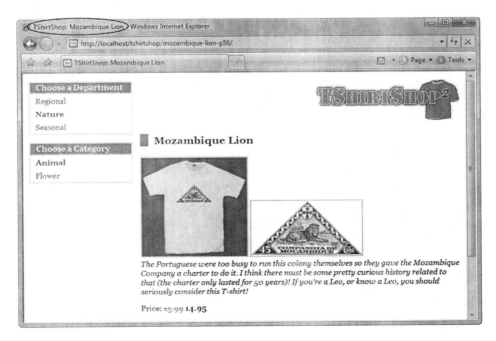

Figure 7-5. *Creating customized product titles*

How It Works: Creating Page Titles

In this exercise, we updated the StoreFront class to use data gathered using the GetDepartmentName(), GetCategoryName(), and GetProductName() of the Catalog class to build the wanted titles for the department, category, and product pages. The Smarty template was also updated to display the newly built title instead of the default one. We'll not belabor on the details, as the code is pretty much straightforward.

Updating Catalog Pagination

Just as search engines assume that pages that are not linked well from external sources are less important than those that are, they may make the assumption that pages buried within a web site's internal link structure are not very important.

Our current system for navigating pages of products is a perfect example of burying pages down the link hierarchy. To navigate between product pages, we currently only offer Previous and Next links. This doesn't make it easy for visitors to navigate directly to the various product pages, and it doesn't make it any easier for search engines either.

Consider the example of the fourth page of products in the Regional category. Currently, that page can be reached by humans or by search engines like this:

```
Home -> Regional -> Page 2 -> Page 3 -> Page 4
```

The fourth page of products is harder to reach not only by humans (who need to click at least four times), but also by search engines. Let's fix this problem by going through a short exercise.

Exercise: SEO Pagination

1. In the ProductsList class from the presentation/products_list.php file, modify the init() method of the ProductList class as shown:

```
/* If there are subpages of products, display navigation
   controls */
if ($this->mrTotalPages > 1)
{
  // Build the Next link
  if ($this->mPage < $this->mrTotalPages)
  {
    if (isset($this->_mCategoryId))
      $this->mLinkToNextPage =
        Link::ToCategory($this->_mDepartmentId, $this->_mCategoryId,
                         $this->mPage + 1);
    elseif (isset($this->_mDepartmentId))
      $this->mLinkToNextPage =
        Link::ToDepartment($this->_mDepartmentId, $this->mPage + 1);
  }
```

```
    // Build the Previous link
    if ($this->mPage > 1)
    {
      if (isset($this->_mCategoryId))
        $this->mLinkToPreviousPage =
          Link::ToCategory($this->_mDepartmentId, $this->_mCategoryId,
                           $this->mPage - 1);
      elseif (isset($this->_mDepartmentId))
        $this->mLinkToPreviousPage =
          Link::ToDepartment($this->_mDepartmentId, $this->mPage - 1);
    }

    // Build the pages links
    for ($i = 1; $i <= $this->mrTotalPages; $i++)
      if (isset($this->_mCategoryId))
        $this->mProductListPages[] =
          Link::ToCategory($this->_mDepartmentId, $this->_mCategoryId, $i);
      elseif (isset($this->_mDepartmentId))
        $this->mProductListPages[] =
          Link::ToDepartment($this->_mDepartmentId, $i);
      else
        $this->mProductListPages[] = Link::ToIndex($i);
  }
```

2. Open the presentation/templates/products_list.tpl file, and modify it as highlighted:

```
{* products_list.tpl *}
{load_presentation_object filename="products_list" assign="obj"}
{if count($obj->mProductListPages) > 0}
<p>

  {if $obj->mLinkToPreviousPage}
  <a href="{$obj->mLinkToPreviousPage}">Previous page</a>
  {/if}
```

```
{section name=m loop=$obj->mProductListPages}
  {if $obj->mPage eq $smarty.section.m.index_next}
  <strong>{$smarty.section.m.index_next}</strong>
  {else}
  <a href="{$obj->mProductListPages[m]}">{$smarty.section.m.index_next}</a>
  {/if}
{/section}

{if $obj->mLinkToNextPage}
<a href="{$obj->mLinkToNextPage}">Next page</a>
{/if}

</p>
{/if}
{if $obj->mProducts}
<table class="product-list" border="0">
  <tbody>
  {section name=k loop=$obj->mProducts}
    {if $smarty.section.k.index % 2 == 0}
    <tr>
    {/if}
```

3. Load TShirtShop, and navigate to the Regional department. In Figure 7-6, you can see the new pagination links.

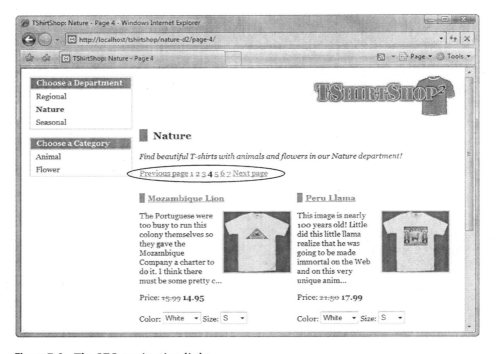

Figure 7-6. *The SEO pagination links*

How It Works: Pagination

With this little trick implemented, your catalog is now easily browsable by both human visitors and electronic visitors. Users will certainly appreciate the aid in quickly navigating to individual product pages, and search engines will find those pages much easier to find and index as well.

Correctly Signaling 404 and 500 Errors

It is important to use the correct HTTP status code when something special happens to the visitor's request. You've already seen that, when performing redirects, knowledge of HTTP status codes can make an important difference to your search engine optimization efforts. This time we will talk about 404 and 500.

The 404 status code is used to tell the visitor that he or she has requested a page that doesn't exist on the destination web site. Browsers and web servers have templates that users get when you make such a request—you know, you've seen them.

Hosting services let you specify a custom page to be displayed when such a 404 error occurs. This is obviously beneficial for your site, as you can provide some custom feedback to your visitor depending on what he or she was searching for. Sometimes, however, the 404 status code isn't automatically set for you, so you need to do it in your 404 script. If, for some reason, your site reacts to 404 errors by sending pages with the 200 OK status code, search engines will think that you have many different URLs hosting the same content, and your site may get penalized.

The 500 status message is used to communicate that the web server or the application is having internal errors. In the following exercise, we'll customize the TShirtShop to use the 404 and 500 status codes correctly.

Exercise: Using the 500 HTTP Status Code

1. Open business\error_handler.php, and modify the Handler() method as shown in the following code snippet:

```
/* Warnings don't abort execution if IS_WARNING_FATAL is false
   E_NOTICE and E_USER_NOTICE errors don't abort execution */
if (($errNo == E_WARNING && IS_WARNING_FATAL == false) ||
    ($errNo == E_NOTICE || $errNo == E_USER_NOTICE))
// If the error is nonfatal ...
{
  // Show message only if DEBUGGING is true
  if (DEBUGGING == true)
    echo '<div class="error_box"><pre>' . $error_message . '</pre></div>';
}
else
// If error is fatal ...
{
  // Show error message
```

```php
      if (DEBUGGING == true)
        echo '<div class="error_box"><pre>' . $error_message . '</pre></div>';
      else
      {
        // Clean output buffer
        ob_clean();

        // Load the 500 page
        include '500.php';

        // Clear the output buffer and stop execution
        flush();
        ob_flush();
        ob_end_clean();
        exit();
      }

      // Stop processing the request
      exit();
    }
  }
```

2. In the root folder of your application, create a file named 500.php, and type the following code:

```php
<?php
  // Set the 500 status code
  header('HTTP/1.0 500 Internal Server Error');

  require_once 'include/config.php';
  require_once PRESENTATION_DIR . 'link.php';
?>
<!DOCTYPE html PUBLIC "-//W3C//DTD XHTML 1.0 Transitional//EN"
  "http://www.w3.org/TR/xhtml1/DTD/xhtml1-transitional.dtd">
<html>
  <head>
    <title>
      TShirtShop Application Error (500): Demo Product Catalog from
      Beginning PHP and MySQL E-Commerce
    </title>
    <link href="<?php echo Link::Build('styles/tshirtshop.css'); ?>"
      type="text/css" rel="stylesheet" />
  </head>
  <body>
    <div id="doc" class="yui-t7">
      <div id="bd">
```

```
        <div id="header" class="yui-g">
          <a href="<?php echo Link::Build(''); ?>">
            <img src="<?php echo Link::Build('images/tshirtshop.png'); ?>"
             alt="tshirtshop logo" />
          </a>
        </div>
        <div id="contents" class="yui-g">
          <h1>
            TShirtShop is experiencing technical difficulties.
          </h1>
          <p>
            Please
            <a href="<?php echo Link::Build(''); ?>">visit us</a> soon,
            or <a href="<?php echo ADMIN_ERROR_MAIL; ?>">contact us</a>.
          </p>
          <p>Thank you!</p>
          <p>The TShirtShop team.</p>
        </div>
      </div>
    </div>
  </body>
</html>
```

3. Add the highlighted lines of code at the end of your .htaccess file:

```
</IfModule>

# Set the default 500 page for Apache errors
ErrorDocument 500 /tshirtshop/500.php
```

■**Caution** Be sure to modify the URL to the location of your 500.php file.

---

4. Let's test our new 500.php file by creating an error in our web site. Open include\config.php, and set the DEBUGGING const to false to disable the debug mode (otherwise, our site won't throw 500 errors):

```
// These should be true while developing the web site
define('IS_WARNING_FATAL', true);
define('DEBUGGING', false);
```

5. Next, open index.php, and add a reference to a nonexistent file:

```
// URL correction
Link::CheckRequest();
require_once('inexistent_file.php');
```

6. Now, load your application. If everything works as expected, you should get the 500 page shown in Figure 7-7.

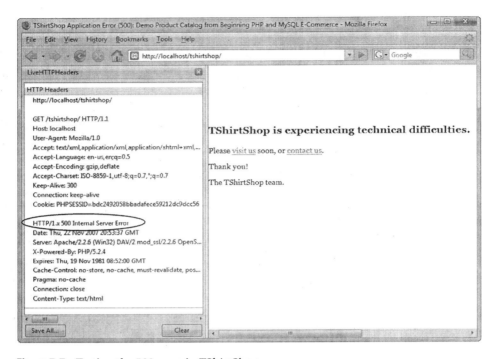

Figure 7-7. *Testing the 500 page in TShirtShop*

How It Works: Handling 500 Errors

As you can now see, if an application error happens, the visitor is shown a proper error page. The status code is properly set to 500, so the search engines will know the web site is experiencing difficulties and won't index the 500 error page. Instead, the previously indexed version of your page, which supposedly contains contained the correct content, is kept in the index. This is very important, because unless the 500 status code is used properly, your entire site could be wiped out of the search engine index, by replacing all the pages with the text you can see in Figure 7-7.

■**Note** Before moving on to the next exercise, be sure to set the DEBUGGING constant back to true, so that TShirtShop will show debugging data when an error happens, instead of throwing the 500 page. Also, remove the reference to inexistent_file.php.

Exercise: Using the 404 HTTP Status Code

1. Modify the CheckRequest() method in presentation/link.php by adding the highlighted code:

```
/* Remove the virtual location from the requested URL
   so we can compare paths */
$requested_url = self::Build(str_replace(VIRTUAL_LOCATION, '',
                                         $_SERVER['REQUEST_URI']));


// 404 redirect if the requested product, category or department
// doesn't exist
if (strstr($proper_url, '/-'))
{
  // Clean output buffer
  ob_clean();

  // Load the 404 page
  include '404.php';

  // Clear the output buffer and stop execution
  flush();
  ob_flush();
  ob_end_clean();
  exit();
}

// 301 redirect to the proper URL if necessary
if ($requested_url != $proper_url)
{
```

2. Open presentation/products_list.php, and add the following code to the init() function:

```
        elseif (isset($this->_mDepartmentId))
          $this->mProductListPages[] =
            Link::ToDepartment($this->_mDepartmentId, $i);
        else
          $this->mProductListPages[] = Link::ToIndex($i);
}

/* 404 redirect if the page number is larger than
   the total number of pages */
if ($this->mPage > $this->mrTotalPages)
{
  // Clean output buffer
  ob_clean();

  // Load the 404 page
  include '404.php';
```

```
    // Clear the output buffer and stop execution
    flush();
    ob_flush();
    ob_end_clean();
    exit();
  }

    // Build links for product details pages
    for ($i = 0; $i < count($this->mProducts); $i++)
    {
```

3. In your tshirtshop folder, create a file named 404.php, and type in the following code:

```php
<?php
  // Set the 404 status code
  header('HTTP/1.0 404 Not Found');

  require_once 'include/config.php';
  require_once PRESENTATION_DIR . 'link.php';
?>
<!DOCTYPE html PUBLIC "-//W3C//DTD XHTML 1.0 Transitional//EN"
 "http://www.w3.org/TR/xhtml1/DTD/xhtml1-transitional.dtd">
<html>
  <head>
    <title>
      TShirtShop Page Not Found (404): Demo Product Catalog from
      Beginning PHP and MySQL E-Commerce
    </title>
    <link href="<?php echo Link::Build('styles/tshirtshop.css'); ?>"
     type="text/css" rel="stylesheet" />
  </head>
  <body>
    <div id="doc" class="yui-t7">
      <div id="bd">
        <div id="header" class="yui-g">
          <a href="<?php echo Link::Build(''); ?>">
            <img src="<?php echo Link::Build('images/tshirtshop.png'); ?>"
             alt="tshirtshop logo" />
          </a>
        </div>
        <div id="contents" class="yui-g">
          <h1>
            The page that you have requested doesn't exist on TShirtShop.
          </h1>
          <p>
            Please visit the
            <a href="<?php echo Link::Build(''); ?>">TShirtShop catalog</a>
            if you're looking for T-shirts,
```

```
        or <a href="<?php echo ADMIN_ERROR_MAIL; ?>">email us</a>
        if you need further assistance.
      </p>
      <p>Thank you!</p>
      <p>The TShirtShop team.</p>
    </div>
  </div>
  </body>
</html>
```

4. Modify .htaccess by adding this highlighted code:

```
# Set the default 500 page for Apache errors
ErrorDocument 500 /tshirtshop/500.php

# Set the default 404 page
ErrorDocument 404 /tshirtshop/404.php
```

■**Caution** Be sure to check these are the correct locations of your 404.php and 500.php files.

---

5. Load http://localhost/tshirtshop/seasonal-d3/page-5/. Because the Seasonal department has only four pages of products, TShirtShop should throw the 404 page as shown in Figure 7-8.

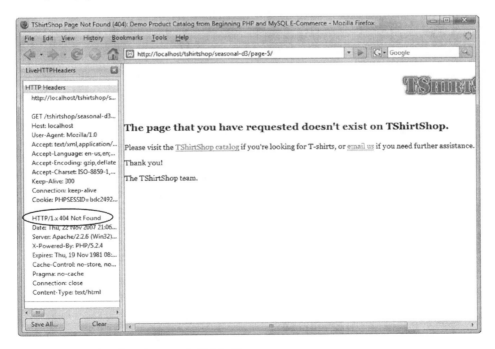

Figure 7-8. *Testing the 404 page in TShirtShop*

How It Works: 404 and 500

In this exercise, and in the previous one, you've learned how to work with the 404 and 500 status codes using the .htaccess configuration file and with PHP code. For 404, the usefulness of both techniques is more obvious. If the user requests a page that doesn't match any existing location of your web site, Apache will use the 404 page that you configured in .htaccess. However, if the user requests a technically valid page but one whose contents don't exist, such as category subpage whose Page value is larger than the largest existing page, we need to throw the 404 page ourselves using PHP code. To test the first scenario, just load a page such as http://localhost/ tshirtshop/does_not_exist.php. The second scenario was tested in the last step of the exercise, and the output is shown in Figure 7-8.

Summary

We're certain you've enjoyed this chapter! With only a few changes in its code, TShirtShop is now ready to face its online competition, with a solid search-engine-optimized foundation. Of course, the search engine optimization efforts don't end here.

When adding each new feature of the web site, we'll make sure to follow general SEO guidelines, so when we launch the web site, the search engines will be our friends, not our enemies.

In following chapters, we'll continue making small SEO improvements. For now, the foundations have been laid, and we're ready to continue implementing another exciting feature in TShirtShop: product searching!

■ ■ ■

Searching the Catalog

"What are you looking for?" This is a question you're often asked when visiting a retail store. Offering assistance in finding the products customers are searching for can bring significant profits to a business, and this rule applies to web stores as well. In this chapter, we'll add the product searching feature to our TShirtShop, which will help visitors find the products they're looking for.

You'll see how easy it is to add this feature to TShirtShop by integrating the new components into the existing architecture. In this chapter, you will

- Analyze the various ways in which the product catalog can be searched.

- Create the necessary MySQL data structures that support product searching.

- Write the data and business tiers used to implement the search feature.

- Build the user interface for the catalog search feature using Smarty componentized templates.

Choosing How to Search the Catalog

As always, there are a few things we need to think about before starting to code. When designing each new feature, we begin by analyzing that feature from the end user's perspective.

For the visual part of the catalog search feature, we'll use a text box in which the visitor can enter one or more words to search for in the product names and descriptions. The text entered by the visitor can be searched for in several ways:

Exact-match search: If the visitor enters a search string composed of more than one word, they will be searched for in the catalog as is, without splitting up the words and searching for them separately.

All-words search: The search string entered by the visitor is split into individual words, causing a search for each product that contains all the words entered by the visitor. This is like the exact-match search in that it still searches for all the entered words, but in this case, the order of the words is not important.

Any-words search: This kind of search returns the products that contain at least one of the words of the search string.

This simple classification isn't by any means complete. The search engine can be as complex as the one offered by modern Internet search engines, which provide many options and features and show a ranked list of results, or as simple as searching the database for the exact string provided by the visitor.

TShirtShop will support the any-words and all-words search modes. We don't include the exact-match search, because it's not really useful for our kind of web site. This decision leads to the visual design of the search feature; see Figure 8-1.

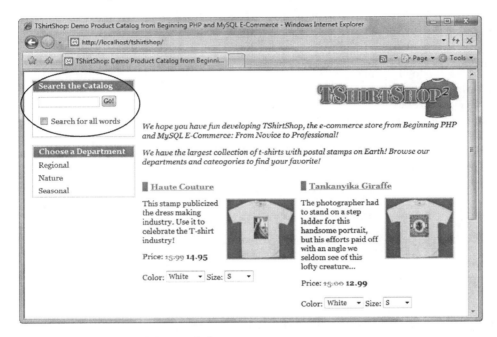

Figure 8-1. *The design of the search feature*

The text box is there, as expected, along with a check box that allows the visitor to choose between an all-words search and an any-words search.

You also need to decide how the search results are displayed. What should the search results page look like? You want to display, after all, a list of products that match the search criteria.

The simplest solution to display the search results would be to reuse the products_list componentized template you built in the previous chapter. A sample search page will look like the one shown in Figure 8-2.

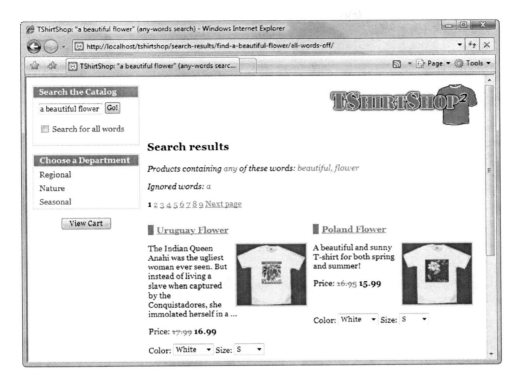

Figure 8-2. *Sample search results*

Figure 8-2 also shows the URLs used for search results pages. This is more a user optimization than search engine optimization, because we'll restrict search engines from browsing search result pages to avoid duplicate content problems. These URLs, however, can be easily bookmarked by visitors and are easily hackable (the visitor can edit the URL in the address bar manually)—both details make the visitor's live browsing of your site more pleasant.

One last detail you can notice in Figure 8-2 is that the site employs paging. If there are a lot of search results, you'll only present a fixed (but configurable) number of products per page and allow the visitor to browse through the pages using navigational links.

Let's begin implementing the functionality starting, as usual, with the data tier.

Teaching the Database to Search Itself

You have two main options to implement searching in the database:

- Implement searching using WHERE and LIKE.

- Search using the full-text search feature in MySQL.

Let's analyze these options.

Searching Using WHERE and LIKE

The straightforward solution, frequently used to implement searching, consists of using LIKE in the WHERE clause of the SELECT statement. Let's take a look at a simple example that will return the products that have the word "flower" somewhere in their descriptions:

```
SELECT name FROM product WHERE description LIKE '%flower%'
```

The LIKE operator matches parts of strings, and the percent wildcard (%) is used to specify any string of zero or more characters. That's why in the previous example, the pattern %flower% matches all records whose description column has the word "flower" somewhere in it. This search is case-insensitive.

If you want to retrieve all the products that contain the word "flower" somewhere in the product's name or description, the query will look like this:

```
SELECT name
FROM    product
WHERE   description LIKE '%flower%' OR name LIKE '%flower%';
```

This method of searching has the great advantage that it works on any type of MySQL tables (such as InnoDB table type), but has three important drawbacks:

Speed: Because we need to search for text somewhere inside the description and name fields, the entire database must be searched on each query. This is called a full-table scan, because the database engine cannot use any regular indexes to speed up the process of finding the results. This can significantly slow down the overall performance, especially if you have a large number of products in the database.

Quality of search results: This method doesn't make it easy for you to implement various advanced features, such as returning the matching products sorted by search relevance.

Advanced search features: This method does not allow visitors to perform searches that use the Boolean operators (AND, OR), inflected forms of words (such as plurals and various verb tenses), or words located in close proximity.

So how can you do better searches that implement these features? If you have a large database that needs to be searched frequently, how can you search this database without killing your server?

The answer is by using MySQL's full-text search capabilities.

Searching Using the MySQL Full-Text Search Feature

Searching using LIKE, as explained earlier, is very inefficient because of the full-table scan operation the database must perform when searching for a word. If you search for "flower" in product descriptions, each product description is read and analyzed. This is the worst-case scenario, as far as database operations are concerned.

■**Tip** Typical table indexes applied on text-based columns (such is `varchar`) improve the performance of searches that look for an exact value or for strings that start with a certain letter or word. This is because a typical index works by sorting the strings in alphabetical order, parsing them *from left to right*—just like names in a phone book are sorted, for example. These indexes speed up searches when you know the letters (or characters) the search string starts with, but they are useless when you're looking for words that reside inside a string.

The good news is that MySQL has a feature named FULLTEXT indexes, which are specifically designed to allow for efficient and powerful text searches. FULLTEXT indexes are similar to normal indexes, but they parse the whole content of string columns (such as product names and descriptions).

A FULLTEXT index will speed up dramatically operations of searching for a particular word (or set of words) *inside* a product description, for example. This index allows performing such operations without performing the full-table scans that happens when LIKE is used.

MySQL full-text search is much faster and smarter than the previously mentioned method (using the LIKE operator). Here are its main advantages:

- *Search results are ordered* based on search relevance.

- *Small words are ignored.* Words that aren't at least four characters long—such as "and", "so", and so on—are removed by default from the search query.

- *Advanced features* such as MySQL full-text searches can also be performed in Boolean mode. This mode allows you to search words based on AND/OR criteria, such as "+beautiful +flower", which retrieves all the rows that contain both the words "beautiful" and "flower".

- *Faster searches* are possible. Because of the use of the special search indexes, the search operation is much faster than when using the LIKE method.

■**Tip** Learn more about the full-text searching capabilities of MySQL at `http://dev.mysql.com/doc/refman/5.1/en/fulltext-search.html`.

As explained in Chapter 4, the main disadvantage of the full-text search feature is that it only works with the MyISAM table type. The alternative table type you could use is InnoDB, which is more advanced and supports features such as foreign keys, ACID transactions, and more but doesn't support the full-text feature.

▨Note ACID is an acronym that describes the four essential properties for database transactions: Atomicity, Consistency, Isolation, and Durability. We won't use database transactions in this book, but you can learn more about them from other sources, such as *The Programmer's Guide to SQL* (Apress, 2003). The database transactions chapter of that book can be downloaded freely from `http://www.cristiandarie.ro/downloads/`.

In the following few pages, you'll first create FULLTEXT indexes in your database and then learn how to use them to search your catalog.

Creating Data Structures That Enable Searching

In our scenario, the table that we'll use for searches is product, because that's what our visitors will be looking for. Before you can make it searchable using FULLTEXT indexes, you need to make sure its table type is MyISAM (this should be the case if you've correctly followed the instructions in the book). If you've used any other table type when creating it, please convert it now by executing this SQL statement after connecting to your tshirtshop database:

```
ALTER TABLE product ENGINE = MYISAM;
```

To make the product table searchable, we must add a full-text index on the (name, description) pair of columns, as follows:

1. Load phpMyAdmin, select the tshirtshop database from the Database box, and click the SQL tab.

2. In the form, type the following command, which adds a new full-text index named idx_ft_product_name_description:

```
-- Create full-text search index
CREATE FULLTEXT INDEX `idx_ft_product_name_description`
        ON `product` (`name`, `description`);
```

After clicking the Go button, you should be informed that the command executed successfully.

Because we want TShirtShop to allow visitors to search for products that contain certain words in their names or descriptions, we created a full-text index on the (name, description) pair of fields of the product table (this is different than having two full-text indexes, one on name and one on description).

Creating this full-text index enables you to do full-text searches on the indexed fields. To have phpMyAdmin confirm the existence of the new full-text index, click the Structure tab, and click the Structure icon for the product table. In the new window, under the Indexes section (see Figure 8-3), you now see a new index of type FULLTEXT on the name and description columns.

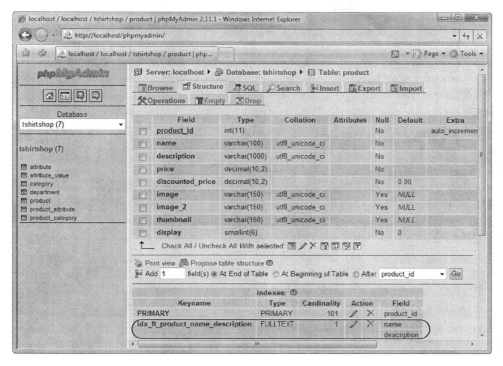

Figure 8-3. *The full-text index in phpMyAdmin*

■**Tip** It's worth noting that phpMyAdmin confirms that we have a single FULLTEXT index on two table columns, rather than two separate FULLTEXT indexes.

Teaching MySQL to Do Any-Words Searches

The general MySQL syntax for performing a full-text search looks like this:

```
SELECT <column_list>
FROM    <table>
WHERE   MATCH <column or list of columns> AGAINST <search criteria>
```

■**Tip** The official documentation for the full-text search feature can be found at http://dev.mysql.com/doc/refman/5.1/en/fulltext-search.html.

The column or list of columns on which you do the search must be full-text indexed. If there is a list of columns, there must be a full-text index that applies to that group of columns, just as our idx_ft_product_name_description index applies to both name and description.

How can you use this full-text index to perform an any-words search on your products? Suppose you want to search for the words "beautiful" and/or "flower" in their (name, description) pair. The following SQL statement achieves this:

```
SELECT name, description FROM product
WHERE MATCH (name, description) AGAINST ("beautiful flower");
```

Executing this query when the tshirtshop database contains the sample data would return 33 product records.

When performing such searches, you usually want to retrieve the results sorted in descending order by relevancy. This is can be done using the ORDER BY clause and providing the MATCH rule as an argument. Always remember to use the DESC option, so that the most relevant result is placed at the top.

```
SELECT name, description FROM product
WHERE MATCH (name, description) AGAINST ("beautiful flower")
ORDER BY MATCH (name, description) AGAINST ("beautiful flower") DESC
```

The query has 33 results using our sample data, shown partially in Figure 8-4. The results represent the records ordered based on search relevance value, the most relevant results being shown first (the list in Figure 8-4 was generated by executing the query and clicking the "Print view (with full texts)" link that shows up at the bottom of the phpMyAdmin page).

For example, products that contain both the words "beautiful" and "flower" (or contain more instances of them) appear higher in the list than products that contain only one of the words.

name	description
Uruguay Flower	The Indian Queen Anahi was the ugliest woman ever seen. But instead of living a slave when captured by the Conquistadores, she immolated herself in a fire and was reborn the most beautiful of flowers: the ceibo, national flower of Uruguay. Of course, you won't need to burn to wear this T-shirt, but you may cause some pretty hot glances to be thrown your way!
Poland Flower	A beautiful and sunny T-shirt for both spring and summer!
Costa Rica Flower	This national flower of Costa Rica is one of our most beloved flower T-shirts (you can see one on Jill, above). You will surely stand out in this T-shirt!
Afghan Flower	This beautiful image was issued to celebrate National Teachers Day. Perhaps you know a teacher who would love this T-shirt?
Albania Flower	Well, these crab apples started out as flowers, so that's close enough for us! They still make for a uniquely beautiful T-shirt.
Romania Flower	Also known as the spring pheasant's eye, this flower belongs on your T-shirt this summer to help you catch a few eyes.
Israel Flower	This plant is native to the rocky and sandy regions of the western United States, so when you come across one, it really stands out. And so will you when you put on this beautiful T-shirt!
Bulgarian Flower	For your interest (and to impress your friends), this beautiful stamp was issued to honor the George Dimitrov state printing works. You'll need to know this when you wear the T-shirt.
Congo Flower	The Congo is not at a loss for beautiful flowers, and we've picked a few of them for your T-shirts.
Austria Flower	Have you ever had nasturtiums on your salad? Try it--they're almost as good as having them on your T-shirt!
Ghana Flower	This is one of the first gingers to bloom in the spring--just like you when you wear this T-shirt!

Figure 8-4. *Sample search results*

FINE-TUNING MYSQL FULLTEXT SEARCHING

By default, words that aren't at least four characters long are not indexed (and as a result they are never included in any searches), but you can change this behavior if you want. The minimum length for words to be included in FULLTEXT indexes is established by the `ft_min_word_len` server variable.

For example, if you want three-character words to be searchable, all you have to do is to set the `ft_min_word_len` variable in your MySQL server configuration file like this:

```
[mysqld]
  ft_min_word_len=3
```

The configuration file where you should store this setting is usually `/opt/lampp/etc/my.cnf` in Unix and `C:\xampp\mysql\bin\my.cnf` or `C:\Windows\php.ini` in Windows. You can find detailed instructions on how to modify this value and perform other FULLTEXT fine-tuning operations in the article at `http://dev.mysql.com/doc/refman/5.0/en/fulltext-fine-tuning.html`.

After changing the value of `ft_min_word_len`, you must restart your MySQL server. After restarting the server, you can query your MySQL server for the values of your variables to make sure the changes have taken effect using a query such as

```
SHOW VARIABLES LIKE 'ft_%';
```

After changing the value of `ft_min_word_len`, you must rebuild your FULLTEXT indexes as well. You can do this by either dropping and re-creating the index or using REPAIR TABLE like this:

```
REPAIR TABLE product QUICK;
```

Note that you only need to REPAIR the tables on which you have FULLTEXT indexes. If, for some reason, you prefer to re-create the index (we advise using REPAIR TABLE though), you can do so like this:

```
ALTER TABLE product
     DROP INDEX idx_ft_product_name_description;
CREATE FULLTEXT INDEX idx_ft_product_name_description
     ON product (name, description);
```

Teaching MySQL to Do All-Words Searches

We've already seen that an *any-words* search will return all the products that contain "flower *or* "beautiful" (or both words) in their names or descriptions. On the other hand, the results of an *all-words* search should contain only the products that contain *all* of the words you're searching for ("beautiful" *and* "flower," in this case). For all-words searches, you need to use the Boolean mode of the full-text search feature, which allows using AND/OR logic in the search criteria.

The new query would look like this:

```
SELECT   name, description FROM product
WHERE    MATCH (name, description) AGAINST ("+beautiful +flower" IN BOOLEAN MODE)
ORDER BY MATCH (name, description) AGAINST ("+beautiful +flower" IN BOOLEAN MODE)
DESC;
```

Sorting in descending order by the match value isn't required but is highly desirable, since you usually want to receive the search results in descending order by relevance. The leading plus sign marks the required words, so it needs to be added for every word in an all-word search. Compared to the any-words search, this query returns only seven products, which you can see in Figure 8-5.

name	description
Afghan Flower	This beautiful image was issued to celebrate National Teachers Day. Perhaps you know a teacher who would love this T-shirt?
Albania Flower	Well, these crab apples started out as flowers, so that's close enough for us! They still make for a uniquely beautiful T-shirt.
Bulgarian Flower	For your interest (and to impress your friends), this beautiful stamp was issued to honor the George Dimitrov state printing works. You'll need to know this when you wear the T-shirt.
Congo Flower	The Congo is not at a loss for beautiful flowers, and we've picked a few of them for your T-shirts.
Israel Flower	This plant is native to the rocky and sandy regions of the western United States, so when you come across one, it really stands out. And so will you when you put on this beautiful T-shirt!
Poland Flower	A beautiful and sunny T-shirt for both spring and summer!
Uruguay Flower	The Indian Queen Anahi was the ugliest woman ever seen. But instead of living a slave when captured by the Conquistadores, she immolated herself in a fire and was reborn the most beautiful of flowers: the ceibo, national flower of Uruguay. Of course, you won't need to burn to wear this T-shirt, but you may cause some pretty hot glances to be thrown your way!

Figure 8-5. *Results of an all-words search*

MORE FULLTEXT FINE-TUNING: QUERY EXPANSION

The full-text search with query expansion feature was introduced in MySQL 4.1.1 and allows MySQL to find products that match not only the words searched for but also related words.

When searching with query expansion, MySQL performs the search twice behind the scenes. First, it finds the words that are most relevant to those you're searching for. Then these words are appended to your initial query string, and the search is performed again.

This method increases the number of search results, but also increases the chance of getting non-relevant products. You can see the official documentation of this feature at http://dev.mysql.com/doc/refman/5.1/en/fulltext-query-expansion.html.

To enable query expansion, you need to add WITH QUERY EXPANSION to the search criteria as shown in the following code snippet:

```
SELECT   name, description FROM product
WHERE    MATCH (name, description) AGAINST ("flower" WITH QUERY EXPANSION)
ORDER BY MATCH (name, description) AGAINST ("flower" WITH QUERY EXPANSION) DESC;
```

Search for "flower" with query expansion retrieves 75 results. Executing the same search without query expansion, you get only 15 results. The data tier code presented in the following pages doesn't use query expansion, but you can add it very easily if you want to.

Writing the Stored Procedures for Searching Functionality

You are ready now to implement your web site's search functionality. If you'd like to learn more about the inner workings of the MySQL full-text, consult its official documentation at

http://dev.mysql.com/doc/refman/5.1/en/fulltext-search.html

Exercise: Writing the Database Searching Code

1. Use phpMyAdmin to execute the following code, which creates the `catalog_count_search_result` stored procedure into your `tshirtshop` database. Don't forget to set $$ as the delimiter before executing the code.

```
-- Create catalog_count_search_result stored procedure
CREATE PROCEDURE catalog_count_search_result(
  IN inSearchString TEXT, IN inAllWords VARCHAR(3))
BEGIN
  IF inAllWords = "on" THEN
    PREPARE statement FROM
      "SELECT   count(*)
       FROM     product
       WHERE    MATCH (name, description) AGAINST (? IN BOOLEAN MODE)";
  ELSE
    PREPARE statement FROM
      "SELECT   count(*)
       FROM     product
       WHERE    MATCH (name, description) AGAINST (?)";
  END IF;

  SET @p1 = inSearchString;

  EXECUTE statement USING @p1;
END$$
```

2. Now, follow the same procedure to execute this code, which creates the `catalog_ search` stored procedure into your `tshirtshop` database:

```
-- Create catalog_search stored procedure
CREATE PROCEDURE catalog_search(
  IN inSearchString TEXT, IN inAllWords VARCHAR(3),
  IN inShortProductDescriptionLength INT,
  IN inProductsPerPage INT, IN inStartItem INT)
BEGIN
  IF inAllWords = "on" THEN
    PREPARE statement FROM
      "SELECT   product_id, name,
                IF(LENGTH(description) <= ?,
                  description,
                  CONCAT(LEFT(description, ?),
                       '...')) AS description,
                price, discounted_price, thumbnail
       FROM     product
       WHERE    MATCH (name, description)
                AGAINST (? IN BOOLEAN MODE)
```

```
                ORDER BY MATCH (name, description)
                         AGAINST (? IN BOOLEAN MODE) DESC
            LIMIT    ?, ?";
        ELSE
          PREPARE statement FROM
            "SELECT   product_id, name,
                      IF(LENGTH(description) <= ?,
                         description,
                         CONCAT(LEFT(description, ?),
                                '...')) AS description,
                      price, discounted_price, thumbnail
            FROM      product
            WHERE     MATCH (name, description) AGAINST (?)
            ORDER BY MATCH (name, description) AGAINST (?) DESC
            LIMIT    ?, ?";
        END IF;

        SET @p1 = inShortProductDescriptionLength;
        SET @p2 = inSearchString;
        SET @p3 = inStartItem;
        SET @p4 = inProductsPerPage;

        EXECUTE statement USING @p1, @p1, @p2, @p2, @p3, @p4;
    END$$
```

How It Works: The Catalog Search Functionality

In this exercise, you created the database functionality that supports the product-searching business tier logic, which consists of two stored procedures:

- `catalog_count_search_result`: This stored procedure counts the number of search results. This is required so that the presentation tier will know how many search results pages to display.

- `catalog_search`: This stored procedure performs the actual product search.

Although they can look intimidating at first, mostly because of their size, these stored procedures simply put the full-text search theory you learned earlier in this chapter to good use. Additionally, `catalog_search` implements the paging techniques that are also present in the other procedures that return lists of products.

Implementing the Business Tier

The business tier of the search feature consists of a single method named Search, which calls the two stored procedures you implemented earlier to retrieve the list of searched products. Let's implement this method first, and then we'll discuss how it works.

Exercise: Implementing the Business Tier

1. The full-text search feature of MySQL ignores words that are shorter than a specified length. We want to inform the visitor which words have been used for searching and which words were ignored. To support this feature, we first need to find out the length that is already specified in our database by interrogating the MySQL `ft_min_word_len` variable. Use phpMyAdmin to execute the following SQL statement in the tshirtshop database:

```
SHOW VARIABLES LIKE 'ft_min_word_len';
```

If you haven't changed the value, `ft_min_word_len` should be 4 (see Figure 8-6).

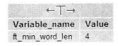

Figure 8-6. *Looking up the* ft_min_word_len *variable in phpMyAdmin*

2. Let's now save the value of the `ft_min_word_len` you just found to the configuration file, making it easily available from the application code. Open `include/config.php`, and add the following code:

```
/* Minimum word length for searches; this constant must be kept in sync
   with the ft_min_word_len MySQL variable */
define('FT_MIN_WORD_LEN', 4);
```

3. Open `business/catalog.php`, and add the code of the `Search()` method:

```
// Search the catalog
public static function Search($searchString, $allWords,
                              $pageNo, &$rHowManyPages)
{
  //The search result will be an array of this form
  $search_result = array ('accepted_words' => array (),
                          'ignored_words' => array (),
                          'products' => array ());

  // Return void if the search string is void
  if (empty ($searchString))
    return $search_result;

  // Search string delimiters
  $delimiters = ',.; ';

  /* On the first call to strtok you supply the whole
     search string and the list of delimiters.
     It returns the first word of the string */
  $word = strtok($searchString, $delimiters);

  // Parse the string word by word until there are no more words
```

```php
while ($word)
{
  // Short words are added to the ignored_words list from $search_result
  if (strlen($word) < FT_MIN_WORD_LEN)
    $search_result['ignored_words'][] = $word;
  else
    $search_result['accepted_words'][] = $word;

  // Get the next word of the search string
  $word = strtok($delimiters);
}

// If there aren't any accepted words return the $search_result
if (count($search_result['accepted_words']) == 0)
  return $search_result;

// Build $search_string from accepted words list
$search_string = '';

// If $allWords is 'on' then we append a ' +' to each word
if (strcmp($allWords, "on") == 0)
  $search_string = implode(" +", $search_result['accepted_words']);
else
  $search_string = implode(" ", $search_result['accepted_words']);

// Count the number of search results
$sql = 'CALL catalog_count_search_result(:search_string, :all_words)';
$params = array(':search_string' => $search_string,
                ':all_words' => $allWords);

// Calculate the number of pages required to display the products
$rHowManyPages = Catalog::HowManyPages($sql, $params);
// Calculate the start item
$start_item = ($pageNo - 1) * PRODUCTS_PER_PAGE;

// Retrieve the list of matching products
$sql = 'CALL catalog_search(:search_string, :all_words,
                            :short_product_description_length,
                            :products_per_page, :start_item)';

// Build the parameters array
$params = array (':search_string' => $search_string,
                 ':all_words' => $allWords,
                 ':short_product_description_length' =>
                   SHORT_PRODUCT_DESCRIPTION_LENGTH,
                 ':products_per_page' => PRODUCTS_PER_PAGE,
                 ':start_item' => $start_item);
```

```
    // Execute the query
    $search_result['products'] = DatabaseHandler::GetAll($sql, $params);

    // Return the results
    return $search_result;
  }
```

How It Works: The Business Tier Search Method

The Search() method removes words that are shorter than the length specified by ft_min_word_len. The minimum word length is stored in the FT_MIN_WORD_LEN constant. The FT_MIN_WORD_LEN should be kept in sync with the ft_min_word_len MySQL server variable.

The reason to know this value in our PHP code is that we want to tell the visitor which words have been removed when doing searches. First, we find out which words are removed by comparing their length with the FT_MIN_WORD_LEN. This way, we split the searched words into two sets—the accepted words and ignored words—and put them in an associative array in which we'll also store the search results and return it as the method's result.

The Search() method of the business tier is called from the presentation tier with the following parameters (notice that all of them except the first one are the same as the parameters of the data tier Search() method):

- $searchString contains the search string entered by the visitor.

- $allWords is "on" for all-words searches.

- $pageNo represents the page of products being requested.

- $rHowManyPages represents the total number of results pages.

The function starts by declaring an associative array named $search_result, which will store the results of the product search.

```
// Search the catalog
public static function Search($searchString, $allWords,
                             $pageNo, &$rHowManyPages)
{
  //The search result will be an array of this form
  $search_result = array ('accepted_words' => array (),
                          'ignored_words' => array (),
                          'products' => array ());
```

As you can see, the array contains three other arrays, with self-descriptive names. The accepted_words array will store the words that will be used for searching, and ignored_words will be populated with the words that will be ignored from searching. The presentation tier will use this data to inform the visitor which words have been searched for and which have been ignored. The products array will store the list of products that match the search string.

Next, Search() verifies that the search string isn't empty. If it is, the empty $search_result array is returned, indicating that no search results have been found:

```
// Return void if the search string is void
if (empty ($searchString))
  return $search_result;
```

Once we've made sure the search string isn't empty, we start filtering the words. Words that are shorter than the FT_MIN_WORD_LEN are sent to the ignored_words array, and they are ignored by MySQL when performing the search. The other words are saved to the accepted_words, array; they will be used for searching. Because MySQL doesn't inform you which words have been used for searching and which have been ignored, we need check the ignored and accepted words in the business tier. When splitting the search string into individual words, we consider that the possible word separators are the comma (,), the dot (.), the semicolon (;) and the space. Any other character the visitor types in the search box will be considered part of a word. The highlighted code that follows is the one that breaks the search string into words and saves them into the accepted words and ignored words arrays:

```
// Search string delimiters
$delimiters = ',.; ';

/* On the first call to strtok you supply the whole
   search string and the list of delimiters.
   It returns the first word of the string */
$word = strtok($searchString, $delimiters);

// Parse the string word by word until there are no more words
while ($word)
{
  // Short words are added to the ignored_words list from $search_result
  if (strlen($word) < FT_MIN_WORD_LEN)
    $search_result['ignored_words'][] = $word;
  else
    $search_result['accepted_words'][] = $word;

  // Get the next word of the search string
  $word = strtok($delimiters);
}
```

Once this operation is done, we check again if we still have words to search for. This time, we check that the accepted_words array is not empty. If it is, then we have nothing to search for, and so we return the empty $search_result array:

```
// If there aren't any accepted words return the $search_result
if (count($search_result['accepted_words']) == 0)
  return $search_result;
```

Now that we know we have at least one word to search for, it's time to prepare the search string that we'll send to the database. As you know from the full-text search theory, when making All-Words searches, we use Boolean searching, and we must prefix each searched word with a plus sign (+). For an all-words Boolean search for "beautiful flower", the search string we send to the database is "+beautiful +flower". For any-words searches, we simply send "beautiful flower". The following code creates and populates the $search_string variable, which contains exactly the string that MySQL needs to search for:

```
// Build $search_string from accepted words list
$search_string = '';
```

```
// If $allWords is 'on' then we append a ' +' to each word
if (strcmp($allWords, "on") == 0)
  $search_string = implode(" +", $search_result['accepted_words']);
else
  $search_string = implode(" ", $search_result['accepted_words']);
```

The following code in Search() is the typical code that requests a page of products, and you're familiar with it from the chapters where you created the product catalog. The function ends by returning $search_result, which contains the search results, and the lists of accepted and ignored words, which represents all the data you want to show your visitor when a search is performed:

```
// Execute the query
$search_result['products'] = DatabaseHandler::GetAll($sql, $params);

// Return the results
return $search_result;
}
```

Implementing the Presentation Tier

The catalog-searching feature has two separate interface elements that you need to implement:

- A componentized template named search_box, whose role is to provide the means to enter the search string for the visitor (refer to Figure 8-1)

- A componentized template named search_results, which displays the products matching the search criteria (refer to Figure 8-2)

You'll create the two componentized templates in two separate exercises.

Creating the Search Box

Follow the steps in the exercise to build the search_box componentized template and integrate it into TShirtShop.

Exercise: Creating the search_box Componentized Template

1. Create a new template file named search_box.tpl in the presentation/templates folder, and add the following code to it:

```
{* search_box.tpl *}
{load_presentation_object filename="search_box" assign="obj"}
{* Start search box *}
<div class="box">
  <p class="box-title">Search the Catalog</p>
  <form class="search_form" method="post" action="{$obj->mLinkToSearch}">
    <p>
      <input maxlength="100" id="search_string" name="search_string"
      value="{$obj->mSearchString}" size="19" />
```

```
      <input type="submit" value="Go!" /><br />
    </p>
    <p>
      <input type="checkbox" id="all_words" name="all_words"
      {if $obj->mAllWords == "on"} checked="checked" {/if}/>
      Search for all words
    </p>
  </form>
</div>
{* End search box *}
```

2. Create the SearchBox presentation object in a file named search_box.php in the presentation folder,
   with the following code:

```php
<?php
// Manages the search box
class SearchBox
{
  // Public variables for the smarty template
  public $mSearchString = '';
  public $mAllWords = 'off';
  public $mLinkToSearch;

  // Class constructor
  public function __construct()
  {
    $this->mLinkToSearch = Link::ToSearch();

    if (isset ($_GET['Search']))
    {
      $this->mSearchString = trim($_POST['search_string']);
      $this->mAllWords = isset ($_POST['all_words']) ?
                          $_POST['all_words'] : 'off';

      // Clean output buffer
      ob_clean();

      // Redirect 302
      header('HTTP/1.1 302 Found');
      header('Location: ' .
              Link::ToSearchResults($this->mSearchString, $this->mAllWords));

      // Clear the output buffer and stop execution
      flush();
      ob_flush();
      ob_end_clean();
      exit();
    }
```

```
    elseif (isset ($_GET['SearchResults']))
    {
      $this->mSearchString = trim(str_replace('-', ' ', $_GET['SearchString']));
      $this->mAllWords = isset ($_GET['AllWords']) ? $_GET['AllWords'] : 'off';
    }

    if (isset ($_GET['ProductId']) &&
        isset ($_SESSION['link_to_continue_shopping']))
    {
      $continue_shopping =
        Link::QueryStringToArray($_SESSION['link_to_continue_shopping']);

      if (isset ($continue_shopping['SearchResults']))
      {
        $this->mSearchString =
          trim(str_replace('-', ' ', $continue_shopping['SearchString']));
        $this->mAllWords = $continue_shopping['AllWords'];
      }
    }
  }
}
?>
```

3. Open presentation/link.php, and add the following two methods to the Link class:

```
// Create link to the search page
public static function ToSearch()
{
  return self::Build('index.php?Search');
}

// Create link to a search results page
public static function ToSearchResults($searchString, $allWords,
                                       $page = 1)
{
  $link = 'search-results/find';

  if (empty($searchString))
    $link .= '/';
  else
    $link .= '-' . self::CleanUrlText($searchString) . '/';

  $link .= 'all-words-' . $allWords . '/';

  if ($page > 1)
    $link .= 'page-' . $page . '/';

  return self::Build($link);
}
```

4. In the same file, modify the following CheckRequest() method as highlighted. You implemented this function in Chapter 7 to redirect incoming requests to their proper versions, but we don't want it to verify search queries or search results pages, which have no "proper" version.

```
// Redirects to proper URL if not already there
public static function CheckRequest()
{
  $proper_url = '';

  if (isset ($_GET['Search']) || isset($_GET['SearchResults']))
  {
    return ;
  }
  // Obtain proper URL for category pages
  elseif (isset ($_GET['DepartmentId']) && isset ($_GET['CategoryId']))
  {
    if (isset ($_GET['Page']))
```

5. Add the following styles, needed in the search_box template, to styles/tshirtshop.css:

```
div.yui-b div form {
  padding: 5px 10px;
}

input, select, textarea {
  font-family: "georgia";
  font-size: 85%;
}
```

6. Modify the presentation/templates/store_front.tpl file to load the search_box template:

```
...
        <div class="yui-b">
          {include file="search_box.tpl"}
          {include file="departments_list.tpl"}
          {include file=$obj->mCategoriesCell}
        </div>
...
```

7. Load your project in a browser, and you'll see the search box resting nicely in its place (refer to Figure 8-1).

How It Works: The search_box Componentized Template

At this point, your search box is functional. However, before you can fully test the searching feature, you also need to implement the search results page. You will do this in the next exercise; until then, make sure you understand how the search box works.

The search_box.tpl template contains the HTML layout of the box—no mysteries here. On the other hand, the presentation object that supports this template deserves some attention. The SearchBox class in search_box.php has two functions:

- When the visitor types a search string and submits the form, the search box, via status code 302, redirects the request to a URL that can be bookmarked by the visitor, such as http://localhost/tshirtshop/ search-results/find-beautiful-flower/all-words-off/. Unless such a mechanism is implemented, the search results would be displayed on the page the visitor was seeing when he or she performed the search.

- If the page that is currently loaded is a search results page, or a product details page that was reached from a search results page, the search box is filled with the keywords that were searched by the visitor.

The location to which the request is redirected when a search is performed is calculated using the Link::ToSearchResults() method. Note that a 302 redirect is used. This is the status code that specifies a temporary page relocation, although in this case, the status code used doesn't really matter, because search engines wouldn't submit the form anyway. The purpose of the redirect isn't for search engine optimization but to give users a way to bookmark search results pages and offer other web sites the means to link to these pages:

```
if (isset ($_GET['Search']))
{
  $this->mSearchString = trim($_POST['search_string']);
  $this->mAllWords = isset ($_POST['all_words']) ?
                   $_POST['all_words'] : 'off';

  // Clean output buffer
  ob_clean();

  // Redirect 302
  header('HTTP/1.1 302 Found');
  header('Location: ' .
         Link::ToSearchResults($this->mSearchString, $this->mAllWords));

  // Clear the output buffer and stop execution
  flush();
  ob_flush();
  ob_end_clean();
  exit();
}
```

Of course, when implementing the search results page in the next exercise, we'll need to learn how to interpret the search results links. Currently, the any-words search for "beautiful flower" link is: http://localhost/tshirtshop/ search-results/find-beautiful-flower/all-words-off/. If this were an all-words search, the last bit of the URL would be all-words-on instead of all-words-off. The second page of the results would contain /page-2/ at the end of the URL.

If we're on the search results page, we retrieve the search string and the AllWords value from the query string. These will be read and displayed by the search_box.tpl template:

```
elseif (isset ($_GET['SearchResults']))
{
  $this->mSearchString = trim(str_replace('-', ' ', $_GET['SearchString']));
  $this->mAllWords = isset ($_GET['AllWords']) ? $_GET['AllWords'] : 'off';
}
```

In the end, SearchBox verifies the current page is a product details page that was reached from a search results page. If that is the case, the search box is also populated with the keywords searched by the visitor:

```
if (isset ($_GET['ProductId']) &&
    isset ($_SESSION['link_to_continue_shopping']))
{
  $continue_shopping =
    Link::QueryStringToArray($_SESSION['link_to_continue_shopping']);

  if (isset ($continue_shopping['SearchResults']))
  {
    $this->mSearchString =
      trim(str_replace('-', ' ', $continue_shopping['SearchString']));
    $this->mAllWords = $continue_shopping['AllWords'];
  }
}
```

Displaying the Search Results

In the next exercise, you'll create the componentized template that displays the search results. To make your life easier, we'll reuse the product_list componentized template to display the list of products. This is the componentized template that we are currently using to list products for the main page, for departments, and for categories. Of course, if you want to have the search results displayed in another format, you must create another componentized template.

You'll need to modify the templates logic file of the products list (products_list.php) to recognize when it's being called to display search results and display the correct list of products. Let's create the search_results template and update the templates logic of the products_list componentized template in the following exercise.

Exercise: Creating the search_results Componentized Template

1. Create a new template file in the presentation/templates directory named search_results.tpl, and add the following code to it:

```
{* search_results.tpl *}
<h1>Search results</h1>
{include file="products_list.tpl"}
```

2. Modify the presentation/products_list.php file by adding the following lines at the beginning of the ProductsList class constructor, __construct():

```
// Retrieve the search string and AllWords from the query string
if (isset ($_GET['SearchResults']))
{
  $this->mSearchString = trim(str_replace('-', ' ', $_GET['SearchString']));
  $this->mAllWords = isset ($_GET['AllWords']) ? $_GET['AllWords'] : 'off';
}
```

3. Add the $mSearchDescription, $mAllWords, and $mSearchString members to the ProductsList class, located in the same file:

```php
<?php
class ProductsList
{
  // Public variables to be read from Smarty template
  public $mPage = 1;
  public $mrTotalPages;
  public $mLinkToNextPage;
  public $mLinkToPreviousPage;
  public $mProductListPages = array();
  public $mProducts;
  public $mSearchDescription;
  public $mAllWords = 'off';
  public $mSearchString;

  // Private members
  private $_mDepartmentId;
  private $_mCategoryId;
```

4. Modify the init() method in ProductsList class like this:

```php
  public function init()
  {
    /* If searching the catalog, get the list of products by calling
       the Search business tier method */
    if (isset ($this->mSearchString))
    {
      // Get search results
      $search_results = Catalog::Search($this->mSearchString,
                                        $this->mAllWords,
                                        $this->mPage,
                                        $this->mrTotalPages);
      // Get the list of products
      $this->mProducts = $search_results['products'];
      // Build the title for the list of products
      if (count($search_results['accepted_words']) > 0)
        $this->mSearchDescription =
          '<p class="description">Products containing <font class="words">'
          . ($this->mAllWords == 'on' ? 'all' : 'any') . '</font>'
          . ' of these words: <font class="words">'
          . implode(', ', $search_results['accepted_words']) .
          '</font></p>';
      if (count($search_results['ignored_words']) > 0)
        $this->mSearchDescription .=
          '<p class="description">Ignored words: <font class="words">'
          . implode(', ', $search_results['ignored_words']) .
          '</font></p>';
```

```
          if (!(count($search_results['products']) > 0))
            $this->mSearchDescription .=
              '<p class="description">Your search generated no results.</p>';
      }
      /* If browsing a category, get the list of products by calling
         the GetProductsInCategory business tier method */
      elseif (isset ($this->_mCategoryId))
          $this->mProducts = Catalog::GetProductsInCategory(
          $this->_mCategoryId, $this->mPage, $this->mrTotalPages);
...
```

5. Continue by updating the init() method as highlighted, to add navigation links on search results pages:

```
...
      /* If there are subpages of products, display navigation
         controls */
      if ($this->mrTotalPages > 1)
      {
        // Build the Next link
        if ($this->mPage < $this->mrTotalPages)
        {
          if (isset($_GET['SearchResults']))
            $this->mLinkToNextPage =
              Link::ToSearchResults($this->mSearchString, $this->mAllWords,
                                    $this->mPage + 1);
          elseif (isset($this->_mCategoryId))
            $this->mLinkToNextPage =
              Link::ToCategory($this->_mDepartmentId, $this->_mCategoryId,
                               $this->mPage + 1);
          elseif (isset($this->_mDepartmentId))
            $this->mLinkToNextPage =
              Link::ToDepartment($this->_mDepartmentId, $this->mPage + 1);
        }

        // Build the Previous link
        if ($this->mPage > 1)
        {
          if (isset($_GET['SearchResults']))
            $this->mLinkToPreviousPage =
              Link::ToSearchResults($this->mSearchString, $this->mAllWords,
                                    $this->mPage - 1);
          elseif (isset($this->_mCategoryId))
            $this->mLinkToPreviousPage =
              Link::ToCategory($this->_mDepartmentId, $this->_mCategoryId,
                               $this->mPage - 1);
          elseif (isset($this->_mDepartmentId))
            $this->mLinkToPreviousPage =
```

```
          Link::ToDepartment($this->_mDepartmentId, $this->mPage - 1);
      }

      // Build the pages links
      for ($i = 1; $i <= $this->mrTotalPages; $i++)
        if (isset($_GET['SearchResults']))
          $this->mProductListPages[] =
            Link::ToSearchResults($this->mSearchString, $this->mAllWords, $i);
        elseif (isset($this->_mCategoryId))
          $this->mProductListPages[] =
            Link::ToCategory($this->_mDepartmentId, $this->_mCategoryId, $i);
        elseif (isset($this->_mDepartmentId))
          $this->mProductListPages[] =
            Link::ToDepartment($this->_mDepartmentId, $i);
        else
          $this->mProductListPages[] = Link::ToIndex($i);
    }
...
    /* 404 redirect if the page number is greater than
       the total number of pages */
    if ($this->mPage > $this->mrTotalPages && !empty($this->mrTotalPages))
    {
      // Clean output buffer
      ob_clean();
...
```

6. Add the following lines at the beginning of presentation/templates/products_list.tpl:

```
{* products_list.tpl *}
{load_presentation_object filename="products_list" assign="obj"}
{if $obj->mSearchDescription != ""}
  <p class="description">{$obj->mSearchDescription}</p>
{/if}
```

7. Open .htaccess, and type the following RewriteRule lines, which redirect the search results pages:

```
# Redirect department pages
RewriteRule ^.*-d([0-9]+)/page-([0-9]+)/?$ index.php?DepartmentId=$1&Page=$2 [L]
RewriteRule ^.*-d([0-9]+)/?$ index.php?DepartmentId=$1 [L]

# Redirect search results
RewriteRule ^search-results/find-(.*)/all-words-(on|off)/page-([0-9]+)/?$
index.php?SearchResults&SearchString=$1&AllWords=$2&Page=$3 [L]
RewriteRule ^search-results/find-?(.*)/all-words-(on|off)/?$
index.php?SearchResults&SearchString=$1&AllWords=$2&Page=1 [L]

# Redirect subpages of the home page
RewriteRule ^page-([0-9]+)/?$ index.php?Page=$1 [L]
```

8. Modify the `presentation/store_front.php` file to load the `search_results` componentized template when a search is performed by adding the highlighted lines of code in the `init()` method:

```
...
    // Load product details page if visiting a product
    if (isset ($_GET['ProductId']))
      $this->mContentsCell = 'product.tpl';

    // Load search result page if we're searching the catalog
    elseif (isset ($_GET['SearchResults']))
      $this->mContentsCell = 'search_results.tpl';

    // Load the page title
    $this->mPageTitle = $this->_GetPageTitle();
...
```

9. Also, in `store_front.php`, add the highlighted lines of code in the `_GetPageTitle()` method to show a custom title when we're viewing the search results page:

```
...
    elseif (isset ($_GET['ProductId']))
    {
      $page_title = 'TShirtShop: ' .
        Catalog::GetProductName($_GET['ProductId']);
    }
    elseif (isset ($_GET['SearchResults']))
    {
      $page_title  = 'TShirtShop: "';

      // Display the search string
      $page_title .= trim(str_replace('-', ' ', $_GET['SearchString'])) . '" (';

      // Display "all-words search " or "any-words search"
      $all_words = isset ($_GET['AllWords']) ? $_GET['AllWords'] : 'off';

      $page_title .= (($all_words == 'on') ? 'all' : 'any') .
                     '-words search';

      // Display page number
      if (isset ($_GET['Page']) && ((int)$_GET['Page']) > 1)
        $page_title .= ', page ' . ((int)$_GET['Page']);

      $page_title .= ')';
    }
    else
    {
      if (isset ($_GET['Page']) && ((int)$_GET['Page']) > 1)
        $page_title .= ' - Page ' . ((int)$_GET['Page']);
    }
```

```
    return $page_title;
  }
...
```

10. Open `presentation/product.php`, and add the highlighted code to the `init()` method of the `Product` class. This enables the continue shopping functionality when we reach a product page from the search results page.

```
    elseif (isset ($continue_shopping['DepartmentId']))
      $this->mLinkToContinueShopping =
        Link::ToDepartment((int)$continue_shopping['DepartmentId'], $page);
    elseif (isset ($continue_shopping['SearchResults']))
      $this->mLinkToContinueShopping =
        Link::ToSearchResults(
          trim(str_replace('-', ' ', $continue_shopping['SearchString'])),
          $continue_shopping['AllWords'], $page);
    else
      $this->mLinkToContinueShopping = Link::ToIndex($page);
  }
```

11. Add the following style to `styles/tshirtshop.css` file:

```
.words {
color: #ff0000;
}
```

12. Load your project in your favorite browser, make an all-words search for "christmas", browse to the second page of results, and expect to see a page such as that in Figure 8-7.

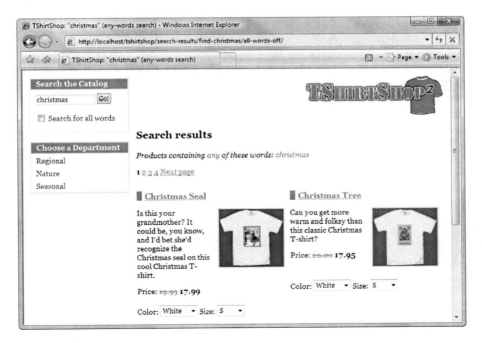

Figure 8-7. *Sample TShirtShop search results page*

How It Works: The Searchable Product Catalog

Congratulations, you have a searchable product catalog! There was quite a bit to write, but the code wasn't *that* complicated, was it?

The list of products is displayed by the products_list template you built in Chapter 5, but now it recognizes if the Search element is in the query string, in which case it uses the Search() method of the business tier to get the list of products for the visitor.

The Search() method of the business tier returns an array that contains, apart from the list of returned products, the list of words that were used for searching and the list of words that were ignored (words shorter than a predefined number of characters). These details are shown to the visitor.

The novelty in this exercise is in the .htaccess rules. As you know, when the visitor submits a new search query, the request is redirected to a keyword-rich URL that represents the results page that your visitors can bookmark. The rewrite rules read the keyword-rich URLs to their dynamic counterparts:

```
# Redirect search results
RewriteRule ^search-results/find-(.*)/all-words-(on|off)/page-([0-9]+)/?$
index.php?SearchResults&SearchString=$1&AllWords=$2&Page=$3 [L]
RewriteRule ^search-results/find-?(.*)/all-words-(on|off)/?$
index.php?SearchResults&SearchString=$1&AllWords=$2&Page=1 [L]
```

The first of these rules matches paged search results URLs, and the second rule matches nonpaged search results URLs.

Summary

In this chapter, you implemented the search functionality of TShirtShop by using the full-text searching functionality of MySQL. The search mechanism integrated very well with the current web site structure and the paging functionality built in Chapter 4. The most interesting new detail you learned in this chapter was about performing full-text searches with MySQL. This was also the first time the business tier had some functionality of its own, instead of simply passing data back and forth between the data tier and the presentation tier.

In Chapter 9, you'll learn how to sell your products using PayPal.

■■■

Receiving Payments Using PayPal

Let's make some money! Your e-commerce web site needs a way to receive payments from customers. The preferred solution for established companies is to open a merchant account, but many small businesses choose to start with a solution that's simpler to implement, where they don't have to process credit card or payment information themselves.

A number of companies and web sites can help individuals or small businesses that don't have the resources to process credit cards and wire transactions. These companies can be used to mediate the payment between online businesses and their customers. Many of these payment-processing companies are relatively new, and handling of any individual's financial details is very sensitive. Additionally, a quick search on the Internet will produce reports from both satisfied and unsatisfied customers for almost all of these companies. For these reasons, we are not recommending any specific third-party company.

Instead, this chapter lists some of the companies currently providing these services, and then demonstrates some of the functionality they provide using PayPal as an example. You'll learn how to integrate PayPal with TShirtShop in the first two phases of development. In this chapter, you will

- Learn how to create a new PayPal Website Payments Standard account.

- Learn how to integrate PayPal in Phase I of development, where you'll need a shopping cart and custom checkout mechanism.

- Learn how to integrate PayPal in Phase II of development, where you'll have your own shopping cart, so you'll guide the visitor directly to a payment page.

■Note This chapter is not a PayPal manual but a quick guide to using PayPal. For detailed information about the services provided, visit PayPal (http://www.paypal.com) or the Internet payment service provider you decide to use.

Considering Internet Payment Service Providers

Take a look at this list of Internet payment service provider web sites. This is a diverse group, each having its own advantages. Some of the providers transfer money person to person, where payments need to be verified manually; others offer sophisticated integration with your web site. Some work anywhere on the globe, whereas others work only for a single country.

The following list is not complete. You can find many other such companies by doing a Google search for "Internet payment service providers".

- *2Checkout*: http://www.2checkout.com

- *AnyPay*: http://www.anypay.com

- *CCNow*: http://www.ccnow.com

- *Electronic Transfer*: http://www.electronictransfer.com

- *Moneybookers*: http://www.moneybookers.com

- *MultiCards*: http://www.multicards.com

- *Pay By Web*: http://www.paybyweb.com

- *Paymate*: https://www.paymate.com.au

- *PayPal*: http://www.paypal.com

- *PaySystems*: http://www.paysystems.com

- *ProPay*: http://www.propay.com

- *QuickPayPro*: http://www.quickpaypro.com

- *WorldPay*: http://www.worldpay.com

Apart from being popular, PayPal offers services that fit very well into our web site for the first two phases of development. PayPal is available in a number of countries—the most up-to-date list can be found at http://www.paypal.com.

For the first phase of development (the current phase)—where you have only a searchable product catalog—with only a few lines of HTML code, PayPal enables you to add a shopping cart with checkout functionality. For the second phase of development, in which you will implement your own shopping cart, PayPal has a feature called Single Item Purchases that can be used to send the visitor directly to a payment page without the intermediate shopping cart. You'll use this feature of PayPal in Chapter 14.

For a summary of the features provided by PayPal, point your browser to http://www.paypal.com, and click the Merchant Services link. That page contains a few other useful links that will show you the main features available from PayPal.

Getting Started with PayPal

Probably the best description of this service is the one found on its web site: "PayPal is an account-based system that lets anyone with an e-mail address securely send and receive online payments using their credit card or bank account."

Instead of paying the merchant directly, the visitor pays PayPal using a credit card or bank account. The merchant company then uses its PayPal account to get the money received from the customers. At the time of this writing, no cost is involved in creating a new PayPal account, and the service is free for the buyer. The fees involved when receiving money are shown at `http://www.paypal.com/cgi-bin/webscr?cmd=_display-fees-outside`.

PAYPAL LINKS AND RESOURCES

Check out these resources when you need more information than this short chapter provides:

- *The Website Payments Standard Integration Guide* contains information previously contained in separate manuals, such as the *Shopping Cart* manual and *the Instant Payments Notification* manual. Get it at `https://www.paypal.com/en_US/pdf/PP_WebsitePaymentsStandard_IntegrationGuide.pdf`.

- *The PayPal Developer Network* is the official resource for PayPal developers, which you can access at `https://www.paypal.com/pdn`.

- *PayPalDev*, according to the site, is an independent forum for PayPal developers. Access it at `http://www.paypaldev.org/`. You'll also find numerous links to various PayPal resources.

In the following exercise, you'll create a new PayPal account and integrate it with TShirtShop (the steps to create a PayPal account are also described in more detail in the PayPal manuals mentioned earlier).

Exercise: Creating the PayPal Account

1. Browse to `http://www.paypal.com` using your favorite web browser.

2. Click the Sign Up link.

3. PayPal supports three account types: Personal, Premier, and Business. To receive credit card payments, you need to open a Premier or Business account. Choose your country from the combo box, and click Continue.

4. Provide all of the requested information, and you will receive an e-mail asking you to revisit the PayPal site to confirm the details you have entered.

How It Works: The PayPal Account

After the PayPal account is set up, the e-mail address you provided will be your PayPal ID.

A lot of functionality is available within the PayPal service—because the site is easy to use and many of the functions are self-explanatory, we won't describe everything here. Remember that sites like PayPal are there for your business, so they're more than happy to assist with any of your queries.

Now, let's see how you can actually use the new account for the web site.

Integrating the PayPal Shopping Cart and Checkout

The first phase is to integrate the shopping cart and checkout functionality from PayPal. In the second phase of development, after you create your own shopping cart, you'll need to rely only on PayPal's checkout mechanism.

To accept payments, you need to add two important elements to the user interface part of the site: Add to Cart buttons for each product and a View Cart button somewhere on the page. PayPal makes adding these buttons a piece of cake.

The functionality of these buttons is performed by secure links to the PayPal web site, which can be implemented as either forms or specially crafted URLs. Let's take a look at both methods. The following is an example of using forms that represent the Add to Cart button for a product named Mistletoe T-Shirt that costs $17.99:

```
<form target="paypal" action="https://www.paypal.com/cgi-bin/webscr"
 method="post">
  <input type="hidden" name="cmd" value="_cart" />
  <input type="hidden" name="business" value="youremail@example.com" />
  <input type="hidden" name="item_name" value="Mistletoe T-Shirt" />
  <input type="hidden" name="on0" value="Size" />
  <select name="os0">
    <option value="S">S</option>
    <option value="M">M</option>
    <option value="L">L</option>
    <option value="XL">XL</option>
    <option value="XXL">XXL</option>
  </select>
  <input type="hidden" name="on1" value="Color" />
  <select name="os1">
    <option value=" White">White</option>
    <option value=" Black">Black</option>
    <option value="Red">Red</option>
    <option value="Orange">Orange</option>
    <option value="Yellow">Yellow</option>
    <option value="Green">Green</option>
    <option value="Blue">Blue</option>
    <option value="Indigo">Indigo</option>
    <option value="Purple">Purple</option>
  </select>
  <input type="hidden" name="amount" value="17.99" />
  <input type="hidden" name="currency_code" value="USD" />
  <input type="hidden" name="add" value="1" />
  <input type="hidden" name="shopping_url"
   value="http://www.example.com/mistletoe-t-shirt-p84/" />
  <input type="hidden" name="return" value="http://www.example.com" />
  <input type="hidden" name="cancel_return" value="http://www.example.com" />
  <input type="submit" name="submit" value="Add to Cart" />
</form>
```

If you load this form in a web browser, you get a form like the one shown in Figure 9-1.

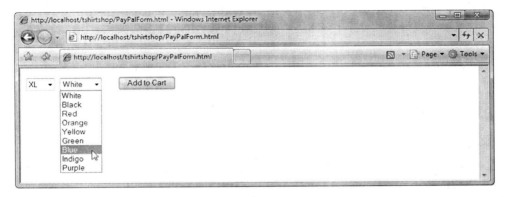

Figure 9-1. *The PayPal Add to Cart form and button*

Tip Although we won't use them for our site, it's good to know that PayPal provides button generators based on certain data you provide (like product name and product price), giving you an HTML code block similar to the one shown previously.

Yes, it's just that simple to manufacture an Add to Cart link! The form fields except on0, os0, on1, and os1, have predefined meaning, and their names are self-explanatory. The on0 and os0, and on1 and os1 elements can be used to define custom product attributes; in our case, we used them to define Size and Color. Note that PayPal accepts a maximum of two attributes, so you can't add more of them.

The most important parameter is business, which must be the e-mail address you used when you registered the PayPal account (the e-mail address that will receive the money). Consult PayPal's *Website Payments Standard Integration Guide* for more details. We will discuss how to overcome this attribute limit later.

Alternatively, you can create Add to Cart URLs without using forms. This is particularly helpful when your Add to Cart button is already included in a form, since HTML doesn't support nested forms. When using Add to Cart URLs instead of forms, you need to specify the attribute values as query string parameters. Here's an example:

```
https://www.paypal.com/cgi-bin/webscr?cmd=_cart&business=yourmail@example.com&
item_name=Mistletoe+T-Shirt&on0=Size&os0=S&on1=Color&os1=White&amount=17.99&
currency_code=USD&add=1&cancel_return=http://www.example.com&
shopping_url=http://www.example.com/mistletoe-t-shirt-p84/&
return=http://www.example.com
```

■Note When using the URL query string to pass information to the server, you need to carefully encode the parameter values. For example, to pass the "Mistletoe T-Shirt" string as a URL parameter, you need to encode the space, which is not an allowed URL character. The space can be encoded as either %20 or +. PHP conveniently provides the urlencode() function, which we can use to encode strings for URL inclusion.

Loading this URL in your web browser will take you to a PayPal shopping cart page like the one shown in Figure 9-2.

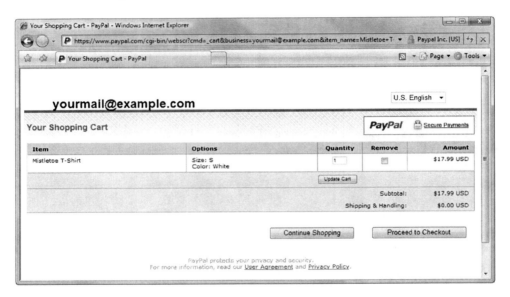

Figure 9-2. *The PayPal shopping cart*

■Caution When receiving a payment, you need to carefully check that the received amount correctly reflects the sum of the ordered products. Since the entire shopping cart data is passed via either forms or URLs, it's very easy for anyone to add a fake product to the shopping cart or an existing product with a modified price. This can be done simply by fabricating one of those PayPal Add to Cart links and navigating to it. You can read a detailed article about this problem at http://www.alphabetware.com/pptamper.asp.

When using shopping cart URLs like PayPal's, you need to control the length of the product names and attributes, although it's unlikely that you could end up with URLs that are so long that they can't be handled by web browsers. The page at http://www.boutell.com/newfaq/misc/urllength.html shows an interesting analysis of maximum URL lengths accepted by the most popular web browsers.

For TShirtShop, we'll be using forms to create the View Cart button and URLs to create the Add to Cart buttons. You can see these buttons in Figure 9-3.

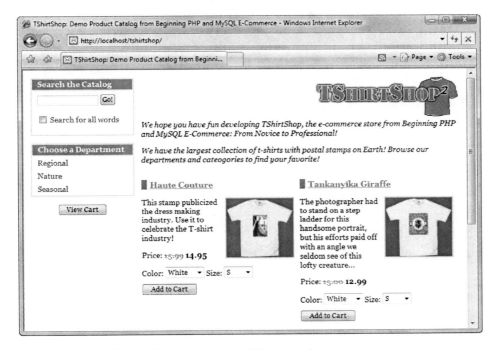

Figure 9-3. *TShirtShop with Add to Cart and View Cart buttons*

To overcome PayPal's limitation of two attributes per product, we include all product attribute values into a single PayPal attribute. The value of this PayPal attribute would be a text containing the selected product's attributes, so your visitor will be shown this data in the PayPal shopping cart. Look ahead at Figure 9-4 to see this in action.

To implement this feature, since we can't use the PayPal form for adding products, the system works like this:

1. Our Add to Cart buttons submit the form to our own application, to a link such as `http://localhost/tshirtshop/add-product-65/`.

2. The URL is rewritten by `mod_rewrite` to a URL such as `index.php?AddProduct=65`.

3. `index.php` creates the PayPal attribute whose value sums up the attributes selected by the visitor for the product. The new attribute value will look like `Size/Color: S/White`, but it will be automatically generated to accommodate any number of attributes.

4. A PayPal Add to Cart URL is created using the newly created attribute.

5. Finally, the visitor is redirected, via the 302 status code, to the new URL.

To sum these rules up: when clicking an Add to Cart button, the visitor's web browser will receive a 302 redirect to a PayPal Add to Cart URL. Next, it will load that URL, which will take the visitor to the PayPal shopping cart, as shown in Figure 9-4.

Figure 9-4. *A PayPal shopping cart containing TShirtShop products*

Now that you have a basic understanding of the steps involved, let's implement this code through an exercise.

Exercise: Integrating the PayPal Shopping Cart and Custom Checkout

1. Open `config.php` from the `include` folder, and add the following constants declarations:

```
// PayPal configuration
define('PAYPAL_URL', 'https://www.paypal.com/cgi-bin/webscr');
define('PAYPAL_EMAIL', 'youremail@example.com');
define('PAYPAL_CURRENCY_CODE', 'USD');
define('PAYPAL_RETURN_URL', 'http://www.example.com');
define('PAYPAL_CANCEL_RETURN_URL', 'http://www.example.com');
```

■**Caution** Make sure you replace youremail@example.com with the e-mail address you submitted when you created your PayPal account! You need to use the correct e-mail address if you want the money to get into your account! Also, replace both instances of www.example.com with the address of your e-commerce store.

2. Open `presentation/products_list.php`, and add the highlighted code to the end of `init()` method as shown:

```
// Build links for product details pages
for ($i = 0; $i < count($this->mProducts); $i++)
{
  $this->mProducts[$i]['link_to_product'] =
    Link::ToProduct($this->mProducts[$i]['product_id']);

  if ($this->mProducts[$i]['thumbnail'])
    $this->mProducts[$i]['thumbnail'] =
      Link::Build('product_images/' . $this->mProducts[$i]['thumbnail']);

  // Create the Add to Cart link
  $this->mProducts[$i]['link_to_add_product'] =
    Link::ToAddProduct($this->mProducts[$i]['product_id']);

  $this->mProducts[$i]['attributes'] =
    Catalog::GetProductAttributes($this->mProducts[$i]['product_id']);
  }
}
```

3. Open `products_list.tpl` from the `presentation/templates` folder, and modify it as shown:

```
<p class="section">
  Price:
  {if $obj->mProducts[k].discounted_price != 0}
    <span class="old-price">{$obj->mProducts[k].price}</span>
    <span class="price">{$obj->mProducts[k].discounted_price}</span>
  {else}
    <span class="price">{$obj->mProducts[k].price}</span>
  {/if}
</p>

{* The Add to Cart form *}
<form class="add-product-form" target="_self" method="post"
 action="{$obj->mProducts[k].link_to_add_product}">

{* Generate the list of attribute values *}
<p class="attributes">

{* Parse the list of attributes and attribute values *}
{section name=l loop=$obj->mProducts[k].attributes}

  {* Generate a new select tag? *}
  {if $smarty.section.l.first ||
      $obj->mProducts[k].attributes[l].attribute_name !==
      $obj->mProducts[k].attributes[l.index_prev].attribute_name}
    {$obj->mProducts[k].attributes[l].attribute_name}:
```

```
              <select name="attr_{$obj->mProducts[k].attributes[l].attribute_name}">
              {/if}

                {* Generate a new option tag *}
                <option value="{$obj->mProducts[k].attributes[l].attribute_value}">
                  {$obj->mProducts[k].attributes[l].attribute_value}
                </option>

              {* Close the select tag? *}
              {if $smarty.section.l.last ||
                  $obj->mProducts[k].attributes[l].attribute_name !==
                  $obj->mProducts[k].attributes[l.index_next].attribute_name}
              </select>
              {/if}

            {/section}
            </p>

            {* Add the submit button and close the form *}
            <p>
              <input type="submit" name="submit" value="Add to Cart" />
            </p>
            </form>

        </td>
      {if $smarty.section.k.index % 2 != 0 && !$smarty.section.k.first ||
          $smarty.section.k.last}
      </tr>
      {/if}
```

4. In presentation/link.php, modify the CheckRequest() method right at the beginning as shown:

```
// Redirects to proper URL if not already there
public static function CheckRequest()
{
  $proper_url = '';

  if (isset ($_GET['Search']) || isset($_GET['SearchResults']) ||
      isset ($_GET['AddProduct']))
  {
    return ;
  }
```

5. Also, in the link.php file, add the following method at the end of the Link class:

```
// Create an Add to Cart link
public static function ToAddProduct($productId)
{
  return self::Build('index.php?AddProduct=' . $productId);
}
```

6. Now, open `product.php` from the `presentation` folder, and add the highlighted code to the `init()` method of the Product class:

```
$this->mProduct['attributes'] =
  Catalog::GetProductAttributes($this->mProduct['product_id']);

$this->mLocations = Catalog::GetProductLocations($this->_mProductId);

// Create the Add to Cart link
$this->mProduct['link_to_add_product'] =
  Link::ToAddProduct($this->_mProductId);

// Build links for product departments and categories pages
for ($i = 0; $i < count($this->mLocations); $i++)
{
  $this->mLocations[$i]['link_to_department'] =
    Link::ToDepartment($this->mLocations[$i]['department_id']);
```

7. In the `product.tpl` from the `presentation/templates` folder, add the highlighted code that adds the Add to Cart button on the product page:

```
<p class="section">
  Price:
  {if $obj->mProduct.discounted_price != 0}
    <span class="old-price">{$obj->mProduct.price}</span>
    <span class="price">{$obj->mProduct.discounted_price}</span>
  {else}
    <span class="price">{$obj->mProduct.price}</span>
  {/if}
</p>

{* The Add to Cart form *}
<form class="add-product-form" target="_self" method="post"
 action="{$obj->mProduct.link_to_add_product}">

{* Generate the list of attribute values *}
<p class="attributes">

{* Parse the list of attributes and attribute values *}
{section name=k loop=$obj->mProduct.attributes}

  {* Generate a new select tag? *}
  {if $smarty.section.k.first ||
      $obj->mProduct.attributes[k].attribute_name !==
      $obj->mProduct.attributes[k.index_prev].attribute_name}
    {$obj->mProduct.attributes[k].attribute_name}:
  <select name="attr_{$obj->mProduct.attributes[k].attribute_name}">
  {/if}
```

```
{* Generate a new option tag *}
<option value="{$obj->mProduct.attributes[k].attribute_value}">
  {$obj->mProduct.attributes[k].attribute_value}
</option>

{* Close the select tag? *}
{if $smarty.section.k.last ||
    $obj->mProduct.attributes[k].attribute_name !==
    $obj->mProduct.attributes[k.index_next].attribute_name}
</select>
{/if}

{/section}
</p>

{* Add the submit button and close the form *}
<p>
  <input type="submit" name="submit" value="Add to Cart" />
</p>
</form>

{if $obj->mLinkToContinueShopping}
<a href="{$obj->mLinkToContinueShopping}">Continue Shopping</a>
{/if}
```

8. In the store_front.php from the presentation folder, add the highlighted code to the StoreFront class as shown:

```
// Page title
public $mPageTitle;
// PayPal continue shopping link
public $mPayPalContinueShoppingLink;

// Class constructor
public function __construct()
{
  $this->mLinkToIndex = Link::ToIndex();
}

public function init()
{
  // Create "Continue Shopping" link for the PayPal shopping cart
  if (!isset ($_GET['AddProduct']))
  {
    /* Store the current request needed for the paypal
       continue shopping functionality */
    $_SESSION['paypal_continue_shopping'] =
      Link::Build(str_replace(VIRTUAL_LOCATION, '',
                              $_SERVER['REQUEST_URI']));
```

```
    $this->mPayPalContinueShoppingLink =
      $_SESSION['paypal_continue_shopping'];
}
// If Add to Cart was clicked, prepare PayPal variables
else
{
  // Clean output buffer
  ob_clean();

  $product_id = 0;

  // Get the product ID to be added to cart
  if (isset ($_GET['AddProduct']))
    $product_id = (int)$_GET['AddProduct'];
  else
    trigger_error('AddProduct not set');

  $selected_attribute_groups = array ();
  $selected_attribute_values = array ();

  // Get selected product attributes if any
  foreach ($_POST as $key => $value)
  {
    // If there are fields starting with "attr_" in the POST array
    if (substr($key, 0, 5) == 'attr_')
    {
      // Get the selected attribute name and value
      $selected_attribute_groups[] = substr($key, strlen('attr_'));
      $selected_attribute_values[] = $_POST[$key];
    }
  }

  // Get product info
  $product = Catalog::GetProductDetails($product_id);

  // Build the PayPal url to add the product to cart
  $paypal_url = PAYPAL_URL . '?cmd=_cart&business=' . PAYPAL_EMAIL .
                '&item_name=' . rawurlencode($product['name']);

  if (count($selected_attribute_groups) > 0)
    $paypal_url .= '&on0=' . implode('/', $selected_attribute_groups) .
                   '&os0=' . implode('/', $selected_attribute_values);

  $paypal_url .=
    '&amount=' . ($product['discounted_price'] == 0 ?
                  $product['price'] : $product['discounted_price']) .
    '&currency_code=' . PAYPAL_CURRENCY_CODE . '&add=1' .
```

```
              '&shopping_url=' .
                rawurlencode($_SESSION['paypal_continue_shopping']) .
              '&return=' . rawurlencode(PAYPAL_RETURN_URL) .
              '&cancel_return=' . rawurlencode(PAYPAL_CANCEL_RETURN_URL);

          // Redirect to the PayPal cart page
          header('HTTP/1.1 302 Found');
          header('Location: ' . $paypal_url);

          // Clear the output buffer and stop execution
          flush();
          ob_flush();
          ob_end_clean();
          exit();
        }

        // Load department details if visiting a department
        if (isset ($_GET['DepartmentId']))
        {
```

9. Open store_front.tpl from the presentation/templates folder, and add the code for View Cart
   button as shown:

```
        <div class="yui-b">
          {include file="search_box.tpl"}
          {include file="departments_list.tpl"}
          {include file=$obj->mCategoriesCell}
          <div class="view-cart">
            <form target="_self" method="post"
             action="{$smarty.const.PAYPAL_URL}">
              <input type="hidden" name="cmd" value="_cart" />
              <input type="hidden" name="business"
               value="{$smarty.const.PAYPAL_EMAIL}" />
              <input type="hidden" name="display" value="1" />
              <input type="hidden" name="shopping_url"
               value="{$obj->mPayPalContinueShoppingLink}" />
              <input type="hidden" name="return"
               value="{$smarty.const.PAYPAL_RETURN_URL}" />
              <input type="hidden" name="cancel_return"
               value="{$smarty.const.PAYPAL_CANCEL_RETURN_URL}" />
              <input type="submit" name="view_cart" value="View Cart" />
            </form>
          </div>
        </div>
```

10. Add the following styles to the `styles/tshirtshop.css` file:

```css
div.yui-b div form.add-product-form
{
  margin: 0;
  padding: 0;
}

.add-product-form p
{
  margin: 0;
  padding: 0 0 10px 0;
}

.view-cart
{
  padding: 10px;
  text-align: center;
}
```

11. Load TShirtShop in a browser, and click one of the Add to Cart buttons, or click the View Cart button. You should get the PayPal shopping cart, which looks like Figure 9-4. Experiment with the PayPal shopping cart to see that it works as advertised.

How It Works: PayPal Integration

You wrote quite a bit of code, but now all your visitors are potential customers! They can use the PayPal shopping cart to purchase your products!

To implement this feature, you first created Add to Cart buttons in the product lists. You modified `presentation/products_list.php` to add the Add to Cart URLs to each product:

```php
$this->mProducts[$i]['link_to_add_product'] =
    Link::ToAddProduct($this->mProducts[$i]['product_id']);
```

Then you modified the template file by adding the buttons:

```html
<form class="add-product-form" target="_self" method="post"
 action="{$obj->mProducts[k].link_to_add_product}">
...
<p>
  <input type="submit" name="submit" value="Add to Cart" />
</p>
</form>
```

You implemented similar changes to `product.php` and `product.tpl`, to create the Add to Cart buttons of the product details pages. To see what happens when one of these buttons is clicked, we used the Firefox `LiveHTTPHeaders` plug-in. We highlighted, in Figure 9-5, the URL loaded when the button was clicked and the URL the request was 302 redirected to.

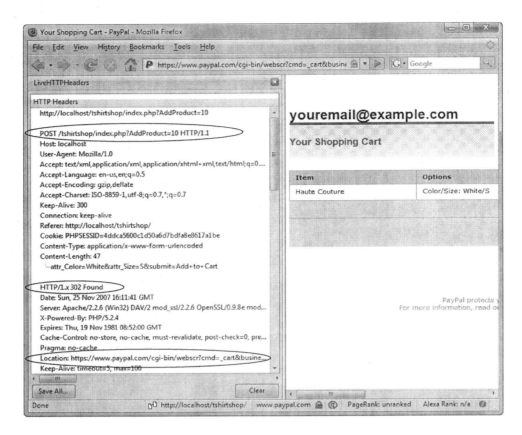

Figure 9-5. *Loading the PayPal shopping cart*

After a customer makes a payment on the web site, an e-mail notification is sent to the e-mail address registered on PayPal and also to the customer. Your PayPal account will reflect the payment, and you can view the transaction information in your account history or as a part of the history transaction log.

After PayPal confirms the payment, you can ship the products to your customer. If you decide to use PayPal for your own web site, make sure you learn about all of its features. For example, you can teach PayPal to automatically calculate shipping costs and tax for each order.

Using the PayPal Single Item Purchases Feature

Single Item Purchases is a PayPal feature that allows you to send the visitor directly to a payment page instead of the PayPal shopping cart. The PayPal shopping cart will become useless in Chapter 12, where you'll create your own shopping cart.

In Chapter 14, you'll implement the Place Order button in the shopping cart, which saves the order into the database and forwards to a PayPal payment page. To call the PayPal payment page (bypassing the PayPal shopping cart), you redirect to a link like the following:

```
https://www.paypal.com/cgi-bin/webscr?cmd=_xclick&business=youremail@example.com&
item_name=Order#123&item_number=123&amount=123&currency_code=USD&
return=www.example.com&cancel_return=www.example.com
```

Review the PayPal *Website Payments Standard Integration Guide* for more details about the service.

Tip You will create your own complete order-processing system in the third phase of development (starting with Chapter 17), where you'll process credit card transactions.

When you implement the PayPal Single Item Purchases in Chapter 14, you'll use code that looks like the following code snippet to create the URL of the PayPal Single Item Purchases page:

```php
// Calculate the total amount for the shopping cart
$this->mTotalAmount = ShoppingCart::GetTotalAmount();

// If the Place Order button was clicked ...
if(isset ($_POST['place_order']))
{
  // Create the order and get the order ID
  $order_id = ShoppingCart::CreateOrder();

  // This will contain the PayPal link
  $redirect =
    PAYPAL_URL . '&item_name=TShirtShop Order ' . urlencode('#') . $order_id .
    '&item_number=' . $order_id .
    '&amount=' . $this->mTotalAmount .
    '&currency_code=' . PAYPAL_CURRENCY_CODE .
    '&return=' . PAYPAL_RETURN_URL .
    '&cancel_return=' . PAYPAL_CANCEL_RETURN_URL;

  // Redirection to the payment page
  header('Location: ' . $redirect);

  exit();
}
```

You'll learn how to work with this feature in Chapter 14.

Summary

In this chapter, you saw how to integrate PayPal into an e-commerce site—a simple payment solution that many small businesses choose so they don't have to process credit card or payment information themselves.

First, we listed some of the alternatives to PayPal, before guiding you through the creation of a new PayPal account. We then covered how to integrate PayPal in Phases I and II of development, first discussing a shopping cart, a custom checkout mechanism.

In the next chapter, we will move on to look at a catalog administration page for TShirtShop.

CHAPTER 10

■■■

Catalog Administration: Departments and Categories

In the previous chapters, you worked with catalog information that already existed in the database. You have probably inserted some records yourself, or maybe you downloaded the department, category, and product information from this book's accompanying source code. Obviously, both ways are unacceptable for a real web site, so you need to write some code to allow easy management of your data. That said, the final detail to take care of before launching a web site is to create its administrative interface. Although visitors will never see this part, it's key to delivering a quality web site to your client.

In this chapter and the following one, you implement a catalog administration page. With this feature, you complete the first stage of your web site's development! Because this page can be implemented in many ways, a serious discussion with the client is required to get the specific list of required features.

In our case, we'll implement a control panel that allows managing the site's departments, categories, products, and the product attributes. In this chapter, we deal with administering departments and categories, leaving the rest for Chapter 11. More specifically, in this chapter we will create features that allow for

- Adding and removing departments

- Modifying existing departments' information (name and description)

- Viewing the list of categories that belong to a department

- Adding and removing categories

- Editing existing categories' information (name and description)

To secure the sensitive pages of your site, such as the administrative section, you'll also do the following:

- Implement a login form where the administrator needs to supply a username and password.

- Learn how to secure the login form and the administrative pages using SSL.

Previewing the Catalog Administration Page

Although the long list of objectives might look intimidating at first, they will be easy to implement. We have already covered most of the theory in the previous chapters, but you'll still learn quite a bit in this chapter.

The first step toward creating the catalog administration page is to create a login mechanism, which will be implemented as the simple login page that you can see in Figure 10-1.

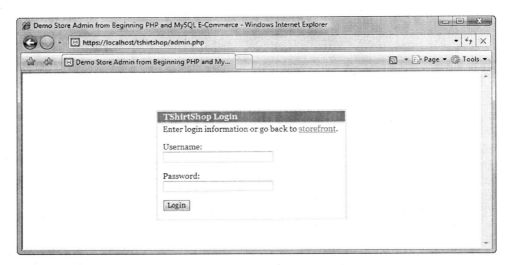

Figure 10-1. *The TShirtShop login page*

Next, you build the management part of the site (commonly referred to as the *control panel*) by creating its main page (admin.php), its associated template (store_admin.tpl), a main menu template (admin_menu.tpl) used to navigate through different administrative sections that we'll extend in the next chapters, a componentized template to manage the authentication (admin_login), and two componentized templates for catalog administration (admin_departments and admin_categories).

After logging in, the administrator is presented with the list of departments (generated by the admin_departments Smarty template, which is loaded from the main administration page, admin.php), as shown in Figure 10-2. Here, the administrator can

- Edit the department's name or description by clicking the Edit button.

- View the categories that belong to a department by clicking the Edit Categories button.

- Completely remove a department from the database by clicking the Delete button (this works only if the department has no related categories).

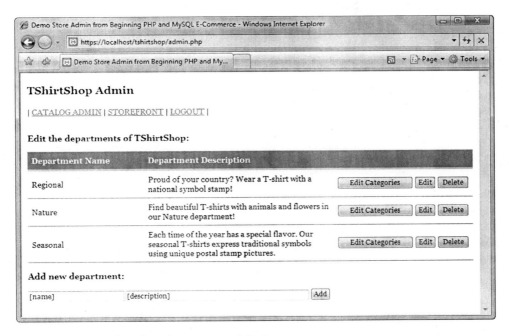

Figure 10-2. *The TShirtShop departments Admin page*

When clicking the Edit button, the corresponding row from the table enters edit mode, and its fields become editable, as shown in Figure 10-3. Also, as you can see, instead of the Edit button, you get Update and Cancel buttons. Clicking Update submits the changes to the database, whereas clicking Cancel simply quits edit mode and reverts the data table to its original state.

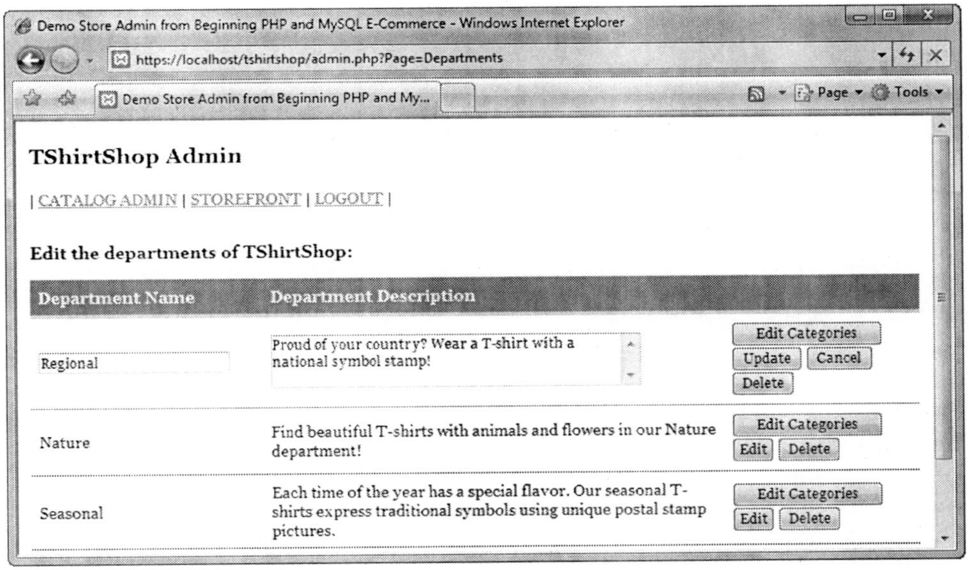

Figure 10-3. *Editing department information*

The administrator can add new departments by entering the new department's name and description in the text boxes below the table and clicking the Add button.

When the administrator clicks the Edit Categories button, the admin.php page is reloaded with an additional parameter in the query string: DepartmentId. This parameter tells admin.php to load the admin_categories Smarty template, which lets the administrator edit the categories that belong to the selected department (see Figure 10-4).

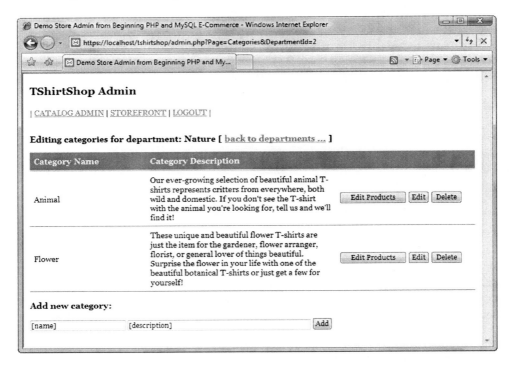

Figure 10-4. *The TShirtShop categories Admin page*

This page works similar to the one for editing departments. You also get a link ("back to departments") that takes you back to the department's administration page.

The navigation logic among the department, category, and product administration pages is done using query string parameters. As you can see in Figure 10-4, when a department is selected, its ID is appended to the query string. You also used this technique when creating the index.php page. There, you decided which componentized template to load (at runtime) by analyzing the query string parameters.

The catalog administration part of the site consists of admin.php and a number of other PHP files and Smarty templates. You'll build these components one at a time. For each component, you'll first implement the presentation layer, then write the business tier code, and finally write the data tier methods.

You'll extend the administrative section of the web site in the following chapters. In Chapter 11, you'll add product administration features, and in later chapters, you'll implement orders and shopping cart administration features, and you'll handle your customers' sensitive data such as credit card data, phone numbers, and so on.

Setting Up the Catalog Administration Page

Before building any administrative pages, we need to put in place a security mechanism for restricting the access to these pages. Only authorized personnel should be able to modify the product catalog!

Security is obviously a large topic, and its complexity depends a lot on the value of the data you're protecting. While we don't have the resources to create such a secure environment as that implemented by banks, for example, when creating an online store, we still have a great responsibility to make sure our data and our customers' data is safe.

Our security implementation deals with these important concepts:

- *Authentication*: This is the process in which users are uniquely identified. The typical way to identify users, which we'll also implement in TShirtShop, is to ask for a username and a password.

- *Authorization*: This concept refers to the process of identifying the resources an authenticated user can access and restricting his or her access accordingly. For example, you can have administrators who can only edit product names and descriptions and administrators who can also view customers' personal data. The administrators of our little shop will have access to all the restricted areas, but as the site gets larger, you may want to delegate administrative tasks to more employees for both management and security reasons.

- *Secure communication channel*: Of course, all of our authentication and authorization efforts are in vain if it's easy for a hacker to implement a *man-in-the-middle* attack, which refers to the scenario where an individual listens to the traffic on a network to intercept sensitive data. Such an attack could be made when an administrator logs in while the attacker listens to the network traffic to intercept the administrator's username and password. To guard against this potential problem, we use the HTTPS protocol, which encrypts the transmitted data and ensures a degree of confidentiality of the transmission.

Using Secure Connections

HTTP isn't a secure protocol, and even if your site protects sensitive areas using passwords (or other forms of authentication), the transmitted data could be intercepted and stolen. To avoid this, you need to set up the application to work with Secure Socket Layer (SSL) connections using the Hypertext Transport Protocol, Secure (HTTPS) protocol.

To be able to accept incoming HTTPS connections, a web server must be configured with a *security certificate*. Security certificates are basically public-private key pairs similar to those used in asynchronous encryption algorithms. You can generate these yourself, but if you're not a trusted certification authority (such as VeriSign or Thawte), this method may be problematic.

Digitally signed SSL certificates that aren't issued by trusted certification authorities will cause browsers to doubt your security. When a user accesses secure pages whose certificate isn't issued by a trusted certification authority, the browser will show a warning message. This isn't disastrous when securing pages that are to be visited by your company personnel but would certainly affect customer confidence if such a warning message shows up, for example, when paying for an order.

If you configured your system using XAMPP, as described in Chapter 1, your Apache web server is already configured with a certificate. If you set up Apache on your own, we recommend you check out the article at http://www.sitepoint.com/article/securing-apache-2-server-ssl. For test purposes, you can also get an SSL-enabled Apache version from http://www.devside.net/web/server/free/download.

For a production scenario, you need to buy a trusted certificate through your web hosting company, or, if you manage the web server yourself, obtain a SSL certificate from a known and respected organization that specializes in web security, such as these:

- VeriSign (http://www.verisign.com/)

- Thawte (http://www.thawte.com/)

- InstantSSL (http://www.instantssl.com/)

Web browsers have built-in root certificates from organizations such as these and are able to authenticate the digital signature of SSL certificates supplied by them. This means that no warning message will appear, and an SSL-secured connection will be available with a minimum of fuss. For example, when loading such a URL in Opera, a little golden lock shows up next to the address bar. Clicking that symbol shows the name of the company that registered the SSL certificate (see Figure 10-5).

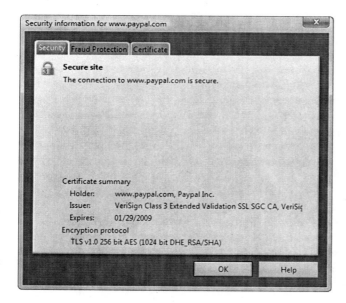

Figure 10-5. *Verifying a web site certificate in Opera*

The certificate that we have from XAMPP, issued by the local machine, is not in the list of trusted certificate providers (obviously). With this setup, web browsers will show a warning message, such as the one displayed by Safari shown in Figure 10-6.

Figure 10-6. *Safari doesn't like untrusted certificates.*

If you click Show Certificate, you can see that the certificate has been issued by localhost for Apache Friends. Apache Friends (http://www.apachefriends.org) is the maker of the XAMPP package.

The warning message you get when using an untrusted certificate varies from browser to browser. In Internet Explorer 7, the message is even more obvious (see Figure 10-7).

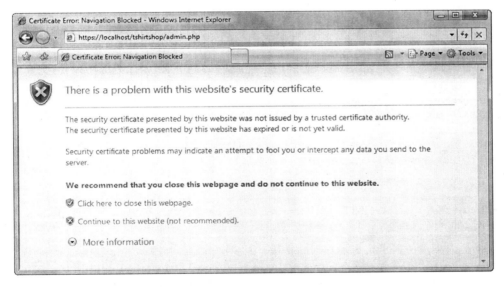

Figure 10-7. *Internet Explorer doesn't like untrusted certificates either.*

Configuring TShirtShop for SSL

If you decide to use SSL, you'll need to install an SSL certificate, as shown in the next few pages. When using SSL, it's also advisable to force any sensitive page to be accessed through SSL; that is, if anyone tries accessing a sensitive page (such as the login page) through http://, the request will be automatically redirected to an https:// URL.

However, if you want to postpone handling SSL and focus on building the administration pages for the moment, you can. To make the solution configurable, we'll add a constant named USE_SSL to the include/config.php file. If its value is yes, the secure areas will be forced to be loaded through HTTPS; otherwise, they'll work via HTTP.

Obtaining an SSL Certificate

Obtaining a certificate is a relatively painless experience. We're covering here the steps required to get a certificate from VeriSign, but the process is similar with the other providers as well. The full instructions are available on the VeriSign web site (http://www.verisign.com/). You can also get test certificates from VeriSign, which are free to use for a trial period. Here are the basic steps:

1. Sign up for a trial certificate on the VeriSign web site.

2. Generate a Certificate Signing Request (CSR) on your web server. This involves filling out various personal information, including the name of your web site, and so on. For this to work, you need to install an SSL module in your web server, as described in the tutorial at http://www.sitepoint.com/article/securing-apache-2-server-ssl.

3. Copy the contents of the generated CSR into the VeriSign request system.

4. Shortly afterward, you will receive a certificate from VeriSign to copy into your web server to install the certificate.

There is a little more to it than that, but as noted previously, detailed instructions are available on the VeriSign web site, and you shouldn't run into any difficulties.

Enforcing SSL Connections

After you've installed the certificate, you can access any web pages on your web server using an SSL connection, simply by replacing the http:// part of the URL used to access the page with https:// (assuming that your firewall is set up to allow an SSL connection, which by default uses port 443).

Obviously, you don't need SSL connections for all areas of the site. If a page can be accessed only via HTTPS, there are two details to keep in mind:

- Search engines don't index HTTPS locations.

- Delivering pages via HTTPS consume web server resources, which must encrypt the transferred data.

So you have two solid reasons for which you should enforce HTTPS connections only for the sensitive areas of your site. In this chapter, we'll enforce SSL for the administrator login page and for the administration pages of your site (in later chapters, when we'll handle payments ourselves, we'll also want to enforce SSL for the checkout, customer login, customer registration, and other administrative pages).

If you want to ensure that all requests to the administrative script (admin.php) are done through HTTPS, you'll simply need to add this code at the beginning of presentation/store_admin.php (we'll take care of it in an exercise, you don't need to type it now):

```
// Class constructor
public function __construct()
{
  $this->mSiteUrl = Link::Build('', 'https');
```

```
// Enforce page to be accessed through HTTPS if USE_SSL is on
if (USE_SSL == 'yes' && getenv('HTTPS') != 'on')
{
  header ('Location: https://' . getenv('SERVER_NAME') .
          getenv('REQUEST_URI'));

  exit();
}
}
```

Note that the secure connection isn't enforced if the USE_SSL constant defined in include/ config.php is set to no. Setting the constant to no may be useful when developing the web site if you don't have access to a real SSL-enabled server.

Authenticating Administrators

Because you only want certain users to access the catalog administration page, you need to implement an *authentication* and *authorization* mechanism that controls access to the sensitive pages in the site. Users who want to access the catalog administration page should first authenticate themselves. After you know who the user is, you decide whether the user is authorized to access the administration page. At this stage, we'll only have two kinds of users: anonymous users, who are regular visitors of your site, and administrators, who can access the administrative parts of the site (later in the book, you'll let visitors create accounts on your web site, but we're not there yet).

In TShirtShop, you'll use an authentication method called *HTTP authentication*, which allows you to control the login process through an HTML form. After the client is authenticated, we save a cookie on the client and use it to authenticate all subsequent requests. If the cookie is not found, the client is shown the HTML login form.

■**Note** We assume the administrator accesses the administrative pages from a client that has cookies enabled.

The username and password combinations can be physically stored in various ways. For example, in Chapter 16, you'll see how to store hashed (encrypted) customer passwords in the database.

■**Tip** *Hashing* is a common method for storing passwords. The hash value of a password is calculated by applying a mathematical function (hash algorithm) to it. When the user tries to authenticate, the password is hashed, and the resulting hash value is compared to the hash value of the original (correct) password. If the two values are identical, then the entered password is correct. The essential property about the hash algorithm is that, theoretically, you cannot obtain the original password from its hash value (the algorithm is one way). In practice, scientists have recently found vulnerabilities with the popular MD5, SHA-0, and SHA-1 hashing algorithms.

A more simple method is to store the username and password combination in your PHP file. This method isn't as flexible as using the database, but it's fast and easy to implement. When storing the username and password data, you can choose to store the password either in clear text or as hashed text with a hashing algorithm such as MD5 or SHA-1.

In the following exercise, you'll simply store the password in clear text, but it's good to know you have other options as well. You'll learn more about hashing in Chapter 16.

Exercise: Implementing the Skeleton of the Admin Page

1. Modify the `presentation/templates/first_page_contents.tpl` file to add a link to the administration page. Note that adding this link is optional, as it only helps with easier access to the page while developing the site. If you decide not to add the link, skip this step and the next one.

```
{* first_page_contents.tpl *}
{load_presentation_object filename="first_page_contents" assign="obj"}
<p class="description">
  We hope you have fun developing TShirtShop, the e-commerce store from
  Beginning PHP and MySQL E-Commerce: From Novice to Professional!
</p>
<p class="description">
  We have the largest collection of t-shirts with postal stamps on Earth!
  Browse our departments and categories to find your favorite!
</p>
<p>Access the <a href="{$obj->mLinkToAdmin}">admin page</a>.</p>
{include file="products_list.tpl"}
```

2. Create a new file named `first_page_contents.php` in the `presentation` folder, and add the following code in it. This is necessary for adding the link on the main page to the administration page.

```php
<?php
class FirstPageContents
{
  public $mLinkToAdmin;

  public function __construct()
  {
    $this->mLinkToAdmin = Link::ToAdmin();
  }
}
?>
```

3. Create a new file named `admin.php` in your site's root folder (`tshirtshop`), and write the following code in it. You'll notice that `admin.php` is quite similar to `index.php`, except that in `admin.php` we don't check the incoming link using `Link::CheckRequest()` and that we load a different template file.

```php
<?php
// Activate session
session_start();
```

```php
// Start output buffer
ob_start();

// Include utility files
require_once 'include/config.php';
require_once BUSINESS_DIR . 'error_handler.php';

// Set the error handler
ErrorHandler::SetHandler();

// Load the application page template
require_once PRESENTATION_DIR . 'application.php';
require_once PRESENTATION_DIR . 'link.php';

// Load the database handler
require_once BUSINESS_DIR . 'database_handler.php';

// Load Business Tier
require_once BUSINESS_DIR . 'catalog.php';

// Load Smarty template file
$application = new Application();

// Display the page
$application->display('store_admin.tpl');

// Close database connection
DatabaseHandler::Close();

// Output content from the buffer
flush();
ob_flush();
ob_end_clean();
?>
```

4. Create the `presentation/templates/store_admin.tpl` template file, which is loaded from the `admin.php` file we just created, and add the following code in it:

```smarty
{load_presentation_object filename="store_admin" assign="obj"}
<!DOCTYPE html PUBLIC "-//W3C//DTD XHTML 1.0 Transitional//EN"
  "http://www.w3.org/TR/xhtml1/DTD/xhtml1-transitional.dtd">
<html>
  <head>
    <title>Demo Store Admin from Beginning PHP and MySQL E-Commerce</title>
    <meta http-equiv="Content-Type" content="text/html; charset=UTF-8" />
    <link href="{$obj->mSiteUrl}styles/tshirtshop.css" type="text/css"
     rel="stylesheet" />
  </head>
```

```html
<body>
  <div id="doc" class="yui-t7">
    <div id="bd">
      <div class="yui-g">
        {include file=$obj->mMenuCell}
      </div>
      <div class="yui-g">
        {include file=$obj->mContentsCell}
      </div>
    </div>
  </div>
</body>
</html>
```

5. Create presentation/store_admin.php, and add the following code in it:

```php
<?php
class StoreAdmin
{
  public $mSiteUrl;
  // Define the template file for the page menu
  public $mMenuCell = 'blank.tpl';
  // Define the template file for the page contents
  public $mContentsCell = 'blank.tpl';

  // Class constructor
  public function __construct()
  {
    $this->mSiteUrl = Link::Build('', 'https');

    // Enforce page to be accessed through HTTPS if USE_SSL is on
    if (USE_SSL == 'yes' && getenv('HTTPS') != 'on')
    {
      header ('Location: https://' . getenv('SERVER_NAME') .
              getenv('REQUEST_URI'));

      exit();
    }
  }

  public function init()
  {
    // If admin is not logged in, load the admin_login template
    if (!(isset ($_SESSION['admin_logged'])) ||
        $_SESSION['admin_logged'] != true)
      $this->mContentsCell = 'admin_login.tpl';
    else
    {
```

```
      // If admin is logged in, load the admin menu page
      $this->mMenuCell = 'admin_menu.tpl';

      // If logging out ...
      if (isset ($_GET['Page']) && ($_GET['Page'] == 'Logout'))
      {
        unset($_SESSION['admin_logged']);
        header('Location: ' . Link::ToAdmin());

        exit();
      }
    }
  }
}
}
?>
```

6. Add the USE_SSL constant, and the administrator login information at the end of include/config.php. If you prefer not to use SSL for now, simply set the USE_SSL constant to no. As you can see, the administrator account is named by default tshirtshopadmin, and its password is also tshirtshopadmin. In a production scenario, you'll want to change these values to something less obvious to a potential hacker.

```
// We enable and enforce SSL when this is set to anything else than 'no'
define('USE_SSL', 'yes');

// Administrator login information
define('ADMIN_USERNAME', 'tshirtshopadmin');
define('ADMIN_PASSWORD', 'tshirtshopadmin');
```

■**Note** As stated earlier, in Chapter 16, you'll learn about hashing and how to work with hashed passwords stored in the database. If you want to use hashing now, you need to store the hash value of the password in the config file instead of storing the password in clear text (tshirtshopadmin, in this case). At login time, you compare the hash value of the string entered by the user to the hash value you saved in config.php. You can calculate the hash value of a string by applying the sha1 function to it (the sha1 function calculates the hash value using the SHA1 algorithm). Don't worry if this sounds too advanced at this moment, Chapter 16 will show you the process in more detail.

7. Now, we'll create the admin_login componentized template, which displays the login box. Start by creating the presentation/templates/admin_login.tpl file, and then add the following code to it:

```
{* admin_login.tpl *}
{load_presentation_object filename="admin_login" assign="obj"}
<div class="login">
  <p class="login-title">TShirtShop Login</p>
  <form method="post" action="{$obj->mLinkToAdmin}">
    <p>
```

```
        Enter login information or go back to
        <a href="{$obj->mLinkToIndex}">storefront</a>.
    </p>
{if $obj->mLoginMessage neq ""}
    <p class="error">{$obj->mLoginMessage}</p>
{/if}
    <p>
      <label for="username">Username:</label>
      <input type="text" name="username" size="35" value="{$obj->mUsername}" />
    </p>
    <p>
      <label for="password">Password:</label>
      <input type="password" name="password" size="35" value="" />
    </p>
    <p>
      <input type="submit" name="submit" value="Login" />
    </p>
  </form>
</div>
```

8. Create a new presentation object file named admin_login.php in the presentation folder, and type the following code:

```php
<?php
// Class that deals with authenticating administrators
class AdminLogin
{
  // Public variables available in smarty templates
  public $mUsername;
  public $mLoginMessage = '';
  public $mLinkToAdmin;
  public $mLinkToIndex;

  // Class constructor
  public function __construct()
  {
    // Verify if the correct username and password have been supplied
    if (isset ($_POST['submit']))
    {
      if ($_POST['username'] == ADMIN_USERNAME
          && $_POST['password'] == ADMIN_PASSWORD)
      {
        $_SESSION['admin_logged'] = true;

        header('Location: ' . Link::ToAdmin());
        exit();
      }
      else
```

```
        $this->mLoginMessage = 'Login failed. Please try again:';
    }

    $this->mLinkToAdmin = Link::ToAdmin();
    $this->mLinkToIndex = Link::ToIndex();
  }
}
?>
```

9. Create `presentation/templates/admin_menu.tpl`, and add the following code:

```
{* admin_menu.tpl *}
{load_presentation_object filename="admin_menu" assign="obj"}
<h1>TShirtShop Admin</h1>
<p> |
  <a href="{$obj->mLinkToStoreAdmin}">CATALOG ADMIN</a> |
  <a href="{$obj->mLinkToStoreFront}">STOREFRONT</a> |
  <a href="{$obj->mLinkToLogout}">LOGOUT</a> |
</p>
```

10. Now, create a new file named `admin_menu.php` in the `presentation` folder, and add the following code:

```php
<?php
class AdminMenu
{
  public $mLinkToStoreAdmin;
  public $mLinkToStoreFront;
  public $mLinkToLogout;

  public function __construct()
  {
    $this->mLinkToStoreAdmin = Link::ToAdmin();
    $this->mLinkToStoreFront = Link::ToIndex();
    $this->mLinkToLogout = Link::ToLogout();
  }
}
?>
```

11. Open `presentation/link.php` file, and modify the Build() method of the Link class as highlighted in the following code snippet. This adds support for secure (HTTPS) links:

```php
public static function Build($link, $type = 'http')
{
  $base = (($type == 'http' || USE_SSL == 'no') ? 'http://' : 'https://') .
          getenv('SERVER_NAME');

  // If HTTP_SERVER_PORT is defined and different than default
  if (defined('HTTP_SERVER_PORT') && HTTP_SERVER_PORT != '80' &&
      strpos($base, 'https') === false)
  {
```

```php
    // Append server port
    $base .= ':' . HTTP_SERVER_PORT;
  }

  $link = $base . VIRTUAL_LOCATION . $link;

  // Escape html
  return htmlspecialchars($link, ENT_QUOTES);
}
```

12. Also in `presentation/link.php`, add the following methods at the end of the `Link` class:

```php
// Create link to admin page
public static function ToAdmin($params = '')
{
  $link = 'admin.php';

  if ($params != '')
    $link .= '?' . $params;

  return self::Build($link, 'https');
}

// Create logout link
public static function ToLogout()
{
  return self::ToAdmin('Page=Logout');
}
```

13. Add the following styles to the `styles/tshirtshop.css` file:

```css
.login {
  color: #333333;
  display: block;
  border: 1px solid #c6e1ec;
  margin: 50px auto;
  width: 325px;
}

.login form p {
  padding: 0 10px;
}

label {
  display: block;
}
```

```css
.error {
  color: #ff0000;
  font-size: 85%;
  font-weight: bold;
}

.login-title {
  background: #0590c7;
  border-bottom: 2px solid #c6e1ec;
  color: #ffffff;
  display: block;
  font-size: 93%;
  font-weight: bold;
  margin: 1px;
  padding: 2px 10px;
}

.no-items-found {
  color: #ff0000;
}

table.tss-table {
  width: 100%;
}

table.tss-table th {
  background: #0590c7;;
  border: none;
  border-bottom: 3px solid #c6e1ec;
  color: #ffffff;
  text-align: left;
}

table.tss-table td {
  border: none;
  border-bottom: 1px solid #0590c7;
}
```

14. Load TShirtShop in your favorite browser, and you'll see the admin page link in the welcome message on the front page. Click it, and an HTML login form will be displayed; Figure 10-8 shows the message you'll get if you type the wrong password. After you supply the correct login information (username: tshirtshopadmin, password: tshirtshopadmin), you'll be redirected to the catalog administration page, which currently contains only the main menu—we'll change this soon.

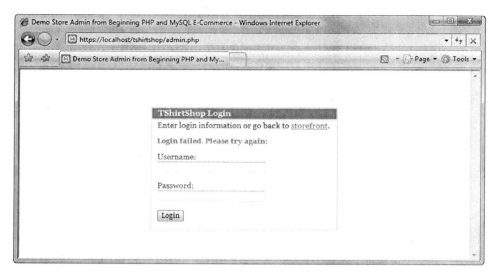

Figure 10-8. *The login page*

How It Works: Authenticating Administrators

The main components you created in this exercise are as follows:

- admin.php is the entry point into the administrative part of the site. You'll continue to develop it in the rest of this chapter. Studying this file, you can see that it doesn't have any visual output. It just prepares the environment and loads the store_admin Smarty componentized template.

- store_admin is a componentized template (made of store_admin.php and store_admin.tpl) that is loaded by admin.php to generate the skeleton for the catalog administration page. Different templates will be plugged in when implementing various administrative features. For example, later in this chapter, you'll add departments and categories administration features.

- admin_login is a componentized template that implements the administrative authentication and authorization feature. The template displays the login form and authenticates the visitor when necessary.

Of all the files you've created, store_admin.php is perhaps the most interesting. First, it checks whether the visitor has been authenticated as the administrator (by checking whether the admin_logged session variable is true). If the visitor is not logged in as the administrator, the admin_login componentized template is loaded:

```
public function init()
{
  // If admin is not logged in, load admin_login template
  if (!(isset ($_SESSION['admin_logged'])) ||
      $_SESSION['admin_logged'] != true)
    $this->mContentsCell = 'admin_login.tpl';
```

The login mechanism in the AdminLogin presentation object stores the current authentication state in the visitor's session under a variable named admin_logged. In the __construct function, we test whether the supplied username and password match the values stored in config.php as ADMIN_USERNAME and ADMIN_PASSWORD; if they match, we set the value of admin_logged to true and redirect to admin.php:

```
// Verify if the correct username and password have been supplied
if (isset ($_POST['submit']))
{
  if ($_POST['username'] == ADMIN_USERNAME
      && $_POST['password'] == ADMIN_PASSWORD)
  {
    $_SESSION['admin_logged'] = true;

    header('Location: ' . Link::ToAdmin());
    exit();
  }
  else
    $this->mLoginMessage = 'Login failed. Please try again:';
}
```

The logout link in admin_menu.tpl simply unsets the admin_logged session variable in store_admin.php and redirects the administrator to admin.php. This way, on the next attempt to access the administration page, the administrator will be redirected to the login page.

```
// If logging out ...
if (isset ($_GET['Page']) && ($_GET['Page'] == 'Logout'))
{
  unset($_SESSION['admin_logged']);
  header('Location: ' . Link::ToAdmin());

  exit();
}
```

Administering Departments

The department administration section allows the user to add, remove, and change department information. To implement this functionality, you'll need to write the necessary code for the presentation, business, and data layers.

One fundamental truth regarding *n*-tiered applications (which applies to this particular case) is that the business and data tiers are ultimately created to support the presentation tier. Drawing on paper and establishing exactly how you want the site to look is a good indication of what the database and business tier will contain (in other words, what functionality needs to be supported by the User Interface, or UI).

Once the functional and technical specifications are done, you will know exactly what to place in each tier, so the order in which you write the code doesn't matter. However, except for the largest projects that really need very careful design and planning, this kind of flexibility rarely happens in practice.

In this book, the usual way to start implementing a feature is with the lower levels (the database and data object). In this chapter, however, we always start development with the presentation tier, which you can now do because you already have a good overview of the architecture and can foresee the implementation details of the business and data tiers. This knowledge is necessary, because when implementing in the presentation tier, you will call methods from both of the other tiers, neither of which you've created. If you don't have a clear idea of how to implement all three tiers, starting with the presentation tier would be a bad idea.

Implementing the Presentation Tier

Take another look at what the admin_departments componentized template looks like in action (Figure 10-9 shows the componentized template running in Safari for Windows).

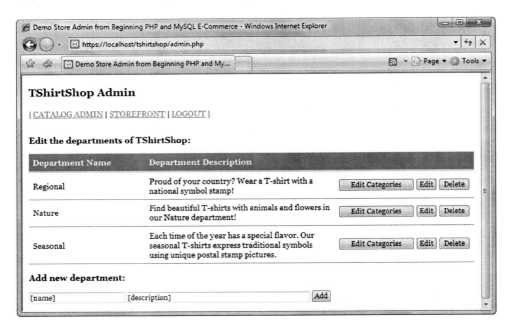

Figure 10-9. *The* admin_departments *componentized template in action*

This componentized template generates a list populated with each department's information, two text boxes, and a button used to add a new department to the list.

When you click a department's Edit button, the name and the description of that department become editable, and the Update and Cancel buttons appear in place of the Edit button, as you saw earlier in Figure 10-3.

Exercise: Implementing the admin_departments Componentized Template

1. Create a new template file named admin_departments.tpl in the presentation/templates folder, and add the following code to it:

```
{* admin_departments.tpl *}
{load_presentation_object filename="admin_departments" assign="obj"}
<form method="post"
 action="{$obj->mLinkToDepartmentsAdmin}">
   <h3>Edit the departments of TShirtShop:</h3>
{if $obj->mErrorMessage}<p class="error">{$obj->mErrorMessage}</p>{/if}
```

```
{if $obj->mDepartmentsCount eq 0}
  <p class="no-items-found">There are no departments in your database!</p>
{else}
  <table class="tss-table">
    <tr>
      <th width="200">Department Name</th>
      <th>Department Description</th>
      <th width="240"> </th>
    </tr>
  {section name=i loop=$obj->mDepartments}
    {if $obj->mEditItem == $obj->mDepartments[i].department_id}
    <tr>
      <td>
        <input type="text" name="name"
         value="{$obj->mDepartments[i].name}" size="30" />
      </td>
      <td>
      {strip}
        <textarea name="description" rows="3" cols="60">
          {$obj->mDepartments[i].description}
        </textarea>
      {/strip}
      </td>
      <td>
        <input type="submit"
         name="submit_edit_cat_{$obj->mDepartments[i].department_id}"
         value="Edit Categories" />
        <input type="submit"
         name="submit_update_dept_{$obj->mDepartments[i].department_id}"
         value="Update" />
        <input type="submit" name="cancel" value="Cancel" />
        <input type="submit"
         name="submit_delete_dept_{$obj->mDepartments[i].department_id}"
         value="Delete" />
      </td>
    </tr>
    {else}
    <tr>
      <td>{$obj->mDepartments[i].name}</td>
      <td>{$obj->mDepartments[i].description}</td>
      <td>
        <input type="submit"
         name="submit_edit_cat_{$obj->mDepartments[i].department_id}"
         value="Edit Categories" />
        <input type="submit"
         name="submit_edit_dept_{$obj->mDepartments[i].department_id}"
         value="Edit" />
```

```
          <input type="submit"
           name="submit_delete_dept_{$obj->mDepartments[i].department_id}"
           value="Delete" />
        </td>
      </tr>
      {/if}
    {/section}
    </table>
  {/if}
    <h3>Add new department:</h3>
    <p>
      <input type="text" name="department_name" value="[name]" size="30" />
      <input type="text" name="department_description" value="[description]"
       size="60" />
      <input type="submit" name="submit_add_dept_0" value="Add" />
    </p>
  </form>
```

2. Create a new presentation object file named admin_departments.php in the presentation folder, and add the following code to it:

```php
<?php
// Class that supports departments admin functionality
class AdminDepartments
{
  // Public variables available in smarty template
  public $mDepartmentsCount;
  public $mDepartments;
  public $mErrorMessage;
  public $mEditItem;
  public $mLinkToDepartmentsAdmin;

  // Private members
  private $_mAction;
  private $_mActionedDepartmentId;

  // Class constructor
  public function __construct()
  {
    // Parse the list with posted variables
    foreach ($_POST as $key => $value)
      // If a submit button was clicked ...
      if (substr($key, 0, 6) == 'submit')
      {
        /* Get the position of the last '_' underscore from submit
           button name e.g strtpos('submit_edit_dept_1', '_') is 17 */
        $last_underscore = strrpos($key, '_');
```

```php
      /* Get the scope of submit button
         (e.g  'edit_dep' from 'submit_edit_dept_1') */
      $this->_mAction = substr($key, strlen('submit_'),
                               $last_underscore - strlen('submit_'));

      /* Get the department id targeted by submit button
         (the number at the end of submit button name)
         e.g '1' from 'submit_edit_dept_1' */
      $this->_mActionedDepartmentId = substr($key, $last_underscore + 1);

      break;
    }

  $this->mLinkToDepartmentsAdmin = Link::ToDepartmentsAdmin();
}

public function init()
{
  // If adding a new department ...
  if ($this->_mAction == 'add_dept')
  {
    $department_name = $_POST['department_name'];
    $department_description = $_POST['department_description'];

    if ($department_name == null)
      $this->mErrorMessage = 'Department name required';

    if ($this->mErrorMessage == null)
    {
      Catalog::AddDepartment($department_name, $department_description);

      header('Location: ' . $this->mLinkToDepartmentsAdmin);
    }
  }

  // If editing an existing department ...
  if ($this->_mAction == 'edit_dept')
    $this->mEditItem = $this->_mActionedDepartmentId;

  // If updating a department ...
  if ($this->_mAction == 'update_dept')
  {
    $department_name = $_POST['name'];
    $department_description = $_POST['description'];
```

```
        if ($department_name == null)
          $this->mErrorMessage = 'Department name required';

        if ($this->mErrorMessage == null)
        {
          Catalog::UpdateDepartment($this->_mActionedDepartmentId,
                            $department_name, $department_description);

          header('Location: ' . $this->mLinkToDepartmentsAdmin);
        }
      }

      // If deleting a department ...
      if ($this->_mAction == 'delete_dept')
      {
        $status = Catalog::DeleteDepartment($this->_mActionedDepartmentId);

        if ($status < 0)
          $this->mErrorMessage = 'Department not empty';
        else
          header('Location: ' . $this->mLinkToDepartmentsAdmin);
      }

      // If editing department's categories ...
      if ($this->_mAction == 'edit_cat')
      {
        header('Location: ' .
                 htmlspecialchars_decode(
                   Link::ToDepartmentCategoriesAdmin(
                     $this->_mActionedDepartmentId)));

        exit();
      }

      // Load the list of departments
      $this->mDepartments = Catalog::GetDepartmentsWithDescriptions();
      $this->mDepartmentsCount = count($this->mDepartments);
    }
  }
?>
```

3. Open presentation/link.php, and add the following method at the end of Link class:

```
    // Create link to the departments administration page
    public static function ToDepartmentsAdmin()
    {
      return self::ToAdmin('Page=Departments');
    }
```

4. Modify the init() method of the StoreAdmin class located in presentation/store_admin.php file to load the newly created admin_departments componentized template:

```
// If logging out ...
if (isset ($_GET['Page']) && ($_GET['Page'] == 'Logout'))
{
  unset($_SESSION['admin_logged']);
  header('Location: ' . Link::ToAdmin());

  exit();
}

// If Page is not explicitly set, assume the Departments page
$admin_page = isset ($_GET['Page']) ? $_GET['Page'] : 'Departments';

// Choose what admin page to load ...
if ($admin_page == 'Departments')
  $this->mContentsCell = 'admin_departments.tpl';
      }
    }
  }
}
?>
```

How It Works: The admin_departments Componentized Template

You wrote a lot of code in this exercise, and you still can't test anything! This is one of the tough parts of creating the UI first. Let's see how the admin_departments.tpl template works.

Here's a scheme of the {section} construct used to build the rows of the department table:

```
{section name=i loop=$obj->mDepartments}
  {if $obj->mEditItem == $obj->mDepartments[i].department_id}
    <!--
      Here goes a form where the administrator can edit the department name
      and description with Update/Cancel, Edit Categories, and Delete buttons.
    //-->
  {else}
    <!--
      Here goes a form that displays the department name and description, and
      also Edit, Edit Categories, and Delete buttons.
    //-->
  {/if}
{/section}
```

By default, the department name and description are not editable, but when you click the Edit button of one department, $obj->mEditItem is set to the department_id value of the clicked department, and the Smarty presentation logic generates editable text boxes instead of labels. This will allow the administrator to edit the selected department's details (in edit mode, Update/Cancel buttons appear instead of the Edit button, as you saw in the earlier figures).

The presentation object of admin_departments—AdminDepartments—contains the logic that makes the departments administration page work. If loaded as a result of the user clicking one of the buttons (such as the Edit or Delete buttons), it checks what button was clicked and reacts accordingly. The buttons follow a special naming convention that makes them identifiable from the code.

All button names start with submit and end with the ID of the department. In the middle of the name is the code for the button type, which specifies what operation to do with the mentioned department. This code can be one of the following:

- add_dept for the Add buttons

- edit_dept for the Edit buttons

- update_dept for the Update buttons

- delete_dept for the Delete buttons

- edit_cat for the Edit Categories buttons

The object recognizes which button was clicked and knows what to do after parsing the list of posted variables and reading the clicked button's name. A button named submit_edit_dept_1 tells the presentation object to enter edit mode for the department with a department_id value of 1.

Note that with the Add department button, the department's ID specified in the button name becomes irrelevant, because its value is automatically generated by the database (department_id is an AUTO_INCREMENT column).

Depending on the type of the clicked button, one of the corresponding business tier methods is called. Let's consider these methods next.

Implementing the Business Tier

You called four middle tier methods from the AdminDepartments class. Now it's time to add their business tier counterparts:

- GetDepartmentsWithDescriptions returns the list of departments to be displayed in the department's administration page.

- AddDepartment adds a new department using the provided name and description. Its ID is automatically generated by the database (the department_id column in the department table is an AUTO_INCREMENT column).

- UpdateDepartment changes a department's details. Its parameters are the department's department_id value, its new name, and its new description.

- DeleteDepartment deletes the department specified by the department_id parameter.

Exercise: Implementing the Business Tier

Now it's time to implement these four new methods. Add this code to the Catalog class in business/ catalog.php:

```php
// Retrieves all departments with their descriptions
public static function GetDepartmentsWithDescriptions()
{
  // Build the SQL query
  $sql = 'CALL catalog_get_departments()';

  // Execute the query and return the results
  return DatabaseHandler::GetAll($sql);
}


// Add a department
public static function AddDepartment($departmentName, $departmentDescription)
{
  // Build the SQL query
  $sql = 'CALL catalog_add_department(:department_name,
                                      :department_description)';

  // Build the parameters array
  $params = array (':department_name' => $departmentName,
                   ':department_description' => $departmentDescription);

  // Execute the query
  DatabaseHandler::Execute($sql, $params);
}


// Updates department details
public static function UpdateDepartment($departmentId, $departmentName,
                                        $departmentDescription)
{
  // Build the SQL query
  $sql = 'CALL catalog_update_department(:department_id, :department_name,
                                         :department_description)';

  // Build the parameters array
  $params = array (':department_id' => $departmentId,
                   ':department_name' => $departmentName,
                   ':department_description' => $departmentDescription);

  // Execute the query
  DatabaseHandler::Execute($sql, $params);
}
```

```
// Deletes a department
public static function DeleteDepartment($departmentId)
{
  // Build the SQL query
  $sql = 'CALL catalog_delete_department(:department_id)';

  // Build the parameters array
  $params = array (':department_id' => $departmentId);

  // Execute the query and return the results
  return DatabaseHandler::GetOne($sql, $params);
}
```

Implementing the Data Tier

You'll add four stored procedures to the data tier that correspond to the four business tier methods you wrote earlier. Let's see what this is all about.

Exercise: Adding Data Tier Stored Procedures to the Database

1. Use phpMyAdmin to execute and create the stored procedures described in the following steps. Also, don't forget to set $$ as the delimiter before executing the code.

2. Execute this code, which creates the catalog_get_departments stored procedure in your tshirtshop database. catalog_get_departments is the simplest stored procedure you'll write here. It returns the list of departments with their IDs, names, and descriptions. It is similar to the catalog_get_departments_list stored procedure called to fill the departments list from the storefront, but this one also returns the descriptions.

```
-- Create catalog_get_departments stored procedure
CREATE PROCEDURE catalog_get_departments()
BEGIN
  SELECT    department_id, name, description
  FROM      department
  ORDER BY  department_id;
END$$
```

3. Execute the following code, which creates the catalog_add_department stored procedure in your tshirtshop database. This procedure inserts a new department into the database.

```
-- Create catalog_add_department stored procedure
CREATE PROCEDURE catalog_add_department(
  IN inName VARCHAR(100), IN inDescription VARCHAR(1000))
BEGIN
  INSERT INTO department (name, description)
        VALUES (inName, inDescription);
END$$
```

4. Execute this code, which creates the catalog_update_department stored procedure in your tshirtshop database. This stored procedure updates the name and description of an existing department using the UPDATE SQL statement.

```
-- Create catalog_update_department stored procedure
CREATE PROCEDURE catalog_update_department(IN inDepartmentId INT,
  IN inName VARCHAR(100), IN inDescription VARCHAR(1000))
BEGIN
  UPDATE department
  SET    name = inName, description = inDescription
  WHERE  department_id = inDepartmentId;
END$$
```

5. Execute the following code, which creates the catalog_delete_department stored procedure in your tshirtshop database. This procedure deletes an existing department from the database, but only if no categories are related to it.

```
-- Create catalog_delete_department stored procedure
CREATE PROCEDURE catalog_delete_department(IN inDepartmentId INT)
BEGIN
  DECLARE categoryRowsCount INT;

  SELECT count(*)
  FROM   category
  WHERE  department_id = inDepartmentId
  INTO   categoryRowsCount;

  IF categoryRowsCount = 0 THEN
    DELETE FROM department WHERE department_id = inDepartmentId;

    SELECT 1;
  ELSE
    SELECT -1;
  END IF;
END$$
```

6. Finally, load the admin.php page in your browser, and admire your results. You should be able to add, delete, and edit departments, as shown in Figures 10-2, 10-3, and 10-9.

Administering Categories

Because the categories administration page is based on the same steps and concepts as the departments administration page, we'll quickly list the steps you need to follow.

When you have completed the following exercise, you will be able to make changes and additions to your product categories by clicking the Edit Categories button in the departments page. In the categories page, clicking an Edit button enters the category in edit mode (see Figure 10-10).

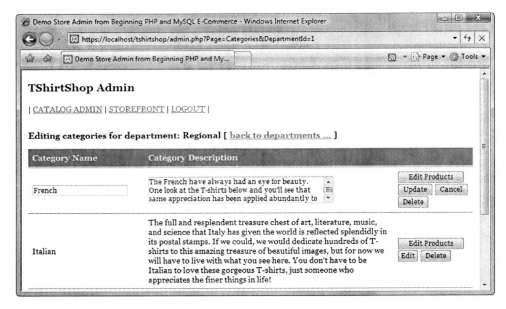

Figure 10-10. *Editing the French category*

Exercise: Administering Categories

1. Create a new template file named admin_categories.tpl in the presentation/templates folder file, and add the following code to it:

```
{* admin_categories.tpl *}
{load_presentation_object filename="admin_categories" assign="obj"}
<form method="post"
 action="{$obj->mLinkToDepartmentCategoriesAdmin}">
  <h3>
    Editing categories for department: {$obj->mDepartmentName} [
    <a href="{$obj->mLinkToDepartmentsAdmin}">back to departments ...</a> ]
  </h3>
{if $obj->mErrorMessage}<p class="error">{$obj->mErrorMessage}</p>{/if}
{if $obj->mCategoriesCount eq 0}
  <p class="no-items-found">There are no categories in this department!</p>
{else}
  <table class="tss-table">
    <tr>
      <th width="200">Category Name</th>
      <th>Category Description</th>
      <th width="240"> </th>
    </tr>
  {section name=i loop=$obj->mCategories}
    {if $obj->mEditItem == $obj->mCategories[i].category_id}
    <tr>
```

```
      <td>
        <input type="text" name="name"
         value="{$obj->mCategories[i].name}" size="30" />
      </td>
      <td>
        {strip}
        <textarea name="description" rows="3" cols="60">
          {$obj->mCategories[i].description}
        </textarea>
        {/strip}
      </td>
      <td>
        <input type="submit"
         name="submit_edit_prod_{$obj->mCategories[i].category_id}"
         value="Edit Products" />
        <input type="submit"
         name="submit_update_cat_{$obj->mCategories[i].category_id}"
         value="Update" />
        <input type="submit" name="cancel" value="Cancel" />
        <input type="submit"
         name="submit_delete_cat_{$obj->mCategories[i].category_id}"
         value="Delete" />
      </td>
    </tr>
    {else}
    <tr>
      <td>{$obj->mCategories[i].name}</td>
      <td>{$obj->mCategories[i].description}</td>
      <td>
        <input type="submit"
         name="submit_edit_prod_{$obj->mCategories[i].category_id}"
         value="Edit Products" />
        <input type="submit"
         name="submit_edit_cat_{$obj->mCategories[i].category_id}"
         value="Edit" />
        <input type="submit"
         name="submit_delete_cat_{$obj->mCategories[i].category_id}"
         value="Delete" />
      </td>
    </tr>
    {/if}
  {/section}
  </table>
{/if}
  <h3>Add new category:</h3>
  <input type="text" name="category_name" value="[name]" size="30" />
  <input type="text" name="category_description" value="[description]"
```

```
  size="60" />
 <input type="submit" name="submit_add_cat_0" value="Add" />
</form>
```

2. Create a new presentation object file named admin_categories.php in the presentation folder, and add the following to it:

```php
<?php
// Class that deals with categories admin
class AdminCategories
{
  // Public variables available in smarty template
  public $mCategoriesCount;
  public $mCategories;
  public $mErrorMessage;
  public $mEditItem;
  public $mDepartmentId;
  public $mDepartmentName;
  public $mLinkToDepartmentsAdmin;
  public $mLinkToDepartmentCategoriesAdmin;

  // Private members
  private $_mAction;
  private $_mActionedCategoryId;

  // Class constructor
  public function __construct()
  {
    if (isset ($_GET['DepartmentId']))
      $this->mDepartmentId = (int)$_GET['DepartmentId'];
    else
      trigger_error('DepartmentId not set');

    $department_details = Catalog::GetDepartmentDetails($this->mDepartmentId);
    $this->mDepartmentName = $department_details['name'];

    foreach ($_POST as $key => $value)
      // If a submit button was clicked ...
      if (substr($key, 0, 6) == 'submit')
      {
        /* Get the position of the last '_' underscore from submit
           button name e.g strtpos('submit_edit_cat_1', '_') is 16 */
        $last_underscore = strrpos($key, '_');

        /* Get the scope of submit button
           (e.g 'edit_cat' from 'submit_edit_cat_1') */
        $this->_mAction = substr($key, strlen('submit_'),
                                 $last_underscore - strlen('submit_'));
```

```php
      /* Get the category id targeted by submit button
         (the number at the end of submit button name)
         e.g '1' from 'submit_edit_cat_1' */
      $this->_mActionedCategoryId = (int)substr($key, $last_underscore + 1);

      break;
    }

  $this->mLinkToDepartmentsAdmin = Link::ToDepartmentsAdmin();

  $this->mLinkToDepartmentCategoriesAdmin =
    Link::ToDepartmentCategoriesAdmin($this->mDepartmentId);
}

public function init()
{
  // If adding a new category ...
  if ($this->_mAction == 'add_cat')
  {
    $category_name = $_POST['category_name'];
    $category_description = $_POST['category_description'];

    if ($category_name == null)
      $this->mErrorMessage = 'Category name is empty';

    if ($this->mErrorMessage == null)
    {
      Catalog::AddCategory($this->mDepartmentId, $category_name,
                           $category_description);

      header('Location: ' .
             htmlspecialchars_decode(
               $this->mLinkToDepartmentCategoriesAdmin));
    }
  }

  // If editing an existing category ...
  if ($this->_mAction == 'edit_cat')
  {
    $this->mEditItem = $this->_mActionedCategoryId;
  }

  // If updating a category ...
  if ($this->_mAction == 'update_cat')
  {
    $category_name = $_POST['name'];
    $category_description = $_POST['description'];
```

```php
      if ($category_name == null)
        $this->mErrorMessage = 'Category name is empty';

      if ($this->mErrorMessage == null)
      {
        Catalog::UpdateCategory($this->_mActionedCategoryId, $category_name,
                                $category_description);

        header('Location: ' .
               htmlspecialchars_decode(
                  $this->mLinkToDepartmentCategoriesAdmin));
      }
    }

    // If deleting a category ...
    if ($this->_mAction == 'delete_cat')
    {
      $status = Catalog::DeleteCategory($this->_mActionedCategoryId);

      if ($status < 0)
        $this->mErrorMessage = 'Category not empty';
      else
        header('Location: ' .
               htmlspecialchars_decode(
                  $this->mLinkToDepartmentCategoriesAdmin));
    }

    // If editing category's products ...
    if ($this->_mAction == 'edit_prod')
    {
      header('Location: ' .
             htmlspecialchars_decode(
                Link::ToCategoryProductsAdmin($this->mDepartmentId,
                                              $this->_mActionedCategoryId)));

      exit();
    }

    // Load the list of categories
    $this->mCategories =
      Catalog::GetDepartmentCategories($this->mDepartmentId);
    $this->mCategoriesCount = count($this->mCategories);
  }
}
?>
```

3. Now, open presentation/link.php, and add the following method at the end of the Link class:

```
// Create link to the categories administration page
public static function ToDepartmentCategoriesAdmin($departmentId)
{
  $link = 'Page=Categories&DepartmentId=' . $departmentId;

  return self::ToAdmin($link);
}
```

4. Open business/catalog.php to add the following business tier methods to the Catalog class:

```
// Gets categories in a department
public static function GetDepartmentCategories($departmentId)
{
  // Build the SQL query
  $sql = 'CALL catalog_get_department_categories(:department_id)';

  // Build the parameters array
  $params = array (':department_id' => $departmentId);

  // Execute the query and return the results
  return DatabaseHandler::GetAll($sql, $params);
}

// Adds a category
public static function AddCategory($departmentId, $categoryName,
                                   $categoryDescription)
{
  // Build the SQL query
  $sql = 'CALL catalog_add_category(:department_id, :category_name,
                                    :category_description)';

  // Build the parameters array
  $params = array (':department_id' => $departmentId,
                   ':category_name' => $categoryName,
                   ':category_description' => $categoryDescription);

  // Execute the query
  DatabaseHandler::Execute($sql, $params);
}

// Updates a category
public static function UpdateCategory($categoryId, $categoryName,
                                      $categoryDescription)
{
  // Build the SQL query
  $sql = 'CALL catalog_update_category(:category_id, :category_name,
                                       :category_description)';
```

```
    // Build the parameters array
    $params = array (':category_id' => $categoryId,
                     ':category_name' => $categoryName,
                     ':category_description' => $categoryDescription);

    // Execute the query
    DatabaseHandler::Execute($sql, $params);
  }

  // Deletes a category
  public static function DeleteCategory($categoryId)
  {
    // Build the SQL query
    $sql = 'CALL catalog_delete_category(:category_id)';

    // Build the parameters array
    $params = array (':category_id' => $categoryId);

    // Execute the query and return the results
    return DatabaseHandler::GetOne($sql, $params);
  }
```

5. Modify the init() method of the StoreAdmin class located in presentation/store_admin.php, to
load the newly added componentized templates:

```
    // Choose what admin page to load ...
    if ($admin_page == 'Departments')
      $this->mContentsCell = 'admin_departments.tpl';
    elseif ($admin_page == 'Categories')
      $this->mContentsCell = 'admin_categories.tpl';
```

6. Use phpMyAdmin to execute the following code, which creates the data tier stored procedures into your
tshirtshop database. Don't forget to set $$ as the delimiter.

```
-- Create catalog_get_department_categories stored procedure
CREATE PROCEDURE catalog_get_department_categories(IN inDepartmentId INT)
BEGIN
  SELECT   category_id, name, description
  FROM     category
  WHERE    department_id = inDepartmentId
  ORDER BY category_id;
END$$

-- Create catalog_add_category stored procedure
CREATE PROCEDURE catalog_add_category(IN inDepartmentId INT,
  IN inName VARCHAR(100), IN inDescription VARCHAR(1000))
BEGIN
  INSERT INTO category (department_id, name, description)
         VALUES (inDepartmentId, inName, inDescription);
END$$
```

```
-- Create catalog_update_category stored procedure
CREATE PROCEDURE catalog_update_category(IN inCategoryId INT,
  IN inName VARCHAR(100), IN inDescription VARCHAR(1000))
BEGIN
    UPDATE category
    SET    name = inName, description = inDescription
    WHERE  category_id = inCategoryId;
END$$

-- Create catalog_delete_category stored procedure
CREATE PROCEDURE catalog_delete_category(IN inCategoryId INT)
BEGIN
  DECLARE productCategoryRowsCount INT;

  SELECT      count(*)
  FROM        product p
  INNER JOIN  product_category pc
                ON p.product_id = pc.product_id
  WHERE       pc.category_id = inCategoryId
  INTO        productCategoryRowsCount;

  IF productCategoryRowsCount = 0 THEN
    DELETE FROM category WHERE category_id = inCategoryId;

    SELECT 1;
  ELSE
    SELECT -1;
  END IF;
END$$
```

7. Load admin.php in your browser, choose a department, and click its Edit Categories button. The categories componentized template should load, displaying a page like the one shown in Figure 10-4. Editing the categories should work as shown in Figure 10-10.

How It Works: Administering Categories

The code for managing categories follows the same patterns as the code for managing departments. In short, you completed these tasks:

- You created the admin_categories Smarty componentized template, which is made of two pieces: the template (admin_categories.tpl) and its associated presentation object (admin_categories.php). These two files implement the presentation tier of the categories administration feature.

- You updated the store_admin Smarty componentized template (more specifically, its presentation object) to load the admin_categories template when a category is selected. As you know from the beginning of the chapter, store_admin is the componentized template loaded by admin.php; its role is to decide what administration template to load.

- You created the business tier methods that support the necessary category administration features: adding, editing, and removing categories.

- You created the database stored procedures that are called by their business tier counterparts to effectively add, edit, or remove categories.

Have a close look at the new code that you added to make sure you understand exactly how it works before moving on to implement products and attributes management features in Chapter 11.

Summary

You've done quite a lot of coding in this chapter. You implemented a number of componentized templates, along with their middle tier methods and stored procedures for the data tier. You learned how to implement a simple authentication scheme, so only administrators are allowed to access the catalog administration page, and you implemented the department and category administration features of TShirtShop. In Chapter 11, you'll finish the administration page by adding management features for products and their attributes.

CHAPTER 11

■■■

Catalog Administration: Products and Attributes

Your administrators are now able to edit the departments and categories of your e-commerce web site. In this chapter, we add the missing features relating to managing products and their attributes. More specifically, we will implement features in this chapter that will allow the site administrator to accomplish the following:

- Manage product attributes, specifically list attribute values, add and delete attributes, and assign attributes to products.

- View the list of products in a specific category.

- Edit product details, such as the product's name, description, price, or whether or not it is on promotion.

- Assign an existing product to an additional category (a product can belong to multiple categories) or move it to another category.

- Remove a product from a category.

- Delete a product from the catalog.

- Allow administrators to access the department, category, or product administration pages right from the catalog.

There's quite a bit to go through but not much more than what you had to endure in the previous chapter. Feel free to look ahead at the figures to see the visual appearance of the new features. Let's start!

Administering Product Attributes

The first feature we'll create in this chapter is the product attributes management page. This page is accessible through a new link in the administration menu that reads "PRODUCT ATTRIBUTES ADMIN." Clicking that link takes you to the page shown in Figure 11-1.

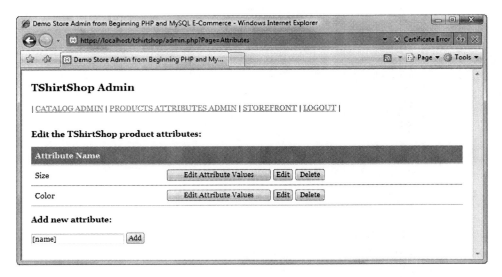

Figure 11-1. *Editing product attributes*

As you know from Chapter 6, where we added support for product attributes, each attribute can have a number of possible attribute values. For example, for the Color attribute, possible values can include Green, Pink, Black, and so on. When a product supports an attribute, we must also specify the possible attribute values that the customer must choose when making a purchase. Clicking the Edit Attribute Values link for an attribute takes you to a page where you can manage the possible values for that attribute, as shown in Figure 11-2.

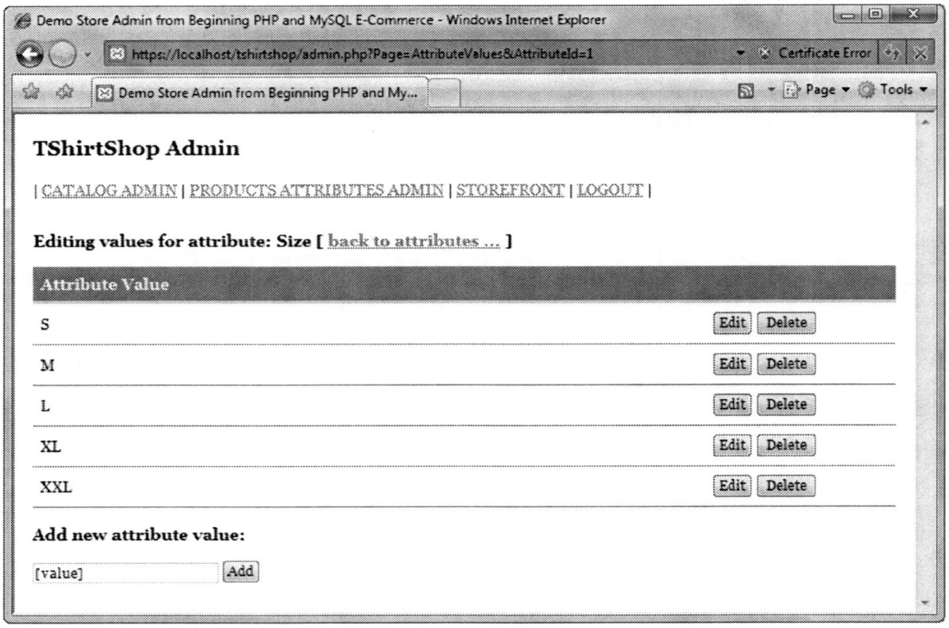

Figure 11-2. *Editing product attribute values*

Let's implement these features through an exercise, and we'll discuss the details afterward.

Exercise: Implementing admin_products

1. Create a new template file named `admin_attributes.tpl` in the `presentation/templates` folder file, and add the following code to it:

```
{* admin_attributes.tpl *}
{load_presentation_object filename="admin_attributes" assign="obj"}
<form method="post"
 action="{$obj->mLinkToAttributesAdmin}">
  <h3>Edit the TShirtShop product attributes:</h3>
{if $obj->mErrorMessage}<p class="error">{$obj->mErrorMessage}</p>{/if}
{if $obj->mAttributesCount eq 0}
  <p class="no-items-found">
    There are no products attributes in your database!
  </p>
{else}
  <table class="tss-table">
    <tr>
      <th>Attribute Name</th>
      <th width="240"> </th>
    </tr>
  {section name=i loop=$obj->mAttributes}
    {if $obj->mEditItem == $obj->mAttributes[i].attribute_id}
    <tr>
      <td>
        <input type="text" name="name"
         value="{$obj->mAttributes[i].name}" size="30" />
      </td>
      <td>
        <input type="submit"
         name="submit_edit_attr_val_{$obj->mAttributes[i].attribute_id}"
         value="Edit Attribute Values" />
        <input type="submit"
         name="submit_update_attr_{$obj->mAttributes[i].attribute_id}"
         value="Update" />
        <input type="submit" name="cancel" value="Cancel" />
        <input type="submit"
         name="submit_delete_attr_{$obj->mAttributes[i].attribute_id}"
         value="Delete" />
      </td>
    </tr>
    {else}
    <tr>
      <td>{$obj->mAttributes[i].name}</td>
      <td>
```

```
        <input type="submit"
         name="submit_edit_val_{$obj->mAttributes[i].attribute_id}"
         value="Edit Attribute Values" />
        <input type="submit"
         name="submit_edit_attr_{$obj->mAttributes[i].attribute_id}"
         value="Edit" />
        <input type="submit"
         name="submit_delete_attr_{$obj->mAttributes[i].attribute_id}"
         value="Delete" />
      </td>
    </tr>
    {/if}
  {/section}
  </table>
{/if}
  <h3>Add new attribute:</h3>
  <p>
    <input type="text" name="attribute_name" value="[name]" size="30" />
    <input type="submit" name="submit_add_attr_0" value="Add" />
  </p>
</form>
```

2. Create a new presentation object file named admin_attributes.php in the presentation folder, and add the following code to it:

```php
<?php
// Class that supports attributes admin functionality
class AdminAttributes
{
  // Public variables available in smarty template
  public $mAttributesCount;
  public $mAttributes;
  public $mErrorMessage;
  public $mEditItem;
  public $mLinkToAttributesAdmin;

  // Private members
  private $_mAction;
  private $_mActionedAttributeId;

  // Class constructor
  public function __construct()
  {
    // Parse the list with posted variables
    foreach ($_POST as $key => $value)
      // If a submit button was clicked ...
      if (substr($key, 0, 6) == 'submit')
      {
```

```
      /* Get the position of the last '_' underscore from submit
         button name e.g strpos('submit_edit_attr_1', '_') is 17 */
      $last_underscore = strrpos($key, '_');

      /* Get the scope of submit button
         (e.g 'edit_dep' from 'submit_edit_attr_1') */
      $this->_mAction = substr($key, strlen('submit_'),
                              $last_underscore - strlen('submit_'));

      /* Get the attribute id targeted by submit button
         (the number at the end of submit button name)
         e.g '1' from 'submit_edit_attr_1' */
      $this->_mActionedAttributeId = substr($key, $last_underscore + 1);

      break;
    }

  $this->mLinkToAttributesAdmin = Link::ToAttributesAdmin();
}

public function init()
{
  // If adding a new attribute ...
  if ($this->_mAction == 'add_attr')
  {
    $attribute_name = $_POST['attribute_name'];

    if ($attribute_name == null)
      $this->mErrorMessage = 'Attribute name required';

    if ($this->mErrorMessage == null)
    {
      Catalog::AddAttribute($attribute_name);

      header('Location: ' . $this->mLinkToAttributesAdmin);
    }
  }

  // If editing an existing attribute ...
  if ($this->_mAction == 'edit_attr')
    $this->mEditItem = $this->_mActionedAttributeId;

  // If updating an attribute ...
  if ($this->_mAction == 'update_attr')
  {
    $attribute_name = $_POST['name'];
```

```
      if ($attribute_name == null)
        $this->mErrorMessage = 'Attribute name required';

      if ($this->mErrorMessage == null)
      {
        Catalog::UpdateAttribute($this->_mActionedAttributeId,
                                  $attribute_name);

        header('Location: ' . $this->mLinkToAttributesAdmin);
      }
    }

    // If deleting an attribute ...
    if ($this->_mAction == 'delete_attr')
    {
      $status = Catalog::DeleteAttribute($this->_mActionedAttributeId);

      if ($status < 0)
        $this->mErrorMessage =
          'Attribute has one or more values and cannot be deleted';
      else
        header('Location: ' . $this->mLinkToAttributesAdmin);
    }

    // If editing an attribute value ...
    if ($this->_mAction == 'edit_val')
    {
      header('Location: ' .
             htmlspecialchars_decode(
               Link::ToAttributeValuesAdmin(
                 $this->_mActionedAttributeId)));

      exit();
    }

    // Load the list of attributes
    $this->mAttributes = Catalog::GetAttributes();
    $this->mAttributesCount = count($this->mAttributes);
  }
}
?>
```

3. Create a new template file named admin_attribute_values.tpl in the presentation/templates folder file, and add the following code to it:

```
{* admin_attribute_values.tpl *}
{load_presentation_object filename="admin_attribute_values" assign="obj"}
<form method="post"
```

```
   action="{$obj->mLinkToAttributeValuesAdmin}">
    <h3>
      Editing values for attribute: {$obj->mAttributeName} [
      <a href="{$obj->mLinkToAttributesAdmin}">back to attributes ...</a> ]
    </h3>
{if $obj->mErrorMessage}<p class="error">{$obj->mErrorMessage}</p>{/if}
{if $obj->mAttributeValuesCount eq 0}
    <p class="no-items-found">There are no values for this attribute!</p>
{else}
    <table class="tss-table">
      <tr>
        <th>Attribute Value</th>
        <th width="170"> </th>
      </tr>
    {section name=i loop=$obj->mAttributeValues}
      {if $obj->mEditItem == $obj->mAttributeValues[i].attribute_value_id}
      <tr>
        <td>
          <input type="text" name="value"
           value="{$obj->mAttributeValues[i].value}" size="30" />
        </td>
        <td>
          <input type="submit"
           name="submit_update_val_{$obj->mAttributeValues[i].attribute_value_id}"
           value="Update" />
          <input type="submit" name="cancel" value="Cancel" />
          <input type="submit"
           name="submit_delete_val_{$obj->mAttributeValues[i].attribute_value_id}"
           value="Delete" />
        </td>
      </tr>
      {else}
      <tr>
        <td>{$obj->mAttributeValues[i].value}</td>
        <td>
          <input type="submit"
           name="submit_edit_val_{$obj->mAttributeValues[i].attribute_value_id}"
           value="Edit" />
          <input type="submit"
           name="submit_delete_val_{$obj->mAttributeValues[i].attribute_value_id}"
           value="Delete" />
        </td>
      </tr>
      {/if}
    {/section}
    </table>
{/if}
```

```
<h3>Add new attribute value:</h3>
<input type="text" name="attribute_value" value="[value]" size="30" />
<input type="submit" name="submit_add_val_0" value="Add" />
</form>
```

4. Create a new presentation object file named admin_attribute_values.php in the presentation folder, and add the following to it:

```php
<?php
// Class that deals with attribute values admin
class AdminAttributeValues
{
  // Public variables available in smarty template
  public $mAttributeValuesCount;
  public $mAttributeValues;
  public $mErrorMessage;
  public $mEditItem;
  public $mAttributeId;
  public $mAttributeName;
  public $mLinkToAttributeAdmin;
  public $mLinkToAttributeValuesAdmin;

  // Private members
  private $_mAction;
  private $_mActionedAttributeValueId;

  // Class constructor
  public function __construct()
  {
    if (isset ($_GET['AttributeId']))
      $this->mAttributeId = (int)$_GET['AttributeId'];
    else
      trigger_error('AttributeId not set');

    $attribute_details = Catalog::GetAttributeDetails($this->mAttributeId);
    $this->mAttributeName = $attribute_details['name'];

    foreach ($_POST as $key => $value)
      // If a submit button was clicked ...
      if (substr($key, 0, 6) == 'submit')
      {
        /* Get the position of the last '_' underscore from submit
           button name e.g strtpos('submit_edit_val_1', '_') is 16 */
        $last_underscore = strrpos($key, '_');

        /* Get the scope of submit button
           (e.g  'edit_cat' from 'submit_edit_val_1') */
        $this->_mAction = substr($key, strlen('submit_'),
                                 $last_underscore - strlen('submit_'));
```

```
      /* Get the attribute value id targeted by submit button
         (the number at the end of submit button name)
         e.g '1' from 'submit_edit_val_1' */
      $this->_mActionedAttributeValueId =
        (int)substr($key, $last_underscore + 1);

    break;
  }

  $this->mLinkToAttributesAdmin = Link::ToAttributesAdmin();

  $this->mLinkToAttributeValuesAdmin =
    Link::ToAttributeValuesAdmin($this->mAttributeId);
}

public function init()
{
  // If adding a new attribute value ...
  if ($this->_mAction == 'add_val')
  {
    $attribute_value = $_POST['attribute_value'];

    if ($attribute_value == null)
      $this->mErrorMessage = 'Attribute value is empty';

    if ($this->mErrorMessage == null)
    {
      Catalog::AddAttributeValue($this->mAttributeId, $attribute_value);

      header('Location: ' .
             htmlspecialchars_decode(
               $this->mLinkToAttributeValuesAdmin));
    }
  }

  // If editing an existing attribute value ...
  if ($this->_mAction == 'edit_val')
  {
    $this->mEditItem = $this->_mActionedAttributeValueId;
  }

  // If updating an attribute value ...
  if ($this->_mAction == 'update_val')
  {
    $attribute_value = $_POST['value'];

    if ($attribute_value == null)
      $this->mErrorMessage = 'Attribute value is empty';
```

```php
      if ($this->mErrorMessage == null)
      {
        Catalog::UpdateAttributeValue(
          $this->_mActionedAttributeValueId, $attribute_value);

        header('Location: ' .
               htmlspecialchars_decode(
                 $this->mLinkToAttributeValuesAdmin));
      }
    }

    // If deleting an attribute value ...
    if ($this->_mAction == 'delete_val')
    {
      $status =
        Catalog::DeleteAttributeValue($this->_mActionedAttributeValueId);

      if ($status < 0)
        $this->mErrorMessage = 'Cannot delete this attribute value. ' .
                               'One or more products are using it!';
      else
        header('Location: ' .
               htmlspecialchars_decode(
                 $this->mLinkToAttributeValuesAdmin));
    }

    // Load the list of attribute values
    $this->mAttributeValues =
      Catalog::GetAttributeValues($this->mAttributeId);
    $this->mAttributeValuesCount = count($this->mAttributeValues);
  }
}
?>
```

5. Open the `presentation/templates/admin_menu.tpl` file, and add the following highlighted code to add a link to the attributes admin page:

```
<p> |
  <a href="{$obj->mLinkToStoreAdmin}">CATALOG ADMIN</a> |
  <a href="{$obj->mLinkToAttributesAdmin}">PRODUCTS ATTRIBUTES ADMIN</a> |
  <a href="{$obj->mLinkToStoreFront}">STOREFRONT</a> |
  <a href="{$obj->mLinkToLogout}">LOGOUT</a> |
</p>
```

6. Open the `presentation/admin_menu.php` file, and add the following highlighted code:

```php
<?php
class AdminMenu
{
```

```
  public $mLinkToStoreAdmin;
  public $mLinkToAttributesAdmin;
  public $mLinkToStoreFront;
  public $mLinkToLogout;

  public function __construct()
  {
    $this->mLinkToStoreAdmin = Link::ToAdmin();
    $this->mLinkToAttributesAdmin = Link::ToAttributesAdmin();
    $this->mLinkToStoreFront = Link::ToIndex();
    $this->mLinkToLogout = Link::ToLogout();
  }
}
?>
```

7. Now, open the presentation/link.php file, and add the following methods at the end of the Link class:

```
// Create link to the attributes administration page
public static function ToAttributesAdmin()
{
  return self::ToAdmin('Page=Attributes');
}

// Create link to the attribute values administration page
public static function ToAttributeValuesAdmin($attributeId)
{
  $link = 'Page=AttributeValues&AttributeId=' . $attributeId;

  return self::ToAdmin($link);
}
```

8. Open business/catalog.php to add the following business tier methods to the Catalog class. These methods are needed for attributes management:

```
// Retrieves all attributes
public static function GetAttributes()
{
  // Build the SQL query
  $sql = 'CALL catalog_get_attributes()';

  // Execute the query and return the results
  return DatabaseHandler::GetAll($sql);
}

// Add an attribute
public static function AddAttribute($attributeName)
{
  // Build the SQL query
  $sql = 'CALL catalog_add_attribute(:attribute_name)';
```

```php
    // Build the parameters array
    $params = array (':attribute_name' => $attributeName);

    // Execute the query
    DatabaseHandler::Execute($sql, $params);
  }

  // Updates attribute name
  public static function UpdateAttribute($attributeId, $attributeName)
  {
    // Build the SQL query
    $sql = 'CALL catalog_update_attribute(:attribute_id, :attribute_name)';

    // Build the parameters array
    $params = array (':attribute_id' => $attributeId,
                     ':attribute_name' => $attributeName);

    // Execute the query
    DatabaseHandler::Execute($sql, $params);
  }

  // Deletes an attribute
  public static function DeleteAttribute($attributeId)
  {
    // Build the SQL query
    $sql = 'CALL catalog_delete_attribute(:attribute_id)';

    // Build the parameters array
    $params = array (':attribute_id' => $attributeId);

    // Execute the query and return the results
    return DatabaseHandler::GetOne($sql, $params);
  }

  // Retrieves details for the specified attribute
  public static function GetAttributeDetails($attributeId)
  {
    // Build SQL query
    $sql = 'CALL catalog_get_attribute_details(:attribute_id)';

    // Build the parameters array
    $params = array (':attribute_id' => $attributeId);

    // Execute the query and return the results
    return DatabaseHandler::GetRow($sql, $params);
  }
```

```php
// Gets atribute values
public static function GetAttributeValues($attributeId)
{
  // Build the SQL query
  $sql = 'CALL catalog_get_attribute_values(:attribute_id)';

  // Build the parameters array
  $params = array (':attribute_id' => $attributeId);

  // Execute the query and return the results
  return DatabaseHandler::GetAll($sql, $params);
}

// Adds an attribute value
public static function AddAttributeValue($attributeId, $attributeValue)
{
  // Build the SQL query
  $sql = 'CALL catalog_add_attribute_value(:attribute_id, :value)';

  // Build the parameters array
  $params = array (':attribute_id' => $attributeId,
                   ':value' => $attributeValue);

  // Execute the query
  DatabaseHandler::Execute($sql, $params);
}

// Updates an attribute value
public static function UpdateAttributeValue(
                       $attributeValueId, $attributeValue)
{
  // Build the SQL query
  $sql = 'CALL catalog_update_attribute_value(
              :attribute_value_id, :value)';

  // Build the parameters array
  $params = array (':attribute_value_id' => $attributeValueId,
                   ':value' => $attributeValue);

  // Execute the query
  DatabaseHandler::Execute($sql, $params);
}

// Deletes an attribute value
public static function DeleteAttributeValue($attributeValueId)
{
  // Build the SQL query
  $sql = 'CALL catalog_delete_attribute_value(:attribute_value_id)';
```

```
    // Build the parameters array
    $params = array (':attribute_value_id' => $attributeValueId);

    // Execute the query and return the results
    return DatabaseHandler::GetOne($sql, $params);
  }
```

9. Modify the init() method of the StoreAdmin class located in the presentation/store_admin.php file to load the newly added componentized templates:

```
    // Choose what admin page to load ...
    if ($admin_page == 'Departments')
      $this->mContentsCell = 'admin_departments.tpl';
    elseif ($admin_page == 'Categories')
      $this->mContentsCell = 'admin_categories.tpl';
    elseif ($admin_page == 'Attributes')
      $this->mContentsCell = 'admin_attributes.tpl';
    elseif ($admin_page == 'AttributeValues')
      $this->mContentsCell = 'admin_attribute_values.tpl';
```

10. Use phpMyAdmin to execute the following code, which creates the data tier stored procedures into your tshirtshop database. Don't forget to set the $$ delimiter. (Remember, if you want to see the list of all stored procedures in the tshirtshop database, you can use the SHOW PROCEDURE STATUS command.)

```
-- Create catalog_get_attributes stored procedure
CREATE PROCEDURE catalog_get_attributes()
BEGIN
  SELECT attribute_id, name FROM attribute ORDER BY attribute_id;
END$$


-- Create catalog_add_attribute stored procedure
CREATE PROCEDURE catalog_add_attribute(IN inName VARCHAR(100))
BEGIN
  INSERT INTO attribute (name) VALUES (inName);
END$$


-- Create catalog_update_attribute stored procedure
CREATE PROCEDURE catalog_update_attribute(
  IN inAttributeId INT, IN inName VARCHAR(100))
BEGIN
  UPDATE attribute SET name = inName WHERE attribute_id = inAttributeId;
END$$


-- Create catalog_delete_attribute stored procedure
CREATE PROCEDURE catalog_delete_attribute(IN inAttributeId INT)
BEGIN
  DECLARE attributeRowsCount INT;

  SELECT count(*)
  FROM   attribute_value
```

```
  WHERE   attribute_id = inAttributeId
  INTO    attributeRowsCount;

  IF attributeRowsCount = 0 THEN
    DELETE FROM attribute WHERE attribute_id = inAttributeId;

    SELECT 1;
  ELSE
    SELECT -1;
  END IF;
END$$

-- Create catalog_get_attribute_details stored procedure
CREATE PROCEDURE catalog_get_attribute_details(IN inAttributeId INT)
BEGIN
  SELECT attribute_id, name
  FROM    attribute
  WHERE   attribute_id = inAttributeId;
END$$

-- Create catalog_get_attribute_values stored procedure
CREATE PROCEDURE catalog_get_attribute_values(IN inAttributeId INT)
BEGIN
  SELECT    attribute_value_id, value
  FROM      attribute_value
  WHERE     attribute_id = inAttributeId
  ORDER BY attribute_id;
END$$

-- Create catalog_add_attribute_value stored procedure
CREATE PROCEDURE catalog_add_attribute_value(
  IN inAttributeId INT, IN inValue VARCHAR(100))
BEGIN
  INSERT INTO attribute_value (attribute_id, value)
        VALUES (inAttributeId, inValue);
END$$

-- Create catalog_update_attribute_value stored procedure
CREATE PROCEDURE catalog_update_attribute_value(
  IN inAttributeValueId INT, IN inValue VARCHAR(100))
BEGIN
    UPDATE attribute_value
    SET    value = inValue
    WHERE  attribute_value_id = inAttributeValueId;
END$$

-- Create catalog_delete_attribute_value stored procedure
CREATE PROCEDURE catalog_delete_attribute_value(IN inAttributeValueId INT)
```

```
BEGIN
  DECLARE productAttributeRowsCount INT;

  SELECT      count(*)
  FROM        product p
  INNER JOIN  product_attribute pa
                ON p.product_id = pa.product_id
  WHERE       pa.attribute_value_id = inAttributeValueId
  INTO        productAttributeRowsCount;

  IF productAttributeRowsCount = 0 THEN
    DELETE FROM attribute_value WHERE attribute_value_id = inAttributeValueId;

    SELECT 1;
  ELSE
    SELECT -1;
  END IF;
END$$
```

11. Load the TShirtShop administration page, and ensure that the attributes administrative features (shown in Figures 11-1 and 11-2) function correctly.

How It Works: Attributes Administration

Admittedly, writing catalog administration code can become a little bit boring, as it's not particularly challenging but involves writing a lot of code. Nevertheless, a functional control panel is necessary for the well-being of such a web site (since you're reading this book, you can always use its code download if you want).

The important tasks you went through in this exercise follow:

- Creating the admin_attributes componentized template, which is made of admin_attributes.tpl and admin_attributes.php. This is the template that implements the page shown in Figure 11-1.

- Creating the admin_attribute_values componentized template, which is made of admin_attribute_values.tpl and admin_attribute_values.php. This is the template that implements the attribute values management feature presented in Figure 11-2.

- Coding the necessary housekeeping, such as adding links to the new feature in the admin_menu template (which contains links to all the administrative parts of the site), and the new link building functions in the Link class.

- Writing the business tier code and database stored procedures that support adding, removing and editing attributes and attribute values.

Administering Products

If there is such a thing as a nonboring administrative feature, products management must be it. Not only do products have pictures (and we all know that pictures are less boring than text), but they also have additional details that can be managed, such as the categories they're part of and whether or not they are on promotion.

Because managing products is a bit more complex than managing departments or categories, we'll support this feature through two administrative pages. The first is called Products Admin, and it's the page that shows the list of products that belong to a category. This page shows up when you click the Edit Products button in the list of categories, and you can admire it in Figure 11-3.

Once this page is functional, we'll create the Product Details Admin page, which is accessible through the Edit buttons you can see in Figure 11-3. But more on this later—for now, let's focus on creating the products administration page.

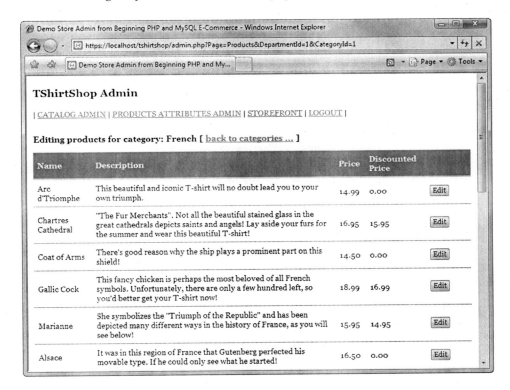

Figure 11-3. *Editing products*

Exercise: Administering Products

1. Create a new template file named `admin_products.tpl` in the `presentation/templates` folder file, and add the following code to it:

```
{* admin_products.tpl *}
{load_presentation_object filename="admin_products" assign="obj"}
<form method="post"
 action="{$obj->mLinkToCategoryProductsAdmin}">
  <h3>
    Editing products for category: {$obj->mCategoryName} [
    <a href="{$obj->mLinkToDepartmentCategoriesAdmin}">
```

```
                    back to categories ...</a> ]
        </h3>
    {if $obj->mErrorMessage}<p class="error">{$obj->mErrorMessage}</p>{/if}
    {if $obj->mProductsCount eq 0}
      <p class="no-items-found">There are no products in this category!</p>
    {else}
      <table class="tss-table">
        <tr>
          <th>Name</th>
          <th>Description</th>
          <th>Price</th>
          <th>Discounted Price</th>
          <th width="80"> </th>
        </tr>
      {section name=i loop=$obj->mProducts}
        <tr>
          <td>{$obj->mProducts[i].name}</td>
          <td>{$obj->mProducts[i].description}</td>
          <td>{$obj->mProducts[i].price}</td>
          <td>{$obj->mProducts[i].discounted_price}</td>
          <td>
            <input type="submit"
            name="submit_edit_prod_{$obj->mProducts[i].product_id}"
            value="Edit" />
          </td>
        </tr>
      {/section}
      </table>
    {/if}
      <h3>Add new product:</h3>
      <input type="text" name="product_name" value="[name]" size="30" />
      <input type="text" name="product_description" value="[description]"
       size="60" />
      <input type="text" name="product_price" value="[price]" size="10" />
      <input type="submit" name="submit_add_prod_0" value="Add" />
    </form>
```

2. Create a new presentation object file named admin_products.php in the presentation folder, and add the following to it:

```php
<?php
// Class that deals with products administration from a specific category
class AdminProducts
{
  // Public variables available in smarty template
  public $mProductsCount;
  public $mProducts;
  public $mErrorMessage;
```

```php
public $mDepartmentId;
public $mCategoryId;
public $mCategoryName;
public $mLinkToDepartmentCategoriesAdmin;
public $mLinkToCategoryProductsAdmin;

// Private attributes
private $_mAction;
private $_mActionedProductId;

// Class constructor
public function __construct()
{
  if (isset ($_GET['DepartmentId']))
    $this->mDepartmentId = (int)$_GET['DepartmentId'];
  else
    trigger_error('DepartmentId not set');

  if (isset ($_GET['CategoryId']))
    $this->mCategoryId = (int)$_GET['CategoryId'];
  else
    trigger_error('CategoryId not set');

  $category_details = Catalog::GetCategoryDetails($this->mCategoryId);
  $this->mCategoryName = $category_details['name'];

  foreach ($_POST as $key => $value)
    // If a submit button was clicked ...
    if (substr($key, 0, 6) == 'submit')
    {
      /* Get the position of the last '_' underscore from submit button name
         e.g strtpos('submit_edit_prod_1', '_') is 17 */
      $last_underscore = strrpos($key, '_');

      /* Get the scope of submit button
         (e.g  'edit_dep' from 'submit_edit_prod_1') */
      $this->_mAction = substr($key, strlen('submit_'),
                              $last_underscore - strlen('submit_'));

      /* Get the product id targeted by submit button
         (the number at the end of submit button name)
         e.g '1' from 'submit_edit_prod_1' */
      $this->_mActionedProductId = (int)substr($key, $last_underscore + 1);

      break;
    }
```

```
    $this->mLinkToDepartmentCategoriesAdmin =
      Link::ToDepartmentCategoriesAdmin($this->mDepartmentId);

    $this->mLinkToCategoryProductsAdmin =
      Link::ToCategoryProductsAdmin($this->mDepartmentId, $this->mCategoryId);
  }

  public function init()
  {
    // If adding a new product ...
    if ($this->_mAction == 'add_prod')
    {
      $product_name = $_POST['product_name'];
      $product_description = $_POST['product_description'];
      $product_price = $_POST['product_price'];

      if ($product_name == null)
        $this->mErrorMessage = 'Product name is empty';

      if ($product_description == null)
        $this->mErrorMessage = 'Product description is empty';

      if ($product_price == null || !is_numeric($product_price))
        $this->mErrorMessage = 'Product price must be a number!';

      if ($this->mErrorMessage == null)
      {
        Catalog::AddProductToCategory($this->mCategoryId, $product_name,
          $product_description, $product_price);

        header('Location: ' .
               htmlspecialchars_decode(
                 $this->mLinkToCategoryProductsAdmin));
      }
    }

    // If we want to see a product details
    if ($this->_mAction == 'edit_prod')
    {
      header('Location: ' .
             htmlspecialchars_decode(
                 Link::ToProductAdmin($this->mDepartmentId,
                                      $this->mCategoryId,
                                      $this->_mActionedProductId)));

      exit();
    }
```

```
    $this->mProducts = Catalog::GetCategoryProducts($this->mCategoryId);
    $this->mProductsCount = count($this->mProducts);
  }
}
?>
```

3. Open the presentation/link.php file, and add the following method at the end of the Link class:

```
// Create link to a products administration page
public static function ToCategoryProductsAdmin($departmentId, $categoryId)
{
  $link = 'Page=Products&DepartmentId=' . $departmentId .
          '&CategoryId=' . $categoryId;

  return self::ToAdmin($link);
}
```

4. Modify the init() method of the StoreAdmin class in store_admin.php to load the admin_products componentized template:

```
        // Choose what admin page to load ...
        if ($admin_page == 'Departments')
          $this->mContentsCell = 'admin_departments.tpl';
        elseif ($admin_page == 'Categories')
          $this->mContentsCell = 'admin_categories.tpl';
        elseif ($admin_page == 'Attributes')
          $this->mContentsCell = 'admin_attributes.tpl';
        elseif ($admin_page == 'AttributeValues')
          $this->mContentsCell = 'admin_attribute_values.tpl';
        elseif ($admin_page == 'Products')
          $this->mContentsCell = 'admin_products.tpl';
```

5. Add the following business tier code to the Catalog class inside of business/catalog.php:

```
// Gets products in a category
public static function GetCategoryProducts($categoryId)
{
  // Build the SQL query
  $sql = 'CALL catalog_get_category_products(:category_id)';

  // Build the parameters array
  $params = array (':category_id' => $categoryId);

  // Execute the query and return the results
  return DatabaseHandler::GetAll($sql, $params);
}

// Creates a product and assigns it to a category
public static function AddProductToCategory($categoryId, $productName,
                        $productDescription, $productPrice)
```

```
{
  // Build the SQL query
  $sql = 'CALL catalog_add_product_to_category(:category_id, :product_name,
                  :product_description, :product_price)';

  // Build the parameters array
  $params = array (':category_id' => $categoryId,
                   ':product_name' => $productName,
                   ':product_description' => $productDescription,
                   ':product_price' => $productPrice);

  // Execute the query
  DatabaseHandler::Execute($sql, $params);
}
```

6. Use phpMyAdmin to execute and create the following stored procedures. Don't forget to set $$ as the delimiter before executing the code.

```
-- Create catalog_get_category_products stored procedure
CREATE PROCEDURE catalog_get_category_products(IN inCategoryId INT)
BEGIN
  SELECT     p.product_id, p.name, p.description, p.price,
             p.discounted_price
  FROM       product p
  INNER JOIN product_category pc
                 ON p.product_id = pc.product_id
  WHERE      pc.category_id = inCategoryId
  ORDER BY   p.product_id;
END$$


-- Create catalog_add_product_to_category stored procedure
CREATE PROCEDURE catalog_add_product_to_category(IN inCategoryId INT,
  IN inName VARCHAR(100), IN inDescription VARCHAR(1000),
  IN inPrice DECIMAL(10, 2))
BEGIN
  DECLARE productLastInsertId INT;

  INSERT INTO product (name, description, price)
         VALUES (inName, inDescription, inPrice);

  SELECT LAST_INSERT_ID() INTO productLastInsertId;

  INSERT INTO product_category (product_id, category_id)
         VALUES (productLastInsertId, inCategoryId);
END$$
```

7. You can now load your administration page, navigate to a category, and click the Edit Products button. You should get a page similar to the one shown in Figure 11-3.

How It Works: Product Administration

So, now you can see the products that belong to a category. You can't edit product details yet, but having them listed is an important step to getting there. You can also add a new product to the selected category by using the text boxes located below the list of products.

You implemented these features in the typical fashion:

- You implemented the core functionality using a Smarty componentized template named `admin_products`. This is formed of the template file `admin_products.tpl` and its associated presentation object in `admin_products.php`.

- You integrated the new feature into the administration site by linking it from `store_admin`.

- You wrote the supporting business tier methods and data tier stored procedures that can add a new product to the database and read the existing products.

Administering Product Details

The products list you built earlier is wonderful, but it lacks a few important features. The final componentized template you're implementing, `admin_product_details`, shows up when the user clicks the Edit button for a product in the list of products. The template enables you to

- View the product's picture

- Remove the product from a category

- Remove the product from the database completely

- Assign the current product to an additional category

- Move the current product to another category

- Change the product's price and discounted price

- Change the product name or description

When it comes to product removal, things aren't so straightforward. You can either unassign the product from a category by removing the record from the `product_category` table, or you can effectively remove the product from the `product` table. Because products are accessed in the catalog by selecting a category, you must make sure there are no orphaned products (products that don't belong to any category).

There will be two delete buttons: a "Remove from category" button, which allows removing the product from a single category, and a "Remove from catalog" button, which completely removes the product from the catalog by deleting its entries in the `product` and `product_category` tables. If the product belongs to multiple categories, only the "Remove from category" button will be active. If the product belongs to a single category, only the "Remove from catalog" button will be available. This way, we offer the necessary features to administrators, and we avoid creating orphaned products that don't belong to any categories.

Take a peek at the product details administration page in Figures 11-4 and 11-5, and go ahead and implement it by going through (another exciting) step-by-step exercise.

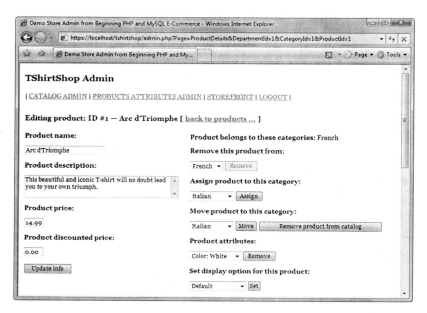

Figure 11-4. *Administering product details*

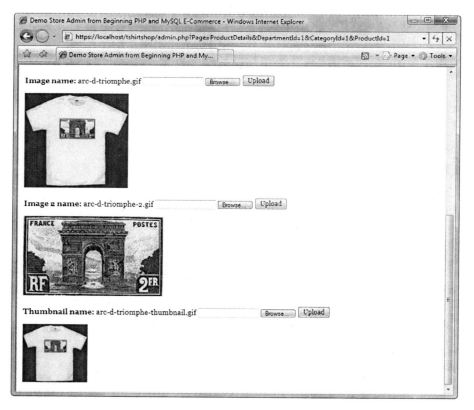

Figure 11-5. *Viewing and editing product pictures*

Product Details: Implementing the Presentation Tier

Note that, because there's quite a bit of code to write, we're implementing (and **explaining**) the presentation tier, business tier, and data tier for the product details administration feature in separate step-by-step exercises. As we've done for all the administrative features, we start the implementation with the presentation tier.

Exercise: Implementing Product Details Presentation Tier

1. Open tshirtshop.css from the styles folder, and add the following style definitions:

```css
.borderless-table {
  width: 100%;
}

.borderless-table td {
  border: none;
  padding-left: 0;
}

.bold-text {
  font-size: 93%;
  font-weight: bold;
}
```

2. Create presentation/templates/admin_product_details.tpl, and add the following code in it:

```
{* admin_product_details.tpl *}
{load_presentation_object filename="admin_product_details" assign="obj"}
<form enctype="multipart/form-data" method="post"
 action="{$obj->mLinkToProductDetailsAdmin}">
  <h3>
    Editing product: ID #{$obj->mProduct.product_id} &mdash;
    {$obj->mProduct.name} [
    <a href="{$obj->mLinkToCategoryProductsAdmin}">
      back to products ...</a> ]
  </h3>
  {if $obj->mErrorMessage}<p class="error">{$obj->mErrorMessage}</p>{/if}
  <table class="borderless-table">
    <tbody>
      <tr>
        <td valign="top">
          <p class="bold-text">
            Product name:
          </p>
          <p>
            <input type="text" name="name"
            value="{$obj->mProduct.name}" size="30" />
```

```
      </p>
      <p class="bold-text">
        Product description:
      </p>
      <p>
        {strip}
        <textarea name="description" rows="3" cols="60">
          {$obj->mProduct.description}
        </textarea>
        {/strip}
      </p>
      <p class="bold-text">
        Product price:
      </p>
      <p>
        <input type="text" name="price"
         value="{$obj->mProduct.price}" size="5" />
      </p>
      <p class="bold-text">
        Product discounted price:
      </p>
      <p>
        <input type="text" name="discounted_price"
         value="{$obj->mProduct.discounted_price}" size="5" />
      </p>
      <p>
        <input type="submit" name="UpdateProductInfo"
         value="Update info" />
      </p>
    </td>
    <td valign="top">
      <p>
        <font class="bold-text">Product belongs to these categories:</font>
        {$obj->mProductCategoriesString}
      </p>
      <p class="bold-text">
        Remove this product from:
      </p>
      <p>
        {html_options name="TargetCategoryIdRemove"
         options=$obj->mRemoveFromCategories}
        <input type="submit" name="RemoveFromCategory" value="Remove"
        {if $obj->mRemoveFromCategoryButtonDisabled}
        disabled="disabled" {/if}/>
      </p>
      <p class="bold-text">
        Assign product to this category:
```

```
</p>
<p>
  {html_options name="TargetCategoryIdAssign"
   options=$obj->mAssignOrMoveTo}
  <input type="submit" name="Assign" value="Assign" />
</p>
<p class="bold-text">
  Move product to this category:
</p>
<p>
  {html_options name="TargetCategoryIdMove"
   options=$obj->mAssignOrMoveTo}
  <input type="submit" name="Move" value="Move" />
  <input type="submit" name="RemoveFromCatalog"
   value="Remove product from catalog"
   {if !$obj->mRemoveFromCategoryButtonDisabled}
   disabled="disabled" {/if}/>
</p>
{if $obj->mProductAttributes}
<p class="bold-text">
  Product attributes:
</p>
<p>
  {html_options name="TargetAttributeValueIdRemove"
   options=$obj->mProductAttributes}
  <input type="submit" name="RemoveAttributeValue"
   value="Remove" />
</p>
{/if}
{if $obj->mCatalogAttributes}
<p class="bold-text">
  Assign attribute to product:
</p>
<p>
  {html_options name="TargetAttributeValueIdAssign"
   options=$obj->mCatalogAttributes}
  <input type="submit" name="AssignAttributeValue"
   value="Assign" />
</p>
{/if}
<p class="bold-text">
  Set display option for this product:
</p>
<p>
  {html_options name="ProductDisplay"
   options=$obj->mProductDisplayOptions
   selected=$obj->mProduct.display}
```

```
              <input type="submit" name="SetProductDisplayOption" value="Set" />
            </p>
          </td>
        </tr>
      </tbody>
    </table>
    <p>
      <font class="bold-text">Image name:</font> {$obj->mProduct.image}
      <input name="ImageUpload" type="file" value="Upload" />
      <input type="submit" name="Upload" value="Upload" />
    </p>
    {if $obj->mProduct.image}
    <p>
      <img src="product_images/{$obj->mProduct.image}"
        border="0" alt="{$obj->mProduct.name} image" />
    </p>
    {/if}
    <p>
      <font class="bold-text">Image 2 name:</font> {$obj->mProduct.image_2}
      <input name="Image2Upload" type="file" value="Upload" />
      <input type="submit" name="Upload" value="Upload" />
    </p>
    {if $obj->mProduct.image_2}
    <p>
      <img src="product_images/{$obj->mProduct.image_2}"
        border="0" alt="{$obj->mProduct.name} image 2" />
    </p>
    {/if}
    <p>
      <font class="bold-text">Thumbnail name:</font> {$obj->mProduct.thumbnail}
      <input name="ThumbnailUpload" type="file" value="Upload" />
      <input type="submit" name="Upload" value="Upload" />
    </p>
    {if $obj->mProduct.thumbnail}
    <p>
      <img src="product_images/{$obj->mProduct.thumbnail}"
        border="0" alt="{$obj->mProduct.name} thumbnail" />
    </p>
    {/if}
  </form>
```

3. Open business/catalog.php to add the $mProductDisplayOptions member to the Catalog class
   needed for admin_products as highlighted:

```
<?php
// Business tier class for reading product catalog information
class Catalog
```

```
{
  // Defines product display options
  public static $mProductDisplayOptions = array ('Default',       // 0
                                                 'On Catalog',     // 1
                                                 'On Department',  // 2
                                                 'On Both');       // 3

  // Retrieves all departments
  public static function GetDepartments()
  {
```

4. Create the presentation/admin_product_details.php presentation object, and add the following in it:

```php
<?php
// Class that deals with product administration
class AdminProductDetails
{
  // Public attributes
  public $mProduct;
  public $mErrorMessage;
  public $mProductCategoriesString;
  public $mProductDisplayOptions;
  public $mProductAttributes;
  public $mCatalogAttributes;
  public $mAssignOrMoveTo;
  public $mRemoveFromCategories;
  public $mRemoveFromCategoryButtonDisabled = false;
  public $mLinkToCategoryProductsAdmin;
  public $mLinkToProductDetailsAdmin;

  // Private attributes
  private $_mProductId;
  private $_mCategoryId;
  private $_mDepartmentId;

  // Class constructor
  public function __construct()
  {
    // Need to have DepartmentId in the query string
    if (!isset ($_GET['DepartmentId']))
      trigger_error('DepartmentId not set');
    else
      $this->_mDepartmentId = (int)$_GET['DepartmentId'];

    // Need to have CategoryId in the query string
    if (!isset ($_GET['CategoryId']))
      trigger_error('CategoryId not set');
```

```
    else
      $this->_mCategoryId = (int)$_GET['CategoryId'];

    // Need to have ProductId in the query string
    if (!isset ($_GET['ProductId']))
      trigger_error('ProductId not set');
    else
      $this->_mProductId = (int)$_GET['ProductId'];

    $this->mProductDisplayOptions = Catalog::$mProductDisplayOptions;

    $this->mLinkToCategoryProductsAdmin =
      Link::ToCategoryProductsAdmin($this->_mDepartmentId, $this->_mCategoryId);

    $this->mLinkToProductDetailsAdmin =
      Link::ToProductAdmin($this->_mDepartmentId,
                           $this->_mCategoryId,
                           $this->_mProductId);
  }

  public function init()
  {
    // If uploading a product picture ...
    if (isset ($_POST['Upload']))
    {
      /* Check whether we have write permission on the
         product_images folder */
      if (!is_writeable(SITE_ROOT . '/product_images/'))
      {
        echo "Can't write to the product_images folder";

        exit();
      }

      // If the error code is 0, the file was uploaded ok
      if ($_FILES['ImageUpload']['error'] == 0)
      {
        /* Use the move_uploaded_file PHP function to move the file
           from its temporary location to the product_images folder */
        move_uploaded_file($_FILES['ImageUpload']['tmp_name'],
                           SITE_ROOT . '/product_images/' .
                           $_FILES['ImageUpload']['name']);

        // Update the product's information in the database
        Catalog::SetImage($this->_mProductId,
                          $_FILES['ImageUpload']['name']);
      }
```

```php
  // If the error code is 0, the file was uploaded ok
  if ($_FILES['Image2Upload']['error'] == 0)
  {
    /* Use the move_uploaded_file PHP function to move the file
       from its temporary location to the product_images folder */
    move_uploaded_file($_FILES['Image2Upload']['tmp_name'],
                       SITE_ROOT . '/product_images/' .
                       $_FILES['Image2Upload']['name']);

    // Update the product's information in the database
    Catalog::SetImage2($this->_mProductId,
                       $_FILES['Image2Upload']['name']);
  }

  // If the error code is 0, the file was uploaded ok
  if ($_FILES['ThumbnailUpload']['error'] == 0)
  {
    // Move the uploaded file to the product_images folder
    move_uploaded_file($_FILES['ThumbnailUpload']['tmp_name'],
                       SITE_ROOT . '/product_images/' .
                       $_FILES['ThumbnailUpload']['name']);

    // Update the product's information in the database
    Catalog::SetThumbnail($this->_mProductId,
                          $_FILES['ThumbnailUpload']['name']);
  }
}

// If updating product info ...
if (isset ($_POST['UpdateProductInfo']))
{
  $product_name = $_POST['name'];
  $product_description = $_POST['description'];
  $product_price = $_POST['price'];
  $product_discounted_price = $_POST['discounted_price'];

  if ($product_name == null)
    $this->mErrorMessage = 'Product name is empty';

  if ($product_description == null)
    $this->mErrorMessage = 'Product description is empty';

  if ($product_price == null || !is_numeric($product_price))
    $this->mErrorMessage = 'Product price must be a number!';

  if ($product_discounted_price == null ||
      !is_numeric($product_discounted_price))
    $this->mErrorMessage = 'Product discounted price must be a number!';
```

```php
    if ($this->mErrorMessage == null)
      Catalog::UpdateProduct($this->_mProductId, $product_name,
        $product_description, $product_price, $product_discounted_price);
  }

  // If removing the product from a category ...
  if (isset ($_POST['RemoveFromCategory']))
  {
    $target_category_id = $_POST['TargetCategoryIdRemove'];
    $still_exists = Catalog::RemoveProductFromCategory(
                      $this->_mProductId, $target_category_id);

    if ($still_exists == 0)
    {
      header('Location: ' .
            htmlspecialchars_decode(
              $this->mLinkToCategoryProductsAdmin));

      exit();
    }
  }

  // If setting product display option ...
  if (isset ($_POST['SetProductDisplayOption']))
  {
    $product_display = $_POST['ProductDisplay'];
    Catalog::SetProductDisplayOption($this->_mProductId, $product_display);
  }

  // If removing the product from catalog ...
  if (isset ($_POST['RemoveFromCatalog']))
  {
    Catalog::DeleteProduct($this->_mProductId);

    header('Location: ' .
          htmlspecialchars_decode(
            $this->mLinkToCategoryProductsAdmin));

    exit();
  }

  // If assigning the product to another category ...
  if (isset ($_POST['Assign']))
  {
    $target_category_id = $_POST['TargetCategoryIdAssign'];
    Catalog::AssignProductToCategory($this->_mProductId,
                                    $target_category_id);
  }
```

```php
// If moving the product to another category ...
if (isset ($_POST['Move']))
{
  $target_category_id = $_POST['TargetCategoryIdMove'];
  Catalog::MoveProductToCategory($this->_mProductId,
    $this->_mCategoryId, $target_category_id);

  header('Location: ' .
         htmlspecialchars_decode(
            Link::ToProductAdmin($this->_mDepartmentId,
                                 $target_category_id,
                                 $this->_mProductId)));

  exit();
}

// If assigning an attribute value to the product ...
if (isset ($_POST['AssignAttributeValue']))
{
  $target_attribute_value_id = $_POST['TargetAttributeValueIdAssign'];
  Catalog::AssignAttributeValueToProduct($this->_mProductId,
                                         $target_attribute_value_id);
}

// If removing an attribute value from the product ...
if (isset ($_POST['RemoveAttributeValue']))
{
  $target_attribute_value_id = $_POST['TargetAttributeValueIdRemove'];
  Catalog::RemoveProductAttributeValue($this->_mProductId,
                                       $target_attribute_value_id);
}

// If moving the product to another category ...
if (isset ($_POST['Move']))
{
  $target_category_id = $_POST['TargetCategoryIdMove'];
  Catalog::MoveProductToCategory($this->_mProductId,
    $this->_mCategoryId, $target_category_id);

  header('Location: ' .
         htmlspecialchars_decode(
            Link::ToProductAdmin($this->_mDepartmentId,
                                 $target_category_id,
                                 $this->_mProductId)));

  exit();
}
```

```php
    // Get product info
    $this->mProduct = Catalog::GetProductInfo($this->_mProductId);
    $product_categories = Catalog::GetCategoriesForProduct($this->_mProductId);

    $product_attributes =
      Catalog::GetProductAttributes($this->_mProductId);

    for ($i = 0; $i < count($product_attributes); $i++)
      $this->mProductAttributes[$product_attributes[$i]['attribute_value_id']] =
        $product_attributes[$i]['attribute_name'] . ': ' .
        $product_attributes[$i]['attribute_value'];

    $catalog_attributes =
      Catalog::GetAttributesNotAssignedToProduct($this->_mProductId);

    for ($i = 0; $i < count($catalog_attributes); $i++)
      $this->mCatalogAttributes[$catalog_attributes[$i]['attribute_value_id']] =
        $catalog_attributes[$i]['attribute_name'] . ': ' .
        $catalog_attributes[$i]['attribute_value'];

    if (count($product_categories) == 1)
      $this->mRemoveFromCategoryButtonDisabled = true;

    // Show the categories the product belongs to
    for ($i = 0; $i < count($product_categories); $i++)
      $temp1[$product_categories[$i]['category_id']] =
        $product_categories[$i]['name'];

    $this->mRemoveFromCategories = $temp1;
    $this->mProductCategoriesString = implode(', ', $temp1);
    $all_categories = Catalog::GetCategories();

    for ($i = 0; $i < count($all_categories); $i++)
      $temp2[$all_categories[$i]['category_id']] =
        $all_categories[$i]['name'];

    $this->mAssignOrMoveTo = array_diff($temp2, $temp1);
  }
}
?>
```

5. Open the presentation/link.php file, and add the following method at the end of the Link class:

```php
    // Create link to product details administration page
    public static function ToProductAdmin($departmentId, $categoryId, $productId)
    {
      $link = 'Page=ProductDetails&DepartmentId=' . $departmentId .
              '&CategoryId=' . $categoryId . '&ProductId=' . $productId;
```

```
        return self::ToAdmin($link);
    }
```

6. Modify the init() method in StoreAdmin class in store_admin.php to load the admin_product_details componentized template:

```
        // Choose what admin page to load ...
        if ($admin_page == 'Departments')
          $this->mContentsCell = 'admin_departments.tpl';
        elseif ($admin_page == 'Categories')
          $this->mContentsCell = 'admin_categories.tpl';
      elseif ($admin_page == 'Attributes')
          $this->mContentsCell = 'admin_attributes.tpl';
        elseif ($admin_page == 'AttributeValues')
          $this->mContentsCell = 'admin_attribute_values.tpl';
        elseif ($admin_page == 'Products')
          $this->mContentsCell = 'admin_products.tpl';
        elseif ($admin_page == 'ProductDetails')
          $this->mContentsCell = 'admin_product_details.tpl';
```

How It Works: Creating admin_product

Even though you can't execute the page yet, it's worth taking a look at the new elements the new template contains. The admin_product_details.tpl template contains a single form with the enctype="multipart/form-data" attribute. This attribute is needed for uploading product pictures and works in conjunction with the HTML code that enables file uploading:

```
...
    <input name="ImageUpload" type="file" value="Upload" />
    <input type="submit" name="Upload" value="Upload" />
...
```

The reaction to clicking one of the three upload buttons corresponding to the product images is implemented in the init() method from the AdminProductDetails class (in presentation/admin_product_details.php):

```
    // If uploading a product picture ...
    if (isset ($_POST['Upload']))
    {
      /* Check whether we have write permission on the
         product_images folder */
      if (!is_writeable(SITE_ROOT . '/product_images/'))
      {
        echo "Can't write to the product_images folder";

        exit();
      }

      // If the error code is 0, the file was uploaded ok
      if ($_FILES['ImageUpload']['error'] == 0)
      {
```

```
    /* Use the move_uploaded_file PHP function to move the file
       from its temporary location to the product_images folder */
    move_uploaded_file($_FILES['ImageUpload']['tmp_name'],
                       SITE_ROOT . '/product_images/' .
                       $_FILES['ImageUpload']['name']);

    // Update the product's information in the database
    Catalog::SetImage($this->_mProductId,
                      $_FILES['ImageUpload']['name']);
  }

  // If the error code is 0, the file was uploaded ok
  if ($_FILES['Image2Upload']['error'] == 0)
  {
    /* Use the move_uploaded_file PHP function to move the file
       from its temporary location to the product_images folder */
    move_uploaded_file($_FILES['Image2Upload']['tmp_name'],
                       SITE_ROOT . '/product_images/' .
                       $_FILES['Image2Upload']['name']);

    // Update the product's information in the database
    Catalog::SetImage2($this->_mProductId,
                       $_FILES['Image2Upload']['name']);
  }

  // If the error code is 0, the file was uploaded ok
  if ($_FILES['ThumbnailUpload']['error'] == 0)
  {
    // Move the uploaded file to the product_images folder
    move_uploaded_file($_FILES['ThumbnailUpload']['tmp_name'],
                       SITE_ROOT . '/product_images/' .
                       $_FILES['ThumbnailUpload']['name']);

    // Update the product's information in the database
    Catalog::SetThumbnail($this->_mProductId,
                          $_FILES['ThumbnailUpload']['name']);
  }
}
```

The $_FILES superglobal variable is a two-dimensional array that stores information about your uploaded file (or files). If the $_FILES['ImageUpload']['error'] variable is set to 0, the main image of the product has uploaded successfully and must be handled. The $_FILES['ImageUpload']['tmp_name'] variable stores the temporary file name of the uploaded file on the server, and the $_FILES['ImageUpload']['name'] variable stores the name of the file as specified when uploaded to the server.

■**Note** A complete description of the $_FILES superglobal is available at http://www.php.net/manual/ en/features.file-upload.php.

The move_uploaded_file() PHP function is used to move the file from the temporary location to the product_images folder:

```
/* Use the move_uploaded_file PHP function to move the file
   from its temporary location to the product_images folder */
move_uploaded_file($_FILES['ImageUpload']['tmp_name'],
                   SITE_ROOT . '/product_images/' .
                   $_FILES['ImageUpload']['name']);
```

After uploading a product picture, the file name must be stored in the database (otherwise, the file upload has no effect):

```
// Update the product's information in the database
Catalog::SetImage($this->_mProductId,
                  $_FILES['ImageUpload']['name']);
```

As you can see, it's pretty simple to handle file uploads with PHP.

Product Details: Implementing the Business Tier

To implement the business tier, you'll need to add the following methods to the Catalog class:

- UpdateProduct updates a product's details: name, description, price, and discounted price.

- DeleteProduct completely removes a product from the catalog.

- RemoveProductFromCategory is called when the "Remove from category" button is clicked to unassign the product from a category.

- GetCategories returns all the categories from our catalog.

- GetProductInfo returns the product details.

- GetCategoriesForProduct is used to get the list of categories that are related to the specified product.

- SetProductDisplayOption sets the product's display setting.

- AssignProductToCategory assigns a product to a category.

- MoveProductToCategory moves a product from one category to another.

- GetAttributesNotAssignedToProduct returns all the attribute values from the table of attribute_values that have *not* been assigned to a product.

- *AssignAttributeValueToProduct* assigns an attribute value to a product.

- *RemoveProductAttributeValue* removes the association between a product and an attribute value from the product_attribute table.

- *SetImage1* changes the image file name in the database for a certain product.

- *SetImage2* changes the second image file name in the database for a certain product.

- *SetThumbnail* changes the thumbnail image file name for a certain product.

Exercise: Implementing the Business Tier Methods

Because the functionality is better expressed by the data tier functions that the methods call, we'll discuss them in more detail when we implement the data tier. For now, simply add the following code to the Catalog class, in business/catalog.php:

```php
// Updates a product
public static function UpdateProduct($productId, $productName,
                   $productDescription, $productPrice,
                   $productDiscountedPrice)
{
  // Build the SQL query
  $sql = 'CALL catalog_update_product(:product_id, :product_name,
                   :product_description, :product_price,
                   :product_discounted_price)';

  // Build the parameters array
  $params = array (':product_id' => $productId,
                   ':product_name' => $productName,
                   ':product_description' => $productDescription,
                   ':product_price' => $productPrice,
                   ':product_discounted_price' => $productDiscountedPrice);

  // Execute the query
  DatabaseHandler::Execute($sql, $params);
}

// Removes a product from the product catalog
public static function DeleteProduct($productId)
{
  // Build SQL query
  $sql = 'CALL catalog_delete_product(:product_id)';

  // Build the parameters array
  $params = array (':product_id' => $productId);
```

```
    // Execute the query
    DatabaseHandler::Execute($sql, $params);
}

// Unassigns a product from a category
public static function RemoveProductFromCategory($productId, $categoryId)
{
    // Build SQL query
    $sql = 'CALL catalog_remove_product_from_category(
                    :product_id, :category_id)';

    // Build the parameters array
    $params = array (':product_id' => $productId,
                     ':category_id' => $categoryId);

    // Execute the query and return the results
    return DatabaseHandler::GetOne($sql, $params);
}

// Retrieves the list of categories a product belongs to
public static function GetCategories()
{
    // Build SQL query
    $sql = 'CALL catalog_get_categories()';

    // Execute the query and return the results
    return DatabaseHandler::GetAll($sql);
}

// Retrieves product info
public static function GetProductInfo($productId)
{
    // Build SQL query
    $sql = 'CALL catalog_get_product_info(:product_id)';

    // Build the parameters array
    $params = array (':product_id' => $productId);

    // Execute the query and return the results
    return DatabaseHandler::GetRow($sql, $params);
}

// Retrieves the list of categories a product belongs to
public static function GetCategoriesForProduct($productId)
{
    // Build SQL query
    $sql = 'CALL catalog_get_categories_for_product(:product_id)';
```

```php
  // Build the parameters array
  $params = array (':product_id' => $productId);

  // Execute the query and return the results
  return DatabaseHandler::GetAll($sql, $params);
}

// Assigns a product to a category
public static function SetProductDisplayOption($productId, $display)
{
  // Build SQL query
  $sql = 'CALL catalog_set_product_display_option(
              :product_id, :display)';

  // Build the parameters array
  $params = array (':product_id' => $productId,
                   ':display' => $display);

  // Execute the query
  DatabaseHandler::Execute($sql, $params);
}

// Assigns a product to a category
public static function AssignProductToCategory($productId, $categoryId)
{
  // Build SQL query
  $sql = 'CALL catalog_assign_product_to_category(
              :product_id, :category_id)';

  // Build the parameters array
  $params = array (':product_id' => $productId,
                   ':category_id' => $categoryId);

  // Execute the query
  DatabaseHandler::Execute($sql, $params);
}

// Moves a product from one category to another
public static function MoveProductToCategory($productId, $sourceCategoryId,
                                             $targetCategoryId)
{
  // Build SQL query
  $sql = 'CALL catalog_move_product_to_category(:product_id,
              :source_category_id, :target_category_id)';

  // Build the parameters array
  $params = array (':product_id' => $productId,
```

```
                                ':source_category_id' => $sourceCategoryId,
                                ':target_category_id' => $targetCategoryId);

  // Execute the query
  DatabaseHandler::Execute($sql, $params);
}

// Gets the catalog attributes that are not assigned to the specified product
public static function GetAttributesNotAssignedToProduct($productId)
{
  // Build the SQL query
  $sql = 'CALL catalog_get_attributes_not_assigned_to_product(:product_id)';

  // Build the parameters array
  $params = array (':product_id' => $productId);

  // Execute the query and return the results
  return DatabaseHandler::GetAll($sql, $params);
}

// Assign an attribute value to the specified product
public static function AssignAttributeValueToProduct($productId,
                                                     $attributeValueId)
{
  // Build SQL query
  $sql = 'CALL catalog_assign_attribute_value_to_product(
                :product_id, :attribute_value_id)';

  // Build the parameters array
  $params = array (':product_id' => $productId,
                   ':attribute_value_id' => $attributeValueId);

  // Execute the query
  DatabaseHandler::Execute($sql, $params);
}

// Removes a product attribute value
public static function RemoveProductAttributeValue($productId,
                                                   $attributeValueId)
{
  // Build SQL query
  $sql = 'CALL catalog_remove_product_attribute_value(
                :product_id, :attribute_value_id)';

  // Build the parameters array
  $params = array (':product_id' => $productId,
                   ':attribute_value_id' => $attributeValueId);
```

```php
    // Execute the query
    DatabaseHandler::Execute($sql, $params);
  }

  // Changes the name of the product image file in the database
  public static function SetImage($productId, $imageName)
  {
    // Build SQL query
    $sql = 'CALL catalog_set_image(:product_id, :image_name)';

    // Build the parameters array
    $params = array (':product_id' => $productId, ':image_name' => $imageName);

    // Execute the query
    DatabaseHandler::Execute($sql, $params);
  }

  // Changes the name of the second product image file in the database
  public static function SetImage2($productId, $imageName)
  {
    // Build SQL query
    $sql = 'CALL catalog_set_image_2(:product_id, :image_name)';

    // Build the parameters array
    $params = array (':product_id' => $productId, ':image_name' => $imageName);

    // Execute the query
    DatabaseHandler::Execute($sql, $params);
  }

  // Changes the name of the product thumbnail file in the database
  public static function SetThumbnail($productId, $thumbnailName)
  {
    // Build SQL query
    $sql = 'CALL catalog_set_thumbnail(:product_id, :thumbnail_name)';

    // Build the parameters array
    $params = array (':product_id' => $productId,
                     ':thumbnail_name' => $thumbnailName);

    // Execute the query
    DatabaseHandler::Execute($sql, $params);
  }
```

Product Details: Implementing the Data Tier

In the data tier, you add the stored procedures that correspond to the business tier methods in the Catalog class you have just seen.

Exercise: Adding the Stored Procedures

1. Use phpMyAdmin to execute and create the stored procedures described in the following steps, and don't forget to set $$ as the delimiter before executing the code.

2. Execute the following code, which creates the catalog_update_product stored procedure to your tshirtshop database. The catalog_update_product stored procedure updates the details of a product using the data received through the inProductId, inName, inDescription, inPrice, and inDiscountedPrice input parameters.

```
-- Create catalog_update_product stored procedure
CREATE PROCEDURE catalog_update_product(IN inProductId INT,
    IN inName VARCHAR(100), IN inDescription VARCHAR(1000),
    IN inPrice DECIMAL(10, 2), IN inDiscountedPrice DECIMAL(10, 2))
BEGIN
  UPDATE product
  SET    name = inName, description = inDescription, price = inPrice,
         discounted_price = inDiscountedPrice
  WHERE  product_id = inProductId;
END$$
```

3. Execute the following code, which creates the catalog_delete_product stored procedure to your tshirtshop database. The catalog_delete_product stored procedure completely removes a product from the catalog by deleting its entries in the product_attribute, product_category, and product tables.

```
-- Create catalog_delete_product stored procedure
CREATE PROCEDURE catalog_delete_product(IN inProductId INT)
BEGIN
  DELETE FROM product_attribute WHERE product_id = inProductId;
  DELETE FROM product_category WHERE product_id = inProductId;
  DELETE FROM product WHERE product_id = inProductId;
END$$
```

4. Execute the following code, which creates the catalog_remove_product_from_category stored procedure in your tshirtshop database. The catalog_remove_product_from_category stored procedure verifies how many categories the product exists in. If the product exists in more than one category, it just removes the product from the specified category (ID received as a parameter). If the product is associated with a single category, it is removed completely from the database.

```
-- Create catalog_remove_product_from_category stored procedure
CREATE PROCEDURE catalog_remove_product_from_category(
  IN inProductId INT, IN inCategoryId INT)
```

```
BEGIN
  DECLARE productCategoryRowsCount INT;

  SELECT count(*)
  FROM    product_category
  WHERE   product_id = inProductId
  INTO    productCategoryRowsCount;

  IF productCategoryRowsCount = 1 THEN
    CALL catalog_delete_product(inProductId);

    SELECT 0;
  ELSE
    DELETE FROM product_category
    WHERE   category_id = inCategoryId AND product_id = inProductId;

    SELECT 1;
  END IF;
END$$
```

5. Execute the following code, which creates the catalog_get_categories stored procedure in your tshirtshop database; catalog_get_categories simply returns all the categories from your catalog.

```
-- Create catalog_get_categories stored procedure
CREATE PROCEDURE catalog_get_categories()
BEGIN
  SELECT    category_id, name, description
  FROM      category
  ORDER BY category_id;
END$$
```

6. Execute the following code, which creates the catalog_get_product_info stored procedure in your tshirtshop database. The catalog_get_product_info stored procedure retrieves the product name, description, price, discounted price, image, the second image, thumbnail, and display option for the product identified by the product ID (inProductId).

```
-- Create catalog_get_product_info stored procedure
CREATE PROCEDURE catalog_get_product_info(IN inProductId INT)
BEGIN
  SELECT product_id, name, description, price, discounted_price,
         image, image_2, thumbnail, display
  FROM    product
  WHERE   product_id = inProductId;
END$$
```

7. Execute this code, which creates the catalog_get_categories_for_product stored procedure in your tshirtshop database. The catalog_get_categories_for_product stored procedure returns a list of the categories that belong to the specified product. Only their IDs and names are returned, because this is the only information we're interested in.

```
-- Create catalog_get_categories_for_product stored procedure
CREATE PROCEDURE catalog_get_categories_for_product(IN inProductId INT)
BEGIN
  SELECT   c.category_id, c.department_id, c.name
  FROM     category c
  JOIN     product_category pc
             ON c.category_id = pc.category_id
  WHERE    pc.product_id = inProductId
  ORDER BY category_id;
END$$
```

8. Execute this code, which creates the catalog_set_product_display_option stored procedure in your tshirtshop database:

```
-- Create catalog_set_product_display_option stored procedure
CREATE PROCEDURE catalog_set_product_display_option(
  IN inProductId INT, IN inDisplay SMALLINT)
BEGIN
  UPDATE product SET display = inDisplay WHERE product_id = inProductId;
END$$
```

9. Execute the following code, which creates the catalog_assign_product_to_category stored procedure in your tshirtshop database. The catalog_assign_product_to_category stored procedure associates a product with a category by adding a (product_id, category_id) value pair into the product_category table.

```
-- Create catalog_assign_product_to_category stored procedure
CREATE PROCEDURE catalog_assign_product_to_category(
  IN inProductId INT, IN inCategoryId INT)
BEGIN
  INSERT INTO product_category (product_id, category_id)
         VALUES (inProductId, inCategoryId);
END$$
```

10. Execute the following code, which creates the catalog_assign_product_to_category stored procedure in your tshirtshop database. The catalog_move_product_to_category stored procedure removes a product from a category and places it in another one.

```
-- Create catalog_move_product_to_category stored procedure
CREATE PROCEDURE catalog_move_product_to_category(IN inProductId INT,
  IN inSourceCategoryId INT, IN inTargetCategoryId INT)
BEGIN
  UPDATE product_category
  SET    category_id = inTargetCategoryId
  WHERE  product_id = inProductId
         AND category_id = inSourceCategoryId;
END$$
```

11. Execute the following code, which creates the `catalog_get_attributes_not_assigned_to_product` stored procedure in your `tshirtshop` database. This procedure returns all attribute values that weren't already associated with the product in the `product_attribute` table.

```
-- Create catalog_get_attributes_not_assigned_to_product stored procedure
CREATE PROCEDURE catalog_get_attributes_not_assigned_to_product(
  IN inProductId INT)
BEGIN
  SELECT     a.name AS attribute_name,
             av.attribute_value_id, av.value AS attribute_value
  FROM       attribute_value av
  INNER JOIN attribute a
               ON av.attribute_id = a.attribute_id
  WHERE      av.attribute_value_id NOT IN
             (SELECT attribute_value_id
              FROM   product_attribute
              WHERE  product_id = inProductId)
  ORDER BY   attribute_name, av.attribute_value_id;
END$$
```

12. Execute the following code, which creates the `catalog_assign_attribute_value_to_product` stored procedure in your `tshirtshop` database. This procedure assigns an attribute value to a product by adding a new record to the `product_attribute` table.

```
-- Create catalog_assign_attribute_value_to_product stored procedure
CREATE PROCEDURE catalog_assign_attribute_value_to_product(
  IN inProductId INT, IN inAttributeValueId INT)
BEGIN
  INSERT INTO product_attribute (product_id, attribute_value_id)
         VALUES (inProductId, inAttributeValueId);
END$$
```

13. Execute the following code, which creates the `catalog_remove_product_attribute_value` stored procedure in your `tshirtshop` database. This procedure unassigns an attribute value from a product by deleting the necessary record from the `product_attribute` table.

```
-- Create catalog_remove_product_attribute_value stored procedure
CREATE PROCEDURE catalog_remove_product_attribute_value(
  IN inProductId INT, IN inAttributeValueId INT)
BEGIN
  DELETE FROM product_attribute
  WHERE       product_id = inProductId AND
              attribute_value_id = inAttributeValueId;
END$$
```

14. Execute this code, which creates the `catalog_set_image`, `catalog_set_image_2`, and `catalog_set_thumbnail` stored procedures into your `tshirtshop` database. We need these functions to change the primary, secondary and/or thumbnail image of a product when uploading a new picture.

```
-- Create catalog_set_image stored procedure
CREATE PROCEDURE catalog_set_image(
  IN inProductId INT, IN inImage VARCHAR(150))
BEGIN
  UPDATE product SET image = inImage WHERE product_id = inProductId;
END$$

-- Create catalog_set_image_2 stored procedure
CREATE PROCEDURE catalog_set_image_2(
  IN inProductId INT, IN inImage VARCHAR(150))
BEGIN
  UPDATE product SET image_2 = inImage WHERE product_id = inProductId;
END$$

-- Create catalog_set_thumbnail stored procedure
CREATE PROCEDURE catalog_set_thumbnail(
  IN inProductId INT, IN inThumbnail VARCHAR(150))
BEGIN
  UPDATE product
  SET    thumbnail = inThumbnail
  WHERE  product_id = inProductId;
END$$
```

15. Load your product details page, and ensure everything works the way it should. You have a lot of functionality to test! Figures 11-4 and 11-5 show the product details admin page in action.

How It Works: Administering Product Details

No administrative feature is fun to implement, but what you've accomplished so far is quite impressive. Your shop administrators can now edit a product's name, description, and price; delete products from the database or from just a category; assign a product to one or more categories; and manage product attributes and pictures.

At this moment you're offering all the important features that are necessary to administer a web site like TShirtShop. We will, however, add yet another feature that will make the life of our shop administrators much easier: in-store administration links.

Creating In-Store Administration Links

Right now, the administration page delivers all the important requirements: administrators can manage the catalog departments, categories, products, and their attributes. In the last part of this chapter, we implement an additional feature, which makes the administrator's task a little bit easier. This feature consists of Edit buttons, such as the Edit Department Details and Edit Product Details buttons you can see in Figure 11-6. These buttons show up only if the visitor is authenticated as an administrator and take him or her directly to the item administrative page.

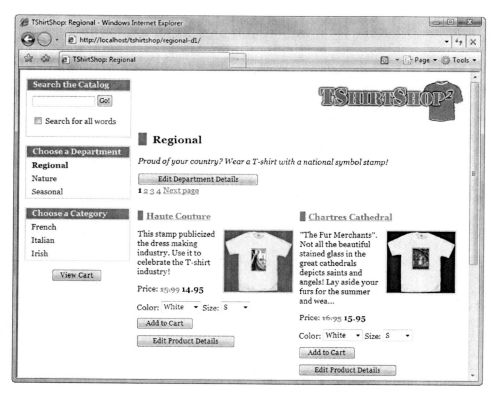

Figure 11-6. *Edit Department Details and Edit Product Details buttons in TShirtShop*

Exercise: Implementing In-Store Administration Links

1. Open the `tshirtshop.css` file from the `styles` folder, and add the following style definitions:

```
div.yui-b div form.edit-form
{
  margin: 0;
  padding: 0;
}

.edit-form
{
  margin: 0;
  padding: 0 0 10px 0;
}
```

2. Open `presentation/templates/department.tpl`, and edit it like this:

```
{* department.tpl *}
{load_presentation_object filename="department" assign="obj"}
<h1>{$obj->mName}</h1>
```

```
<p class="description">{$obj->mDescription}</p>
{if $obj->mShowEditButton}
<form action="{$obj->mEditActionTarget}" method="post" class="edit-form">
  <input type="submit" name="submit_{$obj->mEditAction}"
   value="{$obj->mEditButtonCaption}" />
</form>
{/if}
{include file="products_list.tpl"}
```

3. Add the following highlighted members to the Department class in presentation/department.php:

```
// Deals with retrieving department details
class Department
{
  // Public variables for the smarty template
  public $mName;
  public $mDescription;
  public $mEditActionTarget;
  public $mEditAction;
  public $mEditButtonCaption;
  public $mShowEditButton;
```

4. Also in presentation/department.php, add the following piece of code at the end of the constructor of the Department class. This makes the Edit button show up if the user is an administrator.

```
    /* If CategoryId is in the query string we save it
       (casting it to integer to protect against invalid values) */
    if (isset ($_GET['CategoryId']))
      $this->_mCategoryId = (int)$_GET['CategoryId'];

    // Show Edit button if the user is administrator
    if (!(isset ($_SESSION['admin_logged'])) ||
        $_SESSION['admin_logged'] != true)
      $this->mShowEditButton = false;
    else
      $this->mShowEditButton = true;
  }
```

5. Still in presentation/department.php, add the following highlighted piece of code at the end of the init() method:

```
    // If visiting a category ...
    if (isset ($this->_mCategoryId))
    {
      $category_details =
        Catalog::GetCategoryDetails($this->_mCategoryId);

      $this->mName = $this->mName . ' &raquo; ' .
                     $category_details['name'];
      $this->mDescription = $category_details['description'];
```

```
          $this->mEditActionTarget =
            Link::ToDepartmentCategoriesAdmin($this->_mDepartmentId);
          $this->mEditAction = 'edit_cat_' . $this->_mCategoryId;
          $this->mEditButtonCaption = 'Edit Category Details';
        }
        else
        {
          $this->mEditActionTarget = Link::ToDepartmentsAdmin();
          $this->mEditAction = 'edit_dept_' . $this->_mDepartmentId;
          $this->mEditButtonCaption = 'Edit Department Details';
        }
      }
    }
  }
  ?>
```

6. Add the following piece of code to presentation/templates/product.tpl:

```
{* Add the submit button and close the form *}
<p>
  <input type="submit" name="submit" value="Add to Cart" />
</p>
</form>

{* Show edit button for administrators *}
{if $obj->mShowEditButton}
<form action="{$obj->mEditActionTarget}" target="_self"
 method="post" class="edit-form">
  <p>
    <input type="submit" name="submit_edit" value="Edit Product Details" />
  </p>
</form>
{/if}

{if $obj->mLinkToContinueShopping}
<a href="{$obj->mLinkToContinueShopping}">Continue Shopping</a>
{/if}
```

7. Add these members to the Product class in presentation/product.php:

```
// Handles product details
class Product
{
  // Public variables to be used in Smarty template
  public $mProduct;
  public $mProductLocations;
  public $mLinkToContinueShopping;
  public $mLocations;
  public $mEditActionTarget;
  public $mShowEditButton;
```

8. Add this code at the end of the constructor of the Product class, in presentation/product.php. This code ensures the Edit button shows up only if the user is an administrator:

```
else
  trigger_error('ProductId not set');

// Show Edit button for administrators
if (!(isset ($_SESSION['admin_logged'])) ||
    $_SESSION['admin_logged'] != true)
  $this->mShowEditButton = false;
else
  $this->mShowEditButton = true;
}
```

9. In the same file, add the highlighted piece of code at the end of the init() method of the Product class. This creates the link to the edit product administration page.

```
// Build links for product departments and categories pages
for ($i = 0; $i < count($this->mLocations); $i++)
{
  $this->mLocations[$i]['link_to_department'] =
    Link::ToDepartment($this->mLocations[$i]['department_id']);

  $this->mLocations[$i]['link_to_category'] =
    Link::ToCategory($this->mLocations[$i]['department_id'],
                     $this->mLocations[$i]['category_id']);
}

// Prepare the Edit button
$this->mEditActionTarget =
  Link::Build(str_replace(VIRTUAL_LOCATION, '', getenv('REQUEST_URI')));

if (isset ($_SESSION['admin_logged']) &&
    $_SESSION['admin_logged'] == true &&
    isset ($_POST['submit_edit']))
{
  $product_locations = $this->mLocations;

  if (count($product_locations) > 0)
  {
    $department_id = $product_locations[0]['department_id'];
    $category_id = $product_locations[0]['category_id'];

    header('Location: ' .
           htmlspecialchars_decode(
           Link::ToProductAdmin($department_id,
                                $category_id,
                                $this->_mProductId)));
```

```
        }
      }
    }
  }
  ?>
```

10. Add the following piece of code to presentation/templates/products_list.tpl. This adds the Edit buttons to the product lists.

```
{* Add the submit button and close the form *}
<p>
  <input type="submit" name="submit" value="Add to Cart" />
</p>
</form>

{* Show Edit button for administrators *}
{if $obj->mShowEditButton}
  <form action="{$obj->mEditActionTarget}" target="_self"
   method="post" class="edit-form">
    <input type="hidden" name="product_id"
     value="{$obj->mProducts[k].product_id}" />
    <input type="submit" name="submit" value="Edit Product Details" />
  </form>
{/if}

    </td>
  {if $smarty.section.k.index % 2 != 0 && !$smarty.section.k.first ||
     $smarty.section.k.last}
    </tr>
  {/if}
{/section}
```

11. Open presentation/products_list.php, and add the following members to the ProductsList class:

```
public $mAllWords = 'off';
public $mSearchString;
public $mEditActionTarget;
public $mShowEditButton;

// Private members
private $_mDepartmentId;
private $_mCategoryId;
```

12. Add the following piece of code to the end of the __construct() method of the ProductsList class:

```
if ($this->mPage < 1)
  trigger_error('Incorrect Page value');

// Save page request for continue shopping functionality
$_SESSION['link_to_continue_shopping'] = $_SERVER['QUERY_STRING'];
```

```
        // Show Edit button for administrators
        if (!(isset ($_SESSION['admin_logged'])) ||
            $_SESSION['admin_logged'] != true)
          $this->mShowEditButton = false;
        else
          $this->mShowEditButton = true;
    }
```

13. Also in `presentation/products_list.php`, add the following piece of code at the beginning of the `init()` method of `ProductsList`:

```
    public function init()
    {
      // Prepare the Edit button
      $this->mEditActionTarget =
        Link::Build(str_replace(VIRTUAL_LOCATION, '', getenv('REQUEST_URI')));

      if (isset ($_SESSION['admin_logged']) &&
          $_SESSION['admin_logged'] == true &&
          isset ($_POST['product_id']))
      {
        if (isset ($this->_mDepartmentId) && isset ($this->_mCategoryId))
          header('Location: ' .
                  htmlspecialchars_decode(
                  Link::ToProductAdmin($this->_mDepartmentId,
                                       $this->_mCategoryId,
                                       (int)$_POST['product_id'])));
        else
        {
          $product_locations =
            Catalog::GetProductLocations((int)$_POST['product_id']);

          if (count($product_locations) > 0)
          {
            $department_id = $product_locations[0]['department_id'];
            $category_id = $product_locations[0]['category_id'];

            header('Location: ' .
                    htmlspecialchars_decode(
                    Link::ToProductAdmin($department_id,
                                         $category_id,
                                         (int)$_POST['product_id'])));
          }
        }
      }
    }
```

```
/* If searching the catalog, get the list of products by calling
   the Search business tier method */
if (isset ($this->mSearchString))
{
  // Get search results
  $search_results = Catalog::Search($this->mSearchString,
                                    $this->mAllWords,
                                    $this->mPage,
                                    $this->mrTotalPages);
```

14. Open `presentation/store_front.php`, and add the following piece of code at the beginning of the `init()` method of the `StoreFront` class:

```
public function init()
{
  $_SESSION['link_to_store_front'] =
    Link::Build(str_replace(VIRTUAL_LOCATION, '', getenv('REQUEST_URI')));

  // Create "Continue Shopping" link for the PayPal shopping cart
  if (!isset ($_GET['AddProduct']))
  {
```

15. Open `presentation/admin_menu.php`, and modify the constructor of the `AdminMenu` class like this:

```
public function __construct()
{
  $this->mLinkToStoreAdmin = Link::ToAdmin();
  $this->mLinkToAttributesAdmin = Link::ToAttributesAdmin();

  if (isset ($_SESSION['link_to_store_front']))
    $this->mLinkToStoreFront = $_SESSION['link_to_store_front'];
  else
    $this->mLinkToStoreFront = Link::ToIndex();

  $this->mLinkToLogout = Link::ToLogout();
}
```

16. Navigate TShirtShop while logged in as administrator, and notice the Edit buttons that show up, as shown in Figures 11-6 and 11-7.

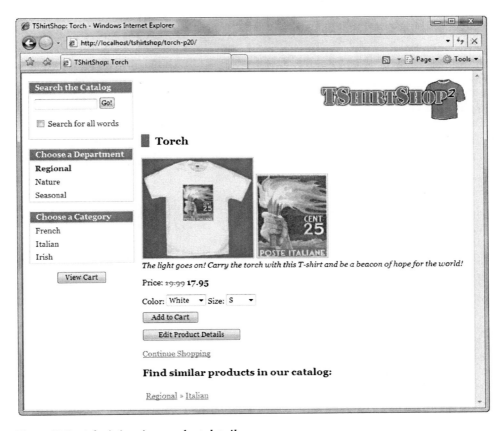

Figure 11-7. *Administering product details*

How It Works: In-Store Administration Links

In this exercise, we created Edit buttons throughout the product catalog that are displayed only when the current user is logged in as an administrator. This way, an administrator who notices, say, a product description that needs to be updated can click the Edit button for that product right from the catalog, rather than having to browse the administration pages to find that product.

Implementing this feature wasn't probably the most exciting coding exercise you've ever completed, but it's a really useful feature that your clients will certainly appreciate!

Summary

In this chapter, you implemented the administrative features for your products, including features for adding or editing product attributes, assigning products to categories, uploading product pictures, and so on. You've also updated TShirtShop to include edit buttons in the catalog pages, so administrators can much more easily access the administration pages for updating the catalog information.

Now that the dry part of developing the administration end of our site is finished, we are finally ready to move on the really exciting features. In Chapter 12, you'll implement your own shopping cart in TShirtShop, replacing the PayPal shopping cart you've been using so far.

## PART 2

Phase II
of Development

CHAPTER 12

■■■

Creating Your Own Shopping Cart

Welcome to the second stage of development! During this stage, you'll start improving and adding new features to the already existing, fully functional e-commerce site.

So, what exactly can you improve? Well, the answer to this question isn't hard to find if you take a quick look at the popular e-commerce sites on the Web. They personalize the experience for the user, provide product recommendations, remember customers' preferences, and boast many other features that make the site easy to remember and hard to leave without first purchasing something.

In the first stage of development, you extensively relied on a third-party payment processor (PayPal) that supplied an integrated shopping cart, so you didn't record any shopping cart or order information in the database. Right now, your site isn't capable of displaying a list of "most wanted" products or any other information about the products that have been sold through the web site because, at this stage, you aren't tracking the products sold. Saving order information in the database is one of our priorities now because most of the features you want to implement next rely on having this information.

At the end of this chapter you'll have a functional shopping cart, but the visitor will not yet be able to order the products contained in it. You'll add this functionality in Chapter 14, when you implement a custom checkout system that integrates with your new shopping cart. Specifically, in this chapter you'll learn how to

- Analyze the elements of a shopping cart.

- Create the database structure that stores shopping cart records.

- Implement the data tier, business tier, and presentation tier components of the shopping cart.

- Update the PayPal Add to Cart buttons you created in Chapter 9 to work with the new shopping cart.

- Create a shopping cart summary box to remind users of the products in their carts and of the total amounts.

- Implement a shopping cart administration page that allows site administrators to delete shopping carts that weren't updated in a specified number of days.

Designing the Shopping Cart

In this chapter we will implement a custom shopping cart, which stores data in the local `tshirtshop` database. This will provide you with much more flexibility than the PayPal shopping cart, over which you have no control and which cannot be easily saved into your database for further processing and analysis. With the custom shopping cart, when the visitor clicks the Add to Cart button for a product, the product is still added to the visitor's shopping cart, but this cart and product information will be stored directly in the `tshirtshop` database rather than the inaccessible PayPal database. When the visitor clicks the View Cart button, a page like the one shown in Figure 12-1 appears.

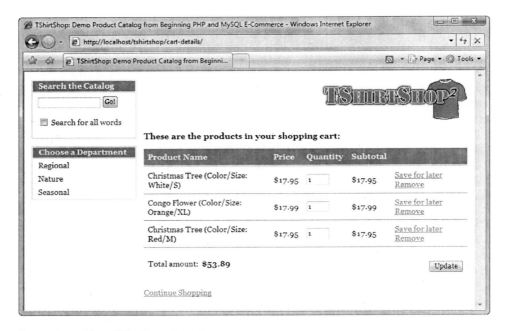

Figure 12-1. *The TShirtShop shopping cart*

Our shopping cart will have a "Save for later" feature, which allows the visitor to order only a subset of the products in the cart and save the other items for purchase at a later time. When a product is saved for later, it's moved to a separate list of the shopping cart and is not included in the order when the visitor checks out (see Figure 12-2).

In all the other pages except the shopping cart page, the visitor will be able to see a shopping cart summary in the left part of the screen, as shown in Figure 12-3.

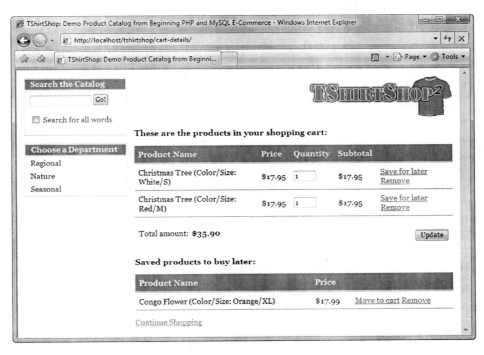

Figure 12-2. *The TShirtShop "Save for later" feature*

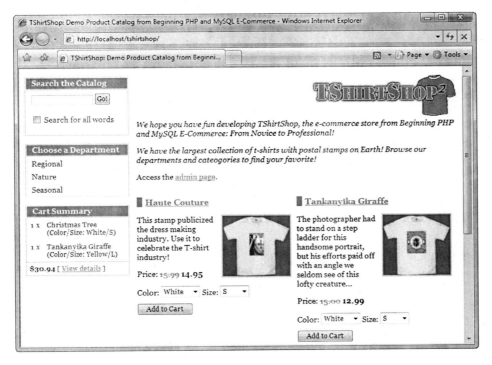

Figure 12-3. *The TShirtShop shopping cart summary*

Before starting to write the code for the shopping cart, let's take a closer look at what we're going to do.

First, note that you won't have any user personalization features at this stage of the site. It doesn't matter who buys your products at this point; you just want to know what products were sold and when. When you add user customization features in the later chapters, your task will be fairly simple: when the visitor authenticates, the visitor's temporary (anonymous) shopping cart will be associated with the visitor's account. Because you work with temporary shopping carts, even after implementing the customer account system, the visitor isn't required to supply additional information (log in) earlier than necessary.

We use cookies to keep track of shopping carts. When the visitor clicks the Add to Cart button, the server first verifies whether a shopping cart cookie already exists on the visitor's computer. If it does, the specified product is added to the existing cart. Otherwise, the server generates a unique cart ID, saves it to the client's cookie, and then adds the product to the newly generated shopping cart.

Storing Shopping Cart Information

You will store all the information from the shopping carts in a single table named shopping_cart. Follow the next exercise to create the shopping_cart table.

Exercise: Creating the shopping_cart Table

1. Load phpMyAdmin, select your tshirtshop database, and open a new SQL query page.

2. Execute the following code, which creates the shopping_cart table in your tshirtshop database:

```
-- Create shopping_cart table
CREATE TABLE `shopping_cart` (
   `item_id`      INT            NOT NULL  AUTO_INCREMENT,
   `cart_id`      CHAR(32)       NOT NULL,
   `product_id`   INT            NOT NULL,
   `attributes`   VARCHAR(1000)  NOT NULL,
   `quantity`     INT            NOT NULL,
   `buy_now`      BOOL           NOT NULL  DEFAULT true,
   `added_on`     DATETIME       NOT NULL,
   PRIMARY KEY (`item_id`),
   KEY `idx_shopping_cart_cart_id` (`cart_id`)
);
```

How It Works: The shopping_cart Table

Let's look at each field in shopping_cart:

- item_id is the primary key of the table. Its value uniquely identifies a shopping cart record.

- cart_id is a CHAR(32) value that uniquely identifies a visitor's shopping cart (as opposed to just one shopping cart record).

- product_id references the ID of an existing product.

- `attributes` is a varying character field that stores the attributes that were selected by the visitor when adding the product to the shopping cart. A possible value of this field can be, for example, `"Color/Size: White/XL"`.

- `quantity` stores the product quantity in the shopping cart.

- `buy_now` is a Boolean field with the default value of `true` that supports the "Save for later" feature. When the customer checks out, only the products that have this value set to `true` are added to the order, whereas the "Save for later" products remain in the shopping cart.

- `added_on` is a date field that is populated with the date the product was added to the cart. This value is used to calculate the age of a shopping cart, which gives us the ability to delete old shopping carts from the database.

The value of the first field, `item_id`, is calculated every time a new record is created in the table. No surprises here—you have worked with `AUTO_INCREMENT` columns before.

The value of `cart_id` represents the ID of the shopping cart. This value is calculated by the business tier each time a new shopping cart is created. The `cart_id` field contains a value that uniquely identifies a visitor's shopping cart.

It's important to understand that a visitor can have several products in the shopping cart, that each product can have different attribute configurations, and that a customer can purchase the same product several times, each with different attributes. For example, a visitor can have a Black/L Torch t-shirt and a Pink/M Torch t-shirt in the cart. For this reason, the only combination of fields that guarantees the uniqueness of the cart items is (`cart_id, product_id, attributes`), which could serve as the table primary key.

But wait! MySQL has a limitation regarding the size of the columns that form a primary key. Trying to create the primary key as specified earlier triggers the following error: "#1071 – Specified key was too long; max key length is 999 bytes." What the error basically says is that the cumulated size of the columns forming the primary key cannot exceed 999 bytes, and in our case the three fields exceed 3,000 bytes (a UT8-encoded character takes three bytes). This means that if you want to create the primary key of the three fields, you'd have to limit the size of attributes to 269 characters. This limitation may or may not be acceptable to you, depending on what you're selling, and even if it is OK today, you might need larger attributes tomorrow!

Our workaround is to create an artificial primary key value—`item_id`—and then use that field as the primary key. This solution of adding a new field breaks the rules of the third normal form, or simply said, it's not a perfect database design; however, with some careful planning, it allows us to implement a functional shopping cart.

Implementing the Data Tier

Now we'll create the stored procedures that support the necessary shopping cart operations. We'll create these procedures in the `tshirtshop` database:

- `shopping_cart_add_product` adds a product to the shopping cart.

- `shopping_cart_update` modifies shopping cart products' quantities and subsequent pricing.

- `shopping_cart_remove_product` deletes a product from the visitor's shopping cart.

- `shopping_cart_get_products` gets the list of products in the specified shopping cart and is called when you want to show the user the shopping cart.

- `shopping_cart_get_saved_products` gets the list of products saved to buy later and is called when the user requests the shopping cart details page.

- `shopping_cart_get_total_amount` returns the total costs of the products in the specified product cart.

- `shopping_cart_save_product_for_later` saves a product to a shopping cart for later purchase.

- `shopping_cart_move_product_to_cart` moves a product from the "Save for later" list back to the "main" shopping cart.

Now let's create each method one at a time in the following exercise.

Exercise: Implementing the Stored Procedures

1. Use phpMyAdmin to create the stored procedures described in the following steps. Don't forget to set the $$ delimiter before executing the code of each step.

2. Create the `shopping_cart_add_product` stored procedure in your `tshirtshop` database by executing this code:

```
-- Create shopping_cart_add_product stored procedure
CREATE PROCEDURE shopping_cart_add_product(IN inCartId CHAR(32),
  IN inProductId INT, IN inAttributes VARCHAR(1000))
BEGIN
  DECLARE productQuantity INT;

  -- Obtain current shopping cart quantity for the product
  SELECT quantity
  FROM   shopping_cart
  WHERE  cart_id = inCartId
         AND product_id = inProductId
         AND attributes = inAttributes
  INTO   productQuantity;

  -- Create new shopping cart record, or increase quantity of existing record
  IF productQuantity IS NULL THEN
    INSERT INTO shopping_cart(cart_id, product_id, attributes,
                              quantity, added_on)
           VALUES (inCartId, inProductId, inAttributes, 1, NOW());
  ELSE
    UPDATE shopping_cart
    SET    quantity = quantity + 1, buy_now = true
    WHERE  cart_id = inCartId
           AND product_id = inProductId
           AND attributes = inAttributes;
  END IF;
END$$
```

The `shopping_cart_add_product` stored procedure is called when the visitor clicks the Add to Cart button for one of the products. If the selected product already exists in the shopping cart, its quantity is increased by one; otherwise, one new unit is added to the shopping cart (a new `shopping_cart` record is created).

The procedure receives three parameters: `inCartId`, `inProductId`, and `inAttributes`. It first determines whether the product already exists in the shopping cart by looking for `cart_id`, `product_id`, and `attributes`. If this combination exists in the `shopping_cart` table, it means the visitor already has the product in its shopping cart, so you update the existing quantity by adding one unit. Otherwise, `shopping_cart_add_product` creates a new record for the product in `shopping_cart` with a default quantity of 1. The `NOW()` MySQL function is used to retrieve the current date to populate the `added_on` field.

3. Execute the following code, which creates the `shopping_cart_update` stored procedure in your `tshirtshop` database:

```
-- Create shopping_cart_update_product stored procedure
CREATE PROCEDURE shopping_cart_update(IN inItemId INT, IN inQuantity INT)
BEGIN
  IF inQuantity > 0 THEN
    UPDATE shopping_cart
    SET    quantity = inQuantity, added_on = NOW()
    WHERE  item_id = inItemId;
  ELSE
    CALL shopping_cart_remove_product(inItemId);
  END IF;
END$$
```

The `shopping_cart_update` stored procedure updates the quantity of one item. This stored procedure is called when the visitor clicks the Update button in the shopping cart page *and is called once for each item that needs to be updated*.

The procedure receives two parameters: `inItemId` and `inQuantity`. If `inQuantity` is zero or less, `shopping_cart_update` is smart enough to remove the mentioned item from the shopping cart. Otherwise, it updates the quantity of the item in the shopping cart and also updates `added_on` to accurately reflect the time the record was last modified. Updating `added_on` is useful for the catalog administration page, where this field is used to calculate the shopping cart age and remove old shopping carts. For this purpose, we consider that an item whose quantity has been modified is a "new item."

4. Execute the following code, which creates the `shopping_cart_remove_product` stored procedure in your `tshirtshop` database:

```
-- Create shopping_cart_remove_product stored procedure
CREATE PROCEDURE shopping_cart_remove_product(IN inItemId INT)
BEGIN
  DELETE FROM shopping_cart WHERE item_id = inItemId;
END$$
```

The `shopping_cart_remove_product` stored procedure removes an item from the shopping cart when a visitor clicks the Remove button for one of the items in the shopping cart.

5. Execute this code, which creates the shopping_cart_get_products stored procedure in your tshirtshop database:

```
-- Create shopping_cart_get_products stored procedure
CREATE PROCEDURE shopping_cart_get_products(IN inCartId CHAR(32))
BEGIN
  SELECT     sc.item_id, p.name, sc.attributes,
             COALESCE(NULLIF(p.discounted_price, 0), p.price) AS price,
             sc.quantity,
             COALESCE(NULLIF(p.discounted_price, 0),
                      p.price) * sc.quantity AS subtotal
  FROM       shopping_cart sc
  INNER JOIN product p
               ON sc.product_id = p.product_id
  WHERE      sc.cart_id = inCartId AND sc.buy_now;
END$$
```

The shopping_cart_get_products stored procedure returns the items in the shopping cart mentioned by the inCartId parameter. Because the shopping_cart table stores the product_id for each product it stores, you need to join the shopping_cart and product tables to get the information you need.

Note that some of the items can have discounted prices. When an item has a discounted price (which happens when its discounted_price value is different from 0), then its discounted price should be used for calculations. Otherwise, its list price should be used. The following expression returns discounted_price if different from 0; otherwise, it returns price.

```
COALESCE(NULLIF(p.discounted_price, 0), p.price)
```

Note This is the first time you've worked with the COALESCE and NULLIF conditional expressions, so we'll now explain what they do. COALESCE can receive any number of parameters, and it returns the first one that is not NULL. NULLIF receives two parameters and returns NULL if they're equal; otherwise, it returns the first of the parameters. In our case, we use NULLIF to test whether the p.discounted_price is 0; if this condition is true, NULLIF returns false, and the COALESCE function will return p.price. If p.discounted_price is different from 0, the whole expression returns p.discounted_price.

---

6. Execute the following code, which creates the shopping_cart_get_saved_products stored procedure in your tshirtshop database:

```
-- Create shopping_cart_get_saved_products stored procedure
CREATE PROCEDURE shopping_cart_get_saved_products(IN inCartId CHAR(32))
BEGIN
  SELECT     sc.item_id, p.name, sc.attributes,
             COALESCE(NULLIF(p.discounted_price, 0), p.price) AS price
  FROM       shopping_cart sc
  INNER JOIN product p
               ON sc.product_id = p.product_id
  WHERE      sc.cart_id = inCartId AND NOT sc.buy_now;
END$$
```

The `shopping_cart_get_saved_products` stored procedure returns the items saved for later in the shopping cart specified by the `inCartId` parameter.

7. Execute the following code, which creates the `shopping_cart_get_total_amount` stored procedure in your `tshirtshop` database:

```
-- Create shopping_cart_get_total_amount stored procedure
CREATE PROCEDURE shopping_cart_get_total_amount(IN inCartId CHAR(32))
BEGIN
  SELECT     SUM(COALESCE(NULLIF(p.discounted_price, 0), p.price)
                  * sc.quantity) AS total_amount
  FROM       shopping_cart sc
  INNER JOIN product p
                ON sc.product_id = p.product_id
  WHERE      sc.cart_id = inCartId AND sc.buy_now;
END$$
```

The `shopping_cart_get_total_amount` stored procedure returns the total value of the items in the shopping cart before applicable taxes and shipping charges. This is called when displaying the total amount for the shopping cart. If the cart is empty, `total_amount` will be 0.

8. Execute the following code, which creates the `shopping_cart_save_product_for_later` stored procedure in your `tshirtshop` database:

```
-- Create shopping_cart_save_product_for_later stored procedure
CREATE PROCEDURE shopping_cart_save_product_for_later(IN inItemId INT)
BEGIN
  UPDATE shopping_cart
  SET    buy_now = false, quantity = 1
  WHERE  item_id = inItemId;
END$$
```

The `shopping_cart_save_product_for_later` stored procedure saves a shopping cart item to the "Save for later" list so the visitor can buy it later (the item isn't sent to checkout when placing the order). This is accomplished by setting the value of the `buy_now` field to `false`.

9. Execute this code, which creates the `shopping_cart_move_product_to_cart` stored procedure in your `tshirtshop` database:

```
-- Create shopping_cart_move_product_to_cart stored procedure
CREATE PROCEDURE shopping_cart_move_product_to_cart(IN inItemId INT)
BEGIN
  UPDATE shopping_cart
  SET    buy_now = true, added_on = NOW()
  WHERE  item_id = inItemId;
END$$
```

The `shopping_cart_move_product_to_cart` stored procedure sets the buy_now state for a shopping cart item to `true`, so the visitor can buy the product when placing the order.

Implementing the Business Tier

To implement the business tier for the shopping cart, we'll create a file named shopping_cart.php, which contains the ShoppingCart class. This class has the following methods:

- SetCartId() generates a new shopping cart ID and saves it on the visitor's browser as a cookie and in the session.

- GetCartId() returns the shopping cart ID.

- AddProduct() adds a new product to the visitor's shopping cart.

- Update() modifies a product quantity in the visitor's shopping cart or deletes the product from the cart if the quantity is zero or negative.

- RemoveProduct() removes a product from the shopping cart.

- GetCartProducts() retrieves all the products in the shopping cart.

- GetTotalAmount() returns the total amount of the products in the cart.

- SaveProductForLater() saves a product in the cart for later.

- MoveProductToCart() moves a product from the "Save for later" list back to the "main" shopping cart.

Let's write the code.

Exercise: Implementing the Shopping Cart Business Logic

1. First, add the following two lines at the end of your include/config.php file. These constants are used to differentiate between current shopping cart items and items that are saved for later.

```
// Shopping cart item types
define('GET_CART_PRODUCTS', 1);
define('GET_CART_SAVED_PRODUCTS', 2);
```

2. Create a new file called shopping_cart.php in the business folder. Add the following code to the file, and then we'll comment on it afterward:

```php
<?php
// Business tier class for the shopping cart
class ShoppingCart
{
  // Stores the visitor's Cart ID
  private static $_mCartId;

  // Private constructor to prevent direct creation of object
  private function __construct()
  {
  }
```

```php
/* This will be called by GetCartId to ensure we have the
   visitor's cart ID in the visitor's session in case
   $_mCartID has no value set */
public static function SetCartId()
{
  // If the cart ID hasn't already been set ...
  if (self::$_mCartId == '')
  {
    // If the visitor's cart ID is in the session, get it from there
    if (isset ($_SESSION['cart_id']))
    {
      self::$_mCartId = $_SESSION['cart_id'];
    }
    // If not, check whether the cart ID was saved as a cookie
    elseif (isset ($_COOKIE['cart_id']))
    {
      // Save the cart ID from the cookie
      self::$_mCartId = $_COOKIE['cart_id'];
      $_SESSION['cart_id'] = self::$_mCartId;

      // Regenerate cookie to be valid for 7 days (604800 seconds)
      setcookie('cart_id', self::$_mCartId, time() + 604800);
    }
    else
    {
      /* Generate cart id and save it to the $_mCartId class member,
         the session and a cookie (on subsequent requests $_mCartId
         will be populated from the session) */
      self::$_mCartId = md5(uniqid(rand(), true));

      // Store cart id in session
      $_SESSION['cart_id'] = self::$_mCartId;

      // Cookie will be valid for 7 days (604800 seconds)
      setcookie('cart_id', self::$_mCartId, time() + 604800);
    }
  }
}

// Returns the current visitor's card id
public static function GetCartId()
{
  // Ensure we have a cart id for the current visitor
  if (!isset (self::$_mCartId))
    self::SetCartId();

  return self::$_mCartId;
}
```

```php
// Adds product to the shopping cart
public static function AddProduct($productId, $attributes)
{
  // Build SQL query
  $sql = 'CALL shopping_cart_add_product(
                  :cart_id, :product_id, :attributes)';

  // Build the parameters array
  $params = array (':cart_id' => self::GetCartId(),
                   ':product_id' => $productId,
                   ':attributes' => $attributes);

  // Execute the query
  DatabaseHandler::Execute($sql, $params);
}

// Updates the shopping cart with new product quantities
public static function Update($itemId, $quantity)
{
  // Build SQL query
  $sql = 'CALL shopping_cart_update(:item_id, :quantity)';

  // Build the parameters array
  $params = array (':item_id' => $itemId,
                   ':quantity' => $quantity);

  // Execute the query
  DatabaseHandler::Execute($sql, $params);
}

// Removes product from shopping cart
public static function RemoveProduct($itemId)
{
  // Build SQL query
  $sql = 'CALL shopping_cart_remove_product(:item_id)';

  // Build the parameters array
  $params = array (':item_id' => $itemId);

  // Execute the query
  DatabaseHandler::Execute($sql, $params);
}

// Gets shopping cart products
public static function GetCartProducts($cartProductsType)
{
  $sql = '';
  // If retrieving "active" shopping cart products ...
```

```
  if ($cartProductsType == GET_CART_PRODUCTS)
  {
    // Build SQL query
    $sql = 'CALL shopping_cart_get_products(:cart_id)';
  }
  // If retrieving products saved for later ...
  elseif ($cartProductsType == GET_CART_SAVED_PRODUCTS)
  {
    // Build SQL query
    $sql = 'CALL shopping_cart_get_saved_products(:cart_id)';
  }
  else
    trigger_error($cartProductsType. ' value unknown', E_USER_ERROR);

  // Build the parameters array
  $params = array (':cart_id' => self::GetCartId());

  // Execute the query and return the results
  return DatabaseHandler::GetAll($sql, $params);
}

/* Gets total amount of shopping cart products before tax and/or
   shipping charges (not including the ones that are being
   saved for later) */
public static function GetTotalAmount()
{
  // Build SQL query
  $sql = 'CALL shopping_cart_get_total_amount(:cart_id)';

  // Build the parameters array
  $params = array (':cart_id' => self::GetCartId());

  // Execute the query and return the results
  return DatabaseHandler::GetOne($sql, $params);
}

// Save product to the Save for Later list
public static function SaveProductForLater($itemId)
{
  // Build SQL query
  $sql = 'CALL shopping_cart_save_product_for_later(:item_id)';

  // Build the parameters array
  $params = array (':item_id' => $itemId);

  // Execute the query
  DatabaseHandler::Execute($sql, $params);
}
```

```
// Get product from the Save for Later list back to the cart
public static function MoveProductToCart($itemId)
{
  // Build SQL query
  $sql = 'CALL shopping_cart_move_product_to_cart(:item_id)';

  // Build the parameters array
  $params = array (':item_id' => $itemId);

  // Execute the query
  DatabaseHandler::Execute($sql, $params);
  }
}
?>
```

3. Include a reference to shopping_cart.php in index.php:

```
// Load Business Tier
require_once BUSINESS_DIR . 'catalog.php';
require_once BUSINESS_DIR . 'shopping_cart.php';
```

How It Works: The Business Tier of the Shopping Cart

When a visitor adds a product or requests any shopping cart operation, we generate a shopping cart ID for the visitor if there isn't one. You take care of this in the SetCartId() method that generates a cart ID to the $_mCartId member of the ShoppingCart class. The shopping cart ID is also saved in the visitor's session and in a persistent cookie.

SetCartId() starts by verifying that the $_mCartId member was already set, in which case we don't need to read it from external sources:

```
public static function SetCartId()
{
  // If the cart ID hasn't already been set ...
  if (self::$_mCartId == '')
  {
```

If we don't have the ID in the member variable, the next place to look is the visitor's session:

```
    // If the visitor's cart ID is in the session, get it from there
    if (isset ($_SESSION['cart_id']))
    {
      self::$_mCartId = $_SESSION['cart_id'];
    }
```

If the ID couldn't be found in the session either, we check whether it was saved as a cookie. If yes, we save the value both to the session and to the $_mCartId member, and we regenerate the cookie to reset its expiration date:

```
    // If not, check whether the cart ID was saved as a cookie
    elseif (isset ($_COOKIE['cart_id']))
    {
      // Save the cart ID from the cookie
```

```
    self::$_mCartId = $_COOKIE['cart_id'];
    $_SESSION['cart_id'] = self::$_mCartId;

    // Regenerate cookie to be valid for 7 days (604800 seconds)
    setcookie('cart_id', self::$_mCartId, time() + 604800);
  }
```

Finally, if the cart ID can't be found anywhere, a new one is generated and saved to the session, to the $_mCartId member, and to the persistent cookie:

```
    else
    {
      /* Generate cart id and save it to the $_mCartId class member,
         the session and a cookie (on subsequent requests $_mCartId
         will be populated from the session) */
      self::$_mCartId = md5(uniqid(rand(), true));

      // Store cart id in session
      $_SESSION['cart_id'] = self::$_mCartId;

      // Cookie will be valid for 7 days (604800 seconds)
      setcookie('cart_id', self::$_mCartId, time() + 604800);
    }
  }
}
```

Three functions are used to generate the cart ID: md5(), uniqid(), and rand(). The call to md5(uniqid(rand(), true)) generates a unique, difficult-to-predict, 32-byte value, which represents the cart ID.

■**Note** If you're interested to know the details about generating the cart ID, here they are. The md5() function uses the Message-Digest algorithm 5 (MD5) to calculate the hash value of a value it receives as a parameter. The hash value is 32 characters long. The uniqid() function returns a unique identifier based on the current time in microseconds; its first parameter is the prefix to be appended to its generated value, in this case, the rand() function that returns a pseudo-random value between 0 and RAND_MAX, which is platform dependent. If the second parameter of uniqid() is true, uniqid() adds an additional combined linear congruential generator (combined LCG) entropy at the end of the return value, which should make the results even "more unique."

In short, uniquid(rand(), true) generates a "very unique" value, which is passed through md5() to ensure that it becomes a random sequence of characters that is 32 characters long.

The SetCartId method is used only by the GetCartId() method that returns the cart ID. GetCartId() first checks to see whether $_mCartId has been set, and if not, it calls SetCartId() before returning the value of $_mCartId:

```
// Returns the current visitor's cart id
public static function GetCartId()
```

```
{
  // Ensure we have a cart id for the current visitor
  if (!isset (self::$_mCartId))
    self::SetCartId();

  return self::$_mCartId;
}
```

This value is saved to the cart_id field in the shopping_cart table, which is a CHAR(32) field especially to fit the value returned by the md5() function.

Let's also take a look at the GetCartProducts() method. This method returns the products in the shopping cart. It receives $cartProductsType as a parameter, which determines whether you're looking for the current shopping cart products or for the products saved for later.

If $cartProductsType is equal to the GET_CART_PRODUCTS constant, GetCartProducts() will return the shopping cart products. If $cartProductsType is equal to the GET_CART_SAVED_PRODUCTS constant, GetCartProducts() will return the "Save for later" products. If $cartProductsType is neither GET_CART_PRODUCTS nor GET_CART_SAVED_PRODUCTS, the method will raise an error.

All the other business tier methods you've written basically call their associated data tier functions to perform the various shopping cart tasks.

Implementing the Presentation Tier

Now let's build the user interface of the shopping cart. After updating the storefront, you'll have Add to Cart buttons for each product and a View Cart link in the cart summary box on the left part of the page. If the visitor's cart is empty, the link isn't displayed anymore, as you can see in Figure 12-4.

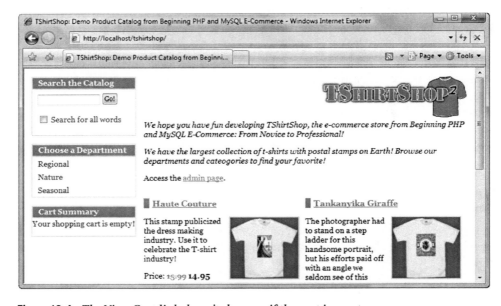

Figure 12-4. *The View Cart link doesn't show up if the cart is empty.*

If you added PayPal integration as presented in Chapter 9, you already have these buttons on your site, and you'll update their functionality here.

When clicking View Cart, the cart details componentized template is loaded in store_ front.tpl. You can see this componentized component in action in Figure 12-1. The mechanism for loading the cart details componentized template is the same one you already used in store_front.php to load other components. When the Add to Cart button is clicked, index.php is reloaded with an additional parameter (CartAction) in the query string:

```
http://localhost/tshirtshop/index.php?CartAction=1&ItemId=10
```

When clicking View Cart, the CartAction parameter added to the query string doesn't take any value.

The shopping cart has five cart actions, which are described using the following self-explanatory constants in the configuration file (include/config.php): ADD_PRODUCT, REMOVE_ PRODUCT, UPDATE_PRODUCTS_QUANTITIES, SAVE_PRODUCT_FOR_LATER, and MOVE_PRODUCT_TO_CART.

Before moving on, let's recap the main steps you'll take to implement the whole UI of the shopping cart:

1. Modify the Add to Cart buttons to use the custom shopping cart.

2. Add a shopping cart summary box to store_front.tpl instead of the View Cart button.

3. Modify the CheckRequest() method from the Link class from the presentation/link.php file to recognize the CartAction query string parameter.

4. Implement the cart_details componentized template.

Updating the Add to Cart Buttons

You need to change the code of products_list.tpl so that each displayed product includes an Add to Cart button with a link like the ones shown earlier (a link to index.php with an additional CartAction parameter in the query string).

Exercise: Adding Products to the New Shopping Cart

1. Add the following code at the end of include/config.php:

```
// Cart actions
define('ADD_PRODUCT', 1);
define('REMOVE_PRODUCT', 2);
define('UPDATE_PRODUCTS_QUANTITIES', 3);
define('SAVE_PRODUCT_FOR_LATER', 4);
define('MOVE_PRODUCT_TO_CART', 5);
```

2. If you implemented the PayPal shopping cart, you need to delete the code from presentation/store_ front.php that redirects to a PayPal link when an Add to Cart button is clicked. Open presentation/ store_front.php, and *delete* the following code from the init() method:

```
// Create "Continue Shopping" link for the PayPal shopping cart
if (!isset ($_GET['AddProduct']))
{
```

```
      /* Store the current request needed for the paypal
         continue shopping functionality */
      $_SESSION['paypal_continue_shopping'] =
        Link::Build(str_replace(VIRTUAL_LOCATION, '',
                                 $_SERVER['REQUEST_URI']));
      ...
      ...
      // Redirect to the PayPal cart page
      header('HTTP/1.1 302 Found');
      header('Location: ' . $paypal_url);

      // clear the output buffer and stop execution
      flush();
      ob_flush();
      ob_end_clean();
      exit();
    }
```

3. Open presentation/link.php, and modify the code of the CheckRequest() method of the Link class as highlighted:

```
// Redirects to proper URL if not already there
public static function CheckRequest()
{
  $proper_url = '';

  if (isset ($_GET['Search']) || isset($_GET['SearchResults']) ||
      isset ($_GET['CartAction']))
  {
    return ;
  }
```

4. Also in presentation/link.php, delete the ToAddProduct() method, and add a method named ToCart() that creates the Add Product and View Cart links:

```
// Create a shopping cart link
public static function ToCart($action = 0, $target = null)
{
  $link = '';

  switch ($action)
  {
    case ADD_PRODUCT:
      $link = 'index.php?CartAction=' . ADD_PRODUCT . '&ItemId=' . $target;
      break;
    default:
      $link = 'cart-details/';
  }
```

```
    return self::Build($link);
  }
```

5. Open `presentation/products_list.php`, and find the following code from the `init()` method of the `ProductList` class:

```
// Create the Add to Cart link
$this->mProducts[$i]['link_to_add_product'] =
  Link::ToAddProduct($this->mProducts[$i]['product_id']);
```

Replace it with the following code that builds the Add to Cart links for our shopping cart:

```
// Create the Add to Cart link
$this->mProducts[$i]['link_to_add_product'] =
  Link::ToCart(ADD_PRODUCT, $this->mProducts[$i]['product_id']);
```

6. Open `presentation/product.php`, and find the following code from the `init()` method of the `Product` class:

```
// Create the Add to Cart link
$this->mProduct['link_to_add_product'] =
  Link::ToAddProduct($this->_mProductId);
```

Replace it with the following code that builds the Add to Cart links for our shopping cart:

```
// Create the Add to Cart link
$this->mProduct['link_to_add_product'] =
  Link::ToCart(ADD_PRODUCT, $this->_mProductId);
```

How It Works: Adding Products Links

You created Add to Cart buttons that link to `index.php` with an additional `CartAction` parameter to the original query string. After making this change, execute the page to make sure you have your button in place, although you can't really test how it works until finishing the presentation tier.

If you browse now to your favorite department or category and click the Add to Cart button of one of the products, you're taken to a URL such as this:

`index.php?CartAction=1&ItemId=10`

The `CartAction` parameter appended at the beginning of the query string specifies the shopping cart action requested by the visitor. When adding a new product, the action is coded with 1. At this moment, the new link gets you to the home page because your site doesn't know yet how to interpret the `CartAction` query string parameter.

Displaying the Cart Summary

Instead of PayPal's View Cart buttons, we want to have a cart summary component with a "View details" link, as shown in Figure 12-3. Implement the `cart_summary` componentized template by following the steps of the next exercise.

Exercise: Displaying the Cart Summary

1. Let's start by removing the View Cart button. Locate and delete the following code in `presentation/templates/store_front.tpl`:

```
<div class="view-cart">
  <form target="_self" method="post"
   action="{$smarty.const.PAYPAL_URL}">
    <input type="hidden" name="cmd" value="_cart" />
    <input type="hidden" name="business"
     value="{$smarty.const.PAYPAL_EMAIL}" />
    <input type="hidden" name="display" value="1" />
    <input type="hidden" name="shopping_url"
     value="{$obj->mPayPalContinueShoppingLink}" />
    <input type="hidden" name="return"
     value="{$smarty.const.PAYPAL_RETURN_URL}" />
    <input type="hidden" name="cancel_return"
     value="{$smarty.const.PAYPAL_CANCEL_RETURN_URL}" />
    <input type="submit" name="view_cart" value="View Cart" />
  </form>
</div>
```

2. In the same file, add a reference to the cart summary component:

```
{include file="search_box.tpl"}
{include file="departments_list.tpl"}
{include file=$obj->mCategoriesCell}
{include file=$obj->mCartSummaryCell}
```

3. Open `presentation/store_front.php`, and update it as highlighted in the following code snippet. This way, the `StoreFront` class will recognize the `CartAction` query string parameter.

```php
<?php
class StoreFront
{
  public $mSiteUrl;
  // Define the template file for the page contents
  public $mContentsCell = 'first_page_contents.tpl';
  // Define the template file for the categories cell
  public $mCategoriesCell = 'blank.tpl';
  // Define the template file for the cart summary cell
  public $mCartSummaryCell = 'blank.tpl';
  // Page title
  public $mPageTitle;
  ...
  public function init()
  {
    ...
    // Load product details page if visiting a product
```

```
      if (isset ($_GET['ProductId']))
        $this->mContentsCell = 'product.tpl';

      // Load search result page if we're searching the catalog
      elseif (isset ($_GET['SearchResults']))
        $this->mContentsCell = 'search_results.tpl';

      // Load shopping cart or cart summary template
      if (isset ($_GET['CartAction']))
        $this->mContentsCell = 'cart_details.tpl';
      else
        $this->mCartSummaryCell = 'cart_summary.tpl';

      // Load the page title
      $this->mPageTitle = $this->_GetPageTitle();
    }
```

4. Create a new presentation object file named presentation/cart_summary.php, and add the following code to it:

```
<?php
// Class that deals with managing the shopping cart summary
class CartSummary
{
  // Public variables to be used in Smarty template
  public $mTotalAmount;
  public $mItems;
  public $mLinkToCartDetails;
  public $mEmptyCart;

  // Class constructor
  public function __construct()
  {
    /* Calculate the total amount for the shopping cart
       before applicable taxes and/or shipping charges */
    $this->mTotalAmount = ShoppingCart::GetTotalAmount();

    // Get shopping cart products
    $this->mItems = ShoppingCart::GetCartProducts(GET_CART_PRODUCTS);

    if (empty($this->mItems))
      $this->mEmptyCart = true;
    else
      $this->mEmptyCart = false;

    $this->mLinkToCartDetails = Link::ToCart();
  }
}
?>
```

5. Create a new file in the `presentation/templates` folder named `cart_summary.tpl`, and write the following code to it:

```
{* cart_summary.tpl *}
{load_presentation_object filename="cart_summary" assign="obj"}
{* Start cart summary *}
<div class="box">
  <p class="box-title">Cart Summary</p>
{if $obj->mEmptyCart}
  <p class="empty-cart">Your shopping cart is empty!</p>
{else}
  <table class="cart-summary">
    <tbody>
  {section name=i loop=$obj->mItems}
      <tr>
        <td width="30" valign="top" align="right">
          {$obj->mItems[i].quantity} x
        </td>
        <td>
          {$obj->mItems[i].name} ({$obj->mItems[i].attributes})
        </td>
      </tr>
  {/section}
      <tr>
        <td colspan="2" class="cart-summary-subtotal">
          <span class="price">${$obj->mTotalAmount}</span>
          <span>
            [ <a href="{$obj->mLinkToCartDetails}">View details</a> ]
          </span>
        </td>
      </tr>
    </tbody>
  </table>
{/if}
</div>
{* End cart summary *}
```

6. Open `.htaccess`, and add the following lines:

```
# Rewrite cart details pages
RewriteRule ^cart-details/?$ index.php?CartAction [L]
```

7. Add the following styles to the `tshirtshop.css` file from the `styles` folder:

```
.empty-cart {
  margin: 0px;
  padding: 5px 10px;
}
```

```
table.cart-summary {
  font-size: 85%;
  margin: 0px;
  padding: 0px 5px;
}

table.cart-summary td {
  border: none;
}

table.cart-summary td.cart-summary-subtotal {
  border-top: 1px solid #C6E1EC;
  padding: 5px 5px;
}
```

How It Works: Displaying the Cart Summary

If you reload TShirtShop, you'll now see the cart summary box on the left side of the page. At this point, you still can't add new products to your cart because you need to create the cart details page. You'll be able to fully test your cart summary component after you implement the cart details page in the next exercise.

Displaying the Cart Details

Right now, clicking the Add to Cart and View Cart buttons generates an error because you haven't written the cart_details componentized template yet, which displays the visitor's shopping cart details. To create the new componentized template, you first create a new template named cart_details.tpl in the presentation/templates folder. Next, you create the cart_details.php presentation object file that will keep your CartDetails class behind the cart_details.tpl template.

Exercise: Displaying the Cart Details

1. Modify presentation/store_front.php to manage the Continue Shopping functionality in the cart details page. Add the following code in the init() method from the StoreFront class:

```php
public function init()
{
  $_SESSION['link_to_store_front'] =
    Link::Build(str_replace(VIRTUAL_LOCATION, '', getenv('REQUEST_URI')));

  // Build the "continue shopping" link
  if (!isset ($_GET['CartAction']))
    $_SESSION['link_to_last_page_loaded'] = $_SESSION['link_to_store_front'];

  // Load department details if visiting a department
  if (isset ($_GET['DepartmentId']))
```

2. Create a new presentation object file named presentation/cart_details.php, and add the following code to it:

```php
<?php
// Class that deals with managing the shopping cart
class CartDetails
{
  // Public variables available in smarty template
  public $mCartProducts;
  public $mSavedCartProducts;
  public $mTotalAmount;
  public $mIsCartNowEmpty = 0; // Is the shopping cart empty?
  public $mIsCartLaterEmpty = 0; // Is the 'saved for later' list empty?
  public $mLinkToContinueShopping;
  public $mUpdateCartTarget;

  // Private attributes
  private $_mItemId;
  private $_mCartAction;

  // Class constructor
  public function __construct()
  {
    if (isset ($_GET['CartAction']))
      $this->_mCartAction = $_GET['CartAction'];
    else
      trigger_error('CartAction not set', E_USER_ERROR);

    // These cart operations require a valid product id
    if ($this->_mCartAction == ADD_PRODUCT ||
        $this->_mCartAction == REMOVE_PRODUCT ||
        $this->_mCartAction == SAVE_PRODUCT_FOR_LATER ||
        $this->_mCartAction == MOVE_PRODUCT_TO_CART)
    {
      if (isset ($_GET['ItemId']))
        $this->_mItemId = $_GET['ItemId'];
      else
        trigger_error('ItemId must be set for this type of request',
                      E_USER_ERROR);
    }

    $this->mUpdateCartTarget = Link::ToCart(UPDATE_PRODUCTS_QUANTITIES);

    // Setting the "Continue shopping" link target
    if (isset ($_SESSION['link_to_last_page_loaded']))
      $this->mLinkToContinueShopping = $_SESSION['link_to_last_page_loaded'];
  }
```

```php
public function init()
{
  switch ($this->_mCartAction)
  {
    case ADD_PRODUCT:
      $selected_attributes = array ();
      $selected_attribute_values = array ();

      // Get selected product attributes if any
      foreach ($_POST as $key => $value)
      {
        // If there are fields starting with "attr_" in the POST array
        if (substr($key, 0, 5) == 'attr_')
        {
          // Get the selected attribute name and value
          $selected_attributes[] = substr($key, strlen('attr_'));
          $selected_attribute_values[] = $_POST[$key];
        }
      }

      $attributes = '';

      if (count($selected_attributes) > 0)
        $attributes = implode('/', $selected_attributes) . ': ' .
                      implode('/', $selected_attribute_values);

      ShoppingCart::AddProduct($this->_mItemId, $attributes);

      header('Location: ' . $this->mLinkToContinueShopping);

      break;
    case REMOVE_PRODUCT:
      ShoppingCart::RemoveProduct($this->_mItemId);

      header('Location: ' . Link::ToCart());

      break;
    case UPDATE_PRODUCTS_QUANTITIES:
      for($i = 0; $i < count($_POST['itemId']); $i++)
        ShoppingCart::Update($_POST['itemId'][$i], $_POST['quantity'][$i]);

      header('Location: ' . Link::ToCart());

      break;
    case SAVE_PRODUCT_FOR_LATER:
      ShoppingCart::SaveProductForLater($this->_mItemId);
```

```
        header('Location: ' . Link::ToCart());

      break;
    case MOVE_PRODUCT_TO_CART:
      ShoppingCart::MoveProductToCart($this->_mItemId);

      header('Location: ' . Link::ToCart());

      break;
    default:
      // Do nothing
      break;
  }

  /* Calculate the total amount for the shopping cart
     before applicable taxes and/or shipping */
  $this->mTotalAmount = ShoppingCart::GetTotalAmount();

  // Get shopping cart products
  $this->mCartProducts =
    ShoppingCart::GetCartProducts(GET_CART_PRODUCTS);

  // Gets the Saved for Later products
  $this->mSavedCartProducts =
    ShoppingCart::GetCartProducts(GET_CART_SAVED_PRODUCTS);

  // Check whether we have an empty shopping cart
  if (count($this->mCartProducts) == 0)
    $this->mIsCartNowEmpty = 1;

  // Check whether we have an empty Saved for Later list
  if (count($this->mSavedCartProducts) == 0)
    $this->mIsCartLaterEmpty = 1;

  // Build the links for cart actions
  for ($i = 0; $i < count($this->mCartProducts); $i++)
  {
    $this->mCartProducts[$i]['save'] =
      Link::ToCart(SAVE_PRODUCT_FOR_LATER,
                   $this->mCartProducts[$i]['item_id']);

    $this->mCartProducts[$i]['remove'] =
      Link::ToCart(REMOVE_PRODUCT,
                   $this->mCartProducts[$i]['item_id']);
  }
```

```php
    for ($i = 0; $i < count($this->mSavedCartProducts); $i++)
    {
      $this->mSavedCartProducts[$i]['move'] =
        Link::ToCart(MOVE_PRODUCT_TO_CART,
                     $this->mSavedCartProducts[$i]['item_id']);

      $this->mSavedCartProducts[$i]['remove'] =
        Link::ToCart(REMOVE_PRODUCT,
                     $this->mSavedCartProducts[$i]['item_id']);
    }
  }
}
?>
```

3. Create a new file named cart_details.tpl in the presentation/templates folder, and add the following code to it:

```smarty
{* cart_details.tpl *}
{load_presentation_object filename="cart_details" assign="obj"}
{if $obj->mIsCartNowEmpty eq 1}
<h3>Your shopping cart is empty!</h3>
{else}
<h3>These are the products in your shopping cart:</h3>
<form class="cart-form" method="post" action="{$obj->mUpdateCartTarget}">
  <table class="tss-table">
    <tr>
      <th>Product Name</th>
      <th>Price</th>
      <th>Quantity</th>
      <th>Subtotal</th>
      <th> </th>
    </tr>
  {section name=i loop=$obj->mCartProducts}
    <tr>
      <td>
        <input name="itemId[]" type="hidden"
         value="{$obj->mCartProducts[i].item_id}" />
        {$obj->mCartProducts[i].name}
        ({$obj->mCartProducts[i].attributes})
      </td>
      <td>${$obj->mCartProducts[i].price}</td>
      <td>
        <input type="text" name="quantity[]" size="5"
         value="{$obj->mCartProducts[i].quantity}" />
      </td>
      <td>${$obj->mCartProducts[i].subtotal}</td>
      <td>
        <a href="{$obj->mCartProducts[i].save}">Save for later</a>
```

```
            <a href="{$obj->mCartProducts[i].remove}">Remove</a>
          </td>
        </tr>
      {/section}
      </table>
      <table class="cart-subtotal">
        <tr>
          <td>
            <p>
              Total amount: 
              <font class="price">${$obj->mTotalAmount}</font>
            </p>
          </td>
          <td align="right">
            <input type="submit" name="update" value="Update" />
          </td>
        </tr>
      </table>
    </form>
    {/if}
    {if ($obj->mIsCartLaterEmpty eq 0)}
    <h3>Saved products to buy later:</h3>
    <table class="tss-table">
      <tr>
        <th>Product Name</th>
        <th>Price</th>
        <th> </th>
      </tr>
      {section name=j loop=$obj->mSavedCartProducts}
      <tr>
        <td>
          {$obj->mSavedCartProducts[j].name}
          ({$obj->mSavedCartProducts[j].attributes})
        </td>
        <td>
          ${$obj->mSavedCartProducts[j].price}
        </td>
        <td>
            <a href="{$obj->mSavedCartProducts[j].move}">Move to cart</a>
            <a href="{$obj->mSavedCartProducts[j].remove}">Remove</a>
        </td>
      </tr>
      {/section}
    </table>
    {/if}
    {if $obj->mLinkToContinueShopping}
    <p><a href="{$obj->mLinkToContinueShopping}">Continue Shopping </a></p>
    {/if}
```

4. Open presentation/link.php, and modify the ToCart() method from the Link class as highlighted here:

```php
// Create a shopping cart link
public static function ToCart($action = 0, $target = null)
{
  $link = '';

  switch ($action)
  {
    case ADD_PRODUCT:
      $link = 'index.php?CartAction=' . ADD_PRODUCT . '&ItemId=' . $target;
      break;
    case REMOVE_PRODUCT:
      $link = 'index.php?CartAction=' .
              REMOVE_PRODUCT . '&ItemId=' . $target;
      break;
    case UPDATE_PRODUCTS_QUANTITIES:
      $link = 'index.php?CartAction=' . UPDATE_PRODUCTS_QUANTITIES;
      break;
    case SAVE_PRODUCT_FOR_LATER:
      $link = 'index.php?CartAction=' .
              SAVE_PRODUCT_FOR_LATER . '&ItemId=' . $target;
      break;
    case MOVE_PRODUCT_TO_CART:
      $link = 'index.php?CartAction=' .
              MOVE_PRODUCT_TO_CART . '&ItemId=' . $target;
      break;
    default:
      $link = 'cart-details/';
  }

  return self::Build($link);
}
```

5. Add the following styles to the tshirtshop.css file from the styles folder:

```css
.cart-subtotal td {
  border: none;
  margin: 10px 0px;
  width: 100%;
}

.yui-b div form.cart-form {
  margin: 0;
  padding: 0;
}
```

You just finished the visitor's part of the code for this chapter, so now it's time to try it and make sure everything works as expected. Test it by adding products to the shopping cart, changing the quantity, and removing items.

How It Works: The Shopping Cart

The actions that the shopping cart can execute are defined by the constants defined in `include/config.php`: ADD_PRODUCT, REMOVE_PRODUCT, UPDATE_PRODUCTS_QUANTITIES, SAVE_PRODUCT_FOR_LATER, and MOVE_PRODUCT_TO_CART. Note that we didn't define any variable for viewing the shopping cart, so if `CartAction` does not take any value or its value is not equal to one of the action variables, it will simply display the shopping cart content.

Every shopping cart action, except viewing and updating the shopping cart, relies on the `ItemId` query string parameter (an error is raised if it isn't set). If the proper conditions are met, the business tier method that corresponds to the visitor's action is called.

Administering the Shopping Cart

Now that you've finished writing the shopping cart, you need to take two more issues into account, both related to administration:

- How to delete from the catalog a product that exists in shopping carts.

- How to count or remove old shopping cart elements by building a simple shopping cart administration page. This is important because without this feature, the shopping_cart table keeps growing, filled with old temporary (and useless) carts.

Deleting Products Residing in the Shopping Cart

The catalog administration pages enable you to completely delete products from the catalog. Before removing a product, you should also remove its appearances in visitors' shopping carts.

Update the `catalog_delete_product` function from the `tshirtshop` database by following these steps:

1. Use phpMyAdmin to execute the code described in the following steps. Also, don't forget to set $$ as the delimiter before executing the code at each step.

2. Execute the following code, which deletes the old `catalog_delete_product` stored procedure from the `tshirtshop` database:

```
-- Drop the old catalog_delete_product stored procedure
DROP PROCEDURE catalog_delete_product$$
```

3. Execute this code, which creates the new `catalog_delete_product` stored procedure in your tshirtshop database:

```
-- Create catalog_delete_product stored procedure
CREATE PROCEDURE catalog_delete_product(IN inProductId INT)
BEGIN
  DELETE FROM product_attribute WHERE product_id = inProductId;
  DELETE FROM product_category WHERE product_id = inProductId;
  DELETE FROM shopping_cart WHERE product_id = inProductId;
  DELETE FROM product WHERE product_id = inProductId;
END$$
```

Building the Shopping Cart Admin Page

The second problem with the shopping cart is that at this moment no mechanism exists to delete the old records from the shopping_cart table. On a high-activity web site, the shopping_cart table can grow very large.

With the current version of the code, shopping cart IDs are stored at the client browser for seven days. As a result, you can assume that any shopping carts that haven't been updated in the last ten days are invalid and can be safely removed.

In the following exercise, you'll quickly implement a simple shopping cart administration page, where the administrator can see how many old shopping cart entries exist and can delete them if necessary. Figure 12-5 shows this page.

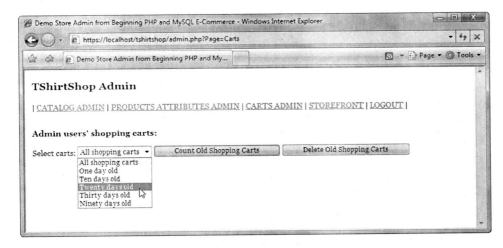

Figure 12-5. *Administering shopping carts*

The most interesting aspect you need to understand is the SQL logic that deletes all shopping carts that haven't been updated in a certain amount of time. This isn't as simple as it sounds—at first sight, you might think all you have to do is delete all the records in shopping_cart whose added_on is older than a specified date. However, this strategy doesn't work with shopping carts that are modified over time (say the visitor has been adding items to the cart each week in the past three months). If the last change to the shopping cart is recent, none of its elements should be deleted, even if some are very old. In other words, you should either remove all elements in a shopping cart or remove none of them. The age of a shopping cart is given by the age of its most recently modified or added product.

That being said, implement the new functionality by following this exercise.

Exercise: Creating the Shopping Cart Admin Page

1. Use phpMyAdmin to execute and create the stored procedures described in the following step. Also, don't forget to set $$ as the delimiter before executing the code.

2. Add the following data tier stored procedures to the tshirtshop database:

```
-- Create shopping_cart_count_old_carts stored procedure
CREATE PROCEDURE shopping_cart_count_old_carts(IN inDays INT)
BEGIN
  SELECT COUNT(cart_id) AS old_shopping_carts_count
  FROM    (SELECT    cart_id
           FROM      shopping_cart
           GROUP BY cart_id
           HAVING    DATE_SUB(NOW(), INTERVAL inDays DAY) >= MAX(added_on))
         AS old_carts;
END$$

-- Create shopping_cart_delete_old_carts stored procedure
CREATE PROCEDURE shopping_cart_delete_old_carts(IN inDays INT)
BEGIN
  DELETE FROM shopping_cart
  WHERE  cart_id IN
          (SELECT cart_id
           FROM    (SELECT    cart_id
                    FROM      shopping_cart
                    GROUP BY cart_id
                    HAVING    DATE_SUB(NOW(), INTERVAL inDays DAY) >=
                              MAX(added_on))
                  AS sc);
END$$
```

3. Add the following business tier method to business/shopping_cart.php:

```
// Count old shopping carts
public static function CountOldShoppingCarts($days)
{
  // Build SQL query
  $sql = 'CALL shopping_cart_count_old_carts(:days)';

  // Build the parameters array
  $params = array (':days' => $days);

  // Execute the query and return the results
  return DatabaseHandler::GetOne($sql, $params);
}

// Deletes old shopping carts
public static function DeleteOldShoppingCarts($days)
{
  // Build SQL query
  $sql = 'CALL shopping_cart_delete_old_carts(:days)';

  // Build the parameters array
  $params = array (':days' => $days);
```

```
   // Execute the query
   DatabaseHandler::Execute($sql, $params);
 }
```

4. Include a reference to shopping_cart.php in admin.php:

```
// Load Business Tier
require_once BUSINESS_DIR . 'catalog.php';
require_once BUSINESS_DIR . 'shopping_cart.php';
```

5. Create a new presentation object file named presentation/admin_carts.php, and add the following code to it:

```php
<?php
// Class that supports cart admin functionality
class AdminCarts
{
  // Public variables available in smarty template
  public $mMessage;
  public $mDaysOptions = array (0  => 'All shopping carts',
                                1  => 'One day old',
                                10 => 'Ten days old',
                                20 => 'Twenty days old',
                                30 => 'Thirty days old',
                                90 => 'Ninety days old');
  public $mSelectedDaysNumber = 0;
  public $mLinkToCartsAdmin;

  // Private members
  public $_mAction = '';

  // Class constructor
  public function __construct()
  {
    foreach ($_POST as $key => $value)
      // If a submit button was clicked ...
      if (substr($key, 0, 6) == 'submit')
      {
        // Get the scope of submit button
        $this->_mAction = substr($key, strlen('submit_'), strlen($key));

        // Get selected days number
        if (isset ($_POST['days']))
          $this->mSelectedDaysNumber = (int) $_POST['days'];
        else
          trigger_error('days value not set');
      }
```

```
      $this->mLinkToCartsAdmin = Link::ToCartsAdmin();
    }

    public function init()
    {
      // If counting shopping carts ...
      if ($this->_mAction == 'count')
      {
        $count_old_carts =
          ShoppingCart::CountOldShoppingCarts($this->mSelectedDaysNumber);

        if ($count_old_carts == 0)
          $count_old_carts = 'no';

        $this->mMessage = 'There are ' . $count_old_carts .
                          ' old shopping carts (selected option: ' .
                          $this->mDaysOptions[$this->mSelectedDaysNumber] .
                          ').';
      }

      // If deleting shopping carts ...
      if ($this->_mAction == 'delete')
      {
        $this->mDeletedCarts =
          ShoppingCart::DeleteOldShoppingCarts($this->mSelectedDaysNumber);

        $this->mMessage = 'The old shopping carts were removed from the
          database (selected option: ' .
          $this->mDaysOptions[$this->mSelectedDaysNumber] .').';
      }
    }
  }
?>
```

6. Create a new file in the presentation/templates folder named admin_carts.tpl, and type the following code:

```
{* admin_carts.tpl *}
{load_presentation_object filename="admin_carts" assign="obj"}
<form action="{$obj->mLinkToCartsAdmin}" method="post">
  <h3>Admin users&#039; shopping carts:</h3>
  {if $obj->mMessage}<p>{$obj->mMessage}</p>{/if}
  <p>
    Select carts:
    {html_options name="days" options=$obj->mDaysOptions
                  selected=$obj->mSelectedDaysNumber}
    <input type="submit" name="submit_count" value="Count Old Shopping Carts" />
    <input type="submit" name="submit_delete"
```

```
      value="Delete Old Shopping Carts" />
  </p>
</form>
```

7. Open `presentation/link.php`, and add following code at the end of the Link class:

```php
// Create link to shopping carts administration page
public static function ToCartsAdmin()
{
  return self::ToAdmin('Page=Carts');
}
```

8. Modify `presentation/templates/admin_menu.tpl` by adding the following highlighted link code to the carts admin page:

```html
<p> |
  <a href="{$obj->mLinkToStoreAdmin}">CATALOG ADMIN</a> |
  <a href="{$obj->mLinkToAttributesAdmin}">PRODUCTS ATTRIBUTES ADMIN</a> |
  <a href="{$obj->mLinkToCartsAdmin}">CARTS ADMIN</a> |
  <a href="{$obj->mLinkToStoreFront}">STOREFRONT</a> |
  <a href="{$obj->mLinkToLogout}">LOGOUT</a> |
</p>
```

9. Open `presentation/admin_menu.php`, and add the following code that creates the new menu link:

```php
<?php
class AdminMenu
{
  public $mLinkToStoreAdmin;
  public $mLinkToAttributesAdmin;
  public $mLinkToCartsAdmin;
  public $mLinkToStoreFront;
  public $mLinkToLogout;

  public function __construct()
  {
    $this->mLinkToStoreAdmin = Link::ToAdmin();
    $this->mLinkToAttributesAdmin = Link::ToAttributesAdmin();
    $this->mLinkToCartsAdmin = Link::ToCartsAdmin();

    if (isset ($_SESSION['link_to_store_front']))
      $this->mLinkToStoreFront = $_SESSION['link_to_store_front'];
```

10. Add the highlighted code at the end of the `init()` method of the StoreAdmin class in `presentation/store_admin.php`, which loads `presentation/templates/admin_carts.tpl`:

```php
      elseif ($admin_page == 'Products')
        $this->mContentsCell = 'admin_products.tpl';
      elseif ($admin_page == 'ProductDetails')
        $this->mContentsCell = 'admin_product_details.tpl';
      elseif ($admin_page == 'Carts')
```

```
                    $this->mContentsCell = 'admin_carts.tpl';
                }
            }
        }
    ?>
```

How It Works: The Shopping Cart Admin Page

The hard work of the shopping cart admin page is done by the two stored procedures you've added to the tshirtshop database: shopping_cart_count_old_carts and shopping_cart_delete_old_carts. They both receive as a parameter the number of days that determine when a shopping cart is old, and they use the same logic to calculate the shopping cart elements that are old and should be removed.

The age of a shopping cart is given by the age of the most recently added or changed item and is calculated using the GROUP BY SQL clause. The following is the condition that establishes whether a cart should be considered old:

```
WHERE   cart_id IN
          (SELECT cart_id
            FROM   (SELECT   cart_id
                    FROM     shopping_cart
                    GROUP BY cart_id
                    HAVING   DATE_SUB(NOW(), INTERVAL inDays DAY) >=
                             MAX(added_on))
                AS sc);
```

The two nested subqueries are necessary to overcome a MySQL limitation that doesn't allow selecting from a table that is being updated.

Summary

In this chapter, you learned how to store the shopping cart information in the database, and you learned a few other things in the process as well. Probably the most interesting was the way you can store the shopping cart ID as a cookie on the client, because you haven't done anything similar so far in this book.

After working through the process of creating the shopping cart, starting with the database and ending with the presentation tier, we also touched on the new administrative challenges.

In Chapter 13, you'll use a technology named AJAX to upgrade the functionality of your product catalog and shopping cart. In Chapter 14, you'll extend the shopping cart by creating a checkout system, and you will start storing the details of your customers' shopping carts in the database. This will allow you to implement fancy features such as dynamic product recommendations, a topic that will be covered in Chapter 15.

CHAPTER 13

■ ■ ■

Implementing AJAX Features

In this chapter we'll enhance our fully functional shopping cart using the technology that made web development headlines in 2005. This technology is called AJAX, and it allows you to make your web applications easier and more pleasant to use for your visitors.

Although AJAX isn't a huge subject, at least compared to other programming fields, it doesn't have a trivial learning curve either. We're going to be here with you the whole way, but you should know there are several AJAX books on the market, including two written specifically for PHP developers: *AJAX and PHP: Building Responsive Web Applications* (Cristian Darie, Bogdan Brinzarea, Filip Chereches-Tosa, and Mihai Bucica, Packt Publishing, 2006.) and *Beginning AJAX with PHP: From Novice to Professional* (Lee Babin. Apress, 2006.).

In this chapter we'll take you through a very concise AJAX tutorial, and then we'll update TShirtShop to

- Allow adding new products to the shopping cart without completely reloading the web page when the Add to Cart buttons are clicked. This way, clicking an Add to Cart button will update the shopping cart much faster, without freezing the web page while the action happens.

- Improve the responsiveness of the shopping cart actions, such as changing the product quantity, removing products, or saving them to the "Save for later" section.

Admittedly, these might not seem like huge feature improvements. However, they're the kind of nice touches that improve a user's experience on your site, and they can differentiate a modern web site from one that feels like it was created in the last century.

AJAX Quick Start

The great advantage AJAX can bring to a web application is that it improves the *responsiveness* of the application. Responsiveness is a term we use when speaking about how fast an application responds to a user's request. In the world of web development, this includes the time it takes for a web site (the server) to respond to a clicked link or to update a page with new data.

The term AJAX was coined by Jesse James Garrett (http://www.jjg.net/about/) in 2005 as an acronym for Asynchronous JavaScript and XML. What's in a name? If you say "not much," we agree, at least in this case. AJAX is a programming technique that uses JavaScript on the client side to make background server calls and retrieve additional data as needed, updating certain portions of the web page without causing full page reloads. AJAX is often cited in the context of Web 2.0 (http://en.wikipedia.org/wiki/Web_2) as being one of the technologies that allows for creating next-generation web sites, which provide a friendly environment that facilitates online information sharing and collaboration.

Technically, the only "new" thing about AJAX is the name. The technologies required to create AJAX web applications have been around for a while. To perform asynchronous server calls (send server requests in the background), we use the XMLHttpRequest object of JavaScript (together with a few other lesser-known techniques). To update the visitor's page in response to the data retrieved from the server, we use the Document Object Model (DOM) eventually together with Cascading Style Sheets (CSS) for a modern presentation layer. And to encode the information passed back and forth from the server, XML (the format implied by the AJAX acronym) or other data formats can be used, with a popular alternative to XML being JavaScript Object Model (JSON). We'll discuss each of these shortly, but first we'll show a visual representation of how an AJAX-enabled web page works. See Figure 13-1.

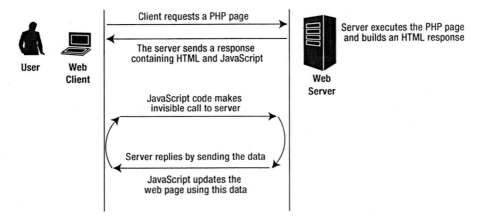

Figure 13-1. *Asynchronous server call using AJAX*

JavaScript

JavaScript is a programming language supported by all modern web browsers, which makes it ideal for implementing various features at the client (web browser) level. JavaScript code can be included in (or referenced from) HTML pages, and it can execute when the page loads or when certain events on the page happen (such as a button being clicked). Some of the first uses of JavaScript were to add (more or less) useful graphical effects to web pages (remember the falling snow and the flying bats?), but in the meantime both the language and the skills (and tastes) of the people using it have improved.

Although familiarity with JavaScript will certainly help you, we'll teach you everything you need to improve your shop. For a comprehensive JavaScript reference, you should check out *JavaScript: The Definitive Guide* (David Flangan. O'Reilly, 2006.) or check one of the several free tutorials on the Web, such as those at these URLs:

- http://www.echoecho.com/javascript.htm

- http://www.webteacher.com/javascript/

- http://www.w3schools.com/js/default.asp

- http://en.wikipedia.org/wiki/JavaScript

DOM

The DOM is an application programming interface (API) that allows for reading and manipulating hierarchical structures such as HTML and XML documents. Most languages contain a DOM component; in the context of AJAX programming, the DOM interface of JavaScript allows you to read, parse, alter, and create HTML elements of the web page. More often than not, after receiving the server response to the asynchronous call you've made, you'll want to modify the page accordingly to inform the visitor of the results.

JavaScript provides the default document object that is a DOM representation of the current page. For example, you can use document.write() to add content to the <body> element of the page, and you can use document.getElementById() to get an element of the page. For example, take the following piece of code that edits the content of the <div> element named cart-summary:

```
document.getElementById("cart-summary").innerHTML = response;
```

> **Caution** There's one obvious detail you must always keep in mind when modifying the contents of a page using JavaScript: clients that don't support JavaScript won't benefit from the new features. The important features of the web site must *not* rely on JavaScript being enabled; in other words, the implementations must be *degradable*. A particular case of visitors that don't execute JavaScript code is web spiders, such as those from Google, Yahoo, or MSN, indexing your web site. You must not display any important content using JavaScript because it would be completely invisible to web spiders, which is not something you can typically afford when you run an online business.

To learn more about the DOM, we recommend you check out the following resources:

- http://www.quirksmode.org/dom/intro.html (a DOM tutorial)

- http://www.javascriptkit.com/javatutors/dom.shtml (a DOM tutorial)

- http://www.topxml.com/learning/games/b/default.asp (a useful and entertaining DOM game)

- http://krook.org/jsdom/ (a DOM reference)

XMLHttpRequest

XMLHttpRequest is the object you can use from your JavaScript code to make asynchronous HTTP server requests. This allows you to initiate HTTP requests and receive responses from the server in the background, without requiring the user to submit the page to the server. Typically, when the response is received from the server, the DOM is used to alter the page accordingly. This allows you to implement responsive functionality and visual effects backed with live data from the server, without the user experiencing significant visual interruptions. This is AJAX.

XMLHttpRequest was implemented by Microsoft in 1999 as an ActiveX object in Internet Explorer, and it eventually became the *de facto* standard for all browsers, with it being supported as a native object by all modern web browsers except Internet Explorer 6.

Let's see how `XMLHttpRequest` works. You need to learn how to create the object, how to initialize it by setting the appropriate parameters, how to start the server request, and how to read the results.

Creating the XMLHttpRequest Object

In Internet Explorer 6 and older, `XMLHttpRequest` is implemented as an ActiveX control, and you create it like this:

```
xmlHttp = new ActiveXObject("Microsoft.XMLHttp");
```

In Internet Explorer 7 and other web browsers—including Firefox, Opera, and Safari—`XMLHttpRequest` is a native object, so you create instances of it like this:

```
xmlHttp = new XMLHttpRequest();
```

To create `XMLHttpRequest` objects for all browsers, we'll use the following JavaScript function, which creates an `XMLHttpRequest` instance by using the native object if available or the `Microsoft.XMLHttp` ActiveX control for visitors who use Internet Explorer 6 or older:

```
// Creates an XMLHttpRequest instance
function createXmlHttpRequestObject()
{
  // xmlHttp will store the reference to the XMLHttpRequest object
  var xmlHttp;
  // Try to instantiate the native XMLHttpRequest object
  try
  {
    // Create an XMLHttpRequest object
    xmlHttp = new XMLHttpRequest();
  }
  catch(e)
  {
    // Assume IE6 or older
    try
    {
      xmlHttp = new ActiveXObject("Microsoft.XMLHttp");
    }
    catch(e) { }
  }
  // Return the created object or display an error message
  if (!xmlHttp)
    alert("Error creating the XMLHttpRequest object.");
  else
    return xmlHttp;
}
```

■**Note** `Microsoft.XMLHttp` is the oldest version of the ActiveX XMLHttp library, but the library comes in many more flavors and versions than you could imagine. Each piece of Microsoft software, including Internet Explorer and MDAC, has shipped with new versions of this ActiveX control, each with its own name. In our code we'll implement a technique that automatically detects the latest XMLHttp version installed on a user machine, but only if it is using Internet Explorer 6 or older. Otherwise, the native `XMLHttpRequest` object is still used.

`createXmlHttpRequestObject()` uses the JavaScript `try-catch` construct, which is a powerful exception-handling technique that was initially implemented in object-oriented programming (OOP) languages and now is also supported by PHP 5. An *exception* is an object that represents an error that has happened in your code at runtime. Exceptions can be caught and dealt with, in which case they don't block the execution of the code when they are raised.

■**Note** An exception propagates through the call stack of your program, from the place it was raised up to the environment on which it runs. The call stack is the list of methods being executed. So if a function `A()` calls a function `B()` that at its turn calls a function `C()`, then the call stack will be formed from all three methods. If an exception happens in `C()`, you can handle it using a `try-catch` block in function `C()` before the exception is passed out of the function. If the exception isn't caught and handled in `C()`, it propagates to `B()`, and so on. The final layer is the web browser, which may display an unpleasant error message to your visitor, depending on how it's configured.

Using the `try-catch` syntax, you can catch the exception and handle it locally so that the error won't be propagated to the user's browser. The `try-catch` syntax is as follows:

```
try
{
  // Code that might generate an exception
}
catch (e)
{
  // Execution is passed to this block when an exception is thrown in the try block
  // (exception details are available through the e parameter)
}
```

If an error happens while executing the code inside the `try` block, the execution is passed immediately to the `catch` block. If no error happens inside the `try` block, then the code in the `catch` block never executes.

The way you handle each exception depends very much on the situation at hand. Sometimes you will simply ignore the error; other times you will flag it somehow in the code, or you will display an error message to your visitor. In our particular case, when we want to create an `XMLHttpRequest` object, we will first try to create the object as if it were a native browser object, like this:

```
// Try to instantiate the native XMLHttpRequest object
try
{
  // Create an XMLHttpRequest object
  xmlHttp = new XMLHttpRequest();
}
```

Internet Explorer 7, Firefox, Opera, Safari, and other browsers will execute this piece of code just fine, and no error will be generated, because XMLHttpRequest is supported natively. However, Internet Explorer 6 and its older versions won't recognize the XMLHttpRequest object, an exception will be generated, and the execution will be passed to the catch block. For Internet Explorer 6 and older versions, the XMLHttpRequest object needs to be created as an ActiveX control:

```
catch(e)
{
  // Assume IE6 or older
  try
  {
    xmlHttp = new ActiveXObject("Microsoft.XMLHttp");
  }
  catch(e) { }
}
```

There are more techniques for creating the XMLHttpRequest object. For example, another technique is to use a JavaScript feature called *object detection*. This feature allows you to check whether a particular object is supported by the browser, and it works like this:

```
if (window.XMLHttpRequest)
{
  xmlHttp = new XMLHttpRequest();
}
```

At the end of createXmlHttpRequestObject, we test that xmlHttp contains a valid XMLHttpRequest instance:

```
// Return the created object or display an error message
if (!xmlHttp)
  alert("Error creating the XMLHttpRequest object.");
else
  return xmlHttp;
```

Here we used the reverse effect of JavaScript's object detection feature, which says that JavaScript will evaluate a valid object instance, such as xmlHttp, to true. The negation of this expression—!xmlHttp—returns true if xmlHttp is false, null, or undefined. (In JavaScript, undefined is a special "value" that is automatically assigned to a variable or object that has not been assigned a value.)

Using XMLHttpRequest

Once the XMLHttpRequest object has been created, you can start using it to initiate synchronous or asynchronous server requests. Table 13-1 describes the public methods and properties of this object.

Table 13-1. *The* XMLHttpRequest *API*

Method/Property	Description
abort	Stops the current request
getAllResponseHeaders()	Returns the response headers as a string
getResponseHeader("headerLabel")	Returns a single response header as a string
open("method", "URL"[, asyncFlag[, "userName"[, "password"]]])	Initializes the request parameters
send(content)	Performs the HTTP request
setRequestHeader("label", "value")	Sets an HTTP request header
onreadystatechange	Sets the callback function that handles request state changes
readyState	Returns the status of the request: 0 = uninitialized 1 = loading 2 = loaded 3 = interactive 4 = complete
responseText	Returns the server response as a string
responseXml	Returns the server response as an XML document that can be manipulated using JavaScript's DOM functions
status	Returns the status code of the request
statusText	Returns the status message of the request

The methods you will use with every server request are open() and send(). The open() method configures the request *without sending it*. It has two required parameters and a few optional ones. The first parameter specifies the method used to send data to the server page; the usual values are GET and POST. The second parameter is URL, which specifies where you want to send the request. The URL can be complete or relative. If the URL doesn't specify a resource accessible via HTTP, the first parameter is ignored.

The third parameter of open(), called async, specifies whether the request should be handled asynchronously. true means that your code processing carries on after send() returns without waiting for a response from the server; false means the script waits for a response before continuing processing. To enable asynchronous processing (which is the heart of the AJAX mechanism), you will need to set async to true and handle the onreadystatechange event to process the response from the server.

After configuring the connection with open(), you execute it using send(). When making a GET request, you send the parameters using the URL query string, as in http://localhost/ajax/test.php?param1=x&param2=y. This server request passes two parameters to the server—a parameter called param1 with the value x and a parameter called param2 with the value y:

```
// Call the server to execute the server-side operation
xmlHttp.open("GET", "http://localhost/ajax/test.php?param1=x&param2=y", true);
xmlHttp.onreadystatechange = handleRequestStateChange;
xmlHttp.send(null);
```

When using POST, you send the query string as a parameter of the send() method, instead of joining it on to the base URL, like this:

```
// Call the server page to execute the server-side operation
xmlHttp.open("POST", "http://localhost/ajax/test.php", true);
xmlHttp.onreadystatechange = handleRequestStateChange;
xmlHttp.send("param1=x&param2=y");
```

The two code samples should have the same effect. In practice, there are a few differences between POST and GET that you should know about:

- Using GET can help with debugging because you can simulate GET requests with a web browser, so you can easily see with your own eyes what your server script generates.

- POST is required when sending large blocks of data, which cannot be handled by GET.

- GET is meant to be used for retrieving data from the server, while POST is meant to submit changes. In the real world, it's good to obey these rules; otherwise, strange things can happen. For example, search engines send GET requests to read data from the Web, but they never post any data. If you use GET to submit changes and a search engine becomes aware of the address of the server script, that search engine could start modifying your data—and you certainly don't want that!

The minimal implementation of a function named process() that makes asynchronous server calls using GET looks like this:

```
function process()
{
  // Call the server to execute the server-side operation
  xmlHttp.open("GET", "server_script.php", true);
  xmlHttp.onreadystatechange = handleRequestStateChange;
  xmlHttp.send(null);
}
```

This implementation has the following potential problems:

- process() may be executed even if xmlHttp doesn't contain a valid XMLHttpRequest instance. This may happen if, for example, the user's browser doesn't support XMLHttpRequest. This would cause an unhandled exception to happen. Our other efforts to handle errors don't help very much if we aren't consistent and do something about the process function as well.

- process() isn't protected against other kinds of errors that could happen. For example, as you will see later in this chapter, some browsers will generate a security exception if they don't like the server you want to access with the XMLHttpRequest object.

A better version of process() looks like this:

```
// Performs a server request and assigns a callback function
function process()
{
  // Continue only if xmlHttp isn't void
  if (xmlHttp)
  {
    // Try to connect to the server
    try
    {
      // Initiate server request
      xmlHttp.open("GET", "server_script.php", true);
      xmlHttp.onreadystatechange = handleRequestStateChange;
      xmlHttp.send(null);
    }
    // Display an error in case of failure
    catch (e)
    {
      alert("Can't connect to server:\n" + e.toString());
    }
  }
}
```

If xmlHttp is null (or false), we don't display yet another error message, because we assume such a message was already displayed by the createXmlHttpRequestObject function. We make sure to signal any other connection problems, though.

Handling the Server Response

When making an asynchronous request, such as in the code snippets presented earlier, the execution of xmlHttp.send() doesn't freeze waiting for the server response; instead, the JavaScript code continues executing. The process() function shown earlier defines a function named handleRequestStateChange() as the callback method that should handle request state changes.

The readyState property can have one the following values representing the possible states of the request:

```
0 = uninitialized
1 = loading
2 = loaded
3 = interactive
4 = complete
```

Usually the handleRequestStateChange() method is called multiple times, when the request enters a new stage, but you can't rely on the web browser to raise the readystatechange event for all the mentioned states except state 4, which signals the request has completed.

The names of the states are self-explanatory except for state 3. The interactive state is an intermediate state when the response has been partially received. In our AJAX applications we will use only the complete state, which marks that a response has been fully received from the server.

The following code snippet shows the typical implementation of handleRequestStateChange and highlights the portion where you actually get to read the response from the server:

```
// Function executed when the state of the request changes
function handleRequestStateChange()
{
  // Continue if the process is completed
  if (xmlHttp.readyState == 4)
  {
    // Continue only if HTTP status is "OK"
    if (xmlHttp.status == 200)
    {
      // Retrieve the response
      response = xmlHttp.responseText;
      // Do something with the response
      // ...
    }
  }
}
```

Before attempting to read the received data, we also verify that the response status code is 200. Sending such a code indicates the status of the request is part of the HTTP protocol, and 200 is the status code that specifies that the request completed successfully. Other popular HTTP status codes are 404, which indicates that the requested resource couldn't be found, and 500, which indicates a server error.

Once again we can use try-catch blocks to handle errors that could happen while initiating a connection to the server or while reading the response from the server. An improved version of the handleRequestStateChange() function looks like this:

```
// Function executed when the state of the request changes
function handleRequestStateChange()
{
  // Continue if the process is completed
  if (xmlHttp.readyState == 4)
  {
    // Continue only if HTTP status is "OK"
    if (xmlHttp.status == 200)
    {
      try
      {
        // Retrieve the response
        response = xmlHttp.responseText;
        // Do something with the response
        // ...
      }
      catch(e)
      {
        // Display error message
        alert("Error reading the response: " + e.toString());
```

```
      }
    }
    else
    {
      // Display status message
      alert("There was a problem retrieving the data:\n" + xmlHttp.statusText);
    }
  }
}
```

In practice, we will be displaying more user-friendly error messages. Moreover, whenever possible, we'll make our code *degradable* so that when an error happens inside the JavaScript code, the functionality is instead performed using a typical form submit. Let's see how.

Writing Degradable Code

Ideally, a modern web application should use AJAX to enhance existing features whenever possible, while keeping the web site functional even when JavaScript isn't available. In our particular case, we want to let our visitors add products to their shopping carts and edit their shopping carts even if they have JavaScript disabled or if their web browser doesn't support JavaScript.

When a visitor clicks the Add to Cart button, we first try to make a background AJAX call to add the product to the visitor's cart and update the cart summary box accordingly. If an error happens when trying to make the call or if JavaScript is disabled, we submit the form to the server and add the product to the visitor's cart in a non-AJAX fashion. This way, we'll offer a better web experience to most of our users, while permitting the others to use our store as well.

This is easier to implement than it sounds. Take a look at the following code, which represents the AJAXified "Save for later" and Remove links in the shopping cart.

```
<a href="{$obj->mCartProducts[i].save}"
    onclick="return executeCartAction(this);">Save for later</a>
<a href="{$obj->mCartProducts[i].remove}"
    onclick="return executeCartAction(this);">Remove</a>
```

In both cases, a JavaScript function is executed as a result of the click event. If that function returns false, the link isn't followed anymore. If the function returns true or it's not executed at all, the link is followed, and the shopping cart gets modified using in a non-AJAX fashion.

The Add to Cart buttons are handled similarly, except in this case the JavaScript function is called when submitting the form:

```
onsubmit="return addProductToCart(this);">
```

Figure 13-2 describes what happens when a visitor clicks an Add to Cart button. The process is similar to that of updating shopping cart items, which we'll also implement in this chapter. As you can see, no matter whether the visitor has JavaScript or not, the same end result is achieved. The difference lies in the responsiveness; in the AJAX scenario the user doesn't have to wait a few seconds for the page to reload.

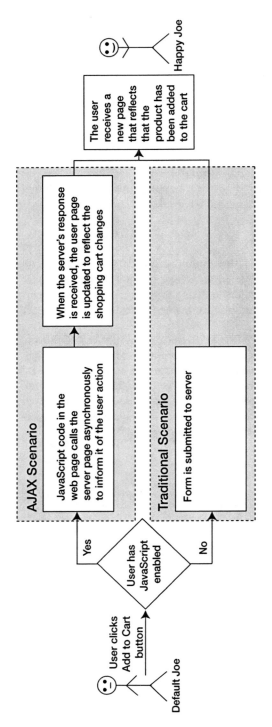

Figure 13-2. *Degradable AJAX feature*

Is AJAX Always Suitable?

We end the theoretical part of the chapter with a warning: AJAX can improve your visitors' experience with your web site, but it can also worsen it when used inappropriately. Usually, AJAX is best used in addition to the traditional web development paradigms, rather than changing or replacing them.

For example, unless your application has really special requirements, it's wise to let your users navigate your content using good old hyperlinks. Web browsers have a long history of dealing with content navigation, and web users have a long history of using browsers' navigational features.

AJAX can bring the following benefits to your projects:

- It makes it possible to create better and more responsive web applications.

- It encourages the development of patterns and frameworks that help developers avoid reinventing the wheel when performing common tasks.

- It makes use of existing technologies and features supported by all modern web browsers.

- It makes use of many existing developer skills.

The following are potential problems with AJAX:

- *It's unavailable to some users*: JavaScript can be disabled at the client side, which makes the AJAX features nonfunctional.

- *It's easy to use AJAX for the wrong purposes*: Increased awareness of usability, accessibility, web standards, and search engine optimization will help you make better decisions when designing and implementing web sites.

- *It can make your content invisible to search engines*: Search engines cannot index content dynamically generated by JavaScript in an AJAX application, because they don't execute any JavaScript code when indexing the web site. If search engine optimization is important for your web site, you shouldn't use AJAX for content delivery and navigation. In our case, we don't want search engines to index the shopping cart page or the cart summary box, so we're not affected by this limitation.

- *It can cause impaired browser bookmarking and page navigation*: Typically AJAX applications run inside a web page whose URL doesn't change in response to user actions, in which case you can bookmark only the entry page. The Back and Forward buttons in browsers don't produce the same result as with classic web sites, unless your AJAX application is specifically programmed to do so. To enable AJAX page bookmarking and the Back and Forward browser buttons, you can use frameworks such as Really Simple History by Brad Neuberg (http://codinginparadise.org/projects/dhtml_history/README.html). This framework enables bookmarking by dynamically adding page anchors using your JavaScript code, such as in http://www.example.com/my-ajax-app.html#Page2. You also need to create supporting code that loads and saves the state of your application through the anchor parameter. However, supporting bookmaking and navigation this way adds a significant level of complexity to your code that increases the chances of errors and browser compatibility problems.

With these warnings out of the way, it's time to start updating TShirtShop with the new AJAX features.

Creating the AJAX Shopping Cart

We'll AJAXify the shopping cart in two steps. First we'll implement the AJAX features to the Add to Cart buttons, which update the shopping cart and the cart summary box without reloading the page. Then we'll enhance the shopping cart page.

Figure 13-3 shows the shopping cart summary box while being updated after clicking an Add to Cart button. Note the "Updating..." text that shows up in the cart summary box to indicate the cart is being updated. Figure 13-4 shows the shopping cart while removing a product.

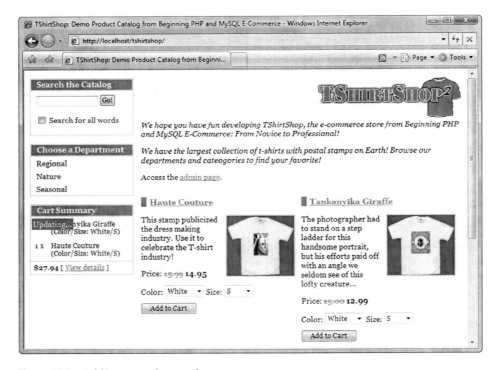

Figure 13-3. *Adding a product to the cart*

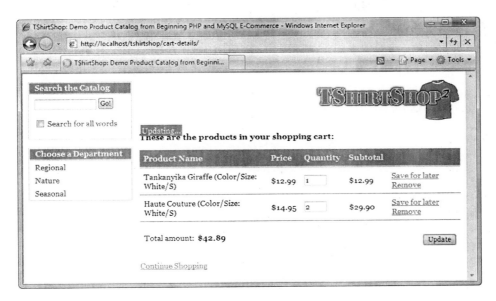

Figure 13-4. *Updating the shopping cart*

Enhancing the Add to Cart Feature with AJAX

You saw in Figure 13-2 what we're about to create here. The implementation is relatively simple. You'll update the product.tpl and products_list.tpl templates to call a JavaScript function named addProductToCart() when an Add to Cart button is clicked to submit the form.

Then you'll create ajax.js, a rather large JavaScript file that contains all the code required to support the new client functionality. It contains the following functions:

- createXmlHttpRequestObject() creates the XMLHttpRequest object.

- handleError(message) displays the error messages generated by the other functions or degrades to classical non-AJAX behavior, depending on the value of a variable named showErrors.

- addProductToCart() is called from the HTML page to add a product to the cart.

- handleAddProductToCart() is the callback function for the Add to Cart server calls.

- postAddProductToCartProcess() reads the Add to Cart server response and updates the cart summary box.

You'll also update your project in various places to utilize or support the new features. Let's go through the exercise that follows, and we'll discuss the process in more detail afterward.

1. Open presentation\templates\product.tpl, add the highlighted code, and modify the name of the input element to add_to_cart:

```
{* The Add to Cart form *}
<form class="add-product-form" target="_self" method="post"
 action="{$obj->mProduct.link_to_add_product}"
 onsubmit="return addProductToCart(this);">

{* Generate the list of attribute values *}
<p class="attributes">

{* Parse the list of attributes and attribute values *}
{section name=k loop=$obj->mProduct.attributes}

...

{/section}
</p>

{* Add the submit button and close the form *}
<p>
  <input type="submit" name="add_to_cart" value="Add to Cart" />
</p>
</form>
```

2. Open presentation\templates\products_list.tpl, and modify it as shown here:

```
{* The Add to Cart form *}
<form class="add-product-form" target="_self" method="post"
 action="{$obj->mProducts[k].link_to_add_product}"
 onsubmit="return addProductToCart(this);">

{* Generate the list of attribute values *}
<p class="attributes">

{* Parse the list of attributes and attribute values *}
{section name=l loop=$obj->mProducts[k].attributes}

...

{/section}
</p>

{* Add the submit button and close the form *}
<p>
  <input type="submit" name="add_to_cart" value="Add to Cart" />
```

```
      </p>
    </form>
```

3. Create a new folder in your project's root folder (tshirtshop) named scripts, add a new file named ajax.js in it, and type the following code:

```javascript
// Holds an instance of XMLHttpRequest
var xmlHttp = createXmlHttpRequestObject();

// Display error messages (true) or degrade to non-AJAX behavior (false)
var showErrors = true;

// Contains the link or form clicked or submitted by the visitor
var actionObject = '';

// Creates an XMLHttpRequest instance
function createXmlHttpRequestObject()
{
  // Will store the XMLHttpRequest object
  var xmlHttp;

  // Create the XMLHttpRequest object
  try
  {
    // Try to create native XMLHttpRequest object
    xmlHttp = new XMLHttpRequest();
  }
  catch(e)
  {
    // Assume IE6 or older
    var XmlHttpVersions = new Array(
      "MSXML2.XMLHTTP.6.0", "MSXML2.XMLHTTP.5.0", "MSXML2.XMLHTTP.4.0",
      "MSXML2.XMLHTTP.3.0", "MSXML2.XMLHTTP", "Microsoft.XMLHTTP");

    // Try every id until one works
    for (i = 0; i < XmlHttpVersions.length && !xmlHttp; i++)
    {
      try
      {
        // Try to create XMLHttpRequest object
        xmlHttp = new ActiveXObject(XmlHttpVersions[i]);
      }
      catch (e) {} // Ignore potential error
    }
  }
```

```
    // If the XMLHttpRequest object was created successfully, return it
    if (xmlHttp)
    {
      return xmlHttp;
    }
    // If an error happened, pass it to handleError
    else
    {
      handleError("Error creating the XMLHttpRequest object.");
    }
}

// Displays an the error message or degrades to non-AJAX behavior
function handleError($message)
{
    // Ignore errors if showErrors is false
    if (showErrors)
    {
      // Display error message
      alert("Error encountered: \n" + $message);
      return false;
    }
    // Fall back to non-AJAX behavior
    else if (!actionObject.tagName)
    {
      return true;
    }
    // Fall back to non-AJAX behavior by following the link
    else if (actionObject.tagName == 'A')
    {
      window.location = actionObject.href;
    }
    // Fall back to non-AJAX behavior by submitting the form
    else if (actionObject.tagName == 'FORM')
    {
      actionObject.submit();
    }
}

// Adds a product to the shopping cart
function addProductToCart(form)
{
    // Display "Updating" message
    document.getElementById('updating').style.visibility = 'visible';

    // Degrade to classical form submit if XMLHttpRequest is not available
    if (!xmlHttp) return true;
```

```
// Create the URL we open asynchronously
request = form.action + '&AjaxRequest';
params  = '';

// obtain selected attributes
formSelects = form.getElementsByTagName('SELECT');
if (formSelects)
{
  for (i = 0; i < formSelects.length; i++)
  {
    params += '&' + formSelects[i].name + '=';
    selected_index = formSelects[i].selectedIndex;
    params += encodeURIComponent(formSelects[i][selected_index].text);
  }
}

// Try to connect to the server
try
{
  // Continue only if the XMLHttpRequest object isn't busy
  if (xmlHttp.readyState == 4 || xmlHttp.readyState == 0)
  {
    // Make a server request to validate the extracted data
    xmlHttp.open("POST", request, true);
    xmlHttp.setRequestHeader("Content-Type",
                             "application/x-www-form-urlencoded");
    xmlHttp.onreadystatechange = addToCartStateChange;
    xmlHttp.send(params);
  }
}
catch (e)
{
  // Handle error
  handleError(e.toString());
}

// Stop classical form submit if AJAX action succeeded
return false;
}

// Function that retrieves the HTTP response
function addToCartStateChange()
{
  // When readyState is 4, we also read the server response
  if (xmlHttp.readyState == 4)
  {
    // Continue only if HTTP status is "OK"
```

```
        if (xmlHttp.status == 200)
        {
          try
          {
            updateCartSummary();
          }
          catch (e)
          {
            handleError(e.toString());
          }
        }
        else
        {
          handleError(xmlHttp.statusText);
        }
      }
    }


    // Process server's response
    function updateCartSummary()
    {
      // Read the response
      response = xmlHttp.responseText;

      // Server error?
      if (response.indexOf("ERRNO") >= 0 || response.indexOf("error") >= 0)
      {
        handleError(response);
      }
      else
      {
        // Extract the contents of the cart_summary div element
        var cartSummaryRegEx = /^<div class="box" id="cart-summary">➥
        ([\s\S]*)<\/div>$/m;
        matches = cartSummaryRegEx.exec(response);
        response = matches[1];

        // Update the cart summary box and hide the Loading message
        document.getElementById("cart-summary").innerHTML = response;
        // Hide the "Updating..." message
        document.getElementById('updating').style.visibility = 'hidden';
      }
    }
```

4. Open presentation\templates\store_front.tpl, and add a reference to your JavaScript file, ajax.js:

```
<html>
  <head>
```

```
    <title>{$obj->mPageTitle}</title>
    <meta http-equiv="Content-Type" content="text/html; charset=UTF-8" />
    <link href="{$obj->mSiteUrl}tshirtshop.css" type="text/css"
     rel="stylesheet" />
    <script type="text/javascript"
     src="{$obj->mSiteUrl}scripts/ajax.js"></script>
  </head>
```

5. Modify index.php as highlighted:

```
// Load Business Tier
require_once BUSINESS_DIR . 'catalog.php';
require_once BUSINESS_DIR . 'shopping_cart.php';

// URL correction
Link::CheckRequest();

// Load Smarty template file
$application = new Application();

// Handle AJAX requests
if (isset ($_GET['AjaxRequest']))
{
  // Headers are sent to prevent browsers from caching
  header('Expires: Fri, 25 Dec 1980 00:00:00 GMT'); // Time in the past
  header('Last-Modified: ' . gmdate('D, d M Y H:i:s') . ' GMT');
  header('Cache-Control: no-cache, must-revalidate');
  header('Pragma: no-cache');
  header('Content-Type: text/html');

  if (isset ($_GET['CartAction']))
  {
    $cart_action = $_GET['CartAction'];

    if ($cart_action == ADD_PRODUCT)
    {
      require_once PRESENTATION_DIR . 'cart_details.php';

      $cart_details = new CartDetails();
      $cart_details->init();

      $application->display('cart_summary.tpl');
    }
  }
  else
    trigger_error('CartAction not set', E_USER_ERROR);
}
```

```
else
{
  // Display the page
  $application->display('store_front.tpl');
}

// Close database connection
DatabaseHandler::Close();
```

6. Open presentation\cart_details.php, and make the following changes in the switch block in the init() method:

```
if (count($selected_attributes) > 0)
  $attributes = implode('/', $selected_attributes) . ': ' .
                implode('/', $selected_attribute_values);

ShoppingCart::AddProduct($this->_mItemId, $attributes);

if (!isset ($_GET['AjaxRequest']))
  header('Location: ' . $this->mLinkToContinueShopping);
else
  return;

break;
case REMOVE_PRODUCT:
  ShoppingCart::RemoveProduct($this->_mItemId);

  if (!isset ($_GET['AjaxRequest']))
    header('Location: ' . Link::ToCart());

break;
case UPDATE_PRODUCTS_QUANTITIES:
  for($i = 0; $i < count($_POST['itemId']); $i++)
    ShoppingCart::Update($_POST['itemId'][$i], $_POST['quantity'][$i]);

  if (!isset ($_GET['AjaxRequest']))
    header('Location: ' . Link::ToCart());

break;
case SAVE_PRODUCT_FOR_LATER:
  ShoppingCart::SaveProductForLater($this->_mItemId);

  if (!isset ($_GET['AjaxRequest']))
    header('Location: ' . Link::ToCart());

break;
case MOVE_PRODUCT_TO_CART:
  ShoppingCart::MoveProductToCart($this->_mItemId);
```

```
        if (!isset ($_GET['AjaxRequest']))
          header('Location: ' . Link::ToCart());

        break;
      default:
        // Do nothing
        break;
    }
```

7. Modify the CheckRequest() method of the Link class, in link.php, as highlighted. We don't validate the URL when responding to an AJAX request.

```
// Redirects to proper URL if not already there
public static function CheckRequest()
{
  $proper_url = '';

  if (isset ($_GET['Search']) || isset($_GET['SearchResults']) ||
      isset ($_GET['CartAction']) || isset ($_GET['AjaxRequest']))
  {
    return ;
  }
```

8. Open presentation\templates\cart_summary.tpl, and make the changes shown here:

```
{* cart_summary.tpl *}
{load_presentation_object filename="cart_summary" assign="obj"}
{* Start cart summary *}
<div class="box" id="cart-summary">
  <p class="box-title">Cart Summary</p>
  <div id="updating">Updating...</div>
{if $obj->mEmptyCart}
  <p class="empty-cart">Your shopping cart is empty!</p>
{else}
```

9. Add the following style definition to the tshirtshop.css file from the styles folder:

```
#updating {
  background-color: #ff0000;
  border: none;
  color: #ffffff;
  margin: 2px;
  padding: 2px;
  visibility: hidden;
  position: absolute;
  width: 70px;
}
```

10. Load your catalog, and ensure that the Add to Cart buttons work fine using the new AJAX code.

How It Works

We've modified the name of the submit HTML element to `add_to_cart` so that we can submit it from JavaScript:

```
{/section}
</p>

{* Add the submit button and close the form *}
<p>
  <input type="submit" name="add_to_cart" value="Add to Cart" />
</p>
</form>
```

We have a variable named `showErrors`, whose value affects the way errors are handled. If this variable is `true`, debugging error messages are displayed using `alert()`. This isn't a very user-friendly method of handling errors, but it helps with debugging. If `showErrors` is `false`, no errors are shown. Instead, when a JavaScript error happens, the behavior is degraded to a classical form submit.

```
// Display error messages (true) or degrade to non-AJAX behavior (false)
var showErrors = true;
```

This variable is used in the `handleError()` function, which is called every time an error happens in the JavaScript code. If `showErrors` is `true`, this function simply displays the error details:

```
// Displays an error message or degrades to non-AJAX behavior
function handleError($message)
{
  // Ignore errors if showErrors is false
  if (showErrors)
  {
    // Display error message
    alert("Error encountered: \n" + $message);
    return false;
  }
```

If `showErrors` is `false`, we don't display error details. Instead, we try to execute the action requested by the visitor in a non-AJAX fashion. Here we use `actionObject`, which represents the form submitted by the visitor or the action link clicked by the visitor. If `actionObject` isn't set, it means the error happened in the JavaScript function referenced in the `onclick` or `onsubmit` attribute. In that case, we simply need to return `true`, which causes the original requested action to happen:

```
  // Fall back to non-AJAX behavior
  else if (!actionObject.tagName)
  {
    return true;
  }
```

If `actionObject` is a link, it means the error happened after the visitor clicked a link, in which case we redirect the request to that URL:

```
  // Fall back to non-AJAX behavior by following the link
  else if (actionObject.tagName == 'A')
```

```
{
  window.location = actionObject.href;
}
```

If `actionObject` is a form, it means the error happened after the visitor submitted a form, in which case we redirect the request to that URL:

```
  // Fall back to non-AJAX behavior by submitting the form
  else if (actionObject.tagName == 'FORM')
  {
    actionObject.submit();
  }
}
```

The index.php script was updated to respond to AJAX requests as well. When making an asynchronous request to index.php, the AjaxRequest parameter is added to the query string so that index.php knows to react accordingly. First it sets the appropriate header values to make sure the response isn't cached:

```
if (isset ($_GET['AjaxRequest']))
{
  // Headers are sent to prevent browsers from caching
  header('Expires: Fri, 25 Dec 1980 00:00:00 GMT'); // Time in the past
  header('Last-Modified: ' . gmdate('D, d M Y H:i:s') . ' GMT');
  header('Cache-Control: no-cache, must-revalidate');
  header('Pragma: no-cache');
  header('Content-Type: text/html');
```

Then the existing code that adds a new product to the cart is used to perform the requested action. The cart_summary.tpl template is sent to the output, and the JavaScript will use it to update the cart summary box using the JavaScript DOM functions:

```
  if (isset ($_GET['CartAction']))
  {
    $cart_action = $_GET['CartAction'];

    if ($cart_action == ADD_PRODUCT)
    {
      require_once PRESENTATION_DIR . 'cart_details.php';

      $cart_details = new CartDetails();
      $cart_details->init();

      $application->display('cart_summary.tpl');
    }
  }
  else
    trigger_error('CartAction not set', E_USER_ERROR);
}
```

The updateCartSummary() JavaScript function in ajax.js is responsible for reading the HTML code generated by cart_summary.tpl and injecting it into the cart summary box. The function first verifies that the request has not resulted in an error, in which case the handleError() function is called to either display the error or fall back to non-AJAX behavior:

```
// Process server's response
function updateCartSummary()
{
  // Read the response
  response = xmlHttp.responseText;

  // Server error?
  if (response.indexOf("ERRNO") >= 0 || response.indexOf("error") >= 0)
  {
    handleError(response);
  }
```

If the response doesn't contain an error, it's assumed to contain the HTML contents of the new cart summary box. This response will be something like this:

```
{* Start cart summary *}
<div class="box" id="cart-summary">
  <p class="box-title">Cart Summary</p>
  <div id="updating">Updating...</div>
...
</div>
```

Our JavaScript code must take the contents of the root <div> element and inject them into the page under the cart-summary <div> element. For this we used a regular expression named cartSummaryRegEx:

```
  else
  {
    // Extract the contents of the cart_summary div element
    var cartSummaryRegEx = /^<div class="box" id="cart-summary">➡
([\s\S]*)<\/div>$/m;
    matches = cartSummaryRegEx.exec(response);
    response = matches[1];
```

Alternatively, we could have used the XML DOM or the substring feature of string. The substring method is the fastest and easiest to implement, but it has the disadvantage that it's not flexible. If the format of the output or the name of the <div> element changes, it will not work anymore. Here's a possible implementation:

```
response = response.substring(25, response.length - 7);
```

After obtaining the string, updateCartSummary() uses it to replace the contents of the cart-summary element of the page, effectively updating the cart summary. The "Loading..." text is also hidden:

```
    // Update the cart summary box and hide the Loading message
    document.getElementById("cart-summary").innerHTML = response;
    // Hide the "Updating..." message
    document.getElementById('updating').style.visibility = 'hidden';
  }
}
```

Enhancing the Shopping Cart with AJAX

The enhanced shopping cart will use AJAX for updating the shopping cart. When removing products from the shopping cart, saving products for buying later, or updating product quantities, the action will happen in the background. During the asynchronous request, an "Updating..." label shows up to indicate visually that the shopping cart is being updated (see Figure 13-4).

Just like with adding products to cart, the shopping cart is updated in a degradable fashion. If the visitor disables JavaScript, the features will still work but will use the classical form submit instead of AJAX.

Follow the steps of this exercise to implement your AJAX shopping cart.

AJAXifying the Shopping Cart

1. Let's start by modifying the template file, `presentation\templates\cart_details.tpl`, to call JavaScript functions on button clicks. Open the file, and apply the highlighted changes:

```
{* cart_details.tpl *}
{load_presentation_object filename="cart_details" assign="obj"}
<div id="updating">Updating...</div>
{if $obj->mIsCartNowEmpty eq 1}
<h3>Your shopping cart is empty!</h3>
{else}
<h3>These are the products in your shopping cart:</h3>
<form class="cart-form" method="post" action="{$obj->mUpdateCartTarget}"
 onsubmit="return executeCartAction(this);">
  <table class="tss-table">
    <tr>
      <th>Product Name</th>
      <th>Price</th>
      <th>Quantity</th>
      <th>Subtotal</th>
      <th> </th>
    </tr>
    {section name=i loop=$obj->mCartProducts}
    <tr>
      <td>
        <input name="itemId[]" type="hidden"
         value="{$obj->mCartProducts[i].item_id}" />
        {$obj->mCartProducts[i].name}
        ({$obj->mCartProducts[i].attributes})
      </td>
      <td>${$obj->mCartProducts[i].price}</td>
      <td>
        <input type="text" name="quantity[]" size="5"
         value="{$obj->mCartProducts[i].quantity}" />
      </td>
      <td>${$obj->mCartProducts[i].subtotal}</td>
      <td>
```

```
          <a href="{$obj->mCartProducts[i].save}"
            onclick="return executeCartAction(this);">Save for later</a>
          <a href="{$obj->mCartProducts[i].remove}"
            onclick="return executeCartAction(this);">Remove</a>
        </td>
      </tr>
    {/section}
    </table>
    <table class="cart-subtotal">
      <tr>
        <td>
          <p>
            Total amount: 
            <font class="price">${$obj->mTotalAmount}</font>
          </p>
        </td>
        <td align="right">
          <input type="submit" name="update" value="Update" />
        </td>
      </tr>
    </table>
  </form>
{/if}
{if ($obj->mIsCartLaterEmpty eq 0)}
<h3>Saved products to buy later:</h3>
<table class="tss-table">
  <tr>
    <th>Product Name</th>
    <th>Price</th>
    <th> </th>
  </tr>
  {section name=j loop=$obj->mSavedCartProducts}
  <tr>
    <td>
      {$obj->mSavedCartProducts[j].name}
      ({$obj->mSavedCartProducts[j].attributes})
    </td>
    <td>
      ${$obj->mSavedCartProducts[j].price}
    </td>
    <td>
        <a href="{$obj->mSavedCartProducts[j].move}"
          onclick="return executeCartAction(this);">Move to cart</a>
        <a href="{$obj->mSavedCartProducts[j].remove}"
          onclick="return executeCartAction(this);">Remove</a>
    </td>
  </tr>
```

```
     {/section}
  </table>
  {/if}
  {if $obj->mLinkToContinueShopping}
  <p><a href="{$obj->mLinkToContinueShopping}">Continue Shopping </a></p>
  {/if}
```

2. Open ajax.js, and add these functions:

```
// Called on shopping cart update actions
function executeCartAction(obj)
{
  // Display "Updating..." message
  document.getElementById('updating').style.visibility = 'visible';

  // Degrade to classical form submit if XMLHttpRequest is not available
  if (!xmlHttp) return true;

  // Save object reference
  actionObject = obj;

  // Initialize response and parameters
  response = '';
  params = '';

  // If a link was clicked we get its href attribute
  if (obj.tagName == 'A')
  {
    url = obj.href + '&AjaxRequest';
  }
  // If the form was submitted we get its elements
  else
  {
    url = obj.action + '&AjaxRequest';
    formElements = obj.getElementsByTagName('INPUT');

    if (formElements)
    {
      for (i = 0; i < formElements.length; i++)
      {
        params += '&' + formElements[i].name + '=';
        params += encodeURIComponent(formElements[i].value);
      }
    }
  }
}
```

```
    // Try to connect to the server
    try
    {
      // Make server request only if the XMLHttpRequest object isn't busy
      if (xmlHttp.readyState == 4 || xmlHttp.readyState == 0)
      {
        xmlHttp.open("POST", url, true);
        xmlHttp.setRequestHeader("Content-Type",
                                 "application/x-www-form-urlencoded");
        xmlHttp.onreadystatechange = cartActionStateChange;
        xmlHttp.send(params);
      }
    }
    catch (e)
    {
      // Handle error
      handleError(e.toString());
    }

    // Stop classical form submit if AJAX action succeeded
    return false;
  }

  // Function that retrieves the HTTP response
  function cartActionStateChange()
  {
    // When readyState is 4, we also read the server response
    if (xmlHttp.readyState == 4)
    {
      // Continue only if HTTP status is "OK"
      if (xmlHttp.status == 200)
      {
        try
        {
          // Read the response
          response = xmlHttp.responseText;

          // Server error?
          if (response.indexOf("ERRNO") >= 0 || response.indexOf("error") >= 0)
          {
            handleError(response);
          }
```

```
      else
      {
        // Update the cart
        document.getElementById("contents").innerHTML = response;
        // Hide the "Updating..." message
        document.getElementById('updating').style.visibility = 'hidden';
      }
    }
    catch (e)
    {
      // Handle error
      handleError(e.toString());
    }
  }
  else
  {
    // Handle error
    handleError(xmlHttp.statusText);
  }
 }
}
```

3. Change index.php as highlighted:

```
  if ($cart_action == ADD_PRODUCT)
  {
    require_once PRESENTATION_DIR . 'cart_details.php';

    $cart_details = new CartDetails();
    $cart_details->init();

    $application->display('cart_summary.tpl');
  }
  else
  {
    $application->display('cart_details.tpl');
  }
}
else
  trigger_error('CartAction not set', E_USER_ERROR);
```

4. Load your shopping cart, and ensure it works as expected.

How It Works: The AJAX Shopping Cart

Because you wrote the code AJAX code earlier in this chapter, the task in this exercise was fairly easy. To upgrade the shopping cart, you needed to follow three easy steps.

First you modified the shopping cart template (cart_details.tpl) by defining the handler for the click event of your "Save for later" links and Remove buttons and the handler for the submit event of the form. This way, when JavaScript is available and these buttons or links are clicked, the JavaScript event handlers execute before the browser has the chance to submit the form or follow the clicked link.

Then you created the necessary JavaScript code that implements the event handlers:

- executeCartAction() is called from the shopping cart page to perform cart actions.
- handleExecuteCartAction() is the callback function for the cart action server calls.
- postExecuteCartActionProcess() reads the cart action server response and updates the page accordingly.

Finally, you updated index.php to return the HTML code of the shopping cart when it is requested by AJAX, and voilà! Your shopping cart is now faster and more user-friendly.

Summary

AJAX is cool, and so is our newly AJAX-enabled site! This wasn't a short and easy chapter, but what you've achieved (and learned!) will prove to be very useful in the future. Of course, the range of AJAX features you can add to your web site is very wide, but right now you have the foundations implemented, and your customers will certainly appreciate the AJAX touch you've added to your store.

CHAPTER 14

■ ■ ■

Accepting Customer Orders

Your new, shiny, AJAXified shopping cart is fully functional, except that it doesn't allow your visitors to actually place orders, which is rather troubling since that is the point of all this! We'll deal with that issue in this chapter in two separate stages:

- First, we'll implement the visitor side of the order-placement mechanism. More precisely, we'll add a Place Order button to the shopping cart page that creates a PayPal order containing the products in the shopping cart (remember, at this stage, we still don't handle financial transactions ourselves).

- Next, we'll implement a simple order administration page, so the site administrator can view and handle pending orders.

The code for each part of the site will be presented in the usual way, starting with the database tier, continuing with the business tier, and finishing with the presentation tier (user interface).

Implementing an Order-Placement System

The entire order-placement system is related to the Place Order button mentioned earlier. Figure 14-1 shows how this button will look after you update the `cart_details` componentized template in this chapter.

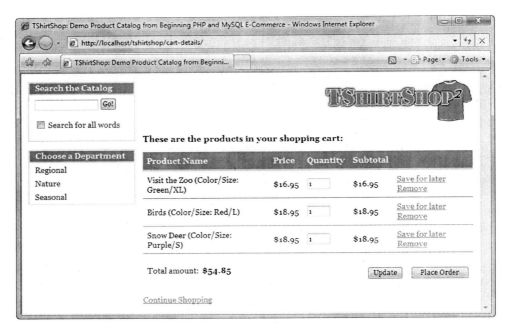

Figure 14-1. *The shopping cart with a Place Order button*

Yes, this button looks quite boring for something that we can honestly say is the center of this chapter's universe. However, a lot of logic is hidden behind it, so let's talk about what should happen when the customer clicks that button. Remember that, at this stage, we don't care who places the order, but we do want to store the order details in our database. This will allow us to implement the cross-selling ("customers who bought this also bought") feature in Chapter 15.

Basically, three things need to happen when Place Order is clicked:

- First, you must store the order somewhere in the database. You'll create a couple of new tables (orders and order_detail) and write the code that saves the ordered products to these tables.

- Next, we must clear the shopping cart. After an order is placed, the shopping cart should be empty. There's a chance customers will cancel their orders at the checkout stage—we don't want their carts hanging around and bloating our database with canceled orders. PayPal and other payment processors offer mechanisms for programmatic notification when an order has been paid for.

- Finally, we send the visitor to the PayPal payment page to pay for the order.

■**Note** Since we're in development Phase I, we still don't process payments ourselves but use a third-party payment processor. Now, we no longer need the PayPal shopping cart, because we implemented our own in the previous couple of chapters. Instead, we'll use PayPal's Single Item Purchases option, which takes the visitor from our shopping cart to the PayPal payment page.

A problem that arises when using a third-party payment processor is that the customer can cancel the order while at the checkout page, which is still at PayPal. This can result in orders that are saved to the database for which no payment was completed. Obviously, we need a payment confirmation system, along with a database structure that is able to store status information about each order.

The confirmation system that we'll implement is simple. Every payment processor, including PayPal, can be configured to send a confirmation message after a payment has been processed. We'll allow the site administrator to manually check, in the administration page, which orders have been paid for and take the appropriate measures.

Note PayPal and its competitors offer automated systems that inform your web site when a payment has been completed or canceled. However, this book doesn't investigate the intimate details of any of these payment systems—you'll need to do your homework and study the documentation of the service of your choice. The PayPal Instant Payment Notification documentation is included in the *Order Management Integration Guide*, which at the time of this writing can be downloaded at `https://www.paypal.com/en_US/pdf/ PP_OrderManagement_IntegrationGuide.pdf`.

Storing the Order Details

As pointed out earlier, we start implementing the new feature by creating the necessary data structures. This should not surprise you at this point. You know that deciding what information to use and how to store it helps a great deal when analyzing a new feature and represents the technical foundation of that feature's implementation.

There are two types of information that we want to store when an order is placed:

- *Details about the order as a whole*: What date was the order created? Have the products have been shipped and, if so, when were they shipped? And what's the order's status now? We'll store this data in a table named orders, where each record represents an order.

- *Product details for the order*: What products were ordered in which order? We'll store this data in a table named order_detail, where each record represents an ordered product. Many records of this table will be associated with one record in the orders table, forming a one-to-many relationship between the tables (you might want to revisit Chapter 5, where the table relationships are explained).

Tip So far, we have been consistent about naming our tables in singular form (shopping_cart, department, and so on). However, here, we make an exception for the orders table, because ORDER is an SQL keyword. For the purposes of this book, we prefer to break the naming convention to avoid any confusion while writing the SQL code, and generally speaking, it isn't good practice to use SQL keywords as object names.

The orders table stores information regarding the order as a whole, while order_detail contains the products that belong to each order. We'll create the tables in the following exercise.

Exercise: Creating the orders and the order_detail Tables

1. Load phpMyAdmin, select your `tshirtshop` database, and open a new SQL query page.

2. Execute this code, which creates the `orders` table in your `tshirtshop` database:

```
-- Create orders table
CREATE TABLE `orders` (
  `order_id`         INT            NOT NULL  AUTO_INCREMENT,
  `total_amount`     NUMERIC(10, 2) NOT NULL  DEFAULT 0.00,
  `created_on`       DATETIME       NOT NULL,
  `shipped_on`       DATETIME,
  `status`           INT            NOT NULL  DEFAULT 0,
  `comments`         VARCHAR(255),
  `customer_name`    VARCHAR(100),
  `shipping_address` VARCHAR(255),
  `customer_email`   VARCHAR(50),
  PRIMARY KEY (`order_id`)
);
```

3. Execute the following code, which creates the `order_detail` table in your `tshirtshop` database:

```
-- Create order_detail table
CREATE TABLE `order_detail` (
  `item_id`      INT            NOT NULL  AUTO_INCREMENT,
  `order_id`     INT            NOT NULL,
  `product_id`   INT            NOT NULL,
  `attributes`   VARCHAR(1000)  NOT NULL,
  `product_name` VARCHAR(100)   NOT NULL,
  `quantity`     INT            NOT NULL,
  `unit_cost`    NUMERIC(10, 2) NOT NULL,
  PRIMARY KEY (`item_id`),
  KEY `idx_order_detail_order_id` (`order_id`)
);
```

Now that you've created the tables, let's take a closer look at their structure and relationships.

How It Works: The orders Table

The `orders` table contains two categories of information: data about the order itself (the first six fields) and data about the customer who made the order (the last three fields). Storing customer data in the `orders` table (in the `customer_name`, `shipping_address`, and `customer_email` fields) is optional. The site administrator can use this feature if it helps with order management tasks, but at this stage, who placed the order doesn't really matter, only what products have been sold. In the Phase III of development (see Chapter 16), we'll move to a full professional implementation and store customer information in its own data table.

The field names are self-explanatory. `order_id` is the primary key of the table. `total_amount` stores the total value of the order. `created_on` and `shipped_on` specify when the order was created and shipped (the latter supports NULL values, which just means the order hasn't been shipped yet).

The status field contains an integer that can have these values:

- 0: The order has been *placed*. This is the initial status of an order after the Place Order button is clicked in the shopping cart.

- 1: The order is *verified*. The administrator marks the order as verified after the payment was confirmed.

- 2: The order is *completed*. The administrator marks the order as completed after the products have been shipped. At the same time, the shipped_on field is also populated.

- 3: The order is *canceled*. Typically, the administrator marks the order as canceled if the order has been placed (by clicking the Place Order button) but the payment wasn't processed, or in other scenarios that require canceling the order.

Figure 14-2 shows some sample records from the orders table.

order_id	total_amount	created_on	shipped_on	status	comments	customer_name	shipping_address	customer_email
1	30.94	2007-12-09 17:50:04	2007-12-09 20:31:00	2				
2	37.00	2007-12-09 19:56:17	NULL	1				
3	54.85	2007-12-09 20:03:03	NULL	0				

Figure 14-2. *Sample data in the* orders *table*

How It Works: The order_detail Table

Let's take a look at Figure 14-3 to see some examples of records in the order_detail table.

item_id	order_id	product_id	attributes	product_name	quantity	unit_cost
1	1	87	Color/Size: White/S	Christmas Tree	1	17.95
2	1	51	Color/Size: Yellow/L	Tankanyika Giraffe	1	12.99
3	2	94	Color/Size: Orange/M	Swede Santa	1	18.50
4	2	85	Color/Size: Red/L	Altar Piece	1	18.50
5	3	36	Color/Size: Green/XL	Visit the Zoo	1	16.95
6	3	97	Color/Size: Red/L	Birds	1	18.95
7	3	80	Color/Size: Purple/S	Snow Deer	1	18.95

Figure 14-3. *Sample data in the* order_detail *table*

Each record in order_detail represents an ordered product that belongs to the order specified by order_id. When forming the primary key of this table, we face the same limitation that we had when creating the shopping_cart table. Normally, the primary key could be formed from (order_id, product_id, attributes), but since this not possible, we created an additional field named item_id to act as the primary key.

We also store the product name, attributes, quantity, and price (unit_cost). You might be wondering why we record this data, since we already have the product_id field, which can lead to that data. It's important to understand that the data we record for an order is stored for historical purposes. Product IDs, names, and prices may change, but to prevent these changes from affecting the details of an order placed in the past, we must be sure we record them in a table unaffected by product changes. We store product_id, because it's the only programmatic way to link back to the original product information (if the product still exists).

Implementing the Data Tier

At this stage, you need to add two additional data tier stored procedures in the tshirtshop database. The first and most important is shopping_cart_create_order, which takes the products from the shopping cart and creates an order with them. The second stored procedure is shopping_cart_empty, which empties the visitor's cart after the order has been placed.

In the following exercise, we'll implement these stored procedures starting with shopping_cart_empty, because it is called from shopping_cart_create_order.

Exercise: Creating the Stored Procedures

1. Use phpMyAdmin to create the stored procedures described in the following steps. Don't forget to set the $$ delimiter before executing the code of each step.

2. Execute the following code, which creates the shopping_cart_empty stored procedure in your tshirtshop database. When a customer places an order, shopping_cart_create_order will call shopping_cart_empty to delete the products from the customer's shopping cart.

```
-- Create shopping_cart_empty stored procedure
CREATE PROCEDURE shopping_cart_empty(IN inCartId CHAR(32))
BEGIN
  DELETE FROM shopping_cart WHERE cart_id = inCartId;
END$$
```

3. Execute the following code, which creates the shopping_cart_create_order stored procedure in your tshirtshop database. This stored procedure gets called when the customer decides to buy the products in the shopping cart and clicks the Place Order button. The role of shopping_cart_create_order is to create a new order based on the products in the customer's shopping cart. This implies adding a new record to the orders table and a number of records (one record for each product) in the order_detail table.

```
-- Create shopping_cart_create_order stored procedure
CREATE PROCEDURE shopping_cart_create_order(IN inCartId CHAR(32))
BEGIN
  DECLARE orderId INT;

  -- Insert a new record into orders and obtain the new order ID
  INSERT INTO orders (created_on) VALUES (NOW());
  -- Obtain the new Order ID
  SELECT LAST_INSERT_ID() INTO orderId;

  -- Insert order details in order_detail table
  INSERT INTO order_detail (order_id, product_id, attributes,
                            product_name, quantity, unit_cost)
  SELECT    orderId, p.product_id, sc.attributes, p.name, sc.quantity,
            COALESCE(NULLIF(p.discounted_price, 0), p.price) AS unit_cost
```

```
FROM          shopping_cart sc
INNER JOIN    product p
                 ON sc.product_id = p.product_id
WHERE         sc.cart_id = inCartId AND sc.buy_now;

-- Save the order's total amount
UPDATE orders
SET    total_amount = (SELECT SUM(unit_cost * quantity)
                       FROM   order_detail
                       WHERE  order_id = orderId)
WHERE  order_id = orderId;

-- Clear the shopping cart
CALL shopping_cart_empty(inCartId);

-- Return the Order ID
SELECT orderId;
END$$
```

How It Works: Implementing shopping_cart_empty and shopping_cart_create_order

The first step in implementing shopping_cart_create_order involves creating the new record in the orders table. You need to do this at the outset to find out what order_id was generated for the new order. Remember that the order_id field is an AUTO_INCREMENT column and is automatically generated by the database, so you need to retrieve its value after inserting a record into orders:

```
-- Insert a new record into orders and obtain the new order ID
INSERT INTO orders (created_on) VALUES (NOW());
-- Obtain the new Order ID
SELECT LAST_INSERT_ID() INTO orderId;
```

This is the basic mechanism of extracting the newly generated ID. After the INSERT statement, you can obtain the last value generated for an AUTO_INCREMENT by reading LAST_INSERT_ID(). The functionality is pretty straightforward, but for more details, you can check its official documentation page at http://dev.mysql.com/doc/refman/5.1/en/getting-unique-id.html.

You read the value of LAST_INSERT_ID(), and save it to a variable named orderId. Using the orderId value, you add the order_detail records by gathering information from the product and shopping_cart tables. You get the list of the products and their quantities from shopping_cart, get their names and prices from product, and save these records one by one to the order_detail table.

```
-- Insert order details in order_detail table
INSERT INTO order_detail (order_id, product_id, attributes,
                          product_name, quantity, unit_cost)
SELECT     orderId, p.product_id, sc.attributes, p.name, sc.quantity,
           COALESCE(NULLIF(p.discounted_price, 0), p.price) AS unit_cost
FROM       shopping_cart sc
INNER JOIN product p
              ON sc.product_id = p.product_id
WHERE      sc.cart_id = inCartId AND sc.buy_now;
```

■**Tip** When joining shopping_cart and product, you get the product_id from product, but you could also get it from shopping_cart; the result would be the same, because the table join is made on the product_id column.

The stored procedure also calculates the total amount of the order by multiplying each product's price by its quantity. This value is then saved as the order's total_amount:

```
-- Save the order's total amount
UPDATE orders
SET    total_amount = (SELECT SUM(unit_cost * quantity)
                       FROM   order_detail
                       WHERE  order_id = orderId)
WHERE  order_id = orderId;
```

In the end, the function empties the visitor's shopping cart by calling the shopping_cart_empty stored procedure and returns the order's ID:

```
-- Clear the shopping cart
CALL shopping_cart_empty(inCartId);

-- Return the Order ID
SELECT orderId;
```

Implementing the Business Tier

The business tier of the order placing feature is made of a single method, CreateOrder. Add this method to the ShoppingCart class inside business/shopping_cart.php:

```
// Create a new order
public static function CreateOrder()
{
  // Build SQL query
  $sql = 'CALL shopping_cart_create_order(:cart_id)';

  // Build the parameters array
  $params = array (':cart_id' => self::GetCartId());

  // Execute the query and return the results
  return DatabaseHandler::GetOne($sql, $params);
}
```

The method calls the shopping_cart_create_order data tier stored procedure, which creates a new order from the shopping cart ID it receives and returns the order_id of the newly created order.

Implementing the Presentation Tier

Finally, you'll see the code you've written put into action. The Place Order button is the only addition on the visitor side of the interface for the custom checkout. Let's first place the button on the `cart_details` template file and then implement its functionality.

Exercise: Placing Orders

1. Modify `presentation/templates/cart_details.tpl` by adding a new button just after the Update button, as highlighted in the following code snippet:

```
<table class="cart-subtotal">
  <tr>
    <td>
      <p>
        Total amount: 
        <font class="price">${$obj->mTotalAmount}</font>
      </p>
    </td>
    <td align="right">
      <input type="submit" name="update" value="Update" />
    </td>
    <td align="right">
      <input type="submit" name="place_order" value="Place Order"
        onclick="placingOrder=true;" />
    </td>
  </tr>
</table>
```

2. Now, we also need to make a small change to `ajax.js`, to ensure that the new button isn't handled by JavaScript code. If you remember, in Chapter 13, we added the `onsubmit` event handler to the shopping cart form, so shopping cart actions are handled asynchronously, using AJAX, whenever possible. We don't want this to happen for the Place Order button. This button must submit the form to the server, which redirects the request to the checkout page. Modify `ajax.js` as highlighted:

```
// Holds an instance of XMLHttpRequest
var xmlHttp = createXmlHttpRequestObject();

// Display error messages (true) or degrade to non-AJAX behavior (false)
var showErrors = true;

// Contains the link or form clicked or submitted by the visitor
var actionObject = '';

// This is true when the Place Order button is clicked, false otherwise
var placingOrder = false;

// Creates an XMLHttpRequest instance
function createXmlHttpRequestObject()
```

3. At onsubmit time, we read the value of placingOrder. This is true after the Place Order button is clicked; therefore, we return true so that the form will be submitted in the usual way. We also make sure not to send the place_order form element during cart-update AJAX requests. Modify the executeCartAction() function in ajax.js as highlighted:

```
// Called on shopping cart update actions
function executeCartAction(obj)
{
  // Degrade to classical form submit for Place Order action
  if (placingOrder) return true;

  // Display "Updating..." message
  document.getElementById('updating').style.visibility = 'visible';

  // Degrade to classical form submit if XMLHttpRequest is not available
  if (!xmlHttp) return true;

  // Save object reference
  actionObject = obj;

  // Initialize response and parameters
  response = '';
  params = '';

  // If a link was clicked we get its href attribute
  if (obj.tagName == 'A')
  {
    url = obj.href + '&AjaxRequest';
  }
  // If the form was submitted we get its elements
  else
  {
    url = obj.action + '&AjaxRequest';
    formElements = obj.getElementsByTagName('INPUT');

    if (formElements)
    {
      for (i = 0; i < formElements.length; i++)
      {
        if (formElements[i].name != 'place_order')
        {
          params += '&' + formElements[i].name + '=';
          params += encodeURIComponent(formElements[i].value);
        }
      }
    }
  }
}
```

4. Let's make the Place Order button work now. Because this feature depends on the company that processes your payments, you might need to adapt it to the behavior of your payment-processing company. Here, we're using PayPal. Start by modifying the PayPal-related constants in config.php as follows. *Don't forget to replace* youremail@example.com *with your PayPal-registered e-mail address.*

```
// PayPal configuration
define('PAYPAL_URL',
       'https://www.paypal.com/xclick/business=youremail@example.com');
define('PAYPAL_CURRENCY_CODE', 'USD');
define('PAYPAL_RETURN_URL', 'http://www.example.com');
define('PAYPAL_CANCEL_RETURN_URL', 'http://www.example.com');
```

5. Add the following highlighted code in the init() method of the CartDetails class in presentation/cart_details.php:

```
/* Calculate the total amount for the shopping cart
   before applicable taxes and/or shipping */
$this->mTotalAmount = ShoppingCart::GetTotalAmount();

// If the Place Order button was clicked ...
if(isset ($_POST['place_order']))
{
  // Create the order and get the order ID
  $order_id = ShoppingCart::CreateOrder();

  // This will contain the PayPal link
  $redirect =
    PAYPAL_URL . '&item_name=TShirtShop Order ' . urlencode('#') . $order_id .
    '&item_number=' . $order_id .
    '&amount=' . $this->mTotalAmount .
    '&currency_code=' . PAYPAL_CURRENCY_CODE .
    '&return=' . PAYPAL_RETURN_URL .
    '&cancel_return=' . PAYPAL_CANCEL_RETURN_URL;

  // Redirection to the payment page
  header('Location: ' . $redirect);
  exit();
}

// Get shopping cart products
$this->mCartProducts =
  ShoppingCart::GetCartProducts(GET_CART_PRODUCTS);
```

6. Your Place Order button is fully functional! Test it by adding some products to your cart and clicking Place Order. Your shopping cart should be cleared, and you should be forwarded to a PayPal payment page like the one shown in Figure 14-4.

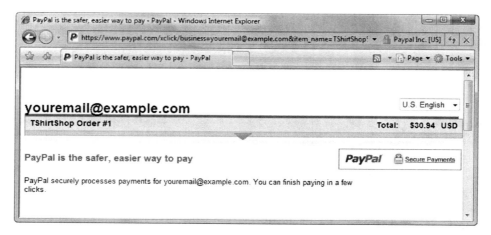

Figure 14-4. *The PayPal payment page*

How It Works: Placing Orders

When a visitor clicks the Place Order button, two important actions happen. First, the order is created in the database by calling the CreateOrder method of the ShoppingCart class. This function calls the shopping_cart_create_order database stored procedure to create a new order with the products in the shopping cart and returns the ID of the new order:

```
// Create the order and get the order ID
$order_id = ShoppingCart::CreateOrder();
```

Second, the visitor is redirected to the payment page, which requests payment for an item named "TShirtShop Order *nnn*" with a value that amounts to the total value of the order.

Administering Orders

Your visitor just placed an order. Now what?

After giving visitors the option to pay for your products, you need to make sure they actually get what they paid for. TShirtShop needs a carefully designed orders administration page, where an administrator can quickly see the status of pending orders.

■**Note** This chapter doesn't intend to help you create a perfect order administration system but rather something that is simple and functional enough to get you on the right track.

The orders administration part of the site will consist of two componentized templates named admin_orders and admin_order_details.

When the administrator clicks the ORDERS ADMIN link, the admin.php page loads the admin_orders componentized template that offers the capability to filter the orders. When first loaded, it offers you various ways of selecting orders, as shown in Figure 14-5.

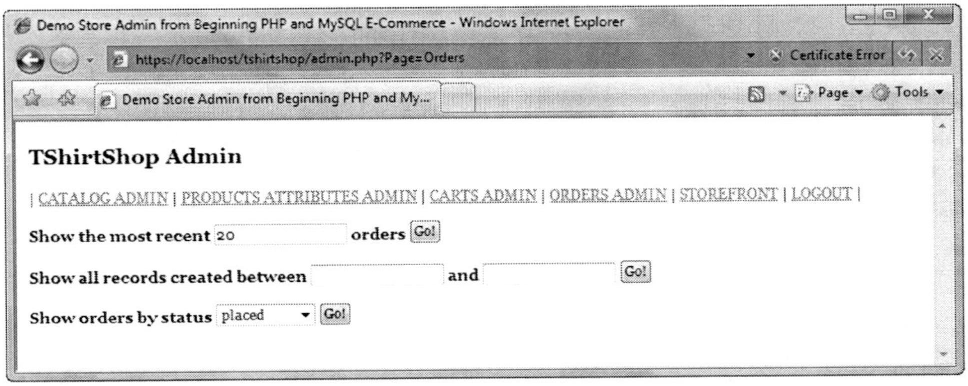

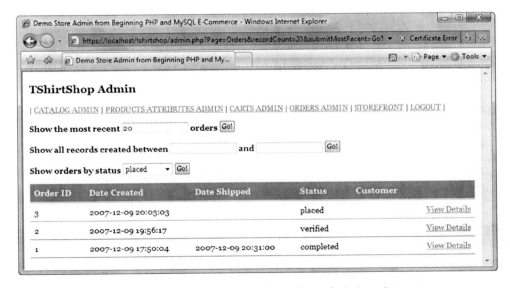

Figure 14-5. *The orders administration page*

After clicking one of the Go buttons, the matching orders appear in a table (see Figure 14-6).

Figure 14-6. *Selecting the most recent orders in the orders administration page*

When you click the View Details button for an order, you are sent to a page where you can view and update order information, as shown in Figure 14-7.

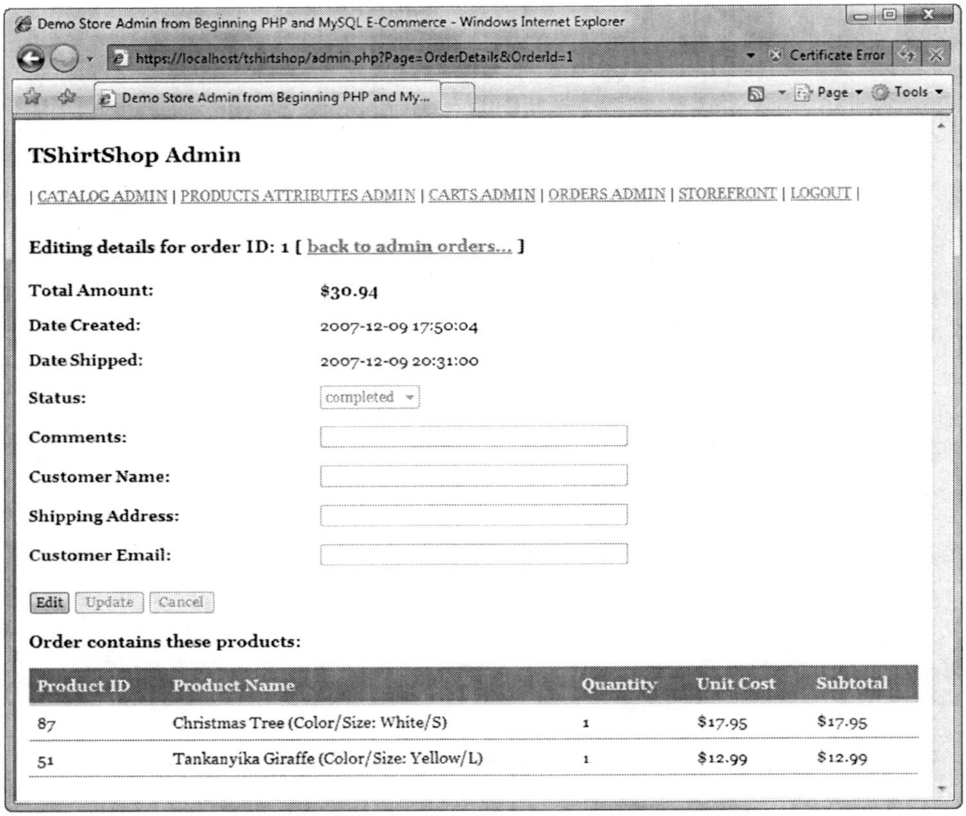

Figure 14-7. *Administering order details*

Before creating the admin_orders and the admin_order_details componentized templates, we need to modify admin.php to load these componentized templates and also modify admin_menu.tpl to display an ORDERS ADMIN link.

Go through the following exercise to prepare the ground for the administrative features we'll create later in the chapter. Note that, after completing the exercise, admin.php will not be functional, as it will reference a new business tier script that we'll create a bit later.

Exercise: Setting Up the ORDERS ADMIN Page

1. Modify admin.php to include a reference to business/orders.php, which we'll create later:

```
// Load Business Tier
require_once BUSINESS_DIR . 'catalog.php';
require_once BUSINESS_DIR . 'shopping_cart.php';
require_once BUSINESS_DIR . 'orders.php';
```

2. In `presentation/store_admin.php`, modify the `StoreAdmin` class by adding the highlighted code at the end of the `init()` method. This code loads `admin_orders.tpl` and `admin_order_details.tpl`:

```
      elseif ($admin_page == 'ProductDetails')
         $this->mContentsCell = 'admin_product_details.tpl';
      elseif ($admin_page == 'Carts')
         $this->mContentsCell = 'admin_carts.tpl';
      elseif ($admin_page == 'Orders')
         $this->mContentsCell = 'admin_orders.tpl';
      elseif ($admin_page == 'OrderDetails')
         $this->mContentsCell = 'admin_order_details.tpl';
    }
  }
}
?>
```

3. Add the following two methods in the `Link` class, which you can find in `presentation/link.php`:

```
  // Create link to orders administration page
  public static function ToOrdersAdmin()
  {
    return self::ToAdmin('Page=Orders');
  }

  // Create link to the order details administration page
  public static function ToOrderDetailsAdmin($orderId)
  {
    $link = 'Page=OrderDetails&OrderId=' . $orderId;

    return self::ToAdmin($link);
  }
```

4. Open `presentation/admin_menu.php`, and modify the `AdminMenu` class adding the highlighted code which creates the ORDERS ADMIN link in the administration menu:

```
<?php
class AdminMenu
{
  public $mLinkToStoreAdmin;
  public $mLinkToAttributesAdmin;
  public $mLinkToCartsAdmin;
  public $mLinkToOrdersAdmin;
  public $mLinkToStoreFront;
  public $mLinkToLogout;

  public function __construct()
  {
    $this->mLinkToStoreAdmin = Link::ToAdmin();
    $this->mLinkToAttributesAdmin = Link::ToAttributesAdmin();
    $this->mLinkToCartsAdmin = Link::ToCartsAdmin();
```

```
    $this->mLinkToOrdersAdmin = Link::ToOrdersAdmin();

    if (isset ($_SESSION['link_to_store_front']))
      $this->mLinkToStoreFront = $_SESSION['link_to_store_front'];
    else
      $this->mLinkToStoreFront = Link::ToIndex();

    $this->mLinkToLogout = Link::ToLogout();
    }
  }
?>
```

5. Modify `presentation/templates/admin_menu.tpl` by adding the highlighted link code to the cart administration page. We also use a style for the menu so that the menu items will fit nicely into the layout.

```
<p class="menu"> |
  <a href="{$obj->mLinkToStoreAdmin}">CATALOG ADMIN</a> |
  <a href="{$obj->mLinkToAttributesAdmin}">PRODUCTS ATTRIBUTES ADMIN</a> |
  <a href="{$obj->mLinkToCartsAdmin}">CARTS ADMIN</a> |
  <a href="{$obj->mLinkToOrdersAdmin}">ORDERS ADMIN</a> |
  <a href="{$obj->mLinkToStoreFront}">STOREFRONT</a> |
  <a href="{$obj->mLinkToLogout}">LOGOUT</a> |
```

6. Open the `tshirtshop.css` file from the `styles` folder, and add the following style definition:

```
.menu {
  font-size: 93%;
}
```

How It Works: Setting Up the Orders Administration Page

There isn't anything to test at this point, because we haven't created any new significant functionality. We only prepared the ground for the implementing the orders and order details administration features. We also added a style to `tshirtshop.css` that will make the administration menu fit nicely on its page. Note that, at the moment, you get an error if you try loading `admin.php`, because we referenced a file that doesn't exist yet—`business/orders.php`. You'll create this file in the next exercise.

Displaying Pending Orders

In the next few pages, you'll implement the `admin_orders` componentized template and its supporting data tier and business tier functionality. `admin_orders` is the componentized template that allows the administrator to view the orders that have been placed on the web site. Because the list of orders will become very long in time, it is important to have a few well chosen filtering options.

The administrator will be able to select the orders using the following criteria:

- Show the most recent orders.

- Show orders that took place in a certain period of time.

- Show orders with a specified status value.

We'll create these features in the following exercise.

Exercise: Implementing the Orders Administration Page

1. We start by creating the necessary stored procedures. Use phpMyAdmin to create the stored procedures described in the following steps. Don't forget to set the $$ delimiter before executing the code of *each* step.

2. Execute the following code, which creates the orders_get_most_recent_orders stored procedure in your tshirtshop database. This procedure returns the most recent orders. The SELECT statement uses the LIMIT clause to limit the number of returned rows to the value of the inHowMany input parameter. The ORDER BY DESC clause, used to sort the results in descending order, is set so the most recent orders will be listed first.

```
-- Create orders_get_most_recent_orders stored procedure
CREATE PROCEDURE orders_get_most_recent_orders(IN inHowMany INT)
BEGIN
  PREPARE statement FROM
    "SELECT   order_id, total_amount, created_on,
              shipped_on, status, customer_name
     FROM     orders
     ORDER BY created_on DESC
     LIMIT    ?";

  SET @p1 = inHowMany;

  EXECUTE statement USING @p1;
END$$
```

3. Execute the following code to create the orders_get_orders_between_dates stored procedure. This procedure returns the orders whose creation date is between inStartDate and inEndDate. The results are sorted descending by creation date.

```
-- Create orders_get_orders_between_dates stored procedure
CREATE PROCEDURE orders_get_orders_between_dates(
   IN inStartDate DATETIME, IN inEndDate DATETIME)
BEGIN
   SELECT   order_id, total_amount, created_on,
            shipped_on, status, customer_name
   FROM     orders
   WHERE    created_on >= inStartDate AND created_on <= inEndDate
   ORDER BY created_on DESC;
END$$
```

4. Execute this code, which creates the orders_get_orders_by_status stored procedure. This procedure returns the orders that have the status value specified by the inStatus parameter.

```
-- Create orders_get_orders_by_status stored procedure
CREATE PROCEDURE orders_get_orders_by_status(IN inStatus INT)
```

```
BEGIN
  SELECT   order_id, total_amount, created_on,
           shipped_on, status, customer_name
  FROM     orders
  WHERE    status = inStatus
  ORDER BY created_on DESC;
END$$
```

5. The business tier consists of a new class named Orders, whose methods call their data tier counterparts. This class is pretty straightforward with no particularly complex logic, so we'll just list the code. Create the business/orders.php file, and add the following code to it:

```php
<?php
// Business tier class for the orders
class Orders
{
  public static $mOrderStatusOptions = array ('placed',     // 0
                                              'verified',  // 1
                                              'completed', // 2
                                              'canceled'); // 3

  // Get the most recent $how_many orders
  public static function GetMostRecentOrders($how_many)
  {
    // Build the SQL query
    $sql = 'CALL orders_get_most_recent_orders(:how_many)';

    // Build the parameters array
    $params = array (':how_many' => $how_many);

    // Execute the query and return the results
    return DatabaseHandler::GetAll($sql, $params);
  }

  // Get orders between two dates
  public static function GetOrdersBetweenDates($startDate, $endDate)
  {
    // Build the SQL query
    $sql = 'CALL orders_get_orders_between_dates(:start_date, :end_date)';

    // Build the parameters array
    $params = array (':start_date' => $startDate, ':end_date' => $endDate);

    // Execute the query and return the results
    return DatabaseHandler::GetAll($sql, $params);
  }

  // Gets orders by status
```

```
  public static function GetOrdersByStatus($status)
  {
    // Build the SQL query
    $sql = 'CALL orders_get_orders_by_status(:status)';

    // Build the parameters array
    $params = array (':status' => $status);

    // Execute the query and return the results
    return DatabaseHandler::GetAll($sql, $params);
  }
}
?>
```

6. Now, it's time to implement the admin_orders componentized template. Create a new file named admin_orders.tpl in the presentation/templates folder with the following code in it:

```
{* admin_orders.tpl *}
{load_presentation_object filename="admin_orders" assign="obj"}
{if $obj->mErrorMessage}<p class="error">{$obj->mErrorMessage}</p>{/if}
<form method="get" action="{$obj->mLinkToAdmin}">
  <input name="Page" type="hidden" value="Orders" />
  <p>
    <font class="bold-text">Show the most recent</font>
    <input name="recordCount" type="text" value="{$obj->mRecordCount}" />
    <font class="bold-text">orders</font>
    <input type="submit" name="submitMostRecent" value="Go!" />
  </p>
  <p>
    <font class="bold-text">Show all records created between</font>
    <input name="startDate" type="text" value="{$obj->mStartDate}" />
    <font class="bold-text">and</font>
    <input name="endDate" type="text" value="{$obj->mEndDate}" />
    <input type="submit" name="submitBetweenDates" value="Go!" />
  </p>
  <p>
    <font class="bold-text">Show orders by status</font>
    {html_options name="status" options=$obj->mOrderStatusOptions
      selected=$obj->mSelectedStatus}
    <input type="submit" name="submitOrdersByStatus" value="Go!" />
  </p>
</form>
{if $obj->mOrders}
<table class="tss-table">
  <tr>
    <th>Order ID</th>
    <th>Date Created</th>
    <th>Date Shipped</th>
```

```
      <th>Status</th>
      <th>Customer</th>
      <th> </th>
    </tr>
    {section name=i loop=$obj->mOrders}
      {assign var=status value=$obj->mOrders[i].status}
    <tr>
      <td>{$obj->mOrders[i].order_id}</td>
      <td>{$obj->mOrders[i].created_on|date_format:"%Y-%m-%d %T"}</td>
      <td>{$obj->mOrders[i].shipped_on|date_format:"%Y-%m-%d %T"}</td>
      <td>{$obj->mOrderStatusOptions[$status]}</td>
      <td>{$obj->mOrders[i].customer_name}</td>
      <td align="right">
        <a href="{$obj->mOrders[i].link_to_order_details_admin}">View Details</a>
      </td>
    </tr>
    {/section}
  </table>
{/if}
```

7. Create a new file named `presentation/admin_orders.php`, and add the following code to it:

```php
<?php
/* Presentation tier class that supports order administration
   functionality */
class AdminOrders
{
  // Public variables available in smarty template
  public $mOrders;
  public $mStartDate;
  public $mEndDate;
  public $mRecordCount = 20;
  public $mOrderStatusOptions;
  public $mSelectedStatus = 0;
  public $mErrorMessage = '';
  public $mLinkToAdmin;

  // Class constructor
  public function __construct()
  {
    /* Save the link to the current page in the link_to_orders_admin
       session variable; it will be used to create the
       "back to admin orders ..." link in admin order details pages */
    $_SESSION['link_to_orders_admin'] =
      Link::Build(str_replace(VIRTUAL_LOCATION, '', getenv('REQUEST_URI')));

    $this->mLinkToAdmin = Link::ToAdmin();
```

```php
    $this->mOrderStatusOptions = Orders::$mOrderStatusOptions;
}

public function init()
{
  // If the "Show the most recent x orders" filter is in action ...
  if (isset ($_GET['submitMostRecent']))
  {
    // If the record count value is not a valid integer, display error
    if ((string)(int)$_GET['recordCount'] == (string)$_GET['recordCount'])
    {
      $this->mRecordCount = (int)$_GET['recordCount'];
      $this->mOrders = Orders::GetMostRecentOrders($this->mRecordCount);
    }
    else
      $this->mErrorMessage = $_GET['recordCount'] . ' is not a number.';
  }

  /* If the "Show all records created between date_1 and date_2"
     filter is in action ... */
  if (isset ($_GET['submitBetweenDates']))
  {
    $this->mStartDate = $_GET['startDate'];
    $this->mEndDate = $_GET['endDate'];

    // Check if the start date is in accepted format
    if (($this->mStartDate == '') ||
        ($timestamp = strtotime($this->mStartDate)) == -1)
      $this->mErrorMessage = 'The start date is invalid. ';
    else
      // Transform date to YYYY/MM/DD HH:MM:SS format
      $this->mStartDate =
        strftime('%Y/%m/%d %H:%M:%S', strtotime($this->mStartDate));

    // Check if the end date is in accepted format
    if (($this->mEndDate == '') ||
        ($timestamp = strtotime($this->mEndDate)) == -1)
      $this->mErrorMessage .= 'The end date is invalid.';
    else
      // Transform date to YYYY/MM/DD HH:MM:SS format
      $this->mEndDate =
        strftime('%Y/%m/%d %H:%M:%S', strtotime($this->mEndDate));

    // Check if start date is more recent than the end date
    if ((empty ($this->mErrorMessage)) &&
        (strtotime($this->mStartDate) > strtotime($this->mEndDate)))
      $this->mErrorMessage .=
        'The start date should be more recent than the end date.';
```

```
        // If there are no errors, get the orders between the two dates
        if (empty($this->mErrorMessage))
          $this->mOrders = Orders::GetOrdersBetweenDates(
                            $this->mStartDate, $this->mEndDate);
      }

      // If "Show orders by status" filter is in action ...
      if (isset ($_GET['submitOrdersByStatus']))
      {
        $this->mSelectedStatus = $_GET['status'];
        $this->mOrders = Orders::GetOrdersByStatus($this->mSelectedStatus);
      }

      if (is_array($this->mOrders) && count($this->mOrders) == 0)
        $this->mErrorMessage =
          'No orders found matching your searching criteria!';

      // Build View Details link
      for ($i = 0; $i < count($this->mOrders); $i++)
      {
        $this->mOrders[$i]['link_to_order_details_admin'] =
          Link::ToOrderDetailsAdmin($this->mOrders[$i]['order_id']);
      }
    }
  }
}
?>
```

8. Load admin.php into the browser, and provide the username/password combination if asked. Click the
ORDERS ADMIN menu link, then click one of the Go buttons, and you should see results similar to those
shown in Figure 14-5.

How It Works: Retrieving Orders

Each of the Go buttons calls one of the business tier methods (in the Orders class) and populates the table with
the returned orders information.

When processing the request, we test the data the visitor entered to make sure it's valid. When the first Go button
is clicked, we verify that the entered value is a number (how many records to show). We also verify whether the
dates entered in the Start Date and End Date text boxes are valid.

We first process the dates with strtotime that parses a string and transforms it into a Unix timestamp. This
function is useful, because it also accepts entries such as "now", "tomorrow", "last Friday", "next Tuesday", and
so on as input values.

The resulting timestamp is then processed with the strftime function, which transforms it into the YYYY/MM/DD
HH:MM:SS format. Have a look at how these date/time values are parsed:

```
    // Check if the start date is in accepted format
    if (($this->mStartDate == '') ||
        ($timestamp = strtotime($this->mStartDate)) == -1)
```

```
    $this->mErrorMessage = 'The start date is invalid. ';
  else
    // Transform date to YYYY/MM/DD HH:MM:SS format
    $this->mStartDate =
      strftime('%Y/%m/%d %H:%M:%S', strtotime($this->mStartDate));
```

> ■**Note** Check http://www.php.net/strtotime to see what input formats are supported by the strtotime function and http://www.php.net/strftime for more details about strftime. You can find a useful strtotime tutorial at http://www.programmers-corner.com/tutorial/80.

Apart from this detail, the admin_orders.tpl template file is pretty simple and doesn't introduce any new theoretical elements for you.

Displaying Order Details

In this section, you'll create the admin_order_details componentized template, which allows the administrator to edit the details of a particular order. The most common tasks are to mark a placed order as either verified or canceled and to mark a verified order as completed when the shipment is dispatched. Take a look at Figure 14-5 to see the admin_order_details template in action.

The site administrator marks an order as verified when the payment for that order is confirmed by PayPal and marks the order as completed when the order is assembled, addressed, and mailed to the purchaser. The administrator can mark an order as canceled if, for example, PayPal does not confirm the payment in a reasonable amount of time (the exact meaning of "reasonable" is up to the administrator).

The other buttons—Edit, Update, and Cancel—allow the administrator to manually edit any of the details of an order. When the Edit button is clicked, the select box and the text boxes become editable.

Now that you have an idea of what this componentized template will do, let's implement it in the usual style by starting with the data tier.

Exercise: Administering Order Details

1. Use phpMyAdmin to create the three stored procedures described in the following steps: orders_get_order_info, orders_get_order_details, and orders_update_order. Don't forget to set the $$ delimiter before executing the code of *each* step.

2. Execute this code, which creates the orders_get_order_info stored procedure. This stored procedure returns the information necessary to fill the form in the admin_order_details componentized template, such as the total amount, date created, date shipped, and so on. You can see this data in Figure 14-6.

```
-- Create orders_get_order_info stored procedure
CREATE PROCEDURE orders_get_order_info(IN inOrderId INT)
```

```
BEGIN
  SELECT order_id, total_amount, created_on, shipped_on, status,
         comments, customer_name, shipping_address, customer_email
  FROM   orders
  WHERE  order_id = inOrderId;
END$$
```

3. Execute the following code, which creates the orders_get_order_details stored procedure in your tshirtshop database. This procedure returns the products that belong to a particular order. This data is used to populate the table containing the order details, situated at the bottom of the page.

```
-- Create orders_get_order_details stored procedure
CREATE PROCEDURE orders_get_order_details(IN inOrderId INT)
BEGIN
  SELECT order_id, product_id, attributes, product_name,
         quantity, unit_cost, (quantity * unit_cost) AS subtotal
  FROM   order_detail
  WHERE  order_id = inOrderId;
END$$
```

4. Execute this code, which creates the stored procedure orders_update_order stored procedure. This is called when the administrator updates an order in edit mode; it updates the details of an order.

```
-- Create orders_update_order stored procedure
CREATE PROCEDURE orders_update_order(IN inOrderId INT, IN inStatus INT,
  IN inComments VARCHAR(255), IN inCustomerName VARCHAR(50),
  IN inShippingAddress VARCHAR(255), IN inCustomerEmail VARCHAR(50))
BEGIN
  DECLARE currentStatus INT;

  SELECT status
  FROM   orders
  WHERE  order_id = inOrderId
  INTO   currentStatus;

  IF inStatus != currentStatus AND (inStatus = 0 OR inStatus = 1) THEN
    UPDATE orders SET shipped_on = NULL WHERE order_id = inOrderId;
  ELSEIF inStatus != currentStatus AND inStatus = 2 THEN
    UPDATE orders SET shipped_on = NOW() WHERE order_id = inOrderId;
  END IF;

  UPDATE orders
  SET    status = inStatus, comments = inComments,
         customer_name = inCustomerName,
         shipping_address = inShippingAddress,
         customer_email = inCustomerEmail
  WHERE  order_id = inOrderId;
END$$
```

5. The business tier part for the componentized template admin_order_details is very simple and consists of the following methods that you need to add to the Orders class inside of the business/orders.php file:

```
// Gets the details of a specific order
public static function GetOrderInfo($orderId)
{
  // Build the SQL query
  $sql = 'CALL orders_get_order_info(:order_id)';

  // Build the parameters array
  $params = array (':order_id' => $orderId);

  // Execute the query and return the results
  return DatabaseHandler::GetRow($sql, $params);
}

// Gets the products that belong to a specific order
public static function GetOrderDetails($orderId)
{
  // Build the SQL query
  $sql = 'CALL orders_get_order_details(:order_id)';

  // Build the parameters array
  $params = array (':order_id' => $orderId);

  // Execute the query and return the results
  return DatabaseHandler::GetAll($sql, $params);
}

// Updates order details
public static function UpdateOrder($orderId, $status, $comments,
                        $customerName, $shippingAddress, $customerEmail)
{
  // Build the SQL query
  $sql = 'CALL orders_update_order(:order_id, :status, :comments,
              :customer_name, :shipping_address, :customer_email)';

  // Build the parameters array
  $params = array (':order_id' => $orderId,
                   ':status' => $status,
                   ':comments' => $comments,
                   ':customer_name' => $customerName,
                   ':shipping_address' => $shippingAddress,
                   ':customer_email' => $customerEmail);

  // Execute the query
  DatabaseHandler::Execute($sql, $params);
}
```

6. Let's wrap things up and create the user interface now. The presentation tier consists of the componentized template admin_order_details. Create a new template file named admin_order_details.tpl in the presentation/templates folder, and add the following code to it:

```
{* admin_order_details.tpl *}
{load_presentation_object filename="admin_order_details" assign="obj"}
<form method="get" action="{$obj->mLinkToAdmin}">
  <h3>
    Editing details for order ID:
    {$obj->mOrderInfo.order_id} [
    <a href="{$obj->mLinkToOrdersAdmin}">back to admin orders...</a> ]
  </h3>
  <input type="hidden" name="Page" value="OrderDetails" />
  <input type="hidden" name="OrderId"
   value="{$obj->mOrderInfo.order_id}" />
  <table class="borderless-table">
    <tr>
      <td class="bold-text">Total Amount: </td>
      <td class="price">
        ${$obj->mOrderInfo.total_amount}
      </td>
    </tr>
    <tr>
      <td class="bold-text">Date Created: </td>
      <td>
        {$obj->mOrderInfo.created_on|date_format:"%Y-%m-%d %T"}
      </td>
    </tr>
    <tr>
      <td class="bold-text">Date Shipped: </td>
      <td>
        {$obj->mOrderInfo.shipped_on|date_format:"%Y-%m-%d %T"}
      </td>
    </tr>
    <tr>
      <td class="bold-text">Status: </td>
      <td>
        <select name="status"
        {if ! $obj->mEditEnabled} disabled="disabled" {/if} >
          {html_options options=$obj->mOrderStatusOptions
           selected=$obj->mOrderInfo.status}
        </select>
      </td>
    </tr>
    <tr>
      <td class="bold-text">Comments: </td>
      <td>
        <input name="comments" type="text" size="50"
```

```
        value="{$obj->mOrderInfo.comments}"
        {if ! $obj->mEditEnabled} disabled="disabled" {/if} />
    <td>
  </tr>
  <tr>
    <td class="bold-text">Customer Name: </td>
    <td>
      <input name="customerName" type="text" size="50"
      value="{$obj->mOrderInfo.customer_name}"
        {if ! $obj->mEditEnabled} disabled="disabled" {/if} />
    <td>
  </tr>
  <tr>
    <td class="bold-text">Shipping Address: </td>
    <td>
      <input name="shippingAddress" type="text" size="50"
      value="{$obj->mOrderInfo.shipping_address}"
        {if ! $obj->mEditEnabled} disabled="disabled" {/if} />
    </td>
  </tr>
  <tr>
    <td class="bold-text">Customer Email: </td>
    <td>
      <input name="customerEmail" type="text" size="50"
      value="{$obj->mOrderInfo.customer_email}"
        {if ! $obj->mEditEnabled} disabled="disabled" {/if} />
    </td>
  </tr>
</table>
<p>
  <input type="submit" name="submitEdit" value="Edit"
  {if $obj->mEditEnabled} disabled="disabled" {/if} />
  <input type="submit" name="submitUpdate" value="Update"
  {if ! $obj->mEditEnabled} disabled="disabled" {/if} />
  <input type="submit" name="submitCancel" value="Cancel"
  {if ! $obj->mEditEnabled} disabled="disabled" {/if} />
</p>
<h3>Order contains these products:</h3>
<table class="tss-table">
  <tr>
    <th>Product ID</th>
    <th>Product Name</th>
    <th>Quantity</th>
    <th>Unit Cost</th>
    <th>Subtotal</th>
  </tr>
{section name=i loop=$obj->mOrderDetails}
```

```
      <tr>
        <td>{$obj->mOrderDetails[i].product_id}</td>
        <td>
          {$obj->mOrderDetails[i].product_name}
          ({$obj->mOrderDetails[i].attributes})
        </td>
        <td>{$obj->mOrderDetails[i].quantity}</td>
        <td>${$obj->mOrderDetails[i].unit_cost}</td>
        <td>${$obj->mOrderDetails[i].subtotal}</td>
      </tr>
    {/section}
    </table>
</form>
```

7. Create a new file named admin_order_details.php in the presentation folder, and write the following
   code in it:

```php
<?php
// Presentation tier class that deals with administering order details
class AdminOrderDetails
{
  // Public variables available in smarty template
  public $mOrderId;
  public $mOrderInfo;
  public $mOrderDetails;
  public $mEditEnabled;
  public $mOrderStatusOptions;
  public $mLinkToAdmin;
  public $mLinkToOrdersAdmin;

  // Class constructor
  public function __construct()
  {
    // Get the back link from session
    $this->mLinkToOrdersAdmin = $_SESSION['link_to_orders_admin'];

    $this->mLinkToAdmin = Link::ToAdmin();

    // We receive the order ID in the query string
    if (isset ($_GET['OrderId']))
      $this->mOrderId = (int) $_GET['OrderId'];
    else
      trigger_error('OrderId paramater is required');

    $this->mOrderStatusOptions = Orders::$mOrderStatusOptions;
  }
```

```
    // Initializes class members
    public function init()
    {
      if (isset ($_GET['submitUpdate']))
      {
        Orders::UpdateOrder($this->mOrderId, $_GET['status'],
          $_GET['comments'], $_GET['customerName'], $_GET['shippingAddress'],
          $_GET['customerEmail']);
      }

      $this->mOrderInfo = Orders::GetOrderInfo($this->mOrderId);
      $this->mOrderDetails = Orders::GetOrderDetails($this->mOrderId);

      // Value which specifies whether to enable or disable edit mode
      if (isset ($_GET['submitEdit']))
        $this->mEditEnabled = true;
      else
        $this->mEditEnabled = false;
    }
  }
  ?>
```

8. Add some fictional orders to the database, and then load the admin.php file in your browser. Click the ORDERS ADMIN menu link, click a Go button to show some orders, and click the View Details button for one of the orders. The order details administration page will show up, allowing you to edit the order's details, as noted earlier in this chapter.

How It Works: Administering Order Details

The two files you just wrote, admin_order_details.tpl and admin_order_details.php, allow you to view and update the details of a particular order.

The constructor of the AdminOrderDetails class (the __construct method) ensures that there's an OrderId parameter in the query string, because without it, this componentized template doesn't make sense:

```
// Class constructor
public function __construct()
{
  // Get the back link from session
  $this->mLinkToOrdersAdmin = $_SESSION['link_to_orders_admin'];

  $this->mLinkToAdmin = Link::ToAdmin();

  // We receive the order ID in the query string
  if (isset ($_GET['OrderId']))
    $this->mOrderId = (int) $_GET['OrderId'];
  else
    trigger_error('OrderId paramater is required');
```

```
        $this->mOrderStatusOptions = Orders::$mOrderStatusOptions;
    }
```

The `init()` method reacts to user's actions and calls various business tier methods to accomplish the user's requests.

It populates the form with the data it gets from the `Orders::GetOrderInfo()` and the `Orders::GetOrderDetails()` business tier methods.

The `$mEditEnabled` class member enters or exits edit mode, depending on whether or not the `submitEdit` parameter from the query string is set. When entering edit mode, all text boxes and the Update and Cancel buttons become enabled, but the Edit button is disabled. The reverse happens when exiting edit mode, which happens when either the Cancel or Update button is clicked.

Summary

We covered a lot of ground in this chapter. In two separate stages, you implemented a system for taking orders and manually administering them. You added a Place Order button to the shopping cart control to allow the visitor to order the products in the shopping cart. You implemented a simple orders administration page, in which the site administrator can view and handle pending orders.

Because order data is now stored in the database, you can do various statistics and calculations based on the items sold. In the next chapter, you'll learn how to implement a dynamic product recommendations feature, which wouldn't have been possible without the order data stored in the database.

CHAPTER 15

■■■

Product Recommendations

One of the most important advantages of an Internet store, compared to a brick-and-mortar location, is the capability to customize the web site for each visitor based on his or her preferences or on preferences based on data gathered from similar visitors. If your web site knows how to suggest additional products to your visitors in a clever way, they might end up buying more than initially planned. You have undoubtedly already seen this strategy in action on many successful ecommerce sites, and there is a reason for that—it increases profits.

In this chapter, you'll implement a simple but efficient product recommendation system in your TShirtShop web store. You will

- Add product recommendations to the product details pages. These recommendations will promote additional products that were ordered together with a particular product.

- Add product recommendations to the shopping cart pages. These recommendations will promote products that were ordered together with the products in the shopping cart.

Implementing these features isn't particularly difficult, but finding the perfect recommendations mechanism is always an interesting task.

Increasing Sales with Dynamic Recommendations

You can implement a product recommendations system in several ways, depending on your kind of store. Here are a few popular ones:

Up-Selling: Up-selling is the strategy of offering consumers the opportunity to purchase an upgrade or a little something extra based on their requested purchase. Perhaps the most famous example of up-selling—"Would you like to super-size that?"—is mentioned to customers when they order a meal at McDonald's. This seemingly innocent question greatly increases the company's profit margin.

Cross-Selling: Cross-selling is the practice of offering customers complementary products. Continuing with the McDonald's analogy, when someone orders a hamburger, you'll always hear the phrase, "Would you like fries with that?" Because it's widely acknowledged that fries go with burgers, and the consumer is ordering a burger, it's likely that the consumer also likes french fries—the mere mention of french fries is likely to generate a new sale.

Featured products on the home page: TShirtShop already permits the site administrator to choose the products featured on the main page and on the department pages.

461

In this chapter, you'll implement a dynamic recommendations system with both up-selling and cross-selling strategies. Because, at this point, TShirtShop retains which products were sold, you will implement the "customers who bought this product also bought . . ." feature in this chapter. This system has the advantage of needing no manual maintenance. Our site will automatically help us to increase our profits without any further intervention!

As mentioned earlier, we'll implement the dynamic recommendations system in the visitor's shopping cart and in the product details page. After adding the new bits to your shop, the product details page will contain the product recommendations list at the bottom of the page, as shown in Figure 15-1.

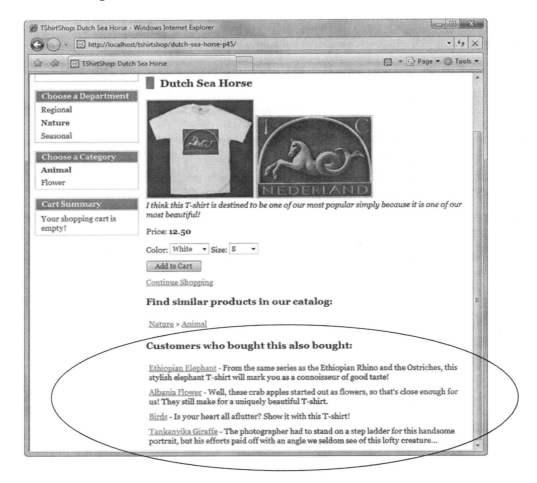

Figure 15-1. *Product recommendations in the product details page*

The shopping cart page gets a similar addition, as shown in Figure 15-2.

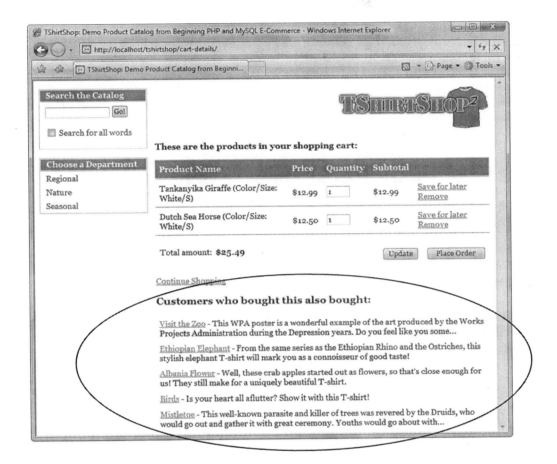

Figure 15-2. *Product recommendations in the shopping cart page*

Selecting Recommendations from the Database

The technical challenge for implementing the new feature lies in writing the database queries that return the product recommendations. Writing a SELECT query that finds the products that were ordered together with another product (to generate product recommendations), or with another set of products (to generate shopping cart recommendations), is not overly complex but not trivial either.

Let's start with the product recommendations. You need to find out what other products were bought by customers who bought the product for which you're calculating the recommendations (in other words, determine the "customer who bought this product also bought . . ." information).

Our order_detail table contains the data for each of our orders. To determine what other products were ordered together with a specific product, we would join two instances of the order_detail table on their order_id fields. Joining multiple instances of a single table is just like joining independent data tables that contain the same data (feel free to review the "Joining Data Tables" section in Chapter 5 for a quick refresher about table joins).

We join two instances of order_detail—which we've named od1 and od2—on their order_id fields and filter on the product_id value in od1 for the product we're looking for. This way, in the od2 side of the relationship, we will have all of the products that were ordered in orders that also contain the product we're filtering for. To more easily understand this, take a look at the diagram in Figure 15-3. In the diagram, we have two orders (1 and 2), each having three products (1, 2, 3, and 2, 5, 7 respectively). Following the relationship between od1 and od2, you can see that is quite easy to find what products were ordered with a particular product.

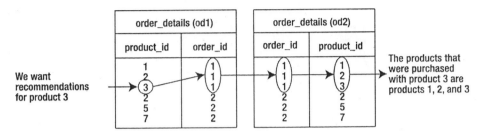

Figure 15-3. *Using order details to find product recommendations*

Let's see how we can implement this relationship with SQL code. The following query retrieves all the products that were ordered together with the product identified by a product_id of 4:

```
SELECT od2.product_id
FROM   order_detail od1
JOIN   order_detail od2
         ON od1.order_id = od2.order_id
WHERE  od1.product_id = 4;
```

This code returns a long list of products, which includes the product with the product_id of 4, such as this one:

```
product_id
----------
         4
         5
        10
        43
         4
         5
        10
        23
        25
        28
         4
        10
        12
        14
        43
```

This result is good to start with, but it's less than perfect. First, it'd be helpful if the list of products was sorted by how *frequently* the products were ordered along with our product. The more times two products are ordered together, the better the cross-selling recommendation will be. We'll show you how to deal with this in a second.

Second, the list shouldn't include the product for which we're calculating the recommendations; it's already been ordered. This problem is simple to solve, by adding one more rule to the WHERE clause:

```
SELECT od2.product_id
FROM    order_detail od1
JOIN    order_detail od2
          ON od1.order_id = od2.order_id
WHERE   od1.product_id = 4 AND od2.product_id != 4;
```

Not surprisingly, executing this query you get a list of products that is similar to the previous one, except it doesn't contain the product with a product_id of 4 anymore:

```
product_id
----------
         5
        10
        43
         5
        10
        23
        25
        28
        10
        12
        14
        43
```

Now, the list of returned products is much shorter, but it contains multiple entries for several products (products that were ordered in several orders that also contain the product identifier 4). To get the most relevant recommendations, we need to find out which products appear more frequently in this list. We do this by grouping the results of the previous query by product_id and sorting in descending order by how many times each product appears in the list (this number is given by the rank calculated column in the following code snippet):

```
SELECT    od2.product_id, COUNT(od2.product_id) AS rank
FROM      order_detail od1
JOIN      order_detail od2
            ON od1.order_id = od2.order_id
WHERE     od1.product_id = 4 AND od2.product_id != 4
GROUP BY od2.product_id
ORDER BY rank DESC;
```

■**Tip** Placing a space between COUNT and the expression that follows makes MySQL generate an error, so be careful.

The query now returns a list with the highest ranking products listed first:

```
product_id    rank
----------    ----
        10       3
         5       2
        43       2
        23       1
        25       1
        28       1
        12       1
        14       1
```

If you don't need to see the rank, you can rewrite this query using the COUNT aggregate function directly in the ORDER BY clause. You can also use the LIMIT keyword to specify how many records you're interested in. If you want the top five products of the list, this query does the trick:

```
SELECT    od2.product_id
FROM      order_detail od1
JOIN      order_detail od2
              ON od1.order_id = od2.order_id
WHERE     od1.product_id = 4 AND od2.product_id != 4
GROUP BY od2.product_id
ORDER BY COUNT(od2.product_id) DESC
LIMIT 5;
```

The results of this query are

```
product_id
----------
        10
         5
        43
        23
        25
```

Note Be aware that you may get different results if you try this query using your database, even if you have the same data as we have. When the sorting criteria that you specify using ORDER BY is not specific enough, the database engine chooses the sorting method that is most convenient for it, which really means that you get the records that are the quickest and easiest for the database to retrieve. For example, as far as the previous query is concerned, you can see there are five product IDs for which the rank is 1 (12, 14, 23, 25, 28). When we executed the query on our test database, we got 23 and 25, but your database may "prefer" other products. To obtain the product recommendations, the only criteria we're interested in is the rank that we calculate; when we have many products with the same rank, it's OK to let the database choose for us.

Because this list of numbers doesn't make much sense to the human eye, you'll also want to know the name and the description of the recommended products. The following query extracts the names by joining the list of recommended product IDs with the product table:

```
SELECT    od2.product_id, od2.product_name
FROM      order_detail od1
JOIN      order_detail od2 ON od1.order_id = od2.order_id
JOIN      product p ON od2.product_id = p.product_id
WHERE     od1.product_id = 4 AND od2.product_id != 4
GROUP BY od2.product_id
ORDER BY COUNT(od2.product_id) DESC
LIMIT 5;
```

Based on the data from the previous fictional results, this query returns something like this:

```
product_id    name
----------    ----------------------
        10    Haute Couture
         5    Marianne
        43    Equatorial Rhino
        23    Italian Airmail
        25    Romulus & Remus
```

Alternatively, you might want to calculate the product recommendations only using data from the orders placed in the last *n* days. For this, you need an additional join with the orders table, which contains the created_on field. The following query calculates product recommendations based on orders placed in the past 30 days:

```
SELECT    od2.product_id, od2.product_name
FROM      order_detail od1
JOIN      order_detail od2 ON od1.order_id = od2.order_id
JOIN      orders o ON od1.order_id = o.order_id
WHERE     od1.product_id = 4 AND od2.product_id != 4
          AND DATE_SUB(NOW(), INTERVAL 30 DAY) < o.created_on
```

```
GROUP BY od2.product_id
ORDER BY COUNT(od2.product_id) DESC
LIMIT 5;
```

■**Note** We won't use this trick at this time in TShirtShop, but it's important to keep it in mind. Over time, as you sell more and more via your site, you will need to limit the number of orders that are used to calculate the recommendations—otherwise, your recommendations will not only be dated but will be calculated on ever larger sets of data. This situation reduces the effectiveness of the recommendations and takes a toll on the site's performance. After all, do we really want to recommend Christmas t-shirts in the month of May? And how will your shoppers feel about having had to wait while your server crunches on outdated recommendations? It's a good bet that they will begin to ignore your recommendations altogether if they are too often irrelevant. If you decide to use this technique, adding an index on the `created_on` field would increase the query performance.

When obtaining shopping cart recommendations, we basically use the same technique as for single product recommendations, except that we add the shopping cart ingredient to the mix. Instead of obtaining the products that were ordered together with another product, we obtain the products that were ordered together with *any* of the products of the shopping cart. This is a more complex calculation indeed, but the return on your time investment is worth it for the potential extra sales!

The last thing to note before writing the code is that our proposed implementation is one of the many possible ones. Generally in programming, and particularly in the world of SQL, a result can be achieved in many ways. The query that returns product recommendations can be rewritten in a number of ways, the most obvious being that of using subqueries instead of table joins.

We implement the data tier logic we've just explained in the two stored procedures: `catalog_get_recommendations` and `shopping_cart_get_recommendations`. In addition to the queries shown earlier, the stored procedures will also retrieve the product names and descriptions, which need to be displayed to the visitor.

Exercise: Adding the Product Recommendation Stored Procedures

1. Use phpMyAdmin to create the stored procedure described in the following steps. Don't forget to set the $$ delimiter before executing the code at *each* step.

2. Execute this code, which creates the `catalog_get_recommendations` stored procedure in your tshirtshop database:

```
-- Create catalog_get_recommendations stored procedure
CREATE PROCEDURE catalog_get_recommendations(
  IN inProductId INT, IN inShortProductDescriptionLength INT)
BEGIN
  PREPARE statement FROM
    "SELECT   od2.product_id, od2.product_name,
```

```
                    IF(LENGTH(p.description) <= ?, p.description,
                        CONCAT(LEFT(p.description, ?), '...')) AS description
        FROM        order_detail od1
        JOIN        order_detail od2 ON od1.order_id = od2.order_id
        JOIN        product p ON od2.product_id = p.product_id
        WHERE       od1.product_id = ? AND
                    od2.product_id != ?
        GROUP BY od2.product_id
        ORDER BY COUNT(od2.product_id) DESC
        LIMIT 5";

    SET @p1 = inShortProductDescriptionLength;
    SET @p2 = inProductId;

    EXECUTE statement USING @p1, @p1, @p2, @p2;
END$$
```

3. Execute the following code, which creates the shopping_cart_get_recommendations stored procedure in your tshirtshop database:

```
-- Create shopping_cart_get_recommendations stored procedure
CREATE PROCEDURE shopping_cart_get_recommendations(
  IN inCartId CHAR(32), IN inShortProductDescriptionLength INT)
BEGIN
  PREPARE statement FROM
    "-- Returns the products that exist in a list of orders
    SELECT    od1.product_id, od1.product_name,
              IF(LENGTH(p.description) <= ?, p.description,
                  CONCAT(LEFT(p.description, ?), '...')) AS description
    FROM      order_detail od1
    JOIN      order_detail od2
                ON od1.order_id = od2.order_id
    JOIN      product p
                ON od1.product_id = p.product_id
    JOIN      shopping_cart
                ON od2.product_id = shopping_cart.product_id
    WHERE     shopping_cart.cart_id = ?
              -- Must not include products that already exist
              -- in the visitor's cart
              AND od1.product_id NOT IN
              (-- Returns the products in the specified
               -- shopping cart
               SELECT product_id
               FROM   shopping_cart
               WHERE  cart_id = ?)
    -- Group the product_id so we can calculate the rank
    GROUP BY od1.product_id
    -- Order descending by rank
```

```
        ORDER BY COUNT(od1.product_id) DESC
        LIMIT    5";

    SET @p1 = inShortProductDescriptionLength;
    SET @p2 = inCartId;

    EXECUTE statement USING @p1, @p1, @p2, @p2;
END$$
```

How It Works: Getting Product Recommendations from the Database

The stored procedures you've just written simply apply the techniques you've learned in the first part of the chapter. In other editions of this book (using PostgreSQL and SQL Server), at this point, we also presented alternative implementations of these stored procedures that used subqueries instead of table joins to obtain the necessary data. In MySQL, using subqueries is not possible because of some limitations of using LIMIT, which are documented at http://dev.mysql.com/doc/refman/5.1/en/subquery-errors.html. If newer versions of MySQL fix these problems, when performance becomes an issue, you could take into consideration making tests using the rewritten versions of these stored procedures. In some cases, the versions that use subqueries offer better performance.

Implementing Product and Shopping Cart Recommendations

In the following exercise, you'll write the code for the business and presentation tiers of the product recommendation system.

The business tier of the product recommendation system consists of two methods both named GetRecommendations. One of them is located in the Catalog class and retrieves recommendations for a product details page, and the other one is located in the ShoppingCart class and retrieves recommendations to be displayed in the visitor's shopping cart.

Exercise: Implementing Product and Shopping Cart Recommendations

1. Add the following method to the Catalog class in business/catalog.php file:

```php
// Get product recommendations
public static function GetRecommendations($productId)
{
  // Build the SQL query
  $sql = 'CALL catalog_get_recommendations(
              :product_id, :short_product_description_length)';

  // Build the parameters array
  $params = array (':product_id' => $productId,
                   ':short_product_description_length' =>
                     SHORT_PRODUCT_DESCRIPTION_LENGTH);
```

```
    // Execute the query and return the results
    return DatabaseHandler::GetAll($sql, $params);
  }
```

2. Open the shopping_cart.php file located in the business folder, and add the following code:

```
// Get product recommendations for the shopping cart
public static function GetRecommendations()
{
  // Build the SQL query
  $sql = 'CALL shopping_cart_get_recommendations(
              :cart_id, :short_product_description_length)';

  // Build the parameters array
  $params = array (':cart_id' => self::GetCartId(),
                   ':short_product_description_length' =>
                     SHORT_PRODUCT_DESCRIPTION_LENGTH);

  // Execute the query and return the results
  return DatabaseHandler::GetAll($sql, $params);
}
```

3. Now, we update the presentation tier by modifying the product and cart_details componentized templates to display the product recommendations. Open the presentation/product.php file, and add a member named $mRecommendations to the Product class:

```
// Public variables to be used in Smarty template
public $mProduct;
public $mProductLocations;
public $mLinkToContinueShopping;
public $mLocations;
public $mEditActionTarget;
public $mShowEditButton;
public $mRecommendations;
```

4. Next, you have to get the recommended products data in $mRecommendations and create links to their product pages. Modify the init() method of the Product class as highlighted here:

```
$this->mLocations = Catalog::GetProductLocations($this->_mProductId);

// Create the Add to Cart link
$this->mProduct['link_to_add_product'] =
  Link::ToCart(ADD_PRODUCT, $this->_mProductId);

// Get product recommendations
$this->mRecommendations =
  Catalog::GetRecommendations($this->_mProductId);

// Create recommended product links
for ($i = 0; $i < count($this->mRecommendations); $i++)
```

```
        $this->mRecommendations[$i]['link_to_product'] =
            Link::ToProduct($this->mRecommendations[$i]['product_id']);

    // Build links for product departments and categories pages
    for ($i = 0; $i < count($this->mLocations); $i++)
    {
```

5. To complete implementing the recommendations system for the product details page, we need to update the product.tpl template. Add the following lines at the end of presentation/templates/product.tpl. After that, you can load TShirtShop and load a product details page. If that product has been ordered with any other products, they'll show up in the recommendations list.

```
{if $obj->mRecommendations}
<h2>Customers who bought this also bought:</h2>
<ol>
    {section name=m loop=$obj->mRecommendations}
    <li>
        {strip}
        <a href="{$obj->mRecommendations[m].link_to_product}">
            {$obj->mRecommendations[m].product_name}
        </a>
        {/strip}
        <span class="list"> - {$obj->mRecommendations[m].description}</span>
    </li>
    {/section}
</ol>
{/if}
```

6. Open tshirtshop.css, and add the following style:

```
.list { color: #000000; }
```

7. Now, let's modify the cart_details componentized template to show product recommendations in the shopping cart page. Open cart_details.php located in the presentation folder to add the $mRecommendation member to the CartDetails class:

```
<?php
// Class that deals with managing the shopping cart
class CartDetails
{
    // Public variables available in smarty template
    public $mCartProducts;
    public $mSavedCartProducts;
    public $mTotalAmount;
    public $mIsCartNowEmpty = 0; // Is the shopping cart empty?
    public $mIsCartLaterEmpty = 0; // Is the 'saved for later' list empty?
    public $mLinkToContinueShopping;
    public $mUpdateCartTarget;
    public $mRecommendations;
```

8. Next, you have to get the recommended products data in $mRecommendations and create links to their product pages. Add the highlighted piece of code at the end of the init() method:

```
for ($i = 0; $i < count($this->mSavedCartProducts); $i++)
{
  $this->mSavedCartProducts[$i]['move'] =
    Link::ToCart(MOVE_PRODUCT_TO_CART,
                 $this->mSavedCartProducts[$i]['item_id']);

  $this->mSavedCartProducts[$i]['remove'] =
    Link::ToCart(REMOVE_PRODUCT,
                 $this->mSavedCartProducts[$i]['item_id']);
}

// Get product recommendations for the shopping cart
$this->mRecommendations =
  ShoppingCart::GetRecommendations();

// Create recommended product links
for ($i = 0; $i < count($this->mRecommendations); $i++)
  $this->mRecommendations[$i]['link_to_product'] =
    Link::ToProduct($this->mRecommendations[$i]['product_id']);
  }
}
?>
```

9. Finally, update the cart_details template to display the list of recommendations. Add the following lines at the end of presentation/templates/cart_details.tpl:

```
{if $obj->mRecommendations}
<h2>Customers who bought this also bought:</h2>
<ol>
  {section name=m loop=$obj->mRecommendations}
  <li>
    {strip}
    <a href="{$obj->mRecommendations[m].link_to_product}">
      {$obj->mRecommendations[m].product_name}
    </a>
    {/strip}
    <span class="list"> - {$obj->mRecommendations[m].description}</span>
  </li>
  {/section}
</ol>
{/if}
```

10. Load TShirtShop, place some orders, and then check the product and shopping cart details pages; they display recommendations based on the ordered products! The results should look like Figures 15-1 and 15-2 shown earlier in this chapter.

Note Remember to place some test orders that contain many products in order to give your recommendations mechanism some data to work with.

Summary

Showing product recommendations is a great way to encourage sales, and we succeeded in implementing this functionality in this short chapter. The greatest challenge was to build the SQL query that gets the list of recommended products, and we analyzed how to create it, step by step. Our site is ready to boost our sales without any further effort on our part!

In the next chapter, we'll enter Phase III of development by adding another service for our customers (and us)—customer accounts functionality.

■■■

## PART 3

Phase III of Development

CHAPTER 16

■ ■ ■

Managing Customer Details

So far in this book you've built a basic but functional site and integrated it with PayPal for accepting payments and confirming orders. In phase III of development, you'll take things a little further. By cutting out PayPal from your ordering process, you can obtain much better control—as well as reduce overhead costs. It isn't as complicated as you might think, but you do have to be careful to do things right.

In this chapter, we'll be laying the groundwork for this by implementing a customer account system.

To make e-commerce sites more user-friendly, you usually store details such as credit card numbers in a database so that users don't have to retype this information each time they place an order. The customer account system you'll implement will store this information and include all the web pages required for entering such details.

As well as implementing these web pages, we'll need to take several other factors into account. First, simply placing credit card numbers, expiry dates, and other important information into a database in plain text isn't ideal because it raises the possibility that this data could be stolen should the server be compromised. This could occur remotely or be perpetrated by individuals within our organization. In addition to enforcing a prohibitively restrictive access policy to such data, it can be a lot easier simply to encrypt sensitive information and retrieve it programmatically when required. We'll create a security library to ease this functionality.

Second, secure communications are important because you'll be capturing sensitive information such as credit card details via the Web. We can't just put a form up for people to access via HTTP and allow them to send it to us, because the information could be intercepted. Instead, we'll use SSL over HTTPS connections. We'll take the TShirtShop application to the point where we can implement a back-end order pipeline in Chapter 18.

In this chapter, you'll learn how to

- Store customer accounts

- Implement the security classes

- Add customer accounts functionality to TShirtShop

- Create the checkout page

Storing Customer Accounts

You can handle customer account functionality in web sites in many ways. In general, however, the methods share the following features:

- Customers log in to access secured areas of the web site.

- Once logged in, the web application remembers the customer until the customer logs out (either manually via a Log Out link or automatically if the session times out or a server error occurs).

- All secure pages in a web application need to check whether a customer is logged in before allowing access.

First we'll look at the general implementation details for the TShirtShop e-commerce site.

The TShirtShop Customer Account Scheme

One simple way to determine whether a customer is logged in is to store the customer ID in the session state. You can then verify whether a value is present at the start of the secured pages and warn the user if not. The login form itself can then authenticate the user and store a value in the session state if successful, ready for later retrieval. To log a user out, you simply remove the ID from the session state.

To log in, a customer needs to supply a username (we'll use the customer's e-mail address here because it is guaranteed to be unique) and a password. Sending this information over the Internet is a sensitive issue because third parties can eavesdrop and capture it. Later in this chapter, we'll look at how to enable secure communications over the Internet. For now, though, we'll concentrate on the authentication side of things, which is unaffected by the type of connection used to transmit the e-mail address and password of the customer.

Another issue related to security concerns storing user passwords. It isn't a good idea to store user passwords in your database in plain text because this information is a potential target for attack. Instead, you should store what is known as the *hash* of the password. A hash is a unique string that represents the password but cannot be converted into the password itself. To validate the password entered by the user, then, you simply need to generate a hash for the password entered and compare it with the hash stored in your database. If the hashes match, then the passwords entered match as well, so you can be sure the customer is genuine.

This leads to another important task—you need to supply a way for new users to register. The result of registration is to add a new customer to your database, including username and password hash information.

To implement this scheme in your application, you'll complete the following tasks:

- Create two new database tables, the first called `customer` to hold customer details and the second called `shipping_region` to store possible shipping regions in which a customer can reside.

- Implement the associated methods in data and business tiers that add, modify, and retrieve information from `customer` and `shipping_region`.

- Modify the `cart_details` componentized template, which will now redirect the user to a checkout page that will be implemented in a new componentized template called `checkout_info`.

- Create a componentized template for customer login called `customer_login`.

- Create a componentized template for customer registration or for editing basic account details called `customer_details`.

- Create a componentized template named `customer_credit_card` that allows customers to enter credit card details.

- Create a componentized template named `customer_address` for customers to enter a shipping address.

Creating customer and shipping_region Tables

Now you can build the `customer` and `shipping_region` tables by following the steps in the next exercise.

Exercise: Creating the Database Tables

1. Load phpMyAdmin, select the `tshirtshop` database, and open a new SQL query page.

2. Execute this code, which creates the `shipping_region` table in your `tshirtshop` database:

```
-- Create shipping_region table
CREATE TABLE `shipping_region` (
  `shipping_region_id` INT          NOT NULL AUTO_INCREMENT,
  `shipping_region`    VARCHAR(100) NOT NULL,
  PRIMARY KEY (`shipping_region_id`)
);
```

3. Now add the values "`Please select`", "`US / Canada`", "`Europe`", and "`Rest of the World`" to the `shipping_region` table. "`Please Select`" should always have a `shipping_region_id` value of 1—this is important! Execute the following SQL code to add the mentioned values to the `shipping_region` table:

```
-- Populate shipping_region table
INSERT INTO `shipping_region` (`shipping_region_id`, `shipping_region`) VALUES
       (1, 'Please Select') , (2, 'US / Canada'),
       (3, 'Europe'),         (4, 'Rest of World');
```

4. Execute the following code, which creates the `customer` table in your `tshirtshop` database:

```
-- Create customer table
CREATE TABLE `customer` (
  `customer_id`   INT          NOT NULL  AUTO_INCREMENT,
  `name`          VARCHAR(50)  NOT NULL,
  `email`         VARCHAR(100) NOT NULL,
  `password`      VARCHAR(50)  NOT NULL,
  `credit_card`   TEXT,
  `address_1`     VARCHAR(100),
  `address_2`     VARCHAR(100),
  `city`          VARCHAR(100),
```

```
    `region`              VARCHAR(100),
    `postal_code`         VARCHAR(100),
    `country`             VARCHAR(100),
    `shipping_region_id`  INTEGER       NOT NULL   DEFAULT 1,
    `day_phone`           VARCHAR(100),
    `eve_phone`           VARCHAR(100),
    `mob_phone`           VARCHAR(100),
    PRIMARY KEY (`customer_id`),
    UNIQUE KEY `idx_customer_email` (`email`),
    KEY `idx_customer_shipping_region_id` (`shipping_region_id`)
);
```

Customers' credit card information will be stored in an encrypted format so that no one will be able to access this information. However, unlike with passwords, you need to be able to retrieve this credit card information when required by the order pipeline, so you can't simply use a hash (the hash algorithm is one-way). You'll implement the credit card data encryption functionality using a number of business tier classes, which you'll see next.

Implementing the Security Classes

So far, two areas need security functionality:

- Password hashing

- Credit card encryption

Both these tasks are carried out by business tier classes that you'll save in the business directory in the following files:

password_hasher.php: Contains the PasswordHasher class, which contains the static method Hash() that returns the hash value for the password supplied.

secure_card.php: Contains the SecureCard class, which represents a credit card. This class can be supplied with credit card information, which is then accessible in encrypted format. This class can also take encrypted credit card data and supply access to the decrypted information.

symmetric_crypt.php: Contains the class SymmetricCrypt, which is used by SecureCard to encrypt and decrypt data. This means that if you ever want to change the encryption method, you need to modify the code here only, leaving the SecureCard class untouched.

We'll look at the code for hashing first, followed by encryption.

Implementing Hashing Functionality in the Business Tier

Hashing is a means by which you can obtain a unique value that represents an object. The algorithm used to convert the source byte array into a hashed byte array varies. The most commonly used hashing algorithm is called Message Digest 5 (MD5, another name for the hash code generated), which generates a 128-bit hash value. Unfortunately, many kinds of attacks are based on word dictionaries constructed against MD5 hashes.

Another popular hashing algorithm is called Secure Hash Algorithm (SHA1), which generates a 160-bit hash value. SHA1 is generally agreed to be more secure (although slower) than MD5. Wikipedia has very useful documentation pages for these hashing functions.

In the TShirtShop implementation, we'll use SHA1, although it is easy to change this if you prefer a different algorithm. Now, we'll implement the PasswordHasher class in the following exercise.

Exercise: Implementing the PasswordHasher Class

To implement the PasswordHasher class, follow these steps:

1. Add the following line at the end of include/config.php. This defines a random value (feel free to change it) to add to the passwords before hashing them.

```
// Random value used for hashing
define('HASH_PREFIX', 'K1-');
```

2. Create a new file named password_hasher.php in the business folder, and write the PasswordHasher class in it:

```php
<?php
class PasswordHasher
{
  public static function Hash($password, $withPrefix = true)
  {
    if ($withPrefix)
      $hashed_password = sha1(HASH_PREFIX . $password);
    else
      $hashed_password = sha1($password);

    return $hashed_password;
  }
}
?>
```

3. Next, write a simple test page to test the PasswordHasher class. Create a new file named test_hasher.php in the tshirtshop folder with the following code in it:

```php
<?php
if (isset ($_GET['to_be_hashed']))
{
  require_once 'include/config.php';
  require_once BUSINESS_DIR . 'password_hasher.php';

  $original_string = $_GET['to_be_hashed'];

  echo 'The hash of "' . $original_string . '" is ' .
      PasswordHasher::Hash($original_string, false);

  echo '<br />';
```

```
      echo '... and the hash of "' . HASH_PREFIX . $original_string .
         '" (secret prefix concatenated with password) is ' .
         PasswordHasher::Hash($original_string, true);
   }
   ?>

   <br /><br />
   <form action="test_hasher.php">
     Write your password:
     <input type="text" name="to_be_hashed" /><br />
     <input type="submit" value="Hash it" />
   </form>
```

4. Load `test_hasher.php` in your favorite browser, enter a password to hash, and admire the results, as shown in Figure 16-1.

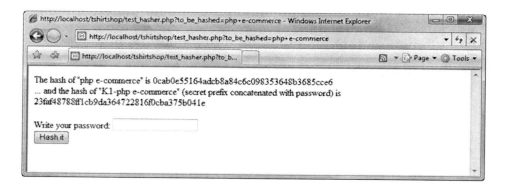

Figure 16-1. *Testing the password hashing functionality*

How It Works: The Hashing Functionality

The code in the `PasswordHasher` class is pretty simple. By default, the static `Hash()` method returns the hash of a string representing the secret prefix concatenated with the password.

You might be wondering what the secret prefix is all about. As you might have already guessed, it has to do with security. If your database is stolen, the thief could try to match the hashed password values with a large dictionary of hashed values that looks something like this:

```
word1      .... sha1(word1)
word2      .... sha1(word2)
...
word10000 .... sha1(word10000)
```

If two hash values match, it means the original strings (which, in our case, are the customers' passwords) also match.

Appending a secret prefix to the password before hashing it reduces the risk of dictionary attacks on the hashed passwords database because the resulting string being hashed (secret prefix + password) is less likely to be found in a large dictionary of "password – hash value" pairs.

The `test_hasher.php` page tests your newly created `PasswordHasher` class.

■**Note** You can also handle hashing at the database level by using the MySQL `PASSWORD()`, `MD5()`, and `SHA1()` encryption functions. For example, you could execute the following MySQL statement to see the MySQL `SHA1()` function in action:

```
SELECT SHA1('freedom');
```

Of course, when relying on MySQL's hashing functionality, the passwords travel in "plain format" to your MySQL server, so if the MySQL server is on another network (which is quite unlikely, however), you must secure the connection between your web server and the MySQL server by using SSL connections. You can avoid this by handling hashing in the PHP code, which also offers better portability because it doesn't rely on MySQL. For more details on MySQL encryption functions, please consult the manual at `http://dev.mysql.com/doc/refman/5.1/en/encryption-functions.html`.

Implementing the Encryption Functionality in the Business Tier

Encryption comes in many shapes and sizes and continues to be a hot topic. There is no definitive solution to encrypting data, although there is plenty of advice on the subject. In general, the two forms of encryption are as follows:

Symmetric encryption: A single key is used both to encrypt and to decrypt data.

Asymmetric encryption: Separate keys are used to encrypt and decrypt data. The encryption key is commonly known as the *public key*, and anyone can use it to encrypt information. The decryption key is known as the *private key* because it can be used only to decrypt data that has been encrypted using the public key. The encryption key (public key) and the decryption key (private key) are mathematically related and are always generated in pairs. The public key and private key can't be obtained one from another. If you have a public key/private key pair, you can send the public key to parties that need to encrypt information for you. You will be the only one who knows the private key associated with that public key and thus the only one able to decrypt the information.

Although asymmetric encryption is more secure, it also requires much more processing power. Symmetric encryption is faster but can be less secure because both the encryptor and the decryptor have knowledge of a single key. With symmetric encryption, the encryptor needs to send the key to the decryptor. With Internet communications, there is often no way of ensuring that this key remains a secret from third parties when it is sent to the encryptor.

Asymmetric encryption gets around this by using key pairs. There is never a need for the decryption key to be divulged, so it's much more difficult for a third party to break the encryption. Because it requires a lot more processing power, however, the practical method of operation is to use asymmetric encryption to exchange a symmetric key over the Internet, which is then used for symmetric encryption safe in the knowledge that this key has not been exposed to third parties.

In the TShirtShop application, things are much simpler than with Internet communications. You just need to encrypt data for storage in the database and decrypt it again when required, so you can use a symmetric encryption algorithm.

■Note Behind the scenes, some asymmetric encryption is also going on, however, because that is the method implemented by HTTPS communication.

As with hashing, you can use several algorithms for both symmetric and asymmetric encryption. PHP's mcrypt library contains implementations of the most important symmetric algorithms. No library in PHP deals with asymmetric encryption, but if you ever need to do asymmetric encryption, you can use the Pretty Good Privacy (PGP) family of software (for more information, see http://www.pgp.com) and GnuPG (http://www.gnupg.org).

Two of the more commonly used asymmetric algorithms are Digital Signature Algorithm (DSA) and Rivest-Shamir-Adleman (RSA), named after its inventors, Ronald Rivest, Adi Shamir, and Leonard Adleman. Of these, DSA can be used only to "sign" data so that its authenticity can be verified, whereas RSA is more versatile (although slower than DSA when used to generate digital signatures). DSA is the current standard for digital authentication used by the U.S. government. Both the DSA and the RSA asymmetric algorithms are implemented in the PGP family of software (PGP and GnuPG).

Some popular symmetric algorithms found in the mcrypt library are Data Encryption Standard (DES), Triple DES (3DES), Ron's Code (RC2, or Rivest's Cipher, depending on who you ask, also from Ronald Rivest), and Rijndael (from the names of its inventors, Joan Daemen and Vincent Rijmen).

DES AND RIJNDAEL

DES has been the standard for some time now, although this is gradually changing. It uses a 64-bit key; however, in practice only 56 of these bits are used (8 bits are "parity" bits), which is not strong enough to avoid being broken using today's computers.

Both Triple DES and RC2 are variations of DES. Triple DES effectively encrypts data using three separate DES encryptions with three keys totaling 168 bits when parity bits are subtracted. The RC2 variant can have key lengths up to 128 bits (longer keys are also possible using RC3, RC4, and so on), so it can be made weaker or stronger than DES depending on the key size.

Rijndael is a completely separate encryption method and is the current Advanced Encryption Standard (AES) standard; several competing algorithms were considered before Rijndael was chosen. This standard is intended to replace DES and is gradually becoming the most used (and secure) symmetric encryption algorithm.

The tasks associated with encrypting and decrypting data are a little more involved than hashing. The mcrypt functions are optimized to work with raw data, so you have some work to do with data conversion. You also have to define both a key and an initialization vector (IV) to perform encryption and decryption. The IV is required because of the nature of encryption: the data blocks are usually encrypted in sequence, and calculating the encrypted values for one sequence of bits involves using some data from the preceding sequence of bits. Because there are no such values at the start of encryption, an IV is used instead. For AES encryption (Rijndael_128), the IV and the key must be 32 bytes long.

▓Note At `http://en.wikipedia.org/wiki/Block_cipher_modes_of_operation`, you can learn more about the various modes of encryption.

The general steps required for encrypting a string are as follows:

1. Create a 32-byte random IV.

2. Convert the IV (which you keep as a hexadecimal string) into a byte array.

3. Encrypt the string using AES encryption by supplying the IV in byte array format.

4. Convert the resulting encrypted data from a byte array into a hexadecimal string.

Decryption follows a similar scheme:

1. Convert the IV (which you keep as a hexadecimal string) into a byte array (the same with the encryption first step).

2. Convert the string to decrypt into a byte array.

3. Decrypt the binary string from the previous step by supplying the IV in a byte array.

In this example's code, you'll use AES, but you can modify the code in the `SymmetricCrypt` class to use any of the supported encryption algorithms.

Exercise: Implementing the SymmetricCrypt Class

1. Add a new file in the business directory called `symmetric_crypt.php` with the following code in it:

```php
<?php
class SymmetricCrypt
{
  // Encryption/decryption key
  private static $_msSecretKey = 'From Dusk Till Dawn';

  // The initialization vector
  private static $_msHexaIv = 'c7098adc8d6128b5d4b4f7b2fe7f7f05';

  // Use the Rijndael Encryption Algorithm
  private static $_msCipherAlgorithm = MCRYPT_RIJNDAEL_128;
```

```php
/* Function encrypts plain-text string received as parameter
   and returns the result in hexadecimal format */
public static function Encrypt($plainString)
{
  // Pack SymmetricCrypt::_msHexaIv into a binary string
  $binary_iv = pack('H*', self::$_msHexaIv);

  // Encrypt $plainString
  $binary_encrypted_string = mcrypt_encrypt(
                             self::$_msCipherAlgorithm,
                             self::$_msSecretKey,
                             $plainString,
                             MCRYPT_MODE_CBC,
                             $binary_iv);

  // Convert $binary_encrypted_string to hexadecimal format
  $hexa_encrypted_string = bin2hex($binary_encrypted_string);

  return $hexa_encrypted_string;
}

/* Function decrypts hexadecimal string received as parameter
   and returns the result in hexadecimal format */
public static function Decrypt($encryptedString)
{
  // Pack Symmetric::_msHexaIv into a binary string
  $binary_iv = pack('H*', self::$_msHexaIv);

  // Convert string in hexadecimal to byte array
  $binary_encrypted_string = pack('H*', $encryptedString);

  // Decrypt $binary_encrypted_string
  $decrypted_string = mcrypt_decrypt(
                         self::$_msCipherAlgorithm,
                         self::$_msSecretKey,
                         $binary_encrypted_string,
                         MCRYPT_MODE_CBC,
                         $binary_iv);

  return $decrypted_string;
  }
}
?>
```

2. Add a test file in the tshirtshop folder called test_encryption.php with the following code:

```php
<?php
if (isset ($_GET['my_string']))
{
  require_once 'include/config.php';
  require_once BUSINESS_DIR . 'symmetric_crypt.php';

  $string = $_GET['my_string'];

  echo 'The string is:<br />' . $string . '<br /><br />';

  $encrypted_string = SymmetricCrypt::Encrypt($string);

  echo 'Encrypted string: <br />' . $encrypted_string . '<br /><br />';

  $decrypted_string = SymmetricCrypt::Decrypt($encrypted_string);

  echo 'Decrypted string:<br />' . $decrypted_string;
}
?>

<br /><br />
<form action="test_encryption.php">
  Enter string to encrypt:
  <input type="text" name="my_string" /><br />
  <input type="submit" value="Encrypt" />
</form>
```

3. Load the newly created test_encryption.php file in your favorite browser, and give a string to encrypt/decrypt (see Figure 16-2).

■**Note** Usually XAMPP comes without the mcrypt library configured; therefore, you'll receive a fatal error about the call to the mcrypt_encrypt() function when testing test_encryption.php. You have to configure PHP to load the mcrypt library. To achieve this, uncomment the following line from php.ini by deleting the ; from the start of the line, as shown here:

extension=php_mcrypt.dll

You'll find the php.ini file in the C:\xampp\apache\bin\ folder on Windows or the /opt/lampp/etc folder on Linux. After modifying php.ini, you need to restart Apache.

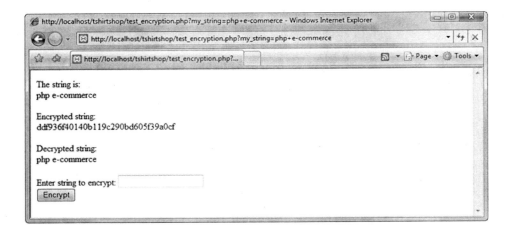

Figure 16-2. *Testing encryption*

▪Caution The decrypted string always has a length that is a multiple of 32 bytes. If the original string is less than 32 bytes, null characters are appended until the string's length becomes a multiple of 32 bytes. You need to be careful with this detail because it means the decrypted value of the string may not be identical to the encrypted value. For our TShirtShop project, because we'll encrypt XML data and the values of interest are between XML tags, we won't need to worry about having additional void characters at the end of the string.

How It Works: Encryption Functionality in the Business Tier

The SymmetricCrypt class has two static methods, Encrypt() and Decrypt(), which encrypt and decrypt data, and a number of encryption configurations parameters stored as static members:

```
// Encryption/decryption key
private static $_msSecretKey = 'From Dusk Till Dawn';

// The initialization vector
private static $_msHexaIv = 'c7098adc8d6128b5d4b4f7b2fe7f7f05';

// Use the Rijndael Encryption Algorithm
private static $_msCipherAlgorithm = MCRYPT_RIJNDAEL_128;
```

The secret key is 16 characters (bytes) long for AES algorithms. Using a smaller key is allowed by the mcrypt library but will reduce the encryption security. The IV should be exactly 16 bytes long for AES and will be kept as a hexadecimal string ($2 \times 16 = 32$ chars long). Both $_msSecretKey and $_msHexaIv variables are set to temporary values here. They could just as easily take any other values, depending on the key you want to use.

Encrypt() starts by converting the IV from its hexadecimal value to a byte array because this is the format expected by the mcrypt_encrypt() function (the one that does the actual encryption):

```
// Pack SymmetricCrypt::_msHexaIv into a binary string
$binary_iv = pack('H*', self::$_msHexaIv);
```

The conversion is done using PHP's pack() function (learn more about it at http://www.php.net/pack).

The call to mcrypt_encrypt() follows:

```
// Encrypt $plainString
$binary_encrypted_string = mcrypt_encrypt(
                            self::$_msCipherAlgorithm,
                            self::$_msSecretKey,
                            $plainString,
                            MCRYPT_MODE_CBC,
                            $binary_iv);
```

This is the call that performs the actual encryption. Its parameters are obvious, and you can find more detail about the mcrypt_encrypt() function at http://www.php.net/mcrypt. The MCRYPT_MODE_CBC specifies the "cipher block chaining" encryption method; this method uses a chaining mechanism in which the encryption of each block of data depends on the encryption results of preceding blocks, except for the first block in which the IV is used instead.

At the end, the encrypted string is transformed into hexadecimal format, which is easier to work with (for example, to save in the database or in a configuration file):

```
// Convert $binary_encrypted_string to hexadecimal format
$hexa_encrypted_string = bin2hex($binary_encrypted_string);
```

The Decrypt() method is similar to the Encrypt() method. First you need the IV to be in a binary form (the same first step you took in the Encrypt() method).

As the Encrypt() method returns the encrypted string as a hexadecimal string, the input parameter of Decrypt() is also a hexadecimal string. You must convert this string to a byte array, which is the format that mcrypt_decrypt() needs:

```
// Convert string in hexadecimal to byte array
$binary_encrypted_string = pack('H*', $encryptedString);
```

```
// Decrypt $binary_encrypted_string
$decrypted_string = mcrypt_decrypt(
                        self::$_msCipherAlgorithm,
                        self::$_msSecretKey,
                        $binary_encrypted_string,
                        MCRYPT_MODE_CBC,
                        $binary_iv);
```

```
    return $decrypted_string;
```

The test_encryption.php test file for this class simply encrypts and decrypts data, demonstrating that things are working properly. The code for this is very simple, so we won't detail it here.

Now that you have the SymmetricCrypt class code, the last step in creating the security-related classes is to add the SecureCard class.

Storing Credit Cart Information Using the SecureCard Class

In the following exercise, you'll build the SecureCard class, which represents the credit card of a customer. This class will use the functionality you implemented in the previous two exercises to ensure that its data will be stored securely in the database.

Exercise: Implementing the SecureCard Class

1. Create a new file named secure_card.php in the business folder, and add the following code to it:

```php
<?php
// Represents a credit card
class SecureCard
{
  // Private members containing credit card's details
  private $_mIsDecrypted = false;
  private $_mIsEncrypted = false;
  private $_mCardHolder;
  private $_mCardNumber;
  private $_mIssueDate;
  private $_mExpiryDate;
  private $_mIssueNumber;
  private $_mCardType;
  private $_mEncryptedData;
  private $_mXmlCardData;

  // Class constructor
  public function __construct()
  {
    // Nothing here
  }

  // Decrypt data
  public function LoadEncryptedDataAndDecrypt($newEncryptedData)
  {
    $this->_mEncryptedData = $newEncryptedData;
    $this->DecryptData();
  }

  // Encrypt data
  public function LoadPlainDataAndEncrypt($newCardHolder, $newCardNumber,
                                          $newIssueDate, $newExpiryDate,
                                          $newIssueNumber, $newCardType)
  {
    $this->_mCardHolder = $newCardHolder;
    $this->_mCardNumber = $newCardNumber;
    $this->_mIssueDate = $newIssueDate;
```

```php
  $this->_mExpiryDate = $newExpiryDate;
  $this->_mIssueNumber = $newIssueNumber;
  $this->_mCardType = $newCardType;
  $this->EncryptData();
}

// Create XML with credit card information
private function CreateXml()
{
  // Encode card details as XML document
  $xml_card_data = &$this->_mXmlCardData;
  $xml_card_data = new DOMDocument();

  $document_root = $xml_card_data->createElement('CardDetails');

  $child = $xml_card_data->createElement('CardHolder');
  $child = $document_root->appendChild($child);
  $value = $xml_card_data->createTextNode($this->_mCardHolder);
  $value = $child->appendChild($value);

  $child = $xml_card_data->createElement('CardNumber');
  $child = $document_root->appendChild($child);
  $value = $xml_card_data->createTextNode($this->_mCardNumber);
  $value = $child->appendChild($value);

  $child = $xml_card_data->createElement('IssueDate');
  $child = $document_root->appendChild($child);
  $value = $xml_card_data->createTextNode($this->_mIssueDate);
  $value = $child->appendChild($value);

  $child = $xml_card_data->createElement('ExpiryDate');
  $child = $document_root->appendChild($child);
  $value = $xml_card_data->createTextNode($this->_mExpiryDate);
  $value = $child->appendChild($value);

  $child = $xml_card_data->createElement('IssueNumber');
  $child = $document_root->appendChild($child);
  $value = $xml_card_data->createTextNode($this->_mIssueNumber);
  $value = $child->appendChild($value);

  $child = $xml_card_data->createElement('CardType');
  $child = $document_root->appendChild($child);
  $value = $xml_card_data->createTextNode($this->_mCardType);
  $value = $child->appendChild($value);

  $document_root = $xml_card_data->appendChild($document_root);
}
```

```php
    // Extract information from XML credit card data
    private function ExtractXml($decryptedData)
    {
      $xml = simplexml_load_string($decryptedData);
      $this->_mCardHolder = (string) $xml->CardHolder;
      $this->_mCardNumber = (string) $xml->CardNumber;
      $this->_mIssueDate = (string) $xml->IssueDate;
      $this->_mExpiryDate = (string) $xml->ExpiryDate;
      $this->_mIssueNumber = (string) $xml->IssueNumber;
      $this->_mCardType = (string) $xml->CardType;
    }

    // Encrypts the XML credit card data
    private function EncryptData()
    {
      // Put data into XML doc
      $this->CreateXml();

      // Encrypt data
      $this->_mEncryptedData =
        SymmetricCrypt::Encrypt($this->_mXmlCardData->saveXML());

      // Set encrypted flag
      $this->_mIsEncrypted = true;
    }

    // Decrypts XML credit card data
    private function DecryptData()
    {
      // Decrypt data
      $decrypted_data = SymmetricCrypt::Decrypt($this->_mEncryptedData);

      // Extract data from XML
      $this->ExtractXml($decrypted_data);

      // Set decrypted flag
      $this->_mIsDecrypted = true;
    }

    public function __get($name)
    {
      if ($name == 'EncryptedData')
      {
        if ($this->_mIsEncrypted)
          return $this->_mEncryptedData;
        else
          throw new Exception('Data not encrypted');
      }
```

```php
    elseif ($name == 'CardNumberX')
    {
      if ($this->_mIsDecrypted)
        return 'XXXX-XXXX-XXXX-' .
          substr($this->_mCardNumber, strlen($this->_mCardNumber) - 4, 4);
      else
        throw new Exception('Data not decrypted');
    }
    elseif (in_array($name, array ('CardHolder', 'CardNumber', 'IssueDate',
                                   'ExpiryDate', 'IssueNumber', 'CardType')))
    {
      $name = '_m' . $name;

      if ($this->_mIsDecrypted)
        return $this->$name;
      else
        throw new Exception('Data not decrypted');
    }
    else
    {
      throw new Exception('Property ' . $name . ' not found');
    }
  }
}
?>
```

2. Create a new file named test_card.php file in the tshirtshop folder:

```php
<?php
require_once 'include/config.php';
require_once BUSINESS_DIR . 'symmetric_crypt.php';
require_once BUSINESS_DIR . 'secure_card.php';

$card_holder = 'John Doe';
$card_number = '1234567890123456';
$expiry_date = '01/09';
$issue_date = '01/06';
$issue_number = 100;
$card_type = 'Mastercard';

echo '<br />Credit card data:<br />' .
     $card_holder . ', ' . $card_number . ', ' .
     $issue_date . ', ' . $expiry_date . ', ' .
     $issue_number . ', ' . $card_type . '<br />';

$credit_card = new SecureCard();
```

```php
    try
    {
      $credit_card->LoadPlainDataAndEncrypt($card_holder, $card_number,
                     $issue_date, $expiry_date, $issue_number, $card_type);

      $encrypted_data = $credit_card->EncryptedData;
    }
    catch(Exception $e)
    {
      echo '<font color="red">Exception: ' . $e->getMessage() . '</font>';

      exit();
    }

    echo '<br />Encrypted data:<br />' . $encrypted_data . '<br />';

    $our_card = new SecureCard();

    try
    {
      $our_card->LoadEncryptedDataAndDecrypt($encrypted_data);

      echo '<br/>Decrypted data:<br/>' .
          $our_card->CardHolder . ', ' . $our_card->CardNumber . ', ' .
          $our_card->IssueDate . ', ' . $our_card->ExpiryDate . ', ' .
          $our_card->IssueNumber . ', ' . $our_card->CardType;
    }
    catch(Exception $e)
    {
      echo '<font color="red">Exception: ' . $e->getMessage() . '</font>';

      exit();
    }
    ?>
```

3. Load test_card.php file in your favorite browser to see the results (see Figure 16-3). You can change the data from this file as you want.

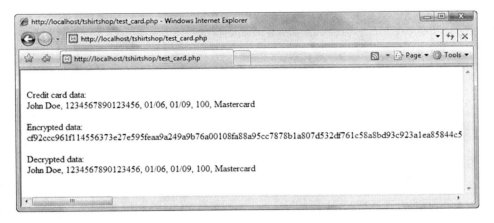

Figure 16-3. *Encrypting and decrypting credit card information*

How It Works: The SecureCard Class

There's a bit more code here than in previous examples, but it's all quite simple. First you have the private member variables to hold the card details as individual strings, as an encrypted string, and in an intermediate XML document. You also have Boolean flags indicating whether the data has been successfully encrypted or decrypted:

```php
<?php
// Represents a credit card
class SecureCard
{
  // Private members containing credit card's details
  private $_mIsDecrypted = false;
  private $_mIsEncrypted = false;
  private $_mCardHolder;
  private $_mCardNumber;
  private $_mIssueDate;
  private $_mExpiryDate;
  private $_mIssueNumber;
  private $_mCardType;
  private $_mEncryptedData;
  private $_mXmlCardData;
```

Next you have two important public methods. Public members are part of the public interface of the class, which provides the functionality for external clients. LoadEncryptedDataAndDecrypt() receives an encrypted string and performs the decryption; LoadPlainDataAndEncrypt() receives the credit card data in plain format and encrypts it:

```
// Decrypt data
public function LoadEncryptedDataAndDecrypt($newEncryptedData)
{
  $this->_mEncryptedData = $newEncryptedData;
  $this->DecryptData();
}

// Encrypt data
public function LoadPlainDataAndEncrypt($newCardHolder, $newCardNumber,
                                        $newIssueDate, $newExpiryDate,
                                        $newIssueNumber, $newCardType)
{
  $this->_mCardHolder = $newCardHolder;
  $this->_mCardNumber = $newCardNumber;
  $this->_mIssueDate = $newIssueDate;
  $this->_mExpiryDate = $newExpiryDate;
  $this->_mIssueNumber = $newIssueNumber;
  $this->_mCardType = $newCardType;
  $this->EncryptData();
}
```

The main work is carried out by the private EncryptData() and DecryptData() methods, which you'll come to shortly. First you have two utility methods for packaging and unpackaging data in XML format (which makes it easier to get at the bits you want when exchanging data with the encrypted format).

XML is a very powerful, tag-based format in which you can store various kinds of information. The SecureCard class stores a customer's credit card data in a structure like the following:

```
<?xml version="1.0"?>
<CardDetails>
  <CardHolder>John Doe</CardHolder>
  <CardNumber>1234567890123456</CardNumber>
  <IssueDate>01/06</IssueDate>
  <ExpiryDate>01/09</ExpiryDate>
  <IssueNumber>100</IssueNumber>
  <CardType>Mastercard</CardType>
</CardDetails>
```

The DOMDocument class is used to work with XML data; this class knows how to create, read, and manipulate XML documents without much effort from the developer. The Document Object Model (DOM) is the most important and versatile tree-model XML-parsing application programming interface (API).

■**Tip** The World Wide Web Consortium manages the DOM standard; its official web page is http://www.w3.org/DOM/.

With the new PHP 5 DOM extension, reading, creating, editing, saving, and searching XML documents from PHP has never been easier. The DOM extension in PHP 5 was entirely rewritten from scratch to fully comply with the DOM specifications. You can see this extension in action in the CreateXml() method, which creates an XML document with the structure shown earlier by creating nodes and setting their values:

```
// Create XML with credit card information
private function CreateXml()
{
  // Encode card details as XML document
  $xml_card_data = &$this->_mXmlCardData;
  $xml_card_data = new DOMDocument();

  $document_root = $xml_card_data->createElement('CardDetails');

  $child = $xml_card_data->createElement('CardHolder');
  $child = $document_root->appendChild($child);
  $value = $xml_card_data->createTextNode($this->_mCardHolder);
  $value = $child->appendChild($value);

  ...

  $document_root = $xml_card_data->appendChild($document_root);
}
```

For reading the XML document, you can use the DOMDocument object, but in the ExtractXml() method, we preferred to use a new and unique feature of PHP 5 called SimpleXML. Although less complex and powerful than DOMDocument, the SimpleXML extension makes parsing XML data a piece of cake by transforming it into a data structure you can simply iterate through:

```
// Extract information from XML credit card data
private function ExtractXml($decryptedData)
{
  $xml = simplexml_load_string($decryptedData);
  $this->_mCardHolder = (string) $xml->CardHolder;
  $this->_mCardNumber = (string) $xml->CardNumber;
  $this->_mIssueDate = (string) $xml->IssueDate;
  $this->_mExpiryDate = (string) $xml->ExpiryDate;
  $this->_mIssueNumber = (string) $xml->IssueNumber;
  $this->_mCardType = (string) $xml->CardType;
}
```

The EncryptData() method starts by using the CreateXml() method to package the details supplied in the SecureCard constructor into XML format:

```
// Encrypts the XML credit card data
private function EncryptData()
{
  // Put data into XML doc
  $this->CreateXml();
```

Next, the XML string contained in the resultant XML document is encrypted into a single string and stored in the $_mEncryptedData member:

```
// Encrypt data
$this->_mEncryptedData =
  SymmetricCrypt::Encrypt($this->_mXmlCardData->saveXML());
```

Finally, the $_mIsEncrypted flag is set to true to indicate that the credit card data has been encrypted:

```
// Set encrypted flag
$this->_mIsEncrypted = true;
}
```

The DecryptData() method gets the XML credit card data from its encrypted form, decrypts it, and populates class attributes with the ExtractXml() method:

```
// Decrypts XML credit card data
private function DecryptData()
{
  // Decrypt data
  $decrypted_data = SymmetricCrypt::Decrypt($this->_mEncryptedData);

  // Extract data from XML
  $this->ExtractXml($decrypted_data);

  // Set decrypted flag
  $this->_mIsDecrypted = true;
}
```

Next, we define a few properties for the class. Starting with PHP 5, you can define a public __get() function that is called automatically whenever you try to call a method or read a member that isn't defined in the class. Take, for example, this code snippet:

```
$card = new SecureCard();
$encrypted = $card->EncryptedData;
```

Because there's no member named EncryptedData in the SecureCard class, the __get() function is called. In __get(), you can check which property is accessed, and you can include code that returns the value for that property. This technique is particularly useful when you want to define "virtual" members of the class whose values need to be calculated on the spot as an alternative to using get functions such as GetEncryptedData().

In our case, the __get() function handles eight "virtual" members. The first is EncryptedData, whose value is returned only if $_mIsEncrypted is true:

```
public function __get($name)
{
  if ($name == 'EncryptedData')
  {
    if ($this->_mIsEncrypted)
      return $this->_mEncryptedData;
```

```
      else
        throw new Exception('Data not encrypted');
    }
```

Then there's CardNumberX, which needs to return a version of the card number where all digits are obfuscated (replaced with X) except the last four. This is handy when showing a user existing details and is becoming standard practice because it lets customers know what card they have stored without exposing the details to prying eyes:

```
    elseif ($name == 'CardNumberX')
    {
      if ($this->_mIsDecrypted)
        return 'XXXX-XXXX-XXXX-' .
          substr($this->_mCardNumber, strlen($this->_mCardNumber) - 4, 4);
      else
        throw new Exception('Data not decrypted');
    }
```

The last six properties (CardHolder, CardNumber, IssueDate, ExpiryDate, IssueNumber, and CardType) are handled in a single block:

```
    elseif (in_array($name, array ('CardHolder', 'CardNumber', 'IssueDate',
                                   'ExpiryDate', 'IssueNumber', 'CardType')))
    {
      $name = '_m' . $name;

      if ($this->_mIsDecrypted)
        return $this->$name;
      else
        throw new Exception('Data not decrypted');
    }
    else
    {
      throw new Exception('Property ' . $name . ' not found');
    }
  }
```

Note that in all cases, the data is accessible only when $_mIsDecrypted is true; otherwise, an exception is thrown.

Also, note that the data isn't accessible after encryption—the data used to initialize a SecureCard object is accessible only in encrypted form. This is more a use-case decision than anything else because this class is really intended for encryption and decryption only, not for persistently representing credit card details. After a SecureCard instance has been used to encrypt card details, we shouldn't subsequently need access to the unencrypted data, only the encrypted string.

■**Note** Before moving on to the client code, it is worth explaining and emphasizing one important design consideration that you have probably already noticed. At no point are any of the card details validated. In fact, this class will work perfectly well with empty strings for any properties. This is so the class can remain as versatile as possible. It is more likely that credit card details will be validated as part of the UI used to enter them, or even not at all. This isn't at all dangerous—if invalid details are used, then the credit card transaction will simply fail, and we handle that using very similar logic to that required when dealing with a lack of funds (that is, we notify the customer of failure and ask them to try another card). Of course, there are also simple data-formatting issues (dates are usually MM/YY, for example), but as noted, these can be dealt with externally to the SecureCard class.

The test page (test_card.php) for this class simply allows you to see how an encrypted card looks. As you can see, quite a lot of data is generated, which is the reason for the rather large column size in the customer database. You can also see that both encryption and decryption are working perfectly, so you can now move on to the customer account section of this chapter.

Adding Customer Accounts Functionality to TShirtShop

Before implementing the visual bits of the customer accounts functionality, let's preview what we're going to do in the final part of this chapter.

We want to have a login form on the front of the site. We also want to let users register on the site and edit their profiles. You'll create a componentized template for the login form and place it just on top of the search box, as shown in Figure 16-4.

Figure 16-4. *TShirtShop with a login box*

The new user registration page looks like Figure 16-5.

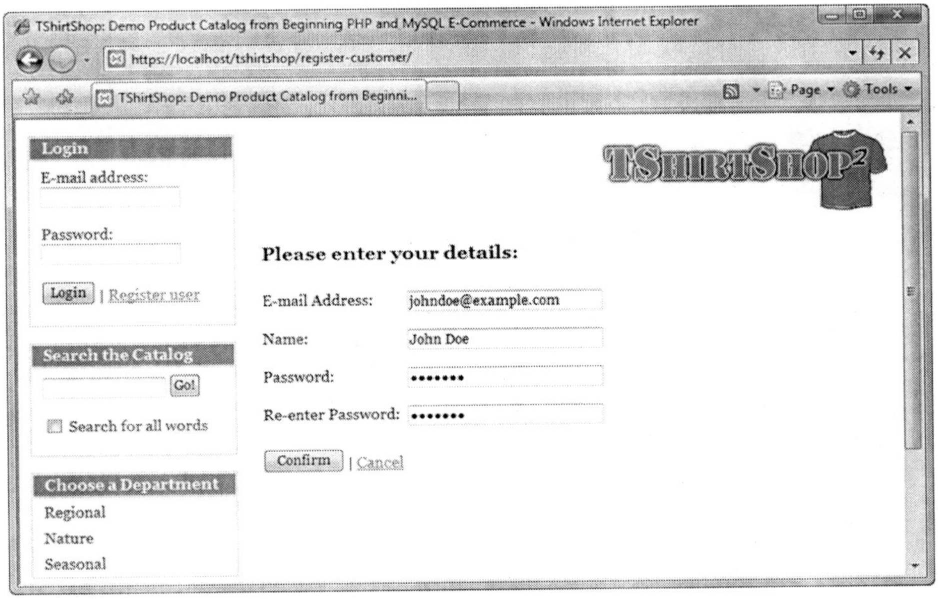

Figure 16-5. *The new user registration page in TShirtShop*

After the user logs in to the site, a new componentized template displays the logged-in user's name and a number of links for manipulating the user's account (see Figure 16-6).

Figure 16-6. *Sample TShirtShop page for a logged-in user*

Clicking the Add CC Details link leads the user to the page shown in Figure 16-7.

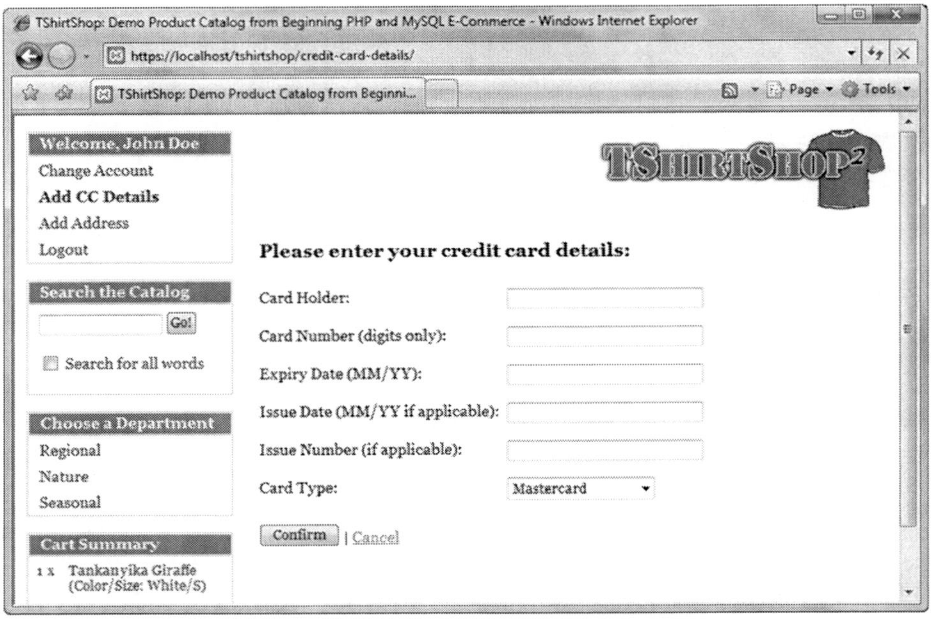

Figure 16-7. *Adding credit card information*

A similar form will be shown to the user when clicking the Add Address link. When the user already has a credit card and an address listed, the Add... links in the Welcome box change into Change... links.

You'll start implementing the new functionality by writing the data tier code that will support the UI.

Implementing the Data Tier

You'll create the usual data tier stored procedures supporting customer accounts functionality in the following exercise, and we'll comment on each one.

Exercise: Creating the Database Functions

1. Use phpMyAdmin to create the stored procedures described in the following steps. Don't forget to set the $$ delimiter before executing the code of each step.

2. Execute this code, which creates the customer_get_login_info stored procedure in your tshirtshop database:

```
-- Create customer_get_login_info stored procedure
CREATE PROCEDURE customer_get_login_info(IN inEmail VARCHAR(100))
BEGIN
  SELECT customer_id, password FROM customer WHERE email = inEmail;
END$$
```

When a user logs in to the site, you must check the user's password. The `customer_get_login_info` stored procedure returns the customer ID and the hashed password for a user with a specific e-mail.

3. Execute the following code, which creates the `customer_add` stored procedure in your `tshirtshop` database:

```
-- Create customer_add stored procedure
CREATE PROCEDURE customer_add(IN inName VARCHAR(50),
  IN inEmail VARCHAR(100), IN inPassword VARCHAR(50))
BEGIN
  INSERT INTO customer (name, email, password)
         VALUES (inName, inEmail, inPassword);

  SELECT LAST_INSERT_ID();
END$$
```

The `customer_add` stored procedure is called when a user registers on the site. This stored procedure returns the customer ID for that user to be saved in the session.

4. Execute this code, which creates the `customer_get_customer` stored procedure in your `tshirtshop` database:

```
-- Create customer_get_customer stored procedure
CREATE PROCEDURE customer_get_customer(IN inCustomerId INT)
BEGIN
  SELECT customer_id, name, email, password, credit_card,
         address_1, address_2, city, region, postal_code, country,
         shipping_region_id, day_phone, eve_phone, mob_phone
  FROM   customer
  WHERE  customer_id = inCustomerId;
END$$
```

The `customer_get_customer` stored procedure returns full customer details for a given customer ID.

5. Execute the following code, which creates the `customer_update_account` stored procedure in your `tshirtshop` database:

```
-- Create customer_update_account stored procedure
CREATE PROCEDURE customer_update_account(IN inCustomerId INT,
  IN inName VARCHAR(50), IN inEmail VARCHAR(100),
  IN inPassword VARCHAR(50), IN inDayPhone VARCHAR(100),
  IN inEvePhone VARCHAR(100), IN inMobPhone VARCHAR(100))
BEGIN
  UPDATE customer
  SET    name = inName, email = inEmail,
         password = inPassword, day_phone = inDayPhone,
         eve_phone = inEvePhone, mob_phone = inMobPhone
  WHERE  customer_id = inCustomerId;
END$$
```

The `customer_update_account` stored procedure updates the customer's account details in the database.

6. Execute this code, which creates the `customer_update_credit_card` stored procedure in your `tshirtshop` database:

```
-- Create customer_update_credit_card stored procedure
CREATE PROCEDURE customer_update_credit_card(
  IN inCustomerId INT, IN inCreditCard TEXT)
BEGIN
  UPDATE customer
  SET    credit_card = inCreditCard
  WHERE  customer_id = inCustomerId;
END$$
```

The `customer_update_credit_card` stored procedure updates the customer's credit card information in the database. It updates only the `credit_card` column for the customer, which contains the encrypted version of the XML document containing the customer's complete credit card details.

7. Execute the following code, which creates the `customer_get_shipping_regions` stored procedure in your `tshirtshop` database:

```
-- Create customer_get_shipping_regions stored procedure
CREATE PROCEDURE customer_get_shipping_regions()
BEGIN
  SELECT shipping_region_id, shipping_region FROM shipping_region;
END$$
```

The `customer_get_shipping_regions` stored procedure returns the shipping regions in the database for the customer address details page.

8. Execute this code, which creates the `customer_update_address` stored procedure in your `tshirtshop` database:

```
-- Create customer_update_address stored procedure
CREATE PROCEDURE customer_update_address(IN inCustomerId INT,
  IN inAddress1 VARCHAR(100), IN inAddress2 VARCHAR(100),
  IN inCity VARCHAR(100), IN inRegion VARCHAR(100),
  IN inPostalCode VARCHAR(100), IN inCountry VARCHAR(100),
  IN inShippingRegionId INT)
BEGIN
  UPDATE customer
  SET    address_1 = inAddress1, address_2 = inAddress2, city = inCity,
         region = inRegion, postal_code = inPostalCode,
         country = inCountry, shipping_region_id = inShippingRegionId
  WHERE  customer_id = inCustomerId;
END$$
```

The `customer_update_address` stored procedure updates the customer's address in the database.

Implementing the Business Tier

In the business folder, create a new file named customer.php that will contain the Customer class. The Customer class is a little longer and mostly accesses the data tier functionality to respond to requests that come from the presentation tier. Write the following code in the business/customer.php file:

```php
<?php
// Business tier class that manages customer accounts functionality
class Customer
{
  // Checks if a customer_id exists in session
  public static function IsAuthenticated()
  {
    if (!(isset ($_SESSION['tshirtshop_customer_id'])))
      return 0;
    else
      return 1;
  }

  // Returns customer_id and password for customer with email $email
  public static function GetLoginInfo($email)
  {
    // Build the SQL query
    $sql = 'CALL customer_get_login_info(:email)';

    // Build the parameters array
    $params = array (':email' => $email);

    // Execute the query and return the results
    return DatabaseHandler::GetRow($sql, $params);
  }

  public static function IsValid($email, $password)
  {
    $customer = self::GetLoginInfo($email);

    if (empty ($customer['customer_id']))
      return 2;

    $customer_id      = $customer['customer_id'];
    $hashed_password = $customer['password'];
```

```php
    if (PasswordHasher::Hash($password) != $hashed_password)
      return 1;
    else
    {
      $_SESSION['tshirtshop_customer_id'] = $customer_id;

      return 0;
    }
  }

  public static function Logout()
  {
    unset($_SESSION['tshirtshop_customer_id']);
  }

  public static function GetCurrentCustomerId()
  {
    if (self::IsAuthenticated())
      return $_SESSION['tshirtshop_customer_id'];
    else
      return 0;
  }

  /* Adds a new customer account, log him in if $addAndLogin is true
     and returns customer_id */
  public static function Add($name, $email, $password, $addAndLogin = true)
  {
    $hashed_password = PasswordHasher::Hash($password);

    // Build the SQL query
    $sql = 'CALL customer_add(:name, :email, :password)';

    // Build the parameters array
    $params = array (':name' => $name, ':email' => $email,
                     ':password' => $hashed_password);

    // Execute the query and get the customer_id
    $customer_id = DatabaseHandler::GetOne($sql, $params);

    if ($addAndLogin)
      $_SESSION['tshirtshop_customer_id'] = $customer_id;

    return $customer_id;
  }
```

```php
public static function Get($customerId = null)
{
  if (is_null($customerId))
    $customerId = self::GetCurrentCustomerId();

  // Build the SQL query
  $sql = 'CALL customer_get_customer(:customer_id)';

  // Build the parameters array
  $params = array (':customer_id' => $customerId);

  // Execute the query and return the results
  return DatabaseHandler::GetRow($sql, $params);
}

public static function UpdateAccountDetails($name, $email, $password,
                         $dayPhone, $evePhone, $mobPhone,
                         $customerId = null)
{
  if (is_null($customerId))
    $customerId = self::GetCurrentCustomerId();

  $hashed_password = PasswordHasher::Hash($password);

  // Build the SQL query
  $sql = 'CALL customer_update_account(:customer_id, :name, :email,
              :password, :day_phone, :eve_phone, :mob_phone)';

  // Build the parameters array
  $params = array (':customer_id' => $customerId, ':name' => $name,
                 ':email' => $email, ':password' => $hashed_password,
                 ':day_phone' => $dayPhone, ':eve_phone' => $evePhone,
                 ':mob_phone' => $mobPhone);

  // Execute the query
  DatabaseHandler::Execute($sql, $params);
}

public static function DecryptCreditCard($encryptedCreditCard)
{
  $secure_card = new SecureCard();
  $secure_card->LoadEncryptedDataAndDecrypt($encryptedCreditCard);

  $credit_card = array();
  $credit_card['card_holder']   = $secure_card->CardHolder;
  $credit_card['card_number']   = $secure_card->CardNumber;
```

```
      $credit_card['issue_date']    = $secure_card->IssueDate;
      $credit_card['expiry_date']   = $secure_card->ExpiryDate;
      $credit_card['issue_number']  = $secure_card->IssueNumber;
      $credit_card['card_type']     = $secure_card->CardType;
      $credit_card['card_number_x'] = $secure_card->CardNumberX;

      return $credit_card;
    }

    public static function GetPlainCreditCard()
    {
      $customer_data = self::Get();

      if (!(empty ($customer_data['credit_card'])))
        return self::DecryptCreditCard($customer_data['credit_card']);
      else
        return array('card_holder'   => '', 'card_number' => '',
                     'issue_date'    => '', 'expiry_date' => '',
                     'issue_number'  => '', 'card_type'   => '',
                     'card_number_x' => '');
    }

    public static function UpdateCreditCardDetails($plainCreditCard,
                                                   $customerId = null)
    {
      if (is_null($customerId))
        $customerId = self::GetCurrentCustomerId();

      $secure_card = new SecureCard();
      $secure_card->LoadPlainDataAndEncrypt($plainCreditCard['card_holder'],
        $plainCreditCard['card_number'], $plainCreditCard['issue_date'],
        $plainCreditCard['expiry_date'], $plainCreditCard['issue_number'],
        $plainCreditCard['card_type']);
      $encrypted_card = $secure_card->EncryptedData;

      // Build the SQL query
      $sql = 'CALL customer_update_credit_card(:customer_id, :credit_card)';

      // Build the parameters array
      $params = array (':customer_id' => $customerId,
                       ':credit_card' => $encrypted_card);

      // Execute the query
      DatabaseHandler::Execute($sql, $params);
    }
```

```php
  public static function GetShippingRegions()
  {
    // Build the SQL query
    $sql = 'CALL customer_get_shipping_regions()';

    // Execute the query and return the results
    return DatabaseHandler::GetAll($sql);
  }

  public static function UpdateAddressDetails($address1, $address2, $city,
                            $region, $postalCode, $country,
                            $shippingRegionId, $customerId = null)
  {
    if (is_null($customerId))
      $customerId = self::GetCurrentCustomerId();

    // Build the SQL query
    $sql = 'CALL customer_update_address(:customer_id, :address_1,
                    :address_2, :city, :region, :postal_code, :country,
                    :shipping_region_id)';

    // Build the parameters array
    $params = array (':customer_id' => $customerId,
                       ':address_1' => $address1, ':address_2' => $address2,
                       ':city' => $city, ':region' => $region,
                       ':postal_code' => $postalCode,
                       ':country' => $country,
                       ':shipping_region_id' => $shippingRegionId);

    // Execute the query
    DatabaseHandler::Execute($sql, $params);
  }
}
?>
```

Implementing the Presentation Tier

The presentation tier for the TShirtShop customer account system consists of the following componentized templates:

customer_login: This is the login box.

customer_logged: After a user is logged, this componentized template takes the place of the customer_login componentized template to show the current logged-in user and displays account management and logout links.

customer_details: This is for registering a new user or for editing the basic details of an existing user.

customer_address: This allows a user to add/edit address information.

customer_credit_card: This allows a user to add/edit credit card information.

Now, take a deep breath, and follow the steps of the next exercise to implement these new componentized templates; we're nearly there!

Exercise: Implementing the Componentized Templates

1. Create a new template file named customer_login.tpl in the presentation/templates folder, and add the following code to it:

```
{* customer_login.tpl *}
{load_presentation_object filename="customer_login" assign="obj"}
<div class="box">
  <p class="box-title">Login</p>
  <form method="post" action="{$obj->mLinkToLogin}">
    {if $obj->mErrorMessage}<p class="error">{$obj->mErrorMessage}</p>{/if}
    <p>
      <label for="email">E-mail address:</label>
      <input type="text" maxlength="50" name="email" size="22"
       value="{$obj->mEmail}" />
    </p>
    <p>
      <label for="password">Password:</label>
      <input type="password" maxlength="50" name="password" size="22" />
    </p>
    <p>
      <input type="submit" name="Login" value="Login" /> |
      <a href="{$obj->mLinkToRegisterCustomer}">Register user</a>
    </p>
  </form>
</div>
```

2. Create a new presentation object file named customer_login.php in the presentation folder, and add the following to it:

```
<?php
class CustomerLogin
{
  // Public stuff
  public $mErrorMessage;
  public $mLinkToLogin;
  public $mLinkToRegisterCustomer;
  public $mEmail = '';
```

```php
  // Class constructor
  public function __construct()
  {
    if (USE_SSL == 'yes' && getenv('HTTPS') != 'on')
      $this->mLinkToLogin =
        Link::Build(str_replace(VIRTUAL_LOCATION, '', getenv('REQUEST_URI')),
                    'https');
    else
      $this->mLinkToLogin =
        Link::Build(str_replace(VIRTUAL_LOCATION, '', getenv('REQUEST_URI')));

    $this->mLinkToRegisterCustomer = Link::ToRegisterCustomer();
  }

  public function init()
  {
    // Decide if we have submitted
    if (isset ($_POST['Login']))
    {
      // Get login status
      $login_status = Customer::IsValid($_POST['email'], $_POST['password']);

      switch ($login_status)
      {
        case 2:
          $this->mErrorMessage = 'Unrecognized Email.';
          $this->mEmail = $_POST['email'];

          break;
        case 1:
          $this->mErrorMessage = 'Unrecognized password.';
          $this->mEmail = $_POST['email'];

          break;
        case 0:
          $redirect_to_link =
            Link::Build(str_replace(VIRTUAL_LOCATION, '',
                                    getenv('REQUEST_URI')));

          header('Location:' . $redirect_to_link);

          exit();
      }
    }
  }
}
?>
```

3. Create a new template file named customer_logged.tpl in the presentation/templates folder, and add the following code to it:

```
{* customer_logged.tpl *}
{load_presentation_object filename="customer_logged" assign="obj"}
<div class="box">
  <p class="box-title">Welcome, {$obj->mCustomerName}</p>
  <ul>
    <li>
      <a {if $obj->mSelectedMenuItem eq 'account'} class="selected" {/if}
         href="{$obj->mLinkToAccountDetails}">
        Change Account
      </a>
    </li>
    <li>
      <a {if $obj->mSelectedMenuItem eq 'credit-card'} class="selected" {/if}
         href="{$obj->mLinkToCreditCardDetails}">
        {$obj->mCreditCardAction} CC Details
      </a>
    </li>
    <li>
      <a {if $obj->mSelectedMenuItem eq 'address'} class="selected" {/if}
         href="{$obj->mLinkToAddressDetails}">
        {$obj->mAddressAction} Address
      </a>
    </li>
    <li>
      <a href="{$obj->mLinkToLogout}">
        Logout
      </a>
    </li>
  </ol>
</div>
```

4. Create a new presentation object file named customer_logged.php in the presentation folder, and add the following to it:

```php
<?php
class CustomerLogged
{
  // Public attributes
  public $mCustomerName;
  public $mCreditCardAction = 'Add';
  public $mAddressAction = 'Add';
  public $mLinkToAccountDetails;
  public $mLinkToCreditCardDetails;
  public $mLinkToAddressDetails;
  public $mLinkToLogout;
  public $mSelectedMenuItem;
```

```
   // Class constructor
   public function __construct()
   {
     $this->mLinkToAccountDetails    = Link::ToAccountDetails();
     $this->mLinkToCreditCardDetails = Link::ToCreditCardDetails();
     $this->mLinkToAddressDetails    = Link::ToAddressDetails();

     $this->mLinkToLogout = Link::Build('index.php?Logout');

     if (isset ($_GET['AccountDetails']))
       $this->mSelectedMenuItem = 'account';
     elseif (isset ($_GET['CreditCardDetails']))
       $this->mSelectedMenuItem = 'credit-card';
     elseif (isset ($_GET['AddressDetails']))
       $this->mSelectedMenuItem = 'address';
   }

   public function init()
   {
     if (isset ($_GET['Logout']))
     {
       Customer::Logout();

       header('Location:' . $_SESSION['link_to_last_page_loaded']);

       exit();
     }

     $customer_data = Customer::Get();
     $this->mCustomerName = $customer_data['name'];

     if (!(empty ($customer_data['credit_card'])))
       $this->mCreditCardAction = 'Change';

     if (!(empty ($customer_data['address_1'])))
       $this->mAddressAction = 'Change';
   }
}
?>
```

5. Create a new template file named customer_details.tpl in the presentation/templates folder, and add the following code to it:

```
{* customer_details.tpl *}
{load_presentation_object filename="customer_details" assign="obj"}
<form method="post" action="{$obj->mLinkToAccountDetails}">
  <h2>Please enter your details:</h2>
  <table class="customer-table">
```

```
<tr>
  <td>E-mail Address:</td>
  <td>
    <input type="text" name="email" value="{$obj->mEmail}"
    {if $obj->mEditMode}readonly="readonly"{/if} size="32" />
    {if $obj->mEmailAlreadyTaken}
    <p class="error">A user with that e-mail address already exists.</p>
    {/if}
    {if $obj->mEmailError}
    <p class="error">You must enter an e-mail address.</p>
    {/if}
  </td>
</tr>
<tr>
  <td>Name:</td>
  <td>
    <input type="text" name="name" value="{$obj->mName}" size="32" />
    {if $obj->mNameError}
    <p class="error">You must enter your name.</p>
    {/if}
  </td>
</tr>
<tr>
  <td>Password:</td>
  <td>
    <input type="password" name="password" size="32" />
    {if $obj->mPasswordError}
    <p class="error">You must enter a password.</p>
    {/if}
  </td>
</tr>
<tr>
  <td>Re-enter Password:</td>
  <td>
    <input type="password" name="passwordConfirm" size="32" />
    {if $obj->mPasswordConfirmError}
    <p class="error">You must re-enter your password.</p>
    {elseif $obj->mPasswordMatchError}
    <p class="error">You must re-enter the same password.</p>
    {/if}
  </td>
</tr>
{if $obj->mEditMode}
<tr>
  <td>Day phone:</td>
```

```
          <td>
            <input type="text" name="dayPhone" value="{$obj->mDayPhone}"
              size="32" />
          </td>
        </tr>
        <tr>
          <td>Eve phone:</td>
          <td>
            <input type="text" name="evePhone" value="{$obj->mEvePhone}"
              size="32" />
          </td>
        </tr>
        <tr>
          <td>Mob phone:</td>
          <td>
            <input type="text" name="mobPhone" value="{$obj->mMobPhone}"
              size="32" />
          </td>
        </tr>
        {/if}
      </table>
      <input type="submit" name="sended" value="Confirm" /> |
      <a href="{$obj->mLinkToCancelPage}">Cancel</a>
    </form>
```

6. Create a new presentation object file named customer_details.php in the presentation folder, and add the following to it:

```php
<?php
class CustomerDetails
{
  // Public attributes
  public $mEditMode = 0;
  public $mEmail;
  public $mName;
  public $mPassword;
  public $mDayPhone = null;
  public $mEvePhone = null;
  public $mMobPhone = null;
  public $mNameError = 0;
  public $mEmailAlreadyTaken = 0;
  public $mEmailError = 0;
  public $mPasswordError = 0;
  public $mPasswordConfirmError = 0;
  public $mPasswordMatchError = 0;
  public $mLinkToAccountDetails;
  public $mLinkToCancelPage;
```

```php
    // Private attributes
    private $_mErrors = 0;

    // Class constructor
    public function __construct()
    {
      // Check if we have new user or editing existing customer details
      if (Customer::IsAuthenticated())
        $this->mEditMode = 1;

      if ($this->mEditMode == 0)
        $this->mLinkToAccountDetails = Link::ToRegisterCustomer();
      else
        $this->mLinkToAccountDetails = Link::ToAccountDetails();

      // Set the cancel page
      if (isset ($_SESSION['customer_cancel_link']))
        $this->mLinkToCancelPage = $_SESSION['customer_cancel_link'];
      else
        $this->mLinkToCancelPage = Link::ToIndex();

      // Check if we have submitted data
      if (isset ($_POST['sended']))
      {
        // Name cannot be empty
        if (empty ($_POST['name']))
        {
          $this->mNameError = 1;
          $this->_mErrors++;
        }
        else
          $this->mName = $_POST['name'];

        if ($this->mEditMode == 0 && empty ($_POST['email']))
        {
          $this->mEmailError = 1;
          $this->_mErrors++;
        }
        else
          $this->mEmail = $_POST['email'];

        // Password cannot be empty
        if (empty ($_POST['password']))
        {
          $this->mPasswordError = 1;
          $this->_mErrors++;
        }
```

```
    else
      $this->mPassword = $_POST['password'];

    // Password confirm cannot be empty
    if (empty ($_POST['passwordConfirm']))
    {
      $this->mPasswordConfirmError = 1;
      $this->_mErrors++;
    }
    else
      $password_confirm = $_POST['passwordConfirm'];

    // Password and password confirm should be the same
    if (!isset ($password_confirm) ||
        $this->mPassword != $password_confirm)
    {
      $this->mPasswordMatchError = 1;
      $this->_mErrors++;
    }

    if ($this->mEditMode == 1)
    {
      if (!empty ($_POST['dayPhone']))
        $this->mDayPhone = $_POST['dayPhone'];

      if (!empty ($_POST['evePhone']))
        $this->mEvePhone = $_POST['evePhone'];

      if (!empty ($_POST['mobPhone']))
        $this->mMobPhone = $_POST['mobPhone'];
    }
  }
}

public function init()
{
  // If we have submitted data and no errors in submitted data
  if ((isset ($_POST['sended'])) && ($this->_mErrors == 0))
  {
    // Check if we have any customer with submitted email...
    $customer_read = Customer::GetLoginInfo($this->mEmail);

    /* ...if we have one and we are in 'new user' mode then
       email already taken error */
    if ((!(empty ($customer_read['customer_id']))) &&
        ($this->mEditMode == 0))
    {
      $this->mEmailAlreadyTaken = 1;
```

```
      return;
    }

    // We have a new user or we are updating an existing user's details
    if ($this->mEditMode == 0)
      Customer::Add($this->mName, $this->mEmail, $this->mPassword);
    else
      Customer::UpdateAccountDetails($this->mName, $this->mEmail,
        $this->mPassword, $this->mDayPhone, $this->mEvePhone,
        $this->mMobPhone);

    header('Location:' . $this->mLinkToCancelPage);

    exit();
  }

  if ($this->mEditMode == 1 && !isset ($_POST['sended']))
  {
    // We are editing an existing customer's details
    $customer_data = Customer::Get();

    $this->mName     = $customer_data['name'];
    $this->mEmail    = $customer_data['email'];
    $this->mDayPhone = $customer_data['day_phone'];
    $this->mEvePhone = $customer_data['eve_phone'];
    $this->mMobPhone = $customer_data['mob_phone'];
  }
 }
}
?>
```

7. Create a new template file named `customer_address.tpl` in the `presentation/templates` folder, and add the following code to it:

```
{* customer_address.tpl *}
{load_presentation_object filename="customer_address" assign="obj"}
<form method="post" action="{$obj->mLinkToAddressDetails}">
  <h2>Please enter your address details:</h2>
  <table class="customer-table">
    <tr>
      <td>Address 1:</td>
      <td>
        <input type="text" name="address1" value="{$obj->mAddress1}"
         size="32" />
        {if $obj->mAddress1Error}
        <p class="error">You must enter an address.</p>
        {/if}
      </td>
    </tr>
```

```
<tr>
  <td>Address 2:</td>
  <td>
    <input type="text" name="address2" value="{$obj->mAddress2}"
    size="32" />
  </td>
</tr>
<tr>
  <td>Town/City:</td>
  <td>
    <input type="text" name="city" value="{$obj->mCity}"
    size="32" />
    {if $obj->mCityError}
    <p class="error">You must enter a city.</p>
    {/if}
  </td>
</tr>
<tr>
  <td>Region/State:</td>
  <td>
    <input type="text" name="region" value="{$obj->mRegion}"
    size="32" />
    {if $obj->mRegionError}
    <p class="error">You must enter a region/state.</p>
    {/if}
  </td>
</tr>
<tr>
  <td>Postal Code/ZIP:</td>
  <td>
    <input type="text" name="postalCode" value="{$obj->mPostalCode}"
    size="32" />
    {if $obj->mPostalCodeError}
    <p class="error">You must enter a postal code/ZIP.</p>
    {/if}
  </td>
</tr>
<tr>
  <td>Country:</td>
  <td>
    <input type="text" name="country" value="{$obj->mCountry}"
    size="32" />
    {if $obj->mCountryError}
    <p class="error">You must enter a country.</p>
    {/if}
  </td>
</tr>
```

```
    <tr>
      <td>Shipping region:</td>
      <td>
        <select name="shippingRegion">
          {html_options options=$obj->mShippingRegions
            selected=$obj->mShippingRegion}
        </select>
        {if $obj->mShippingRegionError}
        <p class="error">You must select a shipping region.</p>
        {/if}
      </td>
    </tr>
  </table>
  <input type="submit" name="sended" value="Confirm" /> |
  <a href="{$obj->mLinkToCancelPage}">Cancel</a>
</form>
```

8. Create a new presentation object file named `customer_address.php` in the presentation folder, and
   add the following to it:

```php
<?php
class CustomerAddress
{
  // Public attributes
  public $mAddress1 = '';
  public $mAddress2 = '';
  public $mCity = '';
  public $mRegion = '';
  public $mPostalCode = '';
  public $mCountry = '';
  public $mShippingRegion = '';
  public $mShippingRegions = array ();
  public $mAddress1Error = 0;
  public $mCityError = 0;
  public $mRegionError = 0;
  public $mPostalCodeError = 0;
  public $mCountryError = 0;
  public $mShippingRegionError = 0;
  public $mLinkToAddressDetails;
  public $mLinkToCancelPage;

  // Private attributes
  private $_mErrors = 0;

  // Class constructor
  public function __construct()
  {
```

```php
// Set form action target
$this->mLinkToAddressDetails = Link::ToAddressDetails();

// Set the cancel page
if (isset ($_SESSION['customer_cancel_link']))
  $this->mLinkToCancelPage = $_SESSION['customer_cancel_link'];
else
  $this->mLinkToCancelPage = Link::ToIndex();

// Check if we have submitted data
if (isset ($_POST['sended']))
{
  // Address 1 cannot be empty
  if (empty ($_POST['address1']))
  {
    $this->mAddress1Error = 1;
    $this->_mErrors++;
  }
  else
    $this->mAddress1 = $_POST['address1'];

  if (isset ($_POST['address2']))
    $this->mAddress2 = $_POST['address2'];

  if (empty ($_POST['city']))
  {
    $this->mCityError = 1;
    $this->_mErrors++;
  }
  else
    $this->mCity = $_POST['city'];

  if (empty ($_POST['region']))
  {
    $this->mRegionError = 1;
    $this->_mErrors++;
  }
  else
    $this->mRegion = $_POST['region'];

  if (empty ($_POST['postalCode']))
  {
    $this->mPostalCodeError = 1;
    $this->_mErrors++;
  }
  else
    $this->mPostalCode = $_POST['postalCode'];
```

```
      if (empty ($_POST['country']))
      {
        $this->mCountryError = 1;
        $this->_mErrors++;
      }
      else
        $this->mCountry = $_POST['country'];

      if ($_POST['shippingRegion'] == 1)
      {
        $this->mShippingRegionError = 1;
        $this->_mErrors++;
      }
      else
        $this->mShippingRegion = $_POST['shippingRegion'];
    }
  }

  public function init()
  {
    $shipping_regions = Customer::GetShippingRegions();

    foreach ($shipping_regions as $item)
      $this->mShippingRegions[$item['shipping_region_id']] =
        $item['shipping_region'];

    if (!isset ($_POST['sended']))
    {
      $customer_data = Customer::Get();

      if (!(empty ($customer_data)))
      {
        $this->mAddress1       = $customer_data['address_1'];
        $this->mAddress2       = $customer_data['address_2'];
        $this->mCity           = $customer_data['city'];
        $this->mRegion         = $customer_data['region'];
        $this->mPostalCode     = $customer_data['postal_code'];
        $this->mCountry        = $customer_data['country'];
        $this->mShippingRegion = $customer_data['shipping_region_id'];
      }
    }
    elseif ($this->_mErrors == 0)
    {
      Customer::UpdateAddressDetails($this->mAddress1, $this->mAddress2,
        $this->mCity, $this->mRegion, $this->mPostalCode,
        $this->mCountry, $this->mShippingRegion);
```

```
            header('Location:' . $this->mLinkToCancelPage);

            exit();
        }
    }
}
?>
```

9. Create a new template file named customer_credit_card.tpl in the presentation/templates folder, and add the following code to it:

```
{* customer_credit_card.tpl *}
{load_presentation_object filename="customer_credit_card" assign="obj"}
<form method="post" action="{$obj->mLinkToCreditCardDetails}">
  <h2>Please enter your credit card details:</h2>
  <table class="customer-table">
    <tr>
      <td>Card Holder:</td>
      <td>
        <input type="text" name="cardHolder" size="32"
         value="{$obj->mPlainCreditCard.card_holder}" />
        {if $obj->mCardHolderError}
        <p class="error">You must enter a card holder.</p>
        {/if}
      </td>
    </tr>
    <tr>
      <td>Card Number (digits only):</td>
      <td>
        <input type="text" name="cardNumber" size="32"
         value="{$obj->mPlainCreditCard.card_number}" />
        {if $obj->mCardNumberError}
        <p class="error">You must enter a card number.</p>
        {/if}
      </td>
    </tr>
    <tr>
      <td>Expiry Date (MM/YY):</td>
      <td>
        <input type="text" name="expDate" size="32"
         value="{$obj->mPlainCreditCard.expiry_date}" />
        {if $obj->mExpDateError}
        <p class="error">You must enter an expiry date</p>
        {/if}
      </td>
    </tr>
    <tr>
      <td>Issue Date (MM/YY if applicable):</td>
```

```
      <td>
        <input type="text" name="issueDate" size="32"
        value="{$obj->mPlainCreditCard.issue_date}" />
      </td>
    </tr>
    <tr>
      <td>Issue Number (if applicable):</td>
      <td>
        <input type="text" name="issueNumber" size="32"
        value="{$obj->mPlainCreditCard.issue_number}" />
      </td>
    </tr>
    <tr>
      <td>Card Type:</td>
      <td>
        <select name="cardType">
          {html_options options=$obj->mCardTypes
            selected=$obj->mPlainCreditCard.card_type}
        </select>
        {if $obj->mCardTypesError}
        <p class="error">You must enter a card type.</p>
        {/if}
      </td>
    </tr>
  </table>
  <input type="submit" name="sended" value="Confirm" /> |
  <a href="{$obj->mLinkToCancelPage}">Cancel</a>
</form>
```

10. Create a new presentation object file named `customer_credit_card.php` in the presentation folder, and add the following to it:

```php
<?php
class CustomerCreditCard
{
  // Public attributes
  public $mCardHolderError;
  public $mCardNumberError;
  public $mExpDateError;
  public $mCardTypesError;
  public $mPlainCreditCard;
  public $mCardTypes;
  public $mLinkToCreditCardDetails;
  public $mLinkToCancelPage;

  // Private attributes
  private $_mErrors = 0;
```

```php
public function __construct()
{
  $this->mPlainCreditCard = array('card_holder' => '',
    'card_number' => '', 'issue_date' => '', 'expiry_date' => '',
    'issue_number' => '', 'card_type' => '', 'card_number_x' => '');

  // Set form action target
  $this->mLinkToCreditCardDetails = Link::ToCreditCardDetails();

  // Set the cancel page
  if (isset ($_SESSION['customer_cancel_link']))
    $this->mLinkToCancelPage = $_SESSION['customer_cancel_link'];
  else
    $this->mLinkToCancelPage = Link::ToIndex();

  $this->mCardTypes = array ('Mastercard' => 'Mastercard',
    'Visa' => 'Visa', 'Mastercard' => 'Mastercard',
    'Switch' => 'Switch', 'Solo' => 'Solo',
    'American Express' => 'American Express');

  // Check if we have submitted data
  if (isset ($_POST['sended']))
  {
    // Initialization/validation stuff
    if (empty ($_POST['cardHolder']))
    {
      $this->mCardHolderError = 1;
      $this->_mErrors++;
    }
    else
      $this->mPlainCreditCard['card_holder'] = $_POST['cardHolder'];

    if (empty ($_POST['cardNumber']))
    {
      $this->mCardNumberError = 1;
      $this->_mErrors++;
    }
    else
      $this->mPlainCreditCard['card_number'] = $_POST['cardNumber'];

    if (empty ($_POST['expDate']))
    {
      $this->mExpDateError = 1;
      $this->_mErrors++;
    }
    else
      $this->mPlainCreditCard['expiry_date'] = $_POST['expDate'];
```

```
          if (isset ($_POST['issueDate']))
            $this->mPlainCreditCard['issue_date'] = $_POST['issueDate'];

          if (isset ($_POST['issueNumber']))
            $this->mPlainCreditCard['issue_number'] = $_POST['issueNumber'];

          $this->mPlainCreditCard['card_type'] = $_POST['cardType'];

          if (empty ($this->mPlainCreditCard['card_type']))
          {
            $this->mCardTypeError = 1;
            $this->_mErrors++;
          }
        }
      }

      public function init()
      {
        if (!isset ($_POST['sended']))
        {
          // Get credit card information
          $this->mPlainCreditCard = Customer::GetPlainCreditCard();
        }
        elseif ($this->_mErrors == 0)
        {
          // Update credit card information
          Customer::UpdateCreditCardDetails($this->mPlainCreditCard);

          header('Location:' . $this->mLinkToCancelPage);

          exit();
        }
      }
    }
  }
?>
```

11. Open `presentation/link.php`, and add the following four methods to the `Link` class:

```
// Creates a link to the register customer page
public static function ToRegisterCustomer()
{
  return self::Build('register-customer/', 'https');
}


// Creates a link to the update customer account details page
public static function ToAccountDetails()
{
  return self::Build('account-details/', 'https');
}
```

```
// Creates a link to the update customer credit card details page
public static function ToCreditCardDetails()
{
  return self::Build('credit-card-details/', 'https');
}

// Creates a link to the update customer address details page
public static function ToAddressDetails()
{
  return self::Build('address-details/', 'https');
}
```

12. Also in the Link class modify the CheckRequest() method as highlighted here:

```
// Redirects to proper URL if not already there
public static function CheckRequest()
{
  $proper_url = '';

  if (isset ($_GET['Search']) || isset($_GET['SearchResults']) ||
      isset ($_GET['CartAction']) || isset ($_GET['AjaxRequest']) ||
      isset ($_POST['Login']) || isset ($_GET['Logout']) ||
      isset ($_GET['RegisterCustomer']) ||
      isset ($_GET['AddressDetails']) ||
      isset ($_GET['CreditCardDetails']) ||
      isset ($_GET['AccountDetails']))
  {
    return ;
  }
  // Obtain proper URL for category pages
  elseif (isset ($_GET['DepartmentId']) && isset ($_GET['CategoryId']))
```

13. Open .htaccess, and add the highlighted RewriteRule lines:

```
# Rewrite cart details pages
RewriteRule ^cart-details/?$ index.php?CartAction [L]

# Rewrite register customer pages
RewriteRule ^register-customer/?$ index.php?RegisterCustomer [L]

# Rewrite address details pages
RewriteRule ^address-details/?$ index.php?AddressDetails [L]

# Rewrite credit card details pages
RewriteRule ^credit-card-details/?$ index.php?CreditCardDetails [L]

# Rewrite account details pages
RewriteRule ^account-details/?$ index.php?AccountDetails [L]
</IfModule>
```

```
# Set the default 500 page for Apache errors
ErrorDocument 500 /tshirtshop/500.php
```

14. Update `index.php` by adding a reference to the password hasher, symmetric crypting, secure card, and customer accounts business tier classes as highlighted here:

```
// Load Business Tier
require_once BUSINESS_DIR . 'catalog.php';
require_once BUSINESS_DIR . 'shopping_cart.php';
require_once BUSINESS_DIR . 'password_hasher.php';
require_once BUSINESS_DIR . 'symmetric_crypt.php';
require_once BUSINESS_DIR . 'secure_card.php';
require_once BUSINESS_DIR . 'customer.php';
```

15. Open `presentation/store_front.php`, and add a new member to the `StoreFront` class as highlighted here:

```
<?php
class StoreFront
{
  public $mSiteUrl;
  // Define the template file for the page contents
  public $mContentsCell = 'first_page_contents.tpl';
  // Define the template file for the categories cell
  public $mCategoriesCell = 'blank.tpl';
  // Define the template file for the cart summary cell
  public $mCartSummaryCell = 'blank.tpl';
  // Define the template file for the login or logged cell
  public $mLoginOrLoggedCell = 'customer_login.tpl';
  // Page title
  public $mPageTitle;
  // PayPal continue shopping link
  public $mPayPalContinueShoppingLink;
```

16. Modify the `init()` method of the `StoreFront` class by adding the new interface elements at the end of the method:

```
    // Load shopping cart or cart summary template
    if (isset ($_GET['CartAction']))
      $this->mContentsCell = 'cart_details.tpl';
    else
      $this->mCartSummaryCell = 'cart_summary.tpl';

    if (Customer::IsAuthenticated())
      $this->mLoginOrLoggedCell = 'customer_logged.tpl';

    if (isset ($_GET['RegisterCustomer']) ||
        isset ($_GET['AccountDetails']))
      $this->mContentsCell = 'customer_details.tpl';
    elseif (isset ($_GET['AddressDetails']))
      $this->mContentsCell = 'customer_address.tpl';
```

```
    elseif (isset ($_GET['CreditCardDetails']))
      $this->mContentsCell = 'customer_credit_card.tpl';

    // Load the page title
    $this->mPageTitle = $this->_GetPageTitle();
  }
```

17. Modify the same init() method of the StoreFront class again:

```
public function init()
{
  $_SESSION['link_to_store_front'] =
    Link::Build(str_replace(VIRTUAL_LOCATION, '', getenv('REQUEST_URI')));

  // Build the "continue shopping" link
  if (!isset ($_GET['CartAction']) && !isset($_GET['Logout']) &&
      !isset($_GET['RegisterCustomer']) &&
      !isset($_GET['AddressDetails']) &&
      !isset($_GET['CreditCardDetails']) &&
      !isset($_GET['AccountDetails']))
    $_SESSION['link_to_last_page_loaded'] = $_SESSION['link_to_store_front'];

  // Build the "cancel" link for customer details pages
  if (!isset($_GET['Logout']) &&
      !isset($_GET['RegisterCustomer']) &&
      !isset($_GET['AddressDetails']) &&
      !isset($_GET['CreditCardDetails']) &&
      !isset($_GET['AccountDetails']))
    $_SESSION['customer_cancel_link'] = $_SESSION['link_to_store_front'];

  // Load department details if visiting a department
  if (isset ($_GET['DepartmentId']))
```

18. Update presentation/templates/store_front.tpl by adding the following:

```
<div class="yui-b">
  {include file=$obj->mLoginOrLoggedCell}
  {include file="search_box.tpl"}
  {include file="departments_list.tpl"}
  {include file=$obj->mCategoriesCell}
```

19. Add the following styles to the tshirtshop.css file, from the styles folder:

```
.customer-table td {
  border: none;
  padding-left: 0;
  vertical-align: top;
}
```

20. You can now load the web site to check that the functionality shown in Figures 16-4 through 16-7 works.

Creating the Checkout Page

You are now ready to create the checkout page. This page looks similar to the shopping cart (the cart_details componentized template) because it displays the ordered items, but it also displays information such as the shipping address and the type of the credit card. The checkout page is accessible through the Checkout link that we'll add to the shipping cart. This button will be disabled if the visitor doesn't have the shipping and credit card data on record.

Let's take a look now at what you'll be doing (see Figure 16-8).

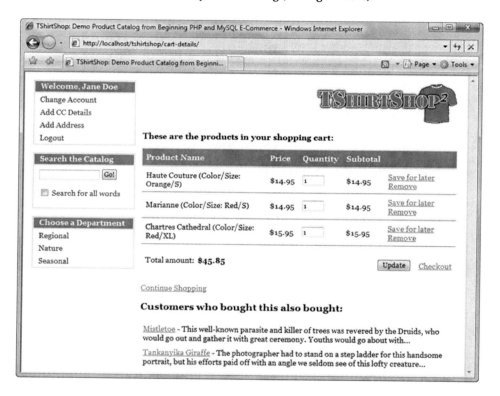

Figure 16-8. *The checkout page*

If the user tries to check out without entering all their personal data, the Place Order button won't be active, and the user will be notified through an error message such as the one shown in Figure 16-9.

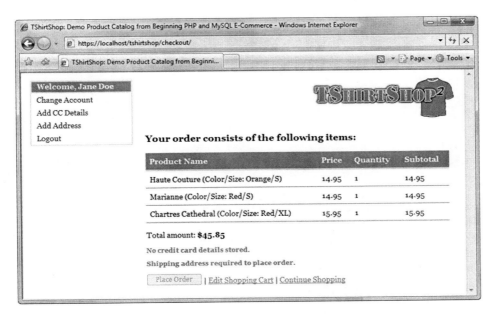

Figure 16-9. *Customers with incomplete details cannot place orders*

At this point, the customer also has the option to change the credit card or address details, using the functionality you implemented earlier.

Let's implement the checkout_info componentized template you saw in Figure 16-9.

Exercise: Implementing the checkout_info Componentized Template

1. Create a new file named checkout_info.tpl in the presentation/templates folder, and add the following code to it:

```
{* checkout_info.tpl *}
{load_presentation_object filename="checkout_info" assign="obj"}
<form method="post" action="{$obj->mLinkToCheckout}">
  <h2>Your order consists of the following items:</h2>
  <table class="tss-table">
    <tr>
      <th>Product Name</th>
      <th>Price</th>
      <th>Quantity</th>
      <th>Subtotal</th>
    </tr>
    {section name=i loop=$obj->mCartItems}
    <tr>
      <td>{$obj->mCartItems[i].name} ({$obj->mCartItems[i].attributes})</td>
      <td>{$obj->mCartItems[i].price}</td>
```

```
              <td>{$obj->mCartItems[i].quantity}</td>
              <td>{$obj->mCartItems[i].subtotal}</td>
          </tr>
        {/section}
        </table>
        <p>Total amount: <font class="price">${$obj->mTotalAmount}</font></p>
        {if $obj->mNoCreditCard == 'yes'}
        <p class="error">No credit card details stored.</p>
        {else}
        <p>{$obj->mCreditCardNote}</p>
        {/if}
        {if $obj->mNoShippingAddress == 'yes'}
        <p class="error">Shipping address required to place order.</p>
        {else}
        <p>
          Shipping address: <br />
           {$obj->mCustomerData.address_1}<br />
          {if $obj->mCustomerData.address_2}
             {$obj->mCustomerData.address_2}<br />
          {/if}
           {$obj->mCustomerData.city}<br />
           {$obj->mCustomerData.region}<br />
           {$obj->mCustomerData.postal_code}<br />
           {$obj->mCustomerData.country}<br /><br />
          Shipping region: {$obj->mShippingRegion}
        </p>
        {/if}
        <input type="submit" name="place_order" value="Place Order"
          {$obj->mOrderButtonVisible} /> |
        <a href="{$obj->mLinkToCart}">Edit Shopping Cart</a> |
        <a href="{$obj->mLinkToContinueShopping}">Continue Shopping</a>
      </form>
```

2. Create the presentation/checkout_info.php file, and fill it with the following code:

```php
<?php
// Class that supports the checkout page
class CheckoutInfo
{
  // Public attributes
  public $mCartItems;
  public $mTotalAmount;
  public $mCreditCardNote;
  public $mOrderButtonVisible;
  public $mNoShippingAddress = 'no';
  public $mNoCreditCard = 'no';
  public $mPlainCreditCard;
  public $mShippingRegion;
```

```php
public $mLinkToCheckout;
public $mLinkToCart;
public $mLinkToContinueShopping;

// Class constructor
public function __construct()
{
  $this->mLinkToCheckout = Link::ToCheckout();
  $this->mLinkToCart = Link::ToCart();
  $this->mLinkToContinueShopping = $_SESSION['link_to_last_page_loaded'];
}

public function init()
{
  // Set members for use in the Smarty template
  $this->mCartItems = ShoppingCart::GetCartProducts(GET_CART_PRODUCTS);
  $this->mTotalAmount = ShoppingCart::GetTotalAmount();
  $this->mCustomerData = Customer::Get();

  // If the Place Order button was clicked, save the order to database ...
  if(isset ($_POST['place_order']))
  {
    // Create the order and get the order ID
    $order_id = ShoppingCart::CreateOrder();

    // This will contain the PayPal link
    $redirect =
      PAYPAL_URL . '&item_name=TShirtShop Order ' .
      urlencode('#') . $order_id .
      '&item_number=' . $order_id .
      '&amount=' . $this->mTotalAmount .
      '&currency_code=' . PAYPAL_CURRENCY_CODE .
      '&return=' . PAYPAL_RETURN_URL .
      '&cancel_return=' . PAYPAL_CANCEL_RETURN_URL;

    // Redirection to the payment page
    header('Location: ' . $redirect);

    exit();
  }

  // We allow placing orders only if we have complete customer details
  if (empty ($this->mCustomerData['credit_card']))
  {
    $this->mOrderButtonVisible = 'disabled="disabled"';
    $this->mNoCreditCard = 'yes';
  }
```

```
      else
      {
        $this->mPlainCreditCard = Customer::DecryptCreditCard(
                              $this->mCustomerData['credit_card']);

        $this->mCreditCardNote = 'Credit card to use: ' .
                             $this->mPlainCreditCard['card_type'] .
                             '<br />Card number: ' .
                             $this->mPlainCreditCard['card_number_x'];
      }

      if (empty ($this->mCustomerData['address_1']))
      {
        $this->mOrderButtonVisible = 'disabled="disabled"';
        $this->mNoShippingAddress = 'yes';
      }
      else
      {
        $shipping_regions = Customer::GetShippingRegions();

        foreach ($shipping_regions as $item)
          if ($item['shipping_region_id'] ==
              $this->mCustomerData['shipping_region_id'])
            $this->mShippingRegion = $item['shipping_region'];
      }
    }
  }
}
?>
```

3. Create the checkout_not_logged.tpl file in the presentation/templates folder, and add the following code. This is the page that we're displaying to an unauthenticated user trying to load the checkout page. (Unauthenticated users don't see the Checkout link in the shopping cart, but they can try to load the checkout URL nevertheless.)

```
{* checkout_not_logged.tpl *}
<h3>
  You must be logged in to CHECKOUT <br />
  If you don't have an account please register <br />
</h3>
```

4. Open presentation/link.php, and add the following method to the end of the Link class:

```
// Creates a link to the checkout page
public static function ToCheckout()
{
  return self::Build('checkout/', 'https');
}
```

5. In the same file, modify the CheckRequest() method from the Link class as highlighted here so it won't verify checkout requests:

```
if (isset ($_GET['Search']) || isset($_GET['SearchResults']) ||
    isset ($_GET['CartAction']) || isset ($_GET['AjaxRequest']) ||
    isset ($_POST['Login']) || isset ($_GET['Logout']) ||
    isset ($_GET['RegisterCustomer']) ||
    isset ($_GET['AddressDetails']) ||
    isset ($_GET['CreditCardDetails']) ||
    isset ($_GET['AccountDetails']) || isset ($_GET['Checkout']))
{
  return ;
}
// Obtain proper URL for category pages
elseif (isset ($_GET['DepartmentId']) && isset ($_GET['CategoryId']))
```

6. Open the .htaccess file from the project root folder, and add the highlighted rewrite rule:

```
# Rewrite account details pages
RewriteRule ^account-details/?$ index.php?AccountDetails [L]

# Rewrite checkout pages
RewriteRule ^checkout/?$ index.php?Checkout [L]
</IfModule>

# Set the default 500 page for Apache errors
ErrorDocument 500 /tshirtshop/500.php
```

7. Open presentation/store_front.php, and modify the init() method of the StoreFront class as shown here to correctly build the "continue shopping" links. $_SESSION['link_to_last_page_loaded'] and $_SESSION['customer_cancel_link'] shouldn't point to the checkout page.

```
// Build the "continue shopping" link
if (!isset ($_GET['CartAction']) && !isset($_GET['Logout']) &&
    !isset($_GET['RegisterCustomer']) &&
    !isset($_GET['AddressDetails']) &&
    !isset($_GET['CreditCardDetails']) &&
    !isset($_GET['AccountDetails']) &&
    !isset($_GET['Checkout']))
  $_SESSION['link_to_last_page_loaded'] = $_SESSION['link_to_store_front'];

// Build the "cancel" link for customer details pages
if (!isset($_GET['Logout']) &&
    !isset($_GET['RegisterCustomer']) &&
    !isset($_GET['AddressDetails']) &&
    !isset($_GET['CreditCardDetails']) &&
    !isset($_GET['AccountDetails']))
  $_SESSION['customer_cancel_link'] = $_SESSION['link_to_store_front'];
```

```
// Load department details if visiting a department
if (isset ($_GET['DepartmentId']))
{
  $this->mContentsCell = 'department.tpl';
  $this->mCategoriesCell = 'categories_list.tpl';
}
```

8. In the same file (presentation/store_front.php), add a new member to the StoreFront class:

```
// Define the template file for the cart summary cell
public $mCartSummaryCell = 'blank.tpl';
// Define the template file for the login or logged cell
public $mLoginOrLoggedCell = 'customer_login.tpl';
// Controls the visibility of the shop navigation (departments, etc)
public $mHideBoxes = false;
// Page title
public $mPageTitle;
// PayPal continue shopping link
public $mPayPalContinueShoppingLink;
```

9. Also in the StoreFront class, modify the init() method adding the highlighted code to the end of the method as shown here:

```
if (isset ($_GET['RegisterCustomer']) ||
    isset ($_GET['AccountDetails']))
  $this->mContentsCell = 'customer_details.tpl';
elseif (isset ($_GET['AddressDetails']))
  $this->mContentsCell = 'customer_address.tpl';
elseif (isset ($_GET['CreditCardDetails']))
  $this->mContentsCell = 'customer_credit_card.tpl';

if (isset ($_GET['Checkout']))
{
  if (Customer::IsAuthenticated())
    $this->mContentsCell = 'checkout_info.tpl';
  else
    $this->mContentsCell = 'checkout_not_logged.tpl';

  $this->mHideBoxes = true;
}

// Load the page title
$this->mPageTitle = $this->_GetPageTitle();
}
```

10. Modify presentation/templates/store_front.tpl to show only the login or logged-in box on the left when showing the checkout page by adding the highlighted code:

```
            <div class="yui-b">
              {include file=$obj->mLoginOrLoggedCell}
              {if !$obj->mHideBoxes}
                {include file="search_box.tpl"}
                {include file="departments_list.tpl"}
                {include file=$obj->mCategoriesCell}
                {include file=$obj->mCartSummaryCell}
              {/if}
            </div>
          </div>
        </div>
      </body>
    </html>
```

11. Modify your presentation/templates/cart_details.tpl file to redirect the user to the checkout_info page instead of PayPal. The Place Order button becomes the Checkout link:

```
    ...
    <table class="cart-subtotal">
      <tr>
        <td>
          <p>
            Total amount: 
            <font class="price">${$obj->mTotalAmount}</font>
          </p>
        </td>
        <td align="right">
          <input type="submit" name="update" value="Update" />
        </td>
        {if $obj->mShowCheckoutLink}
        <td align="right">
          <a href="{$obj->mLinkToCheckout}">Checkout</a>
        </td>
        {/if}
      </tr>
    </table>
  </form>
{/if}
    ...
```

12. Modify the CartDetails class in presentation/cart_details.php by adding two new public members:

```
    ...
    public $mRecommendations;
    public $mLinkToCheckout;
    public $mShowCheckoutLink = false;
```

```
// Private attributes
private $_mItemId;
...
```

13. Update the init() method of the CartDetails class by deleting the PayPal code and adding the highlighted code in its place (it's OK to delete it because we have placed the PayPal link code in checkout_info.php):

```
...
    /* Calculate the total amount for the shopping cart
       before applicable taxes and/or shipping */
    $this->mTotalAmount = ShoppingCart::GetTotalAmount();

    // Display Checkout link in the shopping cart
    if ($this->mTotalAmount != 0 && Customer::IsAuthenticated())
    {
      $this->mLinkToCheckout = Link::ToCheckout();
      $this->mShowCheckoutLink = true;
    }

    // Get shopping cart products
    $this->mCartProducts =
      ShoppingCart::GetCartProducts(GET_CART_PRODUCTS);
...
```

14. Now everything is in its place, and you can see the results. Log in to your site, add some products to your shopping cart, and then click the Checkout link on your shopping cart page. Your page will look something like Figure 16-9 shown earlier.

How It Works: The checkout_info Componentized Template

In the init() method of the CheckoutInfo class, you start by checking whether the customer clicked the Place Order button. If so, you save the order in the database and redirect the customer to the home page:

```
// If the Place Order button was clicked, save the order to database ...
if(isset ($_POST['place_order']))
{
  // Create the order and get the order ID
    $order_id = ShoppingCart::CreateOrder();

    // This will contain the PayPal link
    $redirect =
      PAYPAL_URL . '&item_name=TShirtShop Order ' .
      urlencode('#') . $order_id .
      '&item_number=' . $order_id .
      '&amount=' . $this->mTotalAmount .
```

```
                   '&currency_code=' . PAYPAL_CURRENCY_CODE .
                   '&return=' . PAYPAL_RETURN_URL .
                   '&cancel_return=' . PAYPAL_CANCEL_RETURN_URL;

      // Redirection to the payment page
      header('Location: ' . $redirect);

      exit();
    }
```

We also set up some variables for the template to use:

```
    // Set members for use in the Smarty template
    $this->mCartItems = ShoppingCart::GetCartProducts(GET_CART_PRODUCTS);
    $this->mTotalAmount = ShoppingCart::GetTotalAmount();
    $this->mCustomerData = Customer::Get();
```

If the customer didn't enter credit card information or a shipping address yet, a notice is displayed, and the Place Order button is disabled. If credit card information exists for the customer, you decrypt it and prepare to display the credit card type and the last four digits of its number:

```
    // We allow placing orders only if we have complete customer details
    if (empty ($this->mCustomerData['credit_card']))
    {
      $this->mOrderButtonVisible = 'disabled="disabled"';
      $this->mNoCreditCard = 'yes';
    }
    else
    {
      $this->mPlainCreditCard = Customer::DecryptCreditCard(
                          $this->mCustomerData['credit_card']);

      $this->mCreditCardNote = 'Credit card to use: ' .
                          $this->mPlainCreditCard['card_type'] .
                          '<br />Card number: ' .
                          $this->mPlainCreditCard['card_number_x'];
    }

    if (empty ($this->mCustomerData['address_1']))
    {
      $this->mOrderButtonVisible = 'disabled="disabled"';
      $this->mNoShippingAddress = 'yes';
    }
```

The rest of the code is straightforward.

Enforcing SSL Connections

When building the catalog admin pages, you also learned that it's good to use SSL for securing the data that passes between your server and the client's browser. Back then, SSL was semi-optional because the administrative pages could have been restricted for local access only.

However, now that you have customers sending you extremely sensitive data, using SSL isn't optional anymore! Depending on the settings you implemented in Chapter 10, the customer details pages should be protected already. Remember that you have the include/config.php file that you can use to set the behavior of your site regarding SSL.

You still need to *force* the sensitive pages to be accessed through SSL. Say, if someone tried to access http://localhost/tshirtshop/credit-card-details/, the visitor should be redirected automatically to https://localhost/tshirtshop/credit-card-details/.

Obviously, you don't need SSL connections for all areas of the site, and you shouldn't enforce it in all places because that reduces performance and makes your pages invisible to search engines. However, you *do* want to make sure that the checkout, customer login, customer registration, and customer detail modification pages are accessible only via SSL.

Assuming that your site is working correctly with SSL, you should make some updates to ensure that the pages can't be accessed via HTTP. First add the following method at the end of the StoreFront class (in presentation/store_front.php):

```
// Visiting a sensitive page?
private function _IsSensitivePage()
{
  if (isset($_GET['RegisterCustomer']) ||
      isset($_GET['AccountDetails']) ||
      isset($_GET['CreditCardDetails']) ||
      isset($_GET['AddressDetails']) ||
      isset($_GET['Checkout']) ||
      isset($_POST['Login']))
    return true;

  return false;
}
```

Next, add the highlighted code in the __constructor() method of the StoreFront class:

```
// Class constructor
public function __construct()
{
  $is_https = false;

  // Is the page being accessed through an HTTPS connection?
  if (getenv('HTTPS') == 'on')
    $is_https = true;

  // Use HTTPS when accessing sensitive pages
  if ($this->_IsSensitivePage() && $is_https == false &&
      USE_SSL != 'no')
```

```
  {
    $redirect_to =
      Link::Build(str_replace(VIRTUAL_LOCATION, '', getenv('REQUEST_URI')),
                  'https');

    header ('Location: '. $redirect_to);

    exit();
  }

  // Don't use HTTPS for nonsensitive pages
  if (!$this->_IsSensitivePage() && $is_https == true)
  {
    $redirect_to =
      Link::Build(str_replace(VIRTUAL_LOCATION, '', getenv('REQUEST_URI')));

    header ('Location: '. $redirect_to);

    exit();
  }

  $this->mSiteUrl = Link::Build('');
}
```

Right now, trying to load `http://localhost/tshirtshop/credit-card-details/` will redirect you to `https://localhost/tshirtshop/credit-card-details/`, provided you're logged in.

Summary

In this chapter, you implemented a system that lets customers store their own private payment and shipping details at TShirtShop for use during order processing. You looked at many aspects of the customer account system, including encrypting sensitive data and securing web connections for obtaining it.

You started by creating a new customer table in your database, which holds the customer information.

Next, you created the security classes in your business tier, which use encryption algorithms to handle strings of sensitive data, and a secure credit card representation that makes it easy to exchange credit card details between the encrypted and decrypted formats.

After this, you used these security classes to create the login, registration, and customer detail web pages where customers enter their shipping and credit card information into the `tshirtshop` database. And then you implemented a secure customer checkout page with SSL protection.

CHAPTER 17

■■■

Storing Customer Orders

The TShirtShop e-commerce application is shaping up nicely. We've added customer account management capabilities, and we're keeping track of customer addresses and credit card information, which is stored in a secure way. However, we're not currently using this information in our order tracking system, which was created in Phase II of development. We currently don't associate an order with the account of the customer who placed that order.

In this chapter, we'll make the modifications required for customers to place orders that are associated with their user profiles. This feature will allow us to track in our database the orders placed by a particular customer and lay the foundation for implementing the order pipeline and credit card transactions in the following chapters.

Also in this chapter, we'll take a look at dealing with tax and shipping charges. Many options are available for implementing functionality to cope with these, but we'll just examine a simple way of doing things and lay the groundwork for your own further development.

This chapter is divided into three parts as follows:

- Enable customers to place orders through their accounts.

- Modify the orders administration section to integrate the new features.

- Add tax and shipping charges.

In the next chapter, we'll start to implement a more sophisticated order system, and the code we'll write in this chapter will facilitate that. Therefore, we'll be making some modifications that won't seem necessary at this stage, but they'll make your life easier later on.

Adding Orders to Customer Accounts

To enable customers to place orders, we need to make several modifications to our current order placing mechanism. Right now, the orders we store in our database aren't associated with our existing customers. In this section, we'll update TShirtShop to enable our customers to place orders through their accounts (which they can now create).

First, we'll modify the database to make it ready to hold information about customer orders. We'll first modify the `orders` table and then the `shopping_cart_create_order` stored procedure.

■**Caution** The new `orders` table will not be compatible with the data you currently have in this table, and you'll be required to delete all the existing data. If the orders data you currently have in your database is important to you, be sure to back up your database before proceeding.

More specifically, these are the changes we'll make to the `orders` table:

- Clear all the existing data.

- Remove the `customer_name`, `shipping_address`, and `customer_email` fields.

- Add `customer_id`, `auth_code`, and `reference` fields. The `customer_id` field references the `customer` table, specifying the customer who made the order. The other two fields are related to processing credit card data and will be discussed in Chapter 20.

We'll also modify the `shopping_cart_create_order` stored procedure to reflect the changes in the `orders` table. Follow the steps in the exercise to change the `orders` table and the `shopping_cart_create_order` stored procedure.

Exercise: Adding Orders to Customer Accounts

1. Load phpMyAdmin, select the `tshirtshop` database, and open a new SQL query page.

■**Caution** Be sure to back up your data, as you're going to delete the data in the `order_detail` and `orders` tables.

2. Next, use the query page to execute this code, which deletes the data stored in `order_detail` and `orders` tables from your `tshirtshop` database.

```
-- Delete all records from order_detail table
TRUNCATE TABLE order_detail;

-- Delete all records from orders table
TRUNCATE TABLE orders;
```

3. Drop the `customer_name`, `shipping_address`, and `customer_email` fields from the `orders` table; they are no longer required. This data is now held in the `customer` table.

```
-- Drop customer_name, shipping_address and customer_email fields
-- from the orders table
ALTER TABLE `orders` DROP COLUMN `customer_name`,
                     DROP COLUMN `shipping_address`,
                     DROP COLUMN `customer_email`;
```

4. Add the new fields (`customer_id`, `auth_code`, and `reference`), and add a new index on the `customer_id` field that reference an existing customer.

```
-- Adding the three new fields: customer_id, auth_code and reference.
ALTER TABLE `orders` ADD COLUMN `customer_id` INT,
                     ADD COLUMN `auth_code`   VARCHAR(50),
                     ADD COLUMN `reference`   VARCHAR(50);


-- Adding a new index to orders table
CREATE INDEX `idx_orders_customer_id` ON `orders` (`customer_id`);
```

5. Delete the old `shopping_cart_create_order` stored procedure, and create a new one by executing the following code (don't forget to set the delimiter to $$):

```
-- Drop shopping_cart_create_order stored procedure
DROP PROCEDURE shopping_cart_create_order$$

-- Create shopping_cart_create_order stored procedure
CREATE PROCEDURE shopping_cart_create_order(IN inCartId CHAR(32),
  IN inCustomerId INT)
BEGIN
  DECLARE orderId INT;

  -- Insert a new record into orders and obtain the new order ID
  INSERT INTO orders (created_on, customer_id) VALUES (NOW(), inCustomerId);
  -- Obtain the new Order ID
  SELECT LAST_INSERT_ID() INTO orderId;

  -- Insert order details in order_detail table
  INSERT INTO order_detail (order_id, product_id, attributes,
                            product_name, quantity, unit_cost)
  SELECT     orderId, p.product_id, sc.attributes, p.name, sc.quantity,
             COALESCE(NULLIF(p.discounted_price, 0), p.price) AS unit_cost
  FROM       shopping_cart sc
  INNER JOIN product p
               ON sc.product_id = p.product_id
  WHERE      sc.cart_id = inCartId AND sc.buy_now;

  -- Save the order's total amount
  UPDATE orders
  SET    total_amount = (SELECT SUM(unit_cost * quantity)
                         FROM   order_detail
                         WHERE  order_id = orderId)
  WHERE  order_id = orderId;

  -- Clear the shopping cart
  CALL shopping_cart_empty(inCartId);
```

```
      -- Return the Order ID
      SELECT orderId;
    END$$
```

6. Modify the `CreateOrder()` method of the `ShoppingCart` class in `business/shopping_cart.php` as follows:

```
    // Create a new order
    public static function CreateOrder($customerId)
    {
      // Build SQL query
      $sql = 'CALL shopping_cart_create_order(:cart_id, :customer_id)';

      // Build the parameters array
      $params = array (':cart_id' => self::GetCartId(),
                       ':customer_id' => $customerId);

      // Execute the query and return the results
      return DatabaseHandler::GetOne($sql, $params);
    }
```

7. Modify the `init()` method in `presentation/checkout_info.php` as highlighted:

```
    public function init()
    {
      // Set members for use in the Smarty template
      $this->mCartItems = ShoppingCart::GetCartProducts(GET_CART_PRODUCTS);
      $this->mTotalAmount = ShoppingCart::GetTotalAmount();
      $this->mCustomerData = Customer::Get();

      // If the Place Order button was clicked, save the order to database ...
      if(isset ($_POST['place_order']))
      {
        // Create the order and get the order ID
        $order_id = ShoppingCart::CreateOrder(Customer::GetCurrentCustomerId());

        // This will contain the PayPal link
        $redirect =
          PAYPAL_URL . '&item_name=TShirtShop Order ' .
          urlencode('#') . $order_id .
          '&item_number=' . $order_id .
          '&amount=' . $this->mTotalAmount .
          '&currency_code=' . PAYPAL_CURRENCY_CODE .
          '&return=' . PAYPAL_RETURN_URL .
          '&cancel_return=' . PAYPAL_CANCEL_RETURN_URL;
```

8. Place an order or two using the new system to check that the code works. To do this, you'll need to log on and supply enough details to get past the validation on the checkout page.

▓**Note** At this stage, the orders administration page does not work. It needs to be modified to work with our new functionality.

How It Works: Adding Customer Orders to TShirtShop

The code added in this exercise is very simple and hardly merits much attention. The order handling functions in the data and business tiers now take as a parameter a customer ID, which is assigned to the order.

After we've implemented more of the new ordering code, we'll be able to provide more information to customers, such as sending them confirmation e-mails. For now, however, this is as far as we can take things.

Administering Customer Orders

OK, right now, our database associates orders with their customers. Next, we need to update the order administration pages, because the old ones don't work anymore. This involves various modifications to the data and business tiers to provide new data structures and access code in the administration system for orders we developed in Chapter 14. Because the changes are extensive, we'll deal with them separately for the data, business, and presentation tiers.

Modifying the Data Tier

We need to make several changes here. We'll update these stored procedures from the database:

- orders_get_most_recent_orders
- orders_get_orders_between_dates
- orders_get_orders_by_status
- orders_get_order_info
- orders_update_order

We'll create three new stored procedures:

- orders_get_by_customer_id
- orders_get_order_short_details
- customer_get_customers_list

Exercise: Updating the Data Tier

1. Use phpMyAdmin to create the stored procedures described in the following steps. Don't forget to set the $$ delimiter before executing the code of *each* step.

2. Delete the old `orders_get_most_recent_orders` stored procedure, and create a new one by executing this code:

```
-- Drop orders_get_most_recent_orders stored procedure
DROP PROCEDURE orders_get_most_recent_orders$$

-- Create orders_get_most_recent_orders stored procedure
CREATE PROCEDURE orders_get_most_recent_orders(IN inHowMany INT)
BEGIN
  PREPARE statement FROM
    "SELECT     o.order_id, o.total_amount, o.created_on,
                o.shipped_on, o.status, c.name
     FROM       orders o
     INNER JOIN customer c
                  ON o.customer_id = c.customer_id
     ORDER BY   o.created_on DESC
     LIMIT      ?";

  SET @p1 = inHowMany;

  EXECUTE statement USING @p1;
END$$
```

3. Delete the old `orders_get_orders_between_dates` stored procedure, and create a new one by executing this code:

```
-- Drop orders_get_orders_between_dates stored procedure
DROP PROCEDURE orders_get_orders_between_dates$$

-- Create orders_get_orders_between_dates stored procedure
CREATE PROCEDURE orders_get_orders_between_dates(
  IN inStartDate DATETIME, IN inEndDate DATETIME)
BEGIN
  SELECT     o.order_id, o.total_amount, o.created_on,
             o.shipped_on, o.status, c.name
  FROM       orders o
  INNER JOIN customer c
                ON o.customer_id = c.customer_id
  WHERE      o.created_on >= inStartDate AND o.created_on <= inEndDate
  ORDER BY   o.created_on DESC;
END$$
```

4. Delete the old `orders_get_orders_by_status` stored procedure, and create a new one by executing this code:

```
-- Drop orders_get_orders_by_status stored procedure
DROP PROCEDURE orders_get_orders_by_status$$
```

```
-- Create orders_get_orders_by_status stored procedure
CREATE PROCEDURE orders_get_orders_by_status(IN inStatus INT)
BEGIN
  SELECT      o.order_id, o.total_amount, o.created_on,
              o.shipped_on, o.status, c.name
  FROM        orders o
  INNER JOIN customer c
                ON o.customer_id = c.customer_id
  WHERE       o.status = inStatus
  ORDER BY    o.created_on DESC;
END$$
```

5. Delete the old orders_get_order_info stored procedure, and create a new one by executing this code:

```
-- Drop orders_get_order_info stored procedure
DROP PROCEDURE orders_get_order_info$$

-- Create orders_get_order_info stored procedure
CREATE PROCEDURE orders_get_order_info(IN inOrderId INT)
BEGIN
  SELECT order_id, total_amount, created_on, shipped_on, status,
         comments, customer_id, auth_code, reference
  FROM   orders
  WHERE  order_id = inOrderId;
END$$
```

6. Delete the old orders_update_order stored procedure, and create a new one by executing this code:

```
-- Drop orders_update_order stored procedure
DROP PROCEDURE orders_update_order$$

-- Create orders_update_order stored procedure
CREATE PROCEDURE orders_update_order(IN inOrderId INT, IN inStatus INT,
  IN inComments VARCHAR(255), IN inAuthCode VARCHAR(50),
  IN inReference VARCHAR(50))
BEGIN
  DECLARE currentStatus INT;

  SELECT status
  FROM   orders
  WHERE  order_id = inOrderId
  INTO   currentStatus;

  IF  inStatus != currentStatus AND (inStatus = 0 OR inStatus = 1) THEN
    UPDATE orders SET shipped_on = NULL WHERE order_id = inOrderId;
  ELSEIF inStatus != currentStatus AND inStatus = 2 THEN
    UPDATE orders SET shipped_on = NOW() WHERE order_id = inOrderId;
  END IF;
```

```
   UPDATE orders
   SET    status = inStatus, comments = inComments,
          auth_code = inAuthCode, reference = inReference
   WHERE  order_id = inOrderId;
END$$
```

7. Execute this code, which creates the orders_get_orders_by_customer_id stored procedure:

```
-- Create orders_get_by_customer_id stored procedure
CREATE PROCEDURE orders_get_by_customer_id(IN inCustomerId INT)
BEGIN
   SELECT      o.order_id, o.total_amount, o.created_on,
               o.shipped_on, o.status, c.name
   FROM        orders o
   INNER JOIN  customer c
                 ON o.customer_id = c.customer_id
   WHERE       o.customer_id = inCustomerId
   ORDER BY    o.created_on DESC;
END$$
```

8. Execute the following code, which creates the orders_get_order_short_details stored procedure:

```
-- Create orders_get_order_short_details stored procedure
CREATE PROCEDURE orders_get_order_short_details(IN inOrderId INT)
BEGIN
   SELECT      o.order_id, o.total_amount, o.created_on,
               o.shipped_on, o.status, c.name
   FROM        orders o
   INNER JOIN  customer c
                 ON o.customer_id = c.customer_id
   WHERE       o.order_id = inOrderId;
END$$
```

9. Execute this code, which creates the customer_get_customers_list stored procedure:

```
-- Create customer_get_customers_list stored procedure
CREATE PROCEDURE customer_get_customers_list()
BEGIN
   SELECT customer_id, name FROM customer ORDER BY name ASC;
END$$
```

Modifying the Business Tier

We need to make a few changes to the business tier as well. We need to modify the UpdateOrder()
method of the Orders class and add three new methods to the Orders and Customers classes:

- GetByCustomerId()

- GetOrderShortDetails()

- GetCustomersList()

These new methods support the new administrative functionality we'll need in the admin_ orders.tpl presentation tier template. Create them by following the steps of the exercise.

Exercise: Updating the Business Tier

1. Add a new method named GetByCustomerId() to the Orders class in business/orders.php:

```
// Gets all orders placed by a specified customer
public static function GetByCustomerId($customerId)
{
  // Build the SQL query
  $sql = 'CALL orders_get_by_customer_id(:customer_id)';

  // Build the parameters array
  $params = array (':customer_id' => $customerId);

  // Execute the query and return the results
  return DatabaseHandler::GetAll($sql, $params);
}
```

2. Add a new method named GetOrderShortDetails() to the Orders class in business/orders.php:

```
// Get short details for an order
public static function GetOrderShortDetails($orderId)
{
  // Build the SQL query
  $sql = 'CALL orders_get_order_short_details(:order_id)';

  // Build the parameters array
  $params = array (':order_id' => $orderId);

  // Execute the query and return the results
  return DatabaseHandler::GetAll($sql, $params);
}
```

3. Modify the UpdateOrder() method of the Orders class as follows:

```
// Updates order details
public static function UpdateOrder($orderId, $status, $comments,
                                  $authCode, $reference)
{
  // Build the SQL query
  $sql = 'CALL orders_update_order(:order_id, :status, :comments,
                :auth_code, :reference)';
```

```
        // Build the parameters array
        $params = array (':order_id' => $orderId,
                         ':status' => $status,
                         ':comments' => $comments,
                         ':auth_code' => $authCode,
                         ':reference' => $reference);

        // Execute the query
        DatabaseHandler::Execute($sql, $params);
    }
```

4. Add a new method named GetCustomersList() to the Customer class in business/customer.php:

```
    // Gets all customers names with their associated id
    public static function GetCustomersList()
    {
        // Build the SQL query
        $sql = 'CALL customer_get_customers_list()';

        // Execute the query and return the results
        return DatabaseHandler::GetAll($sql);
    }
```

Modifying the Presentation Tier

Now, we need to update the presentation tier to make use of the new data tier and business tier features. We're not going to implement massive changes to the order administration code at this stage, because we'll just end up modifying it later after we've finished the new order processing system.

Figure 17-1 shows the admin_orders template. This page gives administrators various means of filtering current orders.

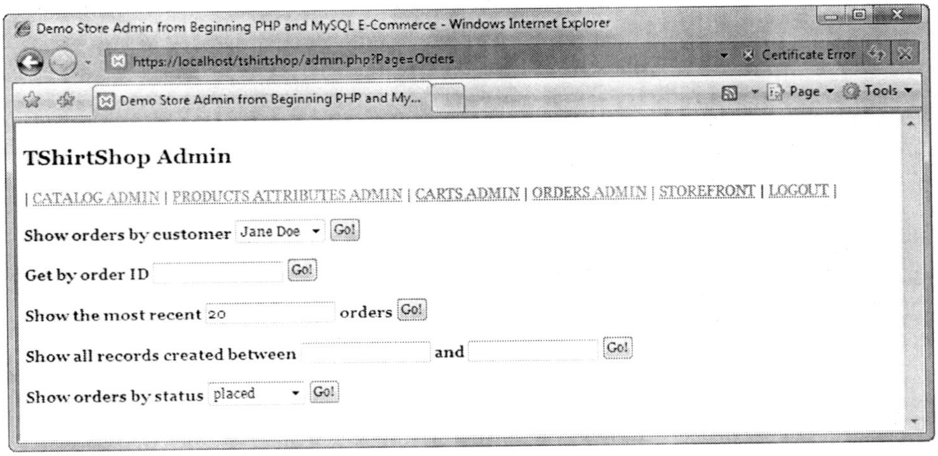

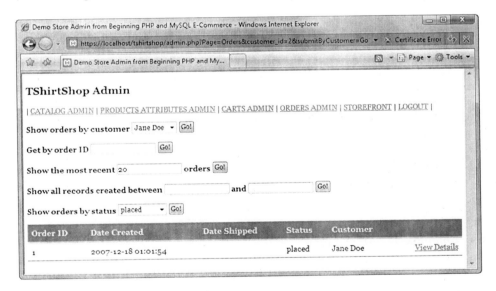

Figure 17-1. *The orders_admin template in action*

No matter what selection method we use, we'll get a list with the orders that match the criteria. In Figure 17-2, we can see the order Jane has just placed.

Figure 17-2. *The orders administration page*

The admin_order_details template looks like the one shown in Figure 17-3. Notice the tax and shipping data, which we'll add later in this chapter.

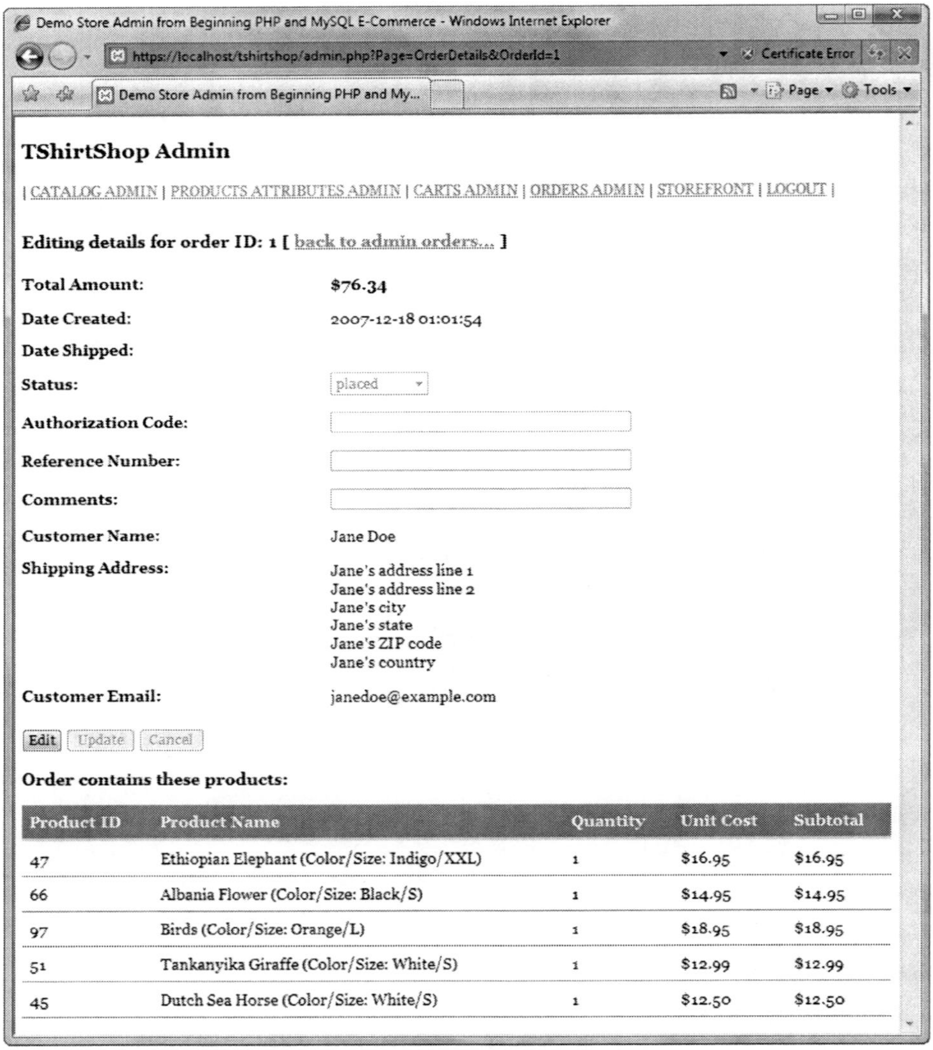

Figure 17-3. *Administering order details*

Exercise: Updating the Presentation Tier

1. Add the highlighted code to presentation/templates/admin_orders.tpl:

```
{* admin_orders.tpl *}
{load_presentation_object filename="admin_orders" assign="obj"}
{if $obj->mErrorMessage}<p class="error">{$obj->mErrorMessage}</p>{/if}
<form method="get" action="{$obj->mLinkToAdmin}">
  <input name="Page" type="hidden" value="Orders" />
```

```
<p>
  <font class="bold-text">Show orders by customer</font>
  <select name="customer_id">
  {section name=i loop=$obj->mCustomers}
    <option value="{$obj->mCustomers[i].customer_id}"
     {if $obj->mCustomers[i].customer_id == $obj->mCustomerId}
       selected="selected"
     {/if}>
       {$obj->mCustomers[i].name}
    </option>
  {/section}
  </select>
  <input type="submit" name="submitByCustomer" value="Go!" />
</p>
<p>
  <font class="bold-text">Get by order ID</font>
  <input name="orderId" type="text" value="{$obj->mOrderId}" />
  <input type="submit" name="submitByOrderId" value="Go!" />
</p>
<p>
  <font class="bold-text">Show the most recent</font>
  <input name="recordCount" type="text" value="{$obj->mRecordCount}" />
...
  {section name=i loop=$obj->mOrders}
    {assign var=status value=$obj->mOrders[i].status}
  <tr>
    <td>{$obj->mOrders[i].order_id}</td>
    <td>{$obj->mOrders[i].created_on|date_format:"%Y-%m-%d %T"}</td>
    <td>{$obj->mOrders[i].shipped_on|date_format:"%Y-%m-%d %T"}</td>
    <td>{$obj->mOrderStatusOptions[$status]}</td>
    <td>{$obj->mOrders[i].name}</td>
    <td align="right">
      <a href="{$obj->mOrders[i].link_to_order_details_admin}">View Details</a>
    </td>
  </tr>
  {/section}
</table>
{/if}
```

2. Add the highlighted members to the AdminOrders class in presentation/admin_orders.php:

```
public $mLinkToAdmin;
public $mCustomers;
public $mCustomerId;
public $mOrderId;
```

3. Add the highlighted code to the init() method of the AdminOrders class in presentation/admin_orders.php:

```php
// If "Show orders by status" filter is in action ...
if (isset ($_GET['submitOrdersByStatus']))
{
  $this->mSelectedStatus = $_GET['status'];
  $this->mOrders = Orders::GetOrdersByStatus($this->mSelectedStatus);
}

// If the "Show orders by customer ID" filter is in action ...
if (isset ($_GET['submitByCustomer']))
{
  if (empty ($_GET['customer_id']))
    $this->mErrorMessage = 'No customer has been selected';
  else
  {
    $this->mCustomerId = $_GET['customer_id'];
    $this->mOrders = Orders::GetByCustomerId($this->mCustomerId);
  }
}

// If the "Get order by ID" filter is in action ...
if (isset ($_GET['submitByOrderId']))
{
  if (empty ($_GET['orderId']))
    $this->mErrorMessage = 'You must enter an order ID.';
  else
  {
    $this->mOrderId = $_GET['orderId'];
    $this->mOrders = Orders::GetOrderShortDetails($this->mOrderId);
  }
}

$this->mCustomers = Customer::GetCustomersList();

if (is_array($this->mOrders) && count($this->mOrders) == 0)
  $this->mErrorMessage =
    'No orders found matching your searching criteria!';
```

4. Add a new member to the AdminOrderDetails class in presentation/admin_order_details.php:

```php
public $mLinkToAdmin;
public $mLinkToOrdersAdmin;
public $mCustomerInfo;
```

5. Modify the line that updates an order in the init() method of AdminOrderDetails as highlighted:

```
// Initializes class members
public function init()
{
  if (isset ($_GET['submitUpdate']))
  {
    Orders::UpdateOrder($this->mOrderId, $_GET['status'],
      $_GET['comments'], $_GET['authCode'], $_GET['reference']);
  }
```

6. Also in the init() method of the AdminOrderDetails class, add a line that reads the data of the customer who made the order:

```
$this->mOrderInfo = Orders::GetOrderInfo($this->mOrderId);
$this->mOrderDetails = Orders::GetOrderDetails($this->mOrderId);
$this->mCustomerInfo = Customer::Get($this->mOrderInfo['customer_id']);

// Value which specifies whether to enable or disable edit mode
if (isset ($_GET['submitEdit']))
```

7. Modify presentation/templates/admin_order_details.tpl as highlighted:

```
<tr>
  <td class="bold-text">Status: </td>
  <td>
    <select name="status"
     {if ! $obj->mEditEnabled} disabled="disabled" {/if} >
      {html_options options=$obj->mOrderStatusOptions
        selected=$obj->mOrderInfo.status}
    </select>
  </td>
</tr>
<tr>
  <td class="bold-text">Authorization Code: </td>
  <td>
    <input name="authCode" type="text" size="50"
    value="{$obj->mOrderInfo.auth_code}"
    {if ! $obj->mEditEnabled} disabled="disabled" {/if} />
  <td>
</tr>
<tr>
  <td class="bold-text">Reference Number: </td>
  <td>
    <input name="reference" type="text" size="50"
    value="{$obj->mOrderInfo.reference}"
    {if ! $obj->mEditEnabled} disabled="disabled" {/if} />
  <td>
</tr>
```

```
<tr>
  <td class="bold-text">Comments: </td>
  <td>
    <input name="comments" type="text" size="50"
     value="{$obj->mOrderInfo.comments}"
     {if ! $obj->mEditEnabled} disabled="disabled" {/if} />
  <td>
</tr>
<tr>
  <td class="bold-text">Customer Name: </td>
  <td>{$obj->mCustomerInfo.name}</td>
</tr>
<tr>
  <td class="bold-text" valign="top">Shipping Address: </td>
  <td>
    {$obj->mCustomerInfo.address_1}<br />
    {if $obj->mCustomerInfo.address_2}
      {$obj->mCustomerInfo.address_2}<br />
    {/if}
    {$obj->mCustomerInfo.city}<br />
    {$obj->mCustomerInfo.region}<br />
    {$obj->mCustomerInfo.postal_code}<br />
    {$obj->mCustomerInfo.country}<br />
  </td>
</tr>
<tr>
  <td class="bold-text">Customer Email: </td>
  <td>{$obj->mCustomerInfo.email}</td>
</tr>
</table>
```

8. Update `admin.php` by adding a reference to the symmetric crypt, secure card, and customer business tier classes:

```
require_once BUSINESS_DIR . 'shopping_cart.php';
require_once BUSINESS_DIR . 'orders.php';
require_once BUSINESS_DIR . 'symmetric_crypt.php';
require_once BUSINESS_DIR . 'secure_card.php';
require_once BUSINESS_DIR . 'customer.php';
```

9. Load the web site to make sure our newly added code works as shown in Figures 17-1, 17-2, and 17-3.

How It Works: Presentation Tier Changes

This was a long exercise, and yet, to get the most out of it, we still need to go through a few more exercises to implement tax and shipping charges. At that moment, our entire customer handling functionality will be completed, and we'll be left with adding only an order pipeline and credit card processing support. Let's now proceed to adding support for tax and shipping charges.

Handling Tax and Shipping Charges

One feature that is common to many e-commerce web sites is the need to add charges for tax and shipping. Obviously, this isn't always the case—digital download sites have no need to charge for shipping, for example, because no physical shipment is involved. However, we'll probably want to include additional charges of one kind or another with our orders.

In fact, adding this functionality can be very simple—or not—depending on how complicated we want to make things. In this chapter, we'll keep things simple and provide basic but extensible functionality for assessing both tax and shipping charges. First, let's discuss the issues.

Tax Issues

The subject of tax and e-commerce web sites has a complicated history. Early on, online vendors could usually get away with just about anything. Taxing was poorly enforced, and many sites simply ignored tax completely. This was especially true for international orders, where it was often possible for customers to avoid paying tax much of the time—unless orders were intercepted by customs officers!

When more people started to become aware of e-commerce web sites, taxation bodies such as the IRS realized that they were losing a lot of money—or at least not getting all that they could—and that tends to upset them. A flurry of activity ensued as various organizations worldwide attempted to hook into this revenue stream. A range of solutions was proposed and implemented with mixed results. Now, things are becoming a little more settled.

The key concept to be aware of when thinking about tax is a nexus, that is, a business with a significant enough presence in a taxing jurisdiction to warrant tax collection. Effectively, this means that when shipping internationally, you may not, in most situations, not be responsible for what happens taxwise, unless your company has a significant presence in the destination country. When shipping internally within a country (or within, say, the European Union), you probably will be responsible. The legislation is a little unclear, and we certainly haven't examined the laws for every country in the world, but this general rule tends to hold true.

The other key issues can be summed up by the following:

- Taxation depends on where you are shipping from and to.

- National rules apply.

- The type of product you are selling is important.

Some countries have it easier than others. Within the United Kingdom, for example, we can charge the current value added tax (VAT) rate on all purchases where it applies (some types of product are exempt or charged at a reduced rate) and be relatively happy that we've done all we can. If we want to take things one step further, we can consider an offshore business to ship our goods (Amazon does it, so why shouldn't we?). The United States (and other countries) has a much more complex system to deal with. Within the United States, sales taxes vary not just from state to state but often within states as well. In fact, pretty much the only time most vendors know exactly what to do is when shipping goods to a customer in the same tax area as their business. At other times, well, to be perfectly honest, your guess is as good as ours.

In this book, the taxation scheme we add is as simple as possible. A database table will include information concerning various tax rates that can be applied, and the choice of these will, for now, depend on the shipping region of the customer. All products are considered to be taxable at the same rate. This does leave a lot to be desired, but at least tax will be calculated and applied. You can replace it with your own specific system later.

Shipping Issues

Shipping is somewhat simpler to deal with than tax, although, again, we can make things as complicated as we want. Because sending out orders from a company that trades via an e-commerce front end is much the same as sending out orders from, say, a mail-order company, the practices are very much in place and relatively easy to understand. There may be new ways of doing things at our disposal, but the general principles are well known.

You may have an existing relationship with a postal service from preonline trading times, in which case, it's probably easiest to keep things as close to the old way of doing things as possible. However, if you're just starting out or revising the way you do things, you have plenty of options to consider.

The simplest option is not to worry about shipping costs at all, which makes sense if there are no costs, for example, in the case of digital downloads. Alternatively, we could simply include the cost of shipping in the cost of our products. Or we could impose a flat fee regardless of the items ordered or the destination. However, some of these options could involve customers either overpaying or underpaying, which isn't ideal.

The other extreme involved is accounting for the weight and dimensions of all the products ordered and calculating the exact cost. This can be simplified slightly because some shipping companies (FedEx, among others) provide useful APIs to help us. In some cases, we can use a dynamic system to calculate the shipping options available (overnight, three to four days, and so on) based on a number of factors, including package weight and delivery location. The exact methods for doing this, however, can vary a great deal among shipping companies, and we'll leave it to you to implement such a solution if you require it.

In this book, we'll again take a simple line. For each shipping region in the database, we'll provide a number of shipping options for the user to choose from, each of which will have an associated cost. This cost is simply added to the cost of the order. This is the reason why, in Chapter 16, we included a `shipping_region` table—its use will soon become apparent.

Implementing Tax and Shipping Charges

As expected, we need to make several modifications to TShirtShop to enable the tax and shipping schemes outlined previously. We have two more database tables to add, `tax` and `shipping`, as well as modifications to make to the `orders` table. We'll need to add new database functions and make some modifications to existing ones. Some of the business tier classes need modifications to account for these changes, and the presentation tier must include a method for users to select a shipping method (the taxing scheme is selected automatically).

Ideally, we would clear the contents of the `orders` and `order_detail` tables or take into consideration the fact that the old orders don't include tax and shipping charges, for which the total amount will be calculated as $0.00.

So, let's get started.

Modifying the Data Tier

In this section, we'll add the new tables and modify the orders table and add or modify old database stored procedures.

Exercise: Creating the Database Structures

1. Load phpMyAdmin, select the tshirtshop database, and open a new SQL query page.

2. Execute this code, which adds the shipping table to the tshirtshop database:

```
-- Create shipping table
CREATE TABLE `shipping` (
    `shipping_id`        INT           NOT NULL AUTO_INCREMENT,
    `shipping_type`      VARCHAR(100)  NOT NULL,
    `shipping_cost`      NUMERIC(10, 2) NOT NULL,
    `shipping_region_id` INT           NOT NULL,
    PRIMARY KEY (`shipping_id`),
    KEY `idx_shipping_shipping_region_id` (`shipping_region_id`)
);
```

3. Execute the following code, which populates the shipping table from the tshirtshop database:

```
-- Populate shipping table
INSERT INTO `shipping` (`shipping_id`,  `shipping_type`,
                        `shipping_cost`, `shipping_region_id`) VALUES
        (1, 'Next Day Delivery ($20)', 20.00, 2),
        (2, '3-4 Days ($10)',          10.00, 2),
        (3, '7 Days ($5)',              5.00, 2),
        (4, 'By air (7 days, $25)',    25.00, 3),
        (5, 'By sea (28 days, $10)',   10.00, 3),
        (6, 'By air (10 days, $35)',   35.00, 4),
        (7, 'By sea (28 days, $30)',   30.00, 4);
```

4. Execute this code, which adds the tax table to the tshirtshop database:

```
-- Create tax table
CREATE TABLE `tax` (
    `tax_id`         INT           NOT NULL  AUTO_INCREMENT,
    `tax_type`       VARCHAR(100)  NOT NULL,
    `tax_percentage` NUMERIC(10, 2) NOT NULL,
    PRIMARY KEY (`tax_id`)
);
```

5. Execute the following code, which populates the tax table from the tshirtshop database:

```
-- Populate tax table
INSERT INTO `tax` (`tax_id`, `tax_type`, `tax_percentage`) VALUES
        (1, 'Sales Tax at 8.5%', 8.50),
        (2, 'No Tax',            0.00);
```

6. Execute this code, which adds the column `shipping_id` and a new index to the `orders` table from the tshirtshop database:

```
-- Adding a new field named shipping_id to orders table
ALTER TABLE `orders` ADD COLUMN `shipping_id` INT;
```

```
-- Adding a new index to orders table
CREATE INDEX `idx_orders_shipping_id` ON `orders` (`shipping_id`);
```

7. Execute the following code, which adds the column `tax_id` and a new index to the `orders` table from the tshirtshop database:

```
-- Adding a new field named tax_id to orders table
ALTER TABLE orders ADD COLUMN tax_id INT;
```

```
-- Adding a new index to orders table
CREATE INDEX `idx_orders_tax_id` ON `orders` (`tax_id`);
```

8. Delete the current `shopping_cart_create_order` stored procedure, and create a new one that takes into consideration the new changes made to the `orders` table (don't forget to set the delimiter to $$):

```
-- Drop shopping_cart_create_order stored procedure
DROP PROCEDURE shopping_cart_create_order$$
```

```
-- Create shopping_cart_create_order stored procedure
CREATE PROCEDURE shopping_cart_create_order(IN inCartId CHAR(32),
  IN inCustomerId INT, IN inShippingId INT, IN inTaxId INT)
BEGIN
  DECLARE orderId INT;

  -- Insert a new record into orders and obtain the new order ID
  INSERT INTO orders (created_on, customer_id, shipping_id, tax_id) VALUES
        (NOW(), inCustomerId, inShippingId, inTaxId);
  -- Obtain the new Order ID
  SELECT LAST_INSERT_ID() INTO orderId;

  -- Insert order details in order_detail table
  INSERT INTO order_detail (order_id, product_id, attributes,
                            product_name, quantity, unit_cost)
  SELECT      orderId, p.product_id, sc.attributes, p.name, sc.quantity,
              COALESCE(NULLIF(p.discounted_price, 0), p.price) AS unit_cost
  FROM        shopping_cart sc
  INNER JOIN  product p
              ON sc.product_id = p.product_id
  WHERE       sc.cart_id = inCartId AND sc.buy_now;

  -- Save the order's total amount
  UPDATE orders
  SET    total_amount = (SELECT SUM(unit_cost * quantity)
                         FROM   order_detail
```

```
                            WHERE   order_id = orderId)
     WHERE   order_id = orderId;

     -- Clear the shopping cart
     CALL shopping_cart_empty(inCartId);

     -- Return the Order ID
     SELECT orderId;
   END$$
```

9. Modify the orders_get_order_info stored procedure by deleting the old version and creating a new one (don't forget to set the delimiter to $$):

```
-- Drop orders_get_order_info stored procedure
DROP PROCEDURE orders_get_order_info$$

-- Create orders_get_order_info stored procedure
CREATE PROCEDURE orders_get_order_info(IN inOrderId INT)
BEGIN
   SELECT     o.order_id, o.total_amount, o.created_on, o.shipped_on,
              o.status, o.comments, o.customer_id, o.auth_code,
              o.reference, o.shipping_id, s.shipping_type, s.shipping_cost,
              o.tax_id, t.tax_type, t.tax_percentage
   FROM       orders o
   INNER JOIN tax t
                 ON t.tax_id = o.tax_id
   INNER JOIN shipping s
                 ON s.shipping_id = o.shipping_id
   WHERE      o.order_id = inOrderId;
END$$
```

10. Execute this code, which adds the orders_get_shipping_info stored procedure to the tshirtshop database:

```
-- Create orders_get_shipping_info stored procedure
CREATE PROCEDURE orders_get_shipping_info(IN inShippingRegionId INT)
BEGIN
   SELECT shipping_id, shipping_type, shipping_cost, shipping_region_id
   FROM   shipping
   WHERE  shipping_region_id = inShippingRegionId;
END$$
```

Modifying the Business Tier

To work with the new database tables and stored procedures, we need to make several changes to business/shopping_cart.php. We must modify CreateOrder() in ShoppingCart to configure tax and shipping for new orders as well.

1. Modify the `CreateOrder()` method in `business/shopping_cart.php` as follows:

```php
// Create a new order
public static function CreateOrder($customerId, $shippingId, $taxId)
{
  // Build SQL query
  $sql = 'CALL shopping_cart_create_order(:cart_id, :customer_id,
                :shipping_id, :tax_id)';

  // Build the parameters array
  $params = array (':cart_id' => self::GetCartId(),
                   ':customer_id' => $customerId,
                   ':shipping_id' => $shippingId,
                   ':tax_id' => $taxId);

  // Execute the query and return the results
  return DatabaseHandler::GetOne($sql, $params);
}
```

2. Add the `GetShippingInfo()` method to the `Orders` class in `business/orders.php`:

```php
// Retrieves the shipping details for a given $shippingRegionId
public static function GetShippingInfo($shippingRegionId)
{
  // Build the SQL query
  $sql = 'CALL orders_get_shipping_info(:shipping_region_id)';

  // Build the parameters array
  $params = array (':shipping_region_id' => $shippingRegionId);

  // Execute the query and return the results
  return DatabaseHandler::GetAll($sql, $params);
}
```

Modifying the Presentation Tier

Finally, we come to the presentation layer. In fact, due to the changes we've made, the only changes to make here are to the checkout and the orders administration pages.

1. Modify `presentation/templates/checkout_info.tpl` as highlighted:

```
  Shipping region: {$obj->mShippingRegion}
</p>
{/if}
```

```
{if $obj->mNoCreditCard!= 'yes' && $obj->mNoShippingAddress != 'yes'}
<p>
  Shipping type:
  <select name="shipping">
  {section name=i loop=$obj->mShippingInfo}
    <option value="{$obj->mShippingInfo[i].shipping_id}">
      {$obj->mShippingInfo[i].shipping_type}
    </option>
  {/section}
  </select>
</p>
{/if}
<input type="submit" name="place_order" value="Place Order"
 {$obj->mOrderButtonVisible} /> |
<a href="{$obj->mLinkToCart}">Edit Shopping Cart</a> |
```

2. Add a new member to the `CheckoutInfo` class in `presentation/checkout_info.php` as follows:

```
public $mLinkToCart;
public $mLinkToContinueShopping;
public $mShippingInfo;
```

3. Modify the `init()` method in the `CheckoutInfo` class in `presentation/checkout_info.php`:

```
// If the Place Order button was clicked, save the order to database ...
if(isset ($_POST['place_order']))
{
  $this->mCustomerData = Customer::Get();
  $tax_id = '';

  switch ($this->mCustomerData['shipping_region_id'])
  {
    case 2:
      $tax_id = 1;

      break;
    default:
      $tax_id = 2;
  }

  // Create the order and get the order ID
  $order_id = ShoppingCart::CreateOrder(
                $this->mCustomerData['customer_id'],
                (int)$_POST['shipping'], $tax_id);

  // This will contain the PayPal link
  $redirect =
    PAYPAL_URL . '&item_name=TShirtShop Order ' .
    urlencode('#') . $order_id .
```

```
                '&item_number=' . $order_id .
                '&amount=' . $this->mTotalAmount .
                '&currency_code=' . PAYPAL_CURRENCY_CODE .
                '&return=' . PAYPAL_RETURN_URL .
                '&cancel_return=' . PAYPAL_CANCEL_RETURN_URL;
```

4. In the same method, add the following code:

```
        foreach ($shipping_regions as $item)
          if ($item['shipping_region_id'] ==
              $this->mCustomerData['shipping_region_id'])
            $this->mShippingRegion = $item['shipping_region'];

        if ($this->mNoCreditCard == 'no' && $this->mNoShippingAddress == 'no')
        {
          $this->mShippingInfo = Orders::GetShippingInfo(
                              $this->mCustomerData['shipping_region_id']);
        }
      }
    }
  }
}
?>
```

5. Update index.php by adding a reference to the orders business tier class, as shown here:

```
require_once BUSINESS_DIR . 'secure_card.php';
require_once BUSINESS_DIR . 'customer.php';
require_once BUSINESS_DIR . 'orders.php';
```

6. Continue modifying the AdminOrderDetails class from the presentation/
   admin_order_details.php file by adding two members:

```
public $mLinkToOrdersAdmin;
public $mCustomerInfo;
public $mTotalCost;
public $mTax = 0.0;
```

7. Add these lines to the AdminOrderDetails class in the init() method:

```
        $this->mOrderInfo = Orders::GetOrderInfo($this->mOrderId);
        $this->mOrderDetails = Orders::GetOrderDetails($this->mOrderId);
        $this->mCustomerInfo = Customer::Get($this->mOrderInfo['customer_id']);
        $this->mTotalCost = $this->mOrderInfo['total_amount'];

        if ($this->mOrderInfo['tax_percentage'] !== 0.0)
          $this->mTax = round((float)$this->mTotalCost *
                            (float)$this->mOrderInfo['tax_percentage'], 2)
                        / 100.00;

        $this->mTotalCost += $this->mOrderInfo['shipping_cost'];
        $this->mTotalCost += $this->mTax;
```

```
    // Format the values
    $this->mTotalCost = number_format($this->mTotalCost, 2, '.', '');
    $this->mTax = number_format($this->mTax, 2, '.', '');

    // Value which specifies whether to enable or disable edit mode
    if (isset ($_GET['submitEdit']))
      $this->mEditEnabled = true;
```

8. Modify the presentation/templates/admin_order_details.tpl template as highlighted:

```html
<input type="hidden" name="Page" value="OrderDetails" />
<input type="hidden" name="OrderId"
 value="{$obj->mOrderInfo.order_id}" />
<table class="borderless-table">
  <tr>
    <td class="bold-text">Total Amount: </td>
    <td class="price">
      ${$obj->mOrderInfo.total_amount}
    </td>
  </tr>
  <tr>
    <td class="bold-text">Tax: </td>
    <td class="price">{$obj->mOrderInfo.tax_type} ${$obj->mTax}</td>
  </tr>
  <tr>
    <td class="bold-text">Shipping: </td>
    <td class="price">{$obj->mOrderInfo.shipping_type}</td>
  </tr>
  <tr>
    <td class="bold-text">Date Created: </td>
    <td>
      {$obj->mOrderInfo.created_on|date_format:"%Y-%m-%d %T"}
    </td>
  </tr>
```

How It Works: Handling Tax and Shipping Issues

Note that this is one of the most crucial pieces of code in this chapter. This is the code where you'll most likely make any modifications to the tax and shipping systems if you decide to implement your own system. The database and business layer changes are far more general—although that's not to say such modifications wouldn't be necessary.

Before testing that the new system is working for tax and shipping charges, use the orders administration page to check that old orders are unaffected. The information retrieved for an old order should be unaffected, because the data is unchanged.

Place a new order, preferably for a customer in the United States/Canada shipping region (as this is currently the only region where tax is applied). Notice that, on the checkout page, you must select a shipping option.

After placing the order, check the new order in the database. The result should look like the page shown in Figure 17-3.

In this chapter, leading up to this example, we've pretty much examined how the tax and shipping charges operate, but let's recap. First, the customer is required to select a shipping region for his or her address. Without this shipping region being selected, visitors cannot place orders, because they cannot select a shipping option. When a visitor places an order, the shipping region selected is attached to the order in the orders table. The tax requirement for the order is also attached, although this requires no user input and is currently selected using a very simple algorithm.

Further Development

There are several ways to proceed from here. Perhaps the first might be to add an administration system for tax and shipping options. This hasn't been implemented here partly because it would be trivial given the experience you've had so far in this book and partly because the techniques laid out here are more of a template for development than a fully developed way of doing things—there are so many options to choose from for both tax and shipping calculations that only the basics are discussed here.

Hooking into online services for tax and shipping cost calculations is an attractive option; for shipping services, this is very much a possibility. In fact, the services offered by shipping companies such as FedEx use a process similar to the credit card gateway companies we'll look at later in this book. Much of the code you would have to write to access shipping services will be very similar to code for credit card processing, although, of course, you'll have to adapt it to get the specifics right. In your case, more major changes may be required, such as adding weights and dimensions to products, but that very much depends on what products you are selling.

Summary

In this chapter, we've extended the TShirtShop site to enable customers to place orders using all the new data and techniques introduced in Chapter 16. Much of the modification made in this chapter lays the groundwork for the order pipeline to be used in the rest of this book. We've also included a quick way to examine customer orders, although this is by no means a fully fleshed-out administration tool—that will come later.

We also implemented a simple system for adding tax and shipping charges to orders. This system is far from being a universal solution, but it works, and it's simple. More importantly, the techniques can easily be built on to introduce more complex algorithms and user interaction to select tax and shipping options and price orders accordingly.

From the next chapter onward, we'll be expanding on the customer ordering system even more by starting to develop a professional order pipeline for order processing.

■ ■ ■

Implementing the Order Pipeline: Part 1

Implementing the order pipeline is the first step we're making for creating a professional order management system. In this and the next chapter, we'll build our own order-processing pipeline that deals with credit card authorization, stock checking, shipping, e-mail notification, and so on. We'll leave the credit card–processing specifics for Chapter 20, but in this chapter, we'll show you where this process fits into the picture.

Order pipeline functionality is an extremely useful capability for an e-commerce site. Order pipeline functions let us keep track of orders at every stage in the process and provide auditing information that we can refer to later or if something goes wrong during the order processing. We can do all this without relying on a third-party accounting system, which can also reduce costs.

The bulk of this chapter deals with what a pipeline system is and constructing this system, which also involves a small amount of modification to the way things currently work and some additions to the database we've been using. However, the code in this chapter isn't much more complicated than the code we've already been using. The real challenges are in designing the system. After designing the order pipeline, the features you'll add to it in this chapter are

- Updating the status of an order

- Setting credit card authentication details

- Setting the order shipment date

- Sending e-mails to customers and suppliers

- Retrieving order details and the customer address

By the end of the next chapter, customers will be able to place orders into our pipeline, and we'll be able to follow the progress of these orders as they pass through various stages. Although no real credit card processing will take place yet, we'll end up with a fairly complete system, including a new administration web page that can be used by suppliers to confirm that they have items in stock and to confirm that orders have been shipped. To start with, however, we need a bit more background about what we're actually trying to achieve.

What Is an Order Pipeline?

Any commercial transaction, whether in a shop on the street, over the Internet, or anywhere else, has several related tasks that must be carried out before it can be considered complete. For example, we can't simply remove an item of clothing from a fashion boutique (without paying) and say that we've bought it—remuneration is an integral part of any purchase. In addition, a transaction completes successfully only if each of the tasks carried out completes successfully. If a customer's credit card is rejected, for example, then no funds can be charged to it, so a purchase can't be made.

The sequence of tasks in a transaction is often thought of in terms of a pipeline. In this analogy, orders start at one end of the pipe and come out of the other end when they are completed. Along the way, they must pass through several pipeline sections, each of which is responsible for a particular task or a related group of tasks. If any pipeline section fails to complete, then the order "gets "stuck" and might require outside interaction before it can move further along the pipeline, or it might be canceled completely.

For example, the simple pipeline shown in Figure 18-1 applies to transactions in a brick-and-mortar store.

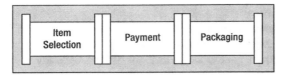

Figure 18-1. *Transactions for a brick-and-mortar store*

The last section, packaging, might be optional and might involve additional tasks such as gift wrapping. The payment stage might also take one of several methods of operation because the customer could pay using cash, credit card, gift certificates, and so on.

When we consider e-commerce purchasing, the pipeline becomes longer, but it isn't really any more complicated.

Designing the Order Pipeline

In the TShirtShop e-commerce application, the pipeline will look like the one in Figure 18-2.

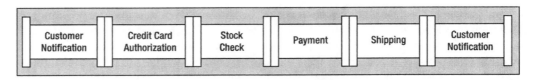

Figure 18-2. *TheTShirtShop order pipeline*

The tasks carried out in these pipeline sections are as follows:

Customer notification: An e-mail notification is sent to the customer stating that order processing has started and confirming the items to be sent and the address to which goods will be sent.

Credit card authorization: The credit card used for purchasing is checked, and the total order amount is set aside (although no payment is taken at this stage).

Stock check: An e-mail is sent to the supplier with a list of the items that have been ordered. Processing continues when the supplier confirms that the goods are available.

Payment: The credit card transaction is completed using the funds set aside earlier.

Shipping: An e-mail is sent to the supplier confirming that payment for the items ordered has been taken. Processing continues when the supplier confirms that the goods have been shipped.

Customer notification: An e-mail is sent notifying the customer that the order has been shipped and thanking the customer for using the TShirtShop web site.

■**Note** In terms of implementation, as you'll see shortly, there are more stages than this because the stock check and shipping stages actually consist of two pipeline sections—one that sends the e-mail and one that waits for confirmation.

As orders flow through this pipeline, entries are added to a new database table called `audit`. These entries can be examined to see what has happened to an order and are an excellent way to identify problems if they occur. Each entry in the `orders` table is also flagged with a status, identifying which point in the pipeline it has reached.

To process the pipeline, we'll create classes representing each stage. These classes carry out the required processing and then modify the status of the order in the `orders` table to advance the order. We'll also need a coordinating class (or processor), which can be called for any order and executes the appropriate pipeline stage class. This processor is called once when the order is placed and, in normal operation, is called twice more—once for stock confirmation and once for shipping confirmation.

To make life easier, we'll also define a common interface supported by each pipeline stage class. This enables the order processor class to access each stage in a standard way. We'll also define several utility functions and expose several common properties in the order processor class, which will be used as necessary by the pipeline stages. For example, the ID of the order should be accessible to all pipeline stages, so to save code duplication, we'll put that information in the order processor class.

Now, let's get on to the specifics. We'll build a number of files in the `business` folder containing all the new classes, which we'll reference from TShirtShop. The new files we'll create are the following:

OrderProcessor: Main class for processing orders.

IPipelineSection: Interface definition for pipeline sections.

PsInitialNotification, PsCheckFunds, PsCheckStock, PsStockOk, PsTakePayment, PsShipGoods, PsShipOk, PsFinalNotification: Pipeline section classes. We'll create these classes in Chapter 19; here we'll use a dummy (PsDummy) class instead.

The progress of an order through the pipeline as mediated by the order processor relates to the pipeline shown earlier (see Figure 18-3).

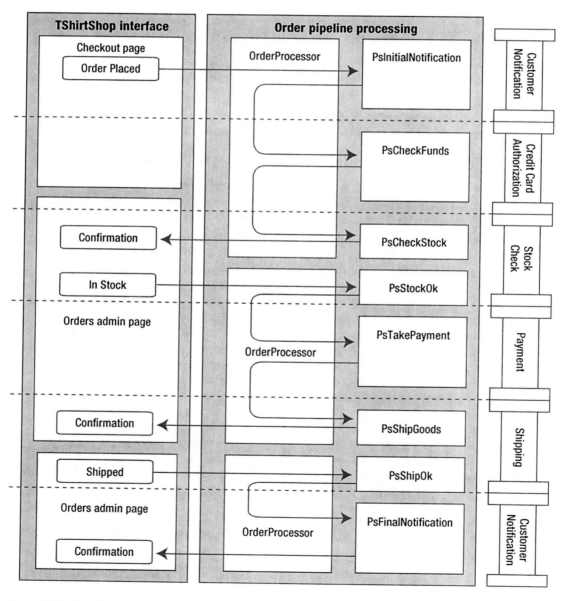

Figure 18-3. *Pipeline processing*

The process shown in this diagram is divided into three sections:

- The customer places order.
- The supplier confirms stock.
- The supplier confirms shipping.

The first stage is as follows:

1. When the customer confirms an order, presentation/checkout_info.php creates the order in the database and calls OrderProcessor to begin order processing.

2. OrderProcessor detects that the order is new and calls PsInitialNotification.

3. PsInitialNotification sends an e-mail to the customer confirming the order and advances the order stage. It also instructs OrderProcessor to continue processing.

4. OrderProcessor detects the new order status and calls PsCheckFunds.

5. PsCheckFunds checks that funds are available on the customer's credit card and stores the details required to complete the transaction if funds are available. If this is successful, then the order stage is advanced, and OrderProcessor is told to continue. Nothing is charged to the customer's credit card yet.

6. OrderProcessor detects the new order status and calls PsCheckStock.

7. PsCheckStock sends an e-mail to the supplier with a list of the items ordered, instructs the supplier to confirm via ORDERS ADMIN from the admin section, and advances the order status.

8. OrderProcessor terminates.

The second stage is as follows:

1. When the supplier logs in to the orders admin page to confirm that the stock is available, presentation/admin_order_details.php calls OrderProcessor to continue order processing.

2. If the supplier confirms that the stock is available, OrderProcessor detects the new order status and calls PsStockOk.

3. PsStockOk advances the order status and tells OrderProcessor to continue.

4. OrderProcessor detects the new order status and calls PsTakePayment.

5. PsTakePayment uses the transaction details stored earlier by PsCheckFunds to complete the transaction by charging the customer's credit card for the order and then advances the order status, telling OrderProcessor to continue.

6. OrderProcessor detects the new order status and calls PsShipGoods.

7. PsShipGoods sends an e-mail to the supplier with a confirmation of the items ordered, instructs the supplier to ship these goods to the customer, and advances the order status.

8. OrderProcessor terminates.

The third stage is as follows:

1. When the supplier confirms that the goods have been shipped, presentation/ admin_order_details.php calls OrderProcessor to continue order processing.

2. OrderProcessor detects the new order status and calls PsShipOk.

3. PsShipOk enters the shipment date in the database, advances the order status, and tells OrderProcessor to continue.

4. OrderProcessor detects the new order status and calls PsFinalNotification.

5. PsFinalNotification sends an e-mail to the customer confirming that the order has been shipped and advances the order stage.

6. OrderProcessor terminates.

If anything goes wrong at any point in the pipeline processing, such as a credit card being declined, an e-mail is sent to an administrator. The administrator then has all the information necessary to check what has happened, get in contact with the customer involved, and cancel or replace the order if necessary.

No point in this process is particularly complicated; it's just that a lot of code is required to put this into action!

Laying the Groundwork

Before we start building the components just described, we need to make a few modifications to the TShirtShop database and web application.

During order processing, one of the most important functions of the pipeline is to maintain an up-to-date audit trail. The implementation of this audit trail involves adding records to a new database table called audit. We'll add the audit table in the following exercise.

To implement the functionality just described, we'll also need to add a new function named orders_create_audit to the tshirtshop database. The orders_create_audit stored procedure adds an entry to the audit table.

We'll also create the OrderProcessor class (the class responsible for moving an order through the pipeline), which contains a lot of code. However, we can start simply and build up additional functionality as needed. To start with, we'll create a version of the OrderProcessor class with the following functionality:

- Dynamically selects a pipeline section supporting the IPipelineSection interface

- Adds basic auditing data

- Gives access to the current order details

- Gives access to the customer for the current order

- Gives access to the administrator mailing

- Mails the administrator in case of error

INTERFACES IN PHP

This is the first time in this book where we're working with interfaces. Interfaces represent a common feature in modern object-oriented languages. An interface represents a set of methods that a class must define when implementing the interface.

When a class implements an interface, it is required to implement all the methods defined by that interface. This way, the interface becomes a contract that guarantees the classes that implement it contain a certain set of methods. For example, in the exercise that follows we'll create an interface named IPipelineSection that contains a single method named Process():

```
interface IPipelineSection
{
  public function Process($processor);
}
```

We'll implement this interface in all the classes that represent pipeline sections (we'll write them in the next chapter), ensuring that each of these classes will include a method named Process(). This way, when working with order pipeline classes, we'll be able to safely call the Process() method on them because we'll be guaranteed this method will be there.

An interface cannot be instantiated like a normal class because it doesn't contain any method implementations, only their signatures. (A method signature is simply a method definition with no code.)

Classes implement interfaces using the implements operator. A class can implement multiple interfaces, but these interfaces must not contain the same method in order to avoid ambiguity.

You can learn more about the support for interfaces in PHP at http://php.net/interfaces.

We'll create a single pipeline section, PsDummy, which uses some of this functionality. PsDummy is used in the code of this chapter in place of the real pipeline section classes, which we'll implement in the next chapter.

Exercise: Implementing the Skeleton of the Order-Processing Functionality

1. Using phpMyAdmin, select the tshirtshop database, and open a new SQL query page.

2. Execute this code, which creates the audit table in the tshirtshop database:

```
-- Create audit table
CREATE TABLE `audit` (
  `audit_id`     INT      NOT NULL AUTO_INCREMENT,
  `order_id`     INT      NOT NULL,
  `created_on`   DATETIME NOT NULL,
  `message`      TEXT     NOT NULL,
  `code`         INT      NOT NULL,
  PRIMARY KEY (`audit_id`),
  KEY `idx_audit_order_id` (`order_id`)
);
```

3. Execute the following code, which creates the `orders_create_audit` stored procedure in the `tshirtshop` database (don't forget to set the delimiter to $$):

```
-- Create orders_create_audit stored procedure
CREATE PROCEDURE orders_create_audit(IN inOrderId INT,
  IN inMessage TEXT, IN inCode INT)
BEGIN
  INSERT INTO audit (order_id, created_on, message, code)
       VALUES (inOrderId, NOW(), inMessage, inCode);
END$$
```

4. Moving to the business tier, add the following method to the `Orders` class in `business/orders.php`:

```
// Creates audit record
public static function CreateAudit($orderId, $message, $code)
{
  // Build the SQL query
  $sql = 'CALL orders_create_audit(:order_id, :message, :code)';

  // Build the parameters array
  $params = array (':order_id' => $orderId,
                   ':message' => $message,
                   ':code' => $code);

  // Execute the query
  DatabaseHandler::Execute($sql, $params);
}
```

5. Add a new file to the `business` directory called `order_processor.php` with the following code:

```
<?php
/* Main class, used to obtain order information,
   run pipeline sections, audit orders, etc. */
class OrderProcessor
{
  public  $mOrderInfo;
  public  $mOrderDetailsInfo;
  public  $mCustomerInfo;
  public  $mContinueNow;

  private $_mCurrentPipelineSection;
  private $_mOrderProcessStage;

  // Class constructor
  public function __construct($orderId)
  {
    // Get order
    $this->mOrderInfo = Orders::GetOrderInfo($orderId);
```

```
  if (empty ($this->mOrderInfo['shipping_id']))
    $this->mOrderInfo['shipping_id'] = -1;

  if (empty ($this->mOrderInfo['tax_id']))
    $this->mOrderInfo['tax_id'] = -1;

  // Get order details
  $this->mOrderDetailsInfo = Orders::GetOrderDetails($orderId);

  // Get customer associated with the processed order
  $this->mCustomerInfo = Customer::Get($this->mOrderInfo['customer_id']);

  $credit_card = new SecureCard();
  $credit_card->LoadEncryptedDataAndDecrypt(
    $this->mCustomerInfo['credit_card']);

  $this->mCustomerInfo['credit_card'] = $credit_card;
}

/* Process is called from presentation/checkout_info.php and
   presentation/admin_orders.php to process an order */
public function Process()
{
  // Configure processor
  $this->mContinueNow = true;

  // Log start of execution
  $this->CreateAudit('Order Processor started.', 10000);

  // Process pipeline section
  try
  {
    while ($this->mContinueNow)
    {
      $this->mContinueNow = false;

      $this->_GetCurrentPipelineSection();
      $this->_mCurrentPipelineSection->Process($this);
    }
  }
  catch(Exception $e)
  {
    $this->MailAdmin('Order Processing error occurred.',
                     'Exception: "' . $e->getMessage() . '" on ' .
                     $e->getFile() . ' line ' . $e->getLine(),
                     $this->_mOrderProcessStage);
```

```php
    $this->CreateAudit('Order Processing error occurred.', 10002);

    throw new Exception('Error occurred, order aborted. ' .
                        'Details mailed to administrator.');
  }

  $this->CreateAudit('Order Processor finished.', 10001);
}

// Adds audit message
public function CreateAudit($message, $code)
{
  Orders::CreateAudit($this->mOrderInfo['order_id'], $message, $code);
}

// Builds e-mail message
public function MailAdmin($subject, $message, $sourceStage)
{
  $to = ADMIN_EMAIL;
  $headers = 'From: ' . ORDER_PROCESSOR_EMAIL . "\r\n";
  $body = 'Message: ' . $message . "\n" .
          'Source: ' . $sourceStage . "\n" .
          'Order ID: ' . $this->mOrderInfo['order_id'];

  $result = mail($to, $subject, $body, $headers);

  if ($result === false)
  {
    throw new Exception ('Failed sending this mail to administrator:' .
                         "\n" . $body);
  }
}

// Gets current pipeline section
private function _GetCurrentPipelineSection()
{
  $this->_mOrderProcessStage = 100;
  $this->_mCurrentPipelineSection = new PsDummy();
}
}
?>
```

6. Create the IPipelineSection interface in a new file named business/i_pipeline_section.php as follows:

```php
<?php
interface IPipelineSection
{
```

```php
    public function Process($processor);
}
?>
```

7. Add a new file in the `business` directory called `ps_dummy.php` with the following code. The `PsDummy` class is used in this chapter for testing purposes in place of the real pipeline sections that we'll implement in the next chapter.

```php
<?php
class PsDummy implements IPipelineSection
{
  public function Process($processor)
  {
    $processor->CreateAudit('PsDoNothing started.', 99999);

    $processor->CreateAudit('Customer: ' .
      $processor->mCustomerInfo['name'], 99999);

    $processor->CreateAudit('Order subtotal: ' .
      $processor->mOrderInfo['total_amount'], 99999);

    $processor->MailAdmin('Test.', 'Test mail from PsDummy.', 99999);

    $processor->CreateAudit('PsDoNothing finished', 99999);
  }
}
?>
```

8. Add the following code to `include/config.php`, customizing the data with your own e-mail addresses:

```php
// Constant definitions for order handling related messages
define('ADMIN_EMAIL', 'Admin@example.com');
define('CUSTOMER_SERVICE_EMAIL', 'CustomerService@example.com');
define('ORDER_PROCESSOR_EMAIL', 'OrderProcessor@example.com');
define('SUPPLIER_EMAIL', 'Supplier@example.com');
```

■**Note** The values of `ADMIN_EMAIL` and `SUPPLIER_EMAIL` will actually be used to send e-mails to. In other words, these must be real e-mail addresses that you can verify. You can leave `CUSTOMER_SERVICE_EMAIL` and `ORDER_PROCESSOR_EMAIL` as they are because they're used in the `FROM` field of the e-mails, and they don't need to be valid e-mail addresses.

9. Add the highlighted lines to `admin.php`:

```php
// Load Business Tier
...
require_once BUSINESS_DIR . 'customer.php';
```

```
require_once BUSINESS_DIR . 'i_pipeline_section.php';
require_once BUSINESS_DIR . 'ps_dummy.php';
require_once BUSINESS_DIR . 'order_processor.php';
```

10. Modify presentation/templates/admin_order_details.tpl by adding the highlighted line:

```
<input type="submit" name="submitCancel" value="Cancel"
 {if ! $obj->mEditEnabled} disabled="disabled" {/if} />
<input type="submit" name="submitProcessOrder" value="Process Order" />
</p>
<h3>Order contains these products:</h3>
```

11. Modify presentation/admin_order_details.php as highlighted here:

```
// Initializes class members
public function init()
{
  if (isset ($_GET['submitUpdate']))
  {
    Orders::UpdateOrder($this->mOrderId, $_GET['status'],
      $_GET['comments'], $_GET['authCode'], $_GET['reference']);
  }

  if (isset ($_GET['submitProcessOrder']))
  {
    $processor = new OrderProcessor($this->mOrderId);
    $processor->Process();
  }

  $this->mOrderInfo = Orders::GetOrderInfo($this->mOrderId);
  $this->mOrderDetails = Orders::GetOrderDetails($this->mOrderId);
```

12. Load the orders administration page in your browser, and select an order to view its details. In the order details page, click the Process Order button (see Figure 18-4).

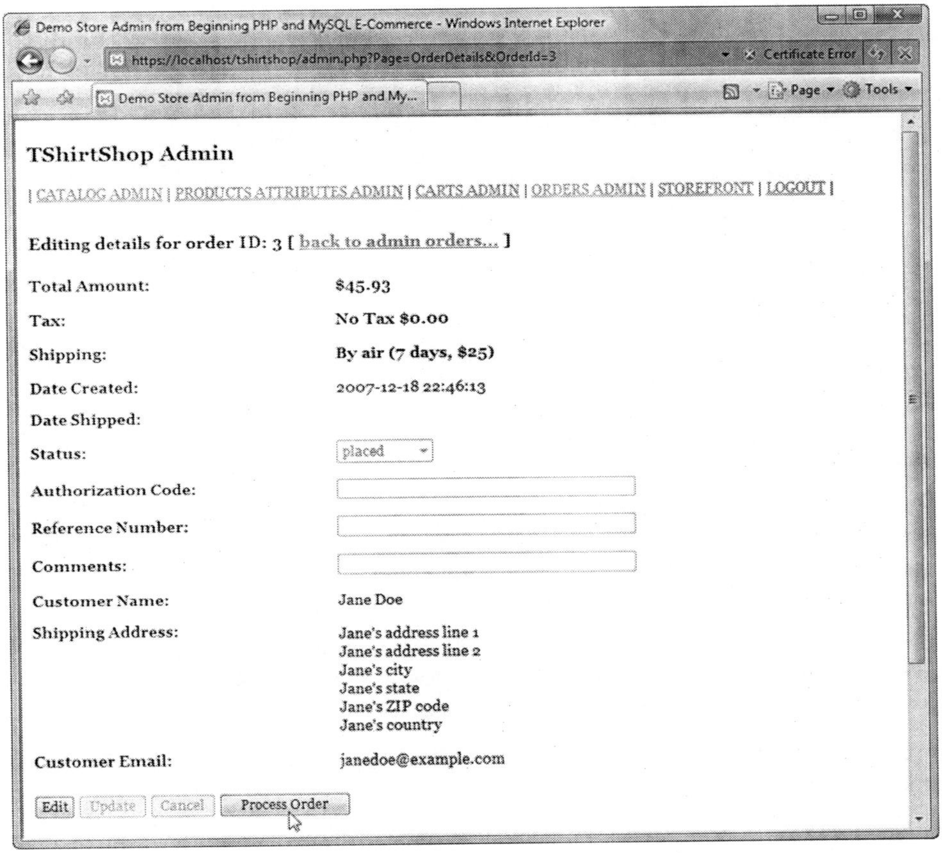

Figure 18-4. *Clicking the Process Order button in the TShirtShop order details page*

■**Note** If you want to be able to send an error e-mail to a localhost mail account (your_name@locahost), then you should have a Simple Mail Transfer Protocol (SMTP) server started on your machine.

On a Red Hat (or Fedora) Linux distribution, you can start an SMTP server with the following command:

```
service sendmail start
```

■**Note** On Windows systems, you should check in Internet Information Services (IIS) Manager for Default SMTP Virtual Server and make sure it's started.

13. Check your inbox for a new e-mail that should read "Test mail from PsDummy."

14. Examine the audit table in the database to see the new entries (see Figure 18-5).

←T→	audit_id ▲	order_id	created_on	message	code
☐ ✎ ✕	15	3	2007-12-18 22:47:41	Order Processor started.	10000
☐ ✎ ✕	16	3	2007-12-18 22:47:41	PsDoNothing started.	99999
☐ ✎ ✕	17	3	2007-12-18 22:47:41	Customer: Jane Doe	99999
☐ ✎ ✕	18	3	2007-12-18 22:47:41	Order subtotal: 45.93	99999
☐ ✎ ✕	19	3	2007-12-18 22:47:41	PsDoNothing finished	99999
☐ ✎ ✕	20	3	2007-12-18 22:47:41	Order Processor finished.	10001

Figure 18-5. audit *table entries from PsDummy*

How It Works: The Skeleton of the Order-Processing Functionality

Entries will be added by OrderProcessor and by individual pipeline stages to indicate successes and failures. These entries can then be examined to see what has happened to an order, which is an important function when it comes to error checking.

The code column is interesting because it allows us to associate specific messages with an identifying number. We can have another database table that matched these code numbers with descriptions, although this isn't really necessary because the scheme used for numbering (as you'll see later in the chapter) is quite descriptive. In addition, we have the message column, which already provides human-readable information.

For demonstration purposes, we set the administrator and supplier e-mail addresses to fictitious e-mail addresses, which should also be the address of the customer used to generate test orders. We should do this to ensure everything is working properly before sending mail to the outside world.

Let's now look at the OrderProcessor class. The main body of the OrderProcessor class is the Process() method, which is now called from presentation/admin_order_details.php to process an order:

```
public function Process()
{
  // Configure processor
  $this->mContinueNow = true;
```

Next we used the CreateAudit() method to add an audit entry indicating that the OrderProcessor has started:

```
// Log start of execution
$this->CreateAudit('Order Processor started.', 10000);
```

■**Note** 10000 is the code to store for the audit entry. We'll look at these codes in more detail shortly.

Next we come to the order processing itself. The model used here is to check the Boolean $mContinueNow field before processing a pipeline section. This allows sections to specify either that processing should continue when they're finished with the current task (by setting $mContinueNow to true) or that processing should pause (by setting $mContinueNow to false). This is necessary because we need to wait for external input at certain points along the pipeline when checking whether the products are in stock and whether the funds are available on the customer's credit card.

The pipeline section to process is selected by the private _GetCurrentPipelineSection() method, which eventually returns a pipeline section class (we'll build these classes in the next chapter) corresponding to the current status of the order. However, at this moment, _GetCurrentPipelineSection() has the job of setting the process stage and returning an instance of PsDummy. In the next chapter, we'll implement classes representing each pipeline section, and we'll return one of those classes instead of PsDummy.

```
// Gets current pipeline section
private function _GetCurrentPipelineSection()
{
  $this->_mOrderProcessStage = 100;
  $this->_mCurrentPipelineSection = new PsDummy();
}
```

Back to Process(), we see this method being called in a try block:

```
// Process pipeline section
try
{
  while ($this->mContinueNow)
  {
    $this->mContinueNow = false;

    $this->_GetCurrentPipelineSection();
    $this->_mCurrentPipelineSection->Process($this);
  }
}
```

Note that $mContinueNow is set to false in the while loop—the default behavior is to stop after each pipeline section. However, the call to the Process() method of the current pipeline section class (which receives a parameter of the current OrderProcessor instance, thus having access to the $mContinueNow member) changes the value of $mContinueNow back to true, in case processing should go to the next pipeline section without waiting for user interaction.

Note that in the previous code snippet, the Process() method is called without knowing what kind of object $this->_mCurrentPipelineSection references. Each pipeline section is represented by a different class, but all these classes need to expose a method named Process(). When such behavior is needed, the standard technique is to create an interface that defines the common behavior we need in that set of classes.

All order pipeline section classes support the simple IPipelineSection interface, defined as follows:

```
<?php
interface IPipelineSection
{
  public function Process($processor);
}
?>
```

All pipeline sections use a Process() method to perform their work. This method requires an OrderProcessor reference as a parameter because the pipeline sections need access to the public fields and methods exposed by the OrderProcessor class.

The last part of the Process() method in OrderProcessor involves catching exceptions. Here, we catch any exceptions that may be thrown by the order pipeline section classes and react to them by sending an e-mail to the administrator using the MailAdmin() method, adding an audit entry, and throwing a new exception that can be caught by PHP pages that use the OrderProcessor class:

```
catch(Exception $e)
{
  $this->MailAdmin('Order Processing error occurred.',
                   'Exception: "' . $e->getMessage() . '" on ' .
                   $e->getFile() . ' line ' . $e->getLine(),
                   $this->_mOrderProcessStage);

  $this->CreateAudit('Order Processing error occurred.', 10002);

  throw new Exception('Error occurred, order aborted. ' .
                      'Details mailed to administrator.');
}
```

Regardless of whether processing is successful, we add a final audit entry saying that the processing has completed:

```
  $this->CreateAudit('Order Processor finished.', 10001);
}
```

Let's now look at the MailAdmin() method that simply takes a few parameters for the basic e-mail properties:

```
// Builds e-mail message
public function MailAdmin($subject, $message, $sourceStage)
{
  $to = ADMIN_EMAIL;
  $headers = 'From: ' . ORDER_PROCESSOR_EMAIL . "\r\n";
  $body = 'Message: ' . $message . "\n" .
          'Source: ' . $sourceStage . "\n" .
          'Order ID: ' . $this->mOrderInfo['order_id'];

  $result = mail($to, $subject, $body, $headers);

  if ($result === false)
  {
    throw new Exception ('Failed sending this mail to administrator:' .
                         "\n" . $body);
  }
}
```

The CreateAudit() method is also a simple one and calls the Orders::CreateAudit() business tier method shown earlier:

```
// Adds audit message
public function CreateAudit($message, $code)
```

```
  {
    Orders::CreateAudit($this->mOrderInfo['order_id'], $message, $code);
  }
```

At this point, it's worth examining the code scheme we've chosen for order-processing audits. In all cases, the audit code will be a five-digit number. The first digit of this number is either 1 if an audit is being added by OrderProcessor or 2 if the audit is added by a pipeline section. The next two digits are used for the pipeline stage that added the audit (which maps directly to the status of the order when the audit was added). The final two digits uniquely identify the message within this scope. For example, so far we've seen the following codes:

- 10000: Order processor started
- 10001: Order processor finished
- 10002: Order processor error occurred

Later, we'll see a lot of these codes that start with 2, as we get on to the pipeline sections and include the necessary information for identifying the pipeline section as noted previously. We hope you'll agree that this scheme allows for plenty of flexibility, although we can, of course, use whatever codes we see fit. As a final note, codes ending in 00 and 01 are used for starting and finishing messages for both the order processor and pipeline stages, whereas 02 and above are for other messages. There is no real reason for this apart from consistency between the components.

The PsDummy class that is used in this skeleton processor performs some basic functions to check that things are working correctly:

```php
<?php
class PsDummy implements IPipelineSection
{
  public function Process($processor)
  {
    $processor->CreateAudit('PsDoNothing started.', 99999);

    $processor->CreateAudit('Customer: ' .
      $processor->mCustomerInfo['name'], 99999);

    $processor->CreateAudit('Order subtotal: ' .
      $processor->mOrderInfo['total_amount'], 99999);

    $processor->MailAdmin('Test.', 'Test mail from PsDummy.', 99999);

    $processor->CreateAudit('PsDoNothing finished', 99999);
  }
}
?>
```

The code here uses the CreateAudit() and MailAdmin() methods of OrderProcessor to generate something to show that the code has executed correctly. Note that the code schemes outlined previously aren't used there because this isn't a real pipeline section!

That was a lot of code to get through, but it did make the client code very simple.

Short of setting all the configuration details, there is very little to do because `OrderProcessor` does a lot of the work for you. Note that the code we have ended up with is, for the most part, a consequence of the design choices made earlier. This is an excellent example of how a strong design can lead you straight to powerful and robust code.

Updating the Orders Processing Code

We need to add a few more bits and pieces to the `OrderProcessor` class, and we will do so by going through a number of short exercises. These exercises implement the features that were listed in the beginning of the chapter:

- Updating the status of an order

- Setting credit card authentication details

- Setting the order shipment date

- Sending e-mails to customers and suppliers

- Retrieving order details and the customer address

We'll start by writing the code that permits updating the status of an order. Each pipeline section needs the capability to change the status of an order, advancing it to the next pipeline section. Rather than simply incrementing the status, this functionality is kept flexible, just in case we end up with a more complicated branched pipeline. This requires a new stored procedure in the database, named `orders_update_status`, and a business tier method, `UpdateOrderStatus()`, which we need to add to the `Orders` class (located in `business/orders.php`).

Exercise: Updating the Status of an Order

1. Start by creating the `orders_update_status` stored procedure in the `tshirtshop` database:

```
-- Create orders_update_status stored procedure
CREATE PROCEDURE orders_update_status(IN inOrderId INT, IN inStatus INT)
BEGIN
  UPDATE orders SET status = inStatus WHERE order_id = inOrderId;
END$$
```

2. Add the `UpdateOrderStatus()` method to the `Orders` class in `business/orders.php`:

```
// Updates the order pipeline status of an order
public static function UpdateOrderStatus($orderId, $status)
{
  // Build the SQL query
  $sql = 'CALL orders_update_status(:order_id, :status)';

  // Build the parameters array
  $params = array (':order_id' => $orderId, ':status' => $status);
```

```
    // Execute the query
    DatabaseHandler::Execute($sql, $params);
}
```

3. The method in OrderProcessor (in business/order_processor.php) that calls this business tier method is also called UpdateOrderStatus(). Add this method to order_processor.php:

```
// Set order status
public function UpdateOrderStatus($status)
{
  Orders::UpdateOrderStatus($this->mOrderInfo['order_id'], $status);
  $this->mOrderInfo['status'] = $status;
}
```

Exercise: Setting Credit Card Authentication Details

1. First add the orders_set_auth_code stored procedure to the database:

```
-- Create orders_set_auth_code stored procedure
CREATE PROCEDURE orders_set_auth_code(IN inOrderId INT,
  IN inAuthCode VARCHAR(50), IN inReference VARCHAR(50))
BEGIN
  UPDATE orders
  SET    auth_code = inAuthCode, reference = inReference
  WHERE  order_id = inOrderId;
END$$
```

2. Add the SetOrderAuthCodeAndReference() method to the Orders class in business/orders.php:

```
// Sets order's authorization code
public static function SetOrderAuthCodeAndReference ($orderId, $authCode,
                                                     $reference)
{
  // Build the SQL query
  $sql = 'CALL orders_set_auth_code(:order_id, :auth_code, :reference)';

  // Build the parameters array
  $params = array (':order_id' => $orderId,
                   ':auth_code' => $authCode,
                   ':reference' => $reference);

  // Execute the query
  DatabaseHandler::Execute($sql, $params);
}
```

3. The code to set these values in the database is the SetOrderAuthCodeAndReference() method, which we need to add to the OrderProcessor class in business/order_processor.php:

```
// Set order's authorization code and reference code
public function SetAuthCodeAndReference($authCode, $reference)
{
  Orders::SetOrderAuthCodeAndReference($this->mOrderInfo['order_id'],
                                       $authCode, $reference);

  $this->mOrderInfo['auth_code'] = $authCode;
  $this->mOrderInfo['reference'] = $reference;
}
```

This code also sets the corresponding elements from the $mOrderInfo array, just in case they are required before the OrderProcessor terminates. In this situation, it wouldn't make much sense to get these values from the database when we already know what the result will be.

In the next chapter, when we deal with credit card usage, we'll need to set data in the auth_code and reference fields in the orders table.

Exercise: Setting the Order Shipment Date

1. When an order is shipped, we should update the shipment date in the database, which can simply be the current date. Add the orders_set_date_shipped stored procedure to the tshirtshop database:

```
-- Create orders_set_date_shipped stored procedure
CREATE PROCEDURE orders_set_date_shipped(IN inOrderId INT)
BEGIN
  UPDATE orders SET shipped_on = NOW() WHERE order_id = inOrderId;
END$$
```

2. Add the new data tier method, SetDateShipped(), to the Orders class in business/orders.php as follows:

```
// Set order's ship date
public static function SetDateShipped($orderId)
{
  // Build the SQL query
  $sql = 'CALL orders_set_date_shipped(:order_id)';

  // Build the parameters array
  $params = array (':order_id' => $orderId);

  // Execute the query
  DatabaseHandler::Execute($sql, $params);
}
```

3. Add the following method to the OrderProcessor class in business/order_processor.php:

```
// Set order's ship date
public function SetDateShipped()
{
  Orders::SetDateShipped($this->mOrderInfo['order_id']);

  $this->mOrderInfo['shipped_on'] = date('Y-m-d');
}
```

Exercise: Sending E-mails to Customers and Suppliers

1. We need two methods to handle sending e-mails to customers and suppliers. Add the MailCustomer()
   method to the OrderProcessor class:

```
// Send e-mail to the customer
public function MailCustomer($subject, $body)
{
  $to = $this->mCustomerInfo['email'];
  $headers = 'From: ' . CUSTOMER_SERVICE_EMAIL . "\r\n";
  $result = mail($to, $subject, $body, $headers);

  if ($result === false)
  {
    throw new Exception ('Unable to send e-mail to customer.');
  }
}
```

2. Add the MailSupplier() method to the OrderProcessor class:

```
// Send e-mail to the supplier
public function MailSupplier($subject, $body)
{
  $to = SUPPLIER_EMAIL;
  $headers = 'From: ' . ORDER_PROCESSOR_EMAIL . "\r\n";
  $result = mail($to, $subject, $body, $headers);

  if ($result === false)
  {
    throw new Exception ('Unable to send e-mail to supplier.');
  }
}
```

Exercise: Retrieving Order Details and the Customer Address

1. We'll need to retrieve a string representation of the order and the customer address. For these tasks, add the `GetCustomerAddressAsString()` method to the `OrderProcessor` class, located in `business/order_processor.php`:

```php
// Returns a string that contains the customer's address
public function GetCustomerAddressAsString()
{
  $new_line = "\n";

  $address_details = $this->mCustomerInfo['name'] . $new_line .
                     $this->mCustomerInfo['address_1'] . $new_line;

  if (!empty ($this->mOrderInfo['address_2']))
    $address_details .= $this->mCustomerInfo['address_2'] . $new_line;

  $address_details .= $this->mCustomerInfo['city'] . $new_line .
                      $this->mCustomerInfo['region'] . $new_line .
                      $this->mCustomerInfo['postal_code'] . $new_line .
                      $this->mCustomerInfo['country'];

  return $address_details;
}
```

2. Add `GetOrderAsString()` to the `OrderProcessor` class:

```php
// Returns a string that contains the order details
public function GetOrderAsString($withCustomerDetails = true)
{
  $total_cost = 0.00;
  $order_details = '';
  $new_line = "\n";

  if ($withCustomerDetails)
  {
    $order_details = 'Customer address:' . $new_line .
                     $this->GetCustomerAddressAsString() .
                     $new_line . $new_line;

    $order_details .= 'Customer credit card:' . $new_line .
                      $this->mCustomerInfo['credit_card']->CardNumberX .
                      $new_line . $new_line;
  }
```

```
    foreach ($this->mOrderDetailsInfo as $order_detail)
    {
      $order_details .= $order_detail['quantity'] . ' ' .
                        $order_detail['product_name'] . '(' .
                        $order_detail['attributes'] . ') $' .
                        $order_detail['unit_cost'] . ' each, total cost $' .
                        number_format($order_detail['subtotal'],
                                      2, '.', '') . $new_line;
      $total_cost += $order_detail['subtotal'];
    }

    // Add shipping cost
    if ($this->mOrderInfo['shipping_id'] != -1)
    {
      $order_details .= 'Shipping: ' . $this->mOrderInfo['shipping_type'] .
                        $new_line;

      $total_cost += $this->mOrderInfo['shipping_cost'];
    }

    // Add tax
    if ($this->mOrderInfo['tax_id'] != -1 &&
        $this->mOrderInfo['tax_percentage'] != 0.00)
    {
      $tax_amount = round((float)$total_cost *
                          (float)$this->mOrderInfo['tax_percentage'], 2)
                          / 100.00;

      $order_details .= 'Tax: ' . $this->mOrderInfo['tax_type'] . ', $' .
                        number_format($tax_amount, 2, '.', '') .
                        $new_line;

      $total_cost += $tax_amount;
    }

    $order_details .= $new_line . 'Total order cost: $' .
                      number_format($total_cost, 2, '.', '');

    return $order_details;
  }
```

How It Works: Order Processor Modifications

You've made several changes to your Orders and OrderProcessor classes, and you've created quite a few
database stored procedures. This is all infrastructure code that supports implementing the order pipeline, which is
a must for a professional e-commerce site.

Summary

We've begun to build the backbone of the application, and we've prepared it for the lion's share of the order pipeline–processing functionality that we'll implement in the next chapter.

Specifically, we've covered the following:

- Modifications to the TShirtShop application to enable our own pipeline processing

- The basic framework for our order pipeline

- The database additions for auditing data and storing additional required data in the orders table

In the next chapter, we'll go on to fully implement the order pipeline.

■ ■ ■

Implementing the Order Pipeline: Part 2

In the previous chapter, we completed the basic functionality of the `OrderProcessor` class, which is responsible for moving orders through the pipeline stages. You saw a quick demonstration of this using a dummy pipeline section, but we haven't yet implemented the pipeline discussed at the beginning of the previous chapter.

In this chapter, we'll add the required pipeline sections so that we can process orders from start to finish, although we won't be adding full credit card transaction functionality until the next chapter.

We'll also look at the web administration of orders by modifying the order administration pages added earlier in the book to take into account the new order-processing system.

Implementing the Pipeline Sections

In the previous chapter, we completed the `OrderProcessor` class, except for one important section—the pipeline stage selection. Rather than forcing the processor to use `PsDummy` (the class we used instead of the real pipeline section classes that we'll build in this chapter), we want to actually select one of the pipeline stages, outlined in Chapter 18, depending on the status of the order.

Let's run through the code for each of the pipeline sections in turn, which will take us to the point where the order pipeline will be complete, apart from actual credit card authorization that we'll implement in Chapter 20. We'll implement eight new classes with the following names:

- `PsInitialNotification`
- `PsCheckFunds`
- `PsCheckStock`
- `PsStockOk`
- `PsTakePayment`
- `PsShipGoods`
- `PsShipOk`
- `PsFinalNotification`

We'll discuss the classes we're creating as we go; we will not be using our typical Exercise format for creating the order pipeline classes in the following pages. Before moving on, remember that this code is available in the source code download section of the Apress web site (http://www.apress.com).

PsInitialNotification

This is the first pipeline stage, which is responsible for sending an e-mail to the customer confirming that the order has been placed. Create a new file named ps_initial_notification.php in the business folder, and start adding code to it as shown here. This class starts off in what will soon become a very familiar fashion:

```php
<?php
class PsInitialNotification implements IPipelineSection
{
  private $_mProcessor;

  public function Process($processor)
  {
    // Set processor reference
    $this->_mProcessor = $processor;

    // Audit
    $processor->CreateAudit('PsInitialNotification started.', 20000);
```

The class implements the IPipelineSection interface, then a private field for storing a reference to the OrderProcessor that invoked the PsInitialNotification, and finally the Process() method implementation. This method starts by storing the reference to OrderProcessor, which some of your pipeline sections will do because using the methods it exposes (either in the Process() method or in other methods) is essential. We also add an audit entry using the codes scheme introduced in Chapter 18 (the initial 2 indicates it's coming from a pipeline section; the next 00 shows that it's the first pipeline section; and the final 00 means that it's the start message for the pipeline section).

The remainder of the Process() method sends the notification e-mail. This requires information from the customer, which we have easy access to. We also use a private method to build a message body, which we'll look at shortly:

```php
    // Send mail to customer
    $processor->MailCustomer(STORE_NAME . ' order received.',
                             $this->GetMailBody());
```

The mail is sent; we add an audit message, change the status of the order, and tell the order processor that it's OK to move straight on to the next pipeline section:

```php
    // Audit
    $processor->CreateAudit('Notification e-mail sent to customer.', 20002);

    // Update order status
    $processor->UpdateOrderStatus(1);
```

```
// Continue processing
$processor->mContinueNow = true;
```

If all goes according to plan, the Process() method finishes by adding a final audit entry:

```
// Audit
$processor->CreateAudit('PsInitialNotification finished.', 20001);
}
```

The GetMailBody() method is used to build a message body to send to the customer. The text uses customer and order data but follows a generally accepted e-commerce e-mail format. Continue by adding this method to the PsInitialNotification class:

```
private function GetMailBody()
{
    $body = 'Thank you for your order! ' .
            'The products you have ordered are as follows:';
    $body.= "\n\n";

    $body.= $this->_mProcessor->GetOrderAsString(false);
    $body.= "\n\n";

    $body.= 'Your order will be shipped to:';
    $body.= "\n\n";

    $body.= $this->_mProcessor->GetCustomerAddressAsString();
    $body.= "\n\n";

    $body.= 'Order reference number: ';
    $body.= $this->_mProcessor->mOrderInfo['order_id'];
    $body.= "\n\n";

    $body.= 'You will receive a confirmation e-mail when this order ' .
            'has been dispatched. Thank you for shopping at ' .
            STORE_NAME . '!';

    return $body;
    }
}
?>
```

When this pipeline stage finishes, processing moves straight on to PsCheckFunds.

PsCheckFunds

This pipeline stage is responsible for making sure that the customer has the required funds available on a credit card. For now, we'll provide a dummy implementation of this and just assume that these funds are available. We'll implement the real functionality in the next chapter, which deals with credit card transactions.

Add the following code to a new file in the business folder named ps_check_funds.php. The code of the Process() method starts almost in the same way as PsInitialNotification:

```php
<?php
class PsCheckFunds implements IPipelineSection
{
  public function Process($processor)
  {
    // Audit
    $processor->CreateAudit('PsCheckFunds started.', 20100);
```

Even though we aren't actually performing a check, set the authorization and reference codes for the transaction to make sure that the code in OrderProcessor works properly:

```php
    /* Check customer funds assume they exist for now
       set order authorization code and reference */
    $processor->SetAuthCodeAndReference('DummyAuthCode',
                                        'DummyReference');
```

We finish up with some auditing and the code required for continuation:

```php
    // Audit
    $processor->CreateAudit('Funds available for purchase.', 20102);

    // Update order status
    $processor->UpdateOrderStatus(2);

    // Continue processing
    $processor->mContinueNow = true;

    // Audit
    $processor->CreateAudit('PsCheckFunds finished.', 20101);
  }
}
?>
```

When this pipeline stage finishes, processing moves on to PsCheckStock.

PsCheckStock

This pipeline stage sends an e-mail instructing the supplier to check stock availability. Add the following code to a new file in the business folder named ps_check_stock.php:

```php
<?php
class PsCheckStock implements IPipelineSection
{
  private $_mProcessor;

  public function Process($processor)
  {
```

```
    // Set processor reference
    $this->_mProcessor = $processor;

    // Audit
    $processor->CreateAudit('PsCheckStock started.', 20200);
```

Mail is sent in a similar way to PsInitialNotification, using a private method to build the body:

```
    // Send mail to supplier
    $processor->MailSupplier(STORE_NAME . ' stock check.',
                             $this->GetMailBody());
```

As before, we finish by auditing and updating the status, although this time, we don't tell the order processor to continue straight away:

```
    // Audit
    $processor->CreateAudit('Notification email sent to supplier.', 20202);

    // Update order status
    $processor->UpdateOrderStatus(3);

    // Audit
    $processor->CreateAudit('PsCheckStock finished.', 20201);
  }
```

The code for building the message body is simple; it just lists the items in the order and tells the supplier to confirm via the TShirtShop web site (using the order administration page, which we'll modify later):

```
  private function GetMailBody()
  {
    $body = 'The following goods have been ordered:';
    $body .= "\n\n";

    $body .= $this->_mProcessor->GetOrderAsString(false);
    $body .= "\n\n";

    $body .= 'Please check availability and confirm via ' .
             Link::ToAdmin();
    $body .= "\n\n";

    $body .= 'Order reference number: ';
    $body .= $this->_mProcessor->mOrderInfo['order_id'];

    return $body;
  }
}
?>
```

When this pipeline stage finishes, processing pauses. Later, when the supplier confirms that stock is available, processing moves on to PsStockOk.

PsStockOk

This pipeline section just confirms that the supplier has the product in stock and moves on. Its Process() method is called for orders whose stock was confirmed and that need to move on to the next pipeline section. Add the following code to a new file in the business folder named ps_stock_ok.php:

```php
<?php
class PsStockOk implements IPipelineSection
{
  public function Process($processor)
  {
    // Audit
    $processor->CreateAudit('PsStockOk started.', 20300);

    /* The method is called when the supplier confirms that stock is
       available, so we don't have to do anything here except audit */
    $processor->CreateAudit('Stock confirmed by supplier.', 20302);

    // Update order status
    $processor->UpdateOrderStatus(4);

    // Continue processing
    $processor->mContinueNow = true;

    // Audit
    $processor->CreateAudit('PsStockOk finished.', 20301);
  }
}
?>
```

When this pipeline stage finishes, processing moves straight on to PsTakePayment.

PsTakePayment

This pipeline section completes the transaction started by PsCheckFunds. As with that section, we only provide a dummy implementation here. Add the following code to a new file in the business folder named ps_take_payment.php:

```php
<?php
class PsTakePayment implements IPipelineSection
{
  public function Process($processor)
  {
    // Audit
    $processor->CreateAudit('PsTakePayment started.', 20400);
```

```
      // Take customer funds assume success for now

      // Audit
      $processor->CreateAudit('Funds deducted from customer credit card account.',
                              20402);

      // Update order status
      $processor->UpdateOrderStatus(5);

      // Continue processing
      $processor->mContinueNow = true;

      // Audit
      $processor->CreateAudit('PsTakePayment finished.', 20401);
   }
}
?>
```

When this pipeline stage finishes, processing moves straight on to PsShipGoods.

PsShipGoods

This pipeline section is remarkably similar to PsCheckStock, as it sends an e-mail to the supplier and stops the pipeline until the supplier has confirmed that stock has shipped. This time, however, we do need customer information, because the supplier needs to know where to ship the order! Add the following code to a new file in the business folder named ps_ship_goods.php:

```
<?php
class PsShipGoods implements IPipelineSection
{
   private $_mProcessor;

   public function Process($processor)
   {
      // Set processor reference
      $this->_mProcessor = $processor;

      // Audit
      $processor->CreateAudit('PsShipGoods started.', 20500);

      // Send mail to supplier
      $processor->MailSupplier(STORE_NAME . ' ship goods.',
                               $this->GetMailBody());

      // Audit
      $processor->CreateAudit('Ship goods e-mail sent to supplier.', 20502);
```

```php
    // Update order status
    $processor->UpdateOrderStatus(6);

    // Audit
    $processor->CreateAudit('PsShipGoods finished.', 20501);
  }
```

As before, a private method called GetMailBody() is used to build the message body for the e-mail sent to the supplier:

```php
  private function GetMailBody()
  {
    $body = 'Payment has been received for the following goods:';
    $body .= "\n\n";

    $body .= $this->_mProcessor->GetOrderAsString(false);
    $body .= "\n\n";

    $body .= 'Please ship to:';
    $body .= "\n\n";

    $body .= $this->_mProcessor->GetCustomerAddressAsString();
    $body .= "\n\n";

    $body .= 'When goods have been shipped, please confirm via ' .
             Link::ToAdmin();
    $body .= "\n\n";

    $body .= 'Order reference number: ';
    $body .= $this->_mProcessor->mOrderInfo['order_id'];

    return $body;
  }
}
?>
```

When this pipeline stage finishes, processing pauses. Later, when the supplier confirms that the order has been shipped, processing moves on to PsShipOk.

PsShipOk

This pipeline section is very similar to PsStockOk, although it has slightly more to do. Because we know that items have shipped, we can add a shipment date value to the orders table. Technically, this isn't really necessary, because all audit entries are dated. However, by adding the entry directly to the orders table, we will have all the information easily accessible in one table. Add the following code to a new file in the business folder named ps_ship_ok.php:

```php
<?php
class PsShipOk implements IPipelineSection
```

```php
{
  public function Process($processor)
  {
    // Audit
    $processor->CreateAudit('PsShipOk started.', 20600);

    // Set order shipment date
    $processor->SetDateShipped();

    // Audit
    $processor->CreateAudit('Order dispatched by supplier.', 20602);

    // Update order status
    $processor->UpdateOrderStatus(7);

    // Continue processing
    $processor->mContinueNow = true;

    // Audit
    $processor->CreateAudit('PsShipOk finished.', 20601);
  }
}
?>
```

When this pipeline stage finishes, processing moves straight on to PsFinalNotification.

PsFinalNotification

This last pipeline section is very similar to the first, because it sends an e-mail to the customer. This time, we're confirming that the order has shipped. Add the following code to a new file in the business folder named ps_final_notification.php:

```php
<?php
class PsFinalNotification implements IPipelineSection
{
  private $_mProcessor;

  public function Process($processor)
  {
    // Set processor reference
    $this->_mProcessor = $processor;

    // Audit
    $processor->CreateAudit('PsFinalNotification started.', 20700);

    // Send mail to customer
    $processor->MailCustomer(STORE_NAME . ' order dispatched.',
                             $this->GetMailBody());
```

```
    // Audit
    $processor->CreateAudit('Dispatch e-mail send to customer.', 20702);

    // Update order status
    $processor->UpdateOrderStatus(8);

    // Audit
    $processor->CreateAudit('PsFinalNotification finished.', 20701);
  }
```

It uses a familiar-looking GetMailBody() method to build the body of the e-mail:

```
private function GetMailBody()
{
    $body = 'Your order has now been dispatched! ' .
            'The following products have been shipped:';
    $body .= "\n\n";

    $body .= $this->_mProcessor->GetOrderAsString(false);
    $body .= "\n\n";

    $body .= 'Your order has been shipped to:';
    $body .= "\n\n";

    $body .= $this->_mProcessor->GetCustomerAddressAsString();
    $body .= "\n\n";

    $body .= 'Order reference number: ';
    $body .= $this->_mProcessor->mOrderInfo['order_id'];
    $body .= "\n\n";

    $body .= 'Thank you for shopping at ' . STORE_NAME . '!';

    return $body;
  }
}
?>
```

When this pipeline section finishes, the order status is changed to 8, which represents a completed order. Further attempts to process the order using OrderProcessor will result in an exception being thrown.

Testing the Pipeline

Now, let's do a simple test to make sure the code we just wrote is working as expected.

Exercise: Testing the Pipeline

1. First, add the STORE_NAME constant to the include/config.php file:

```
// Store name
define('STORE_NAME', 'TShirtShop');
```

2. Add the following highlighted lines in the admin.php file (also feel free to remove the reference to ps_dummy.php, which is no longer required).

```
require_once BUSINESS_DIR . 'order_processor.php';
require_once BUSINESS_DIR . 'ps_initial_notification.php';
require_once BUSINESS_DIR . 'ps_check_funds.php';
require_once BUSINESS_DIR . 'ps_check_stock.php';
require_once BUSINESS_DIR . 'ps_stock_ok.php';
require_once BUSINESS_DIR . 'ps_take_payment.php';
require_once BUSINESS_DIR . 'ps_ship_goods.php';
require_once BUSINESS_DIR . 'ps_ship_ok.php';
require_once BUSINESS_DIR . 'ps_final_notification.php';
```

3. Now, add the highlighted lines in the index.php file:

```
require_once BUSINESS_DIR . 'customer.php';
require_once BUSINESS_DIR . 'orders.php';
require_once BUSINESS_DIR . 'i_pipeline_section.php';
require_once BUSINESS_DIR . 'order_processor.php';
require_once BUSINESS_DIR . 'ps_initial_notification.php';
require_once BUSINESS_DIR . 'ps_check_funds.php';
require_once BUSINESS_DIR . 'ps_check_stock.php';
```

4. Modify the code of the _GetCurrentPipelineSection() method in OrderProcessor (inside business/order_processor.php) as follows:

```
// Gets current pipeline section
private function _GetCurrentPipelineSection()
{
  switch($this->mOrderInfo['status'])
  {
    case 0:
      $this->_mOrderProcessStage = $this->mOrderInfo['status'];
      $this->_mCurrentPipelineSection = new PsInitialNotification();

      break;
    case 1:
      $this->_mOrderProcessStage = $this->mOrderInfo['status'];
      $this->_mCurrentPipelineSection = new PsCheckFunds();

      break;
    case 2:
      $this->_mOrderProcessStage = $this->mOrderInfo['status'];
      $this->_mCurrentPipelineSection = new PsCheckStock();
```

```
        break;
      case 3:
        $this->_mOrderProcessStage = $this->mOrderInfo['status'];
        $this->_mCurrentPipelineSection = new PsStockOk();

        break;
      case 4:
        $this->_mOrderProcessStage = $this->mOrderInfo['status'];
        $this->_mCurrentPipelineSection = new PsTakePayment();

        break;
      case 5:
        $this->_mOrderProcessStage = $this->mOrderInfo['status'];
        $this->_mCurrentPipelineSection = new PsShipGoods();

        break;
      case 6:
        $this->_mOrderProcessStage = $this->mOrderInfo['status'];
        $this->_mCurrentPipelineSection = new PsShipOk();

        break;
      case 7:
        $this->_mOrderProcessStage = $this->mOrderInfo['status'];
        $this->_mCurrentPipelineSection = new PsFinalNotification();

        break;
      case 8:
        $this->_mOrderProcessStage = 100;
        throw new Exception('Order already been completed.');

        break;
      default:
        $this->_mOrderProcessStage = 100;
        throw new Exception('Unknown pipeline section requested.');
    }
  }
```

5. Open business/orders.php, and replace the $mOrdersStatusOptions array of the Orders class to manage the new order status codes. Note that this change affects the old orders, which used different status codes:

```
public static $mOrderStatusOptions = array (
                  'Order placed, notifying customer', // 0
                  'Awaiting confirmation of funds',   // 1
                  'Notifying supplier-stock check',   // 2
                  'Awaiting stock confirmation',      // 3
                  'Awaiting credit card payment',     // 4
                  'Notifying supplier-shipping',      // 5
                  'Awaiting shipment confirmation',   // 6
```

```
             'Sending final notification',    // 7
             'Order completed',               // 8
             'Order canceled');               // 9
```

6. Open `presentation/admin_order_details.php`, and add the highlighted new member to the `AdminOrderDetails` class:

   ```php
   public $mTax = 0.0;
   public $mOrderProcessMessage;
   ```

7. Modify the code of the `init()` method in the `AdminOrderDetails` class located in `presentation/admin_order_details.php` as highlighted. This will handle the functionality necessary when the visitor clicks the Process button.

   ```php
   if (isset ($_GET['submitProcessOrder']))
   {
     $processor = new OrderProcessor($this->mOrderId);


     try
     {
       $processor->Process();
       $this->mOrderProcessMessage = 'Order processed, status now: ' .
                                   $processor->mOrderInfo['status'];
     }
     catch (Exception $e)
     {
       $this->mOrderProcessMessage = 'Processing error, status now: ' .
                                   $processor->mOrderInfo['status'];
     }
   }
   ```

8. Open the `presentation/templates/admin_order_details.tpl` file, and add the highlighted code:

   ```smarty
   {* admin_order_details.tpl *}
   {load_presentation_object filename="admin_order_details" assign="obj"}
   <form method="get" action="{$obj->mLinkToAdmin}">
     <h3>
       Editing details for order ID:
       {$obj->mOrderInfo.order_id} [
       <a href="{$obj->mLinkToOrdersAdmin}">back to admin orders...</a> ]
     </h3>
     {if $obj->mOrderProcessMessage}
     <p><strong>{$obj->mOrderProcessMessage}</strong></p>
     {/if}
     <input type="hidden" name="Page" value="OrderDetails" />
   ```

9. Load TShirtShop; create a new order; and then open that order in the orders administration page. In the orders administration page, click the Process Order button.

10. You should get a customer notification e-mail (see Figure 19-1).

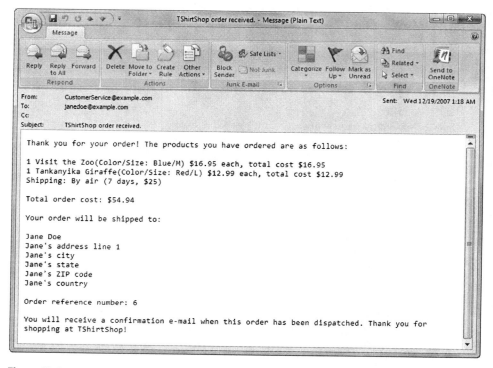

Figure 19-1. *A customer order confirmation e-mail*

11. Check your supplier e-mail for the stock check e-mail (see Figure 19-2).

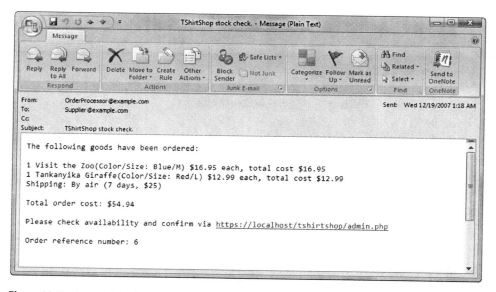

Figure 19-2. *A stock check e-mail*

12. Continue processing in the administration order details page by clicking the Process Order button again, calling the `Process()` method of the `OrderProcessor` class for the second time.

13. Check your supplier e-mail for the e-mail requesting the shipment of the goods (see Figure 19-3).

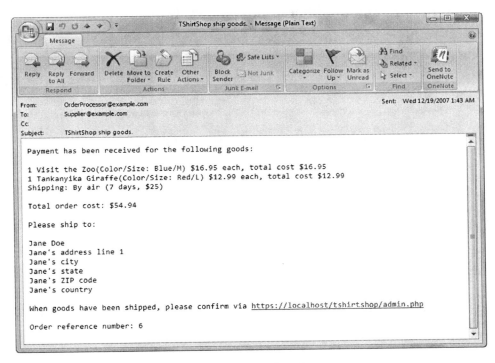

Figure 19-3. *An e-mail requesting the shipment of goods*

14. Continue processing in the administration order details page by clicking Process Order and calling the `Process()` method of the `OrderProcessor` class for the third and last time.

15. Check your e-mail for the shipping confirmation message (see Figure 19-4).

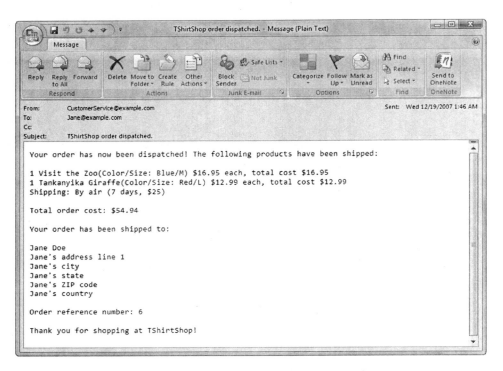

Figure 19-4. *Customer shipping notification e-mail (dispatched.tif)*

16. Examine the new `audit` entries for the order; audit entries are shown in Figure 19-5.

audit_id	order_id	created_on	message	code
34	6	2007-12-19 01:18:20	Order Processor started.	10000
35	6	2007-12-19 01:18:20	PsInitialNotification started.	20000
36	6	2007-12-19 01:18:20	Notification e-mail sent to customer.	20002
37	6	2007-12-19 01:18:20	PsInitialNotification finished.	20001
38	6	2007-12-19 01:18:20	PsCheckFunds started.	20100
39	6	2007-12-19 01:18:20	Funds available for purchase.	20102
40	6	2007-12-19 01:18:20	PsCheckFunds finished.	20101
41	6	2007-12-19 01:18:20	PsCheckStock started.	20200
42	6	2007-12-19 01:18:20	Notification email sent to supplier.	20202
43	6	2007-12-19 01:18:20	PsCheckStock finished.	20201
44	6	2007-12-19 01:18:20	Order Processor finished.	10001
45	6	2007-12-19 01:42:50	Order Processor started.	10000
46	6	2007-12-19 01:42:50	PsStockOk started.	20300
47	6	2007-12-19 01:42:50	Stock confirmed by supplier.	20302
48	6	2007-12-19 01:42:50	PsStockOk finished.	20301
49	6	2007-12-19 01:42:50	PsTakePayment started.	20400
50	6	2007-12-19 01:42:50	Funds deducted from customer credit card account.	20402
51	6	2007-12-19 01:42:50	PsTakePayment finished.	20401
52	6	2007-12-19 01:42:50	PsShipGoods started.	20500
53	6	2007-12-19 01:42:50	Ship goods e-mail sent to supplier.	20502
54	6	2007-12-19 01:42:50	PsShipGoods finished.	20501
55	6	2007-12-19 01:42:50	Order Processor finished.	10001
56	6	2007-12-19 01:46:29	Order Processor started.	10000
57	6	2007-12-19 01:46:29	PsShipOk started.	20600
58	6	2007-12-19 01:46:29	Order dispatched by supplier.	20602
59	6	2007-12-19 01:46:29	PsShipOk finished.	20601
60	6	2007-12-19 01:46:29	PsFinalNotification started.	20700
61	6	2007-12-19 01:46:29	Dispatch e-mail send to customer.	20702
62	6	2007-12-19 01:46:29	PsFinalNotification finished.	20701
63	6	2007-12-19 01:46:29	Order Processor finished.	10001

Figure 19-5. *Audit entries for completed order*

How It Works: The Order Pipeline

We've covered how the order pipeline works, so now we need to explain only the new code added to OrderProcessor. We changed the code in the _GetCurrentPipelineSection() method, which is responsible for selecting the pipeline section that needs to be executed.

The change is simply a switch block that assigns a pipeline section to the $_mCurrentPipelineSection member:

```
// Gets current pipeline section
private function _GetCurrentPipelineSection()
{
  switch($this->mOrderInfo['status'])
  {
    case 0:
      $this->_mOrderProcessStage = $this->mOrderInfo['status'];
      $this->_mCurrentPipelineSection = new PsInitialNotification();
```

```
        break;
      case 1:
        $this->_mOrderProcessStage = $this->mOrderInfo['status'];
        $this->_mCurrentPipelineSection = new PsCheckFunds();

        break;
      case 2:
        $this->_mOrderProcessStage = $this->mOrderInfo['status'];
        $this->_mCurrentPipelineSection = new PsCheckStock();

        break;
      case 3:
        $this->_mOrderProcessStage = $this->mOrderInfo['status'];
        $this->_mCurrentPipelineSection = new PsStockOk();

        break;
      case 4:
        $this->_mOrderProcessStage = $this->mOrderInfo['status'];
        $this->_mCurrentPipelineSection = new PsTakePayment();

        break;
      case 5:
        $this->_mOrderProcessStage = $this->mOrderInfo['status'];
        $this->_mCurrentPipelineSection = new PsShipGoods();

        break;
      case 6:
        $this->_mOrderProcessStage = $this->mOrderInfo['status'];
        $this->_mCurrentPipelineSection = new PsShipOk();

        break;
      case 7:
        $this->_mOrderProcessStage = $this->mOrderInfo['status'];
        $this->_mCurrentPipelineSection = new PsFinalNotification();

        break;
      case 8:
        $this->_mOrderProcessStage = 100;
        throw new Exception('Order already been completed.');

        break;
      default:
        $this->_mOrderProcessStage = 100;
        throw new Exception('Unknown pipeline section requested.');
    }
  }
```

If the order has been completed or an unknown section is requested, we generate an exception.

The test code gives us the additional opportunity of testing this exception generation, because if we run it again, we'll be processing an already completed order. Click the Process Order button for an order that's already complete (has the status 8), and you should get an error e-mail, as shown in Figure 19-6.

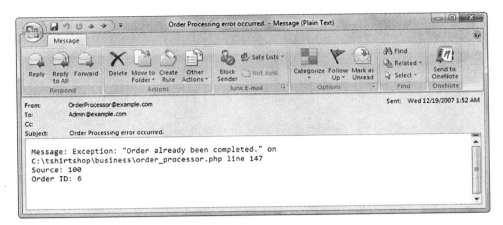

Figure 19-6. *Order processing error e-mail*

The error message mailed to the administrator should be enough to get you started on your way to finding out what happened.

Updating the Checkout Page

In the previous example, we were forced to call the OrderProcessor::Process() method three times in a row from the order details administration page. In practice, this won't happen—the method will be called once by presentation/checkout_info.php when a customer places an order and twice more by the supplier in presentation/admin_order_details.php. We'll need to modify these web pages accordingly.

Follow the steps in this exercise to make checkout_info.php work with the new order pipeline.

Exercise: Updating the Checkout Process

1. Modify the init() method in the CheckoutInfo class in presentation/checkout_info.php by removing the code that redirects to PayPal and replacing it with the highlighted code:

```
// Create the order and get the order ID
$order_id = ShoppingCart::CreateOrder(
            $this->mCustomerData['customer_id'],
            (int)$_POST['shipping'], $tax_id);

// On success head to an order successful page
$redirect_to = Link::ToOrderDone();
```

```
        // Create new OrderProcessor instance
        $processor = new OrderProcessor($order_id);

        try
        {
          $processor->Process();
        }
        catch (Exception $e)
        {
          // If an error occurs, head to an error page
          $redirect_to = Link::ToOrderError();
        }

        // Redirection to the order processing result page
        header('Location: ' . $redirect_to);

        exit();
      }
    ...
```

2. Create a new file named order_done.tpl in the presentation/templates folder, and add the following code to its body:

```
{* order_done.tpl *}
<h3>Thank you for your order!</h3>
<p class="description">
  A confirmation of your order will be sent to your registered email address.
</p>
```

3. If an error occurs when ordering, we need to redirect the customer to another page. Create presentation/templates/order_error.tpl with the following in it:

```
{* order_error.tpl *}
<h3>An error has occurred during the processing of your order.</h3>
<p class="description">
  If you have an inquiry regarding this message please email
  <a href="mailto:{$smarty.const.CUSTOMER_SERVICE_EMAIL}">
  {$smarty.const.CUSTOMER_SERVICE_EMAIL}</a>
</p>
```

4. Add the following methods in the Link class from the presentation/link.php file:

```
// Creates a link to the order done page
public static function ToOrderDone()
{
  return self::Build('order-done/');
}

// Creates a link to the order error page
public static function ToOrderError()
```

```
    {
      return self::Build('order-error/');
    }
```

5. Open the `.htaccess` file from the project root folder, and add the highlighted rewrite rules:

```
    # Rewrite checkout pages
    RewriteRule ^checkout/?$ index.php?Checkout [L]

    # Rewrite order done pages
    RewriteRule ^order-done/?$ index.php?OrderDone [L]

    # Rewrite order error pages
    RewriteRule ^order-error/?$ index.php?OrderError [L]
    </IfModule>

    # Set the default 500 page for Apache errors
    ErrorDocument 500 /tshirtshop/500.php
```

6. Now, modify the `CheckRequest()` method from the `Link` class found in the `presentation/link.php` file, adding the highlighted code:

```
    // Redirects to proper URL if not already there
    public static function CheckRequest()
    {
      $proper_url = '';

      if (isset ($_GET['Search']) || isset($_GET['SearchResults']) ||
          isset ($_GET['CartAction']) || isset ($_GET['AjaxRequest']) ||
          isset ($_POST['Login']) || isset ($_GET['Logout']) ||
          isset ($_GET['RegisterCustomer']) ||
          isset ($_GET['AddressDetails']) ||
          isset ($_GET['CreditCardDetails']) ||
          isset ($_GET['AccountDetails']) || isset ($_GET['Checkout']) ||
          isset ($_GET['OrderDone']) || isset ($_GET['OrderError']))
      {
        return ;
      }
      // Obtain proper URL for category pages
      elseif (isset ($_GET['DepartmentId']) && isset ($_GET['CategoryId']))
```

7. Open `presentation/store_front.php` file, and modify the `init()` method of the `StoreFront` class, adding the highlighted code to load either `order_done.tpl` or `order_error.tpl`, depending on whether the order processed successfully or not:

```
    if (isset ($_GET['Checkout']))
    {
      if (Customer::IsAuthenticated())
        $this->mContentsCell = 'checkout_info.tpl';
      else
        $this->mContentsCell = 'checkout_not_logged.tpl';
```

```
        $this->mHideBoxes = true;
    }

    if (isset($_GET['OrderDone']))
      $this->mContentsCell = 'order_done.tpl';
    elseif (isset($_GET['OrderError']))
      $this->mContentsCell = 'order_error.tpl';

    // Load the page title
    $this->mPageTitle = $this->_GetPageTitle();
  }
```

We can now use the TShirtShop web store to place orders, but they will pause when it gets to stock confirmation. To continue, we'll implement the interface that suppliers and administrators use so we can force orders to continue processing.

Updating the Orders Administration Page

The basic functionality of this page is to allow suppliers and administrators to view a list of orders that need attention and manually advance those orders in the pipeline. This is simply a case of calling the OrderProcess::Process() method as described earlier.

This page could be implemented in many ways. In fact, in some setups, it might be better to implement this as a stand-alone application, for example, if your suppliers are in-house and on the same network. Or, it might be better to combine this approach with Web Services.

To simplify things in this section, we'll supply a single page for both administrators and suppliers. This might not be ideal in all situations, because we might not want to expose all order details and audit information to external suppliers. However, for demonstration purposes, this reduces the amount of code we have to get through. We'll also tie in the security for this page with the administrator forms-based security used earlier in the book, assuming that people with permission to edit the site data will also have permission to administer orders. In a more advanced setup, we could modify this slightly, providing roles for different types of users and restricting the functionality available to users in different roles.

Implementing the Data Tier

We need to add a new stored procedure (orders_get_audit_trail) to the tshirtshop database and update an existing stored procedure (orders_update_order) to take into account the new status codes.

Using phpMyAdmin, select the tshirtshop database, and open a new SQL query page. Now, execute the following code, which creates a new stored procedure called orders_update_order in the tshirtshop database:

```
-- Drop procedure orders_update_order
DROP PROCEDURE orders_update_order$$

-- Update orders_update_order stored procedure
CREATE PROCEDURE orders_update_order(IN inOrderId INT, IN inStatus INT,
  IN inComments VARCHAR(255), IN inAuthCode VARCHAR(50),
```

```
   IN inReference VARCHAR(50))
BEGIN
  DECLARE currentDateShipped DATETIME;

  SELECT shipped_on
  FROM   orders
  WHERE  order_id = inOrderId
  INTO   currentDateShipped;

  UPDATE orders
  SET    status = inStatus, comments = inComments,
         auth_code = inAuthCode, reference = inReference
  WHERE  order_id = inOrderId;

  IF inStatus < 7 AND currentDateShipped IS NOT NULL THEN
    UPDATE orders SET shipped_on = NULL WHERE order_id = inOrderId;
  ELSEIF inStatus > 6 AND currentDateShipped IS NULL THEN
    UPDATE orders SET shipped_on = NOW() WHERE order_id = inOrderId;
  END IF;
END$$
```

Next, execute this code, which creates the orders_get_audit_trail stored procedure in the tshirtshop database:

```
-- Create orders_get_audit_trail stored procedure
CREATE PROCEDURE orders_get_audit_trail(IN inOrderId INT)
BEGIN
  SELECT audit_id, order_id, created_on, message, code
  FROM   audit
  WHERE  order_id = inOrderId;
END$$
```

Implementing the Business Tier

To cater to the new data tier function added in the previous section, we also have to add a new method to the Orders class from business/orders.php. Add the GetAuditTrail() method to the Orders class in business/orders.php as follows:

```
// Gets the audit table entries associated with a specific order
public static function GetAuditTrail($orderId)
{
  // Build the SQL query
  $sql = 'CALL orders_get_audit_trail(:order_id)';

  // Build the parameters array
  $params = array (':order_id' => $orderId);

  // Execute the query and return the results
  return DatabaseHandler::GetAll($sql, $params);
}
```

Implementing the Presentation Tier

We need to update the `admin_order_details` componentized template, which shows the details of an order. Earlier in this book, this componentized template also included the capability to test the order process, but we're removing this here. Instead, we'll provide the capability for orders to be pushed along the pipeline when they are stuck at the "Awaiting confirmation of stock" and "Awaiting confirmation of shipment" stages.

Now, we can also display all the audit information for the order in another new table. Let's look at what we're going to achieve, as shown in Figure 19-7.

We can split the ORDERS ADMIN page into three sections:

- In the first section, we'll change the Process button to a confirmation button for suppliers.

- In the second section, a table is filled with the items data from the order.

- In the third section, a table shows the audit trail for the order.

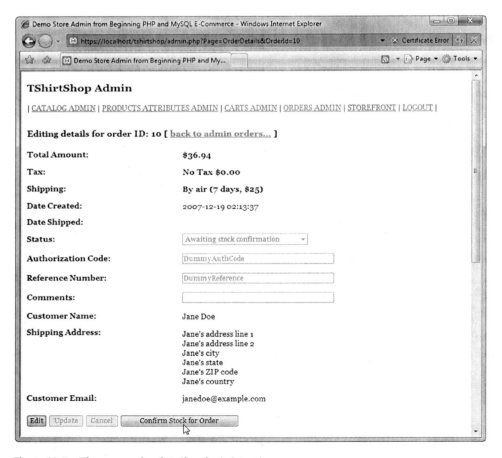

Figure 19-7. *The new order details administration page*

We implement the new functionality in the following exercise.

Exercise: Modifying the Order Details Admin Section

1. Remove the following lines from `presentation/templates/admin_order_details.tpl`:

```
{if $obj->mOrderProcessMessage}
<p><strong>{$obj->mOrderProcessMessage}</strong></p>
{/if}
```

2. Also, in `presentation/templates/admin_order_details.tpl`, replace the Process Order button code with the highlighted code:

```
    <input type="submit" name="submitCancel" value="Cancel"
    {if ! $obj->mEditEnabled} disabled="disabled" {/if} />
    {if $obj->mProcessButtonText}
    <input type="submit" name="submitProcessOrder"
     value="{$obj->mProcessButtonText}" />
    {/if}
</p>
<h3>Order contains these products:</h3>
<table class="tss-table">
```

3. In the same file, add the following highlighted code:

```
{section name=i loop=$obj->mOrderDetails}
  <tr>
    <td>{$obj->mOrderDetails[i].product_id}</td>
    <td>
      {$obj->mOrderDetails[i].product_name}
      ({$obj->mOrderDetails[i].attributes})
    </td>
    <td>{$obj->mOrderDetails[i].quantity}</td>
    <td>${$obj->mOrderDetails[i].unit_cost}</td>
    <td>${$obj->mOrderDetails[i].subtotal}</td>
  </tr>
{/section}
</table>
<h3>Order audit trail:</h3>
<table class="tss-table">
  <tr>
    <th>Audit ID</th>
    <th>Created On</th>
    <th>Code</th>
    <th>Message</th>
  </tr>
{section name=j loop=$obj->mAuditTrail}
  <tr>
    <td>{$obj->mAuditTrail[j].audit_id}</td>
    <td>{$obj->mAuditTrail[j].created_on}</td>
    <td>{$obj->mAuditTrail[j].code}</td>
    <td>{$obj->mAuditTrail[j].message}</td>
```

```
       </tr>
     {/section}
     </table>
   </form>
```

4. Open the presentation/admin_order_details.php file, and remove the definition of the $mOrderProcessMessage member of the AdminOrderDetails class shown here:

```
   public $mOrderProcessMessage;
```

5. Also, in admin_order_details.php, add two new members in the AdminOrderDetails class:

```
   public $mProcessButtonText;
   public $mAuditTrail;
```

6. In the same file, update the init() method of the AdminOrderDetails class as highlighted:

```
   // Initializes class members
   public function init()
   {
     if (isset ($_GET['submitUpdate']))
     {
       Orders::UpdateOrder($this->mOrderId, $_GET['status'],
         $_GET['comments'], $_GET['authCode'], $_GET['reference']);
     }

     if (isset ($_GET['submitProcessOrder']))
     {
       $processor = new OrderProcessor($this->mOrderId);
       $processor->Process();
     }

     $this->mOrderInfo = Orders::GetOrderInfo($this->mOrderId);
     $this->mOrderDetails = Orders::GetOrderDetails($this->mOrderId);
     $this->mCustomerInfo = Customer::Get($this->mOrderInfo['customer_id']);
     $this->mTotalCost = $this->mOrderInfo['total_amount'];
     $this->mAuditTrail = Orders::GetAuditTrail($this->mOrderId);

     if ($this->mOrderInfo['tax_percentage'] !== 0.0)
       $this->mTax = round((float)$this->mTotalCost *
                           (float)$this->mOrderInfo['tax_percentage'], 2)
                     / 100.00;
```

```
    $this->mTotalCost += $this->mOrderInfo['shipping_cost'];
    $this->mTotalCost += $this->mTax;

    // Format the values
    $this->mTotalCost = number_format($this->mTotalCost, 2, '.', '');
    $this->mTax = number_format($this->mTax, 2, '.', '');

    if ($this->mOrderInfo['status'] == 3)
      $this->mProcessButtonText = 'Confirm Stock for Order';
    elseif ($this->mOrderInfo['status'] == 6)
      $this->mProcessButtonText = 'Confirm Shipment for Order';

    // Value which specifies whether to enable or disable edit mode
    if (isset ($_GET['submitEdit']))
      $this->mEditEnabled = true;
    else
      $this->mEditEnabled = false;
  }
```

7. Load TShirtShop; place a new order; and then load the order details administration page to test the new changes. When placing a new order, expect to receive a confirmation message similar to the one shown in Figure 19-8. The site administrator will be able to confirm stock and shipment, as shown in Figure 19-7. The order details administration page now displays the audit trail, as shown in Figure 19-9.

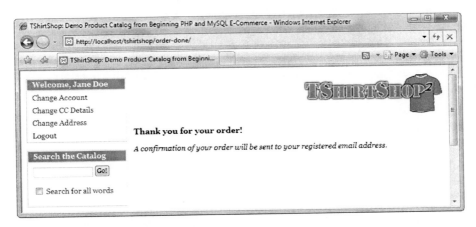

Figure 19-8. *Confirmation that the order has been placed*

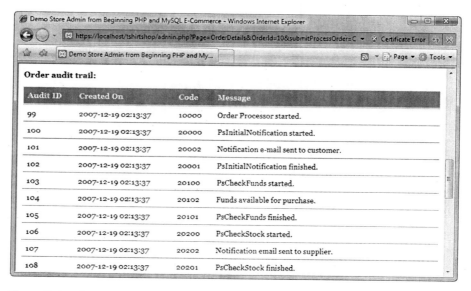

Figure 19-9. *The order's audit trail*

How It Works: Order Details Administration

The init() method found in AdminOrderDetails advances the pipeline to the next section if the Process button is clicked; the presence of this button on the page depends on the value of the $mProcessButtonText member. This value is set to "Confirm Stock" if the current pipeline section is 3 (awaiting stock confirmation), or to "Confirm Shipment" if the current pipeline section is 6 (awaiting shipment confirmation). If the current pipeline section is not set to 3 or 6, it means that the order has been completed successfully, and the button is not shown. The administrator can always check what happened to the order by checking the audit trail that is displayed on the page.

All that remains now is to check that everything is working properly. To do this, use the web interface to place an order, and then review it via the orders details administration section. You should see that the order is awaiting confirmation of stock, as shown earlier in Figure 19-7.

Click the Confirm Stock for Order button, and the order is processed. Because this happens very quickly, we are soon presented with the next stage, where the Confirm Stock for Order button is replaced by a new button named Confirm Shipment, and the audit trail shows a new set of data.

Clicking the Confirm Shipment button completes the order. If we scroll down the page, we can see all audit trail messages that have been stored in the database concerning this order.

Summary

We've taken giant strides toward completing the TShirtShop e-commerce application in this chapter. Now, we have a fully audited, secure backbone for the application.

Specifically, we've covered these enhancements:

- Modifications to the TShirtShop application to enable our own pipeline processing

- The basic framework for the order pipeline

- The database additions for auditing data and storing additional required data in the orders table

- The implementation of most of the order pipeline, apart from those sections that deal with credit cards

The only thing that we need to add before delivering this application to the outside world is credit card processing, which we'll look at in the next chapter.

CHAPTER 20

■■■

Processing Credit Card Transactions

The last thing we need to do before launching the e-commerce site is to enable credit card processing. In this chapter, we examine how we can build this into the pipeline we created in the previous chapter.

We'll start by looking at the theory behind credit card transactions, the sort of organizations that help achieve credit card processing, and the sort of transactions that are possible. Moving on, we'll take two example organizations, DataCash and Authorize.net, and discuss the specifics of their transaction application program interfaces (APIs), the means by which we use their credit card transaction features. After that, we'll build a new class library that helps use one of these transaction APIs via some simple test code.

Finally, we'll integrate the API with the TShirtShop e-commerce application and order-processing pipeline.

Credit Card Transaction Fundamentals

For transactions, banks and other financial institutions use secure networks based on the X.25 protocol rather than Transmission Control Protocol/Internet Protocol (TCP/IP), the primary means by which data is transmitted across the Internet. You don't need to know much about X.25 apart from the fact that it's a different networking protocol that isn't compatible with TCP/IP. As such, X.25 networks are completely separate from the Internet, and although it's possible to get direct access to them, this isn't likely to be a reasonable option. To do so, we might have to enter into some serious negotiation with the owners of the network we want to use. The owners will want to be completely sure that we are reliable customers who are capable of enforcing the necessary safeguards to prevent an attack on *their* system. Accordingly, the network owner won't be handing out these licenses to just anyone—most people can't afford the security measures required (which include locking your servers in a cage, sending daily backup tapes down a secure chute, having three individuals with separate keys to access these tapes, and so on).

The alternative is to access these networks via a gateway provider. This enables us to perform our side of the credit card transaction protocol over the Internet (using a secure protocol), while relying on a chosen gateway to communicate with X.25 networks. Although there is likely to be a cost involved with this, the provider should have a deal with financial institutions to help keep costs low and pass the savings on to us (after the gateway takes its share), so it's likely to be much cheaper than having your own X.25 connection. This method is also likely to be cheaper than using a third-party payment processor, because we only need the minimum functionality since we are handling our own order pipeline. There is no need, for example, to use all the order-auditing functionality offered by a company such as PayPal, because we already have all this functionality in our implementation.

Working with Credit Card Payment Gateways

To work with a gateway organization, we first need to open a merchant bank account. This can be done at most banks; the bank will provide you a merchant ID that you can use when signing up with the gateway. The next step is to find a suitable gateway. This can be a lot of hard work!

Although it isn't hard to find a gateway, the challenge lies in finding a competent one that offers services at an acceptable price and quality. Literally hundreds of companies are eager to take a cut of your sales. A quick search on the Internet for "credit card gateway" will produce a long list. The web sites of these companies are for the most part pure brochureware—you'll find yourself reading through pages of text about how they are the best and most secure at what they do, only to end up with a form to fill in so that a customer service representative can call you to "discuss your needs." In the long run, you can rest assured that at least you will probably only have to go through the procedure once.

You'll probably find that most of the organizations offering this service are offering similar packages. However, some key points to look for include the banks they do business with (your merchant bank account will have to be at one of these), the currencies they deal in, and, of course, the costs.

Table 20-1 shows some of the gateway services available. In this chapter, we'll look at two of the few organizations that are easy to deal with—DataCash and Authorize.net.

Table 20-1. *Gateway Services*

United States Gateways	URL	United Kingdom Gateways	URL
Authorize.net	http://www.authorize.net/	Arcot	http://www.arcot.com/
First Data	http://www.firstdata.com/	WorldPay	http://www.worldpay.com/
Cardservice	http://cardservice.com/	DataCash	http://www.datacash.com/
ICVerify	http://www.icverify.com/		

DataCash and Authorize.net

In this chapter, we'll demonstrate implementing credit card transactions with two online services: DataCash and Authorize.net.

DataCash is a credit card gateway organization based in the United Kingdom. You'll need a UK merchant bank account if you want to use it in the final application. However, you don't have to worry about this for now: it's very easy to get access to a rather useful test account—you don't even need a merchant bank account.

Authorize.net, as mentioned on its official web site at http://www.authorize.net, "provides Internet Protocol (IP) payment gateway services that enable merchants to authorize, settle, and manage credit card or electronic check transactions anytime, anywhere." In other words, Authorize.net also offers the service that we need to process the credit cards ourselves when someone buys one of our t-shirts.

The important point to remember is that the techniques covered in this chapter apply to every credit card gateway. The specifics might change slightly if you switch to a different organization, but you'll have already done most of the hard work.

As you'll see later in this chapter, both Authorize.net and DataCash let us perform test transactions using so-called "magic" credit card numbers (supplied separately by Authorize.net and DataCash), which will accept or decline transactions without performing any actual financial transactions. This is fantastic for development purposes, because we certainly don't want to use our own credit cards for testing!

Understanding Credit Card Transactions

Whichever gateway you use, the basic principles of credit card transactions are the same. First, the sort of transactions we'll be dealing with in an e-commerce web site are known as Card Not Present (CNP) transactions, which means we don't have the credit card in front of us and we can't verify the customer signature. This isn't a problem; after all you've probably been performing CNP transactions for some time now online, over the phone, by mail, and so on. It's just something to be aware of should you see the CNP acronym.

Several advanced services are offered by various gateways, including cardholder address verification, security code checking, fraud screening, and so on. Each of these adds an additional layer of complexity to your credit card processing, and we're not covering those details here. Rather, this chapter provides a starting point from which you can add these services if required. Whether or not you choose these optional extra services depends on how much money is passing through your system and the trade-off between the costs of implementing the services and the potential costs, which could be prevented by these extra services, if something goes wrong. If you are interested in these services, that customer service representative mentioned previously will be happy to explain things.

As it stands now, we can perform several types of transactions:

Authorization: Check a card for adequate funds and perform a deduction.

Preauthorization: Check a card for funds and allocate them if available; this doesn't deduct funds immediately.

Fulfillment: Complete a preauthorized transaction, deducting the funds already allocated.

Refund: Refund a completed transaction or simply put money on a credit card.

Again, the specifics vary, but these are the basic types.

In this chapter, we'll use the preauthorization/fulfillment model, which means we don't take payment until just before we instruct our supplier to ship goods. This structure was hinted at by the structure of the pipeline we created in the previous chapter.

Working with DataCash

Now that we've covered the basics, let's consider how we'll get things working in the TShirtShop application using the DataCash system. The first thing to do is to get a test account with DataCash by following these steps:

1. Go to `http://www.datacash.com/`.

2. Head to the Developers Area ➤ Get a Test Account section of the web site.

3. Enter your details, and submit the form.

4. From the e-mail you receive, make a note of your account username and password, as well as the additional information required for accessing the DataCash reporting system.

■**Note** After you obtain your test account, be sure to download the *DataCash Developer's Guide* at `https://testserver.datacash.com/software/DevelopersGuide.pdf`. This is the official document you can rely on to have accurate and recent information about any DataCash services.

DataCash offers a PHP API composed of a number of PHP classes that you can use to connect to its services. These classes compose the XML messages that interact with the DataCash web service for you. In this chapter, for understanding how the system works even better, we choose to create the XML structures and interact with the DataCash web service directly.

We'll be doing a lot of XML manipulation when communicating with DataCash, because we'll need to create XML documents to send to DataCash and to extract data from XML responses. In the following few pages, we'll take a quick look at the XML required for the operations we'll be performing and the responses we can expect. We'll discuss the communication protocol, which implies discussing the XML files that reflect the following stages of a transaction:

- Preauthentication request

- Response to the preauthentication request

- Fulfillment request

- Fulfillment response

We'll implement these stages into the TShirtShop order pipeline. While reading this chapter, always remember to use the official documentation, which contains the most current and relevant updates, at `https://testserver.datacash.com/software/DevelopersGuide.pdf`.

Preauthentication Request

When we send a preauthentication request to DataCash, we need to include the following information:

- DataCash username (known as the DataCash client)

- DataCash password

- A unique transaction reference number

- The amount of money to be debited

- The currency used for the transaction (U.S. dollars, British pounds, and so on)

- The type of transaction (the code pre for preauthentication and the code fulfill for fulfillment)

- The credit card number

- The credit card expiration date

- The credit card issue date (if applicable to the type of credit card being used)

- The credit card issue number (if applicable to the type of credit card being used)

The unique transaction reference number must be a number between 6 and 12 digits long, which we choose to uniquely identify the transaction with an order. Because we can't use a short number, we can't just use the order ID values we've been using up until now for orders. We can, however, use this order ID as the starting point for creating a reference number by simply adding a high number to it, such as 1,000,000. We can't duplicate the reference number in any future transactions; we must be sure that after a transaction is completed, it won't execute again, which could result in charging the customer twice. This process implies, however, that if a credit card is rejected, we might need to create a whole new order for the customer to generate a new and unique reference number to send to the gateway, but that shouldn't be a problem.

The XML request is formatted in the following way, with the values detailed previously shown in bold:

```
<?xml version="1.0" encoding="UTF-8"?>
<Request>
  <Authentication>
    <password>DataCash password</password>
    <client>DataCash client</client>
  </Authentication>
  <Transaction>
    <TxnDetails>
      <merchantreference>Unique reference number</merchantreference>
      <amount currency='Currency Type'>Cash amount</amount>
    </TxnDetails>
    <CardTxn>
      <method>pre</method>
      <Card>
        <pan>Credit card number</pan>
        <expirydate>Credit card expiry date</expirydate>
      </Card>
    </CardTxn>
  </Transaction>
</Request>
```

Response to the Preauthentication Request

The response to a preauthentication request includes the following information:

- The status code number indicates what happened; the code will be 1 if the transaction was successful or another of several other codes if something else happens. For a complete list of return codes for a DataCash server, see `https://testserver.datacash.com/software/returncodes.shtml`.

- The reason for the status is, basically, a string explaining the status in English. For a status of 1, this string is `ACCEPTED`.

- An authentication code and a reference number are provided for use in completing the transaction in the fulfillment request stage (discussed next).

- The time that the transaction was processed is provided.

- The mode of the transaction, which is `TEST` when using the test account, is also given.

- Confirmation of the type of credit card used is provided.

- Confirmation of the country that the credit card was issued in is included as well.

- And the authorization code used by the bank (for reference only) is also supplied.

The XML for this is formatted as follows:

```xml
<?xml version="1.0" encoding="utf-8"?>
<Response>
  <status>Status code</status>
  <reason>Reason</reason>
  <merchantreference>Authentication code</merchantreference>
  <datacash_reference>Reference number</datacash_reference>
  <time>Time</time>
  <mode>TEST</mode>
  <CardTxn>
    <card_scheme>Card Type</card_scheme>
    <country>Country</country>
    <issuer>Card issuing bank</issuer>
    <authcode>Bank authorization code</authcode>
  </CardTxn>
</Response>
```

Fulfillment Request

For a fulfillment request, we need to send the following information:

- DataCash username (the DataCash client)

- DataCash password

- The type of the transaction (for fulfillment, the code `fulfill`)

- The authentication code received earlier

- The reference number received earlier

We can, optionally, include additional information, such as a confirmation of the amount to be debited from the credit card, although this isn't really necessary.

The fulfillment request XML message is formatted as follows:

```
<?xml version="1.0" encoding="UTF-8"?>
<Request>
  <Authentication>
    <password>DataCash password</password>
    <client>DataCash client</client>
  </Authentication>
  <Transaction>
    <HistoricTxn>
      <reference>Reference Number</reference>
      <authcode>Authentication code</authcode>
      <method>fulfill</method>
    </HistoricTxn>
  </Transaction>
</Request>
```

Fulfillment Response

The response to a fulfillment request includes the following information:

- The status code number indicates what happened; the code will be 1 if the transaction was successful or another of several other codes if something else happens. Again, for a complete list of codes, see https://testserver.datacash.com/software/returncodes.shtml.

- The reason for the status is, basically, a string explaining the status in English. For a status of 1, this string is FULFILLED OK.

- Two copies of the reference code are provided for use by DataCash.

- The time that the transaction was processed is supplied.

- And the mode of the transaction, which is TEST when using the test account, is also provided.

The XML message for the fulfillment response is formatted as follows:

```
<?xml version="1.0" encoding="utf-8"?>
<Response>
  <status>Status code</status>
  <reason>Reason</reason>
  <merchantreference>Reference Code</merchantreference>
  <datacash_reference>Reference Code</datacash_reference>
  <time>Time</time>
  <mode>TEST</mode>
</Response>
```

Exchanging XML Data with DataCash

Because the XML data we need to send to DataCash has a simple and standard structure, we'll build it manually in a string, without using the XML support offered by PHP 5. However, we will take advantage of PHP 5's SimpleXML extension, which makes reading simple XML data a piece of cake.

Although less complex and powerful than DOMDocument, the SimpleXML extension makes parsing XML data easy by transforming it into a data structure we can simply iterate through. You first met the SimpleXML extension in Chapter 6.

▪**Note** For the code that communicates with DataCash, we use the cURL library (http://curl.haxx.se/). Uncomment the following line in php.ini by removing the leading semicolon: extension=php_curl.dll. Then restart Apache.

You'll find the php.ini file in the C:\xampp\apache\bin\ folder on Windows or the /opt/lampp/etc folder on Linux.

For more details about the cURL library, check out the excellent tutorial at http://www.zend.com/pecl/tutorials/curl.php. The official documentation of PHP's cURL support is located at http://www.php.net/curl.

Exercise: Communicating with DataCash

1. Create a new file named datacash_request.php in the business folder, and add the following code to it:

```php
<?php
class DataCashRequest
{
  // DataCash Server URL
  private $_mUrl;

  // Will hold the current XML document to be sent to DataCash
  private $_mXml;

  // Constructor initializes the class with URL of DataCash
  public function __construct($url)
  {
    // Datacash URL
    $this->_mUrl = $url;
  }

  /* Compose the XML structure for the pre-authentication
     request to DataCash */
  public function MakeXmlPre($dataCashClient, $dataCashPassword,
                            $merchantReference, $amount, $currency,
```

```php
                                $cardNumber, $expiryDate,
                                $startDate = '', $issueNumber = '')
{
  $this->_mXml =
    "<?xml version=\"1.0\" encoding=\"UTF-8\"\x3F>
     <Request>
       <Authentication>
         <password>$dataCashPassword</password>
         <client>$dataCashClient</client>
       </Authentication>
       <Transaction>
         <TxnDetails>
           <merchantreference>$merchantReference</merchantreference>
           <amount currency=\"$currency\">$amount</amount>
         </TxnDetails>
         <CardTxn>
           <method>pre</method>
           <Card>
             <pan>$cardNumber</pan>
             <expirydate>$expiryDate</expirydate>
             <startdate>$startDate</startdate>
             <issuenumber>$issueNumber</issuenumber>
           </Card>
         </CardTxn>
       </Transaction>
     </Request>";
}

// Compose the XML structure for the fulfillment request to DataCash
public function MakeXmlFulfill($dataCashClient, $dataCashPassword,
                              $authCode, $reference)
{
  $this->_mXml =
    "<?xml version=\"1.0\" encoding=\"UTF-8\"\x3F>
     <Request>
       <Authentication>
         <password>$dataCashPassword</password>
         <client>$dataCashClient</client>
       </Authentication>
       <Transaction>
         <HistoricTxn>
           <reference>$reference</reference>
           <authcode>$authCode</authcode>
           <method>fulfill</method>
         </HistoricTxn>
       </Transaction>
     </Request>";
}
```

```php
      // Get the current XML
      public function GetRequest()
      {
        return $this->_mXml;
      }

      // Send an HTTP POST request to DataCash using cURL
      public function GetResponse()
      {
        // Initialize a cURL session
        $ch = curl_init();

        // Prepare for an HTTP POST request
        curl_setopt($ch, CURLOPT_POST, 1);

        // Prepare the XML document to be POSTed
        curl_setopt($ch, CURLOPT_POSTFIELDS, $this->_mXml);

        // Set the URL where we want to POST our XML structure
        curl_setopt($ch, CURLOPT_URL, $this->_mUrl);

        /* Do not verify the Common name of the peer certificate in the SSL
           handshake */
        curl_setopt($ch, CURLOPT_SSL_VERIFYHOST, 0);

        // Prevent cURL from verifying the peer's certificate
        curl_setopt($ch, CURLOPT_SSL_VERIFYPEER, 0);

        /* We want cURL to directly return the transfer instead of
           printing it */
        curl_setopt($ch, CURLOPT_RETURNTRANSFER, 1);

        // Perform a cURL session
        $result = curl_exec($ch);

        // Close a cURL session
        curl_close ($ch);

        // Return the response
        return $result;
      }
    }
    ?>
```

2. Define the DataCash URL and login data at the end of your include/config.php file:

```php
// Constant definitions for datacash
define('DATACASH_URL', 'https://testserver.datacash.com/Transaction');
```

```php
define('DATACASH_CLIENT', 'your account client number');
define('DATACASH_PASSWORD', 'your account password');
```

■**Note** Don't forget to use the data from your DataCash account!

---

3. Create the test_datacash.php file in your project's home (the tshirtshop folder), and add the following in it:

```php
<?php
session_start();

if (empty ($_GET['step']))
{
  require_once 'include/config.php';
  require_once BUSINESS_DIR . 'datacash_request.php';

  $request = new DataCashRequest(DATACASH_URL);
  $request->MakeXmlPre(DATACASH_CLIENT, DATACASH_PASSWORD,
                       8880000 + rand(0, 10000), 49.99, 'GBP',
                       '3528000000000007', '11/09');

  $request_xml = $request->GetRequest();
  $_SESSION['pre_request'] = $request_xml;

  $response_xml = $request->GetResponse();
  $_SESSION['pre_response'] = $response_xml;

  $xml = simplexml_load_string($response_xml);
  $request->MakeXmlFulfill(DATACASH_CLIENT, DATACASH_PASSWORD,
                           $xml->merchantreference,
                           $xml->datacash_reference);

  $response_xml = $request->GetResponse();
  $_SESSION['fulfill_response'] = $response_xml;
}
else
{
  header('Content-type: text/xml');

  switch ($_GET['step'])
  {
    case 1:
      print $_SESSION['pre_request'];
```

```
      break;
    case 2:
      print $_SESSION['pre_response'];

      break;
    case 3:
      print $_SESSION['fulfill_response'];

      break;
  }
  exit();
}
?>
<frameset cols="33%, 33%, 33%">
  <frame src="test_datacash.php?step=1">
  <frame src="test_datacash.php?step=2">
  <frame src="test_datacash.php?step=3">
</frameset>
```

4. Load the test_datacash.php file in your browser to see the results. If you use Opera, the output should look like Figure 20-1, because Opera shows only the contents of the XML elements. If you use another web browser, you should see properly formatted XML documents.

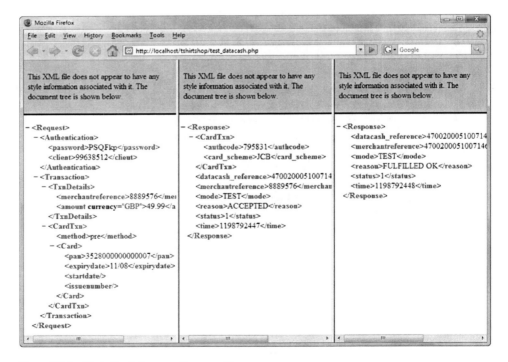

Figure 20-1. *DataCash transaction results*

5. Log on to `https://testserver.datacash.com/reporting2` to see the transaction log for your DataCash account (note that this view takes a while to update, so you might not see the transaction right away). This report is shown in Figure 20-2.

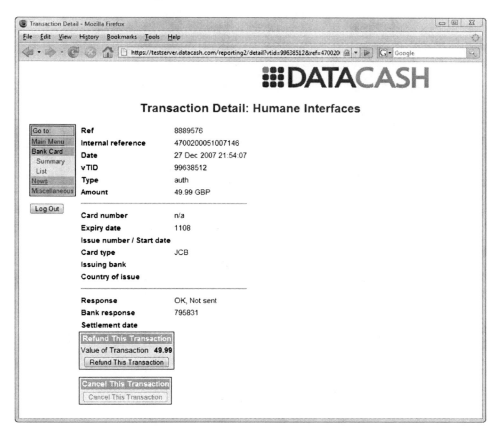

Figure 20-2. *DataCash transaction report details*

How It Works: The Code That Communicates with DataCash

The DataCashRequest class is quite simple. First the constructor sets the HTTPS address where we send your requests:

```
// Constructor initializes the class with URL of DataCash
public function __construct($url)
{
  // Datacash URL
  $this->_mUrl = $url;
}
```

When we want to make a preauthentication request, we first need to call the MakeXmlPre() method to create the required XML for this kind of request. Some XML elements are optional (such as startdate or issuenumber, which get default values if we don't provide our own—see the MakeXmlPre() method), but the other elements are mandatory.

Note If you want to see exactly which elements are mandatory and which are optional for each kind of request, check the XML API frequently asked questions document from DataCash.

The next kind of request we must be able to make to the DataCash system is a fulfill request. The XML for this kind of request is prepared in the MakeXmlFulfill() method.

We then have the GetRequest() method that returns the last XML document built by either MakeXmlPre() or MakeXmlFulfill():

```
// Get the current XML
public function GetRequest()
{
  return $this->_mXml;
}
```

Finally, the GetResponse() method actually sends the latest XML request file, built by a call to either MakeXmlPre() or MakeXmlFulfill() and returns the response XML. Let's take a closer look at this method.

GetResponse() starts by initializing a cURL session and setting the POST method to send your data:

```
// Send an HTTP POST request to DataCash using cURL
public function GetResponse()
{
  // Initialize a cURL session
  $ch = curl_init();

  // Prepare for an HTTP POST request
  curl_setopt($ch, CURLOPT_POST, 1);

  // Prepare the XML document to be POSTed
  curl_setopt($ch, CURLOPT_POSTFIELDS, $this->_mXml);

  // Set the URL where we want to POST our XML structure
  curl_setopt($ch, CURLOPT_URL, $this->_mUrl);

  /* Do not verify the Common name of the peer certificate in the SSL
     handshake */
  curl_setopt($ch, CURLOPT_SSL_VERIFYHOST, 0);

  // Prevent cURL from verifying the peer's certificate
  curl_setopt($ch, CURLOPT_SSL_VERIFYPEER, 0);
```

To return the transfer into a PHP variable, we set the CURLOPT_RETURNTRANSFER parameter to 1, send the request, and close the cURL session:

```
  /* We want cURL to directly return the transfer instead of
     printing it */
  curl_setopt($ch, CURLOPT_RETURNTRANSFER, 1);
```

```
    // Perform a cURL session
    $result = curl_exec($ch);

    // Close a cURL session
    curl_close ($ch);

    // Return the response
    return $result;
  }
```

The test_datacash.php file acts like this: When we load it in the browser, the script makes a preauthentication request and a fulfillment request and then saves the preauthentication request, response, and fulfillment XML data in the session:

```
session_start();

if (empty ($_GET['step']))
{
  require_once 'include/config.php';
  require_once BUSINESS_DIR . 'datacash_request.php';

  $request = new DataCashRequest(DATACASH_URL);
  $request->MakeXmlPre(DATACASH_CLIENT, DATACASH_PASSWORD,
                       8880000 + rand(0, 10000), 49.99, 'GBP',
                       '3528000000000007', '11/09');

  $request_xml = $request->GetRequest();
  $_SESSION['pre_request'] = $request_xml;

  $response_xml = $request->GetResponse();
  $_SESSION['pre_response'] = $response_xml;

  $xml = simplexml_load_string($response_xml);
  $request->MakeXmlFulfill(DATACASH_CLIENT, DATACASH_PASSWORD,
                           $xml->merchantreference,
                           $xml->datacash_reference);

  $response_xml = $request->GetResponse();
  $_SESSION['fulfill_response'] = $response_xml;
}
```

The test_datacash.php page will be loaded three times more, because we have three frames that we want to fill with data:

```
<frameset cols="33%, 33%, 33%">
  <frame src="test_datacash.php?step=1">
  <frame src="test_datacash.php?step=2">
  <frame src="test_datacash.php?step=3">
</frameset>
```

Depending on the step value, we decide which of the previously saved-in-session XML data is displayed in the current frame. If the step value is 1, the prerequest XML code is displayed. If the value is 2, the preresponse XML code is displayed. If the step value is 3, the fulfill response XML is displayed.

```php
else
{
  header('Content-type: text/xml');

  switch ($_GET['step'])
  {
    case 1:
      print $_SESSION['pre_request'];

      break;
    case 2:
      print $_SESSION['pre_response'];

      break;
    case 3:
      print $_SESSION['fulfill_response'];

      break;
  }
  exit();
}
```

Integrating DataCash with TShirtShop

Now that we have a new class that performs credit card transactions, all we need to do is integrate its functionality into the order pipeline we built in the previous chapters. To fully integrate DataCash with TShirtShop, we'll need to update the existing PsCheckFunds and PsTakePayments classes.

We need to modify the pipeline section classes that deal with credit card transactions. We've already included the infrastructure for storing and retrieving authentication codes and reference information, via the OrderProcessor::SetOrderAuthCodeAndReference() method.

Exercise: Implementing the Order Pipeline Classes

1. First, replace the code in business/ps_check_funds.php with the following code that works with DataCash:

```php
<?php
class PsCheckFunds implements IPipelineSection
{
  public function Process($processor)
  {
    // Audit
    $processor->CreateAudit('PsCheckFunds started.', 20100);
```

```php
    $order_total_cost = $processor->mOrderInfo['total_amount'];
    $order_total_cost += $processor->mOrderInfo['shipping_cost'];
    $order_total_cost +=
      round((float)$order_total_cost *
            (float)$processor->mOrderInfo['tax_percentage'], 2) / 100.00;

    $request = new DataCashRequest(DATACASH_URL);
    $request->MakeXmlPre(DATACASH_CLIENT, DATACASH_PASSWORD,
      $processor->mOrderInfo['order_id'] + 1000006,
      $order_total_cost, 'GBP',
      $processor->mCustomerInfo['credit_card']->CardNumber,
      $processor->mCustomerInfo['credit_card']->ExpiryDate,
      $processor->mCustomerInfo['credit_card']->IssueDate,
      $processor->mCustomerInfo['credit_card']->IssueNumber);

    $responseXml = $request->GetResponse();
    $xml = simplexml_load_string($responseXml);

    if ($xml->status == 1)
    {
      $processor->SetAuthCodeAndReference(
        $xml->merchantreference, $xml->datacash_reference);

      // Audit
      $processor->CreateAudit('Funds available for purchase.', 20102);

      // Update order status
      $processor->UpdateOrderStatus(2);

      // Continue processing
      $processor->mContinueNow = true;
    }
    else
    {
      // Audit
      $processor->CreateAudit('Funds not available for purchase.', 20103);

      throw new Exception('Credit card check funds failed for order ' .
                          $processor->mOrderInfo['order_id'] . "\n\n" .
                          'Data exchanged:' . "\n" .
                          $request->GetResponse() . "\n" . $responseXml);
    }

    // Audit
    $processor->CreateAudit('PsCheckFunds finished.', 20101);
  }
}
?>
```

2. Replace the code in business/ps_take_payment.php with the following code:

```php
<?php
class PsTakePayment implements IPipelineSection
{
  public function Process($processor)
  {
    // Audit
    $processor->CreateAudit('PsTakePayment started.', 20400);

    $request = new DataCashRequest(DATACASH_URL);
    $request->MakeXmlFulFill(DATACASH_CLIENT, DATACASH_PASSWORD,
                             $processor->mOrderInfo['auth_code'],
                             $processor->mOrderInfo['reference']);

    $responseXml = $request->GetResponse();
    $xml = simplexml_load_string($responseXml);

    if ($xml->status == 1)
    {
      // Audit
      $processor->CreateAudit(
        'Funds deducted from customer credit card account.', 20402);

      // Update order status
      $processor->UpdateOrderStatus(5);

      // Continue processing
      $processor->mContinueNow = true;
    }
    else
    {
      // Audit
      $processor->CreateAudit('Could not deduct funds from credit card.',
                              20403);

      throw new Exception('Credit card take payment failed for order ' .
                          $processor->mOrderInfo['order_id'] . "\n\n" .
                          'Data exchanged:' . "\n" .
                          $request->GetResponse() . "\n" . $responseXml);
    }

    // Audit
    $processor->CreateAudit('PsTakePayment finished.', 20401);
  }
}
?>
```

3. Add a reference to the business/datacash_request.php file in index.php as highlighted:

```
require_once BUSINESS_DIR . 'ps_check_funds.php';
require_once BUSINESS_DIR . 'ps_check_stock.php';
require_once BUSINESS_DIR . 'datacash_request.php';
```

4. Add a reference to the business/datacash_request.php file in admin.php as highlighted:

```
require_once BUSINESS_DIR . 'ps_ship_ok.php';
require_once BUSINESS_DIR . 'ps_final_notification.php';
require_once BUSINESS_DIR . 'datacash_request.php';
```

Testing DataCash Integration

Now that we have all this in place, it's important to test it with a few orders. We can do this easily by creating a customer with those magic credit card details. As mentioned earlier in this chapter, DataCash supplies these numbers for testing purposes and to obtain specific responses from DataCash. A sample of these numbers is shown in Table 20-2. A full list is available in the Developer's Area of the DataCash web site, under the Magic Card Numbers section.

Table 20-2. *DataCash Credit Card Test Numbers*

Card Type	Card Number	Return Code	Description	Sample Message
Switch	4936000000000000001	1	Authorizes with a random authorization code	AUTH CODE ??????
	4936000000000000019	7	Declines the transaction	DECLINED
	6333000000000005	1	Authorizes with a random authorization code	AUTH CODE ??????
	6333000000000013	7	Declines the transaction	DECLINED
	6333000000123450	1	Authorizes with a random authorization code	AUTH CODE ??????
Visa	4242424242424242	7	Declines the transaction	DECLINED
	4444333322221111	1	Authorizes with a random authorization code	AUTH CODE ??????
	4546389010000131	1	Authorizes with a random authorization code	AUTH CODE ??????

At this moment, we can experiment with the new fully featured e-commerce web site by placing orders with the test credit card numbers, checking the e-mails the web site sends, and finding out how the site reacts in certain situations, such as how it logs errors, how orders are administered using the orders administration page, and so on.

Going Live

Moving from the test account to the live one is now simply a matter of replacing the DataCash login information in `include/config.php` with real-world values. After you set up a merchant bank account, you can use the new details to set up a new DataCash account, obtaining new client and password data along the way. You also need to change the URL for the DataCash server that you send data to, because it needs to be the production server instead of the testing server. Other than removing the test user accounts from the database and moving the web site to an Internet location, this is all you need to do before exposing the newly completed e-commerce application to customers.

Working with Authorize.net

To test Authorize.net, you need to apply for a test account at `http://developer.authorize.net/testaccount/`. The main page where developers can get information on Authorize.net integration is `http://developer.authorize.net/`.

Communicating with Authorize.net is different from communicating with DataCash. Instead of sending and receiving XML files, we send strings consisting of name-value pairs, separated by ampersands (&). Effectively, we use a similar syntax to query strings appended to URLs.

Authorize.net returns the transaction results in the form of a string that contains the return values (without their names) separated by a character that we will specify when making the initial request. In our examples, we'll use the pipe (|) character. The return values come in a predetermined order, and their significance is given by their position in the returned string.

■**Note** The complete documentation for the Authorize.net API can be found in the *Advanced Integration Method (AIM) Implementation Guide: Card-Not-Present Transactions* at `http://www.authorize.net/support/AIM_guide.pdf`. Even more documents are available in the document library at `http://www.authorize.net/resources/documentlibrary/`.

The default transaction type is `AUTH_CAPTURE`, where we request and deduct the funds from the credit card using a single request. For TShirtShop, we'll use two other transaction types: `AUTH_ONLY`, which checks if the necessary funds are available (this happens in the `PsCheckFunds` pipeline stage), and `PRIOR_AUTH_CAPTURE`, which deducts the amount of money that was previously checked using `AUTH_ONLY` (this happens in the `PsTakePayment` pipeline stage).

To perform an `AUTH_ONLY` transaction, we'll first create an array that contains the necessary transaction data:

```
// Auth
$transaction =
  array ('x_invoice_num' => '99999', // Invoice number
         'x_amount'      => '45.99', // Amount
         'x_card_num'    => '4007000000027', // Credit card number
         'x_exp_date'    => '1209', // Expiration date
         'x_method'      => 'CC', // Payment method
         'x_type'        => 'AUTH_ONLY'); // Transaction type
```

For PRIOR_AUTH_CAPTURE transactions, we don't need to specify all this information again; we only need to pass the transaction ID that was returned in response to the AUTH_ONLY request.

```
// Capture
$transaction =
  array ('x_ref_trans_id' => $ref_trans_id, // Transaction id
          'x_method'       => 'CC', // Payment method
          'x_type'         => 'PRIOR_AUTH_CAPTURE'); // Transaction type
```

We'll transform these arrays into a string of name-value pairs and submit them to the Authorize.net server. The response comes in the form of a string whose values are separated by a configurable character. Later, in Figure 20-3, you can see a sample response for an AUTH_ONLY request (in the left part of the window) and a sample response for a PRIOR_AUTH_CAPTURE request (in the right part of the window).

We'll write a simple test with this transaction type before implementing any modifications to TShirtShop. Follow the steps in the exercise to test Authorize.net.

Exercise: Testing Authorize.net

1. Create a new file named authorize_net_request.php in the business folder, and add the following code to it:

```php
<?php
class AuthorizeNetRequest
{
  // Authorize Server URL
  private $_mUrl;

  // Will hold the current request to be sent to Authorize.net
  private $_mRequest;

  // Constructor initializes the class with URL of Authorize.net
  public function __construct($url)
  {
    // Authorize.net URL
    $this->_mUrl = $url;
  }

  public function SetRequest($request)
  {
    $this->_mRequest = '';

    $request_init =
      array ('x_login'        => AUTHORIZE_NET_LOGIN_ID,
              'x_tran_key'     => AUTHORIZE_NET_TRANSACTION_KEY,
              'x_version'      => '3.1',
              'x_test_request' => AUTHORIZE_NET_TEST_REQUEST,
              'x_delim_data'   => 'TRUE',
```

```php
                    'x_delim_char'    => '|',
                    'x_relay_response' => 'FALSE');

    $request = array_merge($request_init, $request);

    foreach($request as $key => $value )
      $this->_mRequest .= $key . '=' . urlencode($value) . '&';
  }

  // Send an HTTP POST request to Authorize.net using cURL
  public function GetResponse()
  {
    // Initialize a cURL session
    $ch = curl_init();

    // Prepare for an HTTP POST request
    curl_setopt($ch, CURLOPT_POST, 1);

    // Prepare the request to be POSTed
    curl_setopt($ch, CURLOPT_POSTFIELDS, rtrim($this->_mRequest, '& '));

    // Set the URL where we want to POST our data
    curl_setopt($ch, CURLOPT_URL, $this->_mUrl);

    /* Do not verify the Common name of the peer certificate in the SSL
       handshake */
    curl_setopt($ch, CURLOPT_SSL_VERIFYHOST, 0);

    // Prevent cURL from verifying the peer's certificate
    curl_setopt($ch, CURLOPT_SSL_VERIFYPEER, 0);

    /* We want cURL to directly return the transfer instead of
       printing it */
    curl_setopt($ch, CURLOPT_RETURNTRANSFER, 1);

    // Perform a cURL session
    $result = curl_exec($ch);

    // Close a cURL session
    curl_close ($ch);

    // Return the response
    return $result;
  }
}
?>
```

2. Add the following at the end of include/config.php file, modifying the constant data with the details of your Authorize.net account:

```php
// Constant definitions for authorize.net
define('AUTHORIZE_NET_URL', 'https://test.authorize.net/gateway/transact.dll');
define('AUTHORIZE_NET_LOGIN_ID', '[Your Login ID]');
define('AUTHORIZE_NET_TRANSACTION_KEY', '[Your Transaction Key]');
define('AUTHORIZE_NET_TEST_REQUEST', 'FALSE');
```

3. Add the following test_authorize_net.php test file in your site root folder:

```php
<?php
session_start();

if (empty ($_GET['step']))
{
  require_once 'include/config.php';
  require_once BUSINESS_DIR . 'authorize_net_request.php';

  $request = new AuthorizeNetRequest(AUTHORIZE_NET_URL);

  // Auth
  $transaction =
    array ('x_invoice_num' => '99999', // Invoice number
           'x_amount'       => '45.99', // Amount
           'x_card_num'     => '4007000000027', // Credit card number
           'x_exp_date'     => '1209', // Expiration date
           'x_method'       => 'CC', // Payment method
           'x_type'         => 'AUTH_ONLY'); // Transaction type

  $request->SetRequest($transaction);
  $auth_only_response = $request->GetResponse();

  $_SESSION['auth_only_response'] = $auth_only_response;

  $auth_only_response = explode('|', $auth_only_response);

  // Read the transaction ID, which will be necessary for taking the payment
  $ref_trans_id = $auth_only_response[6];

  // Capture
  $transaction =
    array ('x_ref_trans_id' => $ref_trans_id, // Transaction id
           'x_method'       => 'CC', // Payment method
           'x_type'         => 'PRIOR_AUTH_CAPTURE'); // Transaction type

  $request->SetRequest($transaction);
  $prior_auth_capture_response = $request->GetResponse();
```

```
        $_SESSION['prior_auth_capture_response'] = $prior_auth_capture_response;
    }
    else
    {
      switch ($_GET['step'])
      {
        case 1:
          print $_SESSION['auth_only_response'];

          break;
        case 2:
          print $_SESSION['prior_auth_capture_response'];

          break;
      }

      exit();
    }
    ?>
    <frameset cols="50%, 50%">
      <frame src="test_authorize_net.php?step=1">
      <frame src="test_authorize_net.php?step=2">
    </frameset>
```

4. Load the test_authorize_net.php page in your favorite browser to see the results (see Figure 20-3).

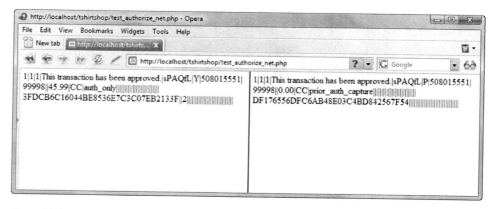

Figure 20-3. *Authorize.net transaction results*

5. Go to Authorize.net, and log in to the Merchant Interface (https://test.authorize.net/). You can see the transaction you've just performed in the Unsettled Transactions section under the Search tab. This report is shown in Figure 20-4.

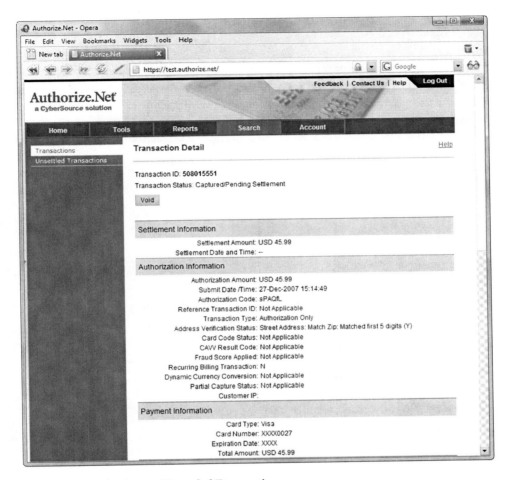

Figure 20-4. *Authorize.net Unsettled Transactions*

How It Works: Authorize.net Transactions

The hard work is done by the AuthorizeNetRequest class, which has two important methods: SetRequest(), used to set up transaction details, and GetResponse(), used to send the request to and retrieve the response from Authorize.net. The following code snippet shows how they are used:

```
// Auth
$transaction =
  array ('x_invoice_num' => '99999', // Invoice number
         'x_amount'      => '45.99', // Amount
         'x_card_num'    => '4007000000027', // Credit card number
         'x_exp_date'    => '1209', // Expiration date
         'x_method'      => 'CC', // Payment method
         'x_type'        => 'AUTH_ONLY'); // Transaction type
```

```
$request->SetRequest($transaction);
$response = $request->GetResponse();
```

> **Note** The credit card data mentioned in this transaction is one of the magic card numbers provided by Authorize.net for testing purposes. Review the *AIM Implementation Guide* for the complete list of such credit card numbers.

We send an array with transaction details as a parameter to SetRequest(), which then joins this array with another array that contains the Authorize.net account details:

```
public function SetRequest($request)
{
  $this->_mRequest = '';

  $request_init =
    array ('x_login'        => AUTHORIZE_NET_LOGIN_ID,
           'x_tran_key'     => AUTHORIZE_NET_TRANSACTION_KEY,
           'x_version'      => '3.1',
           'x_test_request' => AUTHORIZE_NET_TEST_REQUEST,
           'x_delim_data'   => 'TRUE',
           'x_delim_char'   => '|',
           'x_relay_response' => 'FALSE');

  $request = array_merge($request_init, $request);
```

The array data is merged into a name-value string that can be sent to Authorize.net. The values are encoded for inclusion in the URL using the urlencode() function:

```
  foreach($request as $key => $value )
    $this->_mRequest .= $key . '=' . urlencode($value) . '&';
}
```

The GetResponse() method of AuthorizeNetRequest does the actual request, using the cURL library.

```
// Send an HTTP POST request to Authorize.net using cURL
public function GetResponse()
{
  ...

  // Perform a cURL session
  $result = curl_exec($ch);

  // Close a cURL session
  curl_close ($ch);

  // Return the response
  return $result;
```

```
    }
  }
?>
```

When executing the GetResponse() function to perform an AUTH_ONLY transaction, the response will contain a transaction ID. If the authorization is successful, we can then use this transaction ID to perform a PRIOR_AUTH_CAPTURE
transaction, which effectively takes the money from the customer's account.

As explained earlier, the response from Authorize.net comes in the form of a string that contains values delimited
by a configurable character, which, in our case, is the pipe character (|). To read a particular value from the string,
we transform the string into an array using the explode() PHP function (http://www.php.net/manual/en/
function.explode.php):

```
$auth_only_response = $request->GetResponse();

$_SESSION['auth_only_response'] = $auth_only_response;

$auth_only_response = explode('|', $auth_only_response);
```

After this piece of code executes, $auth_only_response will contain an array whose elements are the values
that were delimited by the pipe character in the original string. From this array, we're interested in the seventh
element, which, according to the Authorize.net documentation, is the transaction ID (read the Gateway Response
API details from http://www.authorize.net/support/AIM_guide.pdf for the complete details about the
Authorize.net response).

```
// Read the transaction ID, which will be necessary for taking the payment
$ref_trans_id = $auth_only_response[6];
```

Note The $auth_only_response array created by explode() is zero based, so
$auth_only_response[6] represents the seventh element of the array.

The code that takes the money using this transaction ID is straightforward. Because the transaction has already
been authorized, we only need to specify the transaction ID received after authorization to complete the transaction:

```
// Capture
$transaction =
  array ('x_ref_trans_id' => $ref_trans_id, // Transaction id
         'x_method'       => 'CC', // Payment method
         'x_type'         => 'PRIOR_AUTH_CAPTURE'); // Transaction type

$request->SetRequest($transaction);
$prior_auth_capture_response = $request->GetResponse();
```

Integrating Authorize.net with TShirtShop

As with DataCash, we'll have to modify the PsCheckFunds and PsTakePayment classes to use the
new Authorize.net functionality.

Remember that you can use the files from the Source Code/Download section of the Apress web site (http://www.apress.com/) instead of typing the code yourself.

The final modifications involve changing the pipeline section classes that deal with credit card transactions (PsCheckFunds and PsTakePayment). We've already included the infrastructure for storing and retrieving authentication code and reference information via the OrderProcessor::SetOrderAuthCodeAndReference() method.

Exercise: Implementing the Order Pipeline Classes

1. First, modify business/ps_check_funds.php to work with Authorize.net. You may back up the DataCash version of this file, if you followed the DataCash exercise earlier in this chapter.

```php
<?php
class PsCheckFunds implements IPipelineSection
{
  public function Process($processor)
  {
    // Audit
    $processor->CreateAudit('PsCheckFunds started.', 20100);

    $order_total_cost = $processor->mOrderInfo['total_amount'];
    $order_total_cost += $processor->mOrderInfo['shipping_cost'];
    $order_total_cost +=
      round((float)$order_total_cost *
            (float)$this->mOrderInfo['tax_percentage'], 2) / 100.00;

    $exp_date = str_replace('/', '',
      $processor->mCustomerInfo['credit_card']->ExpiryDate);

    $transaction =
      array (
        'x_invoice_num' => $processor->mOrderInfo['order_id'],
        'x_amount' => $order_total_cost, // Amount to charge
        'x_card_num' => $processor->mCustomerInfo['credit_card']->CardNumber,
        'x_exp_date' => $exp_date, // Expiry (MMYY)
        'x_method' => 'CC',
        'x_type' => 'AUTH_ONLY');

    // Process Transaction
    $request = new AuthorizeNetRequest(AUTHORIZE_NET_URL);
    $request->SetRequest($transaction);

    $response = $request->GetResponse();

    $response = explode('|', $response);
```

```php
      if ($response[0] == 1)
      {
        $processor->SetAuthCodeAndReference($response[4], $response[6]);

        // Audit
        $processor->CreateAudit('Funds available for purchase.', 20102);

        // Update order status
        $processor->UpdateOrderStatus(2);

        // Continue processing
        $processor->mContinueNow = true;
      }
      else
      {
        // Audit
        $processor->CreateAudit('Funds not available for purchase.', 20103);

        throw new Exception('Credit card check funds failed for order ' .
                            $processor->mOrderInfo['order_id'] . ".\n\n" .
                            'Data exchanged:' . "\n" .
                            var_export($transaction, true) . "\n" .
                            var_export($response, true));
      }

      // Audit
      $processor->CreateAudit('PsCheckFunds finished.', 20101);
    }
  }
?>
```

2. Modify business/ps_take_payment.php as follows:

```php
<?php
class PsTakePayment implements IPipelineSection
{
  public function Process($processor)
  {
    // Audit
    $processor->CreateAudit('PsTakePayment started.', 20400);

    $transaction =
      array ('x_ref_trans_id' => $processor->mOrderInfo['reference'],
             'x_method'       => 'CC',
             'x_type'         => 'PRIOR_AUTH_CAPTURE');

    // Process Transaction
    $request = new AuthorizeNetRequest(AUTHORIZE_NET_URL);
    $request->SetRequest($transaction);
```

```php
        $response = $request->GetResponse();

        $response = explode('|', $response);

        if ($response[0] == 1)
        {
          // Audit
          $processor->CreateAudit(
            'Funds deducted from customer credit card account.', 20402);

          // Update order status
          $processor->UpdateOrderStatus(5);

          // Continue processing
          $processor->mContinueNow = true;

          // Audit
          $processor->CreateAudit('PsTakePayment finished.', 20401);
        }
        else
        {
          // Audit
          $processor->CreateAudit(
            'Error taking funds from customer credit card.', 20403);

          throw new Exception('Credit card take payment failed for order ' .
                              $processor->mOrderInfo['order_id'] . ".\n\n" .
                              'Data exchanged:' . "\n" .
                              var_export($transaction, true) . "\n" .
                              var_export($response, true));
        }
      }
    }
  }
?>
```

3. Add a reference to the business/authorize_net_request.php file in index.php as highlighted:

```php
require_once BUSINESS_DIR . 'ps_check_funds.php';
require_once BUSINESS_DIR . 'ps_check_stock.php';
require_once BUSINESS_DIR . 'authorize_net_request.php';
```

4. Add a reference to the business/authorize_net_request.php file in admin.php as highlighted:

```php
require_once BUSINESS_DIR . 'ps_ship_ok.php';
require_once BUSINESS_DIR . 'ps_final_notification.php';
require_once BUSINESS_DIR . 'authorize_net_request.php';
```

Testing Authorize.net Integration

All we have to do now is run some tests with our new web site. Retrieve the list of magic Authorize.net credit card numbers from the *AIM Implementation Guide*, and experiment with doing transactions using them.

Summary

In this chapter, we have completed our e-commerce application by integrating it with credit card authorization. Once you've put your own products in the database, hooked it up with your suppliers, obtained a merchant bank account, and put it on the Web, you're ready to go! OK, so that's still quite a lot of work, but none of it is particularly difficult. The hard work is behind you now!

Specifically, in this chapter, we have looked at the theory behind credit card transactions on the Web and at one full implementation—DataCash. We created a library that can be used to access DataCash and integrated it with our application. We also looked at Authorize.net, and we created code that tests credit card transactions processed via Authorize.net.

CHAPTER 21

■■■

Product Reviews

At this point, we have a complete and functional e-commerce web site. However, this doesn't stop us from adding even more features to make it more useful and pleasant for visitors.

By adding a product reviews system to your web site, you can increase the chances that visitors will return to your site, either to write a review for a product they bought or to see what other people think about that product.

A review system can also help you learn your customers' tastes, which enables you to improve the product recommendations and even make changes in the web site or the structure of the product catalog based on customer feedback.

To make things easy for both the customer and us, we'll add the list of product reviews and the form to add a new product review to the product details pages. The form to add a new product will show up for only registered users, because we decided not to allow anonymous reviews (however, you can easily change this if you like). We'll create the code for this new feature in the usual way, starting from the database and finishing with the user interface (UI).

Planning the Product Reviews Feature

The product reviews feature is simple enough. It is governed by three simple design decisions:

- The list of reviews and the interface elements necessary for adding new reviews should be displayed below the list of product recommendations on the product details pages, as shown in Figure 21-1.

- If the product has no reviews, we should invite the reader to write the first review, as shown in Figure 21-2.

- Only registered users can write product reviews.

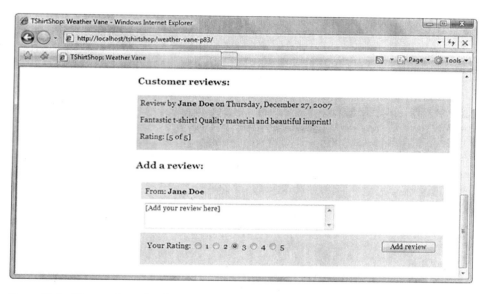

Figure 21-1. *The product details page containing product reviews*

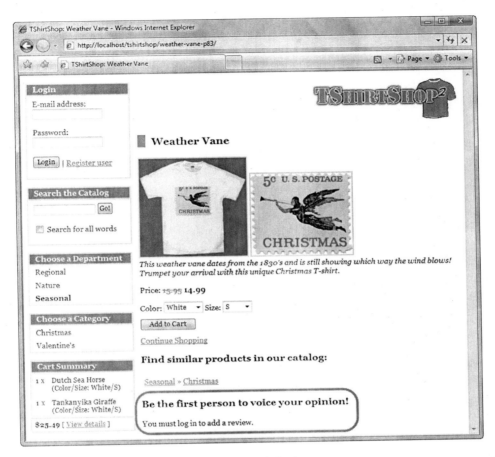

Figure 21-2. *Be the first person to voice your opinion!*

We store the product reviews in a database table named review, which is manipulated by two stored procedures—catalog_get_product_reviews and catalog_create_product_review—whose names are self-describing. The other code we'll write will only package this functionality in a form that is accessible to your visitors.

Implementing Product Reviews

Follow the steps of this exercise to create the database table, stored procedures, business tier, and presentation tier functionality required for the product reviews feature.

Exercise: Implementing Product Reviews

1. Load phpMyAdmin, select the tshirtshop database, and open a new SQL query page. Then, execute this code, which adds the review table in your tshirtshop database:

```
-- Create review table
CREATE TABLE `review` (
  `review_id`    INT      NOT NULL  AUTO_INCREMENT,
  `customer_id`  INT      NOT NULL,
  `product_id`   INT      NOT NULL,
  `review`       TEXT     NOT NULL,
  `rating`       SMALLINT NOT NULL,
  `created_on`   DATETIME NOT NULL,
  PRIMARY KEY (`review_id`),
  KEY `idx_review_customer_id` (`customer_id`),
  KEY `idx_review_product_id` (`product_id`)
);
```

2. Execute the following code, which creates the catalog_get_product_reviews stored procedure in the tshirtshop database (don't forget to set the delimiter to $$). The catalog_get_product_review stored procedure retrieves the reviews for the product identified by the inProductId parameter. We also need the name of the reviewer, so we made an INNER JOIN with the customer table.

```
-- Create catalog_get_product_reviews stored procedure
CREATE PROCEDURE catalog_get_product_reviews(IN inProductId INT)
BEGIN
  SELECT     c.name, r.review, r.rating, r.created_on
  FROM       review r
  INNER JOIN customer c
               ON c.customer_id = r.customer_id
  WHERE      r.product_id = inProductId
  ORDER BY   r.created_on DESC;
END$$
```

3. Execute the following code, which adds the catalog_create_product_review stored procedure in the tshirtshop database (don't forget to set the delimiter to $$). When a registered visitor adds a product review, the catalog_create_product_review stored procedure is called.

```
-- Create catalog_create_product_review stored procedure
CREATE PROCEDURE catalog_create_product_review(IN inCustomerId INT,
  IN inProductId INT, IN inReview TEXT, IN inRating SMALLINT)
BEGIN
  INSERT INTO review (customer_id, product_id, review, rating, created_on)
        VALUES (inCustomerId, inProductId, inReview, inRating, NOW());
END$$
```

4. Add the corresponding business tier methods to the `Catalog` class from the `business/catalog.php` file:

```
// Gets the reviews for a specific product
public static function GetProductReviews($productId)
{
  // Build the SQL query
  $sql = 'CALL catalog_get_product_reviews(:product_id)';

  // Build the parameters array
  $params = array (':product_id' => $productId);

  // Execute the query and return the results
  return DatabaseHandler::GetAll($sql, $params);
}

// Creates a product review
public static function CreateProductReview($customer_id, $productId,
                                          $review, $rating)
{
  // Build the SQL query
  $sql ='CALL catalog_create_product_review(:customer_id, :product_id,
                                            :review, :rating)';
  // Build the parameters array
  $params = array (':customer_id' => $customer_id,
                   ':product_id' => $productId,
                   ':review' => $review,
                   ':rating' => $rating);

  // Execute the query
  DatabaseHandler::Execute($sql, $params);
}
```

5. The UI consists of the reviews componentized template that will be placed on the product details page. Start by creating `presentation/templates/reviews.tpl` and adding the following code to it:

```
{* reviews.tpl *}
{load_presentation_object filename="reviews" assign="obj"}
{if $obj->mTotalReviews != 0}
<h2>Customer reviews:</h2>
<ul class="reviews-list">
  {section name=i loop=$obj->mReviews}
  <li>
    <p>
      Review by <strong>{$obj->mReviews[i].name}</strong> on
      {$obj->mReviews[i].created_on|date_format:"%A, %B %e, %Y"}
    </p>
    <p>{$obj->mReviews[i].review}</p>
    <p>Rating: [{$obj->mReviews[i].rating} of 5]</p>
  </li>
```

```
    {/section}
  </ul>
{else}
<h2>Be the first person to voice your opinion!</h2>
{/if}
{if $obj->mEnableAddProductReviewForm}
{* add review form *}
<h2>Add a review:</h2>
<form method="post" action="{$obj->mLinkToProduct}">
  <table class="review-table">
    <tr>
      <td class="add-review">From: <strong>{$obj->mReviewerName}</strong></td>
    </tr>
    <tr>
      <td>
        <textarea name="review"
         rows="3" cols="65">[Add your review here]</textarea>
      </td>
    </tr>
    <tr>
      <td class="add-review">
        <table class="review-table">
          <tr>
            <td>
              Your Rating:
              <input type="radio" name="rating" value="1" /> 1
              <input type="radio" name="rating" value="2" /> 2
              <input type="radio" name="rating" value="3" checked="checked" /> 3
              <input type="radio" name="rating" value="4" /> 4
              <input type="radio" name="rating" value="5" /> 5
            </td>
            <td align="right">
              <input type="submit" name="AddProductReview" value="Add review" />
            </td>
          </tr>
        </table>
      </td>
    </tr>
  </table>
</form>
{else}
<p>You must log in to add a review.</p>
{/if}
```

6. Create the presentation/reviews.php file, and add the following in it:

```
<?php
// Class that handles product reviews
```

```php
class Reviews
{
  public $mProductId;
  public $mReviews;
  public $mTotalReviews;
  public $mReviewerName;
  public $mEnableAddProductReviewForm = false;
  public $mLinkToProduct;

  public function __construct()
  {
    if (isset ($_GET['ProductId']))
      $this->mProductId = (int)$_GET['ProductId'];
    else
      trigger_error('ProductId not set', E_USER_ERROR);

    $this->mLinkToProduct = Link::ToProduct($this->mProductId);
  }

  public function init()
  {
    // If visitor is logged in ...
    if (Customer::IsAuthenticated())
    {
      // Check if visitor is adding a review
      if (isset($_POST['AddProductReview']))
        Catalog::CreateProductReview(Customer::GetCurrentCustomerId(),
                                     $this->mProductId, $_POST['review'],
                                     $_POST['rating']);

      // Display "add review" form because visitor is registered
      $this->mEnableAddProductReviewForm = true;

      // Get visitor's (reviewer's) name
      $customer_data = Customer::Get();
      $this->mReviewerName = $customer_data['name'];
    }

    // Get reviews for this product
    $this->mReviews = Catalog::GetProductReviews($this->mProductId);

    // Get the number of the reviews
    $this->mTotalReviews = count($this->mReviews);
  }
}
?>
```

7. Open `presentation/templates/product.tpl`, and add the following line at the end of it:

```
{include file="reviews.tpl"}
```

8. Add the following styles at the end of `tshirtshop.css`:

```
.reviews-list li {
  background: #ccddff;
  border-bottom: #fff solid 3px;
  display: block;
  padding: 5px;
}

.review-table {
  width: 100%;
}

.review-table tr td {
  border: none;
}

.add-review {
  background: #e6e6e6;
  padding: 5px;
}
```

9. Load `tshirtshop` in your browser, and click a product to view its product details page. If we're not logged in and the product has no reviews, we'll see the output shown in Figure 21-2. A sample output for a product that has one review was presented in Figure 21-1.

How It Works: The Reviews Componentized Template

The reviews componentized template takes care of both displaying the reviews and adding a new review. The first part of the `reviews.tpl` file determines whether we have any reviews to display for the current product. If we don't, a short message appears encouraging your visitor to write the first review.

```
{if $obj->mTotalReviews != 0}
<h2>Customer reviews:</h2>
[a list with reviews]
{else}
<h2>Be the first person to voice your opinion!</h2>
{/if}
```

The second part of the template displays a form to add a review or a message that invites the visitor to log in to be able to add a review:

```
{if $obj->mEnableAddProductReviewForm}
{* add review form *}
<h2>Add a review:<h2>
[add review form]
```

```
{else}
<p>You must log in to add a review.</p>
{/if}
```

The code from the presentation object is pretty straightforward and should not be a problem for you.

Summary

Yep, it was that simple. Although you might want to add improvements for your own solution (for example, allow the visitors to edit their reviews, or forbid them from adding more reviews), the base is there, and it works as expected.

You're now all set to proceed to the final chapter of this book, where we'll learn how to sell items to your customer from an outside source (we've chosen Amazon.com) by using XML Web Services.

■ ■ ■

## CHAPTER 22

Using Amazon.com Web Services

So far in this book, you've learned how to integrate external functionality provided PayPal, DataCash, and Authorize.net to process payments from your customers. In this chapter, you'll learn new possibilities for integrating features from external sources through web services. Knowing how to interact with third-party web services can offer you an important advantage over your competitors. More specifically, in this chapter you will

- Learn what web services are

- Learn how to connect to the Amazon E-Commerce Service

- Use the Amazon E-Commerce Service to sell Amazon t-shirts through TShirtShop

For more information about accessing web services using PHP, we recommend you check out *Pro PHP XML and Web Services* (Robert Richards. Apress, 2006.), which includes examples of accessing the Amazon.com, Google, eBay, and Yahoo web services.

Introducing Web Services

A *web service* is a piece of functionality that is exposed through a web interface using standard Internet protocols such as HTTP. The messages exchanged by the client and the server are encoded using an XML-based protocol named Simple Object Access Protocol (SOAP) or by using Representational State Transfer (REST) and are sent to the server over the HTTP protocol.

REST uses carefully crafted URLs with specific name-value pairs to call specific methods on the servers. REST is considered to be the easiest way to communicate with the web services that expose this interface. When using REST to access a web service, you simply make an HTTP GET request, and you'll receive the response in XML format.

SOAP is an XML-based standard for encoding the information transferred in a web service request or response. SOAP is fostered by a number of organizations, including powerful companies such as Microsoft, IBM, and Sun.

The beauty of using web services is that the client and the server can use any technology, any language, and any platform. As long as they exchange information with a standard protocol such as SOAP over HTTP, there is no problem if the client is a cell phone and the server is a Java application running on Solaris, for example.

The possibilities are exciting, and we recommend you purchase a book that specializes in web services to discover more about their world. Refer to the list of public web services at `http://www.xmethods.net/` to get an idea of the kinds of external functionality you can integrate into your application.

In this chapter, you'll learn how to integrate Amazon Web Services (AWS) to interact with Amazon and sell Amazon.com products through your TShirtShop web site.

You already have an e-commerce web site that sells t-shirts to its customers. You can go further and make some more money from their passion for t-shirts by incorporating related gifts from Amazon.com into your site. Do you do this for free? Oh no, you'll display Amazon.com's details on your site, but the final checkout will be processed by Amazon.com, and Amazon.com will deliver, in your bank account, a small commission for purchases made from your web site. Sounds like easy money, doesn't it?

In this chapter, you'll learn how to use AWS to add a special department called Amazon T-Shirts to your web store, which you can see in Figure 22-1. This will be a "special" department in that it will be handled differently from others—for example, payment is handled directly by Amazon.com when the visitor wants to buy a product. This chapter explores just a small subset of AWS's capabilities, so if you really want to make a fortune from this service, dig deeper into additional resources to find more substance.

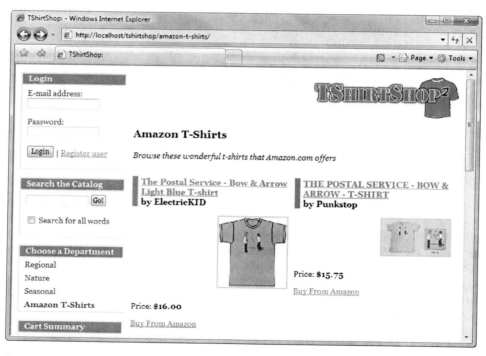

Figure 22-1. *Integrating the Amazon T-Shirts department into TShirtShop*

The rest of the chapter is divided into two parts. In the first part, you'll learn how to access AWS; in the second part, you'll integrate AWS into the TShirtShop web site.

■**Tip** The code in this chapter is independent of the rest of the site, so all you need to get started integrating Amazon.com functionality is the code from the first four chapters (so you have a working product catalog). Of course, with minor adjustments you can also adapt this code to your own personal solutions.

Accessing the Amazon Web Services

Most service providers (including Amazon.com) use SOAP or REST (or both) to expose web services to Internet client programs, and you get the same results with both options. In this chapter, you'll learn how to access AWS using both REST and SOAP.

AWS is the generic name Amazon.com uses for its collection of web services. The particular service we're interested in is the Amazon Associates Web Service (A2S, formerly known as the Amazon E-Commerce Service, or ECS). This web service allows us to query Amazon's catalog, allowing us to obtain product information programmatically. We'll use this web service to retrieve t-shirt product data from Amazon's catalog so that we can use that data to form our Amazon T-Shirts department.

When accessing any Amazon.com web service, including A2S, you can send the request either by using REST or by sending a SOAP message. The web service will return an XML response with the data you requested.

In this chapter, we'll touch just a bit of the functionality provided by the Amazon AWS, and even by A2S in particular. A serious discussion on the subject would need a separate book, but what you'll see in this chapter is enough to get you on the right track. Also, be aware that in this chapter we integrate functionality from Amazon U.S., but using the same AWS account, you can access services from Amazon.fr, Amazon.ca, Amazon.de, Amazon.co.jp, and Amazon.co.uk.

Creating Your Amazon.com Web Services Account

The official AWS web site is located at http://www.amazon.com/webservices. You can find the latest version of the documentation at http://developer.amazonwebservices.com/connect/— be sure to bookmark this URL because you'll find it very useful.

Before moving on, you need to create your account with AWS. To access AWS, you need an *access key ID*, which identifies your account in the AWS system. If you don't already have one, apply now at http://www.amazon.com/gp/aws/registration/registration-form.html. The access key ID is a 20-character alphanumeric string.

■**Note** Before October 11, 2005, Amazon.com used to provide something called a *subscription ID*, instead of an access key ID. The purpose is similar, and if you already have a subscription ID, you can continue using it. For any new applications, Amazon.com encourages you to use the access key ID.

The access key ID gives you access to more Amazon web services and Alexa web services (Alexa is a service owned by Amazon.com), as you can see in Figure 22-2. The access key isn't public information (you're not supposed to share it with anyone), but it isn't very secret information either, because it's free for anyone to get one.

For the paid web services, or for the services that need to be accessed in a secure way, Amazon.com uses another key that is called a *secret access key*, which you also get upon registration. We will not be using the secret access key in this chapter, however. To access A2S, you need only the access key.

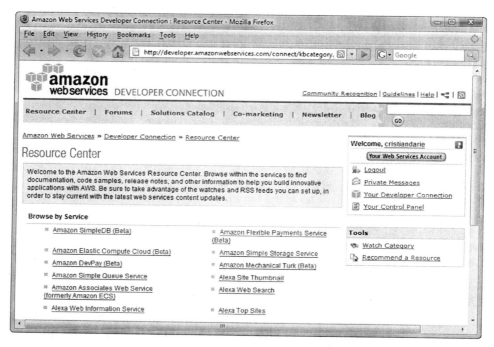

Figure 22-2. *Amazon.com web services*

Obtaining an Amazon.com Associate ID

The access key ID you created earlier is *your key to retrieving data* through the Amazon AWS. This data allows you to compose the Amazon T-Shirts department you saw in Figure 22-1.

If you want to earn commissions for Amazon.com products you sell via your site, you will also need an *associate ID*. The associate ID is used in the Buy From Amazon links you'll display in your special Amazon.com department, and it's the key that Amazon.com uses to identify you as the origin of that sale. So before moving further, if you want to make any money out of your Amazon T-Shirts department, go get your associate ID from http://associates.amazon.com/gp/associates/apply/main.html.

Note that the associate ID and the access key ID are two independent keys you have with Amazon.com, each of them with its own purpose. The associate ID is an ID that you can include in the Amazon.com links in your web site so that Amazon.com knows that the visitors who click those links came from you. The associate ID is not secret, because anyone browsing your web site can see the ID in the Amazon.com links in your site. All you need to sell Amazon.com products through your web site is an associate ID. You don't need an access key ID, which is required only when connecting to Amazon.com web services.

In TShirtShop, we connect to Amazon.com web services (and use the access key ID) to perform searches on Amazon.com's catalog and obtain the products we include in the Amazon T-Shirts department.

Accessing Amazon.com E-Commerce Service Using REST

REST web services are accessed by requesting a properly formed URL. Try the following link in your browser (don't forget to replace the string [Your Access Key ID] with your real access key ID that you obtained earlier):

```
http://webservices.amazon.com/onca/xml?Service=AWSECommerceService
&AWSAccessKeyId=[Your Access Key ID]
&Operation=ItemLookup
&IdType=ASIN
&ItemId=1590598644
```

■**Tip** Make sure you type the entire URL on a single line; we've broken it down here to individual elements to make it easier to read.

Your browser will display an XML structure with information about the book you are reading now. Figure 22-3 shows this XML structure in Firefox, which nicely displays the XML document tree. (We'll discuss displaying the products, visually, in TShirtShop later. For now we are interested in seeing the data that is returned from the request.)

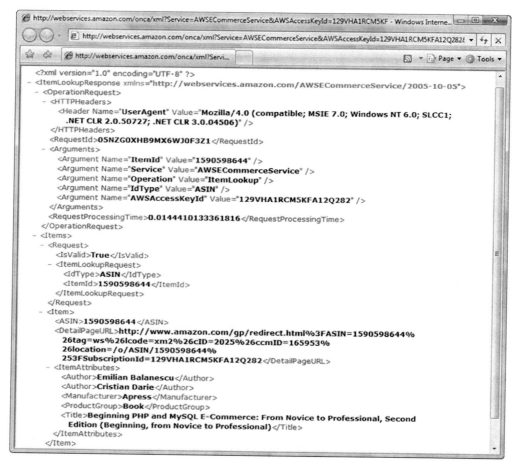

Figure 22-3. *The XML response of an Amazon.com web service request*

Pretty cool, huh? You have just seen REST in action. Every product in the Amazon.com database has a unique identifier called an *Amazon.com standard item number* (ASIN). For books, the ASIN is the book's ISBN (this book has the ASIN 1590598644).

The web service request you just made tells AWS the following: I have an access key ID (AWSAccessKeyId=[Your Access Key ID]), and I want to make an item lookup operation (&Operation=ItemLookup) to learn more about the product with the 1590598644 ASIN (&IdType=ASIN&ItemId=1590598644).

You didn't get much information about this book in this example—no price or availability information and no links to the cover picture or customer reviews. You can fine-tune the data you want to receive using response groups (a *response group* is a set of information about the product).

■ **Note** At the time of writing, AWS lists more than 35 possible response groups. In this book, we'll explain the purpose of only those response groups we're using for TShirtShop; for the complete list, visit the AWS documentation.

So, let's ask for some more data by using response groups. At the end of the link you composed earlier, add the following string to get more specific information about the book: `&ResponseGroup=Request,SalesRank,Small,Images,VariationSummary`. The complete link should look like this:

```
http://webservices.amazon.com/onca/xml?Service=AWSECommerceService
&AWSAccessKeyId=[Your Access Key ID]
&Operation=ItemLookup
&IdType=ASIN
&ItemId=1590598644
&ResponseGroup=Request,SalesRank,Small,Images,VariationSummary
```

The new XML response from Amazon.com includes more details about the Amazon.com item, as shown in Figure 22-4.

Figure 22-4. *The XML response of an Amazon.com web service request*

We have just mixed five response groups: Request, SalesRank, Small, Images, and OfferSummary. To learn more about the response groups, go to http://developer.amazonwebservices.com/connect/kbcategory.jspa?categoryID=5, and click the Latest Tech. Docs button. Alternatively, you can click the Technical Documentation link and then click the link of the latest documentation version. You can download the documentation in PDF format, or you can read it online at http://docs.amazonwebservices.com/AWSEcommerceService/2006-09-13/.

In the AWS documentation, you will find the response groups details in the "API Reference, Response Groups" section. Here's the description for the five response groups used in the previous example:

- The Request response group is a default response group in every kind of operation, and it returns the list of name-value pairs you used to make the request.

- The Sales Rank response group returns data about the current Amazon.com sales rank of the product.

- The Small response group returns general item data (ASIN, item name, URL, and so on) about items included in the response. This is a default response group for an ItemLookup operation (like we have in this example).

- The Images response group gives you the addresses for the three pictures (small, medium, and large) for each item in the response.

- The VariationSummary response group provides detailed price information (lowest price, highest price, lowest sale price, and highest sale price) for each item in the response.

Let's continue by learning how to make a REST request from PHP. To populate the future Amazon T-Shirts department, you'll search the Amazon.com Apparel department for the *postal t-shirt* keywords. One trivial way is to use the PHP file_get_contents() function, as you can see in the following script.

To test accessing web services using REST, create a new file named test_rest.php in your tshirtshop directory, and write the following code in it:

```php
<?php
// Tell the browser it is going to receive an XML document.
header('Content-type: text/xml');

/* DON'T FORGET to replace the string '[Your Access Key ID]' with your
   Access Key ID in the following line */
$url = 'http://webservices.amazon.com/onca/xml?Service=AWSECommerceService' .
       '&AWSAccessKeyId=[Your Access Key ID]' .
       '&Operation=ItemSearch' .
       '&Keywords=postal+t-shirt' .
       '&SearchIndex=Apparel' .
       '&ResponseGroup=Request,Medium,VariationSummary';

echo file_get_contents($url);
?>
```

■**Note** Some PHP installations and web hosting providers might not allow this code to run by default. In that case, you can change this setting in php.ini:

```
allow_url_fopen = On
```

Alternatively, you can add the following line to include/config.php. This second solution is preferred because it affects only your application, and it remains set if you need to move the application to another server.

```
ini_set('allow_url_fopen', 'On');
```

Loading http://localhost/tshirtshop/test_rest.php will show you XML data about Amazon.com's t-shirts (see Figure 22-5).

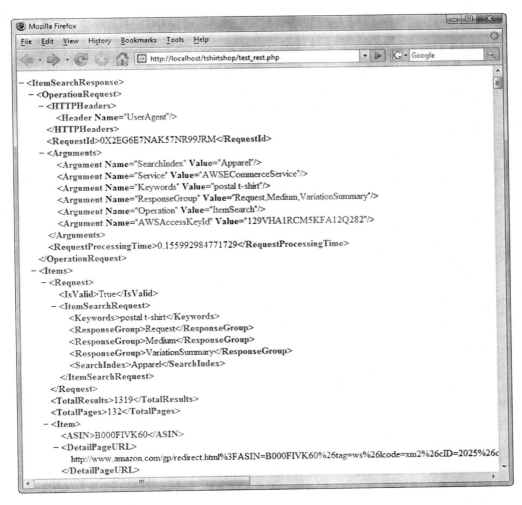

Figure 22-5. *Postal t-shirts from Amazon.com*

To exercise and build more XML links, just study the examples in the "API Reference" section of the AWS documentation. The material will show you how to do a variety of Amazon.com operations using REST.

Accessing Amazon.com E-Commerce Service Using SOAP

Using SOAP, you use a complex API to access the needed Amazon.com functionality. The following code, which performs the same search operation for t-shirts that you did earlier with REST, is using the `AWSECommerceService`, `ItemSearch`, and `ItemSearchRequest` objects from the Amazon.com API to perform the operation.

▪Note To access the Amazon.com server using SOAP, we use the PHP SOAP extension. Make sure the `php_soap.dll` reference in `php.ini` is not commented. You can find the documentation of the PHP SOAP functionality at `http://www.php.net/soap/`.

To test accessing web services using SOAP, create a new file named `test_soap.php` in your tshirtshop directory, and write the following code in it:

```php
<?php
try
{
  // Initialize SOAP client object
  $client = new SoapClient(
    'http://webservices.amazon.com/AWSECommerceService/AWSECommerceService.wsdl');

  /* DON'T FORGET to replace the string '[Your Access Key ID]' with your
     subscription ID in the following line */
  $request = array ('Service' => 'AWSECommerceService',
                    'AWSAccessKeyId' => '[Your Access Key ID]',
                    'Request' => array ('Operation' => 'ItemSearchRequest',
                                        'Keywords' => 'postal+t-shirt',
                                        'SearchIndex' => 'Apparel',
                                        'ResponseGroup' =>
                                          array ('Request',
                                                 'Medium',
                                                 'VariationSummary')));

  $result = $client->ItemSearch($request);
```

```
    echo '<pre>';
    print_r($result);
    echo '</pre>';
}
catch (SoapFault $fault)
{
    trigger_error('SOAP Fault: (faultcode: ' . $fault->faultcode . ', ' .
                  'faultstring: ' . $fault->faultstring . ')', E_USER_ERROR);
}
?>
```

The whole SOAP request code is enclosed in a try block. If the SOAP request fails, it throws an exception of the SoapFault type, which we transform into an error using the trigger_error() function. Read more on the SOAP exception at http://www.php.net/manual/en/function.is-soap-fault.php.

The result of the SOAP request is an object containing the requested data. If you load test_soap.php in your browser (don't forget to put your access key ID in it), it should display the data in a text format that's not easy to read by the human eye.

The code starts by creating a SOAP client object to the Amazon.com SOAP web service:

```
// Initialize SOAP client object
$client = new SoapClient(
    'http://webservices.amazon.com/AWSECommerceService/AWSECommerceService.wsdl');
```

The referenced Web Services Definition Language (WSDL) file describes all the functions and their parameters' types that Amazon.com SOAP server understands. The previously created Amazon.com SOAP client object knows about all these functions, and you can call them now using something like this:

```
$result = $client->ItemSearch($request);
```

Alternatively, you can make the same call, and implicitly obtain the same results, by using the __soapCall() function (http://www.php.net/manual/en/function.soap-soapclient-soap-call.php), like this:

```
$result->__soapCall('ItemSearch', array ($request));
```

The web service request does an ItemSearch operation on the *postal+t-shirt* keywords in the "Apparel" store. The whole request is placed in a try-catch block that catches any potential exceptions and generates an error. Read more on the SoapFault exception class, which contains the details of the SOAP error, at http://www.php.net/manual/en/function.is-soap-fault.php. Loading test_soap.php generates the result shown in Figure 22-6.

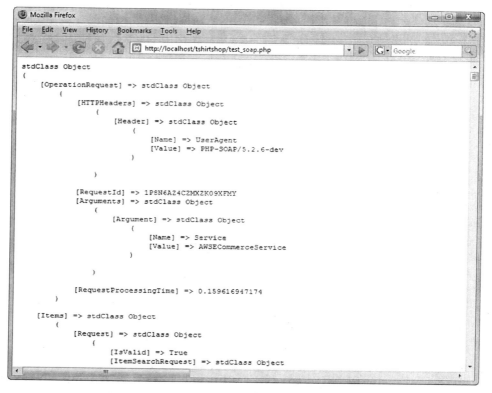

Figure 22-6. *The results of the SOAP request*

Integrating A2S with TShirtShop

The goal is to bring some books related to the words *postal t-shirt* from Amazon.com to your store. You'll build a special department with no categories that will display some book information (cover image, title, authors, and price). Each book will have a Buy from Amazon link that allows your visitor to buy the book from Amazon.com. If you apply for an Amazon.com associates ID account, you'll get a small commission from this. After following the exercises, you'll implement the Amazon.com integration, as shown earlier in Figure 22-1.

The following link engages a REST search for Amazon.com books on the *postal t-shirt* keywords and returns the first ten products data sorted by their sales rank:

```
http://webservices.amazon.com/onca/xml?Service=AWSECommerceService
&Operation=ItemSearch
&AWSAccessKeyId=[Your Access Key ID]
&Keywords=postal+t-shirt
&SearchIndex=Apparel
&ResponseGroup=Request%2CMedium%2CVariationSummary&Sort=salesrank
```

From all the products that will be returned by our request, we will display only the ones that are available for purchase and with cover images.

Implementing the Business Tier

In the business tier, you'll add the code that accesses the A2S system.

Exercise: Adding A2S Communication Code to the Business Tier

1. Add the following code in your `include/config.php` file:

```
// Amazon E-Commerce Service
// define('AMAZON_METHOD', 'REST');
define('AMAZON_METHOD', 'SOAP');
define('AMAZON_WSDL',
   'http://webservices.amazon.com/AWSECommerceService/AWSECommerceService.wsdl');
define('AMAZON_REST_BASE_URL',
   'http://webservices.amazon.com/onca/xml?Service=AWSECommerceService');

// Set Amazon Access Key ID
define('AMAZON_ACCESS_KEY_ID', '[Your Access Key ID]');

// Set Amazon Associates ID
define('AMAZON_ASSOCIATES_ID', '[Your Amazon associate ID]');

// Set Amazon request options
define('AMAZON_SEARCH_KEYWORDS', 'postal t-shirt');
define('AMAZON_SEARCH_NODE', 'Apparel');
define('AMAZON_RESPONSE_GROUPS', 'Request,Medium,VariationSummary');
```

2. Create a new file named `amazon.php` in the business folder, and add the following code to it. The single public method, which will be called from the upper tiers, is `GetProducts()`, whereas the others are private methods for internal use that support the functionality of `GetProducts()`.

```php
<?php
// Class for accessing A2S
class Amazon
{
  public function Amazon()
  {
  }

  // Retrieves Amazon products for sending to presentation tier
  public function GetProducts()
  {
    // Use SOAP to get data
    if (AMAZON_METHOD == 'SOAP')
      $result = $this->_GetDataWithSoap();
    // Use REST to get data
    else
      $result = $this->_GetDataWithRest();
```

```php
    // Initializes Array object
    $results = array ();

    // Format results
    $results = $this->_DataFormat($result);

    // Returns results
    return $results;
  }

  // Call A2S using REST
  private function _GetDataWithRest()
  {
    $params = array ('Operation'     => 'ItemSearch',
                     'SubscriptionId' => AMAZON_ACCESS_KEY_ID,
                     'Keywords'       => AMAZON_SEARCH_KEYWORDS,
                     'SearchIndex'    => AMAZON_SEARCH_NODE,
                     'ResponseGroup'  => AMAZON_RESPONSE_GROUPS,
                     'Sort'           => 'salesrank');

    $query_string = '&';
    foreach ($params as $key => $value)
      $query_string .= $key . '=' . urlencode($value) . '&';

    $amazon_url = AMAZON_REST_BASE_URL . $query_string;

    // Get the XML response using REST
    $amazon_xml = file_get_contents($amazon_url);

    // Unserialize the XML and return
    return simplexml_load_string($amazon_xml);
  }

  // Call A2S using SOAP
  private function _GetDataWithSoap()
  {
    try
    {
      $client = new SoapClient(AMAZON_WSDL);

      /* Set up an array containing input parameters to be
         passed to the remote procedure */
      $request = array ('SubscriptionId' => AMAZON_ACCESS_KEY_ID,
                        'Request' => array ('Operation' =>
'ItemSearchRequest',
                                            'Keywords' =>
                                             AMAZON_SEARCH_KEYWORDS,
                                            'SearchIndex' =>
```

```
AMAZON_SEARCH_NODE,
                                      'ResponseGroup' =>
                                        AMAZON_RESPONSE_GROUPS,
                                      'Sort' => 'salesrank'));

      // Invoke the method
      $result = $client->ItemSearch($request);

      return $result;
    }
    catch (SoapFault $fault)
    {
      trigger_error('SOAP Fault: (faultcode: ' . $fault->faultcode . ', ' .
                    'faultstring: ' . $fault->faultstring . ')',
E_USER_ERROR);
    }
  }

  /* Places an "image not available" picture for products with no image,
     and saves the results in an array with a simple structure for easier
     handling at the upper levels */
  private function _DataFormat($result)
  {
    /* Variable k is the index of the $new_result array, which will
       contain the Amazon products to be displayed in TShirtShop */
    $k = 0;

    $new_result = array ();

    /* Analyze all products retrieved from A2S
       and save them into the $new_result array */
    for ($i = 0; $i < count($result->Items->Item); $i++)
    {
      // Make a temporary copy for product data
      $temp = $result->Items->Item[$i];

      /* Set product's image to images/not_available.jpg,
         if image url is empty */
      if (property_exists($temp, 'MediumImage') &&
          ((string) $temp->MediumImage->URL) != '')
        $new_result[$k]['image'] = (string) $temp->MediumImage->URL;
      else
        $new_result[$k]['image'] = 'images/not_available.jpg';

      // Save asin, brand, name, and price into the $new_result array
      $new_result[$k]['asin'] = (string) $temp->ASIN;
      $new_result[$k]['brand'] = (string) $temp->ItemAttributes->Brand;
      $new_result[$k]['item_name'] = (string) $temp->ItemAttributes->Title;
```

```
      if (property_exists($temp, 'VariationSummary') &&
          property_exists($temp->VariationSummary, 'LowestPrice'))
      {
        $new_result[$k]['price'] =
          (string) $temp->VariationSummary->LowestPrice->FormattedPrice;

        $highest_price = $new_result[$k]['price'];

        if (property_exists($temp->VariationSummary, 'HighestPrice'))
          $highest_price =
            (string) $temp->VariationSummary->HighestPrice->FormattedPrice;

        if ($highest_price !== $new_result[$k]['price'])
          $new_result[$k]['price'] .= ' - ' . $highest_price;
      }
      else
        $new_result[$k]['price'] = '';

      $k++;
    }

    return $new_result;
  }
}
?>
```

How It Works: Communicating with AWS

The only public Amazon.com business-tier method is GetProducts() that takes care to retrieve data. Its functionality is quite clear, because it uses a number of helper methods to get the work done. First, it decides whether it should use SOAP or REST depending on the configuration setting you added to include/config.php:

```
define('AMAZON_METHOD', 'SOAP');
```

The AMAZON_METHOD constant you defined in include/config.php instructs whether AWS will be contacted through REST or SOAP. The value of that constant (which should be REST or SOAP) decides whether _GetDataWithRest() or _GetDataWithSoap() will be used to contact Amazon. No matter which method you choose, the results should be the same:

```
// Retrieves Amazon products for sending to presentation tier
public function GetProducts()
{
  // Use SOAP to get data
  if (AMAZON_METHOD == 'SOAP')
    $result = $this->_GetDataWithSoap();
  // Use REST to get data
  else
    $result = $this->_GetDataWithRest();
```

_GetDataWithSoap() and _GetDataWithRest() return the list of products as an object. Then, we use the _DataFormat() method to parse the data from this object and return that data in the form of an associative array. The _DataFormat() method also places an "image not available" image for the Amazon.com products that don't have a product image.

```
// Initializes Array object
$results = array ();

// Format results
$results = $this->_DataFormat($result);

// Returns results
return $results;
}
```

Let's look now at _GetDataWithRest() and _GetDataWithSoap(), which are the methods that do the actual communication with AWS. _GetDataWithRest() retrieves web service data using REST. It starts by constructing the required query string by joining the individual parameters you want to send to Amazon.com:

```
// Call AWS using REST
private function _GetDataWithRest()
{
  $params = array ('Operation'      => 'ItemSearch',
                   'SubscriptionId' => AMAZON_ACCESS_KEY_ID,
                   'Keywords'       => AMAZON_SEARCH_KEYWORDS,
                   'SearchIndex'    => AMAZON_SEARCH_NODE,
                   'ResponseGroup'  => AMAZON_RESPONSE_GROUPS,
                   'Sort'           => 'salesrank');
  $query_string = '&';
  foreach ($params as $key => $value)
    $query_string .= $key . '=' . urlencode($value) . '&';
```

The complete Amazon.com URL that you need to call is composed of the base URL (which you saved as a constant in include/config.php) to which you append the query string you just built:

```
$amazon_url = AMAZON_REST_BASE_URL . $query_string;
```

Using the file_get_contents() function, you make a simple HTTP GET request to Amazon. It's just like typing the address in your browser:

```
// Get the XML response using REST
$amazon_xml = file_get_contents($amazon_url);
```

The $amazon_xml variable will contain a string with the returned XML data. To further process it, we use the simplexml_load_string() function that parses the XML text and returns a SimpleXMLElement object representing the XML document. Read more details at http://www.php.net/manual/en/function.simplexml-load-string.php.

```
// Unserialize the XML and return
return simplexml_load_string($amazon_xml);
}
```

The _GetDataWithSoap() method has similar functionality as _GetDataWithRest(), but it makes the ItemSearch operation using SOAP. The logic this method uses to contact AWS is the same as in the page you wrote earlier in this chapter.

Implementing the Presentation Tier

Let's create the componentized template that will display the t-shirts and then modify the departments_list componentized template to include this new department.

Exercise: Displaying Amazon.com Products in TShirtShop

1. Add a new file named amazon_products_list.tpl in the presentation/templates folder of your project, and add the following code in it:

```
{* amazon_products_list.tpl *}
{load_presentation_object filename="amazon_products_list" assign="obj"}
<h1>{$obj->mDepartmentName}</h1>
<p class="description">{$obj->mDepartmentDescription}</p>
<table class="product-list">
  <tbody>
{section name=k loop=$obj->mProducts}
  {if $smarty.section.k.index % 2 == 0}
    <tr>
  {/if}
      <td valign="top">
        <h3 class="product-title">
          <a href="{$obj->mProducts[k].link_to_product}">
            {$obj->mProducts[k].item_name}
          </a>
          <br />
          by {$obj->mProducts[k].brand}
        </h3>
        <p>
          {if $obj->mProducts[k].image neq ""}
          <a href="{$obj->mProducts[k].link_to_product}">
            <img src="{$obj->mProducts[k].image}"
             alt="{$obj->mProducts[k].item_name}" width="120" />
          </a>
          {/if}
        </p>
        <p class="attributes">
          {if $obj->mProducts[k].price neq ""}
          Price: <font class="price">{$obj->mProducts[k].price}</font>
          {/if}
        </p>
        <p class="section">
          <a target="_blank" href="{$obj->mProducts[k].link_to_product}">
```

```
        Buy From Amazon
      </a>
    </p>
  </td>
{if $smarty.section.k.index % 2 != 0 && !$smarty.section.k.first ||
   $smarty.section.k.last}
  </tr>
{/if}
{/section}
  </tbody>
</table>
```

2. Create a new file named amazon_products_list.php in the presentation folder, and add the following code in it:

```php
<?php
// Class that handles receiving AWS data
class AmazonProductsList
{
  // Public variables available in smarty template
  public $mProducts;
  public $mDepartmentName;
  public $mDepartmentDescription;

  // Constructor
  public function __construct()
  {
    $this->mDepartmentName = AMAZON_DEPARTMENT_TITLE;
    $this->mDepartmentDescription = AMAZON_DEPARTMENT_DESCRIPTION;
  }

  public function init()
  {
    $amazon = new Amazon();
    $this->mProducts = $amazon->GetProducts();

    for ($i = 0;$i < count($this->mProducts); $i++)
      $this->mProducts[$i]['link_to_product'] =
        'http://www.amazon.com/exec/obidos/ASIN/' .
        $this->mProducts[$i]['asin'] . '/ref=nosim/' . AMAZON_ASSOCIATES_ID;
  }
}
?>
```

3. Add the following two configuration lines at the end of your include/config.php file:

```php
// Amazon.com department configuration options
define('AMAZON_DEPARTMENT_TITLE', 'Amazon T-Shirts');
define('AMAZON_DEPARTMENT_DESCRIPTION',
        'Browse these wonderful t-shirts that Amazon.com offers');
```

4. Modify the `presentation/templates/departments_list.tpl` template file to add the Amazon T-Shirts department. Add the highlighted code shown here:

```
    <li>
      {* Generate a link for a new department in the list *}
      <a {$selected} href="{$obj->mDepartments[i].link_to_department}">
        {$obj->mDepartments[i].name}
      </a>
    </li>
  {/section}
    {assign var=selected value=""}
    {if $obj->mAmazonSelected}
      {assign var=selected value="class=\"selected\""}
    {/if}
    <li>
      <a {$selected} href="{$obj->mLinkToAmazonDepartment}">
        {$obj->mAmazonDepartmentName}
      </a>
    </li>
  </ul>
</div>
{* End departments list *}
```

5. Update `presentation/departments_list.php` as highlighted in this code snippet:

```php
<?php
// Manages the departments list
class DepartmentsList
{
  /* Public variables available in departments_list.tpl Smarty template */
  public $mSelectedDepartment = 0;
  public $mDepartments;
  public $mAmazonSelected = false;
  public $mAmazonDepartmentName;
  public $mLinkToAmazonDepartment;

  // Constructor reads query string parameter
  public function __construct()
  {
    /* If DepartmentId exists in the query string, we're visiting a
       department */
    if (isset ($_GET['DepartmentId']))
      $this->mSelectedDepartment = (int)$_GET['DepartmentId'];
    elseif (isset($_GET['ProductId']) &&
            isset($_SESSION['link_to_continue_shopping']))
    {
      $continue_shopping =
        Link::QueryStringToArray($_SESSION['link_to_continue_shopping']);
```

```
    if (array_key_exists('DepartmentId', $continue_shopping))
      $this->mSelectedDepartment =
        (int)$continue_shopping['DepartmentId'];
  }

    // Set Amazon department name and build the link for department
    $this->mAmazonDepartmentName = AMAZON_DEPARTMENT_TITLE;
    $this->mLinkToAmazonDepartment = Link::ToAmazonDepartment();

    // Check whether the Amazon department is selected
    if ((isset ($_GET['DepartmentId'])) &&
        ((string) $_GET['DepartmentId'] == 'Amazon'))
      $this->mAmazonSelected = true;
  }
...
```

6. Add the following method to the Link class in the presentation/link.php file:

```
// Creates a link to the Amazon T-Shirts department
public static function ToAmazonDepartment()
{
  return self::Build('amazon-t-shirts/');
}
```

7. In the same class, modify the CheckRequest() method as highlighted to exit the function if we request the Amazon T-Shirts department page:

```
...
    // Obtain proper URL for department pages
    elseif (isset ($_GET['DepartmentId']))
    {
      if ((string) $_GET['DepartmentId'] == 'Amazon') return;

      if (isset ($_GET['Page']))
        $proper_url = self::ToDepartment($_GET['DepartmentId'],
                                         $_GET['Page']);
      else
        $proper_url = self::ToDepartment($_GET['DepartmentId']);
    }
...
```

8. Open the .htaccess file from the project root folder, and add the following rewrite definition rule for the Amazon T-Shirts department page:

```
...
# Rewrite order error pages
RewriteRule ^order-error/?$ index.php?OrderError [L]

# Rewrite Amazon t-shirts department pages
RewriteRule ^amazon-t-shirts/?$ index.php?DepartmentId=Amazon [L]
</IfModule>
```

```
# Set the default 500 page for Apache errors
ErrorDocument 500 /tshirtshop/500.php

# Set the default 404 page
ErrorDocument 404 /tshirtshop/404.php
```

9. Update `include/index.php` to reference the new business tier class by adding the following code on top of the line that checks the page requests:

```
require_once BUSINESS_DIR . 'amazon.php';

// URL correction
Link::CheckRequest();

// Load Smarty template file
$application = new Application();
```

10. Open the `presentation/store_front.php` file, and modify the `init()` method from the `StoreFront` class to load the Amazon T-Shirts department when requested:

```
...
    // Load department details if visiting a department
    if (isset ($_GET['DepartmentId']))
    {
      if ((string) $_GET['DepartmentId'] == 'Amazon')
        $this->mContentsCell = 'amazon_products_list.tpl';
      else
      {
        $this->mContentsCell = 'department.tpl';
        $this->mCategoriesCell = 'categories_list.tpl';
      }
    }
...
```

11. Load TShirtShop in your browser, and then click your newly created Amazon T-Shirts department. You should see the new department as shown earlier in Figure 22-1.

How It Works: Displaying Amazon.com Products in TShirtShop

In this exercise, you simply updated TShirtShop to display Amazon.com products by employing the techniques you studied in the first part of the chapter. The new functionality isn't especially complex, but the possibilities are exciting.

To change the access method, modify the following in `include/config.php`:

```
// Amazon E-Commerce Service
define('AMAZON_METHOD', 'REST');
//define('AMAZON_METHOD', 'SOAP');
```

When Buy From Amazon links are clicked, Amazon.com associates that customer and the items purchased to your associate ID (which is mentioned in the links). In the `init()` method from the `AmazonProductsList` class, the `GetProducts()` method from the `Amazon` class is called to get the data to populate the list of products. This data is read to build the Amazon.com links to the retrieved products:

```
public function init()
{
  $amazon = new Amazon();
  $this->mProducts = $amazon->GetProducts();

  for ($i = 0;$i < count($this->mProducts); $i++)
    $this->mProducts[$i]['link'] =
      'http://www.amazon.com/exec/obidos/ASIN/' .
      $this->mProducts[$i]['asin'] .
      '/ref=nosim/' . AMAZON_ASSOCIATES_ID;
}
```

However, you must know that Amazon.com offers many ways in which you can allow your visitors to buy its products. If you log in to the Associates page, you'll see a number of link types you can build and integrate into your web site.

Perhaps the most interesting and powerful is the possibility to create and manage Amazon.com shopping carts from your PHP code by using the Amazon.com API. If you're really into integrating Amazon.com into your web site, you should study the AWS documentation carefully and make the most of it.

Summary

In this chapter, you learned how to access Amazon.com E-Commerce Service using REST and SOAP. You will be able to use the same techniques when accessing any kind of external functionality exposed through these protocols.

Congratulations, you have just finished your journey into learning about building e-commerce web sites with PHP and MySQL. You have the knowledge to build your own customized solutions, perhaps even more interesting and powerful than what we showed you in this book.

Chapters 1 through 11 represented the first stage of development, where you established the basic framework for the site and implemented all the essential site features. After finishing Chapter 11, you could launch the site and start accepting and processing orders from your customers.

Specifically, in Chapters 1 through 3 we talked about e-commerce and the particular e-commerce site that we would build: TShirtShop. We listed the open source programs needed for this project and proceeded with installing and configuring the necessary software. You also learned about the three-tier architecture

In Chapters 4 through 6, we created the tshirtshop database with MySQL and phpMyAdmin and fully implemented a basic product catalog. You learned how to create MySQL stored procedures, how to access them from the business tier of your application, and how to display the database data using presentation objects and Smarty templates.

In Chapters 7 and 8, we developed the code for an online customer to search for products in the tshirtshop database catalog, and we implemented many important search engine optimization improvements. These features are essential for the success of a commercial web site.

In Chapter 9 we discussed how to charge our customers using PayPal. Needless to say, processing payments is necessary for an online store, and starting with a service that does most of the work for you is the simplest way to start charging your customers.

In Chapters 10 and 11 we created the TShirtShop administration functions that allow you to easily edit your catalog's departments and categories, product descriptions and prices, add or remove items from the TShirtShop catalog, and perform many other administrative tasks.

Chapters 12–15 represented the second stage of development, where you replaced PayPal's shopping cart with your own shopping cart solution. Additionally, you added AJAX and dynamic recommendations features, making your site friendlier to your visitors. At the end of this stage of development, your site was once again fully functional and ready to accept your customer's orders.

Specifically, in Chapter 12 we showed you how to design your own customized shopping cart, which you could use instead of PayPal's shopping cart.

In Chapter 13 we described how to use AJAX for your product catalog and customized shopping cart. The improvements to your web site weren't major, but today's educated customers are likely to appreciate the application's better-perceived performance. Additionally, programming AJAX is an important skill that you'll likely find very useful when developing your future web projects.

In Chapter 14 we implemented the order processing mechanism that works with the shopping cart you've implemented in Chapter 12.

In Chapter 15, we showed you how to gather information from each customer order and use it to implement a dynamic cross-selling mechanism using the "Customers who bought this also bought . . ." and the "You might also like . . ." marketing techniques.

Chapters 16–22 consisted of the third stage of development, where you added advanced features to TShirtShop. After completing Chapter 22, your site knows how to process credit card transactions, manage a professional order pipeline, accept product reviews from customers, and integrate with Amazon.com through web services.

Specifically, in Chapter 16 we created the customer accounts feature, so that we can keep track of every individual customer's orders. Storing the customer's personal data, including credit card information, was necessary in order to process credit card transactions. You learned how to use cryptographic functions in order to store the customer's password and credit card information safely in your database.

In Chapters 17–19 you updated your database to keep track of each order using an order pipeline mechanism and started using customers' personal information when storing database orders.

In Chapter 20 you learned how to process credit card transactions using two companies that offer merchant accounts, DataCash and Authorize.net.

In Chapter 21 you implemented a basic product reviews feature, which is a feature customers are accustomed to these days.

Finally, in Chapter 22, you learned how to integrate Amazon.com web services to maximize the revenues your web site produces. At the end of this chapter, TShirtShop is a modern, powerful e-commerce store, ready to take on its online competitors.

We're really glad you've successfully completed the TShirtShop project! We hope you enjoyed reading this book, and we wish you good luck with your own personal PHP and MySQL projects!

Index